Financial Management for Decision Making

Financial Management
for Decision Making

Harold Bierman, Jr.   **Seymour Smidt**

Johnson Graduate School of Management
Cornell University

Macmillan Publishing Company
New York
Collier Macmillan Publishers
London

Macmillan Publishing Company
866 Third Avenue, New York, New York 10022

Collier Macmillan Canada, Inc.

Library of Congress Cataloging in Publication Data

Bierman, Harold.
  Financial management for decision making.

  Includes index.
  1. Corporations—Finance.   2. Decision making.
I. Smidt, Seymour.   II. Title.
HG4026.B534   1986   658.1'5   85-7160
ISBN 0-02-310030-3

Printing: 1 2 3 4 5 6 7 8   Year: 6 7 8 9 0 1 2 3 4 5

ISBN 0-02-310030-3

Preface

This book can be used in the first or the intermediate course in financial management. The book provides a comprehensive introduction to corporate finance, building on the basic capital budgeting framework. Our objective is to stress the theoretical formulations that are most useful in making managerial financial decisions.

Over the past 30 years, there has been a trend in business finance education in the direction of more analytical models. Both theoretical and applied journals of finance have greatly increased the number of articles dealing with quantitative techniques in finance and the modeling of financial decisions. As might be expected, this literature has greatly affected business and governmental financial decision making. The terms *net present value*, *internal rate of return*, and *capital asset pricing model* are today not only used by staff persons, but also by top management. A few years ago the persons in these important managerial positions would have been proud to say that they made the big decisions on the basis of their experience, judgment, and intuition. Now top managers insist more and more on having financial information, properly analyzed, before they exercise their judgments.

Because of this trend toward more analytical models, we think finance students sometimes get a false impression of how financial decisions are made in today's business world. Many of the models are simplifications of the real world. If they were to be applied without modification, it is likely that some of the models would lead to undesirable decisions. However, if used correctly such models will give insights into the weaknesses of other, even more simplified and erroneous decision-making techniques. This book emphasizes that the correct application of financial techniques in business situations improves the likelihood of making good decisions. However, exact answers and correct decisions are not always guaranteed in a complex and uncertain world. After reading this book, we believe students will have a better appreciation for the uses *and* limits of financial analysis.

This book is based on a number of fundamental principles. First, the time value of money and the capital budgeting framework are used as the basic foundation for a large amount of the analysis. Second, decisions are approached on an after-tax basis. Third, we have avoided relatively complex mathematical models which we think are better presented in a more advanced finance course. Fourth, we emphasize decision making throughout. Each topic is approached from the perspective of the specific financial decision in question. In this context, we emphasize the models and methods of analysis that are most useful and practical rather than discussing theory for theory's sake. Finally, once the reader understands the basic concepts and methods, we think it is important to introduce various real-world constraints and complexities. This helps to develop well-rounded managers rather than only technicians.

Part I introduces two of the most important concepts that can be learned in a business school. One is the concept of time value of money, the other is the use of diversification to reduce risk. These two concepts form the basis for much of the material in the following chapters. Also, included is a full chapter on the Capital Asset Pricing Model.

Part II is a comprehensive survey of capital budgeting techniques, first from an assumption of certainty and then uncertainty. Chapter 7 provides especially complete coverage of the crucial issue of determining and using cash flows.

Part III moves to the cost of capital and long-term financing decisions. The use of debt is discussed and other, alternative basic sources of long-term capital. Dividend policy is included in this part because of the importance of dividends to investors and retained earnings to firms as a source of long-term capital.

Part IV deals with short-term financial management topics. Special attention is given to some of the more useful basic quantitative models available to management.

Part V is a collection of special topics in financial management. While none of these topics is essential to most basic finance courses, they are all important and relevant to managerial decisions.

The sequence in which the chapters are read is highly optional. We would strongly recommend that Part I be studied first. After Part I a wide range of alternate paths can be followed. The chapter arrangement is our recommendation only; other alternatives are equally as good.

Each chapter contains a wide range of pedagogical aids and assignment material. Within each chapter we have set off detailed, step-by-step examples of problem-solving techniques. In boxed off sections we have also included brief references to the actual practices of real companies. Each chapter ends with self-review problems. These problems with their detailed solutions serve as a bridge between the text and problems. Finally, we have concentrated on providing a rich selection of problems for assignment, ranging from simple drill exercises to more difficult integrative problems. We have also included at the end of each part a selection of short cases which are intended for those instructors, like ourselves, who want to assign some cases, but do not want to impose the added financial burden of a separate casebook. A solutions manual for all questions, problems, and cases is available from the publisher. Also available is a study guide prepared by John Jahera and Dan Page of Auburn University and a test bank by Gladys Perry of Kenesaw College.

A knowledge of calculus is not essential for an understanding of this book. The mathematics used is basic algebra with some probability and decision theory (such as would be obtained in a beginning statistics or quantitative course). Since our objective is to highlight fundamental concepts, many of the discussions intentionally stop short of known complexities.

Because of the overlap in topic coverage, some material in this book has been adapted from the sixth edition of *The Capital Budgeting Decision*. However, all of the adapted material has been extensively revised for the purposes of this text.

We would like to thank our friend and colleague, Jerry Hass, who is in many senses a co-author of this book.

Finally, we would like to thank the following individuals who provided reviews of the manuscript: John Bildersee, New York University; Trevor Crick, University of Detroit; Zane Dennick-Ream, Miami University; Douglas Emery, University of Missouri, Columbia; Michael Ferri, University of South Carolina; Sidney Finkel, Goldome Federal Savings; David Goldenberg, University of Maryland; William Hardin, University of Arkansas, Fayetteville; James F. Jackson, Oklahoma State University; John Jahera, Auburn University; James Kehr, Miami University; Scott Lummer, Texas A&M University; Gladys Perry, Kenesaw College; Barnard Seligman, Pace University; Paul Vanderheiden, University of Wisconsin, Eau Claire; Brent D. Wilson, Brigham Young University; and Edward Wolfe, Western Kentucky University. The comments of these people were of considerable help and were responsible for significant improvements in the manuscript.

H. B., Jr.
S. S.

Brief Contents

ix

Detailed Contents

Introduction to Financial Management Concepts

Part I introduces two of the primary foundations on which financial decision making is built: the time value of money and the fundamentals of portfolio analysis and diversification.

The arithmetic of the time value of money is used extensively throughout this book to evaluate a wide range of types of business decisions. It is an essential tool for any manager.

Diversification and portfolio analysis enable a decision maker to change the nature of the outcomes so that the well-being of the investor is improved. In Chapter 5 we introduce the capital asset pricing model, which is the theoretical foundation for many practical applications.

Chapter *1*

Financial Management

Major Topics

1. Objectives of a business firm.
2. Time, risk, and the risk-return trade-off.
3. Three basic generalizations that are used throughout the book.
4. The relevance of cash flows and the importance of the time dimension in making decisions.

Corporate Objectives

The motivation for investing in a corporation is the expectation of making a larger risk-adjusted return than can be earned elsewhere. The managers of a corporation have the responsibility of administering the affairs of the firm in a manner consistent with the expectation of returning the investor's original capital plus the return on their capital. The common stockholders are the residual owners, and they earn a return only after the investors in the more senior securities (debt and preferred stock) have received their contractual claims. We will assume that the objective of the firm is to maximize its common stockholders' wealth position. But even this narrow, relatively well-defined definition is apt to give rise to misunderstanding and conflict. It is possible that situations will arise in which one group of stockholders will prefer one financial decision while another group of stockholders will prefer another decision.

For example, imagine a situation in which a business undertakes an investment that its management believes to be desirable, but the immediate effect of the investment will be to depress earnings and lower the common stock price today because the market does not have the same information that the management has. In the future, it is expected that the market will realize that the investment is desirable, and at that time the stock price will reflect the enhanced value. But a stockholder expecting to sell the stock in the near future would prefer that the investment had been rejected, whereas a stockholder holding for the long run might be pleased that the investment was undertaken. Theoretically, the problem can be solved by improving the information available to the market. Then the market price would completely reflect the actions and plans of management. However, in practice, the market does not have access to the same information set as management does.

A corporate objective such as "profit maximization" does not adequately or accurately describe the primary objective of the firm, since profits as conventionally computed do not effectively reflect the cost of the stockholders' capital that is tied up in the investment, nor do they reflect the long-run effect of a decision on the shareholder's wealth. Total sales or share of product market objectives are also inadequate normative descriptions of corporate goals, although achieving these goals may also lead to maximization of the shareholders' wealth position by their positive effect on profits.

It is recognized that a complete statement of the organizational goals of a business enterprise might embrace a much wider range of considerations, including such things as the prestige, income, security, freedom, and power of the management group, and the contribution of the corporation to the overall social environment in which it exists and to the welfare of the labor force it employs. Since the managers of a corporation are acting on behalf of the common stockholders, there is a fiduciary relationship between the managers (and the board of directors) and the stockholders. The common stockholders, the suppliers of the risk capital, have entrusted a part of their wealth position to the firm's management. Thus the success of the firm and the appropriateness of management's decisions must be evaluated in terms of how well this fiduciary responsibility has been met. We define the primary objective of the firm to be the maximization of the value of the common stockholder's ownership rights in the firm but recognize that there are other objectives.

Managerial Finance

The study of managerial finance is concerned with the financial decisions of a firm (as distinct from the study of the structure of markets for obtaining capital). We break the firm's decisions down into three basic types:

1. Investment decisions or, more generally, the allocations of funds among different types of assets or activities.

2. The obtaining of capital in the appropriate mixture of debt and common stock or other securities.
3. The dividend decision (giving of funds back to common stock investors in return for the use of the capital).

We shall find that there are analytical methods of analyzing all of these decisions. In some cases, we can reach fairly definite judgments as to correct and incorrect decisions; in others, we can only identify the relevant quantitative and qualitative considerations.

Business organizations are continually faced with the problem of deciding whether the commitments of resources—time or money—are worthwhile in terms of the expected benefits. If the benefits are likely to accrue reasonably soon after the expenditure is made, and if both the expenditure and the benefits can be measured in dollars, the solution to such a problem is relatively simple. If the expected benefits are likely to accrue over several years, the solution is more complex.

We shall use the term *investment* to refer to commitments of resources made in the hope of realizing benefits that are expected to occur over a reasonably long period of time in the future. Capital budgeting is a many-sided activity that includes searching for new and more profitable investment proposals, investigating engineering and marketing considerations to predict the consequences of accepting the investment, and making economic analyses to determine the profit potential of each investment proposal.

The Finance Managers

Finance managers (financial vice-presidents, controllers, treasurers, etc.) are responsible for a wide range of decisions made in a corporation. The accounts that appear on a balance sheet can be used to describe the tasks of a finance manager. On the asset side, there is the administration of current assets (managing cash, investing in short-term securities, and determining and administering a credit policy) and long-term assets (i.e., making capital budgeting decisions that commit the company to investments in long-lived assets). Shifting to the equity side of the balance sheet, the finance manager is responsible for offering advice as to the best financial structure (determining the relative use of debt, preferred stock, or common stock) and the characteristics of the firm's securities and then implementing the decisions that are made.

Most of the chapters in this book can be related to decisions that involve one or more of the accounts on a balance sheet. There are many types of decisions that the finance manager must solve, such as buy versus lease, dividend payout, and retirement of debt decisions. This book will offer suggestions on how to improve the likelihood of making the correct decision, although frequently it will be seen that absolutely correct choices cannot be made.

To study problems of a manageable size, we shall generally assume that a specific decision does not affect other decisions. This naive assumption may not be valid because of the interrelationships of decisions, but it does enable us to gain understanding. After this understanding is achieved, the complexities can be introduced. We shall learn to walk before we try to run.

Time, Risk, and the Risk-Return Trade-off

The two primary factors that make finance an interesting and complex subject are the elements of *time* and *risk*. Because decisions today often affect cash flow for many future time periods and we are not certain as to the outcomes of our actions, we have to formulate decision rules that take risk and time value into consideration in a systematic fashion. These two problems are as intellectually challenging as any problems that one is likely to encounter in the world of economic activity.

Frequently, the existence of uncertainty means that the decision maker faces alternatives that involve trade-offs of less return and less risk or more return and more risk. A large part of the study of finance has to do with learning how to approach this type of risk-return trade-off choice.

Three Basic Generalizations

We offer three generalizations that are useful in the types of financial decisions that are to be discussed. The first generalization is that investors prefer more return (cash) to less, all other things being equal. Investors who thought that the returns were excessively high could distribute the excess in such a manner that the results would meet their criterion of fairness.

The second generalization is that investors prefer less risk (a possibility of loss) to more risk and have to be paid to undertake risky endeavors. This generalization is contrary to common observations such as the existence of race tracks and gambling casinos (the customers of such establishments are willing to pay for the privilege of undertaking risky investments), but the generalization is useful even if it does not apply to everyone all the time.

The third generalization is that everyone prefers cash to be received today rather than for the same amount to be received in the future. This only requires the reasonable assumption that the funds received today can be invested to earn some positive return. Since this is the situation in the real world, the generalization is reasonable.

These three generalizations are used implicitly and explicitly throughout the book.

Relevance of Cash Flows

Given the objective of stockholder wealth maximization, how should individual financial decisions be evaluated? For the publicly traded firm, it may be convenient to assume that the market value of the stock is a reasonable measure of wealth. The market's assessment of the firm's future is incorporated in the stock price, even though this assessment is not always an accurate forecast of the future. At any moment, the market's assessment of the value of some firms is too high, while its assessment of the value of other firms is too low, compared to the values that ultimately occur through time. Unfortunately, there is no means by which even well-informed and astute investors can identify which firms are overvalued and which are undervalued with 100 percent accuracy. For most investors, who are not in possession of special inside information (information known only to persons working for or with a firm), the market value of a firm is the best available measure of its investment worth. For the privately held firm, for which there is no regularly reported market value, the wealth position of the owner is even more difficult to assess than where there is a market valuation.

Theoretically, alternative actions should be evaluated based on the extent to which they will improve the market value of the stock and those actions leading to a maximization of value should be chosen. Unfortunately, although this evaluation scheme is theoretically correct, it is not operational, for the chain of relationships between a decision and its ultimate impact on the value of common stock equity is long and complicated and is generally not known with certainty. As stated, even the decision time horizon may affect the choice of decision.

We cannot provide unambiguous decision rules for all occasions, but we can suggest that there is an approach that is consistently useful in decision making. Any decision that is expected to alter the anticipated cash flows of the firm is likely to alter the value of the firm's common stock. Cash is the common element in all decisions: For a firm to undertake investments requires it, creditors are paid with it, and stockholders expect to receive it in the form of dividends or when they sell their stock. Any decision can be characterized by the set of incremental cash flows that its acceptance is expected to cause, and thus most decisions can be reduced to evaluating incremental cash flows.

Throughout this book we shall be characterizing alternate courses of action in this fashion and discussing the evaluation of alternate cash flow patterns. It would be an overstatement to say that all decisions can be characterized and evaluated in terms of incremental cash flow, since some aspects of decisions are wholly nonquantifiable, yet the vast majority of business decisions both day to day and strategic can and should be expressed in those terms. Even decisions that have large elements that do not lend themselves to exact cash flow analysis have segments that can be described in cash flow terms. For example, we may not be able to quantify the expected benefits of a research project, but we should be able to define the cash flows of the costs to be incurred. This information may be sufficient to determine if proceeding with the research is desirable.

Cash Flows Versus Earnings

A decision may be characterized by its effect on earnings as well as by its incremental cash flows. The earnings and cash flows would lead to consistent decisions if it were not for the fact that earnings are affected by many accounting conventions, such as expense versus capitalization decisions and the choice of a depreciation method. Thus an investment might generate substantial cash flows in its late years but adversely affect profits during the early years if the initial investment is depreciated more rapidly than is justified by its economic characteristics. If we assume that the firm has sufficient cash inflows with which to meet its cash obligations, the investment may be desirable regardless of its lack of short-run profitability. Of course, long-run profitability is a necessary condition. If all the relevant expenses cannot be covered over the life of the decision, then the effect of the decision on the stockholders' wealth position will be negative.

Since cash flows are easily measured, when properly discounted for time and adjusted for risk, their present value is a good proxy for the present value of profits. We consider cash flows to be a relevant measure of the impact of a decision on the firm and will use cash flows as the primary input in the decision to be analyzed. After the decision has been made, income measures tend to be easier to use as inputs into performance measurement calculations.

Any decisions involving measurable cash flows over one or more periods may be implemented by using the capital budgeting procedures to be developed in this book.

The Capital Market

Corporations at some stage in their life go to the capital market to obtain funds. The market that supplies financial resources is called the capital market and it consists of all savers (banks, insurance companies, pension funds, people, etc). The capital market gathers resources from the savers of society (people who consume less than they earn) and rations these savings out to the organizations that have a need for new capital and that can pay the price that the capital market defines for capital.

The availability of funds (the supply) and the demand for funds determine the cost of funds to the organizations obtaining new capital and the return to be earned by the suppliers of capital. The measure of the cost of new capital becomes very important to a business firm in the process of making decisions involving the use of capital. We shall have occasion to use the market cost of funds (the interest rate) frequently in our analyses, and you should be aware of the relevance of capital market considerations to the decisions of the firm.

Actually, there is not one market cost of funds; rather, there is a series of different but related costs depending on the specific terms on which the capital is obtained and the amount of risk associated with the security. One of the important objectives of this book is to develop an awareness of the cost of the different forms of capital (common stock, preferred stock, debt, retained earnings, etc.) and of the factors that determine these costs. This is a complex matter, since the cost of a specific form of capital for one firm will depend on the returns investors can obtain from other firms, on the characteristics of the assets of the firm that is attempting to raise additional capital, and on the capital structure of the firm. We can expect that the larger the risk, the higher the return that will be needed to attract investors.

Tactical and Strategic Decisions

Investment decisions may be tactical or strategic. A tactical investment decision generally involves a relatively small amount of funds and does not constitute a major departure from what the firm has been doing in the past. The consideration of a new machine tool by Ford Motor Company is a tactical decision, as is a buy or lease decision made by Mobil Oil Company.

Strategic investment decisions involve large sums of money and may also result in a major departure from what the company has been doing in the past. Strategic decisions directly affect the basic course of the company. Acceptance of a strategic investment will involve a significant change in the company's expected profits and in the risks to which these profits will be subject. These changes are likely to lead stockholders and creditors to revise their evaluation of the company. If a private corporation undertook the development of a supersonic commercial transport (costing over $4 billion), this would be a strategic decision. If the company failed in its attempt to develop the commercial plane, the very existence of the company would be jeopardized. Frequently, strategic decisions are based on intuition rather than on detailed quantitative analysis.

The Role of Strategy in Investment Decision Making

The investment strategy of a firm is a statement of the formal criteria it applies in searching for and evaluating investment opportunities. Strategic planning guides the search for projects by identifying promising product lines or geographic areas in which to search for good investment projects. One firm may seek opportunities for rapid growth in emerging high-technology businesses; another may seek opportunities to become the low-cost producer of commodities with well-established technologies and no unusual market problems; a third firm may look for opportunities to exploit its special knowledge of a particular family of chemicals. A strategy should reflect both the special skill and abilities of the firm (its comparative advantage) and the opportunities that are available as a result of dynamic changes in the world economy.

Strategic planning leads to a choice of the forest; project analysis studies and chooses between individual trees. The two activities should complement and reinforce each other. Project analysis may provide a feedback loop to verify the accuracy of the strategic plan. If there are good opportunities where the strategic plan says they should be found, and few promising opportunities in lines of business that the strategy identifies as unattractive, confidence in

---

The Quaker Oats Company

An extract from the company's 1983 Annual Report (Letter to Shareholders from the Chairman and President) follows.

The inside cover of this year's annual report provides visual highlights of our 1983 fiscal year. The strategic steps presented are part of an ongoing process—the shaping of The Quaker Oats Company in an evolutionary way to maximize value for our shareholders. Our Financial Objectives provide the benchmarks for measuring our progress towards that goal over time. The Operating Strategies that flow from these objectives indicate the path we intend to take. The specific steps taken in any one year should clearly be consistent with and contribute to achieving these Objectives and Strategies over the long term. We believe that the Company will maximize value for its shareholders by achieving a balance between solid profitable growth over the long term and consistent favorable returns on investment from year to year.

the strategic plan increases. Alternatively, if attractive projects are not found where the plan had expected them, or if desirable projects appear in lines of business that the strategic plan had identified as unattractive, a reassessment of both the project studies and the strategic plan may be in order.

Conclusions

The study of finance should be an exciting and stimulating experience, since it is an opportunity to eliminate a large number of common misunderstandings and to add to your understanding of financial instruments and decisions. You will be better able to manage your own personal financial affairs.

The basic building blocks of this book are three generalizations that are introduced in this chapter:

1. Investors prefer more expected return to less.
2. Investors prefer less risk to more risk.
3. Investors prefer an amount of cash to be received earlier than the same amount to be received later.

All modern finance is built on these generalizations. Some investors accept or seek risk, but they normally do so with the hope of some monetary gain. They expect to be compensated for the risk they undertake.

Corporations, or more exactly, the managers running the corporations, have many different goals. We have simplified the complex set of objectives that exist to one basic objective, the maximization of the value of the stockholders' ownership rights in the firm. While a simplification, it enables us to make specific recommendations as to how corporate financial decisions should be made.

We shall find that while some financial decisions may be solved exactly, more frequently we shall only be able to define and analyze the problem. We may not always be able to identify the optimum decision with certainty, but we shall generally be able to describe some errors in analysis to avoid. In just about all areas in corporate finance, useful insights for improved decision making can be obtained by applying modern finance theory.

PROBLEMS

1. Can a firm have income without also having a positive cash flow? Explain.

2. If a firm currently earning $1 million can increase its accounting income to $1.1 million (an action consistent with profit maximization), is this a desirable move? Explain.

3. A sales manager is proud of having doubled sales in the past four years. What questions should be asked before praising the manager?

4. A president of an automobile manufacturing firm has the opportunity to double the firm's profits in the next year. To accomplish this profit increase, the quality of the product (currently the prestige car of the world market) must be reduced. No additional investment is required.
   What do you recommend?

5. Name an "economic cost" that is omitted from the accounting income statements that should be of interest to management.

6. Individuals, corporations, cities, and countries (federal governments) all borrow funds. Describe differences in the processes and purposes to which the funds are likely to be placed.

7. Describe several financial decisions you have made recently. Are there corporate counterparts?

8. Make a list of different types of investment or product decisions that a firm is likely to make and describe the nature of the incremental cash flows derived from them.

9. The ABC Company can undertake an investment that is economically desirable. It will adversely affect current earnings, but in management's judgment will benefit future earnings. Management fears that the stock market will interpret the decrease in earnings as a sign of weakness and the common stock price will immediately go down as the lower earnings are reported. Management plans to describe the characteristics of the investment in the annual report and in meetings with security analysts. The company's primary goal is to maximize the well-being of its stockholders.

   (a) What would a decrease in stock price as a result of the investment imply about the stock market?
   (b) What does the decrease in income as a result of the investment imply about the accounting measures?
   (c) Should the company undertake the investment?

10. In a socialist economy would you expect a plant (firm) to earn a profit? Explain.

11. The ABC Company has to make a choice between two strategies:

    Strategy 1: Is expected to result in a market price now of $100 per share of common stock and a price of $120 five years from now.
    Strategy 2: Is expected to result in a market price now of $80 and a price of $140 five years from now.

What do you recommend? Assume that all other things are unaffected by the decision being considered.

12. It has been said that few stockholders would think favorably of a project that promised its first cash flow in 100 years, no matter how large this return.

    Comment on this position.

13. Each of the following is sometimes listed as a reasonable objective for a firm: (a) maximize profit (accounting income), (b) maximize sales (or share of the market), (c) maximize the value of a share of common stock *t* time periods from now, (d) ensure continuity of existence, (e) maximize the rate of growth, (f) maximize future dividends.

    Discuss each item and the extent of its relevance to the making of investment decisions.

14. Discuss the following statement:

    Professionalism in management is regularly equated with hardheaded rationality. We saw it surface at ITT in Harold Geneen's search for the "unshakable facts." It flourished in Vietnam, where success was measured by body counts. Its wizards were the Ford Motor Company's whiz kids, and its grand panjandrum was Robert McNamara. The numerative, rationalist approach to management dominates the business schools. It teaches us that well-trained professional managers can manage anything. It seeks detached, analytical justification for all decisions. It is right enough to be dangerously wrong, and it has arguably led us seriously astray.*

REFERENCES

A number of excellent introductory and intermediate financial management texts are available to be used in conjunction with this book to provide a parallel description of many of the decisions we discuss and to fill the reader in on institutional material. Among them are the following:

Archer, S. H., G. M. Choate, and G. Racette. *Financial Management*. New York: John Wiley & Sons, Inc., 1983.

Brealey, R., and S. Myers. *Principles of Corporate Finance*. New York: McGraw-Hill Book Company, 1984.

Copeland, T. E., and J. F. Weston. *Financial Theory and Corporate Policy*. Reading, Mass: Addison-Wesley Publishing Company, 1983.

Fama, E. F., and M. H. Miller. *The Theory of Finance*. New York: Holt, Rinehart and Winston, 1972.

* Thomas J. Peters and Robert H. Waterman, Jr., *In Search of Excellence* (New York: Harper & Row, 1982) p. 29.

Levy H., and M. Sarnat. *Capital Investment and Financial Decisions*. Englewood Cliffs, N.J.: Prentice-Hall, Inc., 1982.

Schall, L. D., and C. W. Haley. *Financial Management*. New York: McGraw-Hill Book Company, 1983.

Van Horne, James C. *Financial Management and Policy*. Englewood Cliffs, N.J.: Prentice-Hall, Inc., 1983.

For a very complete description of the functions of corporate financial officers, see:

Davey, P. J. *New Patterns in Organizing for Financial Management*. New York: The Conference Board, 1983.

For an excellent summary of modern corporate finance, *see*:

Jensen, M. C., and C. W. Smith, Jr (eds). *The Modern Theory of Corporate Finance*. New York: McGraw-Hill Book Company, 1984.

Chapter 2

The Time Value of Money

Major Topics

1. The importance of time value of money.
2. The calculations for computing the future value and present value of cash flows using discrete and continuous discounting.
3. The basic calculations for annuities and perpetuities.
4. Annual equivalent amounts.
5. Effective and nominal interest rates.

Time Discounting

One of the basic concepts of business economics and managerial decision making is that the value of an amount of money is a function of the time of receipt or disbursement of the cash. A dollar received today is more valuable than a dollar to be received in some future time period. The only requirement for this concept to be valid is that there be a positive rate of interest at which funds can be invested.

The time value of money affects a wide range of business decisions, and a knowledge of how to incorporate time value considerations systematically into a decision is essential to an understanding of finance. This chapter is devoted to describing the mathematical models of compound interest. The objective is to develop skills in finding the present equivalent of a future amount or future amounts and the future equivalent of a present amount. This framework is then applied to a variety of business decisions.

In the next chapter we shall describe investment decision-making techniques for bonds and stocks that build on the time value calculations of this chapter. Later, we use time value in a firm's evaluation of investments in real assets.

The Interest Rate

A dollar available today is more valuable than a dollar available one period from now if investment opportunities exist. There are two primary reasons why real investments can generate an interest return:

1. Some types of capital increase in value through time because of changes in physical characteristics, for example, cattle, wine, and trees.
2. There are many work processes where roundabout methods of production are desirable, leading to increased productivity. If you are going to cut down a large tree, it may be worth investing some time to sharpen your axe. A sharp axe may result in less time being spent cutting down trees (including sharpening time) than working with a dull axe. If you are going to dig a hole, you might want to build or buy a shovel, or even spend the time to manufacture a back-hoe if it is a big hole. The investment increases productivity sufficiently compared to the alternative methods of production without capital so that the new asset can earn a return.

These characteristics of capital lead to a situation in which business entities can pay interest for the use of money. If you invest $1 in an industrial firm, the firm may be able to pay you $1 plus interest if your savings enabled the firm to use some roundabout method of production or to delay the sale of a product while it increased in value.

Future Value

Assume that you have $1.00 now and can invest it to earn r interest. After one period you will have the $1.00 plus the interest earned on the $1. Let FV be the future value and r be the annual interest rate. Then

$$FV = 1 + r$$

Repeating the process, at time 2 you will have

$$FV = (1 + r) + r(1 + r) = (1 + r)^2$$

and the future value of $1.00 invested for n periods is

$$FV = (1 + r)^n$$

If $r = .10$ and $n = 2$, we have

$$FV = (1 + r)^n = (\$1.10)^2 = \$1.21$$

If instead of starting with $1 we start with a present value, PV of $50, the value at time 2 is

$$FV = PV(1 + r)^n \tag{2.1}$$
$$FV = 50(\$1.10)^2 = \$60.50$$

The $50 grows to $55 at time 1. The $55 grows to $60.50 at time 2.

Equation (2.1) is the standard compound interest formula. The term $(1 + r)^n$ is called the accumulation factor.

The power of compounding (earning interest on interest) is dramatic. It can be illustrated by computing how long it takes to double the value of an investment. Table 2.1 shows these periods for different values of r.

A useful rule of thumb in finance is the "double-to-72" rule, where for wide ranges of interest rates, r, the approximate doubling time is $.72/r$. Note how closely the rule approximates the values in Table 2.1. With a .10 time value factor, an investment will double in value every 7.3 years. The rule of thumb gives 7.2 years.

Frequently, to make business decisions instead of computing future values, we shall want to work with present values.

TABLE 2.1   The Power of Compounding

Interest Rate (r)	Time Until Initial Value Is Doubled
.02	35.0 years
.05	14.2
.10	7.3
.15	5.0
.20	3.8

Time Indifference: Present Value

Today over 90 percent of large firms use some form of discounted cash flow (DCF) techniques in their capital budgeting (investment decision making). To perform a DCF analysis, we must find the present value equivalents of future sums of money. For example, if the firm will receive $100 one year from now as a result of a decision, we want to find the present value equivalent of the $100.00. Assuming that the money is worth (can be borrowed or lent at) .10 per year, the $100.00 is worth $90.91 now. The indifference can be shown by noting that $90.91 invested to earn .10 will earn $9.09 interest in one year; thus, the investor starting with $90.91 will have $100.00 at the end of the year. If the investor can both borrow and lend funds at .10, the investor would be indifferent between receiving $100.00 at the end of the year or $90.91 at the beginning of the year.

If the .10 interest rate applies for two time periods, the investor would be indifferent about receiving $82.64 today or $100.00 two years from today. If the $82.64 is invested to earn .10 per year, the investor will have $90.91 after one year and $100.00 at the end of two years.

The unit of time can be different from a year, but the unit of time for which the interest rate is measured must be the same as the unit of time for measuring the timing of the cash flows. For example, the .10 used in the example is defined as the interest rate per year and is applied to a period of one year.

Starting with equation (2.1) we have

$$FV = PV(1 + r)^n \tag{2.1}$$

Dividing both sides of equation (2.1) by $(1 + r)^n$ we obtain

$$PV = \frac{FV}{(1 + r)^n} \tag{2.2}$$

Using C_n to denote the cash flow at the end of period n and r to denote the time value of money, we find that the present value, PV, of C_n is

$$PV = \frac{C_n}{(1 + r)^n} \tag{2.3}$$

or, equivalently,

$$PV = C_n(1 + r)^{-n} \tag{2.4}$$

where $(1 + r)^{-n}$ is the present value of $1 to be received at the end of period n when the time value of money is r. The term $(1 + r)^{-n}$ is called the present value factor, and its value for various combinations of time periods and interest rates is found in Table A of the appendix to the book. Any hand calculator with the capability to compute y^x can be used to compute present value factors directly. If y^x is used, then $y = 1 + r$ and $x = n$. First, y^x is found, and then the reciprocal is taken to determine the present value factor. For example, to find the present value factor for $r = .10$, $n = 5$ using a typical calculator, we would place 1.10 in the calculator, press the y^x button, insert 5, press the "equals" button, and then the reciprocal to find .62092.

EXAMPLE 2.1

What is the present value of $1.00 to be received three time periods from now if the time value of money is .10 per period?

In Table A the .10 column and the line opposite n equal to 3 give .7513. If you invest $.7513 to earn .10 per year, after three years you will have $1.00. Also, $(1.10)^{-3} = .7513$.

What is the present value of $100.00 to be received three time periods from now if the time value of money is .10? Since $(1.10)^{-3} = .7513$ the present value of $100 is

PV $= \$100(.7513) = \$75.13$

If $75.13 is invested at time 0, the following growth takes place:

Time	Investment at Beginning of Period	Interest	Investment at End of Period
0	$75.13	$7.513	$82.643
1	82.643	8.264	90.907
2	90.907	9.091	100.000

If investors can earn .10 per period and can borrow at .10, then they are indifferent between $75.13 received at time 0 or $100 at time 3.

The present value of a series of cash flows is the sum of the present values of each of the components.

EXAMPLE 2.2

What is the present value of two cash flows, $100.00 and $200.00 to be received at the end of one and two periods from now, respectively, if the time value of money is .10?

Period (n)	Cash flow (C_n)	Present Value Factors Using a .10 Interest Rate	Present Value (PV)
1	$100	.9091	$ 90.91
2	200	.8264	165.28
		Present value using .10 =	$256.19

Present Value of an Annuity

Frequently, the evaluation of alternatives will involve a series of equal payments spaced equally through time. Such a series is called an annuity. The present value of an annuity of $1 per period for n periods with the first payment one period from now is the sum of the present values of each dollar to be received:

$$B(n, r) = \frac{1}{(1 + r)} + \frac{1}{(1 + r)^2} + \frac{1}{(1 + r)^3} + \cdots + \frac{1}{(1 + r)^n} \qquad (2.5)$$

where $B(n, r)$ is the symbolic representation for an annuity of n periods and an interest rate of r (first cash flow one period from now). It can be shown (see Appendix 2.1) at the end of this chapter) that

$$B(n, r) = \frac{1 - (1 + r)^{-n}}{r} \qquad (2.6)$$

Equation (2.6) is for an annuity in arrears. Appendix Table B at the end of the book gives the present values of annuities in arrears of $1 per period for different values of r and n. The present value of an annuity can also be computed directly using many hand calculators, or a personal computer.

If C dollars are received each period instead of $1, we can multiply equation (2.6) by C to obtain the present value of C dollars per period. That is, for an annuity for C dollars per period, the present value is

$$PV = C \cdot B(n, r) \qquad (2.7)$$

EXAMPLE 2.3 ─────────────────────────────────────

The ABC Company is to receive $1 a period for three periods, the first payment to be received one period from now. The time value factor is .10. Compute the present value of the annuity.

There are three equivalent solutions:

(a) From Table B,

$$B(3, .10) = 2.4869$$

(b) Using equation (2.6) and Table A,

$$B(3, .10) = \frac{1 - (1 + r)^{-n}}{r} = \frac{1 - .7513}{.10} = \frac{.2487}{.10} = 2.487$$

(c) Adding the first three entries in the .10 column in Table A,

$$(1.10)^{-1} = .9091$$
$$(1.10)^{-2} = .8264$$
$$(1.10)^{-3} = \underline{.7513}$$
$$B(3, .10) = 2.4868$$

If instead of $1 per period, the amount is $100.00, then using equation (2.7) we would multiply $2.487 by $100.00 and obtain $248.70.

An Annuity Due

When the first payment is at time 1, we have an annuity in arrears (also called an ordinary annuity). When the payment occurs at the beginning of each period, we have an annuity due (also called an annuity in advance). Equation (2.6) gives the present value of an annuity in arrears:

$$B(n, r) = \frac{1 - (1 + r)^{-n}}{r} \qquad (2.6)$$

If we have $(n + 1)$ payments with the first payment taking place immediately, we would merely add $1 to the value of equation (2.6). Thus if $B(3, .10)$ equals $2.4868, a four-payment annuity with the first payment at time 0 would have a present value of $3.4868. An n period annuity due is nothing more than an $(n - 1)$ period annuity in arrears plus the initial payment.

Present Value of a Perpetuity

A perpetuity is an annuity that goes on forever (an infinite series). If we let n of equation (2.6) go to infinity so that the annuity becomes a perpetuity, then the $(1 + r)^{-n}$ term goes to zero, and the present value of the perpetuity using equation (2.6) becomes

$$B(\infty, r) = \frac{1}{r} \qquad\qquad (2.8)$$

Thus, if $r = .10$ and the series of cash receipts of $1.00 per period are infinitely long, investors would pay $10.00 for the infinite series. They would not pay $11.00, since they could invest that $11.00 elsewhere and earn $1.10 per period at the going rate of interest, which is better than $1.00 per period. Investors would like to obtain the investment for $9.00, but no rational issuer of the security would commit to pay $1.00 per period in return for $9.00 when $10.00 could be obtained from other lenders for the same commitment.

Although perpetuities are seldom a part of real-life problems, they are useful, since they allow us to determine the value of extreme cases. For example, if $r = .10$, we may not know the present value of $1 per period for 50 time periods, but we do know that it is only a small amount less than $10 since the present value of a perpetuity of $1 per period is $10 and 50 years is close enough to being a perpetuity for us to use 10 as an approximate value:

$$B(\infty, r) = \frac{1}{r} = \frac{1}{.10} = \$10$$

A Flexible Tool

We now have the tools to solve a wide range of time value problems that have not been described. While we could introduce other formulas we prefer to adapt the three basic formulas that have been introduced.

For example, if a $60-per-year annuity for 20 years were to have its first payment at time 10 and if the interest rate is .10, the present value is

$$PV = CB(n, r)(1 + r)^{-t} = 60B(20, .10)(1.10)^{-9}$$

$$= 60(8.5136)(.4241) = \$216.64$$

Note that if the first annuity payment is at time 10, we only have to discount the annuity for nine years to find the present value since $B(n, r)$ gives the annuity value as of time 9.

If one were to invest $216.64 at time 0 to earn .10 per year, then at time 10 one could withdraw $60 and could withdraw $60 a year for 20 years ($1,200 in total). If we turned the problem around, we could determine how much we would have at time 29 if we saved $60 per year for 20 years, with the first amount saved starting at time 10.

$$\text{future value} = \$216.64(1.10)^{29} = \$216.64(15.8631) = \$3,437$$

Equivalently,

$$\text{future value} = \$60B(20, .10)(1.10)^{20} = \$60(8.5136)(6.7275) = \$3,437.$$

Now let us do the same problem but assume the annuity starting at time 10 is a perpetuity. The present value at time 9 is $60/.10 = $600. The present value of the $600 at time 0 is

$$PV = \$600(1.10)^{-9} = \$600(.4241) = \$254.46$$

Another approach to solving for the present value is to compute the present value of a perpetuity and subtract the present value of a nine period annuity:

$$PV = \$600 - \$60B(9, .10) = \$600 - \$60(5.7590) = \$254.46$$

It is important that you realize the extreme flexibility of the basic time discounting tools. These tools are sufficient for solving any time value problem.

Annual Equivalent Amounts

In many situations we will desire to determine the annual equivalent of a given sum. For example, what is the annual equivalent over 20 years of $100,000 received today if the time value of money is 10 percent?

The answer to this question lies in equation (2.7), which, when solved for the annual cash flow, is

$$C = \frac{PV}{B(n, r)} \tag{2.9}$$

That is, to find the annual equivalent, C, of a present sum, PV, that sum is divided by the annuity factor, $B(n, r)$, where r is the time value of money and n is the number of years over which the annual equivalent is to be determined.

Calculations of this type are particularly useful in. the management of financial institutions such as insurance companies or banks, where customers make periodic payments over an extended time period in return for a lump-sum immediate loan.

EXAMPLE 2.4 —————————————————————————————

The ABC Company wishes to borrow $10,000 from the City Bank, repayable in three annual installments (the first one due one year from now). If the bank charges .10 interest, what will be the annual payments?
From equation (2.9),

$$C = \frac{10,000}{B(3, .10)}$$

$$= \frac{10,000}{2.4869} = \$4,021$$

and the loan amortization schedule is

(1)	(2)	(3) Interest	(4)	(5) = (2) + (3) − (4)
Time	Beginning Balance	.10 of (2)	Payment	Ending Balance
0	$10,000	$1,000	$4,021	$6,979
1	6,979	698	4,021	3,656
2	3,656	366	4,021	0

The loan amortization schedule starts with the initial amount owed. Column 2 shows the interest on the amount owed at the beginning of the period (column 2). Column 4 is the payment to pay the debt and column 5 shows the ending debt balance. The ending debt balance is equal to the beginning debt balance plus the period's interest less the debt payment.
The process is repeated for the life of the debt. If the present value of the debt payments is equal to the initial beginning balance (as it will be using the effective cost of debt), the ending balance after the last debt payment will be equal to zero.

Effective and Nominal Interest Rates

In most capital budgeting decisions faced by a firm, the decision makers will use annual cash flows and an annual rate of interest; in other types of financial analysis, particularly with loan and savings transactions, it is sometimes convenient to use months or some other unit of time. Tables A and B are for "periods" of time where the periods may be defined to be any unit of time.

It is useful to distinguish between the effective and the nominal rate of interest in cases where the interest rate is stated in terms of one period of time but applied over a different period of time with compounding (reinvestment of the principal plus accrued interest). For example, if the nominal annual rate of interest is .10 per year and the nominal quarterly effective rate of interest is .025, with interest being compounded quarterly, the effective annual rate is .1038.

Let

r = the effective annual rate

j = the nominal rate for a year

$\dfrac{j}{m}$ = the effective rate for a fraction of a year

m = the number of compoundings in a year, for example for quarterly compoundings $m = 4$

The nominal annual rate is equal to j. For the example, $j = .10$ and $m = 4$, and the effective rate for a quarter is .025. The effective annual rate r may be computed using

$$1 + r = \left(1 + \frac{j}{m}\right)^{m} \tag{2.10}$$

or

$$r = \left(1 + \frac{j}{m}\right)^{m} - 1 \tag{2.11}$$

For the example, we have

$$r = (1.025)^{4} - 1 = 1.1038 - 1 = .1038$$

For example, suppose that a bank pays a nominal 7.75 percent annual interest rate on savings, but compounds quarterly. The nominal rate per quarter is $7.75/4 = 1.9375\%$ per quarter. The annual effective rate is

$$(1.019375)^4 - 1 = .07978$$

or very nearly 8 percent. If a competing bank offers the same nominal rate but compounds daily, the daily effective rate is $7.75/365 = .021233\%$ per day, and the annual effective rate in this case is

$$(1 + .0775/365)^{365} - 1 = .08057$$

In this instance going from quarterly to daily compounding increases the annual effective rate by about .0008 per year. The difference may be negligible to an individual with a savings account of only a few thousand dollars, but it is important to a corporate treasurer responsible for investing temporarily excess funds that may amount to millions of dollars. On $10 million, the interest rate differential amounts to nearly $2,000 per quarter.

As was indicated, the choice of time period varies from one situation to another. Most short-term instruments have interest compounded on a daily basis. A $1,000 90-day loan at nominal 8.5 percent annual interest assuming a 365-day year would require a payment of

$$\$1,000 \left(1 + \frac{.085}{365}\right)^{90} = \$1,021.18$$

Stating this loan as a realized annual interest rate yields

$$\left(1 + \frac{.085}{365}\right)^{365} - 1 = .0887$$

or 8.87 percent per year.

Continuous Cash Flows and Continuous Discounting

While it is generally assumed in this book that cash flows occur instantaneously at the end of a period and that interest is compounded annually, either or both of these assumptions may be varied. Interest may be compounded monthly, weekly, daily, or continuously. Instead of assuming that the cash flows occur at the end of a year, they may also be presumed to occur monthly, weekly, daily, or continuously. We now explain continuous compounding of interest.

Assume that a nominal annual interest rate of .12 is compounded twice during the year. If m is the number of annual compoundings, for $m = 2$ we have

$$\left(1 + \frac{j}{m}\right)^m = \left(1 + \frac{.12}{2}\right)^2 = (1.06)^2 = 1.1236 \tag{2.10}$$

The effective annual interest rate is .1236.

If $m = 12$,

$$\left(1 + \frac{.12}{12}\right)^{12} = (1.01)^{12} = 1.2683$$

If $m = 365$, so that we have daily compounding of interest,

$$\left(1 + \frac{.12}{365}\right)^{365} = (1.000329)^{365} = 1.12747$$

If m is allowed to increase beyond bound (approach infinity), we obtain e^{jn} as the accumulation factor (see Appendix 2.2) where e is equal to 2.71828 and is the base of the natural or Naperian system of logarithms. If $j = .12$ and $n = 1$, we have $e^{.12} = 1.12750$. The use of continuous compounding leads to a larger future value than does the use of discrete compounding.

We can use e^{jn} to find the future value and e^{-jn} to find the present value for n years with interest compounded continuously at an annual rate of j:

$$FV = e^{jn} \tag{2.11}$$

$$PV = e^{-jn} \tag{2.12}$$

EXAMPLE 2.5 ——————————————————————————————

Let

$$j = .02$$

$$n = 1$$

To compute the present value of a dollar to be received at time 1, assuming that interest is compounded continuously,

$$PV = e^{-jn} = e^{-.02}$$

$$PV = e^{-.02} = (2.71828)^{-.02}$$

(2.13)

We can make use of a calculator or table for finding values of e^{-x}.

$$e^{-.02} = .9802.$$

The .9802 resulting from continuous compounding can be compared with .9804, which is the present value of a dollar, using 2 percent compounded annually. The difference between annual compounding and continuous compounding increases as the level of interest rates increase.

Examples of the present values using different interest rates (j) and different time periods (n) follow:

EXAMPLE 2.6

j (continuous interest rate)	n (number of periods)	jn	Present Values (e^{-jn})
.05	1	.05	.951229
.05	2	.10	.904837
.05	3	.15	.860708
.15	1	.15	.860708
.075	2	.15	.860708

.1823   -.833

Any calculator that includes the e^x and $\ln x$ functions can be used to make these calculations.

We can convert from interest rates assuming annual compounding to equivalent interest rates assuming continuous compounding, and vice versa. Suppose that r is the rate assuming annual compounding, and j is the equivalent continuous rate. Then the following relation must hold if we are to have the same present or future value independent of discrete or continuous discounting:

$$(1 + r) = e^j \qquad (2.14)$$

or

$$r = e^j - 1 \qquad (2.15)$$

or

$$j = \ln (1 + r) \qquad (2.16)$$

To convert from a continuous rate j to the corresponding annual compounding rate, we use $r = e^j - 1$. Alternatively, taking the log of both sides of the first relation, we have $j = \ln (1 + r)$. Table 2.2 shows the continuous equivalents of some representative annual rates. For interest rates below 10

TABLE 2.2 Continuous Interest Rates Equivalent to Various Annually Compounded Interest Rates

Annual Rate	Equivalent Continuous Rate $j = \ln (1 + r)$
.01	.00995
.02	.01980
.03	.02956
.04	.03922
.05	.04879
.10	.09531
.15	.13976
.20	.18232
.25	.22314
.30	.26236
.40	.33647
.50	.40547
1.00	.69315
11.00	2.48491
22,025.46	10.00000

percent, the differences between continuous compounding and annual compounding are not of practical significance for most managerial applications. When r or j becomes large, the divergence between their values becomes large.

EXAMPLE 2.7 ————————————————————————————

Compute the annual cost to a corporation for a debt with a .12 nominal cost if the interest is compounded:

(a) Annually.

    .12

(b) Every six months.

$$\left(1 + \frac{.12}{2}\right)^2 - 1 = .1236$$

(c) Every month.

$$(1.01)^{12} - 1 = .1268$$

(d) Continuously.

$$r = e^{.12} - 1 = .1275$$

Continuous Payments

Instead of $1 being received at the end of each year, there may be m payments per year, each payment being an amount of $1/m$ dollars. The total received during each year is $1. If m becomes very large (approaches a limit so that we receive $1 per year in a large number of small installments), the present value of a series of such payments extending over n years, with interest compounded continuously at a rate j, will be

$$\text{present value} = \frac{1 - e^{-jn}}{j} \tag{2.17}$$

Goldome

In September 1984, Goldome, the largest mutual savings bank in the United States, published the following information

Bank	Effective Annual Yield	Interest
Goldome	12.75%	12.00%
Citibank	12.19%	11.50%
Chase	12.02%	11.35%
Dime	12.01%	11.77%
Dollar Dry Dock	11.77%	11.125%

It is not clear how the 12.00% is connected to the 12.75% effective annual yield. But consider that

$$1 + r = e^{j}$$

and

$$1 + r = e^{.12} = 1.1275$$
$$r = .1275$$

and for 11.50 percent

$$r = e^{.115} - 1 = .1219$$

and for 11.35 percent

$$r = e^{.1135} - 1 = .1202.$$

$e = 2.71828$

EXAMPLE 2.8 ———————————————————————————

Compute the present value of $1 per period, assuming that interest is compounded continuously and the cash flows occur continuously.

$$j = .02$$

$$n = 1$$

$$e^{-jn} = e^{-.02} = .9802$$

$$\text{PV} = \frac{1 - e^{-jn}}{j} = \frac{1 - .9802}{.02} \tag{2.17}$$

$$= \frac{.0198}{.02} = .99$$

The .99 should be compared with the .9802, obtained in the preceding example with continuous compounding but one instantaneous payment, and the .9804 of annual compounding and one payment.
If $n = 15$,

$$e^{-jn} = e^{-.02(15)} = e^{-.3} = .7408$$

$$\frac{1 - e^{-jn}}{j} = \frac{1 - .7408}{.02} = 12.959 \tag{2.17}$$

With discrete discounting of instantaneous receipts, and with $r = .02$ and $n = 15$, we have

$$B(15, .02) = \frac{1 - (1 + r)^{-n}}{r} = 12.849 \tag{2.6}$$

Note the two present values are reasonably close since the interest rate is very small.

———————————————————————————————————————

Conclusions

Most investment analyses performed by a company are made on the basis of annual cash flows. Finer divisions of time are usually unwarranted in light of the roughness of the cash flow estimates. Some firms use present value tables that assume the cash flows are distributed evenly over the year or occur at the midpoint of the year in question rather than at the end of the year, as do the present value tables at the end of this book. Such refinements add little to the substance of discounted cash flow analysis and are not likely to alter materially any investment decision obtained from using the "end-of-year" assumption.

Most financial decision making can be reduced to evaluating incremental or alternative cash flows. There are three steps in the analysis. First, the relevant incremental cash flows must be estimated. Second, there must be some means of dealing with uncertainty if the cash flows are not known with certainty. Third, there must be some way to take into consideration the time value of money. The material in this chapter is essential for dealing with the time value of money to determine the present and future values of certain sums of money to be received or paid at various times. In the next chapter, we shall apply the time value concepts to the valuation of debt and common stock.

Review Problem 2.1

(a) If the interest rate per month is .025 compounded monthly, what is the annual equivalent rate?

(b) If \$100 will grow into \$118 in one year, what is the continuous rate of growth?

(c) If \$100 will grow continuously at .20 for one year, what is the discrete annual rate of growth that will lead to the same future value?

(d) What is the continuous equivalent to a .20 discrete rate of discount?

Solution to Review Problem 2.1

(a) $(1.025)^{12} - 1 = .3449$

(b) $100e^j = 118$

$e^j = 1.18$

$j = \ln 1.18 = .1655144$

(c) $1 + r = e^j = e^{.20} = 1.2214$

$r = .2214$

(d) $e^j = 1 + r$

$j = \ln (1 + r) = \ln (1.20) = .18232$

Review Problem 2.2

Exactly 15 years from now, Jones will start receiving a pension of $20,000 a year. The payments will continue forever. How much is the pension worth now, assuming that money is worth .10 per year?

Solution to Review Problem 2.2

The present value at time 14 is $200,000.
The present value at time 0 is

$$200,000(1.10)^{-14} = 200,000(.26333)$$

$$= \$52,666$$

Review Problem 2.3

(a) Twelve rental payments of $1,000 will be paid monthly at the end each month. The monthly interest rate is .01. What is the present value of the payments?
(b) If the payments are at the beginning of each month, what is the present value?

Solution to Review Problem 2.3

(a) $1,000B(12, .01) = \$1,000(11.2551) = \$11,255$
(b) $1,000[B(11, .01) + 1] = \$1,000(10.3676 + 1) = \$11,368$
  or $11,255(1.01) = \$11,368$

PROBLEMS

1. Assume a .05-per-year time value of money. Compute the value of $100 (a) received 1 year from now, (b) received immediately, (c) received at the end of 5 years, (d) received at the beginning of the sixth year, (e) received

at the end of 50 years, (f) received at the end of 50 years, but with an interest rate of .10.

2. Assume that the interest rate is .10. Compute the present value of $1 per year for four years (first payment one year from now) using three different methods (Table A, Table B, and an equation).

3. Assume a .05 time value of money. Compute the value of the following series of payments of $100 a year received for (a) 5 years, the first payment received 1 year from now; (b) 4 years, the first of 5 payments received immediately; (c) 10 years, the first payment received 1 year from now; (d) 9 years, the first of 10 payments received immediately.

4. Assume a .05 time value of money. The sum of $100 received immediately is equivalent to what quantity received in 10 equal annual payments, the first to be received one year from now? What would be the annual amount if the first of 10 payments were received immediately?

5. Assume a .05 time value of money. We have a debt to pay and are given a choice of paying $1,000 now or some amount X five years from now. What is the maximum amount that X can be for us to be willing to defer payment for five years?

6. We can make an immediate payment now of $10,000 or pay equal amounts of R for the next five years (first payment due one year from now). With a time value of money of .05, what is the maximum value of R that we would be willing to accept?

7. If the interest rate per month is .05, compounded quarterly, what is the annual equivalent rate?

8. If a firm borrowed $100,000 for one year and paid back $9,455.96 per month, what is the cost of the debt?

9. A firm can save $10,000 per year for 15 years. If the time value of money is .10, how much better off will the firm be after the 15 years if it accomplishes the saving?

10. If the time value of money is .10, how much do you have to save per year for 20 years to have $50,000 per year for perpetuity? Assume that the first deposit is immediate and that the first payment will be at the beginning of the twenty-first year.

11. If $100 earns .08 per year, how much will the investor have at the end of 10 years? What is the present value of $100 due in 10 years if money is worth .08?

12. What is the present value of $20 per year for perpetuity if money is worth .10?

13. Refer to Problem 12. If the first payment is to be received in 11 years, what is the series of payments worth?

14. You are the loan officer of a bank. The ABC Company wants to borrow $100,000 and repay it with four equal annual payments (first payment due one year from now). You decide that the ABC Company should pay .10 per year on the loan.
    (a) What is the annual payment?
    (b) Complete the following debt amortization table:

Period	Amount Owed (beginning of year)	Interest	Principal	Amount Owed (end of year)
1	$100,000			
2				
3				
4				

(c) What would be the annual payment if the first of four equal payments is due immediately?

15. (a) If the interest rate per month is .02, compounded monthly, what is the annual effective equivalent rate?
    (b) How much do you have to save per year for 20 years in order to have $50,000 per year for perpetuity? $r = .10$. The first $50,000 payment will be received at time 21.
    (c) If $100 will grow into $120 in one year, what is the continuous rate of growth?

16. Assume a .10 interest rate. How much is a perpetuity of $1,000 per year worth?

17. Assume a .10 interest rate (you can borrow and lend at that rate). Specify which you would prefer:
    (a) $10,000 in cash or
        $1,000 per year for perpetuity (first payment received at the end of the first period).
    (b) $10,000 in cash or
        $1,100 per year for perpetuity (first payment received at the end of the first period).
    (c) $10,000 in cash or
        $900 per year for perpetuity (first payment received at the beginning of the first period).

18. (a) What would be the annual payments on an 8 percent per annum installment loan of $1,000 from a credit union with repayment over three years?
    (b) Write out the amortization schedule for the loan.
    (c) Now suppose that the payments were to be made on a semiannual basis; what would the semiannual payments be? Assume the .08 is a nominal rate.
    (d) Is the total paid in case (c) less or more than in the former case? Why?

19. With a continuous discount rate of .08 what is the present value of $400 per year received continuously for five years?

20. Assume that you have just purchased a $75,000 house. One bank will give you a 9 percent mortgage with repayment in equal annual installments over 20 years with $15,000 down payment. Another bank wants 10 percent rate of interest, but will give you a 25-year equal annual installment mortgage with a $15,000 down payment. Assuming that you have the $15,000, what deal will minimize the annual payment?

21. (a) How much do you have to save per year (at the end of each year) for 40 years in order to have $10,000 per year for perpetuity, first receipt starting in year 41? Use .10 as the time value factor.
    (b) If the interest rate being charged is .04 per quarter, compounded quarterly, what is the annual equivalent rate? Use discrete discounting.

22. Exactly 20 years from now Jones will start receiving a pension of $10,000 a year. The payments will continue for 30 years. How much is the pension worth now, assuming money is worth .05 per year?

23. (a) If the interest rate per month is .04 compounded monthly, what is the annual equivalent rate?
    (b) If $100 will grow into $110 in one year, what is the continuous rate of growth?
    (c) If $100 will grow continuously at .20 for one year, what is the discrete annual rate of growth?
    (d) What is the continuous equivalent to a .20 discrete rate of discount?

24. (a) We can make an immediate payment now of $10,000 or pay equal amounts of R for the next four years (first payment due one year from now). With a time value of money of .10, what is the maximum value of payment that we would be willing to make?
    (b) Now assume that the first of the *five* payments is *immediate*. What is the maximum value of payment we would be willing to make?

25. (a) Mr. Jones has 10 years until retirement. He wants to save enough to have $20,000 per year after retirement for perpetuity. Money will earn

.10. How much should he save each year? Assume that the first "draw down" in savings takes place at time 11.

(b) Mr. Smith is spending $12,548 more than he earns each year. He is borrowing at the end of each year at a cost of .10. Assume that he does this for 10 years. How much interest will he be paying each year starting at the end of year 10 (beginning of year 11)?

26. The ABC Company can invest $4,000 and earn $5,000 one year later.
(a) What is the annual return that will be earned if discrete discounting is used?
(b) What is the annual return that will be earned if continuous discounting is used?
(c) Now assume that the return will occur after one week. With discrete discounting, the annual return is _____ . With continuous discounting, the annual return is _____ .

27. The XYZ Company has borrowed $100,000. Payments will be made over a four-year period (first payment at the end of the first year). The bank charges interest of .20 per year.
(a) The annual payment will be _____ .
(b) The debt amortization schedule is

Amount Owed (beginning of period)	Interest	Principal
1. $100,000		
2.		
3.		
4.		

(c) If there are five payments with the first payment made at the moment of borrowing, the annual payment will be _____ .

28. The ABC Company can invest $4,000 in a single positive payment investment and earn .12 per year.
(a) What is the total value of the investment after 15 years if discrete growth is used?
(b) What is the total value of the single positive payment investment after 15 years of continuous growth (at an annual continuous rate of .12)?
(c) With discrete discounting the annual interest rate is .20. With continuous discounting, the annual interest rate that will give the same present value as the .20 discrete rate is _____ .

29. The XYZ Company has borrowed $40,000. Equal payments will be made over a three-year period (first payment at the end of the first year). The bank charges interest of .15 per year.
    (a) The annual payment will be _____ .
    (b) The debt amortization schedule is

Amount Owed (beginning of period)	Interest	Principal Payment
1. $40,000		
2.		
3.		
4.		

    (c) If there are four equal payments with the first payment made at the moment of borrowing, the annual payment will be _____ .

30. (a) An investor will save $1,000 per year for 10 years (first payment at time 1). At time 10, the investor will have _____ , and starting at time 11, the investor will be able to spend _____ per year. The interest rate is .20.
    (b) Mr. Jones has 10 years until retirement. He wants to save enough to have $20,000 per year after retirement for perpetuity. Money will earn .20. How much should he save each year? Assume that the first "draw down" in savings takes place at time 11.

31. Assume that a bank charges .01 interest per month. You borrow $50,000 to be paid by equal payments over a 35-month period, first payment to be due 1 month from now. How much will you have to pay each month? What is the annual effective interest cost?

32. The newspaper headline states "Sal Bando Signs for $1.4 Million." A reading of the article revealed that Sal will receive $100,000 per year for 6 years. He will then receive $40,000 per year for 20 years.

$$6 \times 100,000 = 600,000$$
$$20 \times 40,000 = \underline{800,000}$$
$$\text{Total} = 1,400,000$$

    Assuming that Sal can borrow and lend funds at .10 per year, what is the present value of his contract?

33. The *Ithaca Journal's* headline of March 7, 1984, blared:

Young's Pact Is Ludicrous.

The article stated:

On Monday, Young, the former record-breaking quarterback from Brigham Young University, signed a $40 million, 43-year package with the USFL's Los Angeles Express.

The terms of the contract were $2,500,000 immediately:

$428,571 per year for 7 years (first payment after 1 year)
$932,432 per year for 37 years (first payment at time 8)

We have

$$
\begin{array}{rl}
 & \$\ 2,500,000 \\
7(\$428,571) = & 3,000,000 \\
37(\$932,432) = & \underline{34,500,000} \\
\text{Total} = & \$40,000,000
\end{array}
$$

(a) Assume that Young can borrow and lend at .11 per year, what is the present value of his contract?
(b) Design a contract that would be better for the LA Express but would pay Young more dollars.

REFERENCES

Archer, S. H., G. M. Choate, and G. Racette. *Financial Management*. New York: John Wiley & Sons, Inc., 1983.

Brealey, R., and S. Myers. *Principles of Corporate Finance*. New York: McGraw-Hill Book Company, 1984.

Brigham, E. F., *Financial Management: Theory and Practice*. New York: The Dryden Press, Division of CBS College Publishing, 1982.

Levy H., and M. Sarnat. *Capital Investment and Financial Decisions*. Englewood Cliffs, N.J.: Prentice-Hall, Inc., 1982.

Schall, L. D., and C. W. Haley. *Financial Management*. New York: McGraw-Hill Book Company, 1983.

Van Horne, James C. *Financial Management and Policy*. Englewood Cliffs, N.J.: Prentice-Hall, Inc., 1983.

Appendix 2.1 The Derivation of an Annuity Formula

Let

$$r = \text{the time value of money per period}$$
$$n = \text{the number of time periods}$$
$$B)(n, r) = \text{the present value of an annuity for } n \text{ periods, } r \text{ interest rate, with the first payment one year from time zero}$$

In the following table each entry in column 1 gives the present value of $1 received at the end of the period indicated in the column headed "Time." The sum of the items in this column is $B(n, r)$. Each entry in column 2 of this table gives the item in that row of column 1 multiplied by $(1 + r)$. The sum of the items in this column is $(1 + r)B(n, r)$. Note that $(1 + r)^0 = 1$ and that all except two of the amounts are in both columns. Taking the difference between the sum of the two columns and solving for $B(n, r)$ gives the formula we wish to derive.

Time	(1)	(2)
1	$(1 + r)^{-1}$	$(1 + r)^0$
2	$(1 + r)^{-2}$	$(1 + r)^{-1}$
3	$(1 + r)^{-3}$	$(1 + r)^{-2}$
.	.	.
.	.	.
.	.	.
$n - 1$	$(1 + r)^{-n+1}$	$(1 + r)^{-n+2}$
n	$(1 + r)^{-n}$	$(1 + r)^{-n+1}$
	$B(n, r)$	$(1 + r)B(n, r)$

Column 2 minus column 1 yields

$$(1 + r)B(n, r) - B(n, r) = 1 - (1 + r)^{-n}$$

Simplifying the left-hand side,

$$rB(n, r) = 1 - (1 + r)^{-n}$$

and, dividing by r,

$$B(n, r) = \frac{1 - (1 + r)^{-n}}{r}$$

Appendix Table B gives the values of $B(n, r)$, the present value of an annuity of \$1 per period. If the annuity is for \$$R$, we multiply the value obtained from the table by R.

If n is very large (let n approach infinity), we have the present value for a perpetuity of \$1 per period:

$$B(\infty, r) = \frac{1}{r}$$

Appendix 2.2   Continuous Discounting

Interest may be compounded monthly, weekly, daily, or continuously. Instead of assuming that the cash flows occur at the end of a year, they may also be presumed to occur monthly, weekly, daily, or continuously.

Continuous Compounding

To convert a nominal rate of interest j, which is compounded m times annually, to an effective rate of interest r, compounded annually, we make use of the fact that

$$(1 + r)^{-n} = \left(1 + \frac{j}{m}\right)^{-mn}$$

and solve for r. Because the present value of a dollar may be computed more easily by using $(1 + r)^{-n}$ we can substitute it for the right-hand side of the equation. If m is allowed to increase beyond bound (approach infinity), we have

$$\lim_{m \to \infty} \left(1 + \frac{j}{m}\right)^{-mn} = e^{-jn}$$

where e is approximately equal to 2.71828 and is the base of the natural or Naperian system of logarithms.

Thus the present value of \$1 for n periods with interest compounded continuously may be computed using e^{-jn}.

Continuous Payments

Instead of $1 being received at the end of each year, there may be k payments per year, each payment being an amount of $1/k$ dollars. The total received during each year is $1. The present value of a series of such payments extending over n years, with interest compounded continuously at a rate j, will be

$$\sum_{t=1}^{n \times k} \frac{1}{k} e^{-jt}$$

As we let k become very large (so that we receive the $1 per year in a large number of small installments) the summation approaches a limit, which can be written as follows:

$$\lim_{k \to \infty} \sum_{t=1}^{n \times k} \frac{1}{k} e^{-jt} = \int_0^n e^{-jt} \, dt = \frac{1 - e^{-jn}}{j}$$

Chapter 3

Valuation of Stocks and Bonds

Major Topics

1. The valuation of a conventional bond.
2. The definition of current yield and yield to maturity of a bond.
3. The valuation of a nongrowth stock (e.g., preferred stock).
4. The basic dividend growth model for a common stock.

Bond Valuation

In this chapter we apply the basic time value formulas to compute the value of basic financial securities used to finance corporations. The complexities associated with these securities will be discussed in Part III of this book. Thus the chapter serves two important functions. One is to provide practice in the use of the time value calculations. The second is to introduce the basic financial securities used by corporations and other organizations.

A bond represents the set of promises by a corporation (or other organization) to make one or more contractual payments of cash in the future. A bond is generally characterized by having a maturity that is reasonably far into the future (in excess of five years). Some of the promises made by the corporation (bond indenture provisions) are designed to protect the interests of the investors by maximizing the likelihood that the payments will be made as scheduled.

Since the bond payments are contractual and generally exactly defined, a bond is an excellent device for illustrating present value calculations. The investor knows the cash flows that are to be received if there is no default.

A bond may be a bearer bond or a registered bond. In the case of a bearer bond, interest payments are made when coupons detached from the bond are presented to a paying agent (frequently a bank). Each coupon will indicate the date of payment, the amount of interest, and the paying authority (say, the Chemical Bank). If each coupon for the annual interest of a $1,000 bond is for $150, we would say that the coupon interest rate or contractual interest rate is .15. With a registered bond, the corporation pays interest to the registered owner of the bond.

In recent years, the U.S. government has strongly encouraged the issuance of registered bonds (they are easier to monitor for tax purposes) but the 1984 Tax Act authorized the sales of bearer bonds by U.S corporations to non-U.S. citizens, thus facilitating the raising of capital in foreign capital markets.

Current Yield and Yield to Maturity

A bond will have a face or par value. This value determines how much principal has to be paid at maturity to retire the debt and how much interest will be paid annually.

Although there are many different types of bonds, we shall select one—a conventional bond. A conventional bond is a promise by the borrower to make periodic cash payments called interest and a final principal payment at maturity. This type of bond is called a balloon payment (or bullet) bond.

EXAMPLE 3.1

Assume that a 10 percent bond with a face value of $1,000 pays $100 interest per year at the end of each year for 30 years and will pay the $1,000 principal at maturity. If the current effective interest rate is .10, the present value of the $1,000 principal of the bond, using Tables A and B in the back of the book, is

$$\$1,000 \times (1.10)^{-30} = \$1,000 \times .0573 = \$57$$

(.0573 was obtained from Table A for $r = .10$, $n = 30$). The present value of 30 $100 interest payments is

$$\$100 \times B(30, .10) = \$100 \times 9.4269 = \$943$$

(9.4269 was obtained from Table B for $r = .10$, $n = 30$).

Present value of the bond $= \$57 + \$943 = \$1,000$

Since the interest rate used to accomplish the time discounting is equal to the interest rate paid by the bond, the present value of the bond is equal to the face value. This equality will always hold when the two rates are equal.

If the current effective interest rate used to compute present values were .14 instead of .10, the present value of this same bond using a .14 discount rate would be $720:

principal = $1,000 × .0196 = $ 20
interest = $100 × 7.0027 = $\underline{700}$
                                    $720 ✓

When the current effective interest rate is larger than the interest rate on the bond, the bond will sell at a discount from its face value. A buyer of the bond at $720 would have a "yield to maturity" of .14.

If the current effective interest were .06, we would then have a value of $1,550:

principal = $1,000 × .1741 = $ 174
interest = $100 × 13.7648 = $\underline{1,376}$
                                    $1,550 ✓

A buyer of the bond at $1,550 would have a yield to maturity of .06.

Note the large change in bond value that takes place with this 30-year bond when the interest rate goes from .14 (a value of $720) to .06 (a value of $1,550). If the bond had a maturity one year from now, the value change would only be from $1,100/1.14 to $1,100/1.06. The change would only be from $1,100/1.14 = $964.91 to $1,100/1.06 = $1,037.74.

When the market interest rate is below the contractual interest rate of the bond, the bond will have a value in excess of the face value. If the bond is callable by the issuer at a given price (say, $1,050), we can expect the call price to set a maximum value for the bond value. With a callable bond, the issuer can call the bond, pay the holder the agreed-upon amount (say, $1,050), and avoid an obligation with a present value of $1,550. When the bond is called, the investors give up the bonds, since no further interest will be paid.

With bonds there are always two interest rates that are relevant. One is the contractual rate that is defined by the contract. The contractual rate fixes the dollar payments of interest. The interest payments are determined by multiplying the face value of the bond by the contractual interest rate. The second rate is the effective interest rate. This is a market rate of interest, and it defines the discount rate to be used in computing the present value of the cash flows of the bond. When a new bond is sold, its contractual rate is usually set close to the current market rate, and the bond consequently sells at approximately face value initially. If the market rate subsequently rises or falls, the value of the bond falls or rises (inversely with the interest rate change), since the contractual cash flows are fixed. Thus the bond may subsequently sell at, above, or below face value (par). In Example 3.1, with the contractual rate at .10 but the effective rate rising from .10 to .14, the market price of the bond fell from $1,000 to $720. With an effective market interest rate of .06, the market price of a noncallable bond rose to $1,550.

A Three-Period Example

To illustrate better what happens with a bond selling at a discount, let us assume a .10, three-year $1,000 bond that is selling for $789.35. This is a yield to maturity of .20 (i.e., an investor paying $789.35 will earn .20 per year).

The current yield of a bond is defined to be the interest payment divided by the market price:

$$\text{current yield} = \frac{\$100.00}{\$789.35} = .127$$

The current yield is smaller than the yield to maturity if the bond is selling at a discount. If the bond were selling at a premium, the current yield would be larger than the yield to maturity. At the end of one year (two years until maturity) with no change in interest rate, the bond value will be

$$\text{value at time 1} = \frac{\$100}{1.20} + \frac{\$1,100.00}{1.20^2} = \$847.22$$

The increase in the value of the bond in the first year is

$$\$847.22 - \$789.35 = \$57.87$$

Adding this value change to the $100.00 interest, we obtain $157.87, which is a .20 return on $789.35:

$$\frac{\$157.87}{\$789.35} = .20$$

The investor earns .20 in the first year. At time 2, with no change in interest rates the value of the bond is

$$\text{value at time 2} = \frac{\$1,100.00}{1.20} = \$916.67$$

During period 2 the value of the bond went up:

$$\$916.67 - \$847.22 = \$69.45$$

The $69.45 increase in value added to the $100.00 interest is a .20 return on the beginning-of-the-period investment of $847.22:

$$\frac{\$169.45}{\$847.22} = .20$$

Finally, the value increase in year 3 is $83.33, since the value after the receipt of the interest is $1,000 at time 3 and the total return on the investment in year 3 is again .20:

$$\frac{\$183.33}{\$916.67} = .20$$

The current yield of year 3 is only .109:

$$\frac{\$100.00}{\$916.67} = .109$$

Only considering the cash interest return with a discount bond understates the return actually earned.

All these values were computed using the .20 yield to maturity. If the actual market price at time 1 is different from the value obtained using .20, then the returns earned will differ from those obtained, but the method of calculation would be similar.

For example, if the market price at time 1 were $900.00 rather than $847.22, the increase in value would be

$$\$900.00 - \$789.35 = \$110.65$$

and the total return for year 1 would be

$$\frac{\$110.65 + \$100.00}{\$789.35} = .267$$

The Semiannual Interest Complexity

Long-term bonds frequently will pay interest semiannually. This gives rise to confusion as to what annual return is earned or what the cost is to the issuing corporation.

The return from long-term bonds is usually expressed in nominal rates of one year even though interest is paid semiannually. For example, a $1,000 par (face value) bond paying $45 interest every six months with a nominal interest rate of .09 would have an effective interest rate of

$$r = \left(1 + \frac{.09}{2}\right)^2 - 1 = .092025$$

or just over .0920 if it is sold at face value.

Assume that you can earn .092025 on reinvested funds and that you are given the choice between a .09 $1,000 bond (interest paid semiannually) or a $1,000 bond paying .092025. With this latter bond you will have $1,092.025 at time 1. With the .09 bond you will again have $1,092.025:

$$\frac{1}{2}(\$90)(1.092025)^{1/2} = \$ \quad 47.025$$
$$\text{at time 1} \qquad\qquad\quad = \quad \underline{1{,}045.000}$$
$$\qquad\qquad\qquad\qquad\qquad \$1{,}092.025$$

The .09 bond actually earns more than .09 if the interest is received every six months.

Assume a third bond that pays interest annually at the rate of .09 so that at the end of the year the investor would have $1,090. This is inferior to the .09 bond that pays interest every six months.

If a .09 30-year bond with semiannual interest payments is issued at par, it is conventional practice to describe the yield to maturity as being .09. With semiannual interest payments, it would be more accurate to say that the yield to maturity is .092025.

Bond yield tables that are used to value bonds would indicate that the yield to maturity is .09. You have to remember that this is a nominal rate and that the effective rate is .092025 per year or .045 compounded every six months.

With a 30-year bond we could use 60 time periods and .045 interest rate to compute the present value:

$$\$1{,}000(1.045)^{-60} = \$1{,}000(.07129) = \$ \quad 71.29$$
$$\$45B(60, .045) \quad\; = \$45(20.638022) = \quad \underline{928.71}$$
$$\qquad\qquad\qquad\qquad\quad \text{present value} = \$1{,}000.00$$

If we use .092025, we have to use 30 time periods and annual interest costs of $45(1.092025)^{1/2} + \$45.00 = \$92.025$.

$$\$1.000(1.092025)^{-30} = \$1,000(.07129) = \$\ \ 71.29$$
$$\$92.025B(30,\ .092025) = \$92.025(10.091942) = \underline{\ \ \ \ 928.71}$$
$$\text{present value} = \$1,000.00$$

Note that the market interest rate, the number of time periods, and the annual interest payments all have to be consistent measures that apply to the same unit of time.

A Zero-Coupon Bond

Some bonds only pay interest at the maturity of the bond. These are called zero-coupon bonds or money multiplier notes. They are also called original issue discount (OIDs) notes.

The valuation of a zero-coupon bond is less complex than is that of a conventional bond. If the maturity amount of the bond is $1,000 due in 30 years and if the bond is to yield .10, the present value of the bond is

$$PV = \$1,000(1.10)^{-30} = \$57.31$$

A $1,000 bond (zero coupon) maturing in 30 years and yielding .10 will only cost $57.31 at time 0. You can see why the name "money multiplier" is an apt description.

Needless to say, if the company goes bankrupt in year 29, the investor will not earn .10.

Preferred Stock Valuation

Preferred stock is a security that contracts to pay a dividend. Although the dividend is contractual, there is no legal requirement that the dividend be paid. If it desires, the firm's board of directors may decide not to pay a dividend (the preferred shareholders may accumulate rights to these passed-over dividends).

In the past, the majority of preferred stock issues had constant dividends. With a constant dividend, the cost of preferred stock is defined as the discount rate that equates the future expected preferred dividends (and call price if callable) to the present market price. Let P denote the current price of a share of preferred, D the annual constant dividend payment, and k_p the return required by investors or cost of the preferred stock. The current price of a share, if noncallable, may be defined in terms of D and k_p. If the dividend is assumed to be a perpetuity with first payment one year from now, the value is $P = D/k_p$ and solving for k_p, $k_p = D/P$ under the assumption that the issuing firm expects to pay the dividend for perpetuity. So the current cost of non-callable preferred stock to the issuing corporation is the stock's dividend yield.

Many recent issues of preferred stock have call provisions to provide pro-tection to the issuing firm against decreases in k_p. If interest rates and stock yields should fall after selling a new issue and the issue is not callable, the issuing firm is stuck with perpetual financing at a high cost. For example, if the interest rate on a $100 preferred stock were 10 percent at time of issue (a $10-per-year cash dividend) and if the market currently required a .08 return, the stock would have to be repurchased in the open market for

$$P = \frac{\$10}{.08} = \$125$$

if the firm wished to retire the obligation. If, on the other hand, a call provision is specified at, say, $110, the firm could call the $10 obligation per annum for $110 and replace it with a $110 par value, 8 percent issue paying only $8.80 per annum and issued at par. The company replaces a security promising to pay $10 a year with a security paying $8.80 a year. This is a saving of $1.20 per year. The $110 issue price of the new stock is just enough to retire the out-standing preferred stock.

If there were no call provision and the company paid $125 to retire a share, the new security issued at $125 with a par of $125 and paying .08 would have an annual dividend of $10 and the company's financial position is not im-proved.

Investors desire the preferred stock they buy to be noncallable so that if interest rates fall they may continue to earn a high return. Thus investors will require a higher yield on the callable preferred stock issue than on the non-callable issue. For example, if a noncallable issue were selling for 10 percent, an otherwise comparable callable issue would have to promise to pay a some-what higher dividend than 10 percent if the investor is to pay the same price for both issues.

In the example, if the preferred stock were noncallable and if the fall in interest rates to .08 occurred in the first year, the investor who sells would receive $10 of dividends and $25 of capital gains for a total return on invest-ment of 35 percent. With the preferred stock callable at $110, there would be only $10 of capital gains and the return on investment would be 20 percent.

If the call is expected to take place some time in the future, the expected return from holding the security until the call can be computed. For example, XYZ Corporation has decided to issue preferred stock even though current interest rates are thought to be abnormally high and are expected to fall. The preferred stock will carry a $10 dividend and will be sold for $105 with a call price of $110. The firm expects lower interest rates (say, 8 percent) in approximately two years and therefore expects to call the issue at that time. We can solve by trial and error for the cost of this preferred stock issue or equivalently the return earned by the investor:

$$\$105 = \frac{\$10}{1 + k_p} + \frac{\$10 + \$110}{(1 + k_p)^2}$$

In this case, k_p is approximately 12 percent whereas the nominal dividend yield of $10/$105 is approximately 9.5 percent. The yield with a call provision is greater than the nominal dividend yield but less than it would be without the call. Assume that after two years the stock price goes up to 125. Without a call provision, the two-period economic cost is

$$\$105 = \frac{\$10}{1 + k_p} + \frac{\$10 + \$125}{(1 + k_p)^2}$$

Solving for k_p (by trial and error), we find that k_p is now between 18 and 19 percent. In this example, the call provision reduces the cost of the preferred stock as long as the issue price of $105 is assumed to be independent of the call provision.

We could also compute the cost if the stock is called after period 2, and we would find that the cost is between .12 and .095 depending on when the security is called.

There is a complexity that arises because preferred stock dividends are frequently paid quarterly. If the stock were sold at par, the realized annual rate on a 9 percent annual dividend paid quarterly would be

$$r = \left(1 + \frac{.09}{4}\right)^4 - 1 = .093083$$

or just over 9.3 percent.

Valuation of Common Stock

At the time of issue, the cost of debt is explicitly defined by the future contractual payments of interest and principal to repay the loan. The cost of common stock cannot be explicitly and exactly measured, since the actual return to stockholders not only depends on the earnings of the firm, the investment, and dividend decisions that are made by the firm, but also on the interpretation by the stock market of these events and decisions.

In discussing the cost of equity capital, you should realize that this topic is the mirror image of the decision to invest in common stock. A person understanding the factors affecting the cost of equity capital will have a better understanding of what it means to buy a share of common stock. The theory of stock valuation is a crucial element of the determination of the cost of equity capital.

A Stock Valuation Model

There are several definitions of the cost of equity capital. The standard academic definition is that the cost of equity capital is the rate of discount that equates the present value of all future expected dividends per share to the present price of the common stock. It is the return required by investors so that they are willing to invest in the common stock.

In Chapter 5 we shall discuss one method of determining the required return for a stock. Let us initially define the cost of equity capital, k_e, as the rate of interest or return that investors require to buy the common stock. Mathematically, the cost of equity is the interest rate that equates the next dividend, D_1, and the expected price of the stock at the time, P_1, back to the price of a share today, P, if the next dividend is paid one period in the future. We then have

$$P = \frac{D_1 + P_1}{1 + k_e} = \frac{D_1}{1 + k_e} + \frac{P_1}{1 + k_e} \tag{3.1}$$

The price today is equal to the present value of the next period's dividend plus the next period's price. By the same definition the stock price at time 1 is

$$P_1 = \frac{D_2 + P_2}{1 + k_e} \tag{3.2}$$

so that, substituting equation (3.2) into equation (3.1), we find

$$P = \frac{D_1}{1 + k_e} + \frac{D_2}{(1 + k_e)^2} + \frac{P_2}{(1 + k_e)^2} \tag{3.3}$$

Continuing this substitution process, we obtain

$$P = \sum_{t=1}^{\infty} D_t(1 + k_e)^{-t} \qquad (3.4)$$

Equation (3.4) is a basic dividend valuation model for common stock. It states that the current market value of a share of common stock is equal to the present value of all future dividends, discounted at the cost of equity capital. The cost of equity capital is that rate of return the stock market expects to receive in order to compensate it for the use of funds and the risk associated with the future dividend stream. Equation (3.4) is the simplest general formulation for the valuation of common stock.

Although equation (3.4) could be solved by trial and error for any set of D_t's, over the years substantial effort has been applied to finding closed form models or developing tables (per dollar of initial dividend) for "standard" growth patterns of the dividend stream. We present two models in the next sections to illustrate this methodology but leave extensions to the inquisitive reader.

Note that the future stock prices (capital gains) are not directly in equation (3.4) but rather the future dividends are substituted for these stock prices.

A Closed-Form Stock Price Model

One of the simplest assumptions that can be made about expected dividend behavior is that dividends are expected to grow at a constant rate through time so that $D_t = D_1(1 + g)^{t-1}$. If dividends grow at a rate g in perpetuity and $g < k_e$, then (as shown in Appendix 3.1) we can obtain

$$P = \frac{D_1}{k_e - g} \qquad (3.5)$$

where D_1 is the next period's dividend rate. This is a perpetual growth model where dividend growth is constant each period.

Solving equation (3.5) for the cost of equity capital, we find

$$k_e = \frac{D_1}{P} + g \qquad (3.6)$$

and this is a widely accepted measure of k_e, the cost of stock equity capital. Other methods of estimating the cost of equity capital will be introduced in Chapter 5, but equations (3.5) and (3.6) are widely used because of their simplicity.

EXAMPLE 3.2 ————————————————————————————————————

A common stock is expected to pay a $1-per-share dividend at the end of the year. The stockholders want a return of 15 percent and expect dividends to grow at a rate of 14 percent per period.

D_1 = $1 per year (the next dividend)
 g = .14, growth rate in dividends
 k_e = .15, cost of stock equity capital (the return required by
      stockholders)

Using equation (3.5), we find that the value per share is

$$P = \frac{D_1}{k_e - g} = \frac{\$1}{.15 - .14} = \$100$$

If g were to change from 14 to 10 percent, the value of a share would change to

$$P = \frac{D_1}{k_e - g} = \frac{\$1}{.15 - .10} = \frac{\$1}{.05} = \$20$$

Note that a change in stock price, P, might be caused by a change in D_1, g, or k_e. A decrease in P does not necessarily mean that k_e has increased.

By observing the current annual dividend ($1) and the current price (say, $25) and using an estimate of g (say, 10 percent), we could then estimate k_e using equation (3.6):

$$k_e = \frac{D_1}{P} + g$$

$$= \frac{\$1}{25} + .10 = .04 + .10 = 14\%$$

——

A critic of the dividend valuation model might argue that investors buy price appreciation, not future dividends. For many stocks, investors may expect the first n periods to have very small (or zero) dividends and, nevertheless, the current market price may be very large. The current high price, however, is only justified in a rational market by the expectation of high future dividends (or other forms of cash flow from the firm to investors). The summation of the present value of future dividends does not require that the near-term dividends be large. However, if there are several years of zero dividends and/or changing growth rates through time, then the mathematical formulation of P does not reduce to an expression as simple as $P = D_1/(k_e - g)$.

What would be the value of a stock that promised never to pay a dividend (including a liquidation dividend payoff arising from controlling the firm)? The value of these shares would be zero. There has to be the prospect of dividends (defined to be any cash distribution from the firm to its investors) for stock to have a positive value.

The constant growth rate dividend valuation model assumes that the dividend (D_1) is expected to grow at a constant rate g forever. It may be more realistic to assume that special investment opportunities allowing a high growth rate are available not in perpetuity but only over some finite interval of time, T, and after time the growth rate will be smaller.

A Two-Stage Model*

We will assume dividends grow at a rate g_0 until period T and then grow at g_1 after time T. Define P_{T-1} to be the price at time $T - 1$ and equal to

$$P_{T-1} = \frac{D_T}{k_e - g_1} = \frac{D_1(1 + g_0)^{T-1}}{k_e - g_1}. \tag{3.7}$$

The price today of the stock is

$$P = \sum_{t=1}^{T-1} D_1(1 + g_0)^{t-1}(1 + k_e)^{-t} + (1 + k_e)^{-(T-1)}P_{T-1} \tag{3.8}$$

The value of P_{T-1} is used rather than P_T only to simplify the formulation. Figure 3.1 shows the values being discounted. P is equal to the sum of the present value of the dividends for the first $T - 1$ years $(D_1$ plus $D_1(1 + g_0)$

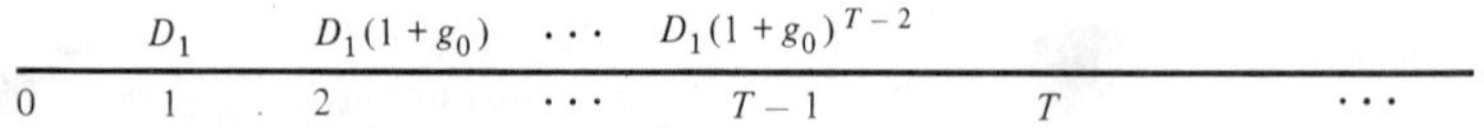

	D_1	$D_1(1+g_0)$	$\cdots$	$D_1(1+g_0)^{T-2}$		
0	1	2	$\cdots$	$T-1$	T	$\cdots$

FIGURE 3.1   Two-Stage Model

*This section may be bypassed with no loss in continuity.

plus $\cdots D_1(1 + g_0)^{T-2}$) plus the present value of P_{T-1}. P_{T-1} is equal to the present value of $D_1(1 + g_0)^{T-1}$ plus $D_1(1 + g_0)^{T-1}(1 + g_1)$, and so on.

The logic of the model may be easier to follow with a numerical example.

EXAMPLE 3.3 ————————————————————————————————

$D_1 = \$1$, $k_e = .15$, $g_0 = .15$, $T = 10$, $g_1 = .02$.

We first solve for

$$D_{10} = D_1(\$1 + g_0)^{T-1} = \$1(1.15)^9 = \$3.518$$

and then for P_{T-1}:

$$P_{T-1} = \frac{\$3.518}{.15 - .02} = \$27.06 \tag{3.9}$$

The stock value now is

$$P = \sum_{t=1}^{9} \$1(1.15)^{t-1}(1.15)^{-t} + (1.15)^{-9}(\$27.06)$$

$$\frac{1.15^9}{1.15^{10}} = \frac{1}{1.15} \tag{3.10}$$

$$= \frac{\$1}{1.15}(9) + .2843(\$27.06) = \$15.52$$

$$7.83 + 7.69$$

We obtain a stock value of $15.52. If the growth rate of .15 had been assumed to continue for perpetuity we would have obtained an infinite value.

————————————————————————————————

Note that the two-period growth model is much more flexible than the constant growth rate model. In particular, there is no restriction on the initial growth rate so that a very large growth rate can be assumed to hold during the first interval and a lower rate in the second time interval to infinity. Of course, the two-period model is not general enough for most cases, and so models with more complex patterns of dividend growth pattern can be used to determine a current value of the stock or an estimate of the cost of equity capital. There is no limit to the number of different expected growth rates that can be used.

In the following example, Emerson has a different actual dividend growth rate each year.

EXAMPLE 3.4 ──

During 1983, the price of Emerson Electric's common stock had a high of $64\frac{5}{8}$ and a low of $49\frac{1}{4}$. The dividend and earnings per share (EPS) record for the past five years was

Year	EPS	Dividends	Annual Dividend Growth
1983	$4.42	$2.10	.05
1982	4.37	2.00	.14
1981	4.16	1.76	.10
1980	3.59	1.60	.11
1979	3.18	1.44	

The average dividend growth from 1979 to 1983 is

$$\$1.44(1 + g)^4 = \$2.10$$

$$g = .10$$

Using the low price of $49\frac{1}{4}$, Emerson's cost of equity is

$$k_e = \frac{D}{P} + g = \frac{\$2.10}{\$49.25} + .10 = .143$$

Using the high price of $64\frac{5}{8}$,

$$k_e = \frac{\$2.10}{\$64.625} + .10 = .132$$

If the market thought the dividend growth rate was different from .10, the estimates of k_e could be significantly wrong.

Assume that you think the growth in dividends will be .12 and that you want a .16 return from investing in Emerson. An estimate of the stock value is

$$P = \frac{D}{k_e - g} = \frac{\$2.10}{.16 - .12} = \$52.50$$

Applying any stock valuation model with confidence is difficult. It is too easy to change the assumptions and obtain a different answer. For example, using a .16 required return and .10 growth rate, we obtain

$$P = \frac{D}{k_e - g} = \frac{\$2.10}{.16 - .10} = \$35.00$$

Conclusions

In this chapter we have valued three different types of financial securities by computing the present value of the cash flows associated with the securities. The formula used to compute present values is $(1 + k)^{-n}$ or its equivalent. The use of this formula assumes that it is correct to adjust for increased risk by increasing k. While it is true that if risk is increased, it is appropriate that k be larger, we should be careful in applying $(1 + k)^{-n}$ to compute present value when risk is large and k is large. In the next chapter we shall discuss risk considerations in greater detail.

Western Union Corporation

The November 29, 1984 issue of *The Wall Street Journal* reported that at their November 1984 meeting the Western Union Corporation's board of directors decided to omit dividends on both the common and preferred stock.

During 1984, the high for the Western Union common stock was $39.75, and the low of $8.875 was reached on December 3, 1984.

Before assuming that the stock price fall was caused entirely by the omission of the dividend, consider the fact that the company reported a net loss of $15.5 million for the third quarter of 1984 and that in November a group of banks canceled a $100 million revolving credit line.*

These three factors resulted in a significant change in the market's expectations of future common stock dividends.

* *The Wall Street Journal*, November 29, 1984, p. 55.

A Review Problem 3.1

A 12 percent bond promises to pay $120 per year for 20 years and also to pay $1,000 at the end of the 20 years. What is the value of the bond if the effective (market) interest rate is
(a) 12 percent?
(b) 9 percent?
(c) 15 percent?
  How does the value of the bond vary with the effective interest rate?

Solution to Review Problem 3.1

Period	Amount	PV Factor	PV	
(a) Years 1–20	$ 120	7.4694	$896.00	
Year 20	1,000	.1037	104.00	
		Total present value =	$1,000.00	using .12
(b) Years 1–20	120	9.1285	$1,095.00	
Year 20	1,000	.1784	178.00	
		Total present value =	$1,273.00	using .09
(c) Years 1–20	120	6.2593	$751.00	
Year 20	1,000	.0611	61.00	
		Total present value =	$812.00	using .15

As the effective interest rate rises, the bond value falls, and visa versa; the relationship is inverse.

Review Problem 3.2

A company's stock is selling at $60 and its dividend for the next year is expected to be $1.50. The expected growth rate is .145 and is expected to continue indefinitely.
(a) What will be the expected dividend after one year has passed?
(b) What will be the price after one year after the dividend?
(c) What is the percentage increase in stock price?
(d) What return will be earned by an investor who buys at $60 and sells after one year after the dividend?
(e) What is the cost of equity?

Solution to Review Problem 3.2

(a) $\$1.50(1.145) = \$1.7175$

(b) $\$60(1.145) = \$68.70$

(c) .145 or 14.5%

(c) $\dfrac{\$8.70 + \$1.50}{\$60} = \dfrac{\$10.20}{\$60} = .17$

(e) $k_e = \dfrac{D}{P} + g = \dfrac{\$1.50}{\$60} + .145 = .025 + .145 = .17$

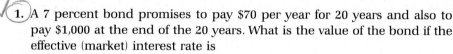

PROBLEMS

1. A 7 percent bond promises to pay $70 per year for 20 years and also to pay $1,000 at the end of the 20 years. What is the value of the bond if the effective (market) interest rate is
   (a) 7 percent?
   (b) 9 percent?
   (c) 5 percent?
   (d) How does the value of the bond vary with the effective interest rate?

2. Assume that the O-I Company has outstanding $10 million of 4 percent bonds maturing in 20 years (paying $400,000 of interest per year). The current interest rate is .10.
   What is the present value of the debt?

3. Assume that the I-O Company has outstanding $10 million of 10 percent bonds maturing in 20 years (paying $1 million of interest per year). The current interest rate is .04.
   (a) What is the present value of the debt?
   (b) If the bonds can be called at a price of $10.5 million, how much would the firm pay to accomplish the refunding? Assume zero taxes.

4. Compute the present value for a bond that promises to pay interest of $150 a year for 30 years and $1,000 at maturity. The first interest payment is one year from now. Use a rate of discount of .15.

5. Estimate the present value of a bond that promises to pay interest of $120 a year for 30 years and $1,000 at maturity. The first interest payment is one year from now. Use a .12 rate of discount. After estimating the present value, compute it using the present value tables.

6. A 20-year $1,000 bond promises to pay .045 interest annually. The current interest rate is .05.

   How much is the bond worth now? How much is the bond worth if the current interest rate were .04?

7. Assume that a $1,000 par bond matures in 40 years. The bonds have a contractual interest rate of 12 percent. Interest is paid annually (first interest one year from now).
   (a) If the market interest rate for comparable bonds is 10 percent, what is the present value of the bonds now?
   (b) What is the worth today of the $1,000 to be received upon maturity 40 years from now?
   (c) If after one year the bond was priced such that it yielded 12 percent, what would be its price?
   (d) If the facts of parts (a) and (c) apply, what will be the net return for the one year for the investor buying the bond at time zero?

8. A preferred stock promises to pay $8 per year. An investor who wants a .12 return will pay what price for this stock?

9. Assume that the stock in Problem 8 is callable at any time at a price of $50.

   If the investor expects the stock to be called at time 2 (in two years), what price will the investor pay?

10. Assume that the stock of Problems 8 and 9 is selling at $50.81.

    If it is expected the stock will be called at time 2, what return is the investor buying the stock expecting?

11. Assume that growth is expected to continue for perpetuity and that $P = D_1/(k_e - g)$ can be used for valuation purposes. The initial dividend is $1 and the cost of equity is .20.
    (a) What is P if $g = .19$?
    (b) What is P if $g = .10$?
    (c) What is P if $g = 0$?
    (d) What is P if $g = -.05$?

12. A company's stock is selling at $50 and its dividend is $4.
    (a) What is k_e if $g = .10$?
    (b) What is k_e if $g = 0$?
    (c) What is k_e if $g = -.05$?

13. A company's stock is selling at $80 and its dividend for the next year is expected to be $4. The expected perpetual growth rate is .10 and the cost of equity is .15.

    (a) What will be the expected dividend after one year has passed?
    (b) What will be the price after one year?
    (c) What is the percentage increase in stock price?

14. Company A has a dividend of $2.10 and earnings of $3.00. The stock is selling at $210. Investors want a .15 return. Dividends and earnings are expected to grow at .14 per year.
    (a) Prepare a table showing the expected dividends and stock prices for the next five years.
    (b) Evaluate the facts of this problem and the resulting table if earnings are expected to remain constant.

15. If you were a corporate treasurer with an excess cash position of $10 million to invest for one year and could purchase either 1-year bonds that have an effective rate today of 5 percent of 20-year bonds with an effective rate today of 7 percent, which would you prefer? How might you choose if you believed the level of effective interest rates was going to remain stable or fall over the next year and were willing to bet on your convictions?

16. David Moore is enthusiastic about the prospects for the Elca Electronics firm. He forecasts a 30 percent growth rate in dividends for the next four years. The last dividend was $1.20 per share. Dividends are paid annually. After four years David forecasts a zero growth rate. For a firm with the risk of Elca, David requires a .15 annual return.
    (a) What is the expected dividend at time 4?
    (b) What is the expected dividend at time 5?
    (c) What is the expected stock price at time 4?
    (d) What is the value of a share of stock today?

17. In 1984 Metromedia Broadcasting Corporation (owner of the Harlem Globetrotters and the Ice Capades as well as less artistic enterprises) offered to its common stock shareholders an exchange offer consisting of $30 plus a subordinated debenture with a $22.50 face value.

    The debentures would mature in 14 years from issuance. They would bear interest beginning in the sixth year (first interest 6 years from date of issue) at a rate of 16 percent per annum and would pay interest semiannually.

    Beginning in the tenth year they would have the "benefit" of a sinking fund. The bonds can be called at face value to satisfy the sinking fund requirement.

    How much are the investors receiving for a share of common stock? Assume that the appropriate annual rate of interest is .1664 for a bond of this risk.

REFERENCES

Acquith, P., and D. W. Mullins, Jr. "The Impact of Initiating Dividend Payments on Shareholders' Wealth." *Journal of Business*, January 1983, 77–96.

Bauman, W. Scott. "Investment Returns and Present Value." *Finanncial Analysts Journal*, November–December 1969, 107–120.

Bierman, H., Jr., and J. Hass. "Normative Stock Price Models" *Journal of Financial and Quantitative Analysis*, September 1971, 1135–1144.

———, D. H., Downes, and J. Hass. "Closed Form Stock Price Models." *Journal of Financial and Quantitative Analysis*, June 1972, 1797–1808.

Brealey, R. A. *An Introduction to Risk and Return for Common Stock*, 2nd ed. Cambridge, Mass.: MIT Press, 1983.

Brigham, Eugene F., and James L. Pappas. "Duration of Growth, Change in Growth Rates, and Corporate Share Prices." *Financial Analysts Journal*, May–June 1966, 157–162.

Clendenin, John C., and Maurice Van Cleave. "Growth and Common Stock Values." *Journal of Finance*, December 1954, 365–376.

Donaldson, G. *Corporate Debt Capacity*. Boston: Harvard Graduate School of Business, 1961.

———. "In Defense of Preferred Stock." *Harvard Business Review*, July–August 1962, 123–136.

Durand, David. "Growth Stocks and the St. Petersburg Paradox." *Journal of Finance*, September 1957, 348–363.

Gordon, Myron J., and E. Shapiro. "Capital Equipment Analysis: The Required Rate of Profit." *Management Science*, October 1956, 102–110.

Sharpe, W. F. *Investments*, 2nd ed. Englewood Cliffs, N.J.: Prentice-Hall, Inc., 1981.

Williams, John Burr. *The Theory of Investment Values*. Cambridge, Mass.: Harvard University Press, 1938.

Appendix 3.1   Derivation of Stock Price Model with Constant Growth Rate

We want to show that

$$P = \frac{D_1}{k_e - g}$$

At time t, $D_t = D_1(1 + g)^{t-1}$. If the current market price is defined as the present value of the future expected dividends,

$$P = \sum_{t=1}^{\infty} D_t(1 + k_e)^{-t}$$

$$= \frac{D_1}{1 + k_e}\left(1 + \frac{1 + g}{1 + k_e} + \left(\frac{1 + g}{1 + k_e}\right)^2 + \cdots\right)$$

If $k_e > g$,

$$P = \frac{D_1}{1 + k_e}\left(\frac{1}{1 - \dfrac{1 + g}{1 + k_e}}\right)$$

$$P = \frac{D_1}{k_e - g}$$

Chapter 4

Fundamentals of Risk and Portfolio Analysis

Major Topics

1. The fundamentals of uncertainty and risk analysis.
2. The use of probabilities in making managerial decisions.
3. The calculation of the fundamental measures of a probability distribution (expected value, variance, and standard deviation).
4. Introduction of portfolio analysis (risk reduction) and the formation of portfolios.
5. Calculation of variances and covariances of investments and portfolios.
6. The efficient frontier; correlation and its importance.
7. The power of diversification.

Uncertainty

Uncertainty is an essential element of most finance decisions. In the present chapter, some essential concepts necessary for dealing with uncertainty are introduced. With uncertainty, more than one outcome can occur after a decision is made. Moreover, the decision maker does not know in advance which outcome will actually occur. In this chapter, we consider methods of describing these uncertain outcomes and methods we can use to affect investment outcomes by a diversification strategy.

Uncertain Events and Forecasts of Outcome

Assume that there is uncertainty regarding the outcome of a decision that has been made. An event will occur and associated with this event will be an outcome. We do not know in advance which of these events will occur. For each possible event, there is one economic outcome.

The uncertainty arises because we do not know with certainty which of the possible events will occur and, thus, cannot be sure which outcome will actually occur. For some purposes it may be useful to combine fundamental occurrences to form a master event. For example, rain or snow may result in the cancellation of a football game; hence we may use an event "bad weather" rather than one event "rain" and another event "snow."

To take a business-oriented case, suppose that a firm is contemplating investing in a plant to produce a product whose demand is very sensitive to general business conditions. If general business conditions are good, the demand for the product is likely to be high and the plant profitable. If general business conditions are poor, the demand is likely to be low and the plant unprofitable. In this case, uncertainty about the cash flows associated with the investment derives from uncertainty about some other event—general business conditions. If the future state of general business conditions could be perfectly forecasted, the outcome of the investment could be predicted.

Table 4.1 illustrates the effect of business conditions and product design on the potential profits from introducing a new product. In this case, the state of business conditions has some effect on the present value of the investment, but product design is more important. If the product design does not appeal to prospective customers, producing the new product will result in a loss, and only the exact size of the loss depends on general business conditions. However, if the product is popular with customers, it will be profitable, but profits will be better if business conditions are favorable than if they are unfavorable.

The classification of events is the first step in focusing attention on what is most relevant for a particular decision. The desirability of an investment is

TABLE 4.1 Conditional Forecasts of Profit of a New Product Investment

Product Design	General Business Conditions	
	Favorable	Unfavorable
Popular design	$1,500,000	$1,400,000
Unpopular design	−250,000	−400,000

likely to be affected more by some events than by others. The purpose of the analysis and the point of view of the analyst will determine which category of events is most useful. If the point of view is that of a manager whose future depends in an important way on the outcome of a particular project, then specific events affecting this project are likely to be more important to that manager. However, if the analysis is done for the benefit of stockholders, then the level of the general business conditions may be more important. The level of the general business conditions will influence many different projects and assets in the same direction and at the same time, and thus greatly affect corporate profitability.

Probability: A Measure of Likelihood

Probability may be described as a measure of the likelihood that an event will occur. If an event is certain to occur, it has a probability of 1 of occurring. If an event is certain not to occur, its probability of occurring is 0. All events have a probability of occurrence somewhere between 0 and 1. By convention, probabilities follow several rules. Among them are (1) the probability assigned to each possible event must be a positive number between 0 and 1, where 0 represents an impossible event and 1 represents a certain event, and (2) if a set of nonoverlapping events covers all possible outcomes, the probabilities of the events must total 1.

Consider events associated with one flip of a coin. With a new, fairly machined coin that has a head on only one side, the probability of landing a head on one fair toss is .5 and the probability of a tail is .5 (these are the only events that can occur if we do not allow the coin to stand on its edge). If we did not know that the coin was fair (e.g., if the coin were worn unevenly), we do not know that probability of landing a head is .5. If, however, we were to take such a two-sided coin and flip it in a fair manner a very large number of times, say, 100,000 times, the ratio of the actual number of heads to the total number of flips would be a reasonable estimate of the probability of the event "heads" for that particular coin. The probability estimate is based on the objective evidence of 100,000 trials and is called an objective probability.

If the concept of probability were applicable only to events that could be repeated a large number of times under controlled circumstances, the concept would be of relatively little use in analyzing business investment decisions. Most business decisions are either unique or are made a small number of times. One does not generally make the same decision in the same circumstances a great many times and observe the outcome of each decision. Even when decisions are repetitive, conditions tend to change. If a person is considering opening a drugstore, there may be considerable evidence that helps to form a judgment about whether a drugstore could be profitable in a particular location. But there is no other location and period of time that is exactly the same in all respects as the location and time this person has in mind, and the prospective investor cannot resort to an objective measure of probability to describe the events associated with the profitability of the drugstore. Probability measures that reflect the state of belief of a person rather than the objective evidence of a large number of trials are called *subjective probabilities*.

Let us consider an election and ask ourselves the meaning of a statement such as the following: Mr. A has a .65 probability of winning this election. The election will not be repeated in exactly the same form, nor has it been held before, although there may be all sorts of evidence relevant to a belief about the outcome. If we say that there is a .65 probability that Mr. A will win the election, this statement implies a comparison of the following sort. Suppose that a jar is filled with 100 beads identical in all respects, except that 65 are blue and 35 are red. We mix the beads thoroughly and randomly draw out one bead. The statement that Mr. A has a .65 probability of winning the election means we believe that we are as likely to draw a blue bead as Mr. A is to win the election.

In the case of any unique event (like an election), all observers will not exactly agree on the probability that any particular candidate will win. The adjective *subjective* applied to probabilities suggests that the probabilities described are opinions or statements of belief held by individuals. Expressing an opinion about the likelihood that an event will occur in terms of a numerical subjective probability facilitates the development of decision-making procedures that are explicit and consistent with the decision maker's beliefs.

Expected Values, Variances, and Standard Deviations

In working with probabilities, the concepts of expected value, variance, and standard deviation are essential. These basic ideas will be introduced with an example.

EXAMPLE 4.1 ——————————————————————————————————

In Table 4.2, column 1 lists six possible events, column 2 shows the profit if the event in question occurs, and column 3 lists the probability of each event. We wish to calculate the "expected" profit. To do this, we multiply the probability in each row by the corresponding profit. The products are shown in column 4 of the table. The sum of the amounts in column 4 is the expected

TABLE 4.2   Calculating the Expected Profit of an Uncertain Investment

(1) Possible Events	(2) Profit for Each Event	(3) Probability of Event	(4) Expectation of Profit (col. 2 × col. 3)
a	− $100	.3	− $30
b	0	.1	0
c	50	.1	5
d	0	.2	0
e	50	.1	5
f	200	.2	40
		1.0 Expected profit =	$20

profit, which is a weighted average. Each possible profit is weighted by the probability that it will occur.

In Table 4.2, two events, b and d, both result in profit values of zero.

If we assume that the only relevant characteristic of an event is the profit associated with it, events that lead to identical profit can be combined (by adding their probabilities). A redescription of the events is shown in Table 4.3. The expected profit is not changed by this recombination of the data; it is still $20.

Further insight into the meaning of an expected value can be obtained if we examine the differences between the profits that can occur and their expected value. In Table 4.4, column 1 lists the possible profit measures and column 3 the corresponding differences, or deviations, of each from the expected value. That is, each value in column 3 is the corresponding value in column 1 minus the expected value of 20. The values in column 4 are these

TABLE 4.3   Calculating the Expected Profit of an Uncertain Investment

(1) Possible Values of Profit	(2) Probability of That Value	(3) Expectation of Profit (col. 2 × col. 1)
− $100	.3	− $30
0	.3	0
50	.2	10
200	.2	40
	1.0 Expected profit =	$20

TABLE 4.4   Calculating the Expected Deviation Between Profit and Expected Profit

(1) Possible Values of Profit	(2) Probability of That Value	(3) Profit Minus Expected Profit $20	(4) Expectation (col. 2 × col. 3)
− $100	.3	− $120	− $36
0	.3	− 20	− 6
50	.2	30	6
200	.2	180	36
	1.0		0

deviations times the corresponding probabilities. The sum of the items in column 4 is the expected value of the deviations, and the sum of these deviations is zero. In fact, it could be proved that the expected deviation must always be zero.

This suggests another interpretation of the expected profit. It is a number in the center of the possible values, in the sense that the sum of positive deviations from the expected profit equals the sum of the negative deviations, provided that both types of deviations are weighted by their respective probabilities.

The variance and its square root, the standard deviation, are commonly used as measures of how concentrated the possible values are around their expected value. The variance is calculated by squaring each deviation and taking the expected value of the squared deviations. The procedure is illustrated in Table 4.5. The first three columns in that table contain the same entries as in Table 4.4. Column 4 of Table 4.5 shows the square of the deviation, and column 5 shows the squared deviation multiplied by its probability. The sum of the items in column 5 is the variance. For some purposes it is more

TABLE 4.5   Calculating the Variance of the Profit

(1) Possible Values of Profit	(2) Probability of That Value	(3) Profit Minus Expected Profit	(4) Squared Deviation	(5) Col. 2 × Col. 4
− $100	.3	− $120	$14,400	$ 4,320
0	.3	− 20	400	120
50	.2	30	900	180
200	.2	180	32,400	6,480
	1.0		Variance =	$11,100

Standard deviation $= \sqrt{\$11,100} = \$105.36$

convenient to work with the standard deviation, since its units, dollars in this case, are the same as the units of the expected value. In this example, the variance of the profit is 11,100 (dollars squared) and the standard deviation is the square root of $11,100, or $105.36.

Random Variables and Their Expected Values

If the specific value of a quantity, such as profit, depends on the outcome of an uncertain event, the quantity is called a *random variable*. The profit of an investment might be denoted by the symbol X, where the specific numerical value of X depends on the outcome of an uncertain event. X is a random variable.

The symbol E is used to denote the process of finding the expected value of a random variable; the specific random variable whose expected value is being taken is placed in parentheses or brackets following the E. Thus, in our example,

$$E(X) = 20$$

summarizes in symbolic terms, the results of the calculations shown in Tables 4.2 and 4.3. Although X is a random variable, note that $E(X)$ is just a number whose value depends on the probabilities and outcomes of all the events that could occur.

Using this notation, we find that the deviation of profit from its expected value could be denoted as

$$X - E(X)$$

In Table 4.5 we illustrated the computation of the variance by squaring each deviation and then calculating the expected value of the squared deviation. In symbols, the variance can be described as

$$E[X - E(X)]^2 = E(X^2) - E(X)^2 = \$11,500 - \$400 = \$11,100$$

In computing a variance it is important to distinguish between

$$E(X)^2 = \$20^2 = \$400$$

and

$$E(X^2) = (100)^2.3 + (50)^2.2 + (200)^2.2 = 3,000 + 500 + 8,000 = \$11,500$$

The first equation indicates that an expected value was found and then squared. The second equation indicates that each possible value of the random variable is first squared and the expected value of these squared quantities is then found. It can be shown that the variance equals $E(X^2) - E(X)^2 = \$11,500 - \$400 = \$11,100$.

We shall sometimes find it convenient to represent the expected value using $\overline{X}$ rather than $E(X)$. Thus we could write $\overline{X}^2 = 400$ instead of $E(X)^2 = 400$.

Next we consider the consequences to expected return and risk of combining investments. This process is called portfolio analysis and is the first step toward achieving diversification.

Diversification

Normally, it is not a desirable strategy for individual investors to put all their investable funds into the one stock or bond they consider the best. The disadvantage of an investor concentrating investments is that if some unfavorable event occurs that greatly affects the one investment, it will have a drastic effect on the inverstor's total financial situation.

Stock market investors typically attempt to spread their investments in common stocks over a number of different companies. When this strategy is followed, an unfavorable event specific to the firm, affecting the value of that company, will have a relatively small effect on the value of the entire portfolio because many of the other investments will be unaffected by the occurrence of such an event.

The collection of marketable stocks and other assets held by an individual investor is referred to as a portfolio. The portfolio problem might be defined as the problem of choosing a collection of securities that, taken together, has desirable characteristics with respect to risk and expected rate of return. Suppose that the investor wants more return and less risk (the investor is risk averse). Assume also that the investor begins with a portfolio that consists entirely of one security and then diversifies the portfolio by adding a second security. How will this second security affect the expected rate of return and the risk of the portfolio? The objective is to construct a portfolio with desirable characteristics with respect to both risk and expected rate of return where there is a trade-off between the two.

The portfolio problem will be developed in a context of investments in stocks and bonds on the one hand and business capital expenditures on the other. However, it is desirable to mention briefly three of the differences between an investment in securities and an investment in real assets.

One difference is the relevant time horizon and transaction costs. The transaction costs associated with purchasing or selling most stocks and bonds are a relatively small fraction of their value. Thus the holder of these assets can make decisions within the framework of a relatively short time horizon. By contrast, the transaction costs associated with buying or selling real assets may be a large fraction of their value. When acquisition of such assets is under consideration, the relevant time horizon is often the life of the asset.

A second difference is the divisibility of the investments. You cannot buy half a steel mill or two-thirds of a lathe, but you can buy securities that represent a very small fraction of a very large collection of real assets. The real assets themselves are not easily divisible into convenient sizes for consumer ownership, but the securities are customarily issued in relatively small denominations so that investors can buy the number of units they desire.

Another important difference is the nature of the dependency of the cash flows from the investments. The expected cash flows from a portfolio consisting of two securities can be obtained by adding the expected cash flows of the two securities. But the expected cash flows from a portfolio consisting of a blast furnance and a rolling mill is often greater than the total amount that could be earned from each of the assets by itself because of economic efficiencies (sometimes called synergy).

Despite the fact that differences exist, the basic principles of portfolio analysis apply to investments in real assets as well as to investments in securities.

The basic assumption of portfolio analysis is that most investors dislike risk. Also, other things being equal, most investors would prefer higher returns to lower returns. Whenever it is possible to reduce risk without reducing expected returns, it follows that investors will attempt to do this. It will be assumed that the standard deviation of the rate of return from a portfolio of securities is a reasonable measure of portfolio risk. Thus there is an incentive to use diversification to reduce the standard deviation of a portfolio. For example, if the rates of return from two securities have the same expected value and their outcomes are statistically independent, it can be shown that a portfolio consisting of both securities in appropriate proportions will have the same expected return and a lower risk than will a portfolio that consists of one of the securities.

Although it is conventional to use expected return to measure the benefits and the standard deviation to measure the risk of a portfolio, it can properly be argued that other statistical measures are of interest to investors. You can look at this simplification as a way of achieving a workable solution to a very complex problem. Choosing the best of a very large number of portfolios for an investor is not an easy task.

Introduction to Portfolio Analysis

With an individual investment we must consider risk or, more specifically, our attitudes toward the undesirable events that might occur. As soon as a firm is considering the purchase of more than one asset, we must consider the risk not of the individual assets but of the entire collection of assets.

Consider investment A. Investment A has an outlay of $400 and benefits of

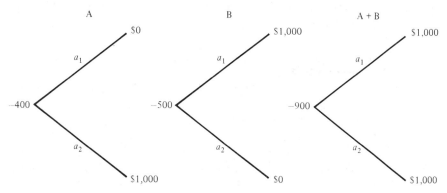

FIGURE 4.1 Forming a Portfolio

$500. The investment is apparently acceptable. Now add the information that the $500 is an expectation and that the outcomes are either $0 if event a_1 with .5 probability occurs or $1,000 if event a_2 with .5 probability occurs. Assume that the payoffs are made immediately.

Many of us would reject investment A because of excessive risk. If you happen to find this investment acceptable, consider adding one or more zeros to each of the dollar amounts to increase the scale of the investment and then decide whether or not you find the investment acceptable.

Now consider a second investment (investment B) that has a $500 outlay immediately followed by $500 of expected benefits. This investment seems to be unacceptable, but again the $500 is an expectation. Assume that the possible outcomes are $0 if event a_2 with .5 probability occurs or $1,000 if event a_1 with .5 probability occurs.

Investment B with a zero return is clearly undesirable if we consider it as an individual investment. When we combine A and B, however, we have an investment that all of us would find acceptable (see Figure 4.1)

The outcomes of the individual investment A and the individual investment B are uncertain. When we combine the investments, however, the uncertainty about the joint outcomes is eliminated. The factor at work to reduce the uncertainty of the sum of the investments is called the covariance. Whether event a_1 occurs or event a_2 occurs, the outcome of A + B is equal to $1,000. For example, if a_1 occurs, the outcome of A is 0, the outcome of B is $1,000, and the outcome of A + B is $1,000.

The Covariance

The covariance is a useful means of measuring how two random variables react to events. When the value of one investment is large, will the other be large or small? Consider the two random variables X and Y.

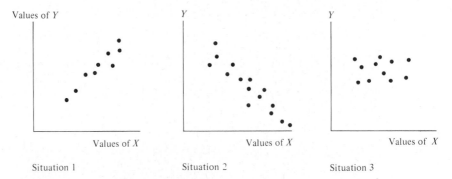

FIGURE 4.2 Examples of Covariance

Three basic relationships are illustrated in Figure 4.2. If we take the product of each pair of values for X and Y in all three situations, we would arrive at a positive amount for the sum or the average of these products. However, in situation 1, the higher the value of X, the higher the value of Y; in situation 2, the higher the value of X, the lower the value of Y; and, in situation 3, the value of Y is not affected by the value of X. We next subtract the mean of X and the mean of Y from the observed values of X and Y. The result is a shifting of the X and Y axes so that the average of the products is positive for situation 1, negative for situation 2, and zero for situation 3. This is shown in Figure 4.3.

The covariance is affected by the scale used to measure the variables. The

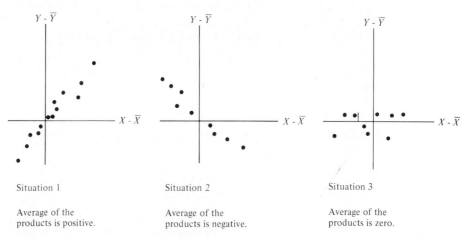

FIGURE 4.3 Examples of Covariance

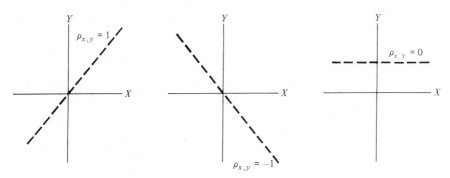

FIGURE 4.4   Correlation Coefficients

correlation coefficient is invariant to scale and is obtained by dividing the covariance by the product of the two standard deviations:

$$\rho_{x,y} = \frac{\text{cov}\,(X,\,Y)}{\sigma_X\sigma_Y}$$

The correlation coefficient $\rho_{X,Y}$ can take on values between -1 and 1 (see Figure 4.4).

The covariance may be written in terms of the correlation coefficient:

$$\text{cov}\,(X,\,Y) = \rho_{X,Y}\sigma_X\sigma_Y$$

The covariance between X and Y may be defined mathematically as

$$\text{cov}\,(X,\,Y) = E[(X - \overline{X})(Y - \overline{Y})]$$

and it can be shown that

$$\text{cov}\,(X,\,Y) = E(XY) - XY$$

If we have two random variables X and Y, the variance of their sum is

$$\text{var}\,(X + Y) = \text{var}\,(X) + \text{var}\,(Y) + 2\,\text{cov}\,(X,\,Y)$$

If we have more than two variables, we have several covariances; for example, with three random variables (X_1, X_2, and X_3),

$$\text{var}\,(X_1 + X_2 + X_3) = \text{var}\,(X_1) + \text{var}\,(X_2) + \text{var}\,(X_3) + 2\,\text{cov}\,(X_1,\,X_2)$$

$$+ 2\,\text{cov}\,(X_1,\,X_3) + 2\,\text{cov}\,(X_2,\,X_3)$$

Note that with three securities there are three different covariances each of which carries a weight of two in the total.

To understand the computation of the variance of the portfolio, it is easiest to use a table of variances and covariances that gives one line and one column for each of the securities. For N securities there are N^2 entries in the table. All entries on the diagonal boxes are variances, and all other entries are covariances. The entries in the upper right-hand half corner (with the table split by the diagonal) mirrors the lower left-hand half. For three securities we have

	1	2	3
1	$var_{1,1}$	$cov_{1,2}$	$cov_{1,3}$
2	$cov_{2,1}$	$var_{2,2}$	$cov_{2,3}$
3	$cov_{3,1}$	$cov_{3,2}$	$var_{3,3}$

With N securities there are N^2 boxes, N variances on the diagonal, and $N^2 - N$ covariances. Since each covariance appears twice ($cov_{i,j} = cov_{j,i}$) and there are N variances, there are $(N^2 - N)/2$ different covariances.

With 100 different assets, there are 10,000 separate entries, 100 variances and 9,900 covariances. Each of 4,950 different covariances are entered into the table twice. Note that there are many more covariances than variances. With many different investments in the portfolio, the covariances tend to be more heavily weighted than the variances (there are more of them).

The Efficient Frontier

Figure 4.5 shows three portfolios. The expected return is measured on Y axis, and the standard deviation of the return is measured on the X axis. Using Figure 4.5 we conclude that

1. Portfolio 2 is better than portfolio 1 (same risk and higher mean return).
2. Portfolio 3 is better than portfolio 1 (same expected return and smaller risk).

Any portfolio that lands within the area bounded by vectors **a** and **b** is better than portfolio 1. It is desirable to move up, to the left, or up and to the left.

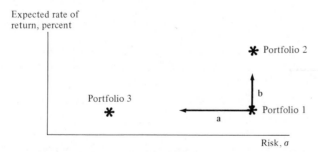

FIGURE 4.5   Choosing Portfolios

If we compare portfolio 2 and 3, we cannot make a definite choice between them. Portfolio 2 has a larger expected return, but it also has more risk. The choice will depend on the investor's preferences.

Taking all portfolios that are not dominated by other portfolios, we can form an efficient frontier of portfolios. All the portfolios on the efficient frontier are eligible for consideration. So far, the portfolios 2 and 3 would be on the frontier but portfolio 1 would not. The choice of a specific portfolio will depend on the investor's preferences.

Forming Portfolios

Portfolios are made up of individual securities or groups of securities that are correlated in some manner. Suppose r_1 and r_2 are random variables measuring the rates of return of two securities whose correlation coefficient is ρ. If $\rho = -1$, r_2 and r_1 are perfectly negatively dependent; that is, an increase in r_1 results in a perfectly predictable decrease in r_2. If $\rho > 0$, there is positive correlation, but knowing r_1 does not allow us to predict the exact value of r_2. If $\rho = 0$, r_1 and r_2 are uncorrelated. If two variables are independent, then $\rho = 0$, but if $\rho = 0$ it does not necessarily mean that the two variables are independent. Figure 4.6 shows a situation in which the two assets A and B are perfectly correlated ($\rho = 1$).

If we start at point A, we have 100 percent invested in asset A. As we substitute asset B for asset A, we move up the line to point B. All combinations of asset A and asset B lie on the line connecting points A and B.

The expected return of the portfolio will be a weighted average of $\bar{r}_1$ and $\bar{r}_2$:

$$\bar{r}_p = x_1\bar{r}_1 + x_2\bar{r}_2$$

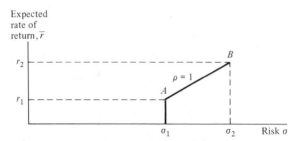

FIGURE 4.6 Perfect Linear Dependence

where x_1 is the proportion invested in asset 1 and x_2 is the proportion invested in asset 2. Appendix 4.2 shows that the standard deviation of the portfolio's return is also a weighted average of the standard deviations of the assets:

$$\sigma_p = x_1\sigma_1 + x_2\sigma_2$$

This simplified expression for the standard deviation of a portfolio can only be used if $\rho = 1$.

If the correlation coefficient is equal to -1, the assets are perfectly negatively correlated. Figure 4.7 shows that when $\rho = -1$, it is possible to attain a zero-risk portfolio. If we start with 100 percent of an investment in asset B, we are at point B. As we substitute some asset A, both the risk and the expected return decrease until point C is reached and the portfolio has zero risk. If still more asset A is introduced, then the investor slides down line CA. There is increasing risk and decreasing expected return.

Any point on line CA is dominated by one or more points on line CB. No investor would want to have an amount of asset A that causes a portfolio to lie on line CA.

The correlation coefficient can take on any value between -1 and $+1$.

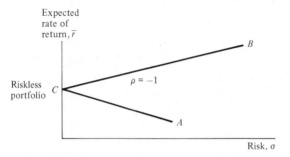

FIGURE 4.7 Perfect Negative Correlation

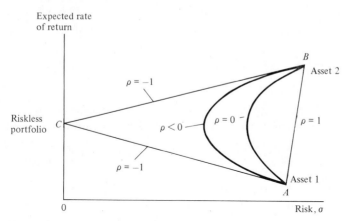

FIGURE 4.8   Two Securities and Different Values of ρ

Figure 4.8 shows the feasible portfolios resulting from different values of ρ. Note that if $\rho = 0$, the locus of feasible portfolios is a curve inside the triangle of *ABC*. If one starts with investment B, substituting any amount of investment A (with $\rho = 0$) will reduce risk. If $\rho < 0$, the risk-reduction potential is even larger.

For any portfolio of two securities with x_1 proportion of the investment in security 1 and x_2 in security 2, with $x_1 + x_2 = 1$,

$$\bar{r}_p = x_1\bar{r}_1 + x_2\bar{r}_2$$

and

$$\sigma_p^2 = x_1^2 \text{ var } (r_1) + x_2^2 \text{ var } (r_2) + 2x_1x_2\rho\sigma_1\sigma_2$$

The construction of an efficient frontier of investments (portfolios) makes use of the concepts illustrated in Figure 4.8. Assets are combined to form new assets that have less risk and an expected return that is larger than the expected return of one of the building block assets. If the correlation coefficient is less than 1, it may be possible to increase the expected return and decrease risk by substituting asset 2 for asset 1. If the correlation coefficient is equal to -1, it is possible for the portfolio to have zero risk.

We want to investigate what happens when we combine two assets that are perfectly negatively correlated. If $\rho = -1$

$$\sigma_p^2 = x_1^2 \text{ var } (r_1) - 2x_1x_2\sigma_1\sigma_2 + x_2^2 \text{ var } (r_2)$$

$$\sigma_p^2 = (x_1\sigma_1 - x_2\sigma_2)^2$$

The variance is equal to zero if:

$$x_1 \sigma_1 = x_2 \sigma_2$$

EXAMPLE 4.2

Let $\bar{r}_1 = .14$, $\sigma_1 = .0735$ and $\bar{r}_2 = .12$, $\sigma_2 = .1470$ with the two investments having a -1 correlation coefficient. Let x_1 be the amount invested in asset 1 and x_2 be the amount invested in asset 2. Table 4.6 shows the results of investing in different mixtures of the two securities.

TABLE 4.6   Two Perfectly Negatively Correlated Assets

x_1	x_2	$\sigma_p = x_1 \sigma_1 - x_2 \sigma_2$
1	0	$\sigma_p = 1(.0735) = .0735$
$\frac{2}{3}$	$\frac{1}{3}$	$\sigma_p = [\frac{2}{3}(.0735) - \frac{1}{3}(.1470)] = (.049 - .049) = 0$
.5	.5	$\sigma_p = [\frac{1}{2}(.0735) - \frac{1}{2}(.1470)] = (.03675 - .0735)$
		$\sigma_p = .03675$
0	1	$\sigma_p = 1(.1470) = .1470$

The Power of Diversification

Independent Investments

We want to show the advantages of diversification if investments are independent and the correlation coefficient is equal to zero.

Consider investment A of Figure 4.9. It has a $400 expected value and is

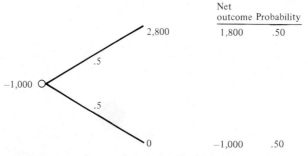

FIGURE 4.9   One Investment: Investment A

desirable to a risk-neutral investor, but a risk-averse investor might reject it because there is a .5 probability of losing $1,000. Any fraction of A can be purchased.

Now assume an investment B that is identical to A except that its outcomes are independent of the outcomes of A. The outcomes of investing $500 in A with .5 probability of winning $1,400 and investing $500 in B are shown in Figure 4.10. Now there is only .25 probability of losing $1,000. Some of the probability of the two extreme outcomes has been shifted to the less extreme outcome of $400. The variance of outcomes has been cut in half.

If there were additional independent investments, we could further reduce the risk. In fact, in this case we could make the probability of a loss approach zero if we had enough independent investments with the same characteristics.

We shall generalize the situation in which we can invest in more than one identical independent investments. For simplification of the conclusions, we assume that all the investments have the same variance:

$$\text{var }(X) = \text{var }(X_1) = \text{var }(X_2) = \cdots = \text{var }(X_n) = 100$$

In Appendix 4.1 it is shown that the variance of the portfolio when one-nth of its value is in each of n independent investments is

$$\text{var }(X_p) = \frac{\text{var }(X)}{n}$$

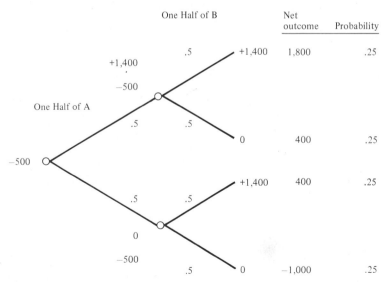

FIGURE 4.10   Two Independent Investments (Half of A and Half of B)

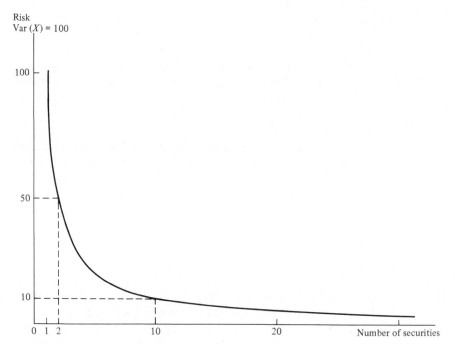

FIGURE 4.11   Risk and Number of Securities: $\rho = 0$

If n approaches infinity, var (X_p) approaches zero. With unsystematic risk, each outcome is independent of the outcomes of the other stocks. As the number of stocks becomes very large, the amount invested in each stock becomes very small and the unsystematic risk in total approaches zero.

If $n = 10$ and var $(X) = 100$;

$$\text{var } (X_p) = \frac{100}{10} = 10$$

If $n = 100$,

$$\text{var } (X_p) = 1$$

Assuming a zero correlation coefficient, we find that the amount of risk reduction is

$$\frac{n-1}{n} \text{ var } (X)$$

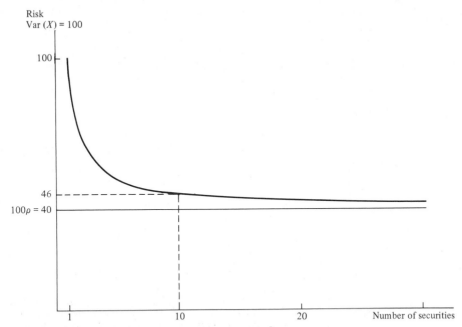

FIGURE 4.12   Risk and Number of Securities: $\rho = .40$

Thus, if $n = 10$,

$$\frac{10 - 1}{10} = .9$$

and the amount of risk reduction is

$$\frac{n - 1}{n} \text{ var } (X) = .9(100) = 90$$

With one security, the risk measure is 100. With the investment spread over 10 securities, the risk is reduced to 10, a reduction of 90. This is illustrated graphically in Figure 4.11 for $\rho = 0$. Figure 4.12 shows the risk with $\rho = .40$.

Positively Correlated Investments

To this point we have assumed $\rho = 0$. We shall continue to assume each security has the same variance equal to var (X), but now we let $\rho \geq 0$. All pairs

TABLE 4.7 Portfolio Variance as Fraction of Individual Security Variance

Number of Securities in the Portfolio	Correlation Between Securities (ρ)					Percentage of Risk Reduction[a]
	1	.8	.5	.1	0	
1	1	1	1	1	1	0
2	1	.9	.75	.55	.50	1/2
10	1	.82	.55	.19	.10	9/10
100	1	.802	.505	.109	.01	99/100
∞	1	.800	.500	.100	.00	1

[a]$(n - 1)/n$.

of investments have the same correlation coefficient. See Appendix 4.3 for the derivation. The risk of a portfolio of n securities is

$$\text{risk} = \frac{1 - \rho}{n} \, \text{var}\,(X) + \rho \, \text{var}\,(X)$$

If n is infinitely large,

$$\text{risk} = \rho \, \text{var}\,(X)$$

Table 4.7 shows the risk for different numbers of securities if the variance of the security is 1. Notice that with $\rho = 1$ there is no risk reduction. With

A Perspective on Investor Diversification

When you look back on the experience of the 1970's, the unpleasant surprises for portfolio managers were less in the unexpected character of the environment than in the unexpected character of the responses to that environment. Stocks were a bad hedge against inflation. High money growth led to high interest rates and vice versa. Bonds yielded less than the inflation rate precisely when inflationary expectations were most intense. The riskless asset—Treasury bills—provided higher returns than most risky assets, but risky stocks outperformed low-risk stocks most of the time.*

* Peter L. Bernstein, "The Concealed Factors," *The Journal of Portfolio Management,* Spring 1980, p. 4.

the other values of ρ there are different amounts of risk. The minimum amount of risk is always ρ var (X). The risk cannot be reduced below the value ρ var (X).

While the amount of risk reduction for a given number of securities depends on the value of ρ, the fraction of risk reduction is equal to $(n - 1)/n$ and is independent of ρ, as long as $\rho \geq 0$.

For $n = 10$, 90 percent of the maximum feasible risk reduction is achieved. Increasing the number of securities to 100 increases the risk reduction to 99

Two Perspectives on Corporate Diversification

We shall remain an independent, fully integrated petro-leum company. We have no plans to diversify outside of the oil industry.

We are large enough in today's environment to remain competitive and efficient and small enough to move quickly in response to opportunities.[*]

- Our long-term economic goal (subject to some qualifications mentioned later) is to maximize the average annual rate of gain in intrinsic business value on a per-share basis. We do not measure the economic significance or performance of Berkshire by its size; we measure by per-share progress. We are certain that the rate of per-share progress will diminish in the future—a greatly enlarged capital base will see to that. But we will be disappointed if our rate does not exceed that of the average large American corporation.

- Our preference would be to reach this goal by directly owning a diversified group of businesses that generate cash and consistently earn above-average returns on capital. Our second choice is to own parts of similar businesses, attained primarily through purchases of marketable common stocks by our insurance subsidiaries. The price and availability of businesses and the need for insurance capital determine any given year's capital allocation.[†]

[*] Leon Hess, Chairman of the Board, Amerada Hess Corporation, *Remarks by Leon Hess*, 1984,
[†] Warren E. Buffett, Chairman of the Board, Berkshire Hathaway, Inc. "Letter to Shareholders," March 14, 1984.

percent of the maximum feasible. If $\rho = 0$, it is possible to reduce the risk to zero.

These formulations all made simplifying assumptions so that we could obtain definite conclusions. If we drop the assumptions, the mathematical presentations and conclusions are more complex and less exact, but the same general type of observations remains. Risk can be reduced by an intelligent theoretically sound diversification policy, but there is a limit to the amount of achievable risk reduction unless the correlation coefficient is equal to or less than zero.

Conclusions

Any asset has an expected return and a variance of returns. This chapter highlights the fact that the correlation of that asset with the other assets held by the investor (or firm) is very important in evaluating the risk of holding the investment from the point of view of the investor (or firm). The covariance is the crucial building block in evaluating the effect on risk of adding an asset to the portfolio of assets. The riskiness of the portfolio is evaluated using the standard deviation of the portfolio's returns.

The main point made in this chapter is that the riskiness of a single investment cannot be evaluated in a meaningful way by looking only at the possible outcomes of the investment taken by itself. In evaluating the riskiness to a corporation of a new asset to be acquired by the corporation, one should take into account how it will affect the dispersion of possible outcomes for the corporation as a whole. Similarly, the common stock of a particular corporation is seldom the sole asset in the portfolio of an investor. The majority of the common stock of large corporations is held by institutions whose portfolios contain dozens and sometimes hundreds of other stocks. Even among individual investors, those who have substantial portfolios are likely to have a significant degree of diversification.

The corporation should take into consideration the nature of the risk associated with the investment and its interaction with the risks of other investments. The process by which risk is incorporated into the decision can be complex. The existence of security markets helps to simplify the decision process tremendously, however. If we assume that the investors are able and willing to diversify, the only risk components that need be taken into account by the corporation (from the point of view of stockholders) are those that the investors cannot eliminate by diversification. This suggests that many investments that have been traditionally considered to be highly risky, such as exploring for new reserves of oil, may turn out to be relatively riskless. Methods of adjusting for risk when a firm is owned by stockholders who have diversified stock portfolios are presented in the next two chapters.

Corporate management may wish to apply a significant risk premium to large investments that could jeopardize the existence of the firm. If managers have special skills and experience that make them more valuable to their present employer than to other firms, and if they derive a large fraction of their income from this employment, they are less able than most stockholders to diversify against events that could threaten the continued existence of the firm.

If we drop the assumption of a large publicly owned firm, we can no longer assume that the investor has attained investment diversification. A major investor in the firm may be adversely affected by a decision that fails to consider nonsystematic risk. The corporation should try to take into consideration the affairs of this investor because the investor may be seeking risk, seeking large gains no matter how risky, or attempting to avoid risk. The decision being made should reflect the owner's preferences.

Review Problem 4.1

With an investment of $5,000 all 10 investments have a variance of 100 and they all have a .5 correlation coefficient. What is the variance of a portfolio of the 10 investments if $500 is invested in each?

Solution to Review Problem 4.1

$$\text{var}\,(X_p) = \frac{1 - \rho}{n}\,\text{var}\,(X) + \rho\,\text{var}\,(X)$$

$$= \frac{.5}{10}\,(100) + .5(100) = 5 + 50 = 55$$

The variance is reduced from 100 to 55, a reduction of 45. The maximum reduction is $100 - 50 = 50$; $45/50 = .9$ of the maximum reduction has been achieved with 10 securities.

Review Problem 4.2

For the two investments shown in Figure 4.1 compute the covariance, the correlation coefficient, and the variance of investing in both investments.

Solution to Review Problem 4.2

Let values of X represent the dollar outcomes of investment A, and values of Y represent the dollar outcomes of B, we would have the following computations:

$$E(X) = E(Y) = .5(1,000) + .5(0) = \$500$$

Event a_i	Probability $P(a_i)$	A X	A X^2	B Y	B Y^2	XY
a_1	.5	\$ 0	\$ 0	\$1,000	\$1,000,000	\$ 0
a_2	.5	\$1,000	\$1,000,000	\$ 0	0	0
			$E(X^2) = \$500,000$		$E(Y^2) = \$500,000$	$E(XY) = 0$

var $(X) = E(X^2) - \bar{X}^2 = 500,000 - 500^2 = 500,000 - 250,000 = 250,000$
var $(Y) = E(Y^2) - \bar{Y}^2 = 500,000 - 500^2 = 500,000 - 250,000 = 250,000$
cov $(X, Y) = E(XY) - \bar{X}\bar{Y} = 0 - (500)(500) = -250,000$
var $(X + Y) = $ var $(X) + $ var $(Y) + 2$ cov $(X, Y) = 250,000 + 250,000$
$\qquad\qquad + 2(-250,000) = 0$

The correlation coefficient is

$$\rho = \frac{\text{cov }(X, Y)}{\sigma_x \sigma_y} = \frac{-250,000}{500 \times 500} = -1$$

Review Problem 4.3

Assume two investments with two possible outcomes:

Event	Probability	Outcome Investment 1	Outcome Investment 2
e_1	.6	.20	0
e_2	.4	.05	.30

Compute the expected rates of return, variances, standard deviations, and the covariance. Also compute the investment split that leads to a zero portfolio variance.

Solution to Review Problem 4.3

Investment 1

e_i	r_1	$p(e_i)$	Expectation	$(r_1 - \bar{r}_1)$	$(r_1 - \bar{r}_1)^2$	$p(r_1 - \bar{r}_1)^2$
e_1	.20	.6	.12	.06	.0036	.00216
e_2	.05	.4	.02	−.09	.0081	.00324
			$\bar{r}_1 = .14$			Var $(r_1) = .00540$
						$\sigma_1 = .0735$

Investment 2

e_i	r_2	$p(e_i)$	Expectation	$(r_2 - \bar{r}_2)$	$(r_2 - \bar{r}_2)^2$	$p(r_2 - \bar{r}_2)^2$
e_1	0	.6	0	−.12	.0144	.00864
e_2	.30	.4	.12	.18	.0324	.01296
			$\bar{r}_2 = .12$			Var $(r_2) = .02160$
						$\sigma_2 = .1470$

Computation of Covariance

e_i	$p(e_i)$	r_1	r_2	$r_1 r_2$	$p(r_1 r_2)$
e_1	.6	.20	0	0	0
e_2	.4	.05	.30	.015	.006
					$E(r_1 r_2) = .006$

$$\text{cov } (r_1, r_2) = E(r_1 r_2) - \bar{r}_1 \bar{r}_2$$

$$= .006 - (.14)(.12) = .006 - .0168 = -.0108$$

The correlation coefficient is

$$\rho = \frac{\text{cov } (r_1, r_2)}{\sigma_1 \sigma_2} = \frac{-.0108}{.0735 \times .4170} = -1.0$$

Since $\rho = -1$, it has been shown that

$$\sigma_p^2 = (x_1 \sigma_1 - x_2 \sigma_2)^2$$

Continuing the example, we can solve for the portfolio that has zero risk. Remember that

$$\sigma_1 = .0735 \qquad \sigma_2 = .147$$

$$\text{var } (r_1) = .0054 \qquad \text{var } (r_2) = .0216$$

Solving for the value of x_1 for which $\sigma_p = 0$,

$$x_1(.0735) - (1 - x_1)(.147) = 0$$

$$x_1 = \tfrac{2}{3}, \quad x_2 = \tfrac{1}{3}$$

With that investment split, we have zero risk:

$$\text{var } (r_p) = \tfrac{4}{9}(.0054) + \tfrac{1}{9}(.0216) - 2(\tfrac{1}{3})(\tfrac{2}{3})(.0735)(.147)$$

$$= .0024 + .0024 - .0048 = 0$$

If we had invested .7 in r_1 and .3 in r_2, we would have

$$\text{var } (r_p) = (.7)^2(.00540) + (.3)^2(.0216) + 2(-.018)(.7)(.3)$$

$$= .002646 + .001944 - .004536 = .000054$$

PROBLEMS

1. Two investments have the following characteristics for an outlay of $800:

	Expected Value	Variance	Standard Deviation
Investment A	$1,000	$100	10
Investment B	2,000	900	30

For an outlay of $800 in each of the two investments ($1,600 in total),
(a) Compute the expected benefits (return).
(b) Compute the variance of the returns if the correlation coefficient is .8.
(c) Compute the variance of the returns if the correlation coefficient is −.8.
(d) Compute the variance of the returns if the investments are independent.

2. The outcomes of investment A are as follows:

Event	Outcome	Probability
e_1	$200	.4
e_2	100	.5
e_3	− 100	.1

Compute the expected value and variance of the investment outcomes.

3. All you are told about an investment is that there is an outlay of $100 and that the returns (net of outlay) have an expectation of $120 and a variance of $7,600.

   Would you accept this investment? Explain.

4. Two investments have the following net returns for the two events indicated:

Event	Probability	Value of Investment A	B
e_1	.6	$600	− $100
e_2	.4	− 400	500

   (a) Compute the expectation and variance of each investment and the covariance of the two investments.
   (b) Compute the correlation coefficient of the two investments.

5. (Problem 4 continued) What is the expected return and variance of the value of investment in both A and B?

6. An investment X has the following net return for the two events indicated:

Event	Probability	Value
e_1	.6	$500
e_2	.4	100

   Compute the expectation and variance of investment in X.

7. A proposed exploratory well for oil will cost $1 million to drill. A large oil deposit would be worth $20 million and a small oil deposit would be worth $2 million; the probabilities of these events are .04 and .10, respectively. If no oil is found, the drillers can collect $200,000 in dry hole money from the owners of nearby leases.

What is the expected profit from drilling and its standard deviation?

8. An investment has the following outcomes and probabilities:

−$ 500	.24
100	.16
500	.36
1,100	.24

Compute the expectation and variance of this investment.

9. The ABC Book Company is considering investing $3 million in an advanced teaching mechanism. If the advanced mechanism is successful, the company expects the investment to have a value of $4 million. If it is unsuccessful, the investment has a negative value of $2 million. The probability of success is .7 and failure .3. A loss of $2 million would be very material to this firm. These results are independent of other projects the firm might do.

   The company is also considering investing $1 million in a new method of producing books. The method has a .4 probability of being workable. If the method works, the value of this investment is computed to be $2 million if the teaching mechanism fails and $0 if the teaching mechanism is successful. If the method of producing books is not successful, there will be a net loss of $1 million resulting from this investment, with a successful teaching mechanism, and the company will break even on this investment if the teaching mechanism is not successful.

	Successful Teaching Mechanism	
Successful Book Method	Yes	No
Yes	0	$2,000,000
No	− $1,000,000	0

Should the company undertake the advanced teaching mechanism or both of the investments?

10. Consider a portfolio consisting of .6 of security A and .4 of security B that have rates of return that are independent.

	Expected Rate of Return	Standard Deviation
Security A	20%	5%
Security B	10	3

(a) The portfolio has an expected rate of return of ＿＿＿＿＿＿ percent and a standard deviation of ＿＿＿＿＿＿ percent.

(b) If the two securities had rates of return that are perfectly positively correlated, then the expected rate of return on the portfolio is ＿＿＿＿＿＿ percent. The standard deviation of the portfolio's return is ＿＿＿＿＿＿ .

(c) If the correlation coefficient of the returns is .7 the variance of the portfolio is ＿＿＿＿＿＿ percent.

11.

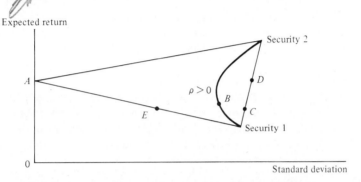

Securities 1 and 2 are to be combined into a portfolio.

(a) If point A results, the correlation coefficient is ＿＿＿＿＿＿ .

(b) If point E results, the correlation coefficient is ＿＿＿＿＿＿ .

(c) If point C results, the correlation is ＿＿＿＿＿＿ .

(d) If point D results, the correlation is ＿＿＿＿＿＿ .

(e) Draw in a curve for the correlation coefficient equal to zero, assuming that portfolio B results from $\rho > 0$.

12. There are two investments with the following characteristics:

Investment	Expected Return	Variance
A	.10	.09
B	.20	.25

The correlation coefficient is $-.5$.

    If .4 is invested in A and .6 in B;

(a) The portfolio's expected return is ＿＿＿＿＿＿ .

(b) The variance of the portfolio's return is ＿＿＿＿＿＿ .

(c) The covariance is ＿＿＿＿＿＿ .

13. Suppose that an investor has the following information for two securities:

Security	$\bar{r}_i$	σ_i
A	.05	.02
B	.12	.06

The correlation coefficient between A and B is .2.

Compute the expected return and variance of the following portfolios.
(a) All invested in A.
(b) All invested in B.
(c) .5 invested in A and .5 invested in B.
(d) .1 invested in A and .9 invested in B.

14. If there are four securities in a portfolio, how many different covariances will there be?

15. Test for $n = 4$ the formula $(n^2 - n)$ as a shortcut for determining the number of covariances that there will be in the formula for the variance of a portfolio and $(n^2 - n)/2$ for the number of different covariances. N is the number of securities in the portfolio.

16. If there are 100 securities in a portfolio, how many covariances will there be? What does this tell you about the importance of the covariances in determining the value of the portfolio's variance?

17. Suppose that an investor has the following information on two securities that have a correlation coefficient $= -1$.

Security	$\bar{r}_i$	σ_i
A	.10	.05
B	.20	.08

(a) What combination of A and B will lead to a portfolio with no variance?
(b) What will be the expected return of that portfolio?

18. Assume that a small firm has enough funds to drill one oil well and that the cost of drilling a well is $1 million. A large firm has enough funds to drill 50 wells.
(a) What is the maximum loss of the small firm?
(b) What is the maximum loss of the large firm?
(c) Which of the two firms has more risk?

19. Assume that the average oil well returns a value of benefits of $1.5 million for every well drilled (a well costs $1 million on the average to drill), resulting in an expected net value of $500,000 per well. Assume that you are in charge of investing $1 million. You have the choice of investing in 1 well and owning it completely or investing in a series of 10 equally

desirable wells and having .1 ownership in each. The probability of a successful well is .1.

What decision would you make? Explain.

20. Assume that you have to predict the number of successful wells for a small firm that will drill 1 well and for a large firm that will drill 100 wells.

Which prediction would you guess will be closest to the actual number of successful wells?

21. (Problem 20 continued)   Assume that you are to estimate the proportion of successes for the two firms.

Which estimate is likely to be closer?

22. An investment firm conducts a contest where the person who recommends 20 stocks that perform the best over a given period wins a prize.

What investment strategy would you recommend to win the contest?

23. Assume that you are approached about the possibility of investing in a Broadway play. After conducting some research, you find that the expected profits are $800,000 per play and that approximately 25 percent of the plays that open on Broadway show a profit.

Explain whether you would be willing to invest in a play being prepared for Broadway.

24. Answer the following two questions as you would if *you* were faced with the betting situations. Assume that the bets are legal and moral.
   (a) *Situation 1:* A fair coin will be tossed fairly. If a head appears, you will receive $5. If a tail appears, you will receive nothing. How much would you pay to participate in this game?
   (b) *Situation 2:* Two evenly matched basketball teams are playing this Saturday. You will receive $5 if you pick the winner, $0 otherwise. How much would you pay for this gamble?

25. In the accompanying table below, X, Y, and Z are three different investments, each with four different outcomes. The decision maker is free to accept or reject each investment.

Find the expected profit and the standard deviation of profit for each of the following:
   (a) X alone   (b) Y alone   (c) Z alone
   (d) X + Y   (e) X + Z

Event	Probability of Event	Profit for Event		
		X	Y	Z
e_1	.25	$1,000	0	$1,000
e_2	.25	1,000	0	0
e_3	.25	0	$1,000	1,000
e_4	.25	0	1,000	0

26. The Boeing Company was faced with a major decision: To what extent should it independently develop a supersonic air transport? The estimates of the cost of developing such a plane ranged from $1 to $4 billion. During the period of decision other companies (in other countries) were acting jointly in the development of such a plane.

    If you were advising the president of Boeing, what would you suggest?

27. Through their subsidiaries the ABC Company and the XYZ Company are both currently distributing automobiles in the country of Acro. The profits per year of the two subsidiaries are currently as follows:

ABC	$10,000,000
XYZ	20,000,000

    The ABC Company is considering establishing a manufacturing plant in Acro. An analyst has projected a profit of $38 million after the plant begins operations (this assumes that the XYZ Company continues to distribute but not manufacture in the country).

    An analyst for the XYZ Company has heard of the plans of the ABC Company. If the plant by ABC is built, the analyst projects XYZ's profits to fall to $4 million. If the XYZ Company builds a plant and the ABC Company does not, she anticipates profits of $38 million and a decrease in the profits of ABC to $4 million.

    If both companies build plants, it is expected that they would both earn $5 million per year.

    What course of action would you recommend for the ABC Company?

REFERENCES

Brealey, R. A. *An Introduction to Risk and Return from Common Stocks.* Cambridge, Mass.: M.I.T. Press, 1969. Second edition, 1983.

Elton, E. J., and M. J. Gruber. *Modern Portfolio Theory and Investment Analysis.* New York: John Wiley & Sons, Inc., 1981.

Fama, E. F. "Risk Return and Equilibrium: Some Clarifying Comments." *Journal of Finance*, March 1968.

Markowitz, H. M. "Portfolio Selection." *Journal of Finance*, March 1952.

———. *Portfolio Selection: Efficient Diversification of Investments.* New York: John Wiley & Sons, Inc., 1959.

———. "Markowitz Revisited." *Financial Analysts Journal*, September-October 1976, 3–8.

Merton, R. C. "An Inter-temporal Capital Asset Pricing Model." *Econometrica*, 1973.

Mossin, J. "Equilibrium in a Capital Assets Market." *Econometrica*, October 1966.

Sharpe, W. F. *Investments*, 2nd ed. Englewood Cliffs, N.J.: Prentice-Hall, Inc., 1981.

Sharpe, W. F. *Portfolio Theory and Capital Markets.* New York: McGraw-Hill Book Company, 1971.

Tobin, J. "Liquidity Preference as Behavior Towards Risk." *Review of Economic Studies*, February 1958.

Appendix 4.1   The Variance of a Portfolio with Independent Investments

Assume there are n independent investments each requiring the same initial outlay, with payoffs of $X_1, X_2, \ldots, X_n$, and variances of $\mathrm{var}(X_1), \mathrm{var}(X_2), \ldots, \mathrm{var}(X_n)$. All of the investments have the same variance, $\mathrm{var}(X)$. Form a portfolio by buying one-nth of the payoff of each investment. The payoff of the portfolio is

$$X_p = \frac{X_1}{n} + \frac{X_2}{n} + \cdots + \frac{X_n}{n}$$

The variance of the portfolio is

$$\mathrm{var}\,(X_p) = \mathrm{var}\left(\frac{X_1}{n} + \frac{X_2}{n} + \cdots + \frac{X_n}{n}\right)$$

We can factor out the $1/n$:

$$= \frac{1}{n^2}\,\mathrm{var}\,(X_1 + X_2 + \cdots + X_n)$$

Since the investments are independent;

$$\mathrm{var}\,(X_1 + X_2 + \cdots + X_n) = \mathrm{var}\,(X_1) + \cdots + \mathrm{var}\,(X_n)$$

and since all the variances are equal

$$\mathrm{var}\,(X_1) + \cdots + \mathrm{var}\,(X_n) = n\,\mathrm{var}\,(X)$$

we now have

$$\mathrm{var}\,(X_p) = \frac{n\,\mathrm{var}\,(X)}{n^2} = \frac{\mathrm{var}\,(X)}{n}$$

Appendix 4.2   Perfectly Correlated ($\rho = 1$)

With $\rho = 1$, we have

$$\text{var}(r_p) = x_1^2 \,\text{var}(r_1) + x_2^2 \,\text{var}(r_2) + 2x_1x_2\sigma_1\sigma_2$$

$$\text{var}(r_p) = (x_1\sigma_1 + x_2\sigma_2)^2$$

$$\sigma_p = x_1\sigma_1 + x_2\sigma_2$$

Appendix 4.3   The Number of Securities and Diversification

Assume now that the n investments referred to in Appendix 4.1 are not independent. Each pair of investments has the same non-negative correlation coefficient, ρ. As before, a portfolio is formed by buying one-nth of the payoff of each of the n investments. The payoff of the portfolio is X_p. We want to show that

$$\text{var}(X_p) = \frac{(1 - \rho) + \rho n}{n} \,\text{var}(X)$$

As explained in the chapter, the variance of a portfolio of n assets consists of the sum of n variances and of $(n^2 - n)$ covariances. Under the present assumptions each variance term is equal to $\dfrac{1}{n^2} \,\text{var}(X)$. A typical covariance term is equal to

$$\text{cov}\left(\frac{1}{n}X_1, \frac{1}{n}X_2\right) = \frac{1}{n^2} \,\text{cov}(X_1, X_2)$$

$$= \frac{1}{n^2} \,\text{var}(X)\rho$$

Therefore the variance of the portfolio is

$$\text{var}(X_p) = n\left[\frac{1}{n^2}\text{var}(X)\right] + (n^2 - n)\left[\frac{1}{n^2}\text{var}(X)\rho\right]$$

$$= \left[\frac{1}{n} + \frac{n\rho - \rho}{n}\right]\text{var}(X)$$

$$= \left[\frac{1 - \rho + n\rho}{n}\right]\text{var}(X)$$

If $\rho = 1$ then

$$\text{var}(X_\rho) = \text{var}(X)$$

and there is no reduction in portfolio variance from adding securities. If $\rho = 0$, then

$$\text{var}(X_p) = \frac{1}{n}\text{var}(X)$$

and it is possible to have the variance of the portfolio approach zero.

Chapter 5

The Capital Asset Pricing Model

Major Topics

1. The use of markets to reduce risk; the capital asset pricing model: the capital market line and the separation theorem.
2. The security characteristic line and the beta measure of an investment.
3. Systematic and unsystematic risk.
4. The security market line (expected return as a function of beta).

A Market Model

The Risk-Free Asset

The previous chapter presented the basic portfolio analysis but left out one crucial element. There was no opportunity to invest in a risk-free asset (or, more exactly, a default-free asset). When that opportunity is included in the analysis, we can derive a theoretical development called the capital asset pricing model (CAPM). The capital asset pricing model is an extension of the portfolio literature of the 1950s and early 1960s. The main change is that the CAPM makes use of the prices that the market is setting for return-risk trade-offs rather than uses subjective measures of attitudes toward risk (such as the risk preferences of specific investors).

The capital asset pricing model is a major contribution to modern business finance theory and practice. Wall Street analysts currently are constructing portfolios using the theories and models presented in this chapter, but even more important than present practice is the fact that the extent of use of the basic concepts in this chapter can be expected to increase in the future. The models will be modified through time to include more and more refinements, but future market models will be built on present understanding.

It is necessary to know the willingness of an investor to exchange risk for expected return before definitive statements can be made concerning the evaluation of risky investment alternatives and to illustrate how market return-risk trade-offs enter into decisions.*

The Assumptions

To understand the CAPM and its limitations, it is necessary to understand the assumptions on which the model is based. It is a single-period model with no assumptions being made about the interaction of return and risk through time. It is assumed that the investor is only interested in the expected return and standard deviation (or variance) of the portfolio's outcomes. This is a theoretical deficiency. For most probability distributions, this ignores other information that an investor might consider to be relevant—the expected value and variance does define exactly a normal probability distribution.

It is assumed that all investors must be persuaded to take more risk by the prospect of a higher expected return (they are risk averse). The actions of an investor do not affect price. The investors are "price takers." The investors can invest at the default-free rate (r_f), and generally we assume that they can borrow at the same rate; this assumption is easily dropped. Investors can sell securities they do not own; that is, they can borrow securities to sell them (this is called a short sale). All investors think the same about the expected return and variance of all securities (they have homogeneous expectations), and they are all perfectly diversified.

The quantity of securities to be purchased is fixed and divisible (securities of any dollar amount can be purchased). There are no transaction costs and taxes.

Many of these assumptions could be dropped, and a model very much like the conventional CAPM would be derived. One important function served by this set of assumptions is a simplification of the model so that we are not distracted by elements that are not crucial to our understanding.

---

* Much of the analysis performed here is based on articles by Markowitz annd Sharpe. See Harry Markowitz, "Portfolio Selection," *Journal of Finance*, March 1952, pp. 77–91; and W. F. Sharpe, "Capital Asset Prices: A Theory of Market Equilibrium Under Conditions of Risk," *Journal of Finance*, September 1964, pp. 425–442.

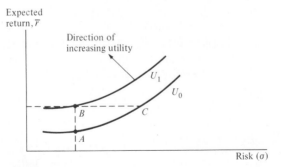

FIGURE 5.1

The Investors

With risk aversion an investor wants a larger expected return as risk (defined as the standard deviation of outcomes) is increased.

We assume utility-maximizing investors who (1) are risk averse, (2) measure the risk of an investment portfolio by the standard deviation of the yield on that investment portfolio, and (3) have indifference curves (different combination of expected return and standard deviation for which the investors are indifferent) that have the shape shown in Figure 5.1.* By definition, any point on the indifference curve U_1 is equally desirable for the investor in question; furthermore, since point B has a higher expected return with no change in risk from point A, a risk-averting investor would find B preferable to A. Finally, point B lies on the indifference curve U_1, and all points on U_1 are preferable to those lying on U_0. Point B is preferred to point C since it has the same expected return and a smaller amount of risk.

Portfolio Analysis with a Riskless Security: The Capital Asset Pricing Model

Up to this point we have indicated that an investor, with a set of expectations, should determine the set of efficient portfolios and proceed to find which portfolio of that set lies on the highest indifference utility curve. All we observe are individual portfolios. We have no information about how the market trades expected return for risk with risky portfolios.

---

* See James Tobin, "Liquidity Preference as a Behavior Towards Risk," *Review of Economic Studies*. February 1958, pp. 65–86, for a discussion of the states of nature and modes of investor behavior that imply this assumption.

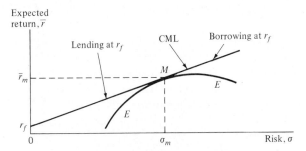

FIGURE 5.2   The Capital Market Line

Fortunately, if we assume the existence of a riskless security and extend portfolio analysis theory to cover that situation, we obtain some useful insights. Government bonds held to maturity are essentially a riskless asset. Therefore, every investor has a riskless security available. "Riskless" as used here refers only to the risk of default and not to other types of risk.

Consider a riskless security earning a pure time value of money rate, r_f (such as the yield of a U.S. Treasury bill). If a portfolio consisting of the riskless security and a risky portfolio of marketable securities $(\bar{r}_m, \sigma_m)$ were purchased, the expected mean and standard deviation of the different portfolios would lie on the straight line connecting the two points r_f and M. This is shown in Figure 5.2. For a proof see Appendix 5.1. Point M is the tangent of the line originating at r_f and the efficient frontier determined without considering the risk-free asset. Although there are other possible portfolios made up of the risk-free asset and efficient portfolios (other points on the efficient frontier EE), none of them is as desirable as the portfolios represented by the line r_fM. The line r_fM is called the capital market line.

If 100 percent of the portfolio is invested in portfolio M, the investor will earn r_m with risk σ_m. If some risk-free asset is substituted for M, the line r_fM defines the feasible combinations of expected return and risk that are possible.

If the investor supplements the investable resources by borrowing at a rate of r_f and investing in portfolio M, the right-hand extension of r_fM defines the expected return-risk possibilities. Since funds are being borrowed at r_f and invested to earn r_m, where r_m is larger than r_f, the borrowing increases the expected profit, but it also increases the portfolio's risk.

Choose any point on curve EE other than M. Note that for the same risk, a higher expected return can be earned by investing in a mix of M and the risk-free asset and being on the line r_fM. The line r_fM offers a set of investment opportunities that is at least as desirable as all points on the efficient frontier (the set of investment opportunities that excludes the risk-free asset).

Different investors (with differing degrees of risk aversion) will have optimal portfolios that lie on different points on the capital market line, but all optimal portfolios will consist of the riskless asset and the portfolio M, which is called the market portfolio.

There are two steps in the determination of the investor's optimum portfolio. Step 1 determines point M, the market portfolio. Assuming that all investors have the same expectations, all investors hold a portion of the same market portfolio. The second step is to determine the optimum point on line $r_f M$. This is the optimum mix of the market portfolio M and the risk-free asset. The theory (originated by Tobin) supporting this two-step process is called the separation theorem.

The market portfolio consists of all risky assets held in the same proportions as their relative total market value. Investors whose common objective is to achieve the maximum amount of diversification would include in their portfolio every security available. Securities are defined here to include common stock and any other security for which there is a market. Thus warrants, convertible bonds, and preferred stock issues would be included in this portfolio.

In deciding how to allocate their assets, the investors do not attempt to anticipate future changes in the value of each security, but use the existing market valuations. Thus, if the outstanding common stock of company X represented .035 percent of the value of the equity of all companies, the stock would represent .035 percent of the value of the portfolio. The investor would literally be buying a share in the capital market; we shall call the resulting investment the market portfolio.

We shall assume that because of the diversification characteristics of the market portfolio and the risk aversion of most investors, the prices of the securities in the market portfolio have adjusted so that an investor could not earn a higher rate of return for the same or a lower level of risk in some other form of investment. The level of risk associated with the market portfolio may be too high or too low for a particular investor, however. Investors can lower the level of risk to which they are exposed and still invest in the market portfolio by buying some of the risk-free asset.

Regardless of the location of the optimal portfolio for each investor along the line, each investor (except those at the two extreme points) is trading off risk for return at a rate equal to the slope of the straight line; that is, the slope of each investor's indifference curve at the point of tangency with the efficient portfolio line is equal to the slope of the line. This marginal trade-off rate (see Appendix 5.1) between expected return and risk is $(\bar{r}_m - r_f)/\sigma_m$. This trade-off is available to each investor.

If the investor can borrow at r_f and is willing to accept more risk than σ_m, then the right-hand extension of the line $r_f M$ applies. Whether the investor borrows (moves to the right of M) or invests in a riskless security (moves to the left of M) depends on the investor's risk preferences. But all investors will have the market portfolio except for those investors who only want the risk free security.

Note that the optimum portfolio is being chosen using the expected return and the standard deviation of the portfolio. When we consider the risk of individual securities, we shall consider the covariance of the security with the market portfolio to be a relevant risk measure.

The Expected Return

Assume that an investor owns the market portfolio. In equilibrium if we add a very small amount of a new security i, the expected return-risk trade-off that results from the inclusion of i must equal the market's current trade-off rate. For this to happen, it can be shown that it is necessary that security i's expected return be equal to

$$\bar{r}_i = r_f + (\bar{r}_m - r_f)\beta_i$$

where

$\bar{r}_i$ = the equilibrium expected return of security i

r_f = the return from the risk-free asset

$\bar{r}_m$ = the expected return from investing in the market

β_i = the beta of security i, where $\beta_i = \text{cov}\,(r_i, r_m)/\sigma_m^2$

The term $(\bar{r}_m - r_f)\beta_i$ is the adjustment to the risk-free r_f for the risk of security i.

The beta measures the amount of systematic risk, that is, the risk arising because of fluctuations in the market return. There is no adjustment for risk specific to the firm (unsystematic risk) in the CAPM, since it is assumed that the unsystematic risk goes to zero given the very large number of investments (the unsystematic components are independent).

The beta of a security measures how the security's return is correlated with the market's return; thus it is a measure of the security's systematic risk.

The Security Characteristic Line

The excess return from investing in the market portfolio compared to investing in the risk-free security is $r_m - r_f$. The excess return from investing in security i is $r_i - r_f$. If the excess return for security i is plotted against the excess market return and a regression line is drawn for these points, we obtain the security characteristic line. This line can be drawn for any security or portfolio of securities. The slope of this line is the beta (β_i) of the security i (see Appendix 5.2) and the intercept is the alpha (α_i). We would expect the intercept to be equal to zero, but when actual regressions are run, α tends to be positive. Alpha measures the security's excess return when the market's excess return is zero.

The alpha of a security is a security's earning rate in excess of the risk-free return when the market earns only the risk-free return (a zero excess return). When the market earns a zero excess return, we would expect any security in equilibrium also to earn a zero excess return (an alpha equal to zero). While the weighted average of the alphas of all securities is equal to zero, some securities will have positive alphas and some will have negative alphas based on the observed returns.

If the market thinks that the empirical data leading to a positive alpha will continue in the future, the security is attractive. It will be purchased, and the price will be driven up and the expected return down so that the expected alpha is equal to zero. Because of market imperfections (including imperfect forecasts), it is not surprising that when time passes and the actual returns are plotted, the alpha of the security will not be exactly equal to zero. The best guess of the alpha of a security, if we think the market is in equilibrium, is zero, but it would be surprising if the actual alpha resulting from the plot of excess returns were zero.

If the CAPM neglects relevant factors that are actually considered by investors, the alpha of a security (or a class of securities) may be expected to be positive or negative because of these neglected factors. For example, the common stock of electric utilities building nuclear generating plants could have negative alphas because the CAPM does not take into consideration specific risk of building nuclear generating plants, but the market does consider this risk.

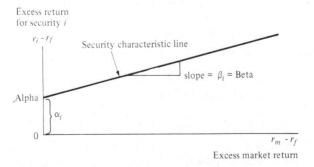

FIGURE 5.3 The Security Characteristic Line

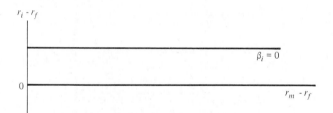

FIGURE 5.4   A Security Characteristic Line with $\beta = 0$

Figure 5.3 shows a security with a positive β. The β can also be zero (the excess return for the security is not correlated with the market's excess return), or negative. Figure 5.4 shows a zero beta characteristic line (the intercept will depend on the value of α). The excess return for a security with a zero beta is not affected by the level of the market return.

If the beta is equal to one and an alpha of zero, we would have for different excess market returns

Excess Market Return	Excess Security Return ($\beta = 1$)
.00	.00
.05	.05
.10	.10
.20	.20
.40	.40

Whatever the excess market return, the security excess return is equal to the excess market return.

If $\alpha = .04$, we would then have

$$(r_i - r_f) = \alpha + (r_m - r_f)\beta$$

and for the excess market returns we would have

Excess Market Return	Excess Security Return $\alpha = .04, \beta = 1$
.00	.04
.05	.09
.10	.14 ·
.20	.24
.40	.44

If $\alpha = 0$ and $\beta = 2$, we would have

Excess Market Return	Excess Security Return $\alpha = 0, \beta = 2$
.00	.00
.05	.10
.10	.20
.20	.40
.40	.80

If $\alpha = 0$ and $\beta = .5$, we would have

Excess Market Return	Excess Security Return $\alpha = 0, \beta = .5$
.00	.00
.05	.025
.10	.05
.20	.10
.40	.20

The following betas were taken from the September 1984 Merrill Lynch publication, *Quantitative Analysis* (remember, betas change through time).

	Beta
Anchor Hocking	1.0
Asarco	1.5
Atlantic City Electric	.7
Chrysler Corp.	1.4
Eastman Kodak	.6
Five-firm average beta	1.04

It can be proven that

$$\beta_i = \frac{\text{cov } (r_i, r_m)}{\text{var } (r_m)} = \frac{\rho_{i,m}\sigma_i}{\sigma_m} \tag{5.1}$$

Example 5.1

Assume that the correlation between a security i and the market is .82. The security has a standard deviation of .045 and the market has a standard deviation of .034. The beta of the security is

$$\beta_i = \frac{\rho_{i,m}\sigma_i}{\sigma_m} = \frac{.82(.045)}{.034} = 1.085$$

The beta coefficient of a stock (β_i) is widely advocated as the appropriate measure of a stock's risk. It includes the stock's correlation with the market ($\rho_{i,m}$) and the standard deviation of the stock (σ_i) compared to the standard deviation of the market (σ_m).

The beta of a portfolio is the weighted average of the betas of the components.

$$\beta_p = \sum_i x_i \beta_i \tag{5.2}$$

For example, if .6 of the portfolio is invested in a security with a beta of 1.3 and .4 is invested in a security with a beta of .9, we have

$$\beta_p = .6(1.3) + .4(.9) = .78 + .36 = 1.14$$

Systematic and Unsystematic Risk

It is conventional theory to separate risk into two components. One component is systematic risk or market risk that represents the change in value resulting from market value changes. Systematic risk can be somewhat reduced by the choice of securities (low-beta securities). Also, reducing systematic risk in this way may increase total risk, since the investor's portfolio will not be perfectly diversified. The second type of risk is residual or unsystematic risk. This risk is specific to the company (or asset) and is independent to what happens to the other securities. If the investor's portfolio consists of a very large number of securities with no security being a large percentage of the portfolio, then this residual risk is equal to var $(X)/n$. If n is very large, this unsystematic risk can be made to approach zero by a strategy of perfect diversification. Figure 5.5 shows the effect on total risk of adding securities.

With a portfolio of 10 securities, 90 percent of the unsystematic risk is eliminated. With a portfolio of 100 securities, 99 percent of the unsystematic risk is eliminated. The systematic risk remains.

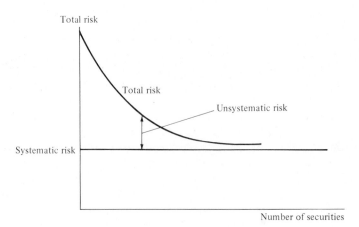

FIGURE 5.5   Risk Reduction by Diversification

If the costs of diversification are relatively low, investors will not be willing to pay more for a security simply because it carries a relatively low burden of unsystematic risk (which can be diversified away). Similarly, securities that carry a large amount of unsystematic risk will not suffer a serious price disadvantage.

To anticipate the conclusions of this chapter; to the extent that security prices are determined by the activities of the investors who can diversify their portfolios at low cost, the prices of securities will be set in such a way that differentials in expected rates of return will reflect primarily differences in the amount of systematic risk to which the securities are exposed.

While a middle manager might find the risk of a specific asset to be of interest, the top management of a firm will want to know the effect of the asset on the overall risk of the firm. At the investor level, investors should be more interested in the effect of the specific asset on the riskiness of their portfolios than the risk of a specific asset. Managers are likely to be interested in the effect of the specific asset on the risk of their careers.

We find it useful to break down risk into two components: (1) risk that can be eliminated by diversification, which is termed unsystematic risk, and (2) risk that is still present when all unsystematic risk has been eliminated, which is termed systematic risk. The latter reflects how the investments in the portfolio are correlated with the market. Only systematic risk is relevant for a perfectly diversified investor.

The beta of a security measures its systematic risk. This is the risk associated with changes in the market's excess return. Since most securities have betas between the values of .8 and 1.2 and most investors want extensive diversification, it is difficult to reduce the systematic risk by changing the composition of the risky securities in the portfolio (by definition the beta of the market is 1.0).

Unsystematic risk can be diversified away because each security's unsystematic risk is independent of the unsystematic risk of other securities. If the portfolio consists of a very large number of securities with no security being a large proportion of the portfolio, the unsystematic risk of the portfolio will approach zero. It does not take many securities for the unsystematic risk of the portfolio to approach zero.

A beta coefficient of unity indicates that a security has the same amount of systematic risk as the market portfolio. A beta coefficient greater (less) than unity indicates the security is riskier (safer) than the market portfolio. Betas based on actual data are prepared by Merrill Lynch, Wells Fargo Bank, and the Value Line investor service as well as others. These are called historical betas. Fundamental betas would be ex ante estimates based on the capital structure and operating characteristics of the firm.

The Security Market Line

Consider what happens to expected return as we move from a security with a low level of systematic risk to a security with a higher level. We find that for any security i the expected return $(\bar{r}_i)$ is

$$\bar{r}_i = r_f + \beta_i(\bar{r}_m - r_f) \tag{3}$$

This relationship is the security market line; it is the major mathematical relationship of the capital asset pricing model. Figure 5.6 shows the security market line. Note that β is measured on the X axis and expected return on the Y axis. M is the market portfolio with a beta of 1. The slope of the line is $(\bar{r}_m - r_f)$. The risk premium is $\beta_i(\bar{r}_m - r_f)$ for a security with beta β_i.

If the risk is $\beta = 1$, then the expected return is $\bar{r}_m$ and the investment is equivalent to the market portfolio. The security market line leads to a conclu-

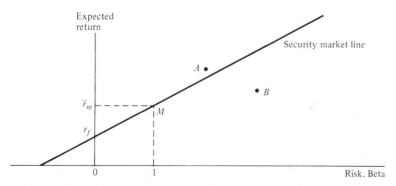

FIGURE 5.6   The Security Market Line

sion that if a security has more systematic risk the market will require a higher return.

Earlier we wrote that

$$\bar{r}_i = r_f + (\bar{r}_m - r_f)\beta_i \tag{5.3}$$

but since

$$\beta_i = \frac{\text{cov}(r_i, r_m)}{\text{var}(r_m)} = \frac{\rho_{i,m}\sigma_i}{\sigma_m} \tag{5.1}$$

we can write the formulation for $\bar{r}_i$ in a variety of forms by substituting for β. In addition, if we define

$$\lambda = \frac{\bar{r}_m - r_f}{\text{var}(r_m)} \tag{5.4}$$

then

$$\bar{r}_i = r_f + \lambda \, \text{cov}(r_i, r_m) \tag{5.5}$$

The equation for $\bar{r}_i$ can be presented in a large number of different forms. All the forms have r_i as a function of r_f, $(\bar{r}_m - r_f)$ and β or the components of β.

Security A of Figure 5.6 is above the security market line. It is a higher expected return than the market requires for its given task. We can expect the price of A to increase so that its expected return decreases and A returns to the security market line. Investors will buy A, drive its price up and its return down.

Security B is below the security market line. We can expect the price of B to decrease as investors avoid it so that its expected return increases and B will then sit on the security market line. In equilibrium, all securities will be on the security market line.

In understanding the several graphs that have been presented, it is useful to keep the following facts in mind:

	X Axis	Y Axis
Capital market line $\left(\text{the slope is } \dfrac{\bar{r}_m - r_f}{\sigma_m}\right)$	Standard deviation	Expected return
Security characteristic line (the slope is the beta)	Excess market return	Excess return for security
Security market line (the slope is $\bar{r}_m - r_f$)	Beta	Expected return

All three of the equations describe relationships that should exist in equilibrium if the capital asset pricing model is correct. The capital market line applies only to portfolios that are a mixture of the market portfolio and the riskless asset. The security market line applies to any security (or portfolio of securities) whose price is in equilibrium. The security characteristic line shows how deviations of the return on the market portfolio from its expected level affects the returns of individual securities or portfolios.

One important factor should be kept in mind. We are interested in what return the market expects to earn for a given amount of risk. To determine this, we need to know the return that is expected to be earned in the market $(\bar{r}_m)$ as well as how the risk of a specific security compares to the risk of the market. The model needs expectations in order to be used correctly. All we shall have are data based on past events that we shall use to estimate the variables that we need. For example, one problem is that the beta will change through time. Also, the value of r_f will depend on the maturity of the government security that is used. It is not easy to use the CAPM in an exact manner.

Use of the CAPM

Even though the assumptions on which the CAPM is based limit the generality of the model, it is still widely used. Among the uses are

1. To estimate the cost of equity capital using

$$\bar{r}_i = r_f + (\bar{r}_m - r_f)\beta_i$$

   These estimates are used both for public utility regulatory proceedings and determining the required return to be earned by operating divisions of corporations.
2. To form portfolios of securities (the weighted average of the betas of all the securities is one relevant risk measure if the investor is imperfectly diversified).
3. To evaluate securities—if the expected return is larger than

$$\bar{r}_i = r_f + (\bar{r}_m - r_f)\beta_i$$

   the security is a "bargain."

If a security has a larger expected return than the return indicated by the CAPM all investors (with homogeneous expectations) will buy it until its expected return is lowered to be equal to

$$\bar{r}_i = r_f + (\bar{r}_m - r_f)\beta_i$$

In like manner if a security i is expected to earn less than

$$r_f + (\bar{r}_m - r_f)\beta_i$$

no one will buy (some will sell it short), its price will decrease, and its expected return will increase.

All securities are contained in the market portfolio in proportion to their market value. The beta of the market portfolio is 1.

The Market Model

Let us assume the following linear relationship:

$$r_i = \alpha_i + r_m\beta_i + e_i$$

where

r_i = the return of security i

α_i = the intercept

r_m = the market return

β_i = the beta of security i

e_i = a random element that affects the return

We assume that the average of the e_i's is equal to zero and that the values of the random elements of different securities are independent of each other

> *Is the capital asset pricing model dead? As long as we have free markets in which investors are risk averse rather than risk-seekers, they will tend to price securities so that the riskier asset classes will have higher expected returns than the less risky classes.*
>
> *Is modern portfolio theory dead? . . . As long as the interaction of individual securities within a portfolio produces results that are different from the performance of a single security, the art of composing a portfolio will remain a different art from the skills employed in security selection as such.*
>
> * Peter L. Bernstein, "Dead—or Alive and Well?" The *Journal of Portfolio Management,* Winter 1981, p. 4.

> ## Hank Cable
>
> Hank Cable, the managing partner of the Common Stock Equity Fund, managed a portfolio of over a billion dollars of common stock equity capital. His take-home pay was heavily affected by his ability to forecast the market turns as well as his ability to pick the "right" stocks.
>
> And what did Hank invest his own savings in? Most anything except common stock. He reasoned, "My wages depend on my ability to perform well in the market. It would be too risky for me to also invest in common stocks."
>
> He diversified!

and that successive values of the random element for a particular security are independent.

If r_i of a security and r_m of the market are measured for a series of periods, then we can obtain an estimate of α and β for that security by the use of a regression analysis (fitting a line to the data).

The market model

$$r_i = \alpha_i + r_m\beta_i + e_i$$

used for empirical analysis should be distinguished from the security market line

$$\bar{r}_i = r_f + (\bar{r}_m - r_f)\beta_i$$

which is the basic fundamental equation for the CAPM.

Conclusions

The theoretical finance literature is being rewritten in terms of the capital asset pricing model. In addition, the practical inhabitants of Wall Street are applying the CAPM theories in making real decisions. The next step will be for finance officers to apply the capital asset pricing model to their decisions.

The capital asset pricing model says that investors have available a market basket of risky securities and the opportunity to invest in securities with no risk of default. Risk preferences of investors dictate a combination of the market basket of the risky securities and the riskless securities. In equilibrium, the return of any security must be such that the investor expects to earn a basic return equal to the return on a default-free security plus an adjustment that is heavily influenced by the "correlation" of the security's return and the market's return. If the return from the investment is positively correlated with the market return, the equilibrium return will be larger than the default-free return. If the correlation is negative, the equilibrium return will be smaller than the default-free return. We cannot prove that investors behave in a manner consistent with the CAPM, but it is likely that the model is a useful representation of how investors act.

It is easy to get lost in a complexity of mathematical symbols and mathematical manipulations. To many readers, the suggested technique will be an example of that situation. However, it is extremely important that you not fail to see the import of the calculations.

Today, industry tends to use a "cost of capital" or a "hurdle rate" to implement the discounted cash flow capital budgeting techniques. Both of these measures are "averages" reflecting average risks and average time value conditions and cannot be sensibly applied to unique "marginal" situations. There is no reason to think that the weighted average cost of capital can be inserted in a compound interest formula and then be applied to any series of future cash flows to obtain a useful measure of net present value that takes both the time value and risk of the investment into consideration.

Now the capital asset pricing model offers hope for accomplishing a systematic calculation of risk-adjusted present value. The measure reflects the investor's alternative investment return-risk trade-off opportunities in the same way as the rate of interest on a government bond reflects investment opportunities when there is no default risk.

Even where there is a reluctance to accept immediately the specific calculations of the type illustrated in this chapter, there will be a change in the way that management will look at alternatives.

One important limitation of the capital asset pricing model for corporate decision making should be kept in mind. The model assumes that the investors are widely diversified, and equally important, it assumes that the managers of the firm are willing to make investment decisions with the objective of maximizing the well-being of this type of investor. This means that unsystematic risk (for which the investor is well diversified) may be ignored in the evaluation of investments.

It is well known that objectives of firms and managers are multidimensional and that there will be a reluctance to ignore risk because it does not affect the well-diversified investor. The so-called "unsystematic" risk is not something that is likely to be ignored by a management that includes among its objectives the continuity of existence of the firm.

The models we have used here are somewhat simplified. Investors are much more complex in their behavior and markets are less than perfect. Nevertheless, we feel the conclusions reached are relevant and will be the foundation for a great deal of the financial investment models of the future. Investment decision making under uncertainty is not an easy task, but uncertainty is a characteristic of the world and the problem must be faced.

Review Problem 5.1

The market portfolio has an historically based expected return of .085 and a standard deviation of .03 during a period when risk-free assets yielded .025. The .06 risk premium is thought to be constant through time. Riskless investments may now be purchased to yield .08.

A security has a standard deviation of .07 and a .75 correlation with the market portfolio. The market portfolio is now expected to have a standard deviation of .035.

(a) What is the market's return-risk trade-off?
(b) What is the security's beta?
(c) What the equilibrium required expected return of the security?

Solution of Review Problem 5.1

(a) Market's return-risk trade-off $= \dfrac{\bar{r}_m - r_f}{\sigma_m}$

$$= \frac{.085 - .025}{.03} = 2$$

(b) $\beta_i = \dfrac{\text{cov}(r_i, r_m)}{\sigma_m^2} = \dfrac{\rho \sigma_i \sigma_m}{\sigma_m^2} = \dfrac{.75 \times .07 \times .035}{.035^2}$

$= 1.5$

(c) $\bar{r}_i = r_f + (\bar{r}_m - r_f)\beta_i = .08 + (.06)1.5$

$= .17$

Note the difficulty of deciding which estimates of market return, risk premium, and market standard deviation to use.

PROBLEMS

For Problems 1 through 8, assume that $\bar{r}_m = .14$, $r_f = .08$, and $\sigma_m = .12$.

1. If an investor put half her funds in the market portfolio and half in Treasury bills,
   (a) What rate of return would you expect her to earn?
   (b) What is the standard deviation of returns from her portfolio?
   (c) Draw a graph (capital market line) with expected return on the vertical axis and standard deviation of return on the horizontal axis.
   (d) Find the slope of the capital market line.

2. If an investor wished to hold a portfolio consisting only of Treasury bills and shares in the market portfolio, and he wanted an expected return of .12 per year, what proportion of his funds should be invested in the market portfolio?

   What is the standard deviation of returns from this portfolio?

3. On January 1, M. B. University had an endowment worth $100 million. Of this amount, $25 million was invested in Treasury bills earning .08, and $75 million was invested in the market portfolio. By the following December 31, MBU had earned $2 million in interest and had received dividends of $3 million. These amounts were considered as "income" and were used to pay the current expenses of the university. Except for "rolling over" Treasury bills, no portfolio transactions were undertaken. Although on December 31 MBU's portfolio still held the same number of shares in the market portfolio, the market value of these shares had declined to $71 million because of a general decline in stock prices.
   (a) What was the expected annual rate of return on MBU's portfolio on January 1 and its standard deviation?
   (b) What was the actual rate of return earned?

4. (Problem 3 continued) What rate of return would be expected from the portfolio held by MBU on December 31?

5. Suppose that an investor could borrow at 8 percent per year as much as $.75 for every dollar of stock that was owned "free and clear."
   Could an investor having $100,000 in cash devise a portfolio consisting only of shares in the market portfolio and Treasury bills for which the expected rate of return was 17 percent?

6. A retired doctor want to hold a portfolio consisting only of riskless debt and stock in the market portfolio. She also wants the assurance that even if the return on the market portfolio were two standard deviations below normal, the rate of return on her portfolio would be −5 percent.
   What portfolio would you recommmend for her?

7. The correlation coefficient between the return of a stock and the return of the market index is .85. The standard deviation of the stock is .20.
   (a) What is the required rate of return of this stock?
   (b) What is the beta coefficient of the common stock?

8. If an investment is expected to temporarily depress both accounting income and the current market price of the stock, should the investment be undertaken if it is expected to have a beneficial long-run effect on stock prices?

9. Assume that the following facts exist:

	Default-Free Investment	Market Investment
Expected return	.07	.10
Standard deviation	0	.02

   Compute the portfolio expected return and risk (standard deviation) if the investment is split .6 in the market portfolio and .4 in the default-free investment.

10. (Problem 9 continued)   For the information given, determine the equation for the capital market line.

11. (Problem 9 continued)   Assume that there is an investment with a covariance of .00064 with the market.
    Determine the expected return required by the market.

12. (Problem 11 continued)   If the investment currently has an expected return of .15, what would you expect to happen?

13. (Problem 11 continued)   If the covariance of the investment with the market were − .00064, what would be the expected return required by the market?

14. If the β of a security is large, what does this imply about the expected change in value of the stock for small changes in the value of the market portfolio?

15. The market portfolio has an expected return of .08 and a standard deviation of .02. Riskless (default-free) investments may be purchased to yield .05.
    Compute the market's trade-off rate between return and risk.

16. (Problem 15 continued). A security has a standard deviation of .06 and has a .2 correlation with the market portfolio.
    What is the equilibrium "required yield" of the security? What is its beta?

17. (Problems 15 and 16 continued)   What is the required yield if the correlation with the market portfolio is 1? If the correlation is $-.4$?

18. Letting I denote an investment proposal, J denote the firm prior to the investment, and M denote the market portfolio, suppose that an investor had the following expectations:

	r_i	σ_i	Correlations (ρ_{ij}'s)		
			I	J	M
I	.04	.08	1.0	$+.8$	$-.5$
J	.05	.05	$+.8$	1.0	$-.2$
M	.12	.06	$-.5$	$-.2$	1.0

The riskless asset yields of 6 percent.
(a) Is the current price of equity in firm J an equilibrium price?
(b) Suppose that the investment outlay is approximately the same size as the current value of the firm. If the investment is undertaken and financed by equity, what effect will the investment have on the expected value and standard deviation of the firm's return?
(c) What factor might lead you to recommend acceptance of the investment despite the fact that it will lower the expected yield on equity and increase the standard deviation of the equity yield.

19. Consider a portfolio consisting of .6 of security A and .4 of security B that have rates of return that are independent:

	Expected Rate of Return	Standard Deviation
Security A	20%	5%
Security B	10	3

(a) The portfolio has an expected rate of return of _____ percent and a standard deviation of _____ percent.
(b) If the two securities had rates of return that are perfectly correlated, then the expected rate of return on the portfolio is _____ percent. The standard deviation of the portfolio's return is _____ _____ .
(c) If the correlation coefficient of the returns is .7, the variance of the portfolio is _____ percent.
(d) If A has a .8 correlation coefficient with the market and if the market has a .10 standard deviation, then A has a beta of _____ .

(e) If the risk-free rate is .11 and the market has an expected return of .14, the expected return of A with market equilibrium would be _____
_____ .

REFERENCES

Baron, David P. "On the Utility Theoretic Foundation of Mean-Variance Analysis," *Journal of Finance*, December 1977, 1683–1698.

Bauman, W. Scott. "Investment Returns and Present Values." *Financial Analysts Journal*, November–December 1969, 107–118.

Bierman, H., and J. E. Hass. "Capital Budgeting Under Uncertainty: A Reformulation." *Journal of Finance*, March 1973, 119–129.

Black, F. "Capital Market Equilibrium with Restricted Borrowing." *Journal of Business*, July 1972.

Fama, E. "Risk, Return, and Equilibrium: Some Clarifying Comments." *Journal of Finance*, March 1968, 29–40.

Hamada, R. S. "Portfolio Analysis, Market Equilibrum and Corporation Finance." *Journal of Finance* March 1969, 13–31.

Levy, Haim, and Marshall Sarnat. "The Portfolio Analysis of Multiperiod Capital Investments Under Conditions of Risk." *The Engineering Economist*, Fall 1970, 1–19.

Lintner, J. "Security Prices, Risk, and Maximal Gains for Diversification." *Journal of Finance*, December 1965, 587–613.

———. "The Valuation of Risk Assets and the Selection of Risky Investment in Stock Portfolios and Capital Budgets." *Review of Economics and Statistics*, February 1965, 13–27.

Litzenberger, R. H., and A. P. Budd. "Corporate Investment Criteria and the Validation of Risk Assets." *Journal of Financial and Quantitative Analysis*, December 1970, 395–419.

Markowitz, H. M. *Portfolio Selection: Efficient Diversification of Investments*, Monograph No. 16, New York: Cowles Foundation, 1959.

Modigliani, Franco, and Gerald A. Pogue. "An Introduction to Risk and Return." *Financial Analysts Journal*, March–April 1974. 68–80, and May–June 1974, 69–86.

Mossin, J. "Equilibrium in a Capital Asset Market." *Econometrica*, October 1966, 768–775.

Mossin, J. *Theory of Financial Markets*. Englewood Cliffs, N.J.: Prentice-Hall, Inc., 1973.

Robichek, A. A. "Risk and the Value of Securities." *Journal of Financial and Quantitative Analysis*, December 1969, 749–756.

———, and S. C. Myers. "Valuation of the Firm: Effects of Uncertainty in a Market Context." *Journal of Finance*, May 1966, 215–227.

Ross, S. A. "The Arbitrage Theory of Capital Asset Pricing." *Journal of Economic Theory*, December 1976, 341–360.

Sharpe, W. F. "Capital Asset Prices: A Theory of Market Equilibrium Under Conditions of Risk." *Journal of Finance*, September 1964, 425–442.

Stapleton, R. C. "Portfolio Analysis, Stock Valuation and Capital Budgeting Decision Rules for Risky Projects," *Journal of Finance*, March 1971, 95–117.

Tobin, J. "Liquidity Preference as Behavior Towards Risk." *Review of Economic Studies*, February 1958, 65–86.

Appendix 5.1   Relationship Between Mean Return and Standard Deviation

We wish to explore the relationship between a portfolio's mean return r_p and its standard deviation σ_p when the portfolio consists of various portions of two securities whose returns have mean $\bar{r}_m$ and r_f and standard deviation σ_m and zero, respectively. The correlation is zero. The return on the portfolio with proportion α of r_f and proportion $(1 - \alpha)$ of r_m is

$$r_p = \alpha r_f + (1 - \alpha) r_m$$

and the portfolio return's mean and standard deviation are

$$\bar{r}_p = \alpha r_f + (1 - \alpha) \bar{r}_m \tag{1}$$

and

$$\sigma_p = (1 - \alpha) \sigma_m \tag{2}$$

Solving equation (1) for α yields

$$\alpha = \frac{\bar{r}_p - \bar{r}_m}{r_f - \bar{r}_m} \tag{3}$$

so that

$$(1 - \alpha) = \frac{r_f - \bar{r}_p}{r_f - \bar{r}_m} \tag{4}$$

Substituting (4) into (2) gives

$$\sigma_p = \left(\frac{r_f - \bar{r}_p}{r_f - \bar{r}_m} \right) \sigma_m \tag{5}$$

Solving for $\bar{r}_p$, we obtain

$$\bar{r}_p \sigma_m = r_f \sigma_m - \sigma_p (r_f - \bar{r}_m)$$

$$\bar{r}_p = r_f + \frac{\bar{r}_m - r_f}{\sigma_m} \sigma_p$$

This is a linear relationship $\bar{r}_p = a + b\sigma_p$, where

$$a = r_f \text{ (the intercept)}$$

$$b = \frac{\bar{r}_m - r_f}{\sigma_m} \text{ (the slope)}$$

Appendix 5.2   The Security Characteristic Line

We want to show for the security characteristic line that

$$\text{slope} = \frac{\text{cov}\,(r_i,\,r_m)}{\text{var}\,(r_m)}$$

(See Figure 5.7.)

$$\text{any value on the line} = r_i - r_f = a + b(r_m - r_f)$$

$$\text{value of } \bar{r}_m = \underline{\bar{r}_i - r_f = a + b(\bar{r}_m - r_f)}$$

$$\text{difference} = r_i - \bar{r}_i = b(r_m - \bar{r}_m)$$

We substitue for $(r_i - \bar{r}_i)$ in

$$\text{cov}\,(r_i,\,r_m) = E(r_i - \bar{r}_i)(r_m - \bar{r}_m) = bE(r_m - \bar{r}_m)^2 = b\,\text{var}\,(r_m)$$

Solving for b yields

$$b = \frac{\text{cov}\,(r_i,\,r_m)}{\text{var}\,(r_m)}$$

Since

$$\beta = \frac{\text{cov}\,(r_i,\,r_m)}{\text{var}\,(r_m)}$$

b is equal to the security's beta.

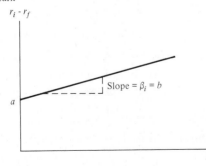

FIGURE 5.7   The Security Characteristic Line

Cases: Part I

The cases that follow all apply to the material covered in Part I. They offer you the opportunity to test your understanding of some basic calculations and also some more advanced issues that have been introduced.

Case 1. Finance of FMC

The following letter was written by the vice-president of finance at FMC Corporation to prospective managerial employees.

QUESTION: What different types of financial processes and decisions are implicitly referred to in the letter?

> FMC Corporation
> Executive Offices
> 200 East Randolph Drive
> Chicago Illinois 60601
> 312-861-6000

In an increasingly competitive business environment, consistently earning a high real return on shareholder's equity has become a substantial challenge. Notwithstanding, management has set high goals for FMC's performance. To reach these goals without shortchanging the company's future requires a thorough understanding of the problems, opportunities, and alternatives facing the company. In this respect FMC relies heavily on financial management.

Decisions that help FMC obtain maximum benefit from its resources require both accurate and relevant financial information. But volatile interest and inflation rates, and a depressed but changing world economy have exposed weaknesses in traditional financial analysis. With FMC's diverse operating environments, addressing these weaknesses requires a creative approach to finance. We pride ourselves in adapting and implementing state-of-the-art techniques across the financial functions including the areas of budgeting, forecasting, reporting, and capital allocation.

In 1983, for example, FMC adopted current cost, or completely inflation adjusted financial statements for all internal performance reporting. Although there are still additional refinements to be made, we feel this system will give management more meaningful and accurate information upon which to base operating decisions.

To maintain FMC's position on the leading edge of financial expertise, we are committed to attracting the highest caliber people and giving them the opportunity to develop and take on increased responsibility. But to be successful in finance at FMC requires more than an understanding of the finance function itself. The finance staff must take a multi-functional, multi-national perspective and understand the operating issues that contribute to financial results.

> Robert B. Hoffman
> Vice-President
> Finance

Case 2.   Time Magazine

The following announcement was made on June 17, 1929:

Perpetual Subscription

In announcing a Perpetual TIME Subscription, the publishers believe their action is without precedent in Publishing history. Life Subscriptions there have been. But the thought of TIME's being limited to a single lifetime is incongruous. TIME is timeless and so, too, is TIME's Perpetual Subscription.

Sixty dollars, payable at the expiration of your present subscription, will bring TIME to you during your lifetime—to your heir and his heir—to the end of TIME.

June 17, 1929

Assume that a year's subscription to *Time* could be purchased for $4 in 1929, that a very safe long-term bond could be purchased to yield .07, and that you could borrow very-long-term funds at .10. Assume, further, that the value of a perpetual subscription to *Time* in June 1986 is $400.

Assume further that the interest earned on the long-term bond (costing $60) during the interim years exactly covers the cost of buying the magazines. Just considering the value of the subscription after 57 years, was it a good buy if

QUESTIONS

(a) You had the cash and the alternative was a long-term investment.
(b) You had to borrow the purchase price at a cost of .10?

Case 3.   Exxon Corporation

The following factors in the 1983 Annual Report apply for the years 1979–1983.

Financial Summary
(Millions of Dollars)

	1979	1980	1981	1982	1983
Sales and other operating revenue					
Petroleum and natural gas	$76,162	$ 98,238	$102,418	$ 92,570	$83,622
Chemicals	5,807	6,928	7,116	6,049	6,392
Other	1,586	3,246	3,686	3,440	3,433
Total sales and other operating revenue	$83,555	$108,412	$113,220	$102,059	$93,447
Earnings					
Petroleum and natural gas	$ 4,629	$ 5,622	$ 5,254	$ 4,456	$ 5,083
Chemicals	456	345	238	93	270
Other operating segments	(58)	(77)	(127)	(206)	37
Unallocated corporate costs	(638)	(468)	(316)	(291)	(322)
Interest (expense)/income, net	(94)	(72)	(223)	134	(90)
Net income	$ 4.295	$ 5,350	$ 4,826	$ 4,186	$ 4,978
Net income per share	$4.87	$6.15	$5.58	$4.82	$5.78
Cash dividends per share	$1.95	$2.70	$3.00	$3.00	$3.10
Net income to average shareholders' equity	20.1%	21.0%	17.8%	14.9%	17.2%
Net income to total revenue	5.1%	4.9%	4.2%	4.0%	5.3%

QUESTIONS

(a) If the 1983 year-end stock price is $39, what is the cost of equity capital for Exxon?
(b) If an investor in the common stock of Exxon wants a return on invest-

ment of .18, what value will a share of stock have for that investor? Use $3.10 as the expected dividend. Use the dividend growth model.

(c) If the stock price is $39, the required return is .18, and the next period's expected dividend is $3.10, what growth rate is implicitly being used?

Case 4. The S Company

The S Company has price/earnings (P/E) ratio of 6. It has an asset with a book value of $50,000,000 that is earning $10,000,000 per year. This .20 return on investment is satisfactory. Also, it is estimated that asset is making a contribution of $10,000,000 × 6 = $60,000,000 to the market value of the common stock. The 6 is the firm's P/E ratio. The firm uses a .12 discount rate. The cash flow is $12,000,000 per year. If .6 of the cash flow is reinvested, the growth rate is estimated to be .04.

The asset has growth potential. A buyer has offered $250,000,000 for the asset.

QUESTION: Should the firm sell?

Case 5. Berkshire Hathaway Inc.

The letters of Warren Buffett, chairman of Berkshire Hathaway, to the firm's stockholders are famous.

There follows an extract from the 1984 letter.

QUESTION: How would you evaluate the references that are applicable to financial management?

To the Shareholders of Berkshire Hathaway Inc.:

This past year our registered shareholders increased from about 1900 to 2900. Most of this growth resulted from our merger with Blue Chip Stamps, but there also was an acceleration in the pace of "natural" increase that has raised us from the 1000 level a few years ago.

With so many new shareholders, it's appropriate to summarize the major business principles we follow that pertain to the manager-owner relationship:

- Although our form is corporate, our attitude is partnership. Charlie Munger and I think of our shareholders as owner-partners, and of ourselves as managing partners. (Because of the size of our shareholdings we also are, for better or worse, controlling partners). We do not view the company itself as the ultimate owner of our business assets but, instead, view the company as a conduit through which our shareholders own the assets.

- In line with this owner-orientation, our directors, are all major shareholders of Berkshire Hathaway. In the case of at least four of the five, over 50% of family net worth is represented by holdings of Berkshire. We eat our own cooking.

- Our long-term economic goal (subject to some qualifications mentioned later) is to maximize the average annual rate of gain in intrinsic business value on a per-share basis. We do not measure the economic significance or performance of Berkshire by its size; we measure by per-share progress. We are certain that the rate of per-share progress will diminish in the future—a greatly enlarged capital base will see to that. But we will be disappointed if our rate does not exceed that of the average large American corporation.

- Our preference would be to reach this goal by directly owning a diversified group of businesses that generate cash and consistently earn above-average returns on capital. Our second choice is to own parts of similar businesses, attained primarily through purchases of marketable common stocks by our insurance subsidiaries. The price and availability of businesses and the need for insurance capital determine any given year's capital allocation.

- Because of this two-pronged approach to business ownership and because of the limitations of conventional accounting, consolidated reported earnings may reveal relatively little about our true economic performance. Charlie and I, both as owners and managers, virtually ignore such consolidated numbers. However, we will also report to you the earnings of each major business we control, numbers we consider of great importance. These figures, along with other information we will supply about the individual businesses, should generally aid you in making judgments about them.

- Accounting consequences do not influence our operating or capital-allocation decisions. When acquisition costs are similar, we much prefer to purchase $2 of earnings that is not reportable by us under standard accounting principles than to purchase $1 of earnings that is reportable. This is precisely the choice that often faces us since entire businesses (whose earnings will be fully reportable) frequently sell for double the pro-rata price of small portions (whose earnings will be largely unreportable). In aggregate and over time, we expect the unreported earnings to be fully reflected in our intrinsic business value through capital gains.

- We rarely use much debt and, when we do, we attempt to structure it on a long-term fixed-rate basis. We will reject interesting opportunities rather than over-leverage our balance sheet. This conservatism has penalized our results but it is the only behavior that leaves us comfortable, considering our fiduciary obligations to policyholders, depositors, lenders and the many equity holders who have committed unusually large portions of their net worth to our case.

- A managerial "wish list" will not be filled at shareholder expense. We will not diversify by purchasing entire businesses at control prices that ignore long-term economic consequences to our shareholders. We will only do with your money what we would do with our own, weighing fully the values you can obtain by diversifying your own portfolios through direct purchases in the stock market.

- We feel noble intentions should be checked periodically against results. We test the wisdom of retaining earnings by assessing whether retention, over time, delivers shareholders at least $1 of market value for each $1 retained. To date, this test has been met. We will continue to apply it on a five-year rolling basis. As our net worth grows, it is more difficult to use retained earnings wisely.

- We will issue common stock only when we receive as much in business value as we give. This rule applies to all forms of issurance—not only mergers or public stock offerings, but stock-for-debt swaps, stock options, and convertible securities as well. We will not sell small portions of your company—and that is what the issuance of shares amounts to—on a basis inconsistent with the value of the entire enterprise.

- You should be fully aware of one attitude Charlie and I share that hurts our financial performance: regardless of price, we have no interest at all in selling any good businesses that Berkshire owns, and are very reluctant to sell sub-par businesses as long as we expect them to generate at least some cash and as long as we feel good about their managers and labor relations. We hope not to repeat the capital-allocation mistakes that led us into such sub-par businesses. And we react with great caution to suggestions that our poor businesses can be restored to satisfactory profitability by major capital expenditures. (The projections will be dazzling—the advocates will be sincere—but, in the end, major additional investment in a terrible industry usually is about as rewarding as struggling in quicksand.) Nevertheless, gin rummy managerial behavior (discard your least promising business at each turn) is not our style. We would rather have our overall results penalized a bit than engage in it.

- We will be candid in our reporting to you, emphasizing the pluses and minuses important in appraising business value. Our guideline is to tell you the business facts that we would want to know if our positions were reversed. We owe you no less. Moreover, as a company with a major communications business, it would be inexcusable for us to apply lesser standards of accuracy, balance and incisiveness when reporting on ourselves than we would expect our news people to apply when reporting on others. We also believe candor benefits us as managers: the CEO who misleads others in public may eventually mislead himself in private.

Despite our policy of candor, we will discusss our activitives in marketable securities only to the extent legally required. Good investment ideas are rare, valuable and subject to competitive appropriation just as good product or business acquisition idea's are. Therefore, we normally will not talk about our investment ideas. This ban extends even to securities we have sold (because we may purchase them again) and to stocks we are incorrectly rumored to be buying. If we deny those reports but say "no comment" on other occasions, the no-comments become confirmation.

Case 6.   Jonathan Elray

Jonathan Elray, president of the Can Division of a *Fortune* 500 firm, has a major decision. He is considering a major investment proposal that requires an outlay of $500 million and would lead to a new container for holding food.

Given the fact that the investment involves a basic commodity with a known demand, it is believed that the beta of the investment is zero. The return from the investment is expected to be independent of the return from the market.

By using r_f to evaluate the investment, the investment is highly acceptable.

There is one aspect of the decision that bothers Jon. The manufacturing process for the new containers uses a new chemical and there is a .3 probability that this chemical is harmful to humans and could not be used to contain food. This expectation was considered in defining the benefits, but since the risk is an unsystematic one, he has still used r_f to evaluate the investment. He knows that only systematic risk is relevant to a well-diversified investor.

The investment cannot be delayed until the health issue is resolved (the competitive edge would be lost).

QUESTION: What should Jon do?

Case 7.   Tax-Deferred Savings Bonds

An investor can buy a U.S. savings bond that allows the deferral of income taxes until the bond matures. The bond pays an interest rate equal to a fraction of the yield of taxable U.S. securities.

To simplify the analysis, we will change the exact terms of the security (which are likely to change in any event). Assume that the bond is sold as a discount bond paying interest only at maturity. The yield of the bond is .85 of the yield of taxable U.S. securities.

The best comparable investment is a tax-exempt discount bond (no tax on the interest) that yields .90 of the yield of taxable U.S. securities.

QUESTIONS

(a) Is the savings bond or the tax-exempt security the better investment?
(b) How low does the yield on the tax-exempt discount bond have to go before a person paying at a .45 tax rate would find the savings bond desirable? Assume a 12-year maturity period and the U.S. taxable securities yield of .10.

Case 8. Mortgage Points

Obtaining a home mortgage from a bank is a financial adventure. A bank will state an interest rate and then as an afterthought will inform you of the number of points you have to pay. For example, 5 points on a $100,000 mortgage leads to a $5,000 payment (i.e., 5 percent of $100,000).

QUESTIONS:

(a) If you assume zero personal taxes, what is the relationship between the real cost of the funds and the interest rate on the mortgage and the points given; that is, what is the effective cost of a mortgage where points are given.
(b) What is the after-tax cost of the mortgage—the after-tax cost with zero points is $(1 - .45).14 = .077$. Assume
  (1) A personal tax rate of .45.
  (2) Expensing of the points for taxes immediately
  (3) Expensing of the interest when it is paid
  (4) A borrowing of $100,000, an interest rate of .14, 5 points, and four equal payments of $34,320.47 per year (first payment one year from now).

Case 9. The Cayuga Fund

The Cayuga Fund manages $1 billion of assets all invested in equity securities. Currently the fund is well diversified; however, management is upset about the volatility of the returns. The fund currently has a beta of 1. The investment committee met on January 5 to determine possible new investment strategies.

Jane Doe, one of the funds' investment managers, has suggested that the beta of the portfolio could be reduced by only investing in securities that have betas of less than 1. With this strategy the market risk could be reduced.

Bob Smith, another investment manager, feels strongly that all firms doing business with the South African government or corporations should be eliminated from the portfolio on moral grounds. He feels equally strongly that nuclear energy is socially undesirable and that corporations associated with it should be eliminated.

Pauline Rogers was persuaded by the arguments offered by Jane and Bob, but she had some other candidates for elimination. She felt strongly that if the nuclear energy firms were eliminated, so should firms engaged in defense contracts, producers and sellers of tobacco products, and owners of gambling establishments or producers of "porno" movies, books, or magazines.

Frank Jones, an old-line fundamentalist, thought that Jane, Bob, and Pauline were going off on a tangent. He thought that the federal government should pass laws if something was illegal, but if an investment was legal, then Cayuga's only function was to balance expected return and risk on behalf of its investors. However, Frank was upset about the larger number of "growth" stocks currently in the portfolio. All of these companies had the common characteristic of not paying a significant percentage of their earnings as dividends. He would divest these stocks from the portfolio. He also did not like companies that engaged in mergers and acquisitions for the stated purpose of risk diversification. It was his opinion that Cayuga did not need corporations to pay premium prices for other corporations when Cayuga could diversify as much as it wished at low cost.

The investors in Cayuga fund are mostly middle-income individuals saving for retirement. Although not the only investment of these individuals, it is probably a major portion of the liquid savings of the investors.

QUESTION: What should be the investment policy of the fund?

Case 10: Bob Jones

Bob Jones had two major problems. He had recently gone to work with the trust department of a major bank, and it was his job to evaluate the common stock of 10 major corporations. He was directed by his boss, Mabel Smith, to use a discounted cash flow dividend valuation model.

He had no problems with the first eight companies. He applied the formula

$$P = \frac{D_1}{k_e - g}$$

and obtained reasonable results that he would be pleased to present at the next investment committee meeting. For these eight companies he used discount rates that ranged from .12 to .16 (depending on risk).

The ninth company he had to analyze was IBM. He computed IBM's expected growth rate to be .20 and its cost of equity to be .15, but when he inserted this information into the formula, he obtained a negative stock price. He knew that it would not be wise for him to tell Mabel that IBM had a negative value, but there was no question that if g was larger than k_e the value of P was negative. He had even checked this out with a friend who taught mathematics.

Bob's tenth company was Teledyne. Here he also had a problem, since the company, though profitable, did not pay a cash dividend. With a zero cash dividend, Bob obtained a zero value for P. Given that Teledyne was a very profitable firm, Bob did not want to tell Mabel that the stock had zero value.

Bob is aware that you are currently taking a finance course, so he has asked you, as a friend, to help him out.

QUESTION: What do you tell Bob that will help him present useful analysis at the next investment committee meeting?

Case 11:   Automobile Financing

In April of 1985 several automobile companies offered to finance automobile purchases at a cost of 8% per year for five-year loans. At the time short-term money cost 14%.

Assume a zero tax rate for the decision maker.

For a car costing $12,000, an amount of $10,000 could be borrowed.

QUESTION: How much of an economic saving is the buyer achieving? (An equivalent question would be "How much of a discount on the purchase is the buyer receiving?) Assume that annual payments are made.

Part *II*

Capital Budgeting

This section deals with capital budgeting under certainty (Chapters 6, 7, 8, and 9) and uncertainty (Chapter 10). Because firms make many decisions involving immediate outlays and long-run benefits, it is desirable that time value be brought into the analysis in a sensible fashion.

One issue that has concerned managers is the situation that occurs when there are projects that require more capital than there is available. This capital rationing problem is discussed in Chapter 8.

Chapter 6

Capital Budgeting: Decisions with Certainty

Major Topics

1. Net present value and internal rate of return and the use of cash flows.
2. The net present value profile.
3. The limitations of payback and return on investment as primary methods of evaluating investments.

A Capital Budgeting Decision

A capital budgeting decision is characterized by costs and benefits that are spread out over several time periods. This leads to a requirement that the time value of money be considered in order to evaluate the alternatives correctly. Although in actual practice we must consider risk as well as time value, in this chapter we restrict the discussion to situations in which the costs and benefits are known with certainty. There are sufficient difficulties in just taking the time value of money into consideration without also incorporating risk factors. Moreover, when the cash flows are finally allowed to be uncertain, we shall suggest the use of a procedure that is based on the initial recommendations made with the certainty assumption, so nothing is lost by making the initial assumption of certainty.

In this chapter we shall describe four of the more commonly used procedures for making capital budgeting decisions. We shall not attempt to describe all the variations that are possible or all the procedures used that are faulty.

139

If you understand the basic elements of a correct procedure, you will soon be able to distinguish between correct and incorrect procedures. The two basic correct capital budgeting techniques presented in this chapter are applicable to a wide range of decisions found throughout the economy both in the profit and not-for-profit sectors.

Rate of Discount

We shall use the term *time value of money* to describe the discount rate. One possibility is to use the rate of interest associated with default-free securities. This rate does not include an adjustment for the risk of default; thus risk, if present, would be handled separately from the time discounting. In many situations it is convenient to use the firm's borrowing rate (the marginal cost of borrowing funds). The objective of the discounting process is to take the time value of money into consideration. We want to find the present equivalent of future sums, neglecting risk considerations. Later, we shall introduce several techniques to adjust for the risk of the investment.

Although the average cost of capital is an important concept that should be understood by all managers and is useful in deciding on the financing mix, we do not advocate its general use in evaluating all investments.

Classification of Cash Flows

We shall define conventional investments as those having one or more periods of outlays followed by one or more periods of cash proceeds. Borrowing money is a kind of "negative investment" or "loan-type of cash flow" in which one or more periods of cash proceeds are followed by one or more periods in which there are cash outlays. Loan-type investments have positive cash flows (cash in flows) followed by periods of negative cash flows (cash outlays). There are also nonconventional investments that are defined to be investments that have one or more periods of outlays interspersed with periods of proceeds. With nonconventional investments, there are more than one sign change in the sequence of the cash flow. With a conventional investment or loan, there is one sign change. The possibilities may be illustrated as follows:

	Sign of Flow for Period			
	0	*1*	*2*	*3*
Conventional investment	−	+	+	+
Loan type of flows	+	−	−	−
Nonconventional investment	−	+	+	−
Nonconventional investment	+	−	−	+

Methods of Classifying Investments

Any useful scheme of evaluating investments must be based on a classification of types of investments. Different kinds of investments raise different problems, are of different relative importance to the firm, and will require different persons to evaluate their significance. By classifying types of investments, each investment proposal will receive attention from persons qualified to analyze it.

Investments may be classified according to the following categories:

1. The kinds of scarce resources used by the investment. For example, does the investment require important amounts of cash, floor space, or the time of key personnel? (Personnel may also be classified: sales, production, research, top management, legal staff, and so on.)

2. The amount of cash investment that is required. For example, with respect to the amount of immediate cash outlays required, we could classify investments as requiring less than $500, between $500 and $50,000, and over $50,000.

3. The way in which benefits from the investment are affected by other possible investments. Some investments stand on their own feet. Others will be improved or will be successful only if supplementary investments are made; still others will be useless if competing investments are accepted. For example, the worth of another fork-lift truck may depend on whether or not the plan for adding an automatic conveyor system is accepted.

4. The form in which the benefits are received. Investments may generate greater cash flows, reduce the risks associated with poor business conditions, reduce the accident rate, improve employee morale, or eliminate a community nuisance such as excessive smoke or noise.

5. Whether the incremental benefits are the result of lower costs (efficiency) or increased sales or whether the investments merely prevent a decline in sales or market share.

6. The functional activity to which the investments are most closely related. For example, an oil company may classify investments according to the following activities: exploration, production, transportation, refining, or marketing.

7. The industry classification of the investment. For example, the manager of a conglomerate may want to know if the investment being considered has to do with its professional football team, steel production, or space activities.

8. The degree of necessity. Some investments are necessary in the sense that if they are not undertaken the entire operation stops (if stoppage is

desirable, the *necessity* may not be absolute). Other investments are highly optional and move the firm in a new direction.

Many other methods of classification could be suggested (e.g., energy saving, new products, maintaining market share, capacity expansion, pollution control). Clearly, no single scheme of classification will be equally valid for all uses or for all companies. The essential task is to develop a classification system for investments that is appropriate to the activity of the business and the organizational structure of the particular company.

We are primarily concerned with investments for which both the resources used and the benefits to be received can be measured to an important degree in terms of cash flows. Second, the analytical methods developed in this book will be most useful for investments that are important enough to the firm to warrant a relatively careful study of their potential profitability. Next, we shall consider a classification of investments that is based on the way the benefits from a given investment are affected by other possible investments.

Dependent and Independent Investments

In evaluating the investment proposals presented to management, it is important to be aware of the possible interrelationships between pairs of investment proposals. A given investment proposal may be economically independent of, or dependent on, another investment proposal. An investment proposal will be said to be *economically independent* of a second investment if the cash flows (or more generally the costs and benefits) expected from the first investment would be the same regardless of whether the second investment were accepted or rejected. If the cash flows associated with the first investment are affected by the decision to accept or reject the second investment, the first investment is said to be economically dependent on the second. It should be clear that when one investment is dependent on another, some attention must be given to the question of whether decisions about the first investment can or should be made separately from decisions about the second.

Economically Independent Investments

In order for investment A to be economically independent of investment B, two conditions must be satisfied. First, it must be technically possible to undertake investment A whether or not investment B is accepted. Thus it is *not* possible to build a school and shopping center on the same site; therefore, the proposal to build the one is not independent of a proposal to build the other. Second, the net benefits to be expected from the first investment must not be affected by the acceptance or rejection of the second. If the estimates of the cash outlays and the cash inflows for investment A are not the same when B is either accepted or rejected, the two investments are not independent. Thus it is technically possible to build a toll bridge and operate a ferry across adjacent points on a river, but the two investments are not independent because the proceeds from one will be affected by the existence of the other. The two investments would not be economically independent in the sense in which we are using the term, even if the traffic across the river at this point were sufficient to operate profitably both the bridge and the ferry.

Sometimes two investments cannot both be accepted because the firm does not have enough cash to finance both. This situation could occur if the amount of cash available for investments were strictly limited by management rather than by the capital market or if increments of funds obtained from the capital market cost more than previous increments. In such a situation, the acceptance of one investment may cause the rejection of the other. But we will not consider the two investments to be economically dependent. To classify this type of investment as dependent would make all investments for such a firm dependent, and this is not a useful definition for our purposes.

Economically Dependent Investments

The dependency relationship can be classified further. If a decision to undertake the second investment will increase the benefits expected from the first (or decrease the costs of undertaking the first without changing the benefits), the second investment is said to be a *complement* of the first. If the decision to undertake the second investment will decrease the benefits expected from the first (or increase the costs of undertaking the first without changing the benefits), the second is said to be a substitute for the first. In the extreme case where the potential benefits to be derived from the first investment will completely disappear if the second investment is accepted, or where it is technically impossible to undertake the first when the second has been accepted, the two investments are said to be mutually exclusive.

It may be helpful to think of the possible relationships between investments as being arrayed along a line segment (see Figure 6.1). At the extreme left, investment A is a prerequisite to investment B. In the center of the line, investment A is independent of investment B. At the extreme right-hand end of

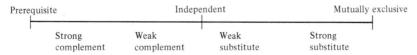

FIGURE 6.1   Investment Relationships

the line, investment A is mutually exclusive with respect to investment B. As we move to the right from the left-hand side of the line, we have varying degrees of complementariness, decreasing to the right. Similarly, the right-hand side of the line represents varying degrees of substitutability, increasing to the right.

Statistical Dependence

It is possible for two or more investments to be economically independent but statistically dependent. Statistical dependence is said to be present if the cash flows from two or more investments would be affected by some external event or happening whose occurrence is uncertain. For example, a firm could produce high-priced yachts and expensive cars. The investment decisions affecting these two product lines are economically independent. However, the fortunes of both activities are closely associated with high business activity and a large amount of discretionary income for the "rich" people. This statistical dependence may affect the risk of investments in these product lines, because the swings of profitability of a firm with these two product lines will be wider than those of a firm with two product lines having less statistical dependence.

Measures of Investment Worth

Here we introduce some methods of evaluating the worth of investments that are in common use or have been frequently recommended as being desirable. If we take a group of investment proposals and rank them by each of these methods, we shall find that each method will frequently give a different ranking to the same set of investment proposals. In fact, it can be said that the different measures will only accidentally give identical rankings to a set of investment proposals. Although we shall not to be able to rank economically independent investments in a useful manner, we shall normally be able to make decisions without such rankings.

Various executives faced with the same set of investment possibilities, but using different measures of investment worth, will tend to make dissimilar investment decisions. Clearly, all the measures that will be described here cannot be equally valid. We shall attempt to determine which of the measures have some legitimate reason for use and to isolate the circumstances under which they will tend to give satisfactory results.

In current business practice, each of the methods selected has its advocates, and frequently they are used in combination with each other. Because investment proposals are rarely accepted by top management solely on the basis of such analyses, it may be argued that the choice of method is of little significance because the investment decision is likely to be influenced by many different factors. Insofar as the executives making the final decision are aware of the risks involved and are intimately familiar with the proposals, know the possible technical or operating problems that may be encountered, and realize the potential erosion of earnings resulting from competitive action or changing technology, this criticism may very well be valid. In most large organizations, however, it is impossible for the top management officials, who must finally approve or disapprove investment proposals, to be intimately familiar with the details of each and every proposal presented to them. To the extent that this intimate knowledge is impossible or impractical, these executives must rely upon the economic evaluations prepared by their subordinates. To make reasonable choices in weighing alternative investments, it is increasingly necessary that various proposals be evaluated as nearly as possible on some uniform, comparable basis. In such circumstances, although the measure of economic worth of an investment should never be the sole factor considered in making a final decision, it should play an important part in the evaluation of the investments under consideration by the firm.

The fact that various measures give different rankings and indicate different accept or reject decisions to identical sets of investment proposals is a matter of concern. Substantial improvements in efficiency and income may result if a more adequate measure can be discovered and widely adopted. Any such progress requires first a more general agreement about the desirable characteristics to be possessed by a good index of the economic worth of an investment. We assume that the objective is to maximize the well-being of the common stockholders.

Incremental Cash Flow

Investments should be analyzed using after-tax incremental cash flows. Although we shall initially assume zero taxes so that we can concentrate on the technique of analysis, it should be remembered that the only relevant cash flows of a period are after all tax effects have been taken into account.

The definition of incremental cash flows is relatively straightforward: If the item changes the bank account or cash balance, it is a cash flow. This definition includes opportunity costs (the value of alternative uses). For example, if a warehouse is used for a new product and the alternative is to rent the space, the lost rentals should be counted as an opportunity cost in computing the incremental cash flows.

It is generally advisable to exclude financial types of cash flows from the investment analysis. One common error in cash flow calculations is to include interest payments on debt in the cash flows and then apply the time-discounting formulas. This results in double counting the time value of money. The time discounting takes interest into consideration. It is not correct to also deduct interest in computing cash flows.

Special Assumptions

The computations of this chapter make several assumptions that are convenient, but are not essential. They simplify the analysis. The assumptions are

1. Capital can be borrowed and lent at the same rate.
2. The cash inflows and outflows occur at the beginning or end of each period rather than continuously during the periods.
3. The cash flows are certain, and no risk adjustment is necessary.

In addition, in choosing the methods of analysis and implementation, it is assumed that the objective is to maximize the well-being of stockholders, and more wealth is better than less.

The Elements of a Cash Flow Projection

To arrive at the set of projected incremental cash flows used in evaluating any investment, it is usually necessary to project the impact of the investment on the revenues and expenses of the company. Some investments will affect only the expense components (i.e., cost-saving investments), whereas others will affect revenues as well as costs. Projecting how various expense and revenue items will be affected if the investment is undertaken is not an easy task, for incremental impacts are often difficult to assess. In some cases, such as the impact of a new product on the sales of an existing product that is considered a substitute, the problem is the uncertain extent of the erosion. In other cases, such as with overhead items, (e.g., accounting services, plant security, a regional warehouse system), the problem arises because there is not a well-defined relationship between the incremental action contemplated with these costs; no exact solution exists to these knotty problems.

An investment in plant or equipment to produce a new product will probably also require an investment in current assets less current liabilities (working capital). There may be an increase in raw material, work-in-process, and finished goods inventories. Also, if there are sales on credit rather than cash, accounts receivable will increase; that is, sales per the income statement will be collected with a lag, and there will be an increase in accounts receivable.

Finally, not all payables will be paid immediately, and this lag will manifest itself in an increase in current liabilities (reducing the need for other financing). Thus a working capital investment (a negative cash flow and a need for capital) usually accompanies the direct investment in plant and equipment.

One can assume that the working capital investment is fully turned into cash at the hypothesized end of the project. That is, it is assumed that inventories are depleted, receivables are collected, and payables are paid. Hence, over the life of the project, the sum of the working capital changes should be zero if this assumption is accepted. However, the commitment of resources to working capital has a cost (the time value of money) even if those resources are ultimately freed.

Two Discounted Cash Flow Methods

We shall first introduce the two primary discounted cash flow investment evaluation procedures, net present value (NPV) and internal rate of return (IRR). After a brief discussion of these two measures of investment worth, we shall describe a series of four hypothetical investments. The four hypothetical investments have been designed so that for two selected pairs it is possible to decide that one investment is clearly preferable to the other. If a measure of investment worth indicates that one investment is better when the other investment is actually better, then clearly there is a danger in using that measure. We shall find that some measures can easily be eliminated as general decision rules because in some situations they give obviously wrong answers and another measure gives the "right" answer. We shall conclude that the net present value method is better than the other possible methods.

Net Present Value

We offer two proposed measures of investment worth that as a group could be called the discounted cash flow, or DCF, measures. Before proceeding to analyze them, it is desirable to explain again the concept of the present value of a future sum because in one way or another this concept is utilized in both these measures.

The present value of $100 payable in two years can be defined as that quantity of money necessary to invest today at compound interest in order to have $100 in two years. The rate of interest at which the money will grow and the frequency at which it will be compounded will determine the present value. We shall assume that funds are compounded annually. The manner in which a rate of interest will be chosen will be discussed later. For the present, assume that we are given a .10 annual rate of interest. Let us examine how the present value of a future sum can be computed by using that rate of interest.

Suppose that an investment promises to return a total of $100 at the end of two years. Because $1.00 invested today at 10 percent compounded annually would grow to $1.21 in two years, we can find the present value at 10 percent of $100 in two years by dividing $100 by 1.21 or by multiplying by the present value factor, .8264. This gives $82.64. Therefore, a sum of $82.64 that earns 10 percent interest compounded annually will be worth $100 at the end of two years. By repeated applications of this method, we can convert any series of current or future cash payments (or outlays) into an equivalent present value. Because tables, hand calculators, and computers are available that give the appropriate conversion factors for various rates of interest, the calculations involved are relatively simple.

The net present value method is a direct application of the present value concept. Its computation requires the following steps: (1) Choose an appropriate rate of discount, (2) compute the present value of the cash proceeds expected from the investment, (3) compute the present value of the cash outlays required by the investment, and (4) add the present value equivalents to obtain the net present value.

The sum of the present values of the proceeds minus the present value of the outlays is the net present value of the investment. The recommended accept or reject criterion is to accept all independent investments whose net present value is greater than or equal to zero and to reject all investments whose net present value is less than zero.

With zero taxes, the net present value of an investment may be described as the maximum amount a firm could pay for the opportunity of making the investment without being financially worse off. With such a payment the investor would be indifferent to undertaking and not undertaking the investment. Because usually no such payment must be made, the expected net present value is an unrealized capital gain from the investment, over and above the cost of the investment used in the calculation. The capital gain will be realized if the expected cash proceeds materialize. Assume an investment that costs $10,000 and returns $12,100 a year later. If the rate of discount is 10 percent, a company could make a maximum immediately outlay of $11,000 in the expectation of receiving the $12,100 a year later. If it can receive the $12,100 with an actual outlay of only $10,000, the net present value of the investment would be $1,000. The $1,000 represents the difference between the actual outlay of $10,000 and the present value of the proceeds $11,000. The company would have been willing to spend a maximum of $11,000 to receive $12,100 a year later.

The following example illustrates the basic computations for discounting cash flows, that is, adjusting future cash flows for the time value of money, using the net present value method.

Assume that there is an investment opportunity with the following cash flows:

	Period		
	0	*1*	*2*
Cash flow	− $12,337	$10,000	$5,000

We want first to compute the net present value of this investment using .10 as the discount rate. Table A in the Appendix of the book gives the present value of $1 due *n* periods from now. The present value of

$1 due 0 periods from now discounted at any interest rate is 1.000.
$1 due 1 period from now discounted at .10 is .9091.
$1 due 2 periods from now discounted at .10 is .8264.

The net present value of the investment is the algebraic sum of the three present values of the cash flows:

Period	*(1)* *Cash Flow*	*(2)* *Present Value Factor*	*(3)* *Present Value* *(col. 1 × col. 2)*
0	− $12,337	1.0000	− $12,337
1	10,000	.9091	9,091
2	5,000	.8264	4,132
		Net present value = $	886

The net present value is positive, indicating that the investment is acceptable. Any investment with a net present value equal to or greater than zero is acceptable using this single criterion. Since the net present value is $886, the firm could pay an amount of $886 in excess of the cost of $12,337 and still break even economically by undertaking the investment. The net present value calculation is a reliable method for evaluating investments.

Internal Rate of Return

Many different terms are used to define the internal rate of return concept. Among these terms are yield, interest rate of return, rate of return, return on investment, present value return on investment, discounted cash flow, investor's method, time-adjusted rate of return, and marginal efficiency of capital. In this book, IRR and internal rate of return are used interchangeably.

The internal rate of return method utilizes present value concepts. The procedure is to find a rate of discount that will make the present value of the cash proceeds expected from an investment equal to the present value of the cash outlays required by the investment. Such a rate of discount may be found by trial and error. For example, with a conventional investment, if we know the cash proceeds and the cash outlays in each future year, we can start with any rate of discount and find for that rate the present value of the cash proceeds and the present value of the outlays. If the net present value of the cash flows is positive, then using some higher rate of discount would make them equal. By a process of trial and error, the approximately correct rate of discount can be determined. This rate of discount is referred to as the internal rate of return of the investment, or its IRR.

The IRR method is commonly used in security markets in evaluating bonds and other debt instruments. The yield to maturity of a bond is the rate of discount that makes the present value of the payments promised to the bondholder equal to the market price of the bond. The yield to maturity on a $1,000 bond having a coupon rate of 10 percent will be equal to 10 percent only if the current market value of the bond is $1,000. If the current market value is greater than $1,000, the IRR to maturity will be something less than the coupon rate; if the current market value is less than $1,000, the IRR will be greater than the coupon rate.

The internal rate of return may also be described as the rate of growth of an investment. This is more easily seen for an investment with one present outlay and one future benefit. For example, assume that an investment with an outlay of $1,000 today will return $1,331 three years from now. This is a .10 internal rate of return, and it is also a .10 growth rate per year:

Time	Beginning-of-Period Investment	Growth of Period	Growth Divided by Beginning-of-Period Investment
0	$1,000	$100	$100/$1,000 = .10
1	1,100	110	$110/$1,100 = .10
2	1,210	121	$121/$1,210 = .10
3	1,331	—	

The internal rate of return of a conventional investment has an interesting interpretation that may be referred to at this point. It represents the highest rate of interest an investor could afford to pay, without losing money, if all the funds to finance the investment were borrowed and the loan (principal and accrued interest) was repaid by application of the cash proceeds from the investment as they were earned.

We shall illustrate the internal rate of return calculation using the example of the previous section where the investment had a net present value of $886 using .10 as the discount rate.

We want to find the rate of discount that causes the sum of the present values of the cash flows to be equal to zero. Assume that our first choice (an arbitrary guess) is .10. In the preceding situation, we found that the net present value using .10 is a positive $886. We want to change the discount rate so that the present value is zero. Should we increase or decrease the rate of discount for our second estimate? Since the cash flows are conventional (negative followed by positive), to decrease the present value of the future cash flows, we should increase the rate of discount (thus causing the present value of the future cash flows that are positive to be smaller).

Let us try .20 as the rate of discount:

Period	Cash Flow	Present Value Factor	Present Value
0	− $12,337	1.0000	− $12,337
1	10,000	.8333	8,333
2	5,000	.6944	3,472
		Net present value =	− $ 532

The net present value is negative, indicating that the .20 rate of discount is too large. We shall try a value between .10 and .20 for our next estimate. Assume that we try .16:

Period	Cash Flow	Present Value Factor	Present Value
0	− $12,337	1.0000	− $12,337
1	10,000	.8621	8,621
2	5,000	.7432	3,716
		Net present value =	0

The net present value is zero using .16 as the rate of discount, which by definition means that .16 is the internal rate of return of the investment.

Although tables give only present value factors for select interest rates, calculators and computers can be used for any interest rate.

Net Present Value Profile

The net present value profile is one of the more useful devices for summarizing the profitability characteristics of an investment. On the horizontal axis we measure different discount rates; on the vertical axis we measure the net present value of the investment. The net present value of the investment is plotted for all discount rates from zero to some reasonably large rate. The plot of net present values will cross the horizontal axis (have zero net present value) at the rate of discount that is called the internal rate of return of the investment.

Figure 6.2 shows the net present value profile for the investment discussed in the previous two sections. If we add the cash flows, assuming a zero rate of discount, we obtain

$$-\$12,337 + \$10,000 + \$5,000 = \$2,663$$

The $2,663 is the intersection of the graph with the Y axis. We know that the graph has a height of $886 at a .10 rate of discount and crosses the X axis at .16, since .16 is the internal rate of return of the investment. For interest rates greater than .16, the net present value is negative.

Note that for a conventional investment (minus cash flows followed by positive cash flows), the net present value profile slopes downward to the right.

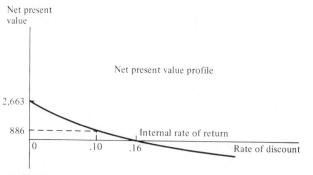

FIGURE 6.2

The net present value profile graph can be used to estimate the internal rate of return by plotting one negative value and one positive value and connecting the two points with a straight line. The intercept with the X axis will give a sensible estimate (not the exact value) of the internal rate of return.

We shall now consider four different investment opportunities and will apply four different investment criteria to these investments.

Four Investments

In Table 6.1 four hypothetical investments are described in terms of the initial cost of each and the net proceeds expected during each year of earning life. The salvage value or terminal value of each is assumed to be zero. We shall illustrate the ranking that may be given to these investments by each measure of investment worth under consideration.

TABLE 6.1   Cash Flows of Hypothetical Investments

| | | Net Cash Proceeds per Year | |
Investment	Initial Cost	Year 1	Year 2
A	$10,000	$10,000	
B	10,000	10,000	$1,100
C	10,000	3,762	7,762
D	10,000	5,762	5,762

To avoid complexities, we will assume that there are zero taxes and no uncertainty. An evaluation of the risk or uncertainty associated with an investment is a crucial part of the investment decision process. Also, all investments must be placed on an after-tax basis. The concepts of risk or uncertainty and taxation are complex, however, and it has seemed advisable to take these problems up separately later in the book.

Ranking by Inspection

It is possible in certain limited cases to determine by inspection which of two or more investments is more desirable. Two situations in which this is true are the following:

1. Two investments have identical cash flows each year through the final year of the short-lived investment, but one continues to earn cash proceeds in subsequent years. The investment with the longer life would

be more desirable. Thus investment B is better than investment A, because all factors are equal except that B continues to earn proceeds after A has been retired.

2. Two investments have the same initial outlay and the same earning life and earn the same total proceeds. If at the end of every year (during their earning life) the total net proceeds of one investment are at least as great as, and for at least one year are greater than, the total for the other investment, then the first investment will always be more profitable. Thus investment D is more desirable than investment C, because D earns $2,000 more in year 1 than investment C does; investment C does not earn this $2,000 until year 2. The earning of $2,000 more in the earlier year leads to the conclusion that investment D is more desirable than investment C.

Payback Period

The payback period is one of the simplest and one of the most frequently used methods of measuring the economic value of an investment. The *payback period* is defined as the length of time required for the stream of cash proceeds produced by an investment to equal the original cash outlay required by the investment. If an investment is expected to produce a stream of cash proceeds that is constant from year to year, the payback period can be determined by dividing the total original cash outlay by the amount of the annual cash proceeds expected. Thus, if an investment required an original outlay of $300 and was expected to produce a stream of cash proceeds of $100 a year for five years, the payback period would be $300 divided by $100, or three years. If the stream of expected proceeds is not constant from year to year, the payback period must be determined by adding up the proceeds expected in successive years until the total is equal to the original outlay.

Ordinarily, the administrator would set some maximum payback period and reject all investment proposals for which the payback period is greater than this maximum. Investigators have reported that maximum payback periods of two, three, four, or five years are frequently used by industrial concerns. The relatively short periods mentioned suggest that different maximum payback periods are required for different types of investments because some kinds of investments (construction, for example) can seldom be expected to have a payback period as short as five years.

Assume that the payback period is also used to rank investment alternatives with those having the shortest payback periods being given the highest ranking. The investments described in Table 6.1 are ranked by this method in Table 6.2.

TABLE 6.2　Payback Period

Investment	Payback Period (years)	Ranking	Calculations of Payback
A	1.0	1	
B	1.0	1	
C	1.8	4	$1 + \dfrac{\$6,238}{\$7,762} = 1.803$
D	1.7	3	$1 + \dfrac{\$4,238}{\$5,762} = 1.736$

Let us check the reasonableness of the ranking given the investments by the cash payback approach. Investments A and B are both ranked as 1 because they both have shorter payback periods than do any of the other investments, namely, one year. But investment A earns total proceeds of $10,000, and this amount merely equals the cost of the investment. Investment B, which has the same rank as A, will not only earn $10,000 in the first year but also $1,100 in the next year. Obviously, investment B is superior to A. Any ranking procedure, such as the payback period, that fails to disclose this fact is deficient.

Consider investments C and D modified so as to cost $11,524. Both would be given identical rankings because both would return their original outlay by the end of the second year. The two investments are in fact similar, with the single exception that out of identical total returns, more proceeds are received in the first year and less in the second year from investment D than is the case with C. To the extent that earnings can be increased by having $2,000 available for reinvestment one year earlier, D is superior to investment C, but both would be given the same ranking by the payback period measure.

Thus the cash payback period measure has two weaknesses: (1) It fails to give any consideration to cash proceeds earned after the payback date, and (2) it fails to take into account the differences in the timing of proceeds earned prior to the payback date. These weaknesses disqualify the cash payback measures as a general method of ranking investments. They are useful as a general measure of risk (all things equal a 2-year payback is less risky than a 10-year payback).

Return on Investment

The methods described in this section are commonly referred to as rate of return analysis or return on investment (ROI) analysis. Terminology is a problem because both these terms are also used to describe other procedures. We shall consistently use internal rate of return only when we refer to a dis-

TABLE 6.3　Average Income on Book Value

Investment	Average Proceeds	Average Depreciation[a]	Average (proceeds less depreciation)	Average Book Value[b]	Income on Book Value (%)	Ranking
A	$10,000	$10,000	$ 0	$5,000	0	4
B	5,550	5,000	550	5,000	11	3
C	5,762	5,000	762	5,000	15	1
D	5,762	5,000	762	5,000	15	1

[a]Assuming straight-line depreciation.
[b]Investment divided by 2.

counted cash flow calculation and return on investment to refer to an income divided by investment calculation.

To get a measure of efficiency, analysts frequently use the ratio of the firm's income to the book value of its assets. Some companies also use this measure as a means of choosing among various proposed internal investments. When this measure is used, the average income is computed after depreciation. If the denominator in the ratio is the book value of the investment, the value of both the numerator and the denominator will depend on the depreciation method used. An alternative procedure is to divide the average income by the cost of the investment (the accrued depreciation is not subtracted).

The ratio of income to book value is a common and useful measure of performance, but it is less useful as a device for ranking investments. Table 6.3 shows that the same ranking of one is given to investments C and D, although D is preferable to C. This procedure fails to rank these investments correctly because it does not take into consideration the timing of the proceeds.

An alternative procedure (see Table 6.4) is to divide income by the cost of the investment (accumulated depreciation not being subtracted). For purposes of measuring performance and computing return on investment, the

TABLE 6.4　Average Income on Cost

Investment	Cost	Average Income	Average Income on Cost (%)	Ranking
A	$10,000	$ 0	0	4
B	10,000	550	5.5	3
C	10,000	762	7.6	1
D	10,000	762	7.6	1

use of undepreciated cost will give lower measures than will the use of book value. Both measures illustrated fail to take into consideration the timing of cash proceeds. It is this failing that leads to incorrect decisions from the use of either of the two methods.

Discounted Cash Flow Methods

We have considered payback and return on investment as methods for measuring the value of an investment. Payback indicated that B is as desirable as A. ROI indicated that C is tied with D. But B is clearly better than A and D is better than C. On the basis of such an example, we have been able to reject payback and ROI as general methods of evaluating investments.

These two measures failed to consider the timing of cash proceeds from the investments. The payback period represents one extreme in this regard because all the proceeds received before the payback period are counted and treated as equals and all the proceeds received after the payback period are ignored completely. With the return on investment, the proceeds were related by simple averaging techniques to such things as the original cost of the investment or its book value. Neither of these methods succeeded in bringing the timing of cash proceeds into the analysis.

We have seen that the measures of investment worth previously considered may give obviously incorrect results because they fail either to consider the entire life of the investment or to give adequate attention to the timing of future cash proceeds. The discounted cash flow concept provides a method of taking into account the timing of cash proceeds and outlays over the entire life of the investment. We now return to the two measures of investment worth already introduced that incorporate present value concepts.

Internal Rate of Return

In Table 6.5 we show the internal rate of return for each of the investments listed in Table 6.1 and the ranking of investments that would result if this method were used.

It is instructive to examine the rankings given by this method applicable to each of the pairs of investments in this list for which we were earlier able to determine the more desirable investment of each pair.

We previously compared two pairs of investments and decided that investment B was preferable to A and D to C. In each case, if preference had been determined by using the internal rate of return of an investment method,

TABLE 6.5   Internal Rate of Return of the Investments

Investment	IRR (%)	Ranking
A	0	4
B	10	1
C	9[a]	3
D	10	1

[a]Approximate measure.

the pairs would be given the correct ranking. This is the first method that we have used that gives the correct rankings of both pairs:

A,   0%   C,   9%
B, 10%   D,   10%

Net Present Value

It is instructive to note the rankings that will be given to the hypothetical investments of Table 6.1 by the net present value method, using two sample rates of discount. In Table 6.6 we present the results of using the net present value method and a 6 percent rate of discount.

In discussing the measures of investment worth that do not use the discounted cash flow method, we pointed out that the relative ranking of certain pairs of these four investments was obvious. That is, it is obvious from examining the cash flows that investment B is preferable to A and D is preferable to C. The reader may note that in each case the net present value method using a 6 percent rate of discount ranks these investment pairs in the correct relative order.

TABLE 6.6   Net Present Values of the Investments— Rate of Discount Is 6 Percent

Investment	Present Value of Cash Flow	Present Value of Outlay	Net Present Value	Ranking
A	$ 9,430	$10,000	− $570	4
B	10,413	10,000	+ 413	3
C	10,457	10,000	+ 457	2
D	10,564	10,000	+ 564	1

**TABLE 6.7   Net Present Values of the Investments—
Rate of Discount Is 30 Percent**

Investment	Present Value of Proceeds	Present Value of Outlay	Net Present Value	Ranking
A	$7,692	$10,000	− $2,308	3
B	8,343	10,000	− 1,657	1
C	7,487	10,000	− 2,513	4
D	7,842	10,000	− 2,158	2

In Table 6.7 the same investments are ranked by the net present value method using a 30 percent rate of discount instead of 6 percent. The relative ranking of investments C and D does not change with the change in the rate of discount. Investment C, which was ranked second when a 6 percent rate of discount was used, is ranked fourth when the 30 percent discount rate is used. The ranking of investment D is changed from first to second by the change in the rate of discount. The higher rate of discount results in the proceeds of the later years being worth less relative to the proceeds of the early years; thus the ranking of B goes from 3 to 1, but D is still ranked ahead of C.

Even with a 30 percent rate of interest, the present value method maintains the correct ordering of each of the two pairs of investments for which an obvious preference can be determined. Thus we still find investment B preferred to A, and D preferred to C. This result is not an accident resulting from the specific choice of hypothetical investments and discount rates used in our examples. Whenever it is possible to determine obvious preferences between pairs of investments by the methods described earlier, the present value method will rank these investments in the correct order, no matter what rate of discount is used to compute the present value, as long as the same rate of discount is used to determine the present value of both the investments.

Summary of Rankings

The rankings given by each measure of investment worth for each of the hypothetical investments described in Table 6.1 are summarized in Table 6.8.

The most striking conclusion to be drawn from Table 6.8 is the tendency for each measure of investment worth to give a different ranking to the identical set of investments. This emphasizes the need to give careful consideration to the choice of measures used to evaluate proposed investments. All four

TABLE 6.8   Summary of Rankings

Measure of Investment Worth	Investment			
	A	B	C	D
Payback period	1[a]	1[a]	4	3
Average income on book value or cost	4	3	1[a]	1[a]
Internal rate of return	4	1[a]	3	1[a]
Net present value				
At 6%	4	3	2	1
At 30%	3	1	4	2

[a]Indicates a tie between two investments.

methods cannot be equally valid. By considering specific pairs of investments, we have shown that the measures of investment worth that do not involve the use of the discounted cash flow method can give rankings of investments that are obviously incorrect. For this reason, these measures will be excluded from further consideration.

The rankings given the investments by the net present value measures are not identical to that given by the internal rate of return of an investment measure. Neither of these rankings can be eliminated as being obviously incorrect; yet, because they are different, they could lead to contradictory conclusions in certain situations. In Chapter 7 we shall continue our investigation in an attempt to determine whether the net present value or the internal rate of return measure is more useful to a decision maker.

Limitation of Investment Rankings

In this chapter we discussed the ranking of four investments and showed that given a carefully defined set of investments we can make definite statements about the relative desirability of two or more investments. If the investments are not restricted to this set, we would find our ability to rank investments very limited.

Except for Chapter 8 of this book, we shall not be concerned with the "ranking" of investments; instead, we shall

1. Make accept or reject decisions for investments that are independent (i.e., if we undertake one investment, the cash flows of undertaking the other investments are not affected).
2. Choose the best of a set of mutually exclusive investments (i.e., if we

undertake one, either we would not want to undertake the other or we would not be able to because of the characteristics of the investments).

Although the objectives are somewhat more modest than the objective of ranking investments, we shall still encounter difficulties. There is nothing in our recommendations, however, that will preclude a manager from applying qualitative criteria to the investments being considered to obtain a ranking. The ranking that is so obtained is likely to be difficult to defend. Fortunately, for a wide range of decision situations, a manager can make decisions without a ranking of investments.

The Rollback Method

Using a simple hand calculator (one where there is no present value button), it is sometimes convenient to use a rollback method of calculation to compute the net present value of an investment. One advantage of this procedure is that the present values at different moments in time are obtained. Consider the following investment:

Time	Cash Flow
0	− $7,000
1	5,000
2	2,300
3	1,100

Assume that the discount rate is .10.

The first step is to place the cash flow of period 3 ($1,100) in the calculator and divide by 1.10 to obtain $1,000, the value at time 2. Add $2,300 and divide the sum by 1.10 to obtain $3,000, the value at time 1. Add $5,000 and divide by 1.10 to obtain $7,273, the value of time 0. Subtract $7,000 to obtain the net present value of $273.

Discounted Payback

Instead of computing the length of time required to recover the original investment, some analysts compute the length of time required until the present value turns from being negative to positive. This computation gives a break-

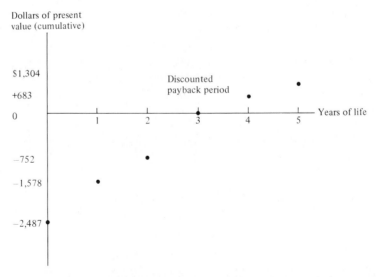

FIGURE 6.3   Discounted Payback Period

even life of the asset or a discounted payback period. If the life of the asset exceeds this break-even life, the asset will have a positive present value. The discounted payback period can be used to make independent investment decisions, since any investment with a discounted payback period will at least earn the required return.

Assume an investment with the following cash flows:

Time	Cash Flow
0	− $2,487
1	1,000
2	1,000
3	1,000
4	1,000
5	1,000

Figure 6.3 shows the cumulative present values (with a discount rate of 10 percent) for the investment. It has a discounted payback period of three years, and Table 6.9 shows the calculations, assuming a 10 percent rate of discount.

TABLE 6.9   Present Values for Different Lives

| | Net Present Value for Life of i | Cash Flows and Present Values for Period | | | | | |
| | | 0 (−$2,487) | 1 ($1,000) | 2 ($1,000) | 3 ($1,000) | 4 ($1,000) | 5 ($1,000) |
Period i							
0	− $2,487	− $2,487					
1	− 1,578	− 2,487	$909				
2	− 752	− 2,487	909	$826			
3	0	− 2,487	909	826	$752		
4	+ 683	− 2,487	909	826	752	$683	
5	+ 1,304	− 2,487	909	826	752	683	$621

What Firms Do

Prior to 1960 very few corporations used discounted cash flow methods for evaluating investments. Recent surveys indicate that the situation has changed. Gitman and Forrester showed in a 1976 study that 67.6 percent of the major U.S. firms responding used internal rate of return as either the primary or secondary method and that 35.7 percent used net present value (see Table 6.10).

In an independent study (see Table 6.11), Scholl, Sundem, and Gaijsbeck found that 86 percent of the major firms responding used internal rate of return or present value, thus confirming the magnitudes of the Gitman–Forrester study (see Table 6.11).

TABLE 6.10   What Firms Do: A Survey in 1976

| | Capital Budgeting Techniques in Use | | | |
| | Primary | | Secondary | |
Technique	Number	Percent	Number	Percent
Internal (or discounted) rate of return	60	53.6%	13	14.0%
Rate of return (average)	28	25.0	13	14.0
Net present value	11	9.8	24	25.8
Payback period	10	8.9	41	44.0
Benefit/cost ratio (profitability index)	3	2.7	2	2.2
Total responses	112	100.0%	93	100.0%

Source: L. J. Gitman and J. R. Forrester, Jr., "A Survey of Capital Budgeting Techniques Used by Major U.S. Firms," *Financial Management*, Fall 1977, pp. 66–71.

TABLE 6.11   Percentage of Firms Using Method

Method	Percentage of Firms
Payback	74%
Accounting return on investment	58
Internal rate of return	65
Net present value	56
Internal rate of return or present value	86
Use only one method (of which 8 percent is a DCF method)	14

Source: L. D. Scholl, G. L. Sundem, W. R. Gaijsbeck, "Survey and Analysis of Capital Budgeting Methods," *Journal of Finance*, March 1978, pp. 281–287. There were 429 firms selected and 189 responses. The firms were large and stable. A major financial officer was sent the survey.

Where We Are Going

There are many different ways of evaluating investments. In some situations, several of the methods will lead to identical decisions. We shall consistently recommend the net present value method as the primary means of evaluating investments.

The net present value method ensures that future cash flows are brought back to a common moment in time called *time 0*. For each future cash flow, a present value equivalent is found. These present value equivalents are summed to obtain a net present value. If the net present value is positive, the investment is acceptable.

The transformation of future flows back to the present is accomplished

---

A Vice-President

The following statement made by a vice-president of a *Fortune* 500 firm highlights the perspective of many managers:

The real challenge is creativity and invention, not analysis. Timely execution of projects by entrepreneurial managers is also more critical than sophistication of analytical budgeting techniques.

using the mathematical relationship $(1 + r)^{-n}$, which we shall call the present value factor for r rate of interest and n time periods.

In cases of uncertainty, additional complexities must be considered, but the basic framework of analysis will remain the net present value method.

Conclusions

An effective understanding of present value concepts is of great assistance in the understanding of a wide range of areas of business decision making. The concepts are especially important in financial decision making, since many decisions reached today affect the firm's cash flows over future time periods.

It should be stressed that this chapter has only discussed how to take the timing of the cash flows into consideration. This limitation in objective (and achievement) should be kept in mind. Risk and tax considerations must still be explained before the real-world decision maker has a tool that can be effectively applied. In addition, there may be qualitative factors that management wants to consider before accepting or rejecting an investment.

It is sometimes stated that refinements in capital budgeting techniques are a waste of effort because the basic information being used is so unreliable. It is claimed that the estimates of cash proceeds are only guesses and that to use anything except the simplest capital budget procedures is as futile as using complicated formulas or observations of past market levels to determine which way the stock market is going to move next.

It is true that in many situations reliable estimates of cash proceeds are difficult to make. Fortunately, there are a large number of investment decisions in which cash proceeds can be predicted with a fair degree of certainty. But even with an accurate, reliable estimate of cash proceeds, the wrong decision is freqently made because incorrect methods are used in evaluating this information.

When it is not possible to make a single estimate of cash proceeds that is certain to occur, it does not follow that incorrect methods of analysis are justified. If the investment is large, the use of a careful and comprehensive analysis is justified, even if this means that the analysis will be more complicated and costly. With small tactical investments, somewhat less involved methods might be used because a more complex analysis would not be necessary, but again there is no need to use inferior methods that decrease the likelihood of making correct investment decisions.

When all the calculations are completed, judgmental insights may be included in the analysis to decide whether to accept or reject a project.

Review Problem 6.1

Assume that a firm has a cost of money of .15. It is considering an investment with the following cash flows:

Time	Cash Flow
0	− $27,000,000
1	+ 12,000,000
2	+ 11,520,000
3	+ 15,552,000

Should the investment be accepted?

Solution to Review Problem 6.1

The net present value using .15 as the discount rate is

Time	Cash Flow	Present Value Factor	Present Value
0	− $27,000,000	1.15^{-0}	− $27,000,000
1	+ 12,000,000	1.15^{-1}	10,435,000
2	+ 11,520,000	1.15^{-2}	8,711,000
3	+ 15,552,000	1.15^{-3}	10,226,000
		Net present value =	$ 2,372,000

The net present value is positive and the investment is acceptable. The internal rate of return is .20.

PROBLEMS

1. Compute the net present value for each of the following cash flows. Assume a cost of money of 10 percent.

			Period			
Investment	0	1	2	3	4	5
A	$(1,000)	$100	$100	$100	$100	$1,100
B	(1,000)	264	264	264	264	264
C	(1,000)					1,611

2. Compute the internal rate of return for each of the cash flows in Problem 1.

3. Compute the payback for each of the cash flows in Problem 1. If the maximum acceptable payback period is four years, which (if any) of the cash flows would be accepted as a desirable investment?

4. Assume a cost of money of 5 percent. Compute the net present values of the cash flows of Problem 1.

5. Assume a cost of money of 15 percent. Compute the net present values of the cash flows of Problem 1. Compare with the results obtained from Problems 1 and 4.

6. The Arrow Company is considering the purchase of equipment that will return cash proceeds as follows:

End of Period	Proceeds
1	$5,000
2	3,000
3	2,000
4	1,000
5	500

Assume a cost of money of 10 percent.
   What is the maximum amount the company could pay for the machine and still be financially no worse off than if it did not buy the machine?

7. (a) An investment with an internal rate of return of .25 has the following cash flows:

Time	Cash Flow
0	C_0
1	+ $8,000
2	+ 10,000

The value of C_0 is ⸺⸺⸺ .

(b) If the firm financed the investment in (a) with debt costing .25, the debt amortization table (using the funds generated by the investment to repay the loan) would be

Time	Amount Owed	Interest	Principal Payment
0			
1			
2			

8. Compute the net present value (use a cost of money of .15) and the internal rate of return for each of the following investments:

	Period		
Investment	0	1	2
A	$(1,000)		$1,322
B	(1,000)	$ 615	615
C	(1,000)	1,150	

9. Recompute the net present values using (a) a cost of money of .20 and (b) a cost of money of .05 for each of the investments of Problem 8.

10. Prepare a schedule showing that, with a rate of growth of .15 per year, $1,000 will grow to $1,322 in two years.

11. Determine the internal rate of return of the following investment:

Period	Cash Flow
0	$(9,120)
1	1,000
2	5,000
3	10,000

12. How much could you pay in excess of the indicated cost for the investment in Problem 11 if the cost of money were .10?

13. Assume that you can only invest in one of the three investments of Problem 8.
    (a) Using the internal rates of return of the three investments, which is preferred?
    (b) Using the net present value method and a cost of money of .05, which is preferred?

14. A company uses a 10 percent discount rate. Assume equal annual cash proceeds.

    What should be the maximum acceptable payback period for equipment whose life is 5 years? What are the maximum acceptable paybacks for lives of 10, 20, and 40 years and infinite life?

15. Assume that the discount rate is 5 percent and answer Problem 14.

16. Assume that $r = .06$. A new machine that costs $7,000 has equal annual cash proceeds over its entire life and a payback period of 7.0 years.

    What is the minimum number of full years of life it must have to be acceptable?

17. Compute the internal rate of return of the following investments:

		Period		
Investment	0	1	2	3
A	− $10,000	$4,747	$4,747	$ 4,747
B	− 10,000			17,280

Compare the two investments.

Which do you prefer? Are you making any assumption about the reinvestment of the cash flows?

18. Determine the internal rate of return of the following investment:

Period	Cash Flow
0	− $15,094
1	10,000
2	10,000
3	1,000

19. Draw the net present value profile for the investment of Problem 18.

    Using a hand calculator and the rollback method described in the chapter, compute the net present value using a discount rate of .10.

20. Assume a discount rate of 3 percent and a machine that generates a constant annual amount of savings.

    What is the maximum acceptable payback period if the life of the machine is (a) 5 year, (b) 10 years, (c) 15 years, and (d) 20 years?

21. Assume interest rates of 6 percent and 12 percent and answer Problem 20.

22. Find the net present value at a 5 percent discount rate for each of the following three investments:

Investment	Period		
	0	*1*	*2*
A	− $18,594	$10,000	$10,000
B	− 18,140	0	20,000
C	− 19,048	20,000	0

23. Assume a discount rate of 5 percent from time 0 to time 1 and of 7 percent from time 1 to time 2.

    Find the net present value of each of the three investments in Problem 22.

24. Assume a discount rate of 5 percent from time 0 to time 1 and of 3 percent from time 1 to time 2.

    Find the net present value of each of the three investments in Problem 22.

25. An investment costing $31,699 will earn cash flows of $10,000 a year for eight years. The rate of discount is 10 percent.

    What is the discounted payback period?

26. Assume that two investments have the following sets of cash flows. Based on the analysis it is decided that A is more desirable.

    Evaluate the conclusion.

	0	*1*	*2*
A	− $19,008	$10,000	$12,000
B	− 19,008	12,000	10,000

	A		B	
	1	*2*	*1*	*2*
Revenue	$10,000	$12,000	$12,000	$10,000
Straight-line depreciation	9,504	9,504	9,504	9,504
Income	$ 496	$ 2,496	$ 2,496	$ 496
Average investment	14,256	4,752	14,256	4,752
ROI	.03	.50	.17	.11
Average ROI		.26		.14

27. The Super Company used a ROFE (return on funds employed) method of evaluating investments. The income of each period is divided by the average assets used during the period. This is done for each period and then an average ROFE is computed of all the ROFEs.

The controller of the Super Company defends the procedure since it is consistent with the performance evaluation procedures that are used after the investment is acquired.

The company is currently evaluating two investments (A and B).

	0	1	2
A	− $20,000	+ $11,000	+ $12,100
B	− 20,000	+ 12,100	+ 11,000

	A		B	
	Year 1	Year 2	Year 1	Year 2
Revenue	$11,000	$12,100	$12,100	$11,000
Depreciation	10,000	10,000	10,000	10,000
Income	$ 1,000	$ 2,100	$ 2,100	$ 1,000
Average investment	15,000	5,000	15,000	5,000
ROFE	.067	.420	.140	.200
Average ROFE		.24		.17

The firm requires a .20 return for an investment to be acceptable. The firm acquired investment A.

Which investment is more desirable?

28. Assume the following set of cash flows and a discount rate of 10 percent. What is the investment's net present value?

Period	Cash Flows
0	− $11,000
1	1,000
2	10,000
3	5,000

29. (Problem 28 continued) If you were to take the cash flows from the investment and use them to repay a 10 percent loan of $11,000 that was

used to finance the investment, how much cash would you have at time 3? What is the present value of this cash amount?

30. (a) If the investment of Problem 28 costs $12,930, what is the investment's internal rate of return?
    (b) If funds were borrowed at 10 percent to finance the investment and if the cash flows were used to repay the debt, how much cash will the firm have at time 3?

31. The ABC Company has determined that its cost of money is .12, however, because of a series of necessary nonproductive (not generating cash flows) investments, it has found that on the average a discretionary investment must earn .15 in order for the firm to break even.

    The firm has a chance to undertake an investment that has an internal rate of return of .14 and no risk. This investment also will not affect the amount of nonproductive investments needed.

    Should the investment be accepted?

32. The ABC Company has signed a contract with the XYZ Company agreeing to share the profits (equally) on a $1 million investment if the profits are in excess of a .24 return. If the investment does not earn in excess of .24, ABC should get all the cash generated.

    It is agreed that the investment is risky.

    The expected cash flows of the investment agreed to by ABC and XYZ are

0	1	2	3	4
− $1,000,000	+ $300,000	+ $300,000	+ $1,200,000	+ $400,000

Devise a procedure in which the profits are split. The ABC Company does not want to have to collect a refund from XYZ in the future, since XYZ's future is uncertain and a refund might not be collectible. The ABC want to recover its investment and the .24 return before splitting with XYZ. Assume that the cash flows shown occur. Illustrate your profit-splitting arrangement.

REFERENCES*

Journals

Specific papers that may be of interest follow.

Bacon, Peter W. "The Evaluation of Mutually Exclusive Investments." *Financial Management*, Summer 1977, 55–58.

Beedles, William L. "A Note on Evaluating Non-Simple Investments." *Journal of Financial and Quantitative Analysis*, March 1978, 173–176.

Bernhard, Richard H. "Mathematical Programming Models for Capital Budgeting—A Survey, Generalization, and Critique." *Journal of Financial and Quantitative Analysis*, June 1969, 111–158.

Brigham, Eugene F., and Richard H. Pettway. "Capital Budgeting by Utilities." *Financial Management*, Autumn 1973, 11–22.

Carter, E. Eugene. "Designing the Capital Budgeting Process." *TIMS Studies in the Management Studies*, 1977, 25–42.

Corr, Arthur V. "Capital Investment Planning." *Financial Executive*, April 1982, 12–15.

Dean, J. "Measuring the Productivity of Capital." *Harvard Business Review*, January–February 1954, 120–130.

Dorfman, Robert. "The Meaning of the Internal Rate of Return." *Journal of Finance*, December 1981, 1010–1023.

Fogler, H. Russell "Ranking Techniques and Capital Rationing." *Accounting Review*, January 1972, 134–143.

Gitman, Lawrence J., and John R. Forrester, Jr. "Forecasting and Evaluation Practices and Performance: A Survey of Capital Budgeting." *Financial Management*, Fall 1977, 66–71.

Hirschleifer, J. "On the Theory of Optimal Investment Decisions." *Journal of Political Economics*, August 1958, 329–352.

Hoskins, Colin G., and Glen A. Mumey, "Payback: A Maligned Method of Asset Ranking?" *Engineering Economist*, Fall 1979, 53–65.

Keane, Simon M. "The Internal Rate of Return and the Reinvestment Fallacy." *Journal of Accounting and Business Studies*, June 1979, 48–55.

Lewellen, Wilbur G., H. P. Lanser, and J. J. McConnell. "Payback Substitutes for Discounted Cash Flow." *Financial Management*, Summer 1973, 17–25.

Lorie, J. H., and L. J. Savage, "Three Problems in Rationing Capital." *Journal of Business*, October 1955, 229–239.

Mao, James C. T. "Survey of Capital Budgeting: Theory and Practice." *Journal of Finance*, May 1970, 349–360.

Rappaport, Alfred, and Robert A. Taggart, Jr. "Evaluation of Capital Expenditure Proposals Under Inflation." *Financial Management*, Spring 1982, 5–13.

---

* *Financial Management*, the *Engineering Economist*, and the *Journal of Business Finance & Accounting* carry a large number of relatively readable papers on capital budgeting. The *Journal of Finance* does also but is somewhat less readable. The *Financial Executive* and the *Harvard Business Review* will have occasional papers.

Sarnat, Marshall, and Haim Levy. "The Relationship of Rules of Thumb to the Internal Rate of Return: A Restatement and Generalization." *Journal of Finance*, June 1969, 479–489.

Schwab, Bernhard, and Peter Lusztig. "A Comparative Analysis of the Net Present Value and the Benefit-Cost Ratios as Measures of the Economic Desirability of Investments." *Journal of Finance*, June 1969, 507–516.

Weaver, James B. "Organizing and Maintaining a Capital Expenditure Program." *Engineering Economist*, Fall 1974, 1–36.

Weingartner, H. Martin. "Capital Budgeting of Interrelated Projects: Survey and Synthesis." *Management Science*, March 1966, 485–516.

———. "Some New Views on the Payback Period and Capital Budgeting Decisions." *Management Science*, August 1969, 594–607.

Books

Archer, S. H., and C. A. D'Ambrosio. *The Theory of Business Finance, A Book of Readings*, 2nd ed. New York: Macmillan Publishing Company, 6th ed. 1976.

Bierman, H., and S. Smidt. *The Capital Budgeting Decision*, New York: Macmillan Publishing Company, 1984.

Bonesss, A. J. *Capital Budgeting*. New York: Praeger Publishers, Inc., 1972.

Brigham, E. F., and R. E. Johnson. *Issues in Managerial Finance*, 2nd ed. Hinsdale, Ill.: The Dryden Press, Division of CBS College Publishing, 1980.

Crum, R. L., and F. G. J. Derkinderen. *Capital Budgeting Under Conditions of Uncertainty*. Boston: Martinus Nijhoff, 1981.

Dean J. *Capital Budgeting*. New York: Columbia University Press, 1951.

Fisher, I. *The Theory of Interest*. New York: Macmillan Publishing Company, 1930.

Grant, E. L., W. G. Ireson, and R. S. Leavenworth. *Principles of Engineering Economy*, 6th ed. New York: Ronald Press, 1976.

Levy, H., and M. Sarnat. *Capital Investment and Financial Decisions*, 2nd ed. Englewood Cliffs, N.J.: Prentice-Hall, Inc., 1983.

Lind, R. C. *Discounting for Time and Risk in Energy Policy*. Baltimore, Md.: The Johns Hopkins University Press, 1982.

Lutz, F., and V. Lutz. *The Theory of Investment of the Firm*. Princeton, N.J.: Princeton University Press, 1951.

Masse, P. *Optimal Investment Decisions: Rules for Action and Criteria for Choices*. Englewood Cliffs, N.J.: Prentice-Hall, Inc., 1962.

Merrett, A. J., and A. Sykes. *The Finance and Analysis of Capital Projects*. New York: John Wiley & Sons, Inc., 1963.

———. *Capital Budgeting & Company Finance*, New York: Longman, Inc., 1966.

Quirin, G. D., and J. C. Wiginton. *Analyzing Capital Expenditures*. Homewood, Ill.: Richard D. Irwin Inc., 1981.

Solomon, E. *The Management of Corporate Capital*. New York: Free Press, Division of Macmillan Publishing Company, 1959.

Wilkes, F. M. *Capital Budgeting Techniques*. New York: John Wiley & Sons, Inc., 1977.

Chapter 7

The Determination and Use
of Cash Flows

Major Topics

1. The determination of cash flows taking into consideration taxes and debt flows.
2. The difference between absolute and relative cash flows.
3. Opportunity costs and cash flow determination.

Cash Flows

We can define an investment as a commitment of resources made in the hope of realizing benefits that are expected to occur some time in the future. According to this definition, neither the resources nor the benefits need be in the form of explicit cash flows. A decision to have an executive spend a month studying the capabilities of various types of electronic data processing equipment would be an investment in the sense of this definition. The executive's time is a scarce resource. The month could have been spent in other activities that are valuable to the firm. In the first instance, at least, the expected benefits will be increased knowledge by management of a relatively new technology. Thus there is no explicit cash outlay or cash inflow, but there is an investment.

In the previous chapter, it was argued that investments ought to be evaluated in terms of the present value of the cash flows expected from them, in preference to any other measures of investment worth that have been sug-

175

gested. We have not given a complete or careful definition of the term cash flows, however. In the present chapter we expect to do this as well as explain some of the difficulties that arise in applying a cash flow analysis to investment proposals.

Cash Flows and Profits

Cash flows are not identical with profits or income. Changes in income can occur without any corresponding changes in cash flows. During a period of investment in plant, receivables, and inventories, a corporation can even experience a decrease in cash at the same time that income is increasing. One main advantage of the cash flow procedure is that it avoids difficult problems underlying the measurement of corporate income, which necessarily accompanies the accrual method of accounting. These accounting problems include the following:

1. In what time period should revenue be recognized?
2. What expenses should be treated as investments and therefore capitalized and depreciated over several time periods?
3. What method of depreciation should be used in measuring income as reported to management and stockholders (as distinct from income measurement for tax purposes)?
4. Should LIFO (last-in, first-out), FIFO (first-in, first-out), or some other method be used to measure inventory flow?
5. What costs are inventoriable? Should fixed, variable, direct, indirect, out-of-pocket, unavoidable, administrative, or selling costs be included in evaluating inventory?

There are disagreements as to the answers in each of these questions. Different approaches may lead to different measures of income. If income is used to evaluate investment worth, investments may look good or bad, depending on how income is measured. The utilization of cash flows minimizes many of these complications.

The Use of Cash Flows

In evaluating an investment, we suggest that the cash flows of the investment be used in the analysis. We are not interested in the conventional "cost" of the investment but, rather, in the cash outlays required and the timing of these cash flows. We are not using the earnings of period 1 but, rather, the cash flows of period 1. These distinctions can be important. A builder may tell us that a construction project will cost $1 million, but this is not sufficient information. We want to know when the outlays will be required. For example, if the outlays are made on completion of the building, the cost is truly $1 million. If the payment is required one year prior to completion, the true cost is $1 million plus the interest on the $1 million for one year. The use of expected earnings to measure the benefits of an investment would require a much more sophisticated accounting system than is currently being used by any corporation. The earnings figures resulting from current accounting practices are not usable for investment evaluation without adjustment. Also, even with improved measures of income, there would remain the question of whether the use of cash flows or earnings is more appropriate. If earnings are measured correctly, both measures should give identical net present values. The advantage of the use of the cash flow is that the receipt of cash is an objective, clearly defined event that leads to a significantly different situation than before the receipt of cash.

A sale on account is an economic event recorded by the accountant and affecting accounting income. But the firm has not yet received the cash, it cannot spend the cash, and the ultimate collection of the cash is uncertain. For purposes of investment analysis, we are more interested in the moment when the cash is to be received. At that moment the firm reaches a new decision point. The cash may be returned to the stockholders by the payment of a dividend. It may be used to retire debt, increase the working capital, or acquire new long-lived assets.

It might be suggested that to be correct, the dollar of cash received in period 1 should be followed to its disposition at the end of the firm's life. However, we find it more convenient to take the receipt of cash associated with a specific asset to be a self-contained event, and we do not normally concern ourselves with the final disposition of the dollar. The assumption that cash flow can be borrowed and lent at a given discount rate allows us to make this simplifying assumption.

Thus for purposes of investment analysis, unlike conventional accounting, we choose the receipt or disbursement of cash to be the crucial event. It should not be thought that a sale on account or other accruals are ignored. A sale on account in period 1 will affect the expected cash collection in period 2; hence, it is brought into the analysis in period 2, the period in which the firm has the cash in hand and has reached a decision point.

Absolute and Relative Cash Flows

When cash flows are being compared with zero cash flows, we shall speak of absolute cash flows. In evaluating the present value of these cash flows, using a 10 percent rate of interest, we are implicitly comparing this investment with an investment that would return 10 percent, thus having a zero net present value.

A second method of analysis would be to compare directly one alternative with the other. In looking at the cash flow estimates, for example, we can subtract the cash flows of one alternative from the cash flows of the second alternative. The incremental cash flows can be called relative cash flows, and we can compute the present value of this series of relative cash flows. It can be shown that the present value of this series of relative cash flows will be the same as the difference between the present values of the absolute cash flows from the two alternatives. Thus the present value method will lead to the same conclusion as to the relative worth of the two alternatives, whichever of the approaches is used.

There is an important difference between the two series of cash flows, however. With the series of absolute cash flows, if the investment were accepted and actually began to operate, we could compare, period by period, the actual cash flows with our previous forecasts. There is not, however, any similarly indentifiable series of cash flows that could be compared with the relative cash flow estimates.

Importance of Considering All Alternatives

Apart from those difficulties in making estimates of relative cash flows that are a by-product of the difficulties of estimating the incremental effects of various actions of the firm, there is an important conceptual danger that must be avoided in estimating relative cash flows. As explained, an estimate of relative cash flows always involves a comparison of two alternatives. The size of the estimated relative cash flows from making a particular investment will depend upon the alternative that is used as a basis of comparison. *This means that almost any investment can be made to seem worthwhile if it is compared with a sufficiently bad alternative.*

In general, an investment should not be accepted unless the present value of its absolute cash flows generated by it are positive. As long as all feasible alternatives are considered (including doing nothing or abandoning what is currently being done), it makes no difference which alternative is tentatively accepted as the standard of comparison. The final answer will be the same in any case. The choice of a standard of comparison may lead to mistaken conclusions only if some advantageous alternatives (such as ceasing production entirely) are excluded from the analysis.

EXAMPLE 7.1   ABSOLUTE AND RELATIVE ————————————
CASH FLOWS

A new modernized store replacing an old store is expected to earn 25 percent. Should it be accepted if the firm has a 10 percent cost of money? The cash flows (a perpetuity) are

0	1	2	
− $1,000,000	+ $250,000	+ $250,000	· · ·

Conclusion: We have to know what the present store is earning. Are the cash flows shown absolute or relative cash flows?

EXAMPLE 7.2   (CONTINUATION OF EXAMPLE 7.1)

Now assume that the cash flows of Example 7.1 are absolute flows and that the old store is currently earning $200,000 a year. The relative cash flows for "new minus old" are

0	1	2	3
− $1,000,000	$50,000	$50,000	· · ·

This is a 5 percent return, and the new store is clearly not acceptable even though it earns $250,000 per year unless we add new information (such as a changing competitive situation) that will adversely affect the $200,000 currently being earned.

EXAMPLE 7.3   (CONTINUATION OF EXAMPLE 7.1)

Now assume that the cash flows of Example 7.1 are relative cash flows and that the old store is losing $200,000 per year. The firm still uses a 10 percent cost of money.

	0	1	2	3
Continue old		− $200,000	− $200,000	· · ·
New	− $1,000,000	50,000	50,000	· · ·
New−old	− $1,000,000	$250,000	$250,000	· · ·

The relative cash flow has a 25 percent internal rate of return.
    The 25 percent return is not valid, since the new is being compared to an

unacceptable alternative. Both alternatives are unacceptable. If there are no better alternatives, the store should be shut down. The undesirability of the new store is illustrated if "new" is compared to "shut down" and if shutdown has zero cash flows. The 5 percent return is not sufficient to justify investment.

	0	1	2	3
New	− $1,000,000	$50,000	$50,000	$50,000
Shut down		0	0	0
New–shut down	− $1,000,000	$50,000	$50,000	$50,000

These examples illustrate the fact that all the alternatives must be considered.

Opportunity Costs

Usually, the cash outlays included in the computation of net cash flows are the outlays incurred because of the investment. Outlays that would be incurred by the firm whether or not the investment is accepted should not be charged to a particular investment project. Thus the practice of allocating a share of general overhead to a new project on the basis of some arbitrary measure, such as direct labor hours or a fraction of net sales, is not recommended unless it is expected that general overhead will actually increase if the project is accepted.

On the other hand, in some instances an investment project may require the use of some scarce resource available to the firm, although the explicit cash outlays associated with using that resource may be nonexistent or may not adequately reflect the value of the resource to the firm. Examples are projects that require a heavy drain on the time of key executive personnel or that use valuable floor space in a plant or store already owned by the business. The costs of using such resources are called opportunity costs, and they are measured by estimating how much the resource (the executives' time or the floor space) would earn for the company if the investments under consideration were rejected.

It may appear that the practice of charging opportunity costs against an investment project when no corresponding cash outlay can be identified is a violation of, or exception to, the procedure of evaluating investments in terms of actual cash flows. Actually, including opportunity costs is not so much an exception to the cash flow procedure as an extension of it. The opportunity cost charged should measure net cash flows that could have been earned if the project under discussion had been rejected. Suppose that one floor of a factory building owned by a business could either be rented out at $1,200 per month or be used to produce a new product. By charging a rental opportunity cost of $1,200 per month against the new product, a more meaningful measure of the cost to the company of producing it is obtained. An alternative procedure would be to estimate the relative cash flow from the new product compared with that produced by renting the extra space and not producing the new product.

In some instances it will be extremely difficult to estimate opportunity costs. The temptation then is to use some other, more easily identifiable basis of charging for the use of such things as floor space or executive time. This temptation must be viewed with some skepticism. The pro rata share of the costs of owning a building may be much higher or much lower than the true opportunity costs of using that space. When there is really no basis for estimating the opportunity costs associated with the use of a factor, such as the time of certain key executives, it may be preferable to note merely that the proposed project is likely to require some amount of attention from such key executives.

The only valid justification for the prorating of the out-of-pocket costs to the proposed project would be if the costs are a reasonable basis for estimating the opportunity cost. For example, if an additional executive can be hired for the same cost as a present executive, the opportunity cost of using some of the time of the present executive should not be greater than this current salary (a new executive could be hired). If it is felt that the managers are currently earning their salaries when they are doing their least profitable tasks, the cost should not be less. Thus we can correctly say that the opportunity cost of an executive's time is equal to the actual salary that would be paid to the next executive who could be hired.

Cash Flow Determination

Acquiring Assets Without Cash Disbursements

The term cash outlay is also applied to a transaction in which an asset is acquired by incurring a long-term debt or by issuing stock. Even though there may be no explicit borrowing of cash, receipt of cash, and disbursement of cash, these transactions are assumed to occur when an asset is acquired via a promise to pay in some distant time period and the transaction is treated as if there has been a cash outlay as well as a source of new capital.

Some investments are acquired by the issuance of common stock. In such a situation there is no disbursement of cash, and there is a tendency to evaluate such opportunities as if there are no cash outlays. This tendency is wrong. The cash that could have been obtained by a public offering of the common stock is an opportunity cost, and in an economic sense it is a cash outlay. The method of analysis for an issuance of stock should be identical to the analysis used when there is an explicit cash outlay. The cost of using common stock capital will be taken into consideration when the cash flows are discounted and adjusted for uncertainty.

Working Capital

In focusing attention on outlays for plant and equipment, it is possible to lose sight of the fact that the working capital needed to operate the investment project should also be included in computing the investment outlays. If residual working capital is recoverable at the termination of operations, this causes the investment to have a net terminal value that should be taken into consideration. Increases in current liabilities are subtracted from the increase in current assets to compute the use of cash. It is assumed that the additional current liabilities do not change the proportion of current liabilities to other sources of capital.

An investment in plant assets will usually lead to funds being tied up in working capital. This will include the cash necessary to meet payroll and other bills, funds invested in the raw material, work-in-process and finished-goods inventories, and receivables from customers. The size of these items will depend on the exact nature of the capital investment, but all the previously mentioned fund requirements will usually accompany an investment in long-lived assets. The one possible exception would be an investment that would decrease the need for working capital by increasing efficiency. Examples of this nature are accounting machines that expedite the billing to customers or storage facilities and inventory control devices that reduce the amount of inventory that must be kept on hand.

A working capital need arising because of the investment (required by the investment increase) has the effect of increasing the investment outflow today. If the investment has a limited life and the working capital is expected to be recovered at the end of the life of the investment, the recovery of the working capital in the last period should be considered as cash proceeds and treated in the same manner as the other cash flows are treated. It should not be thought that ignoring the working capital investment and the recovery of working capital will balance each other out. The factor that must be considered is the required return on the working capital during the period of use.

When an asset is acquired by the incurrence of a noninterest-bearing current liability, there is no cash outlay. It is the timing of the actual cash disbursement that is important. Thus, if the investment results in an increase in inventories of $100 and the source of capital is an increase in current liabilities of $100, the net cash outlay that is required in the period of inventory acquisition is zero. If the $100 increase in inventories required cash outlays of $20 and current liabilities increased by $80, then the net cash outlays in the period of inventory acquisition is $20. A net increase in working capital (leaving out interest-bearing debt) needed by an investment is a use of capital and thus a negative cash flow. If the use of the investment increases the working capital that is available and the firm can use this working capital in other projects, this is a positive cash flow.

The cash flow caused by working capital is equal to the change of the net working capital or in more detail:

$$\text{cash flow used} = \text{increase in working capital assets} - \text{increase in current liabilities that are noninterest bearing}$$

An interesting problem arises with accounts receivable. Assume an investment where a credit sale of $100 with the incremental costs of the sale being $40 is projected for time one. Working capital is expected to increase by $100 at time 1. But the cost of the sale is $40. Is the investment in accounts receivable $100 or $40?

The investment is $40, but the easy and correct solution is to use $100 as the expected use of cash to increase working capital. There will also be $60 of income reported and the net use of cash flow is $40, which agrees with the conclusion reached above that the investment is $40.

Excluding Interest Payments

Cash disbursed for interest is normally excluded from the cash flow computation used in analyzing investments. The interest factor is taken into consideration by the use of the present value procedures. To include the cash disbursement for interest would result in double counting. Assume that the discount factor being used to take into consideration the time value of money is 6 percent. There is an investment that requires an outlay of $1,000 and promises to return $1,080 at the end of one period with certainty. This investment would seem to be desirable. Assume that we can raise money for this investment at a cost of 6 percent, that is, obtain $1,000 now and pay $1,060 a year from now. An incorrect analysis would show the $60 interest as a deduction from the cash flows of period 1:

	Year	
	0	*1*
Investment	− $1,000	$1,080
Interest		− 60
Net cash flows	− $1,000	$1,020

$$\text{NPV} = \frac{\$1,020}{1.06} - \$1,000 = -\$34$$

This analysis of cash flows would incorrectly lead to a reject decision, using higher than a 2 percent rate of interest because of a double counting of interest.

Including All Debt Flows

As stated previously, it is incorrect to include the interest payments in the cash flows. We can choose for certain purposes to include all cash flows of the debt financing associated with an investment, however. Although this practice makes comparisons of different projects more complex, the calculation is sometimes used and should be understood. It is used for evaluating investments from the viewpoint of the residual owner (e.g., real estate projects).

Continuing the preceding example, we find that the cash flows of the investment and the cash flows of the $1,000 debt would be as follows:

	Year	
	0	*1*
Investment	− $1,000	$1,080
Debt financing	1,000	− 1,060
Net cash flows	$ 0	$ 20

An inspection of the table shows that the present value of the net of debt cash flows is positive for any choice of interest rate greater than zero. Whenever we include debt-financing cash flows in the investment analysis, with limitless debt, by a suitable usage of debt we can cause any conventional investment with an internal rate of return greater than the cost of debt to have a positive present value (or equivalently to have a very high internal rate of return). If we were using the internal rate of return method, (IRR), we would say that the internal rate of return resulting after the subtraction of the debt cash flows would be the IRR on the stockholders' investment. In like manner, using the net present value method, we are computing the net present value of the cash flows associated with the stockholders' investment. By combining suitable amounts of debt with the investment cash flows, we can cause investments with IRRs only slightly greater than the cost of debt to have acceptable present values and acceptable IRRs. The method of analysis being illustrated should never be used arbitrarily, that is, for some investments and not for others. It is safer to exclude all debt flows from the cash flow calculation than to include them. Including debt flow adds to the complexity of the analysis.

The computation of the internal rate of return and net present value of the cash flows associated with the stockholders' investment are interesting calculations. They follow naturally from the assumption that the stockholders want to know the expected return (and risk) of their investment. However, they are more complex than the basic investment flows, since their use requires either that the capital structure be kept constant through time or a different discount rate be used each time period. In the preceding example, the acceptance of the investment financed by 100 percent debt would change the capital structure. This factor must be considered in evaluating the cash flow stream.

The Tax Shield of Interest

The interest on debt gives rise to a tax shield. How should this affect the investment analysis?

Consider an investment requiring an immediate outlay of $1,000 that will generate before-tax benefits of $1,090. The tax rate is 46 percent. The asset will be financed 100 percent by debt.

If debt costs 10 percent, an inspection of the cash flows reveals that the investment does not generate enough cash flows to pay the debt. Thus the investment is not acceptable.

$(1 - .46)$
$.54 \times .1 = .054$

The after-tax cost of debt is 5.4 percent. Since the $100 interest tax shield is larger than the $90 of taxable income, there will be no taxes paid. The actual cash flows and a possible net present value (NPV) would be

Time 0	Time 1	Net Present Value (.054)
− $1,000	+ $1,090	$34.16

The calculation using the $1,090 cash flow at time 1 is *incorrect* since it double counts the interest tax shield. The interest tax shield is used to compute the discount rate and in computing the cash flows. The interest tax shield cannot be used both in the discount rate calculation and to compute cash flows. The correct investment cash flows for time 1 are $1,090.00 minus the $41.40 tax on $90.00, or $1,048.60. Discounting this amount by 5.4 percent, we obtain a negative net present value of $5.12, properly indicating that the investment should be rejected.

Salvage and Removal Costs

The salvage and removal costs introduce no real problem if we keep in mind that we are interested in the periods when cash outlays are made or when cash flows into the firm. In the following descriptive material, the term salvage refers to "net salvage"; removal costs have been subtracted.

Let us first consider the salvage value of the new investment. Any funds obtained from selling the new investment when it is retired will increase the flow of cash in the last period. Thus the salvage of the new investment will increase the cash flow of the last period of use.

When the investment is being made to replace an item of equipment currently being used, there are two additional salvage values to be considered: (1) the salvage value now of the old equipment and (2) the salvage value that the old equipment would have had at the end of its physical or useful life (whichever comes first) if it were not replaced now. If the asset is replaced now, the present salvage will have the effect of increasing the cash flow of this period (or decreasing the required cash outlay). However, if the old equipment is being retired now, the salvage that would have been obtained at the end of its life will not be obtained. Thus there is a decrease in the relative cash flows of that last period because of the salvage which will not be obtained at that time. To summarize, the absolute cash flow effects are

> *Salvage value of the new equipment*. Increase the cash flow of the last year of use for the buy alternative.
>
> *Present salvage value of the old equipment*. Increase the cash flow for this year (decrease the cash outlay) for the buy alternative.
>
> *Salvage value of the old equipment at time of normal retirement*. Increase the cash flow of that year (because the salvage value would be obtained if the replacement did not take place). This cash inflow applies to the absolute cash flows of the "continue the old" alternative.

The analysis of the cash flows arising from salvage is complicated by the fact that the cash flow analysis may be made in terms of relative or absolute cash flows. If the cash flows are relative, we compute the cash flows from buying the new equipment minus the cash flows that would occur if the old equipment were retained. To analyze the absolute cash flows of the several alternatives, the cash flows of retaining the old would be computed, as would the cash flows of purchasing the new equipment. The present salvage value of the old equipment and the future salvage value of the new equipment would affect the cash flow of the alternative of purchasing the new equipment. The salvage value on retirement of the old would affect the cash flow of retaining the old equipment.

EXAMPLE 7.4

Assume that the present equipment has a salvage value now of $1,000 and an expected salvage value in five years of $400 (at which time the equipment would be physically unusable). The new equipment will have a salvage value at the time of its expected retirement in year 10 of $650. All figures are on an after-tax basis. The cash flows arising from the salvage values would be as follows:

	Year		
	0	5	10
Absolute flows of			
retaining the old		$400	
purchasing the new	$1,000		$650
Relative flows of			
replacing now	$1,000	$(400)	$650

Terminal Value

Salvage value is one form of terminal value. Another form is the release of cash necessary to operate the investment. Other examples of items that may result in released cash at the cessation of operations are collections of accounts receivable and reduction in required inventories. All these items give rise to outlays of cash when they were purchased and then lagged in their generation of cash. When the outlays of cash cease, because the production is being phased out, the coming periods will have increases in cash flows resulting from the conversion of these noncash current assets into cash; similarly, reductions of current liabilities reduce cash.

Even when $100 of working capital can be converted into $100 of cash, there is a timing cost. Assume that $100 is invested in working capital at time 0 and that the working capital is converted into $100 of cash at the end of the asset's life at time 10. Use a .15 time value factor.

Present value of outlay at time 0	$100
Present value of benefits at time 10	25
Net cost	$ 75

Cash Flow and Uncertainty

Each computation of cash flows makes specific assumptions about the level of business activity, actions of competitors, future availability of improved models of machines, costs of factors of production, future sales, and the like. Because there is a large amount of uncertainty connected with each of these factors, it should be appreciated that computations using the net present value method are indications of value rather than measures with 100 percent certainty and accuracy. A more detailed discussion of the consequences of uncertain estimates and some suggestions for making analyses when basic assumptions are subject to uncertainty are presented in later chapters. It should be stressed that any decision about investments must be based on as complete a consideration of all the relevant factors as it is possible to provide and that the probable net present value of an investment proposal is only one factor, although a very significant one, to be considered in arriving at a final decision.

Income Taxes and Cash Flows

All decisions must be made on an after-tax basis. The income taxes are computed by applying the expected tax rate for each period to the taxable income (excluding interest charges) of that period. The taxable income will not be equal to the cash flow of the period, and frequently the taxable income will be different from the income computed in accordance with generally accepted accounting principles. The taxable income is defined by the tax laws established by government. The accounting income is defined by the accounting authorities (i.e., the Financial Accounting Standards Board). No matter what method is being used to accept or reject investments, it will be necessary to compute the income for tax purposes, so that the tax can be computed.

In the case of corporations subject to income taxes, the timing of revenues and expenses adopted for income tax purposes must be considered in evaluating a potential investment, since the choices will affect the amount and timing of income tax payments. Because income taxes do not affect all investments in the same manner, it is necessary to place cash flows associated with each investment on an after-tax basis before evaluating the investments.

Governments have available many devices for encouraging or discouraging firms to undertake investments. Among the variables are the method of depreciation, the allowed life of assets, the treatment of salvage, and investment tax credits or investment allowances. Instead of investment tax credits, some countries use investment allowances or grants where firms are actually paid a percentage of the cost of the investment. Whatever the terminology, the economic effect of such tax benefits is to reduce the cost of the investment.

Business managers should be knowledgeable as to the nature of the current tax laws and sensitive to changes in the laws. The tax laws are a powerful tool for governments to influence the level of investments. Businesses should make decisions that are consistent with the tax laws under which they will have to operate.

After-Tax Flows

If revenues are $100 and the tax rate is .46, the firm will pay $46 of taxes and will net $54. The calculation is

$$(1 - t)R$$

where t is the tax rate and R is the revenue. A variation would be to write the expression as

$$R - tR$$

where tR is the incremental tax. Note that R is being multiplied by $(1 - t)$ to reduce it to an after-tax cash flow measure.

If out-of-pocket expenses are E, the after-tax cash flow expense is

$$(1 - t)E$$

or equivalently

$$E - tE$$

where tE is the tax savings arising from being able to deduct E from the taxable income. If the out-of-expenses are $100, the after-tax cash flow expense is $54.

If the expense is a noncash utilizing expense then the calculation is modified. Define depreciation expense deductible for taxes to be Dep_t; then the cash flow effect of deducting Dep_t depreciation for taxes

$$tDep_t$$

Thus if there is $100 of depreciation expense taken for taxes, the cash flow effect will be a positive $46.

Measuring the Effects of Depreciation Expense on Cash Flows

Suppose that we are considering the purchase of a new piece of equipment. If there were no income taxes, the cash proceeds resulting from the use of the equipment could be estimated by subtracting the additional cash outlays required to operate the equipment from the additional revenues that result from acquiring it. The depreciation expense does not affect the cash proceeds. That is,

before-tax cash proceeds =
$$\text{revenues} - \text{expenses other than depreciation} \qquad (7.1)$$

The term *cash proceeds* is used here to refer to the proceeds generated by operating the investment. It assumes that all revenues are accompanied by an immediate generation of cash equal to the revenues. It also assumes that there are no changes in net working capital. For a nonprofit hospital or government bureau, this is the only calculation that would be necessary.

Now assume that there are income taxes. It is necessary to subtract the additional income tax liability that occurs because of the investment:

after-tax proceeds = revenues − cash outlays − income tax $\qquad (7.2)$

or equivalently

after-tax proceeds = revenues − expenses other than
$$\text{depreciation} - \text{income tax} \qquad (7.3)$$

The income tax liability is computed by applying the income tax rate to the additional taxable income. It is the amount of tax that actually has to be paid. One allowable deduction for purposes of computing the tax liability is the tax depreciation of the investment. It is possible to express the determination of the income tax in the following way:

$$\text{income tax} = (\text{tax rate}) \times (\text{taxable income}) \tag{7.4}$$

and

$$\text{income tax} = (\text{tax rate}) \times (\text{revenues} - \text{expenses other than depreciation} - \text{tax depreciation}) \tag{7.5}$$

From equation (7.5) it can be seen that the higher the depreciation taken for income tax purposes, the lower the income tax will be and the greater the after-tax cash proceeds. Substituting equation (7.5) in equation (7.3) and simplifying gives equations (7.6) and (7.7).

$$\text{after-tax proceeds} = (1 - \text{tax rate}) \times (\text{revenues} - \text{expenses other than depreciation} - \text{tax depreciation}) + \text{tax depreciation} \tag{7.6}$$

or

$$\text{after-tax proceeds} = (1 - \text{tax rate}) \times (\text{revenues} - \text{expenses other than depreciation}) + (\text{tax rate} \times \text{tax depreciation}) \tag{7.7}$$

Equations (7.6) and (7.7) are mathematically equivalent and therefore give identical answers, although one or the other formula may be easier to use in a particular instance. Equation (7.7) is particularly useful, because it highlights the fact that the cash proceeds of the period are increased by the allowable tax depreciation times the tax rate. Thus we can compute the present value of the "tax savings" by multiplying the depreciation by the expected tax rate of each period and discounting that amount back to the present. For convenience, we assume that the first depreciation deduction and the resulting tax saving takes place exactly one year after the single outlay associated with the investment. This is a simplification since the exact timing of the savings will depend on the timing difference between the investment outlays and the tax payments.

Let

C = the after-tax proceeds
t = the tax rate
R = the revenues
E = the expenses other than depreciation
Dep_t = the depreciation expense taken for taxes

Then rewriting equations (7.6) and (7.7), we have:

$$C = (1 - t)(R - E - Dep_t) + Dep_t \qquad\qquad (7.6a)$$

and

$$C = (1 - t)(R - E) + tDep_t \qquad\qquad (7.7a)$$

Equation (7.7a) highlights the fact that the higher the period's tax depreciation expense, the larger the period's cash flow if the tax expense can be used to shelter taxable income.

EXAMPLE 7.5 ──

Assume that the tax rate is .46, revenue is $150, the out-of-pocket expenses are $50, and the depreciation for taxes is $80. We have

$t = .46$

$R = 150, \quad E = 50, \quad Dep_t = 80$

Using equations (7.6a) and (7.7a), we have

$C = (1 - t)(R - E - Dep_t) + Dep_t$

$\quad = .54(\$150 - \$50 - \$80) + \$80$

$\quad = \$10.80 + \$80.00 = \$90.80$

$C = (1 - t)(R - E) + tDep_t = .54(\$100) + .46(\$80)$

$\quad = \$54 + \$36.80 = \$90.80$

The exact method of computing the cash flows is a matter of taste. A wide range of different methods will be equally correct.

Accelerated Cost Recovery System (ACRS)

In August 1981 the U.S. Congress passed a law that introduced a new method of tax depreciation expense calculation. Even the words "depreciation expenses" were dropped and "recovery allowances" were introduced. The objective of the legislation was to accelerate the tax deductions.

Capital assets were divided into five classes, with four of the classes defined in terms of a number of years. After several subsequent changes in the tax law, we have

Three-year property class—tangible personal and other property with a life of four years or less (certain tools, research and development equipment, light-duty trucks and autos).

Five-year property class—practically all machinery and equipment, petroleum storage facilities, and public utility property with lives between 4.5 and 18.0 years.

Ten-year property class—certain public utility property (with lives between 18.5 and 25.0 years) and a few other selected items (e.g., railroad tank cars).

Fifteen-year property class—exclusive for public utility property with lives greater than 25 years.

Real estate:—mostly written off over 18 years using 200 percent declining balance (for low-income housing) or 175 percent declining balance with a switch to straight line (for other real estate).

When the asset (tangible personal property) is sold, any gain is treated as ordinary income to the extent of any prior capital recovery allowance. For example, if an asset costing $10,000 with a book value of $8,000 after one year is sold for $11,000 there would be $2,000 of ordinary income and $1,000 of capital gain.

The recapture provisions for real property are more complex (there are more exceptions to the treatment of the gain as ordinary income).

In May of 1985 the President of the United States proposed that the ACRS be abandoned in favor of a slower rate of write-off. We can expect the tax law to be revised so that the depreciation tax shields are less generous than those offered by the ACRS provisions in place in 1985. However, the relevant thing to remember is that the present value of the depreciation deductions times the tax rate is the economic value of the depreciation tax savings and this amount effectively reduces the cost of acquiring a depreciable asset.

**TABLE 7.1   ACRS Depreciation Expense Property Placed
in Service After December 31, 1980**

Ownership Year	Three-Year	Five-Year	Ten-Year	Fifteen-Year Utility Property
1	25%	15%	8%	5%
2	38	22	14	10
3	37	21	12	9
4		21	10	8
5		21	10	7
6			9	7
7			9	6
8			9	6
9			9	6
10			9	6
11				6
12				6
13				6
14				6
15				6
	100%	100%	100%	100%

Investment Tax Credit and ACRS

The three-year class has a 6 percent investment credit rather than the 10 percent available for the other classes (only depreciable property is eligible).

The investment tax credit may be recaptured if the asset is disposed of prior to the asset being fully depreciated for three-year property or prior to the completion of 5 full years of use for 5-, 10-, or 15-year property.

In 1982, the law was changed so that any regular investment tax credit that is taken reduces the tax basis for depreciation calculations by 50 percent of the tax credit. In lieu of reducing the tax basis, the investor can reduce the 10 percent credit to 8 percent and the 6 percent credit to 4 percent (for three-year property).

Table 7.1 gives the recovery allowances in effect as a result of the 1981 Tax Act as amended in 1982. The use of this table is mandatory except for real estate. Also, straight-line depreciation may be used. However, if straight-line depreciation is chosen, it must be used for all assets acquired in that year in that class, except for 18-year real estate, where the election may be made on a property-by-property basis.

EXAMPLE 7.6

A piece of new equipment costs $10,000. It can be depreciated for tax purposes in three years, and it has been decided to use the ACRS method. It is expected

TABLE 7.2 Computation of Income Tax

Year	Revenues	Other Costs	Depreciation for Tax Purposes	Taxable Income	Tax Rate (%)	Income Tax
1	$8,000	$4,000	$2,500	$1,500	46	$690
2	8,000	4,000	3,800	200	46	92
3	8,000	4,000	3,700	300	46	138

to have no salvage value on retirement. The company uses straight-line depreciation in its accounting. The equipment is expected to result in an increase in annual revenues (sales are all for cash) of $8,000 and additional annual costs requiring cash outlays of $4,000 (not including depreciation of the equipment). The income tax rate is 46 percent. The cost of money is 10 percent (after tax). The investment tax credit of $400 is taken instead of reducing the tax basis.

The first step is to compute the taxable income and income tax of each year. This is accomplished in Table 7.2.

It should be noted that the use of a tax rate of 46 percent for all years carries an assumption that the tax rate will not be changed. If a change is expected, the tax rates of the future years should be used.

The second step is to compute the cash flows of each year (Table 7.3). It is important to note that the book depreciation does not enter into this computation at all, but the depreciation for tax purposes influences the income tax and thus does indirectly affect the proceeds. Using equation (7.6) to compute the cash flows of year 2, we would have

$$\text{after-tax cash flows} = (1 - .46)(\$8,000 - \$4,000 - \$3,800) + \$3,800$$

$$= \$108 + \$3,800$$

$$= \$3,908$$

TABLE 7.3 Computation of Cash Flows

Year	Revenue	Other Costs	Income Tax	Cash Flows
1	$8,000	$4,000	$690	$3,310
2	8,000	4,000	92	3,908
3	8,000	4,000	138	3,862

TABLE 7.4   Computation of the Present Value of Cash Flows

Year	Cash Flow	Discount Factor (using 10%)	Present Value of the Proceeds
1	$3,310	.9091	$3,009
2	3,908	.8264	3,230
3	3,862	.7513	2,902
			$9,141

Using equation (7.7), we would also have

$$\text{after-tax cash flows} = (1 - .46)(\$8,000 - \$4,000) + (.46 \times \$3,800)$$

$$= \$2,160 + \$1,784$$

$$= \$3,908$$

The next step is to compute the present value of the cash flows, using 10 percent as the rate of discount (see Table 7.4). The present value of the cash flow is $9,141, to which we add the $400 of the investment tax credit to obtain $9,541. This is less than the cash outflows of $10,000; thus the investment is to be rejected.

Analogous calculations can be made for investments where either a .10 or .08 investment tax credit can be taken (the .10 credit will tend to be more desirable).

In May of 1985 President Reagan proposed that the investment tax credit be eliminated. Even if the investment tax credit is eliminated in 1985 or some year shortly after that, it is likely that a new investment tax credit or an investment allowance will be given in the future. Traditionally, the government has used the tax law to influence decisions. Tax credits and allowances are effective ways of stimulating investment and they are likely to be used in the future.

The Tax Rate

Let us assume that the statutory tax rate is 46 percent and that we are making a capital budgeting analysis. What rate should be used for decisions if the actual tax expense divided by reported income for the previous period is 30 percent?

The differences arise because of provisions in the tax code such as tax-exempt interest, investment tax credits, accelerated depreciation, and various other tax avoidance possibilities. A normal tax-paying corporate entity may have any tax rate from 0 to 46 percent. What rate should be used?

We could argue that the rate applicable to the marginal investment should be used. The rate may be zero for the next investment because of a large tax-loss carryover; however, the tax rate might still change to 46 percent on an additional investment that would cause a positive tax payment.

A firm with tax losses that would otherwise not be used would be incorrect if it used 46 percent. If there is expectation that an investment for a zero tax firm will move the firm to a tax status of 46 percent, then there is some tax cost, however. If we would expect the firm to be able to keep itself in a zero tax status at no cost, then the tax rate should be zero. But a zero tax rate tends to be unrealistic, since most companies are only temporarily zero tax and profitable investments tend to cause taxes, either now or in the future. We advocate the use of a marginal tax rate that would be between 0 and 46 percent. The choice of the rate will depend on the incremental effect on taxes of undertaking the investment. Remember that the marginal tax rate could be 46 percent when the average tax on the corporation's reported income is less than 46 percent.

EXAMPLE 7.7

The ABC Company earned $100 million before tax and $90 million after tax. The effective tax rate was .10 of before-tax income and .11 of after-tax income. The low tax rate was caused by investment tax credits and the treatment of foreign taxes. There are no unused tax credits.

What tax rate should be used on the next investment?

If $100 of income will result in $46 of taxes, then a .46 tax rate should be used.

Vice-President, Finance

Implementing capital budgeting techniques depends on judgment and foresight of those looking into the future. Sophisticated analysis seldom compensates for bad judgment.

Vice-President of Finance, a *Fortune* 500 firm

Conclusions

Investment analysis uses cash flows because it is theoretically correct and because it is easier to define and use than accounting incomes.

The cash flow can be defined to be equal to the change in the company's bank account as long as the debt flows and other financing flows are excluded and the opportunity costs are included. If some debt flows are included, then all debt flows must be included and the resulting net cash flow will be the change in the stockholder's position.

Changes in working capital affect the cash flow. A $100 of cash earned will increase working capital and will be a positive cash flow. A $100 of cash required to be on deposit in a bank because of the investment is also an increase in working capital, but this is a negative cash flow because now capital is required to finance the $100 of cash sitting in the bank. Changes in net working capital caused by undertaking an investment change the amount of capital needed.

Review Problem 7.1

The following events are assumed to take place at time 1. Determine the cash flow for investment evaluation purposes. The tax rate is .46.

Credit sales	$ 40,000	
Cash sales	100,000	
Out-of-pocket expenses	75,000	
Income taxes	12,880	(reflects the $7,000 interest expense tax shield and the $30,000 depreciation)
Depreciation (accounting)	20,000	
Depreciation (tax)	30,000	
Change in net working capital (increase)	8,000	(includes $28,000 of accounts receivable that only cost $20,000 incrementally)
Interest expense	7,000	
Principal payment	16,000	

Solution to Review Problem 7.1

Cash from operations:		
Sales		$140,000
Less		
	75,000	
	12,880	87,880
		$ 52,120

To eliminate interest tax savings;

$$\$7,000 \times .46 = \quad \underline{\$\ 3,220} \\ \$55,340$$

Less

Increase in working capital	8,000
Cash flow	$47,340

The tax calculation was

	With Interest	Without Interest
Revenue	$140,000	$140,000
Expenses	75,000	75,000
Dep_t	30,000	30,000
Interest	7,000	
Total expenses	$112,000	$105,000
Taxable income	28,000	35,000
Tax rate	× .46	× .46
Tax	$ 12,880	$ 16,100

$16,100 − $12,880 = $3,220 tax shield of interest

or

$7,000 × .46 = $3,220 tax shield of interest

Note:

(a) Depreciation (accounting) of $20,000 does not affect any of the calculations.
(b) Interest expense is excluded (or eliminated).
(c) Principal payment is excluded.
(d) The difference between book amount of receivables and the cost of receivables does not effect the calculations (two items are affected and they self-balance).

PROBLEMS

1. The following facts relate to an investment that costs $10,000 being considered by the ABC Company:

	Period	
	1	2
Cash revenues	$12,000	$12,000
Depreciation	5,000	5,000
Net income	$ 7,000	$ 7,000

   The company intends to declare dividends of $12,000 in period 1 and $12,000 in period 2 as a result of the investment. The company is not subject to income taxes.

   What are the cash flows of the two years for purposes of the analysis of the investment?

2. For Problem 1, assume that all the sales were made on account and that collection lagged the sale by one period. The company will distribute dividends equal to the cash generation.

   What are the cash flows of each year?

3. An investment will require an increase in the following working capital items:

Cash	$1,000,000
Accounts receivable	3,000,000
Inventories	6,000,000

   It is also expected that current liabilities will increase by $4 million.

   How will the preceding items affect the cash flows of the investment?

4. In computing the cash flows of a period, should interest payments be included or excluded? Explain.

5. The ABC Company is considering an investment in a new product. The information for one year is as follows:

Sales	$200,000
Manufacturing costs of sales	80,000
(includes $20,000 of depreciation)	
Selling and administrative expenses	40,000
(directly associated with the product)	
Equipment purchases	10,000
Decrease in contribution of other products	5,000
Increase in accounts receivable	15,000
Increase in inventories	20,000
Increase in current liabilities	30,000
Income taxes associated with product income	12,000
Interest on bonds expected to be used in financing	18,000

Compute the cash flow that can be used in the present value computations of this investment.

6. A product is currently being manufactured on a machine that has a book value of $10,000 (it was purchased for $50,000 20 years ago). The costs of the product are as follows:

	Unit Costs
Labor, direct	$ 4.00
Labor, variable indirect	5.00
Other variable overhead	2.50
Fixed overhead	2.50
	$14.00

In the past year 10,000 units were produced and sold for $10 per unit. It is expected that the old machine can be used indefinitely in the future, and that the price will continue to be $10 per unit.

An equipment manufacturer has offered to accept the old machine as a trade-in for a new version. The new machine would cost $80,000 after allowing $15,000 for the old equipment. The projected costs associated with the new machine are as follows:

Labor, direct	$ 2.00
Labor, variable indirect	3.50
Other variable overhead	4.00
Fixed overhead	3.25
	$12.75

The fixed overhead costs are allocations from other departments plus the depreciation of the old equipment. Repair costs are the same for both machines.

The old machine could be sold on the open market now for $6,000. Ten years from now it is expected to have a salvage value of $1,000. The new machine has an expected life of 10 years and an expected salvage of $10,000.

There are no corporate income taxes. The appropriate time discount rate for this company is .05. It is expected that future demand of the product will remain at 10,000 units per year.

Evaluate whether, the new equipment should be acquired.

7. The ABC Company is considering an investment in a new product. The information for one year is as follows:

Sales (all on account)	$200,000
Manufacturing costs of sales	90,000
(include $20,000 of depreciation and $6,000 of fixed cost	
allocations from service departments)	
Selling and administrative expenses	40,000
(directly associated with the product)	
Equipment purchases	10,000
(purchased on account and not yet paid)	
Decrease in contribution of other products	5,000
Increase in accounts receivable	15,000
Increase in inventories	20,000
(includes $4,000 depreciation)	
Increase in current liabilities	30,000
Income taxes associated with product income	12,000
Interest on bonds expected to be used in financing	18,000
Increase in accumulated depreciation	19,000

Compute the cash flow that can be used in the present value computations of this investment.

8. Assume that an investment is financed partially by sinking fund bonds and that there is a requirement to place $50,000 per year into a sinking fund.

Does this information affect the computation of the cash flows for the investment analysis? A sinking fund requirement requires that cash or the bonds themselves be set aside for the debt retirement.

9. Compute the cash flow effect (change) caused by the following items. The tax rate is .46. Assume the firm is paying taxes.

(a) Revenues increased by $100 _____ .

(b) Labor expenses increase by $100 _____ .

(c) Tax depreciation expense increases by $100 _____ .

(d) The investment tax credit increases by $100 (nothing else is changed)

_____ .

(e) Accounting depreciation increases by $100 _____ .

10. The A Company is currently earning $13,000,000 per year on $100,000,000 of stockholders' equity, or a return of 13 percent. One plant with a cost base of $10,000,000 earns $800,000 of cash per year, or 8 percent.

   The chairman of the board has set a target ROI of 15 percent. The company has received an offer of $5,000,000 for the plant. The pro forma return on investment (assuming the $5,000,000 from the sale of the plant is returned to investors) is

$$\text{ROI} = \frac{\$12,200,000}{\$90,000,000} = 13.5\%$$

   Should the plant be sold?

11. The X Company will use a .10 discount rate in evaluating an investment that costs $1,500,000. For each year of its 15-year life, the investment will have the following same revenues and out-of-pocket expenses. The firm uses straight-line depreciation. The first year's income statement is

Revenues	$280,000
Out-of-pocket expenses	30,000
Interest	150,000
Depreciation expense	100,000
Income	$ 0

The company has a zero tax rate.

   Should the company undertake the investment?

12. Assume that the cash flows of an investment are

0	− $1,500,000
1–15	250,000

The rate of discount to be used is .10.

   Should the company undertake the investment?

13. The National Money Company, in deciding whether to make or buy, considers only direct labor and direct material as being relevant costs. The sum of these two costs factors is compared with the cost of purchasing the items, and a decision is made on this basis.

    Appraise the make or buy procedure of the National Money Company.

14. The National Money Company has an investment opportunity that offers $1 million of cash flows a year for perpetuity. It requires a cash outlay of $19.6 million for plant and equipment and the necessary inventory. It is estimated that an additional $500,000 of cash will have to be carried as a compensating balance during the period of the investment. The company has a time value of money of .05.

    Is the investment acceptable?

15. To make a new product, inventories must be increased by $5 million.

    Should this be considered a cash outlay?

16. Would you expect the relevant costs for decision making (such as the make or buy decision) to be higher or lower than the accounting costs computed on an absorption costing basis?

17. Assume that the Internal Revenue Code allows a tax credit of .10 of the cost of eligible investments to be deducted from the amount of federal income taxes payable. It also allows the use of accelerated depreciation. The tax base is not reduced by the investment tax credit.

    Assume a marginal income tax rate of .46 and an after-tax discount rate of .12.

    (a) How much is $1 of tax credit worth today?
    (b) How much is the "right" to deduct $1 of depreciation today worth today?
    (c) Assume that we pay $1 million for equipment eligible for the tax credit. The equipment will be depreciated for tax purposes in 10 years. What is the cost of the equipment? What is the cash flow of the period of purchase of the equipment? What do we know about the value of the equipment as of the beginning of the period after the taking of tax credit?

18. Assume a tax rate of .4 and a before-tax rate of discount of .05.
    (a) If the firm is basically profitable, what is the present value of $1 of tax-deductible expense incurred and paid for at the end of period 1?
    (b) If the firm is operating at a loss, what is the present value of $1 of tax-deductible expense incurred and paid for at the end of period 1?

19. Compute the present value of the right to deduct $1 million in depreciation immediately compared with the right to deduct the $1 million in 20 years from now. The tax rate is .4 and the after-tax rate of discount is .05.

20. The AB has a borrowing cost of .10 and a tax rate of .4. It uses an after-tax borrowing rate of .06 to evaluate riskless investments (cash flows are certain). It can invest $1,000 to earn $1,080 of net revenues (before tax) one period hence. The cash flows are certain and the firm has taxable income. The following calculations have been done:

Revenue		$1,080
Depreciation	1,000	
Interest	100	1,100
Tax loss		$ 20
Tax rate		× .4
Tax saving		$ 8

The cash flows used were

Time 0	− $1,000	
Time 1	+ 1,088	(including $8 tax savings)

The present value using .06 as the discount rate is

$$- \$1,000 + \$1,088(1.06)^{-1} = -\$1,000 + \$1,026 = +\$26$$

The investment was accepted.
    Evaluate the decision.

21. Manufacturers of heavy electric generating equipment have been arguing for years over the value of buying in advance of need. The following analysis was presented by one manufacturer in order to persuade utilities to order in advance under a "buy and store" plan.

Cost of boiler if purchased a year early and stored (90 percent of the purchase price would be paid immediately and 10 percent one year later, when the boiler is completed)	$1,000,000
Storage costs for one year (this amount would be paid two years from now)	10,000

It is expected that there will be an 8.5 percent increase in cost ($85,000) if the purchase is delayed one year.

Assuming a short-term interest rate of .04, the interest cost of buying early is $36,000. With a .52 tax rate, the after-tax interest cost is $17,200. Comparing the $85,000 of cost saving with the storage cost plus the interest indicates that it is desirable to purchase early.

Assume that the boiler is to be placed into use two years from now.

The after-tax cost of money of the company considering the purchase is 7 percent.

Prepare an estimate of the incremental after-tax cash flows resulting from ordering a boiler immediately. The estimated cash flows should be suitable for determining the value of advance ordering, using a discounted cash flow approach. Assume that the boiler would be depreciated on a straight-line basis over a 20-year period from the date it is installed and ready to use. The investment tax credit does not apply.

22. The following projections for an investment apply for the year 1984 (the forecasted tax rate is .46):

Revenues (credit sales)	$100,000
Accounting depreciation	30,000
Tax depreciation	40,000
Interest expense	5,000
Principal payment	12,000
Receipt of receivables	93,000
Increase in receivables	7,000
Increase in net working capital (where working capital includes receivables)	29,000

(a) Assuming that the firm is on an accrual basis for taxes, determine the expected tax expense that will be *paid*.

(b) The tax expense to be used for the investment evaluation cash flow calculation is _____ .

(c) Determine the cash flow for purposes of evaluating the investment:

_____ . The cash flow will be discounted using an after-tax discount rate based on using a composite of all types of capital.

23. Assume that the tax law says that you can expense the cost of equipment for tax purposes when the asset is acquired. The tax rate is .46. The ABC Company has the opportunity to invest in a piece of equipment that costs $299,060 and will earn $100,000 per year for five years.

(a) Compute the before-tax internal rate of return.

(b) Compute the after-tax internal rate of return.

(c) Compute the after-tax internal rate of return if the tax rate is .70.

24. The Packaging Company has developed a new product. While the prospects look good, there are considerable production risks, and all things equal, it would prefer to build a pilot plant to test the production process and then build the production plant. The following cash flows have been projected:

0	1	2	3	4
− $4,000,000	+ $100,000	+ $1,000,000	− $25,000,000	+ $5,000,000

Assume that the $5,000,000 of benefits will continue for perpetuity, the $4,000,000 plant will be abandoned at time 3, and the firm uses a 10 percent discount rate. It has a requirement that investments have a payback period of 5 years or less.

If the pilot plant is bypassed, the outlay of $25,000,000 and benefits of $5,000,000 per year will take place (starting in year 1).

What do you recommend?

REFERENCES

See references for Chapter 6.

Chapter 8

Mutually Exclusive Investments and Capital Rationing

Major Topics

1. How net present value and internal rate of return can be used to evaluate mutually exclusive investments.
2. The importance of the reinvestment of cash flows assumption.
3. The index of present value.
4. Capital rationing.
5. The limitations of investment rankings.

Net Present Value

In Chapter 6 we saw that neither of the two discounted cash flow procedures for evaluating an investment is obviously incorrect. In many situations the internal rate of return (IRR) procedure will lead to the same decision as the net present value (NPV) procedure. There are also times when the internal rate of return may lead to different decisions from those obtained by using the net present value procedure. When the two methods lead to different decisions, the net present value method tends to give better decisions.

It is sometimes possible to use the IRR method in such a way that it gives the same results as the NPV method. For this to occur, it is necessary that the rate of discount at which it is appropriate to discount future cash proceeds be the same for all future years. If the appropriate rate of interest varies from year to year, even if that pattern of variation is known in advance, then the two procedures may not give identical answers.

It is easy to use the NPV method correctly. It is much more difficult to use the IRR method correctly. We recommend the use of the net present value method, and in this chapter we shall explain why we believe the internal rate of return method is inferior. In the process we shall show how that method could be used more correctly.

Accept or Reject Decisions

Frequently, the investment decision to be made is whether or not to accept or reject a project where the cash flows of the project do not affect the cash flows of other projects. We speak of this type of investment as being an independent investment. With the internal rate of return procedure, the recommendation with conventional cash flows is to accept an independent investment if its IRR is greater than some minimum acceptable rate of discount. If the cash flow corresponding to the investment consists of one or more periods of cash outlays followed only by periods of cash proceeds, this method will give the same accept or reject decisions as the net present value method, using the same discount rate. Because most independent investments have cash flow patterns that meet the specifications described, it is fair to say that in practice, the internal rate of return and net present value methods tend to give the same recommendations for independent investments.

Consider an investment with an immediate outlay of $100 and benefits of $115 one year from now. Its net present value profile is shown in Figure 8.1. With discount rates of less than 15 percent, the net present value is positive; with rates larger than 15 percent, the net present value is negative. At 15 percent, the net present value is zero; the investment has an internal rate of return of 15 percent.

Figure 8.1 illustrates an investment that has an internal rate of return of 15 percent. If the required rate is less than 15 percent, the investment is acceptable using the IRR method, and the figure shows that the net present value will be positive if the discount rate is less than 15 percent. With a conventional investment, the NPV method and the IRR method will lead to consistent accept and reject decisions.

It is sometimes suggested that one of the advantages of the internal rate of return procedure is that it may be utilized without deciding on a minimum acceptable discount rate, whereas the net present value method requires that this rate be incorporated into the computations. The weakness of this position becomes evident when we consider the accept or reject type of investment

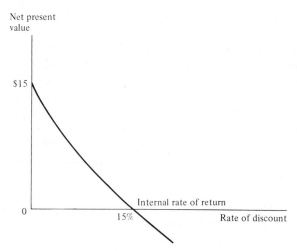

FIGURE 8.1   Net Present Value Profile

decision. To reach a decision, the internal rate of return of an investment must be compared with the minimum acceptable discount rate. The discount rate is no less important to IRR than to net present value, although it enters at an earlier stage in the computations with the net present value method.

Mutually Exclusive Investments

If undertaking any one of a set of investments will decrease the profitability of the other investments, the investments are substitutes. An extreme case of substitution exists if undertaking one of the investments completely eliminates the expected proceeds of the other investments. Such investments are said to be mutually exclusive.

Frequently, a company will have two or more investments, any one of which would be acceptable, but because the investments are mutually exclusive, only one can be accepted. For example, assume that a company is trying to decide where to build a new plant. It may be that either of two locations would be profitable. But the company will have to decide which one is likely to be the more profitable because only one new plant is needed. An oil company may need additional transport facilities for its products. Should it build a pipeline or acquire additional tankers and ship by water? All of these alternatives may result in a net profit to the firm, but the company will wish to choose the one that is more profitable. Suppose that it has decided to build the pipeline. Should a 6- or 10-inch diameter pipeline be installed? Again, the problem is to choose the more profitable of these alternatives. In all these situations, the choice is between mutually exclusive investments.

Mutually exclusive investment alternatives are common in industry. The situation frequently occurs in connection with the engineering design of a new installation. In the process of designing such an installation, the engineers are typically faced at a great many points with alternatives that are mutually exclusive. Thus a measure of investment worth that does not lead to correct mutually exclusive choices will be seriously deficient. In this light, the fact that the two discounted cash flow measures of investment worth may give different rankings to the same set of mutually exclusive investment proposals becomes of considerable importance.

Incremental Benefits: The Scale Problem

The IRR method's recommendations for mutually exclusive investments are less reliable than are those that result from the application of the present value method because the former fails to consider the size of the investment. Let us assume that we must choose one of the following investments for a company whose discount rate is 10 percent: investment A requires an outlay of $10,000 this year and has cash proceeds of $12,000 next year; investment B requires an outlay of $15,000 this year and has cash proceeds of $17,700 next year. The internal rate of return of A is 20 percent and that of B is 18 percent.

A quick answer would be that A is more desirable, based on the hypothesis that the higher the internal rate of return, the better the investment. To see why this answer may be wrong, consider that an internal rate of return of 1,000 percent on an investment of a dime for one year is likely to be a poor substitute for a rate of 15 percent on $1,000 for one year if only one of the investments can be undertaken and if the time factor is less than 15 percent.

When only the IRR of the investment is considered, something significant is left out—and that is the *size* of the investments. The important difference between investments B and A is that B requires an additional outlay of $5,000 and provides additional cash proceeds of $5,700. Table 8.1 shows that the IRR

TABLE 8.1 Two Mutually Exclusive Investments

Investment	Cash Flows		Internal Rate of Return (%)
	0	*1*	
A	− $10,000	$12,000	20
B	− 15,000	17,700	18
Incremental (B–A)	− $ 5,000	+ $ 5,700	14

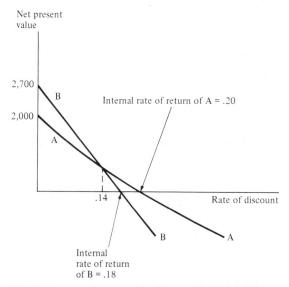

FIGURE 8.2   Two Mutually Exclusive Investments

of the incremental investment is 14 percent, which is clearly worthwhile for a company that can obtain additional funds at 10 percent. The $5,000 saved by investing in A can earn $5,500 (a 10 percent return). This is inferior to the $5,700 earned by investing an additional $5,000 in B.

Figure 8.2 shows both investments. It can be seen that investment B is more desirable (has a higher present value) as long as the discount rate is less than 14 percent.

We can identify the difficulty just described as the scale or size problem that arises when the internal rate of return method is used to evaluate mutually exclusive investments. Because the IRR is a percentage, the process of computation eliminates size, yet size of the investment is important.

Timing

The scale problem is sometimes more difficult to identify than in the preceding example. Assume that there are two mutually exclusive investments both requiring the same initial outlay. This case seems to be different from the one we have just discussed because there is no incremental investment. Actually, the difference is superficial. Consider investments Y and Z described in Table 8.2. Suppose that they are mutually exclusive investments for a company whose cost of money was 5 percent. The internal rate of return of Y is 20 percent,

TABLE 8.2

Investment	Cash Flows for Period			Internal Rate of Return (%)	Net Present Value at 5%
	0	1	2		
Y	− $100.00	$ 20.00	$120.00	20	$27.89
Z	− 100.00	100.00	31.25	25	23.58

whereas that of Z is 25 percent. If we take the present value of each investment at 5 percent, however, we find that the ranking is in the opposite order. The present value of Z is less than the present value of Y. Neither investment can be said to be obviously superior to the other, and both require the same cash outlays at time 0.

Suppose that we attempt to make an incremental comparison, as follows:

Period 0	0	Cash flows identical
Period 1	− $80.00	Cash flow of Y is less than that of Z
Period 2	$88.75	Cash flow of Y exceeds that of Z

We see that the cash flow of Y is $80.00 less in year 1 and $88.75 more than Z in year 2. As before, we can compute the IRR on the incremental cash flow. An outlay of $80.00 that returns $88.75 one year later has a rate of 10.9 percent. An investment such as this would be desirable for a company whose cost of money is less than 10.9 percent. Again we are really dealing with a problem of the scale of the investment, but in this case, the opportunity for the additional investment occurs one year later.

The same result can be reached by a somewhat different route if we ask how much cash the company would have on hand at the end of the second year if it accepted investment Y or if it accepted investment Z. Both investments give some cash proceeds at the end of the first year. The value of the investment at the end of the second year will depend on what is done with cash proceeds of the first year. Assume that the cash proceeds of the first year could be reinvested to yield 5 percent. Then investment Y would result in a total cash accumulation by the end of the year of $141 (105 percent of $20 plus $120). Investment Z would result in a cash accumulation of only $136.25 (105 percent of $100 plus $31.25).

Figure 8.3 shows that investment Y is to be preferred as long as the appropriate discount rate is less than 10.9 percent. If the rate is in excess of 10.9, then Z is to be preferred.

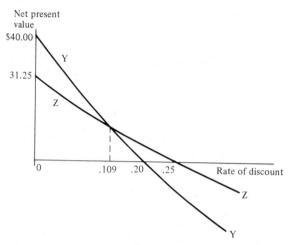

FIGURE 8.3   Two Mutually Exclusive Investments

One disadvantage associated with the use of the internal rate of return method is the necessity of computing the IRR on the incremental cash proceeds in order to determine which of a pair of mutually exclusive investments is preferable. If there are more than two mutually exclusive investments, we shall have to conduct an elimination tournament among the mutually exclusive investments. Taking any pair, we compute the internal rate of return on the incremental cash flow and attempt to decide which of the two investments is preferable. The winner of this round would then be compared in the same manner with one of the remaining investments until the grand champion investment is discovered. If there were 151 investments being considered, there would have to be 150 computations, because 150 investments would have to be eliminated.

Reinvestment Assumption

When it is being used to make decisions, one implicitly assumes that the internal rate of return method implies reinvestment at the internal rate of return (with NPV, the comparable assumption is that funds are invested at the discount rate). The internal rate of return of an investment can be computed without any assumption about the utilization of the funds generated by the investment. For example, an investment generating cash flows that are consumed will have the same internal rate of return as will an investment whose cash flows are invested, if the basic cash flows of the two investments are identical. When we compare alternatives, the reinvestment assumption becomes important.

To illustrate the importance of reinvestment rates, assume that a bank can invest $100 in a 1-month note yielding 26.8 percent on an annual basis (2 percent per month compounded 12 times), or it can invest in a 12-month security yielding only 16 percent. The bank wants to invest the funds for one year.

To make the choice, we have to know or estimate the return to be earned for the 11 months after the 1-month security matures. Assume that after 1 month the bank will be able to earn 1 percent per month, or 12.7 percent per year. The note matures in one month, and at the end of the year, the bank will have

$$\$100(1.02)(1.01)^{11} = \$113.80$$

This total is less than that which the 12-month security yielding 16 percent will return. The reinvestment opportunity must be considered.

If we are comparing two mutually exclusive investments using the internal rate of return, then the relevant opportunity cost for cash will affect the choice. For example, if the alternatives have the same internal rate of return, we would be indifferent if the opportunity cost were equal to the internal rate of return (thus the conclusion that the reinvestment rate is equal to the internal rate of return). If the mutually exclusive investments have different internal rates of return, the opportunity cost (investment rate) is again relevant to the choice and we cannot assume that funds are reinvested at the internal rate of return of either investment. Consider three investments:

	A	B	C
0	− $1,000	− $1,000	− $1,000
1	+ 100		+ 1,100
2	+ 1,100	+ 1,210	

The internal rates of return of the three investments are all 10 percent. This is independent of the cash flow reinvestment. The $100 of time 1 for investment A can be consumed, and the internal rate of return will remain 10 percent. Let us assume that the investor want to consume at time 2. In this case, a comparison of A, B, and C requires a reinvestment assumption. Assume that it is expected that one-period funds can be invested at time 1 to earn 20 percent. The terminal values of the three investments using the forward rate of 20 percent are

A	B	C	
$ 120		$1,100	
+1,100	+$1,210	+ 220	
$1,220	$1,210	$1,320	Values at time 2

Investment C is the best of the three investments if the reinvestment rate for period 2 is larger than .10. Present values, instead of terminal values, can be used to reach an identical decision. Assume that the discount rate for period 2 is .20 and for period 1 it is .10. We obtain the following present values:

$$A: -\$1,000 + \frac{\$100}{1.1} + \frac{\$1,100}{1.1 \times 1.2} = -\$152$$

$$B: - \$1,000 + \frac{\$1,210}{1.1 \times 1.2} = -\$83$$

$$C: - \$1,000 + \frac{\$1,100}{1.1} = 0$$

We conclude that one does not need to know the reinvestment rates to compute the internal rate of return. However, one does need to know the reinvestment rates to compare alternatives.

Loan-Type Flows

So far in this chapter we have discussed the investment type of cash flows. Now let us consider loan-type-cash flows (positive flows followed by negative flows or outlays) from the viewpoint of the borrower. Instead of a negative slope, the net present value profile will now have a positive slope. Consider a borrowing of $10,000 where $12,100 is to be repaid at time 2. The net present value using a zero rate of discount is a negative $2,100, and the present value is zero at 10 percent. Figure 8.4 shows the net present value profile of the borrowed funds. The maximum height of the net present value profile is $10,000, the amount borrowed.

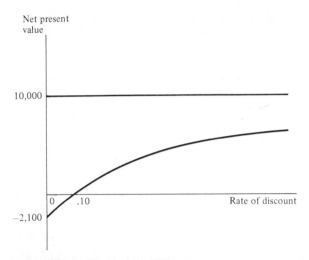

FIGURE 8.4   Loan-Type Flows

The characteristic of loan-type flows is that their net present value increases with higher rates of discount. By contrast, with a pure investment-type cash flow, the net present value decreases with higher rates of discount.

Multiple Internal Rates of Return

When the internal rate of return method is used, the ability to choose the best of two investments depends on whether a given series of incremental cash flows is like a conventional investment—in which case the higher the rate, the better—or whether it is like a loan—in which case the lower rate or interest cost, the better. The following illustrates a case in which the choice is not obvious. The cash flows represented by two mutually exclusive investments, R and S, are given in Table 8.3. The last line, labeled I, shows the incremental

TABLE 8.3

| | Cash Flows for Period | | | Internal Rate |
Investment	0	1	2	of Return
R	− $100	+ $ 30	+ $130	.30
S	0	− 280	+ 350	.25
I	− $100	+ $310	− $220	.10 and 1.00

cash flows (i.e., R–S). The cash flows, R and S, are conventional investments because they have outlays *followed by proceeds*. But for investment I, the outlays of period 0 are followed by proceeds in period 1 and then by further outlays in period 2. With this kind of cash flow, we cannot say, "the higher the internal rate of return, the better," or "the lower the internal rate of return the better."

Suppose that the mutually exclusive investments R and S are available to a company whose cost of money is 15 percent. If the IRR of the incremental cash flows I is 10 percent, should the company accept R or S? If the IRR of the incremental cash flows I is 100 percent, should the company accept R or S? It turns out that the present value of the cash proceeds is equal to the present value of the cash outlays at a 10 percent rate of discount and at a 100 percent rate of discount. The internal rate of return of I is *both* 10 and 100 percent.

Interpretation of Multiple IRRs

To help illustrate the relationship between the internal rate of return of an investment and the present value measure, and to explain why multiple IRRs occur and how they should be interpreted, it is helpful to introduce a graph. In Table 8.3, we described the three series of cash flows, R, S, and I. For R, S, and I in Figure 8.5, the vertical axis represents the net present value of the corresponding cash flow for various possible rates of interest, which are measured along the horizontal axis. By net present value we mean the algebraic sum of the present value of the proceeds and the present value of the outlays.

Because the IRR of a cash flow is defined as the rate of discount that makes the net present value zero, the IRR is the point at which the net present value

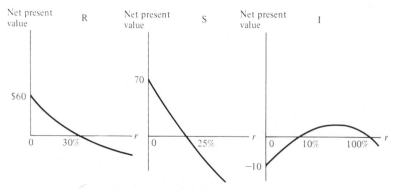

FIGURE 8.5   A Multiple Rate of Return

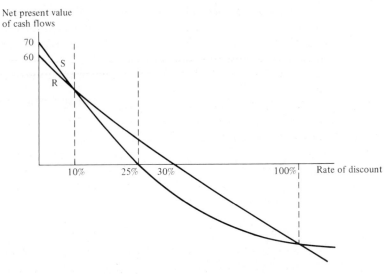

FIGURE 8.6   A Multiple Rate of Return

line crosses the horizontal axis (which measures the rate of discount). For R, the net present value line drops as the rate of discount increases. At discount rates lower than 30 percent, the net present value is positive; at discount rates greater than 30 percent, it is negative. This general configuration typifies those conventional investments in which a series of cash outlays is followed by a series of cash proceeds.

The left-hand part of the graph for I is typical of that of a loan; the right-hand part has the downward slope typical of the ordinary investment. This series of cash flows would be worthwhile at rates of discount between 10 and 100 percent; outside this range it is not advisable.

In this case a simple calculation of the net present value of the investment at the correct rate of discount would have provided the correct answer and would have bypassed the problem of multiple internal rates of return. Figure 8.6 shows that investment R has a higher present value at rates of discount in excess of 10 percent. The two curves cross again at 100 percent, but normally the values at such high interest rates are not relevant.

Why IRR Is Popular

Managers like the IRR, since they consider it important to know the differential between the proposed investment's internal rate of return and the required return. This is a measure of safety that allows an evaluation of the investment's return compared to its risk. If an investment has an IRR of .30 when the required return is .12, this is a large margin that allows for error. A net present value measure does not give the same type of information to management.

Index of Present Value
(or Profitability Index)

Some authors suggest dividing the present value of the cash proceeds by the present value of the investment type of outlays to obtain an index of present value (proceeds per dollar of outlay, both expressed in terms of present value). This calculation is also called the profitability index of an investment.

The index of present value method is a variant of the present value method; its appeal lies in the fact that seemingly it can be used to rank investments. We shall attempt to show that the resulting ranking of mutually exclusive investments is frequently spurious. If our objective is limited to accept or reject decisions, the index of present value (accept all investments with an index greater than 1) will give results identical to those of the present value method.

EXAMPLE 8.1

The cost of money is 10 percent. Assume that an investment has the following cash flows:

0	1	2
−$1,500	$1,000	$1,000

The present value of the $1,000-a-period cash proceeds is $1,736. The index is 1.16.

$$\text{present value index} = \frac{\$1,736}{\$1,500} = 1.16$$

One rule to use with an independent investment is the following: If the index is larger than 1, accept the investment. This rule is sound. If the index is greater than 1, however, the net present value is also positive, and the computation of the present value index is unnecessary.

A second rule is this: Evaluate mutually exclusive investments by their indexes; choose the investment with the highest index. This rule may lead to correct decision, but it may just as well lead to incorrect decisions because of two factors: scale of the investment and classification of cash flows.

EXAMPLE 8.2 (SCALE)

Assume two mutually exclusive investments with the cash flows indicated. Which is the more desirable for a cutoff rate of 10 percent?

Investment	Period			Present Value Index
	0	1	2	
X	− $1,500	$1,000	$1,000	1.16
Y	− 3,100	2,000	2,000	1.12

The index measure indicates that X is preferred to Y. A computation of present values will show that Y is better, however (a net present value of $371 for Y compared to $236 for X). The present value index is a ratio of benefits to outlay. But it fails to consider the scale of the investment in the same manner as do other ratio measures, such as return on investment and internal rate of return. This point can be seen more clearly if we look at the incremental investment consequent on moving from X to Y. We shall label that investment Y–X.

Investment	Period			Present Value Index
	0	1	2	
Y–X	− $1,600	$1,000	$1,000	1.08

The index is greater than 1; thus the incremental investment is desirable. The problem of scale can be solved by comparing pairs of investments, but this is unnecessary because the problem can be solved more easily by using present value. Also the problem of the classification of cash flows still exists.

EXAMPLE 8.3   (CLASSIFICATION OF CASH FLOWS)

The second difficulty with the present value index is that it requires that a distinction be made between deductions from cash proceeds and investment-type outlays). Assume the following two mutually exclusive investments and a 10 percent time value factor:

Investment	Period 0	Period 1	Period 2	Present Value Index
A Net flows	− $1,500	$1,000	$1,000	1.16
B Proceeds		2,000	2,000	1.07
outlays	− 1,500	− 1,000	− 1,000	

Calculations

$$\text{present value index (A)} = \frac{\$1,000.00(1.10)^{-1} + \$1,000.00(1.10)^{-2}}{\$1,500.00}$$

$$= \frac{\$1,735.54}{\$1,500.00} = 1.16$$

$$\text{present value index (B)} = \frac{\$2,000\,(1.7355)}{\$1,500 + \$1,000\,(1.7355)} = \frac{\$3,471.08}{\$3,235.54} = 1.07$$

The index measure chooses A over B. Close inspection of the cash flows of the investments shows that the investment net cash flows are identical for both investments. The cash flow difference is only a matter of classifying the $1,000 outlays of B as investments or as deductions from cash proceeds as with A. Any procedure that depends on arbitrary classifications rests on quicksand. For example, are advertising expenditures an expense or an investment? A partial solution to this problem is to use net cash flows.

A misconception about the present value index is that it will rank independent investments. This ranking is not reliable. If the company does not intend to accept all independent investments with a positive present value (or an index greater than 1), the cost of money used will not be the appropriate rate of discount and the index ranking will not be reliable. It is not claimed here that the net present value method may be used to rank independent investments. It is claimed only that the net present value method will lead to more easily obtained decisions involving choices between mutually exclusive investments and will give equally correct accept or reject decisions when applied to independent investments.

Capital Budgeting Under Capital Rationing

Speak to a manager about problems of implementing capital budgeting methods, and the subject of capital rationing will arise. Under conditions of certainty, if a firm can borrow or lend funds at a given market rate of interest, it should accept independent investments when the investments have positive net present values at this market rate of interest. In this section we consider a situation in which management decides to limit arbitrarily the total amount invested or the kind of investments the firm undertakes, or to set acceptance criteria that lead it to reject some investments that are advantageous when judged by market criteria. For example, instead of using the market interest rate, the firm might use some higher rate such as a cutoff or hurdle rate. This situation is frequently labeled capital rationing. Two possible approaches are offered. The first approach is to make simplifying assumptions where appropriate and to recognize that the answer obtained is an approximation. The second approach is to use mathematical techniques to develop possible solutions, following different possible investment alternatives (including all possible combinations of investments through the succeeding years). This analytical technique may lead to a sound solution to the capital budgeting decision under capital rationing, but it is complex and requires detailed knowledge of future investment alternatives that is frequently not available.

High Hurdle Rates

Two types of capital rationing must be considered. In the first, the firm sets a cutoff rate for investments that is higher than the firm's cost of money. In the second, the firm decides to limit the total amount of funds committed to internal investments in a given year to some fixed sum, even though investments having positive net present values at the firm's cost of money may be rejected as a result of this decision.

Consider the first kind of capital rationing. Suppose that a firm requires that investments must have a positive net present value of 15 percent, even though the firm's cost of money is only 10 percent. In this case, if the same cutoff rate is maintained from year to year, the cutoff rate in future years will be known, and the firm can evaluate all investments *as if* the cost of money were 15 percent.

But, although a definite cutoff rate is available, the logic of using that rate to discount cash flows is no longer completely correct. The rate of discount used should measure the alternative uses of funds available to the firm. In the present instance, however, it indicates only that an investment of $1 now yielding less than 15 percent will not be undertaken.

A Fixed Amount of Investment

In the second type of capital rationing, the cutoff rate is not specified, but the maximum amount that will be invested is determined by top management, because it is unwilling to go to the market to obtain additional funds, even though there are desirable investments. This reluctance to go to the market may result from a wish to prevent outsiders from gaining control of the business or from a feeling that there will be a dilution of earnings if additional equity funds are raised under the given market conditions. The amounts of cash available for investment will vary from period to period, as will the desirability of investments (the demand schedule for investments may shift). This situation may result in the firm's rejecting internal investments with IRRs greater than the borrowing rate. For this reason it will be very difficult to make predictions of future cutoff rates (the opportunity costs for future cash flows).

Ranking Independent Investments

If managment views a situation as being one of capital rationing, it is apt to lead to a request to the investment analyst for the ranking of independent investment. The decision for the independent investments is no longer a matter of accept or reject decisions, but management wants to know the ranking of investments so that it might choose the best set of investments.

There are many procedures that seem to give a reliable ranking of investments, but that apearance is an illusion. There is no sure proof procedure for the ranking of independent investments. The problem is that ranking implies the use of a cutoff rate above the cost of money and a rejection of investments that would be acceptable except for the rationing situation. This implies that the use of the conventional cutoff rate as a discount rate is not valid, since the opportunity cost for funds will be higher. Also, the opportunity cost of future time periods may well be different than that of the present as the capital rationing either becomes more tight or less tight.

The internal rate of return method is intuitively appealing, but we already

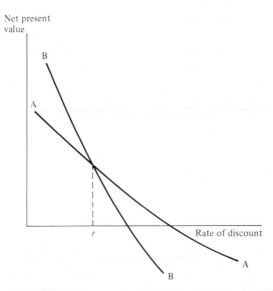

FIGURE 8.7 **Two Mutually Exclusive Invest-ments**

know that an investment with a lower internal rate of return might be more desirable than an investment with a higher internal rate of return. Figure 8.7 shows that investment B is preferred to investment A if the time value factor being used is less than r, even though the internal rate of return of A is larger than that of B.

Another popular method of ranking investments is the index of present value (present value of benefits divided by benefit of outlays). There are several difficulties in using this technique to rank independent investments. For example, the index depends on whether an outlay decreases the numerator (is deducted from benefits) or increases the denominator (increases the outlays). Since the classification is of necessity somewhat arbitrary, this is a severe weakness. A second problem is that the technique does require the use of a rate of discount in a situation where the ultimate choice of investments and rejection of investments will determine the opportunity cost of funds. A third problem is the fact that investments come in different sizes; thus we might not be able to undertake the mix of investments indicated by the ranking. The index of present value fails to consider effectively the size of the investment.

Let us consider the use of net present value as a ranking technique. First, the net present value does not tell us how much capital had to be committed to the investment. Two small investments may well be better than one large investment, even though the large investment has a larger net present value than either of the two small investments (but not larger than their sum).

Second, the net present value is the result of an assumption about the time value of money that with rationing may not be appropriate. Neither of these difficulties is bothersome in the absence of capital rationing, but with capital rationing, they eliminate present value as an effective means of ranking investments.

We can safely use the net present value method to choose the best of a set of mutually exclusive investments only when the rate of discount used is an appropriate opportunity cost. As soon as we use the net present value method to rank independent investments for the purpose of choosing a cutoff rate above the cost of money (some investments with positive present values will be rejected), the rate of discount used in computing the net present values becomes the inappropriate rate to use because the true opportunity cost is higher than the rate chosen.

EXAMPLE 8.4

The time value of money of the firm has been computed to be .10. There are two independent investments, C and D, with the following characteristics:

Investment	Cash Flows for Period		Internal Rate of Return	Present Value (using .10)
	0	1		
C	−$ 5,000	$10,000	1.00	$9,091 − $5,000 = $4,091
D	− 20,000	30,000	.50	$27,273 − $20,000 = $7,273

Using the internal rate of return C is ranked 1 and D is ranked 2. Using the net present values, we would choose D over C. Using the internal rate of return of the rejected investment C (1.00) as the opportunity cost, we find the present values to be

present value of C = $5,000 − $5,000 = 0

present value of D = $15,000 − $20,000 = −$5,000

Now C is better than D.

If we used the internal rate of return of the last investment accepted, D (.50), we would have as present values

present value of C = $6,667 − $5,000 = $1,667

present value of D = $20,000 − $20,000 = 0

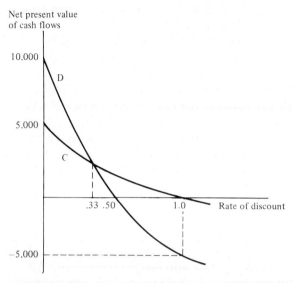

FIGURE 8.8   Two Mutually Exclusive Investments

With rates of interest of .50 and 1.00, we find that C is preferred to D, but with an interest rate of .10, D is preferred to C. Figure 8.8 shows that as long as the appropriate time value factor is less than 33 percent, the investor prefers investment D, but that if the discount factor is greater than 33 percent, investment C is preferred.

The problem becomes even more complex when we consider the opportunity costs of money for many time periods and where we have many sets of mutually exclusive investments. The choice of the best of each set will depend on the opportunity cost that is chosen.

Thus we make no claim that the net present value method can be used to rank independent investments where that ranking will be used to eliminate some independent investments with positive present values.

Recognizing that certain individuals have the audacity to pick the best movie of the year, we should be able to rank investments. And so we can, as long as the ranking is placed in somewhat the same perspective as the best movie contest. A reasonable (not exactly correct) ranking can be obtained using either internal rate of return or index of present value. If desired, the present value of different sets of investments can be computed and an attempt made to maximize present value (but remember, the discount rate should represent the opportunity cost of funds).

In addition to the foregoing complexities, if risk considerations are also

> ## A Major Steel Company
>
> A major steel company faced an important decision. It could spend $800 million to modernize and expand its current plant, or it could spend $1.6 billion to build a new plant. The board of directors was split, and its members were very emotional concerning the choice. There was no difference as to the facts, but there was a great deal of difference of opinion as to what the firm should do.
>
> A consultant was hired. He drew two present value profiles and asked what discount rate was to be used. The economic problem was solved.

brought into the analysis, then we must conclude that the ranking of independent investments for a capital rationing situation is truly more like choosing the best movie than it is an exact scientific technique.

Conclusions

If a corporation knows its cost of money and can either obtain additional funds from the market at the cost of money for desirable internal investments or invest any excess funds externally at that cost of money, then either of the two discounted cash flow procedures can be used to make correct investment decisions.

If the net present value method is used, the rules for making correct investment decisions are quite simple in principle. They are

1. For each investment proposal, compute the net present value of the proposal, using the cost of money as the discount rate.
2. If the choice is between accepting or rejecting the investment, accept it if its net present value is greater than zero and reject it if the net present value is less than zero.
3. If a set of comparable mutually exclusive investment proposals is available and the net present value of each investment is greater than zero, but only one can be accepted, accept the one for which the net present value is the greatest.

The internal rate of return method can also be used to make correct investment choices, provided that the cost of money is the same in all future time periods. If used properly, this method will in fact lead to the same choices as the net present value method. But the rules that must be followed are quite complex if the internal rate of return method is to be used properly. The complexities arise from the following considerations:

1. A single investment may have more than one internal rate of return. The present value of the cash proceeds from an investment may equal the present value of the costs at both x and at y percent. This may mean that the investment is profitable only if the cost of money is between x and y percent, or it may mean that the investment is profitable only if the cost of money is less than x percent or greater than y percent.
2. If a group of two or more mutually exclusive investments is available, a direct comparison of their internal rates of return will not necessarily lead to the correct choice of the best alternative. If the cost of money is the same in all future periods, it is possible to analyze the investment proposals two at a time, decide which one of each pair is more desirable, and then compare the more desirable investment with one of the others to decide which of those two is more desirable, continuing until by a process of elimination the best one can be determined. By contrast, the present value method indicates immediately which one of a group of mutually exclusive proposals is more desirable.
3. In interpreting the internal rate of return of a single investment, it is necessary first to determine whether the cash flows correspond to an ordinary conventional investment or to a loan from the point of view of the borrower.
4. It may not be possible to define the internal rate of return for a cash flow series. In this case it is easiest to interpret the cash flow series using the net present value method.
5. If the cost of money is not expected to be the same in all future time periods, the internal rate of return method can not be used to give the same decisions as the net present value method.

For most purposes, the net present value method is simpler, easier, and more direct. The remainder of this book will proceed in terms of this approach.

The "conflict" between present value and internal rate of return disappears if the graph of present values is used for comparing investments. The internal rate of return is the intersection of the net present value profile graph and the X axis, and the present value is the vertical height from the X axis to the graph. Using the internal rate of return as the rate of discount, the net present value is zero.

Capital rationing in one form or another exists to some extent in most corporations. We may distinguish among minor and severe cases of capital rationing. In the minor cases, the present value rules suggested in this book may be used with confidence. In the more severe forms of capital rationing, the net present value method may still be used, but it is now less correct to use a constant rate of discount for all future years. The rate of discount used for each future year must reflect the cost of obtaining additional funds, the value of external investments available to the firm, or the desires of the owners for present versus future proceeds.

Review Problem 8.1

There are two mutually exclusive investments. Assume an interest cost of 8 percent. Choose the better of the two investments.

		Period		
Investment	*0*	*1*	*2*	*Internal Rate of Return (%)*
A	− $10,000	0	$12,100	10
B	− 10,000	$5,762	5,762	10

Solution of Review Problem 8.1

By inspection, A is more desirable (you can also compute the net present value). The funds are invested longer at the desirable return of .10.

$$NPV(A) = \frac{\$12,100}{(1.08)^2} - \$10,000 = \$374$$

$$NPV(B) = \frac{\$5,762}{(1.08)^2} + \frac{\$5,762}{(1.08)^1} - \$10,000 = \$275$$

PROBLEMS

1. Accept or reject the following independent investment proposals using the internal rate of return and net present value procedures and a cutoff rate of 10 percent.

	Period		
Investment	0	1	2
A	$(10,000)	$ 2,000	$12,000
B	(10,000)	10,500	
C	10,000	(12,000)	

2. (a) There are three mutually exclusive investments. Which of the three investments should be chosen? Assume a cutoff rate of 10 percent.

	Period			Internal Rate
Investment	0	1	2	3	of Return (%)
A	$(1,000)	$ 505	$ 505	$ 505	24
B	(10,000)	2,000	2,000	12,000	20
C	(11,000)	5,304	5,304	5,304	21

(b) Compute the incremental cash flow for investments B and C in Problem 2(a).

Compute the internal rate or rates of return of this incremental cash flow. Is investment B or C more desirable?

3. The Apple Company wishes to choose between two different machines that accomplish essentially the same task (the machines are mutually exclusive). A comparison of the cash flows of the two machines shows that if the less expensive of the two machines is chosen, there will be a saving of $1,000 at the time of purchase, but there will be additional outlays of $333 per year over the five-year life of the machines. The cost of money for the Apple Company is 10 percent.

Compute the internal rate of return of the incremental cash flows and determine whether or not the cheaper of the two machines should be purchased. Make the same decision using the net present value procedure.

4. There are two mutually exclusive investments. Assume a discount rate of 10 percent.

Choose the better of the two investments.

| | Period | | | Internal Rate |
Investment	*0*	*1*	*2*	of Return (%)
A	$(16,050)	$10,000	$10,000	16
B	(100,000)	60,000	60,000	13

5. There are two mutually exclusive investments. Assume an interest cost of 5 percent.

Choose the better of the two investments.

| | Period | | | Internal Rate |
Investment	*0*	*1*	*2*	of Return (%)
A	$(10,000)	$ 0	$12,100	10
B	(10,000)	5,762	5,762	10

6. Assume an interest rate of 15 percent.

Choose the better of the two investments of Problem 5.

7. There are two mutually exclusive investments. Assume an interest rate of 5 percent.

Choose the better of the two investments.

| | Period | | |
Investment	*0*	*1*	*2*
A	− $600	$500	$600
B	− 700	800	400

8. Compute the relative cash flows of investment (B − A) of Problem 7.

Comment on the computation of the internal rate of return of this investment.

9. There is an investment with the following cash flows:

Period

0	1	2
− $50	$150	− $100

Assume an interest rate of .05.
   Is the investment acceptable? What are the internal rates of return of the investment?

10. (a) Compute the internal rates of return of the following two investments:

Period	X	Period	Y
0	− $9,089	0	− $7,118
1	+ 1,000		
2	+ 10,000		
3	+ 1,000	3	+ 10,000

(b) Compute the net present values of the investments if the appropriate rate of discount is .10.

11. (a) Compute the internal rates of return of the following three investments:

	0	1	2
A	− $10,000	$11,500	
B	− 10,000	6,151	$ 6,151
C	− 10,000		13,226

(b) Compute the amount the investor will have at time 2 if the funds received at time 1 can be reinvested to earn .15.
(c) For each of the three investments, graph the present value profile.
(d) Which investment is to be preferred if the rate of discount is .10?

12. The ABC Company is considering undertaking an investment that promises to have the following cash flows:

0	1
− $50	$90

If the firm waits a year, it can invest in an alternative (that is, mutually exclusive) investment that promises to pay

1	2
− $60	$100

Assume a time value of money of .05.

Which investment should the firm undertake? Use the net present value and the internal rate of return methods.

13. The IBC Company is considering undertaking an investment that promises to have the following cash flows:

0	1	2	3
− $100	$150	$50	$50

If it waits a year, it can invest in an alternative (that is, mutually exclusive) investment that promises to pay

1	2	3
− $150	$250	$50

Assume a time value of money of .05.

Which investment should the firm undertake? Use the present value method and the internal rate of return approaches. With the IRR approach, use the incremental cash flows.

14. The Arabian Oil Company is considering an investment that can be undertaken this year or postponed one year. The investment cash flows if undertaken now would be as follows:

Period

0	1
− $100	$200

The cash flows if delayed one period would be as follows:

Period

1	2
− $100	$200

Assume a time value of money of .05. Should the company invest now or delay one year? First use the internal rate of return method and then use the net present value method.

15. The IBC Company is considering undertaking an investment that promises the following cash flows:

0	1	2
− $100	$80	$80

If the company waits a year, it can make the following investment:

1	2
− $220	$280

Assuming a time value of .10, which investment should the firm undertake? Use both the net present value and IRR approaches. With the IRR method use incremental cash flows.

16. Assume that there are two mutually exclusive investments. Which of the two investments would be chosen using the index of present value? Assume a cost of money of 10 percent.
   Evaluate the procedure.

| | Period | |
Investment	0	1
A	− $ 4,000	$11,000
B	− 20,000	33,000

17. Assume that there are two mutually exclusive investments.
   Which of the two investments would be chosen using the index of present value? Assume a cost of money of 10 percent.

| | Period | |
Investment	0	1
A	− $4,000	$11,000
B	− 4,000	− 10,000
		21,000

18. Assume that an investment has the following cash flows:

0	1	2
− $10,000	$21,600	− $11,600

This investment has IRRs of 0 and .16. Assume that the firm has a time value of money of .10 (it can borrow at .10). Divide the investment into two components, a fictitious investment of $10,000 at time 0 returning $11,000 at time 1 and borrowing of $10,600 at time 1 requiring an outlay of $11,600 at time 2.
   Determine whether the basic investment is desirable.

19. Assume that an investment has the following cash flows:

0	1	2
$10,000	− $21,600	$11,600

The investment has IRRs of 0 and .16. Assume that the firm has a time value of .10 (it can borrow at .10). Divide the investment into two components, a fictitious borrowing of $10,000 at time 0 paying $11,000 at time 1 and an investment of $10,600 at time 1 earning $11,600 at time 2.

Determine whether the basic investment is desirable.

20. Assume that an investment has the following cash flows:

0	1	2	3
$10,000	$10,000	$10,000	− $29,000

The firm uses the internal rate of return method of evaluating investments and has a hurdle rate of .10.

Is the investment desirable?

21. There are two mutually exclusive investments with the following cash flows:

	Cash Flows for Period		
Investment	0	1	2
R	− $162,727	$190,909	$60,000
S	− 90,000	20,000	160,000

Which of the two investments do you prefer if the firm's time value of money is (a) .05, (b) .20, (c) .30?

22. The ABC Company can save $200,000 immediately by reducing its finished goods inventory. Lost sales due to stockouts will be $30,000 per year as a result of the reduction, however. This decision offers a 15 percent internal rate of return.

Should the change be accepted if the cost of money of the firm is 10 percent?

23. The controller of the A-Can Company is evaluating the status of a plant. Currently, the plant is losing $1 million per year (cash flow). If the plant is shut down, there will be $5 million of closing costs (out of pocket).

    An alternative is to modernize the plant at a cost of $10 million. This will cause the cash flow per year to be $500,000. Assume that this cash flow will continue for perpetuity as will the $1 million negative cash flow associated with doing nothing.

    What should the company do? The company is not sure which discount rate it should use to evaluate this decision.

24. In 1978 Cornell University's Teagle Hall management instituted a plan that reduced the inventory of gym wear by eliminating the "dead" inventory stored in the lockers. The new system did result in increased labor cost through time, however, since each customer now had to go through the service line twice, whereas before, each customer went through the line once.

    Assuming that the cash flows were computed for the decision to implement the system, and assuming that the internal rate of return was unique and equal to 30 percent, should Cornell have adopted the new system?

    The cash flows were calculated by assuming that students and professors waiting in line have zero value to their time.

25. Is the plant that offers the highest internal rate of return the most desirable plant (in a set of mutually exclusive alternatives)?

26. Consider the following three mutually exclusive investments:

		Investment	
Period	A	B	C
0	− $2,000	− $800	− $1,450
1	200	0	500
2	1,000	600	700
3	1,400	600	700

    (a) If the time value of money is 6 percent, which investment is most desirable?
    (b) Which investment has the highest internal rate of return?

27. Consider the following investment cash flow patterns over time: $-\$100$, 240, $-\$143$ for periods 0 through 2, respectively.

    At what rates of discount will the net present value of the investment equal zero? Solve this problem algebraically (remember that if $a^2X^2 + bX + c = 0$, then $X = \dfrac{-b \pm \sqrt{b^2 - 4ac}}{2a}$.

28. Consider two mutually exclusive investments:

	Period 0	Period 1	Internal Rate of Return (%)
Investment A	$-\$10,000$	$12,500	25
Investment B	$-110,000$	127,500	16

    Which investment should the firm accept? Assume that the firm uses .10 as the rate of discount.

29. There are two mutually exclusive investments. Assume a cost of money of 10 percent.

    Choose the better of the two investments.

	Period			Internal Rate of Return (%)
Investment	0	1	2	
A	$-\$16,050$	$10,000	$10,000	16
B	$-100,000$	60,000	60,000	13

30. A firm has an office building that will earn cash flows of $20 million per year at the end of each year (for perpetuity) if left unchanged. It can tear down the building and put up a new building at a cost of $100 million. The building will have an infinite life.

    There are zero taxes. The firm uses a .10 discount rate. The land can be sold for $42 million, and it is expected that this price will stay constant.

    The depreciated cost (book value) of the present building is $45 million (exclusive of land) and the replacement cost is $86 million.

    (a) What annual (constant) cash flows have to be achieved for the firm to replace the old and build the new? Assume a perpetual life and constant cash flow.

    (b) How (if at all) does the answer to (a) change if the firm can sell now for $250 million (both building and land).

31. The ABC Company has more investment opportunities than it can use (it is unwilling to borrow or issue more common stock). Management estimated that the investment cutoffs for the next two years will be as follows:

Year	Cutoff
0–1	.20
1–2	.30

It is attempting to choose between two mutually exclusive alternatives, both of which will require an initial outlay now and payoff at the end of two periods.

What discount rate should be used in evaluating the mutually exclusive investments? What rate would you use if the investments had a life of one year? **Hint:** $(1 + R_n)^n = (1 + r_1)(1 + r_2) \cdots (1 + r_n)$, where r_i is the value of money of period i and R_n is the equivalent interest rate for the n periods.

32. The president of the ABC Company wants a ranking of three investments. The firm considers its cost of money to be .05. The following three independent investments are ranked.

Investment	Cash Flows of Period 0	1	2	Net Present Value (using .05)	Ranking
A	− $1,000	$1,120		$66.69	3
B	− 1,000		$1,210	97.47	1
C	− 1,000	400	775	83.89	2

The firm has $1,000 of uncommitted funds available (without borrowing) for investment. Based on the preceding ranking, the president decides to accept investment B. It is then revealed that because investment B has a IRR of .10 this could be considered to be the investment cut off rate (other investments already approved having higher IRRs).

Evaluate the decision process.

33. In answering the following questions, assume that a dollar one year from now is worth $.90 today and that a dollar two years from now is worth $.75 today. Dollars can be bought and sold at these prices. There are no transaction costs.

A firm anticipates that it will have a surplus of dollars one year from now but a shortage two years from now.

(a) The present value of the surplus of dollars that is forecast for one year from now is $2,000. What is the amount of the surplus in terms of dollars available in one year?

(b) By how much would the net present value of the firm change if all of the surplus year 1 dollars are sold (now) and the proceeds used to buy more year 2 dollars?

(c) How many year 2 dollars can be obtained in the transaction described in (b)?

(d) What is the present value of an annuity of a dollar per year for two years at these prices?

(e) What is the interest rate the firm would have to pay on a one-year loan, negotiated now, with the funds to be received one year from now, and paid back two years from now? That is, the cash flow from the point of view of the borrower would be as follows:

		Time	
	0	1	2
Amount	$\frac{0}{0}$	$+\$100$	$-\$100(1 + r)$

Find r.

34. The ABC Company prefers to finance investments internally to the extent possible. However it has adopted the following policies that are applied unless there are significant qualitative considerations that justify an exception for a particular project.

(a) Investments are not accepted unless they can earn at least 11.1 percent after taxes on a discounted cash flow basis, even if excess funds are available.

(b) Investments are not rejected if they will earn 25 percent or more after-taxes on a discounted cash flow basis, even if internally generated funds are not available.

The accompanying table shows the cash flows for a series of independent investments. Use the ABC Company's criteria to classify each investment as

A   Must accept

R   Must reject;

U   Uncertain

Show your calculations.

Investments	Cash Flows			Classification
D	− $100	$50	$50	$50
E	− 100			200
F	− 100	80	50	30
G	− 100	30	50	80
H	− 100	10	40	70

35. The Big Manufacturing Company (BMC) has a plant that is currently losing $1 million of cash per year. This loss is expected to continue into the future unless either of two actions is taken.

    The plant can be closed down at a one-time cost of $10 million (there is a large amount of pension obligations). Alternatively, $12 million can be invested to modernize to earn $600,000 of cash flow per year (a perpetuity).

    The analysts of the firm have concluded that the $12 million should not be invested, since the investment will earn only 5 percent per year and the plant should be closed down. The firm has a weighted average cost of capital of 15 percent and a borrowing cost of 12 percent (it has debt outstanding). Its tax rate is zero.

    (a) What should BMC do?

    (b) What should BMC do if the investment opportunity is not available?

REFERENCES

Bacon, P. W. "The Evaluation of Mutually Exclusive Investments." *Financial Management*, Summer 1977, 55–58.

Baumol, W., and R. Quandt. "Investment and Discount Rates Under Capital Rationing—A Programming Approach." *Economic Journal*, June 1965, 317–329.

Bernhard, Richard H. "Mathematical Programming Models for Capital Budgeting—A Survey, Generalization, and Critique." *Journal of Financial and Quantitative Analysis*, June 1969, 111–158.

Burton, R. M., and W. W. Damon. "On the Existence of a Cost of Capital Under Pure Capital Rationing." *Journal of Finance*, September 1974, 1165–1174.

Carleton, W. T., "Linear Programming and Capital Budgeting Models: A New Interpretation." *Journal of Finance*, December 1969, 825–833.

Elton, E. J. "Capital Rationing and External Discount Rates." *Journal of Finance*, June 1970, 573–584.

Forsyth, J. D., and D. C. Owen. "Capital Rationing Methods." In *Capital Budgeting Under Conditions of Uncertainty*, ed. R. L. Crum and F. G. J. Derkinderen. Boston: Martinus Nighoff Publishers, 1981, pp. 213–235.

Hirshleifer, J. "On the Theory of Optimal Investment." *Journal of Politcal Economy*, August 1958, 329–352.

Lorie, J. H., and L. J. Savage. "Three Problems in Rationing Capital." *Journal of Business*, October 1955, 229–239.

Lusztig, P., and B. Schwab. "A Note on the Application of Linear Programming to Capital Budgeting." *Journal of Financial and Quantitative Analysis*, December 1968, 427–431.

Manne, A. S. "Optimal Dividend and Investment Policies for a Self-Financing Business Enterprise." *Management Science*, November 1968, 119–129.

Merville, L. J., and L. A. Tavis, "A Generalized Model for Capital Investment." *Journal of Finance*, March 1973, 109–118.

Myers, S. C. "A Note on Linear Programming and Capital Budgeting." *Journal of Finance*, March 1972, 89–92.

Myers, Stewart C., and Gerald A. Pogue, "A Programming Approach to Corporate Financial Management." *Journal of Finance*, May 1974, 579–599.

Rychel, D. F. "Capital Budgeting with Mixed Integer Linear Programming: An Application." *Financial Management*, Winter 1977, pp. 11–19.

Thompson, H. E. "Mathematical Programming, The Capital Asset Pricing Model and Capital Budgeting of Interrelated Projects." *Journal of Finance*, March 1976, 125–131.

Weingartner, H. M. *Mathematical Programming and the Analysis of Capital Budgeting Problems*. Englewood Cliffs, N.J.: Prentice-Hall, Inc., 1963.

———. "Capital Rationing: n Authors in Search of a Plot." *Journal of Finance*, December 1977, 1403–1431.

Whitmore, G. A., and L. R. Amey. "Capital Budgeting under Rationing: Comments on the Lusztig and Schwab Procedure." *Journal of Financial and Quantitative Analysis*, January 1973, 127–135.

Chapter 9

Annual Equivalent Costs and Replacement Decisions

Major Topics

1. Annual equivalent cost and its use.
2. The comparability of life and investment timing problems.
3. Make or buy decisions.

Annual Equivalent Cost

Investments tend to involve large expenditures that benefit many time periods and to have lives longer or shorter than the time period for which the decision is being made. In these situations we may find it useful to compute the annual equivalent cost of utilizing a long-lived asset. This concept has a large number of potential uses, including computing the cost of making a product and solving the decision problem when different alternatives or components have different lives.

Consider an investment that has an expected life of 20 years and that costs $2 million. It is easy to divide the $2 million by 20 and obtain an annual cost of $100,000 per year. The difficulty is that this cost computation leaves out the capital cost (the interest factor) and is an incomplete calculation.

Assume there is an investment outlay of $2,000,000 and that the investment has a life of 20 years. We would like to replace the $2,000,000 outlay with a series of annual costs that have a present value of $2,000,000 and thus are economically equivalent. Let us assume that the firm has a 10 percent time value of money. Define R to be the annual equivalent cost of the initial outlay. Then,

$$B(20, .10)R = \$2,000,000$$

$$8.5136R = \$2,000,000$$

$$R = \$234,918$$

The firm would be indifferent between the immediate outlay of \$2,000,000 and an annual outlay of \$234,918 occurring at the end of each time period. We would say that the annual equivalent cost is \$234,918 where the cost is measured at the end of each of 20 time periods. Remember that if we had divided the cost by the 20 years of life, we would have obtained an annual cost of \$100,000. The equivalent annual cost is about 2.35 times as large as the incorrect calculation that omits the interest cost.

Make or Buy Decisions

As an example of the use of the annual equivalent cost concept, consider a make or buy decision. The CBD Corporation requires 10,000 units per year of a metal part used in several of its major products. Demand for the part will remain at this level for the next 20 years. CBD has been purchasing the part from a reliable outside supplier at a cost of \$20.00 per unit. The purchasing manager has proposed that the company make the product itself at a saving of \$5.00 per unit and has justified the recommendation with the following data.

	Per Unit	Per Year
Cost of making		
Labor and material	\$ 5.00	\$ 50,000
Depreciation expense	10.00	100,000
Total	\$15.00	\$150,000
Cost of buying	20.00	200,000

The depreciation expense results from the acquisition of a specialized machine at a cost of \$2,000,000 that will be needed if CBD is to make the part itself. The machine has no other applications and would have a life of 20 years. CBD Corporation has a long-term credit arrangement with an insurance company under which it could borrow the \$2,000,000 needed to acquire the machine at an interest cost of 10 percent per year. If CBD borrows, it can arrange whatever repayment terms it wishes for the loan. Or if CBD has available excess funds, those funds could be applied to a partial repayment of existing loans under this agreement, thereby saving interest of 10 percent per year, or the funds could be used for capital outlays earning 10 percent. The cost of funds is 10 percent.

The purchasing manager's analysis of the cost of making is incomplete in that it fails to consider the time value of money. We will assume that the labor and material expense will be incurred at the end of each year so that their present value will be less than the eventual outlay. But the payment for the machine is made at the start, so that the cost is $2,000,000. The present value of making 10,000 units per year is $2,425,680 and the present value of the cost of buying is only $1,702,720.

	Outlays	Present Value Factors	Present Values
Cost of making			
Labor and material	$ 50,000	8.5136	$ 425,680
Equipment cost	2,000,000	1.0000	2,000,000
Total			2,425,680
Cost of buying	200,000	8.5136	1,702,720

While the foregoing analysis is correct, it may not be meaningful to executives who are not familiar with present value calculations. Additionally, the present value calculation does not provide a convenient means of evaluating the savings from buying on a per unit basis.

An alternative approach is to present the analysis in terms of annual equivalent costs. With this approach the annual equivalent cost per unit can be obtained by dividing the total annual equivalent cost by the number of units per year. The resulting annual equivalent cost per unit will be fully comparable to the $20.00 cost per unit of buying. The analysis might be presented as follows:

	Per Unit	Per Year
Cost of making		
Labor and material	$ 5.00	$ 50,000
Equipment ($2,000,000/8.5136)	23.49	234,918
Total	$28.49	$284,918
Cost of buying	20.00	200,000

The annual equivalent cost of the equipment can be explained as the annual payment that would be required to amortize a $2,000,000 loan at 10 percent with 20 equal annual payments. Or the $234,918 can be interpreted as the annual amount by which future debt service payments could have been reduced over the next 20 years if the $2,000,000 had been paid to the equipment supplier at the time of acquisition.

Instead of assuming that the annual expenditure for the equipment takes place at the end of the period, we could assume that the expenditure takes place at the beginning of the period. We would then have for the annual equivalent cost

$$[1 + B(19, .10)]R = \$2,000,000$$

$$9.3649R = \$2,000,000$$

$$R = \$213,563$$

A third possibility is to assume continuous outlays for the equipment. For this purpose, we must use continuous discounting. If the discrete interest rate is $r = .10$ compounded annually, the corresponding equivalent continuous interest rate j can be found from the following equality:

$$1 + r = e^j$$

Taking the natural logarithm of both sides (using a computer or calculator), we find for $r = .10$ that $j = .0953$. A continuous interest rate of .0953 gives the same present value as the discrete rate of .10 used with $(1 + r)^{-n}$. With continuous discounting we then have an annual cost of $223,893:

$$R\left(\frac{1 - e^{-20j}}{j}\right) = \$2,000,000$$

$$R\left(\frac{1 - .1487}{.0953}\right) = \$2,000,000$$

$$R = \frac{\$2,000,000}{8.9328} = \$223,893$$

One important application of annual equivalent costs occurs in situations where mutually exclusive alternatives have different lives. We shall define this to be a problem of "comparability of life."

Comparability

A group of investments will be said to be comparable and mutually exclusive if the profitability of subsequent investment possibilities will be the same, regardless of which investment is accepted or if all are rejected, but only one investment of the group can be accepted. Investment alternatives should be combined into groups that are both mutually exclusive and comparable before a final decision is made.

For example, a new plant could be heated by using forced hot air or steam. These are mutually exclusive alternatives. They are not comparable, however, if an air-conditioning system will be installed at some time in the future. The air-conditioning system would cost less to install in a building already equipped with air vents, and the present value of this difference in expected costs should be taken into account when choosing the heating system. Including the installation costs of the air-conditioning system will make the two alternatives comparable.

The importance of having mutually exclusive investments comparable is a matter of degree. In choosing a heating system for a new plant, the importance of the fact that future installation of air conditioning would be more expensive with steam heating will depend on the likelihood that air conditioning will eventually be required, the lapse of time until it may be required, the extent of the extra installation costs, and so on. In deciding whether a group of mutually exclusive alternatives is sufficiently comparable for practical purposes, one must apply a reasonable approach.

Mutually Exclusive Alternatives with Different Lives

Must mutually exclusive investment alternatives have the same lives in order to be comparable? The answer is no. In some instances, investment alternatives with different lives will be comparable; in other instances, equal future time periods are necessary to achieve comparability.

An example of comparable mutually exclusive alternatives not having the same life occurs in connection with deciding how to exploit a new patented product. One alternative is to sell the patent rights to another firm. This results in a single, lump-sum payment. The patent may also be exploited by manufacturing and selling the product.

In this example the two choices are comparable, although the expected cash proceeds from one would extend only one year and from the second for a longer period of time. The two alternatives should be compared using the net present value of each over its own life. For example, if selling the patent rights would generate immediate cash proceeds of $2 million and manufacturing and selling the product would produce cash flows having a net present value of $1.5 million over a 12-year period, the immediate sale is more desirable. We are assuming that at the expiration of life of each asset, the firm will invest in assets that earn the time value of money.

When mutually exclusive investments have unequal lives and there is a necessity to make the alternatives comparable, we have a choice of assumptions that we can make:

1. We can assume that the firm will reinvest in assets of exactly the same characteristics as those currently being used.
2. We can make specific assumptions about the reinvestment opportunities that will become available in the future.

The present value method will lead to a correct decision with both assumptions as long as the facts of the decision are consistent with the method chosen.

In theory the second alternative is both the preferred and the easiest to describe. While it is easy in theory, it is difficult to implement in practice because it requires a great deal of forecasting about the future.

As an example, suppose that there are two mutually exclusive investments, A and B, with the following characteristics:

	Cash Flows for Period			
Investment	0	1	2	3
A	− $10,000	$12,000		
B	− 10,000	5,000	$5,000	$5,000

A and B may be different types of equipment that perform the same task, with A having a life of one year and B a life of three years. With a cost of money of 10 percent, the net present values of the cash flows of A and B are as follows:

Investment	Net Present Value of Cash Flows
A	$ 909
B	2,434

NPV of
cash flows

Investment B would seem to be the more desirable investment; however, this analysis is incomplete if we assume that after one year the equipment of type A (or similar equipment) will again be purchased. Where it is assumed that investment A will be repeated at the beginning of periods 2 and 3 (assumption 1), the following cash flows would occur for investment A:

Investment	Period			
	0	1	2	3
A	− $10,000	− $10,000	− $10,000	
		12,000	12,000	$12,000
Total	− $10,000	$ 2,000	$ 2,000	$12,000

The present value of the cash flows as now presented is $2,488 for investment A; thus A is marginally more desirable than B. When the mutually exclusive investments have unequal lives, we may want to take into consideration the possibility of reinvesting in a similar type of equipment. If we choose assumption 2, we have to forecast the nature of the equipment available after one period and after two periods for investment A.

In most situations, the lowest common multiple of the lives of the two investments results in a length of time longer than the life of the longest-lived alternative. For example, if there are two types of equipment, one of which has a life of 3 years and the other of 8 years, the lowest common multiple of lives is 24 years. In a situation such as this, the equivalent cost per year, the cost for perpetuity, or the present value of the costs for 24 years can be computed. The equipment with the lowest cost would be the most desirable alternative. The two methods of computation being discussed will lead to the same decision.

EXAMPLE 9.1

Assume that two pieces of equipment have the following characteristics:

Equipment	Expected Life (years)	Initial Cost	Operating Cost per Year
X	3	$10,000	$2,000
Y	8	30,000	1,500

This problem can be solved by taking the lowest common multiple of 8 and 3, 24 years, and by computing the costs for a 24-year period.

Annual Equivalent Cost

An alternative procedure for solving Example 9.1 is to compute the annual equivalent cost of an outlay off $10,000 every 3 years, and the annual equivalent cost of an outlay of $30,000 every 8 years.

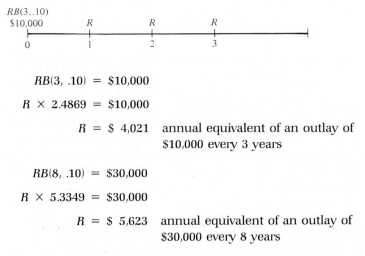

$$RB(3, .10) = \$10,000$$

$$R \times 2.4869 = \$10,000$$

$$R = \$\ 4,021 \quad \text{annual equivalent of an outlay of } \$10,000 \text{ every 3 years}$$

$$RB(8, .10) = \$30,000$$

$$R \times 5.3349 = \$30,000$$

$$R = \$\ 5,623 \quad \text{annual equivalent of an outlay of } \$30,000 \text{ every 8 years}$$

The annual equivalent cost of using equipment X is $6,021 (that is, $2,000 + $4,021), and the annual equivalent cost of using equipment Y is $7,123 (that is, $1,500 + $5,623). On the basis of annual equivalent costs, X is the more desirable equipment.

To find the present value of the cost of using each type of equipment for 24 years, we multiply the annual equivalent cost for each type of equipment by the annuity factor for 24 years. Since $B(24, .10) = 8.9847$, the present values are as follows:

X: $6,021 \times 8.9847 = \$54,097$

Y: $7,123 \times 8.9847 = \$63,998$

Since both annual equivalent costs are multiplied by the same annuity factor, the relative merits of the two alternatives are not changed if we compare their present values instead of their annual equivalent costs. X remains more desirable than Y.

To find the cost of using the equipment forever, we multiply the equivalent cost per year by the present value of a perpetuity. The general formula for the present value of a perpetuity of $1 a period is

$$\text{present value of a perpetuity} = \frac{1}{r}$$

where r is the appropriate rate of interest.

Since r is equal to .10, the factor in this example is .10. The present value of using equipment X forever is 10 × $6,021, or $60,210. The present value of using Y is $71,230.

Components of Unequal Lives

An investment alternative (possibly one of several mutually exclusive investments) may be made up of several components of unequal lives. For example, we may have a building with a life of 50 years costing $5 million, a furnace with a life of 25 years costing $4 million (exclusive of lining), and a furnace lining costing $1 million with a life of 4 years. With a time value of money of .05, the annual equivalent cost for each of the first 4 years of operation is

$$\frac{\$5,000,000}{B(50, .05)} = \frac{\$5,000,000}{18.25593} = \$273,884 \quad \text{cost of building}$$

$$\frac{\$4,000,000}{B(25, .05)} = \frac{\$4,000,000}{14.09394} = \$283,810 \quad \text{cost of furnace}$$

$$\frac{\$1,000,000}{B(4, .05)} = \frac{\$1,000,000}{3.54595} = \underline{\$282,012} \quad \text{cost of furnace lining}$$

total annual equivalent cost = $839,705

The expression $1/B(n, r)$ is called a capital recovery factor. When taxes are not a consideration, a simple rule for converting from the initial cost of an item of capital equipment to the corresponding annual equivalent cost is to multiply the initial cost of the equipment by the corresponding capital recovery factor. When this procedure is used to find the annual equivalent cost of a collection of equipment with varying lives, there is the implicit assumption that each item of equipment will be replaced at the end of its useful life by another item having the same annual equivalent cost. This assumption would be satisfied if each item of equipment were replaced by another having the same cost and the same life.

Cost of Excess Capacity

Assume that the ABC Chemical Corporation has extra boiler capacity and is considering the addition of a new product that will take one half of the extra capacity. How is the cost of the boiler brought into the analysis? The quick, easy answer is to say there is no relevant boiler cost since the cost is a sunk cost. Unfortunately, this conclusion may not be correct. Add the information that undertaking the new product and using one half of the excess capacity moves up the expected date of purchase of a new utility system from five to three years in the future. This acceleration of future purchase has costs, and these costs are part of the new product decision.

Assume that the expected cost of the boiler acquisition is $2.595 million and it has an estimated life of 15 years. With a cost of money of .05, the annual equivalent cost per year of use is

$$\frac{\$2,595,000}{B(15, .05)} = \frac{\$2,595,000}{10.38} = \$250,000$$

Without the new product, years 4 and 5 will not have the cost of a new boiler. With the new product there is an additional equivalent cost of $250,000 for years 4 and 5.

Date of purchase

The present value of the additional costs at time 0 is $401,550.

$$.8227 \times \$250,000 = \$205,675$$
$$.7835 \times \$250,000 = \underline{\quad 195,875}$$
$$\text{Present value} = \$401,550$$

An advocate for the new product might argue that the cost should be less because the degree of utilization of the new boiler during the first two years of its use will be very low and there will not be any wear and tear. If we assume no wear and tear (also no obsolescence), there would only be the interest cost of $129,750 (.05 of $2,595,000) occurring four and five years in the future. Just taking interest into account gives a cost of approximately $208,404 present value:

$$.8227 \times \$129,750 = \$106,745$$
$$.7835 \times \$129,750 = \underline{\quad 101,659}$$
$$\text{Present value} = \$208,404$$

Generally, some decrease in value (i.e., depreciation) should be recognized, however. Thus the present value of the cost of adding the product is not exactly defined. One estimate is $401,550, but it could be $208,404 if we assume that the life of the new equipment is not shortened or maintenance increased by the early purchase. Including either of these estimates is better than assuming that there is no cost associated with using the excess capacity.

We may want to perform an analysis in which we did not include the capacity cost but rather considered abandoning the product when capacity was reached and it was time to add new facilities. This possibility should be checked out, but generally it is appropriate to assume that once the product is added, it will be produced in the future. This will tend to occur because of the momentum principle (it is difficult for a firm to change directions) and because, after the costs of getting a product under way have been incurred, there is a good chance that if the original forecasts are realized, an economic analysis would indicate the desirability of continuing the sale of the product and taking advantage of the goodwill that was created.

Investment Timing

We want to consider decisions to determine when a new investment should be undertaken and when an investment should be terminated. In principle, the timing problem could be handled by considering a mutually exclusive set of alternatives: undertaking the investment now or undertaking it one period from now, or two periods from now, and so on. But more efficient techniques for approaching this problem are available.

Frequently, in making investment decisions, the useful life of the investment must be determined. This can be accomplished in at least two ways. First, the desirability of an investment may be affected by the estimate of its useful life. Thus the estimated profits from growing trees are critically affected by assumptions about when they will be harvested. Second, the decision to undertake an investment may require terminating an existing investment. Planting a new crop of trees may require harvesting the existing stand of trees, or buying a new car may require selling the old one. In these cases the salvage value of the existing investment, the costs incurred, and the revenues that might be received if it were not scrapped now will influence the decision of when to undertake the new investment.

The question of when to replace an existing piece of equipment with another machine that will perform the same function is very similar to the question of when to harvest a crop of trees. In the case of trees we are seeking to maximize the net present value of the revenues that we can receive from the land, whereas in the equipment replacement problem, we are seeking to minimize the net present value of the costs that will be incurred from owning and operating a sequence of machines.

In the machine problem, the costs incurred by retaining the existing machine are the costs of operating it for the current period (including any necessary repairs and maintenance), the decline in its salvage value during the current period, and the interest on the current salvage value of the existing machine. If the machine is retained for one additional period, we benefit by delaying for that length of time the costs of acquiring and operating all subsequent replacement machines. The magnitude of the latter cost is measured by the market interest rate times the present value of the costs of acquiring and operating all subsequent replacements. This present value will depend critically on how long each subsequent replacement equipment is retained. Thus the decision about when to replace the current machine requires an estimate of the economic value of its anticipated replacements, just as the decision about when to harvest a crop of trees depends on the future use that will be made of the land occupied by the trees.

EXAMPLE 9.2 ────────────

Trees growing at .15 per year are currently worth $1,000,000. The land on which the trees are growing has alternative uses that are worth $5,000,000 (this value is not expected to change).

Money is worth .10.
Should the trees be harvested now?
If harvested now,

value of harvesting now = $1,000,000 + $5,000,000 = $6,000,000

If harvested one year from now,

$$\text{value of harvesting in one year} = \frac{\$1,000,000(1.15) \;+\; \$5,000,000}{1.10}$$

$$= \$5,590,000$$

Harvesting now is better.

Change the alternative use value of the land to zero. Does this change the decision?

value of harvesting now $= \$1,000,000$

$$\text{value of harvesting in one year} = \frac{\$1,000,000(1.15)}{1.10} = \$1,045,000$$

Delaying a year is now better than harvesting immediately.

The fact that the land had an alternative use worth $5,000,000 caused the harvest to be accelerated. This alternative use can be thought of as being future generations of trees waiting to be planted. The sooner they are planted, the sooner they will have value.

A more complex and more accurate solution would have the alternative use value of the land be a function of the length of time the trees are allowed to grow.

Conclusions

Although techniques such as those we are recommending force one to make difficult estimates in the face of imperfect and incomplete information, they have the advantage of focusing attention on the important unknowns. Simpler techniques achieve their simplicity by using general assumptions about the nature of future opportunities rather than conjectures tailor made to a particular situation. They save time and effort but result in a less precise analysis of the decision-making situation.

Including Debt Financing: An Example

In 1985 a firm that constructed oil refinery plants costing approximately $400 million arranged debt financing for each individual refinery. It used discounted cash flow procedures to evaluate projects and a .15 average cost of capital as the required return.

In the cash flow stream used in the evaluation were all the debt flows associated with the project (interest, principal, and tax effects of interest).

The cash flow stream was for the stockholders' equity (net of debt) and not the investment stream. The use of the .15 average cost of capital to evaluate this stream was not correct.

Review Problem 9.1

The NSV Manufacturing Company currently manufactures a product on a machine that is fully depreciated for tax purposes and has a book value of $10,000 (it was purchased for $30,000 20 years ago). The costs of the product are as follows:

	Unit Costs
Labor, direct	$ 4.00
Labor, variable indirect	2.00
Other variable overhead	1.50
Fixed overhead	2.50
	$10.00

In the past year 10,000 units were produced and sold for $18 per unit. It is expected that with suitable repairs the old machine can be used indefinitely in the future. The repairs are expected to average $25,000 per year.

An equipment manufacturer has offered to accept the old machine as a trade-in for a new version. The new machine would cost $60,000 after allowing $15,000 for the old equipment. The projected costs associated with the new machine are as follows:

Labor, direct	$2.00
Labor, variable indirect	3.00
Other variable overhead	1.00
Fixed overhead	3.25
	$9.25

The fixed overhead costs are allocations from other departments plus the depreciation of the equipment. The old machine could not be sold on the open market. The new machine has an expected life of 10 years and no expected salvage at that time. The current corporate income tax rate is .40. For tax purposes, the cost of the new machine may be depreciated in 10 years. The appropriate after-tax time discount rate for this company is .10. Assume that the present value of depreciation deductions per dollar of cost is .701 (using the sum of the years' digits method). It is expected that future demand of the product will stay steady at 10,000 units per year.

(a) Should the new equipment be acquired?

(b) If the product can be purchased at a cost of $7.80 per unit from a reliable supplier, should it be purchased or made? Explain.

Solution to Review Problem 9.1

Cost of using the old:

$$PV = -.6(\$75{,}000 + \$25{,}000)B(10, .10)$$

$\rightarrow$ *PV annuity*

$$= -.6 \times \$100{,}000 \times 6.1446$$

$$= -\$369{,}000$$

Costs of using the new:

costs

$$PV = -\$60{,}000 - .60(\$60{,}000 \times 6.1446)$$

$$= -\$60{,}000 - \$221{,}000$$

$$= -\$281{,}000$$

Using SYDs depreciation yields

$$\text{tax savings} = \$60{,}000 \times .4 \times .701 = \$17{,}000$$

$$\text{net cost} = \$281{,}000 - \$17{,}000 = -\$264{,}000$$

Replace because $264,000 is less than $369,000.
The annual equivalent after-tax cost of using the new equipment is

$$R = \frac{\$264{,}000}{6.1446} = \$42{,}960 \text{ per year}$$

$$\frac{\$42{,}960}{\$10{,}000} = \$4.30 \text{ per unit}$$

Let X be the maximum before-tax cost per unit we would be willing to pay.
The after-tax cost is $.6X$, where X is the before-tax cost.

$$\$7.80 \times .6 = \$4.68, \text{ after-tax cost of buying}$$

Or the after-tax cost of making is $4.30. The before-tax cost of making is

$$.6X = 4.30$$

$$X = 7.17, \text{ before-tax cost of making}$$

We would not be willing to pay the $7.80 cost per unit described in the problem. Produce the product unless the capacity of the plant can be used on other products, in which case these other products should be considered.

PROBLEMS

1. The Roger Company has the choice between two different types of dies. One type costs less, but it also has a shorter life expectancy. The expected cash flows after taxes for the two different dies are as follows:

			Period		
Die	0	1	2	3	4
A	$(10,000)	$8,000	$8,000		
B	(12,000)	5,000	5,000	$5,000	$5,000

The cost of money of the firm is 10 percent.
  Choose the more desirable die. Explain.

2. Assume that there are two mutually exclusive investments that have the following cash flows:

	Period		Internal Rate of Return (%)
Investment	0	1	
A	$(10,000)	$12,000	20
B	(5,000)	6,100	22

Assume that either investment will require modification to the basic building structure, which will cost $1,000, and that this amount is not included in the preceding computations. The cost of money is 10 percent.
  (a) Compute the actual internal rates of return of the investments.
  (b) Does the additional $1,000 change the ranking of the two investments? Explain.

3. Consider the following two mutually exclusive investments.

	Period		Internal Rate of Return (%)
Investment	0	1	
A	$ (20,000)	$ 30,000	50
B	(100,000)	130,000	30

Assuming a cost of money of .10, which investment is to be preferred?

4. An existing machine must be replaced. Two new models are under consideration. Both cost $15,000. Model X will generate savings of $10,000 per year and has a life of two years. Model Y will generate savings of $18,000; it has a life of one year. The machine will be needed for two years.

Which model should be purchased if the cost of money is .05?

5. Assume that two pieces of equipment have the following characteristics:

Equipment	Expected Life (years)	Initial Cost	Operating Cost per Year
A	9	$20,000	$10,000
B	5	25,000	8,000

At a cost of money of .10, which equipment is the more desirable?

6. The A Corporation's computer currently has excess capacity. The controller would like to prepare and distribute a report that would take approximately one hour a day of the computer's time. The computer could do this task and still have excess capacity. The annual cost of this type of computer is $1 million a year. The discount rate is .05. The long-range planning group estimates that without the report, the corporation would be shifting to a more powerful computer five years from now. With the report, it estimates the shift to be four years from now. The new computer will cost $1.5 million per year. Assume that the computer payments take place at the end of each year.

What is your estimate of the cost of adding the report?

7. The New York State Utility Company is considering the construction of a new utility plant. It has accumulated the following cost information:

	Fossil Plant (oil and gas)	Nuclear Plant
Initial outlay	$60,000,000	$100,000,000
Annual operating cost	15,000,000	20,000,000[a]

[a]This is the projected cost for year 1. It is expected that the operating costs of the nuclear plant will decrease by $2,000,000 per year and level off at $10,000,000. The expected decrease is a result of decreased fuel costs. Both plants have an expected useful life of 50 years.

Assume a time value of money of .05 per year.

(a) Which plant should be built?

(b) Assume that if the nuclear plant is not built, the needed electricity can be purchased at a cost of $16 million per year. Should it be built?

8. (Problem 7(b) continued) Assume that the cost of the needed electricity is $17 million

(a) Should the nuclear plant be built?

(b) Compute the present value today of building (that is, completing) the nuclear plant six years from now when the operation costs would be $10 million per year, compared to buying electricity.

9. The A Corporation is considering the construction of a new plant to build a component part that it is currently purchasing. It has the following information:

	Cost	Expected Life
Plant	$20,000,000	40 years
Utilities	10,000,000	20 years
Equipment	15,000,000	10 years

The operating costs are estimated at $5 million per year, assuming an output of 1 million units of product per year.

The corporation uses a discount rate of .05. It can purchase the product at a cost of $10 per unit.

Should the new plant be built (on a straight economic basis)?

10. A company is considering two alternative marketing strategies for a new product. Introducing the product will require an outlay of $15,000. With a low price, the product will generate cash proceeds of $10,000 per year and will have a life of two years. With a high price, the product will generate cash proceeds of $18,000 but will have a life of only one year. The cost of money for the company is .05.

Which marketing strategy should be accepted?

11. Compare your answers to Problems 4 and 10. Are the relevant cash flows the same in both problems? If not, why?

12. State Electric wants to decide whether to repair or replace electric meters when they break down. A new meter costs $30 and on the average will operate for 12 years without repair. It costs $18 to repair a meter, and a repaired meter will, on the average, operate for 8 years before it again needs a repair. Repairs can be made repeatedly to meters because they

are essentially rebuilt each time they are repaired. It costs $6 to take out and reinstall a meter. The time value of money is .05.

Should the company repair old meters or buy new meters?

13. Assume that an investment requires an initial outlay of $12,337 and that the revenues from the investment are $10,000 in year 1 and $5,000 in year 2. Assume that an interest rate of .05 should be used.

Using annual equivalent revenues and costs, determine whether the investment is acceptable.

14. The following facts apply to an investment that the ABC Company is considering:

>   Plant costs $1 million with a life of 50 years.
>   Equipment costs are $2 million with a life of 20 years.
>   Annual fixed costs are $180,000, of which $100,000 are incremental with the decision (but excluding depreciation) and $80,000 are allocations from other departments and projects. These costs could be avoided if the product is discontinued in the future.
>   The net revenue contribution per unit sold is $2.
>   The cost of money of the firm is .10.
>   It is expected that 1 million units of product will be used per year.

How many units have to be produced and sold per year to break even? If 1 million units are produced, what will be the per unit cost?

15. (Problem 14 continued)   Assume that the plant and equipment described have been purchased. One million units of the product are needed in the coming year. These units can be purchased at a cost of $1.20 per unit from a reliable supplier. The variable manufacturing costs per unit are $.20. If the units are purchased, the plant and equipment will be shut down (this can be done with little additional cost). They have no alternative use.

Should the units be made or bought? Assume that the probability of the product being supplied on time and the quality of the product are the same whether made or bought.

16. (Refers to Problem 15) If the plant requires working capital of $1.5 million (cash outlay), should the units be made or purchased?

17. Assume that the plant and equipment of Problem 14 have been purchased. There is a marginal tax rate of .4 and an after-tax time value factor is .06.

Should the units be made or bought? Assume that there are no other uses for the plant or equipment and that their book value for taxes is $12 million. The annual out-of-pocket costs of making the product are $300,000. The annual costs of buying are $400,000.

If retained, the plant and equipment will be depreciated over 20 years using the straight-line method.

Should the product be made or bought?

18. The Bright Machine Tool Shop is considering replacement of the equipment in a section of its shop. The equipment performs a function that could be completely eliminated. A comparison of the present equipment being used with new equipment indicates that the following relative cash flows would result if the new machine were purchased instead of continuing with the old:

Period

0	1
$(10,000)	$12,000

The internal rate of return of the investment is 20 percent, and the cost of money is 15 percent. The net present value of the investment is $435. Based on the positive net present value, the decision was made to replace the present equipment.

In the period of operation, the machine performed exactly as predicted, and all costs were as predicted. The absolute cash flows were as follows:

Period

0	1
$(10,000)	$11,000

Comment on the investment decision made by the Bright Machine Tool Shop.

19. The Dotted Airline Company is considering replacement of its fleet of 10 two-engined planes with 5 new model jets. One jet can replace two of the present planes. The airplane company has prepared an analysis showing that each new plane will cost $343,000 and will earn cash proceeds of $100,000 per year for five years. Assume that after five years, the salvage value will be zero for both the new and old planes. The analysis was based on the load and operating characteristics of the new plane and the past experience of the airline, as well as on the number of passengers and the routes traveled, adjusted in a reasonable manner for additional passengers who will be attracted by the new planes.

The planes currently being used are considered to be safe workhorses, but are not as glamorous as the new planes. In competition with jets, they are expected to earn net cash proceeds of only $10,000 per yer per plane. There is no discernible trend of earnings. The present planes now have a zero salvage value.

The cost of money of the Dotted Airline is 10 percent. Assume that the company has access to the necessary funds.

Should the Dotted Airline purchase the new jets? Explain. What would be your recommendation if the salvage value is now $40,000 on an old plane?

20. A new piece of equipment being considered costs $75,816 and has a useful life of five years. It will cost $10,000 in out-of-pocket expenses per year to operate. The cost of money is .10. An alternative to the equipment is to use a labor-intensive process that would cost $38,000 per year. This $38,000 includes $15,000 of depreciation expense for the currently used machine (the machine has no other use but does have a replacement cost of $25,000). The tax rate is zero.

(a) Prepare an analysis of the alternatives. What should the firm do?

(b) If the equipment will make 1,000 units of product per year, what will be the cost per unit if the new equipment is purchased?

21. The Ithaca Manufacturing Company has excess capacity and is considering manufacturing a component part that is currently being purchased. The estimate of the cost of producing one unit of product is as follows:

Direct labor	$2.00
Material	3.00
Variable overhead	1.00
Fixed overhead (based on accounting procedures of a generally accepted nature)	2.50
	$8.50

The average increase in net working capital that will be required if the item is produced internally is $50,000.

The firm uses 100,000 of the parts per year. The unit cost of purchasing the parts is $6.05. Assume a zero tax rate.

Should the company make or buy the parts?

22. The XYZ Manufacturing Company is currently manufacturing its product on a machine that is fully depreciated for tax purposes and that has a book value of $10,000 (it was purchased for $30,000 20 years ago). The costs of the product are as follows:

	Unit Costs
Labor, direct	$ 4.00
Labor, indirect	2.00
Variable overhead	1.50
Fixed overhead	2.50
	$10.00

In the past year 1,000 units were produced and sold for $18 per unit. It is expected that the old machine can be used indefinitely in the future. An equipment manufacturer has offered to accept the old machine as a trade-in for a new version. The new machine would cost $60,000 after allowing $15,000 for the old equipment. The projected costs associated with the new machine are as follows:

Labor, direct	$2.00
Labor, indirect	3.00
Variable overhead	1.00
Fixed overhead	3.25
	$9.25

The fixed overhead costs are allocations from other departments plus the depreciation of the equipment.

The old machine could be sold on the open market now for $5,000. Ten years from now it is expected to have a salvage value of $1,000. The new machine has an expected life of 10 years and an expected salvage of $10,000.

The current corporate income tax rate is .40, and the capital gain tax rate is .25. Any salvage from sale will result in a capital gain at the time of retirement. (For tax purposes, the entire cost may be depreciated in 10 years using straight line depreciation.) The appropriate after-tax time discount rate for this company is .10.

It is expected that future demand of the product will stay steady at 1,000 units per year.

(a) Should the equipment be acquired?

(b) If the product can be purchased at a cost of $7.80 per unit from a reliable supplier, should it be purchased or made? Explain.

REFERENCES

See references for Chapter 6.

Chapter 10

Capital Budgeting with Uncertainty

Major Topics

1. Summarizing outcomes: simulation and sensitivity analysis.
2. The interaction of time and risk.
3. Limitations in the use of WACC to evaluate investments.
4. Choice of discount rate (a default-free rate, the borrowing rate, risk-adjusted discount rates).
5. The use of certainty equivalents.
6. Establishing that expected monetary value may be an inadequate basis for making decisions.
7. The concepts of utility functions as useful tools for analyzing decision making.

Summarizing Outcomes

Uncertainty

We first want to be able to summarize the relevant measures of value and risk (the expected return and standard deviation) of the cash flows of an investment or a portfolio of investments and to evaluate the relevance of the measures.

We next need to understand that the investors have attitudes toward risk and that this affects the amount of expected rewards they need to undertake a risky investment.

Finally, we need to understand the interaction of time and risk and the fact that with uncertainty there are no easy answers. If a firm justifies the undertaking or rejection of uncertain investments with a single summary measure of value (such as net present value or internal rate of return or payback or return on investment), that firm is in error. There is no single measure that allows us to make investment decisions with confidence. There are difficulties (measurement difficulties if not theoretical difficulties) with all measures.

What we can accomplish is a better understanding of the measures so that judgment can appropriately enter the decision process. We should use a combination of measures and other information.

Use of Tree Diagrams

In Table 10.1 an uncertain investment is described by listing all the possible events, the probability of each event, and the sequence of cash flows that would occur if the investment were accepted and that event occurred. In this example, there are six possible events, and cash flows can occur in only three different periods, so the complete description is manageable. Nevertheless, the need for methods of summarizing the description of the investment should be apparent.

A common and very useful means of describing the information contained in Table 10.1 is a tree diagram. We shall illustrate how tree diagrams can be used to summarize the interrelationships between sequences of events.

Table 10.1 shows the possible outcomes that are predicted for three periods from accepting an investment. Figure 10.1a shows a tree diagram of the forecasted outcomes at time zero. The two events possible at time 0 are an outlay of $100 or of $200. Each outcome has a probability of one half, which can be determined by summing the probabilities of the corresponding rows in Table 10.1. In the tree diagram each event is depicted by a branch that ends above

Event	Probability of Event	Cash Flows in Period		
		0	1	2
a	.3	− $200	$110	$ 0
b	.1	− 200	110	121
c	.1	− 200	165	121
d	.2	− 100	55	60.5
e	.1	− 100	55	121
f	.2	− 100	110	242

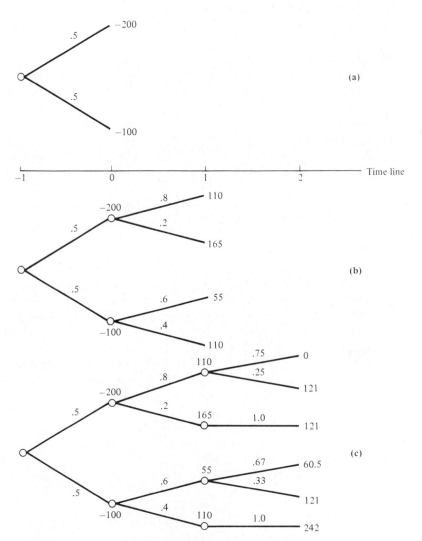

FIGURE 10.1   Tree Diagrams of Investment Outcomes

the point on the time line at which the events will be observable. All mutually exclusive events observable at a given time are arranged vertically above the appropriate point. The cash flow corresponding to the event is shown at the end of each branch, and the probability that the event will occur is displayed in the middle of the branch. The sum of the probabilities of all branches originating from a common point must sum to 1.

In Figure 10.1b events that would be observable at time 1 have been added to the tree diagram. All the outcomes that are possible from a given starting point are shown as branches radiating from that starting point. At the end of each branch are the cash flows that would occur, and in the middle of each branch is the probability of that branch, given the starting point at the left-hand end of the branch.

In Figure 10.1c the tree diagram is completed by adding the outcomes that could occur at time 2. Tree diagram 10.1c and Table 10.1 contain identical information about the investment although the form of the presentation differs.

A limb in the tree diagram consists of a sequence of branches starting at the extreme left of the diagram and ending at the extreme right. Each limb corresponds to a particular sequence of events, one at each point in time. Such a sequence of events is referred to as a *state of nature* or a scenario. In Figure 10.1 each number corresponds to a different state of nature. To determine the probability of a scenario at the end of each path, multiply the probabilities of the corresponding branches. The circles at the beginning of each split in the branches indicates that a stochastic event (an outcome subject to a probability distribution) follows.

In this simplified example, in which there are only three periods and six scenarios, it is possible to depict all the possible outcomes. In practice with a real investment this will not be possible. Suppose that cash flows occur at 10 different times and that there are 10 different outcomes that can occur at each time. Then a total of 10 billion different scenarios is necessary to describe completely an investment. Clearly, a method of summarizing the possible outcomes is necessary. The next sections of the chapter briefly introduce some strategies that have been used to summarize the possible outcomes associated with an uncertain investment.

Period-by-Period Summaries

A common approach for summarizing the cash flows associated with an uncertain investment is for an analyst who has studied the investment to write down a single number for each time period to represent the cash flow that it is "estimated" will be associated with the investment. The estimated cash flow may be labeled an expected cash flow, but in practice, it is more likely to be based on an educated guess by the analyst than a complete risk analysis. Many investment decisions are based on the expected present value with no further formal analysis of uncertainty. That is, the numbers reported will usually represent a judgment as to the magnitude of the cash flows rather than a detailed calculation based on a listing of alternative scenarios.

Another common approach is for the analyst to specify the assumptions that were used. In effect, the analyst describes a particular scenario and estimates the cash flows that would result if that scenario occurred.

TABLE 10.2   Period-by-Period Summary of the Cash Flows of an Uncertain Investment

Line	Item	Periods 0	1	2
1	Best estimate of cash flows	− $150	$100	$100
2	Optimistic cash flow for each period	− 100	165	242
3	Pessimistic cash flow for each period	− 200	55	0

The estimated cash flows may be accompanied by a written report in which the analyst has an opportunity to describe in qualitative terms the conditions under which the estimated cash flows will or will not be realized and the extent of the discrepancies that might possibly occur. Occasionally the single set of estimated cash flows may be supplemented by some effort to indicate other possible outcomes that could occur, perhaps by providing cash flow estimates labeled optimistic or pessimistic. An example of this type of presentation is contained in lines 2 and 3 of Table 10.2. The first line is the "best" estimate of cash flows. The terms used in Table 10.2 do not have exact statistical interpretations.

The estimated cash flows are ordinarily accompanied by a table that gives one or more summary measures of investment worth based on the best estimate of cash flows, as illustrated in Table 10.3.

Sensitivity Analysis

The summary measures included in Table 10.3 may be estimates that are conditional on certain assumptions. For example, the net present value calculation assumes a discount rate of 10 percent. All of the measures calculated

TABLE 10.3   Summary Measures of the Worth of an Uncertain Investment, Based on Best Estimate of Cash Flows

Measure	Value
Net present value at 10%	$23.55
Internal rate of return	21.5%
Payback	1.5 years
Return on average investment	33.3%

TABLE 10.4   Sensitivity Analysis

Assumption Varied	Assumed Level of Variable	Net Present Value
A. Discount rate	20%	$ 2.78
	15	12.57
	10	23.55
	5	35.94
B. Estimated annual proceeds	$120	58.26
(initial outlay is $150)	100	23.55
	80	−11.16
C. Initial outlay	$200	−26.45
(annual proceeds are $100)	150	23.55
	100	73.55

assume that the life of the investment will be two years and that the initial outlay will be $150. The purpose of a sensitivity analysis is to determine how varying the assumptions will affect the measures of investment worth. Ordinarily, the assumptions are varied one at a time. The results of this type of analysis are illustrated in Table 10.4. In the first panel of the table (A), the estimated cash flows are held constant, but the rate of discount used is varied (as when there is a difference of opinion as to what rate should be used). Note that the net present value is positive for the four rates used.

In the second panel (B), the discount rate is assumed to be 10 percent, and the initial outlay is assumed to be $150; holding these assumptions constant, the effect of changing the assumed level of the estimated constant annual proceeds is determined. In the third panel of the table (C), the effect of changing the level of the initial outlay is illustrated if the discount rate is 10 percent and annual proceeds are $100 per period.

Risk Analysis: Simulation

Risk analysis is intended to give the managers a better feel for the possible outcomes that can occur, so that they can use their judgment and experience with regard to whether or not the investment is acceptable. In practice, the possible outcomes are so numerous that listing all of them is not feasible, even with the help of a large-scale computer. Instead, the analysis is based on a sample of the possible outcomes. This approach is called simulation. If the process involves choosing outcomes randomly, the process is sometimes called the Monte Carlo method.

The steps involved in producing a risk analysis can be briefly summarized

TABLE 10.5   Frequency Distribution of Net Present Values of an Uncertain Investment

Possible States of Nature	Probability of State	Net Present Value at 10%
a	.3	− $100
b	.1	0
c	.1	50
d	.2	0
e	.1	50
f	.2	200

as follows. First, a measure of investment worth is selected, for example, net present value or internal rate of return. Second, for each set of decisions a computer program is devised that will sample from all possible outcomes. Outcomes are clustered, and for each outcome selected the probability of the outcome and the value of the investment are computed. Third, the outcomes of the simulation are summarized and presented to management. The final summary might consist of drawing a histogram or calculating the mean and variance (or other measures of central tendency and dispersion) for whatever measure or measures of investment worth have been selected in the first step. This approach is called risk analysis.

Assume that the outcomes for one set of decisions has been simulated a large number of times (say, 100,000). For 30,000 trials outcome a occurred. Table 10.5 assigns a .3 probability to outcome a. Table 10.5 gives the net present value, using a 10 percent discount rate, for each state of nature a to f. This table is consistent with the hypothetical investment of Table 10.1. Table 10.6 illustrates some of the ways a set of net present values could be summarized for management using the information of Table 10.5.

TABLE 10.6   Risk Analyses of an Uncertain Investment Based on Net Present Value Using a 10 Percent Discount Rate

Expected net present value	$ 20.00
Modal net present value	− 100.00
Standard deviation of net present value	105.36
Maximum (with probability .2)	200.00
Minimum (with probability .3)	− 100.00
Probability of zero or less	.6
Probability of $200 or more	.2

A Distribution of Net Present Values

Uncertainty may enter into the investment decision analysis in several ways. We shall focus attention on the uncertainty relative to the cash flows. Assume an investment with an immediate outlay of $800 and a $1,000 inflow at time 1. The firm uses a .10 discount rate.

If there is a probability that the cash flows of the preceding example may be something other than $800 outlay and a $1,000 inflow, then there is uncertainty about the cash flows. It is assumed here that the cash flow distributions are normal. See Figure 10.2.

It is also assumed that the cash outlays for the investment have a standard deviation of $200 ($\sigma = 200$) and that the cash flows at time 1 have a standard deviation of $450. Also, we assume that the cash flows of successive periods are statistically independent.

In summary, there are two independent probability distributions:

Cash Flows

	Mean	σ
Period 0 cash flow	$ (800)	$200
Period 1 cash flow	1,000	450

We want to determine the mean and variance of standard deviation of the probability distribution of the net present value distribution.

The mean of the present value distribution is computed using the means of the other distributions. We shall use $(1 + r)^{-i}$ as the present value factor,

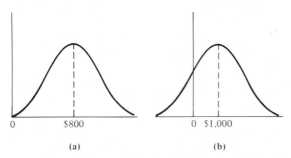

(a)   (b)

FIGURE 10.2   Probability Density Functions for (a) Cash Outlays and (b) Cash Flows of the First Year

where r is the rate of discount and i is the number of periods. The basic formula we use to compute the expected net present value is

$$\text{mean} = \sum_{i=0}^{n} (1 + r)^{-i} \overline{Y}_i$$

where $\overline{Y}_i$ is the mean cash flows of period i. Computation of the mean of the present value distribution using a 10 percent discount rate yields

period 0 cash flows: $-\$800(1 + .10)^{-0} = (\$800)$
period 1 cash flows: $\$1,000(1 + .10)^{-1} = \underline{909}$
mean, net present value distribution $= \$109$

The computation of the variance of the net present value distribution is slightly more complex. It a is a constant, then var $(aX) = a^2$ var (X), and if X_1 and X_2 are independent, var $(X_1 + X_2) =$ var $(X_1) +$ var (X_2). The variance of the net present value distribution is

$$\text{var (NPV)} = \sum_{i=0}^{n} (1 + r)^{-2i} \text{var } (Y_i)$$

where var (Y_i) is the variance of the cash flow of the ith year. Note that the present value factor for each period is squared.

Period	$(1.10)^{-2i}$	Var (Y_i)	$(1.10)^{-2i}$ Var (Y_i)
0	$(1.10)^{-2 \times 0}$	$200^2 = \$\ 40,000$	$\$\ 40,000$
1	$(1.10)^{-2 \times 1}$	$450^2 = \$202,500$	$\underline{167,000}$
			Var (NPV) $= \$207,000$
		$\sigma_Y = \sqrt{\$207,000} = \$455$	

We have now determined the mean ($109) and the standard deviation ($455) of the net present value distribution.

This distribution contains a great deal of information. For example, we can determine the probability of the net present value being zero or less. Since the expected NPV is $109, a zero NPV is .24 standard deviations:

$$\frac{\$109}{\$455} = .24$$

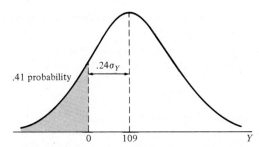

FIGURE 10.3   A Probability Density Function

From a table of normal probability distribution, we find that the probability of zero net present value or less is .41 (.24 standard deviations from the mean). See Figure 10.3.

Tables, a calculator, or a computer give the following probabilities for the selected standard deviations with a normal probability distribution (see Figure 10.3 for the probability being computed).

Number of Standard Deviations	*Probability of the Outcome Being Farther Away from the Mean*
0	.50
.24	.41
.62	.27
.75	.23
1.00	.16
2.00	.02

The probability of different outcomes can be computed. For example, since the mean is $109 and the standard deviation is $455, there is .02 probability that the net present value will exceeed $109 + 2($455) = $1,019. Should the investment be undertaken? That depends on the risk preferences of the management and the owners of the corporation.

The conventional net present value method of evaluating investments makes use of the mean values of the cash flows, and the dispersions of the flows are not generally incorporated into the analysis. This section suggests methods of computing the probability of realizing different amounts of net present value. However, the foregoing analysis does not consider the correlation of the investment with the firm's other assets or with the market portfolio. This omission has to be rectified.

Implicit in the computation of the standard deviation of the net present value distribution is an assumption that the investors have risk preferences.

Risk Preferences

Some people like risk (they gamble at race tracks and the casinos in Atlantic City despite negative expected values); others are risk neutral (they buy risky bonds and stocks but think the expected value is positive); but most persons are risk averse. They want to be paid to accept risk.

Attitudes toward risk are an important factor that must be taken into account when considering investment opportunities that are subject to uncertainty. Let us suppose that a potential investor has $50,000 of cash. The investor considers that the probability is 1 that the assets held in a riskless investment account for one year will be worth $55,000 one year from now. Now suppose that there is an investment opportunity that would require an immediate outlay of $50,000 and would return either $0 (with probability .2) or $100,000 (with probability .8) one year from now. If this opportunity is accepted, the expected cash flow one year from now will be $80,000 (that is, .2 × 0 + .8 × $100,000). The rate of return on the expected cash flows of this one-year investment will be 60 percent. This is an attractive expected rate of return by ordinary standards. However, we cannot use the expected rate of return to decide the acceptability of this investment for this potential investor. It is necessary to establish attitudes toward risk before we can decide whether the investor should accept or reject the investment if it must be financed with the investor's own funds.

One may be tempted to say that a reasonable way to make the decision is to compare the certain cash flow of $55,000 that would be realized if the investor kept the money in a savings account with the average or expected cash flow of $80,000 from accepting the risky investment. The difficulty with this approach is that it buries the fact that at the end of the year, the investor will have $0 or $100,000 from the risky investment compared with $55,000 with the certain investment of $50,000. The question that our potential investor cannot avoid is whether the dissatisfactions associated with the .2 possibility of having $0 next year, when a safe investment would lead to a sure $55,000, outweigh the satisfactions associated with the .8 possibility of having $100,000. Figure 10.4 shows the decision tree for the two choices.

The ability to make a decision under uncertainty depends on such comparisons and requires knowledge of attitudes toward risk. Different investors

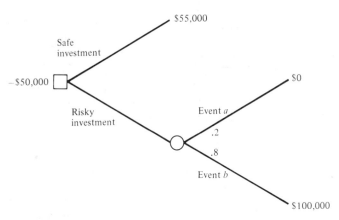

FIGURE 10.4

might answer questions regarding the acceptance of risk differently, in which case we shall say that they have different risk preferences. And the same investor may have different risk preferences at different stages of life or under different circumstances. Other investments already undertaken, the state of health, the number of persons dependent on the outcome, and the chances of being unemployed next year are factors that one must take into account in making the decision.

A description of an investor's risk preferences is called a *utility function*. Just as subjective probabilities can be used to describe a person's attitude about the likelihood that some outcome will occur, so a utility function may describe risk preferences.

A utility function assigns a number to each possible outcome of an uncertain event. The number assigned by a utility function can be interpreted as an index of the relative satisfaction the individual would derive if that outcome actually occurred.

No matter how large the firm, there is some investment opportunity that it would not want to consider on a straight expected monetary value basis. The analysis of risk (i.e., incorporating the consequences of the outcomes) could be performed by a utility analysis or by some other means, but it must be recognized that we cannot inspect one number (say, the internal rate of return of the investment or the expected net present value) to make an investment decision. It is necessary to consider all possible outcomes and the probabilities of these outcomes.

For giant corporations it is sometimes difficult to imagine an investment that we could not judge on a straight expected monetary value basis. But even for such corporations, there are investments (or classes of investments) of such magnitude that they give rise to the likelihood of events that could be disastrous to the firm. Incorporating this information into the analysis, rather than just using the maximization of wealth (or the expected monetary value criterion), can be done by the use of a utility analysis. Assume that an investment has the characteristic of resulting in a doubling of the firm's income or reducing the firm's income to approximately zero. Should this type of investment decision be made on an expected monetary value basis?

The expected value decision criterion may at times be consistent with the wealth maximization objective, but several things should be noted. The consistency holds true only in the long run and assuming that we can repeat the trial many times. We are dealing with averages, and there is very little chance that the average event will actually occur on any trial (there may be no chance). In some cases, following the expected monetary value criterion will lead to bankruptcy (i.e., ruin) and end of the "game." Where the possibility of this unhappy event is present, it is reasonable that this should affect our decision process. The objective "maximize the expected wealth" ignores the fact that this is a maximization of an average amount. This is not a sufficient description of the objectives of the investor. The maximization goal is reasonable, but the things being maximized should not be expected monetary values; rather it should be expected value with risk being considered.

Certainty Equivalents

In 1965 Robichek and Myers suggested the use of certainty equivalents to compensate for risk. This method uses a certainty equivalent of the cash flows of period t, C_t^* rather than the expected value of the cash flow, $\overline{C}_t$, where C_t^* is defined to be the risk-adjusted counterpart of $\overline{C}_t$. The decision can be formulated in present value terms by using a "default-free" rate in the discounting process. Using this method, we would then calculate the net present value of the certainty equivalents,

$$P = \sum_{t=0}^{n} \frac{C_t^*}{(1 + r_f)^t} \tag{10.1}$$

where r_f is a default-free interest rate and n is the economic life of the project. The project would be deemed acceptable if P is positive.

The determination of certainty equivalents for a corporation, even for one-period investments, would not be easy. It would be necessary to determine the appropriate utility functions, and it is not clear that we know how to determine a corporation's untility function. In practice, the certainty equivalent approach is difficult to implement.

Time and Risk

A satisfactory definition of a discount rate to be used for time discounting would be helpful in guiding the internal investment policy of corporate management. The choice of investments frequently represents a strategic decision for the management of a firm, since in large part the choices made now will influence the future course of the firm's development. It is not surprising to find that implicit in any definition of a discount rate to guide investment policy is a judgment on the goals toward which the firm is or should be striving. The goals help to determine the appropriate definition of capital cost.

There are wide-ranging disagreements about the choice of the rate of discount to be used to evaluate investments. It is sometimes argued that the weighted average cost of capital of a firm may be used to evaluate investments whose cash flows are perfectly correlated with the cash flows from the firm's present assets. With perfect correlation betwen the cash flows of two investments, the risk is the same. But if the timing of the cash flows is not also the same, it is not obvious that the same discount rate can be used for both investments.

Consider a situation in which three gambles have payoffs of either $0 or $1,000, both with .5 probability. Thus the expected payoff for all of the gambles is $500. All of the gambles are perfectly correlated, and the outcome of the gambles will be known immediately. Assume that money can be borrowed and lent at a .10 annual rate. Assume that one of the gambles will pay off immediately and is worth $440.00. There is a $60.00 discount for risk.

Now assume that a second gamble with an expected value of benefits of $500 and a certainty equivalent of $440 will pay off one year from now and that an investor is indifferent between this gamble and $400 for certain now. The choice of $400 implies an average cost of capital of .25. (The expected value of the payoff is $500 and a .25 rate of discount would equate the present value of $500 to $400.) The $400 of value can also be obtained by discounting the certainty equivalent $440 (equal to the $500 of expected value minus the $60 discount for risk) by .10.

A third gamble identical to the first in terms of dollar values of the outcomes will pay off 20 years from today. If the discount rate of .25 is applied to the $500 expected value, we obtain $5.75 (.0115 × $500). But the risk does not exist for 20 years. It is resolved immediately. If money can be borrowed and lent at .10, it is not clear that an investor would be indifferent between $5.75 and the gamble.

The cost of capital combines in one discount rate an allowance for the time value of money and an allowance for risk. To apply the same cost of capital to cash flows that occur at different points in time, the magnitude of these risk allowances (i.e., the percent per unit of time) must remain constant over time.

Studies of the term structure of default-free interest rates suggest that the appropriate allowance for the time value of money is not necessarily constant for all future time periods. More important, the rate at which uncertainty increases is often not constant through time. In the previous example, the uncertainty about the gamble was independent of the timing of the payment. The discount rate of 25 percent for the first lottery represents the average value over one year of an allowance for the time value of money and an allowance for the risk of an uncertain event where the payoff is in one year. The present value of $1,000 to be received in one year is $909, using .10 as the discount rate. This is the value of the gamble if the outcome is favorable. Multiplying by .5, we obtain an expected value of $454.55. This is $54.55 more than the $400 value of the asset to the investor. This $54.55 difference represents the present value of the allowance for risk for an investment paying off at time one. Recall that the risk for this investment will be resolved immediately.

Now let us assume the uncertainty is not resolved until time 20 when the payoff takes place. Immediately before the uncertainty is resolved the discount for risk is $60 and the certainty equivalent of the gamble is $440. The present value of the certainty equivalent using 10 percent is

$$\$440(1.10)^{-20} = \$65.40$$

or

$$\$440(1.25)^{-20} = \$5.07$$

if .25 is used.

If $65.40 can be invested to earn .10 and the lottery can be purchased at a cost of $440, one would not pay more than $65.40 at time 0 for the gamble. A purchase of the gamble for less than $65.40 at time 0 would be a bargain if funds can be borrowed at .10. If the gamble were priced at $5.07 and if the $5.07 were borrowed at .10, the cost at time 20 would be

$$\$5.07(1.10)^{20} = \$34.11$$

The value of the lottery at time 20 is $440. If $5.07 is borrowed at time 0 to buy the lottery and the debt repayment to time 20 is $34.11, the lottery can be sold for $440. The purchase at $5.07 would be a bargin, likely to be eliminated by arbitragers. We conclude that a combination of time and risk is very difficult to resolve with a simple mathematical relationship.

Perpetuities and Risk

If the benefits from all investments are perpetuities, the use of different discount rates, where the rates increase with increased risk, may give an evaluation of investments using their present values that is consistent with their risks. For example, if all investments have cash flows of $1,000 per year and if there are three investments with different risks (high, medium, and low), we can use a high discount factor (say, .20) with the high risk, a medium discount factor (say, .10) with the medium risk, and a low discount factor (say, .05) with the low risk. The three different present values we obtain are as follows:

	Discount Factor	Perpetual Cash Flow Present Value Factors	Present Value of $1,000 per Year
High risk	.20	5	$ 5,000
Medium risk	.10	10	10,000
Low risk	.05	20	20,000

There is a $.50 discount per dollar of proceeds for risk as we move from the low-to the medium-risk investment and a $.75 discount per dollar for risk as we move from the low- to the high-risk investment. These risk adjustments may not be correct, but at least the adjustment for risk is in the correct direction, and they apply in the same manner to all investments in the same risk class.

It is less obvious than with common stock, but the cost of corporate debt also includes an adjustment for risk, because there is generally the possibility of default. A bond yield of .15 is partially a result of time preference (say, .10) and partially a result of the risk of default. It may also include an allowance for the risk and dilution of value resulting from changes in the purchasing power of the dollar.

Risk-Adjusted Discount Rates

In capital budgeting practice, a commonly used criterion for making accept or reject decisions is to compare the internal rate of return on cost for an investment with the firm's weighted average cost of capital (WACC). The WACC represents the required rate of return for the firm as whole, and as its name

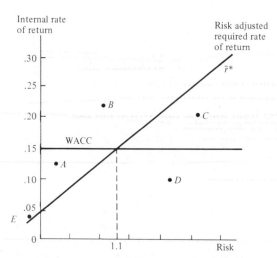

FIGURE 10.5   Risk-Adjusted Required Rate of Return

suggests, it is an average. Those who advocate this procedure recommend accepting the investment if its expected internal rate of return exceeds or is equal to the firm's cost of capital. A variation of this rule is to accept an investment if its expected internal rate of return exceeds the risk-adjusted discount rate appropriate for that specific investment. The WACC is a risk-adjusted discount rate.

Figure 10.5 illustrates a firm or an asset with a WACC of .15 and a risk measure of 1.1. Risk is measured on the X axis. The beta of an asset is one method of measuring risk that was introduced in Chapter 5 when we discussed the capital asset pricing model (CAPM). Other possibilities would be to use the standard deviation or variance of the distribution of net present values.

Figure 10.5 shows both the WACC and the risk-adjusted required-return lines. The two lines imply different investment criteria; in each case, the line is the boundary between the accept region (above the line) and the reject region (below the line).*

For investments B and D, both criteria lead to the same decisions. For investments A, C, and E, contradictory recommendations would result. Investments A and E would be rejected by the WACC criterion—but would be acceptable using the risk-adjusted discount rate approach, even though E yields less than the default-free return. Investment C would be accepted using the WACC but rejected using the risk-adjusted discount rate approach.

---

* The analysis in this section is adapted from Mark E. Rubinstein, "A Mean-Variance Synthesis of Corporate Financial Theory," *Journal of Finance*, Vol. 28 (March 1973), p. 167–181.

Figure 10.5 illustrates one important limitation of a WACC approach that is limited to one rate. It would not take into account variations in the riskiness of different projects. The one-rate approach tends to reject some low-risk projects like A that should be accepted because their rates of return are more than enough to compensate for their risk. The one-rate WACC approach tends to lead to the acceptance of high-risk projects, like C, whose expected rates of return are greater than the one-rate WACC but not enough greater to compensate for the risk of the project.

Default-Free Rate of Discount

Many discount rates may be suggested for use in making investment decisions. The following are the two possibilities we shall consider in this section: (1) interest rate of government securities and (2) interest rate of long-term bonds of the firm.

Before proceeding farther, however, we should establish more clearly the characteristics we seek in selecting an interest rate. The term risk-free might be used to describe the interest rate. This is suggestive, but not strictly accurate. There are risks that cannot in practice be eliminated and that affect all interest-bearing securities to a greater or lesser extent. The interest rates we have in mind are those at which investors can lend money with no significant danger of default or at which they can borrow if their collateral is so good that their creditors feel that there is a negligible chance of default.

Even if the risk of default is practically negligible, there are other risks inherent in fixed money debt instruments as long as there is uncertainty about the future changes that might take place in the economy. We shall describe these risks from the point of view of the lender. The counterparts of these risks also exist for a borrower.

One source of risk arises because of uncertainty about the future price level. Expectations about possible future price levels influence the market determination of interest rates. Lenders will tend to be hurt if the price level rises; hence, they require a higher interest return with an expected price-level increase than with an expected price-level decrease, or with constant prices.

Another source of risk arises because of the possibility of changes in the level and structure of interest rates. Normally, the interest rate on bonds will vary with the number of years to maturity even when there is no risk of default. Bonds that mature in a few years may have higher (or lower) yields than bonds that mature in the more distant future. If there is no risk of default, the lender can always be sure of earning the going yield by buying a bond of given maturity and holding it until it matures. The possibility exists, however, that some other strategy would result in earning a higher yield. If investors want to lend money for a 5-year period and expect a decline in interest rates, they may be able to earn a higher yield by buying a 15- or 20-year bond and selling it after 5 years than by buying a 5-year bond and holding it to maturity. When this strategy is followed, however, there is no longer any guarantee that a certain minimum rate of interest will actually be earned.

In spite of these limitations, the interest rates on government debt constitute a reasonable choice of discount rates representing default-free lending opportunities. These rates represent actual market opportunities at which firms or individuals could lend money with essentially no risk of default. If a default-free rate is used to discount for time, it would then be necessary to subtract from the net present value a dollar amount for the asset's risk. Unfortunately, the value of the amount to be subtracted is not well defined.

The Borrowing Rate

Neither private corporations nor individuals can actually borrow money at default-free rates. The rates at which a corporation could actually borrow for a given term would be higher than the rates at which the government can borrow for loans of the same maturity.

The after-tax borrowing rate sets a minimum return for an investment with certain cash flows. If a firm borrows at .07 after tax, it would not want to invest and earn .06 for certain.

With uncertain cash flows, the use of the after-tax borrowing rate would give a net present value that did not reflect the risk of the asset; thus further adjustments for risk would be necessary.

Changing the Uncertainty

It is possible for a company to follow courses of action that will decrease to some extent the degree of uncertainty connected with its operations. Increasing the information obtained prior to making a decision is one method of decreasing uncertainty. For example, a thorough job of market research may make the outcome of an investment in a new product much less uncertain than if the product were launched without the market research.

Another method of reducing uncertainty in some situations is by increasing the scale of operations. A large oil company faces less risk of complete bust when it drills 50 oil wells than does a small group of investors banded together to drill 1 well. On the other hand, a decentralized company may not make use of this fact if a division manager's performance is measured by using the operating data of the relatively small operation. In this case the division manager may be in the same position as the manager of a small firm who fears risky investments because of the threat of insolvency.

Product diversification may also decrease the uncertainty, especially if two products compete with each other. Thus a combined gas and electric company servicing a metropolitan city would have less uncertainty than would two separate companies, each specializing in either the electric or gas business. If major industrial users switch from electricity to gas, the fortunes of the specialized companies will be drastically affected, whereas if there were only one company there would be less of a change in the company's profits. Product diversification would also decrease uncertainty if the two products were differently affected by changes in business activity or technological change. For example, a combined grocery chain and machine equipment company would have less uncertainty as a result of changes in equipment technology than would a specialized machine equipment manufacturer.

Coping with Risk

Risk means different things to different people. The risk of an investment for an individual decision maker depends heavily on the preferences of that decision maker. For example, if the amount of loss is small relative to the wealth position of the investor, the decision may be based purely on expected present value (discounting at the time value of money). For large possible losses, risk aversion may lead to rejecting an investment despite a positive expected net present value.

A set of mutually exclusive outcomes is associated with any investment made under uncertainty. Each outcome is a unique cash flow pattern over time. Thus the risk of an investment cannot be measured simply by the variability of the cash flows associated with the investment within a period of time, for the interdependence of the cash flows across time is an important aspect of the risk of the investment. The cash flow from the investment in period t is usually not independent of the outcome in period $(t - 1)$. All shortcut methods of risk adjustment in which expected cash flows are reduced to "certainty equivalents" or discounted at risk-adjusted discount rates fail to capture this dimension of risk. A more complete description of the uncertainty of an investment is, however, captured in its distribution of net present values. This distribution depicts the possible set of cash flow outcomes adjusted only for their timing and their probability of occurrence; it is a good picture of the uncertainty of the investment.

In actual practice many decision makers want to know the distribution of internal rates of return rather than the distribution of net present values because the former seems to be easier to understand. But the internal rate of return distribution has no information about the dollar size of either the investment or the potential cash flows; thus we recommend that it not be used by itself.

One of the biggest problems in abandoning the shortcut procedures for handling risk is that a simple decision rule is no longer provided. Simple decision rules such as "accept the investment if its net present value is positive" are no longer applicable. Until more is learned about how an individual or a group perceives risk, the analyst can only describe the various outcomes to which the investor or the firm will be subject and the likelihood of their occurrence if a particular decision or set of decisions is reached.

For a publicly held corporation, there should be no individual investment decision maker imposing a personal risk preference in the decision-making process. The firm's goal should be the maximization of the stockholders' wealth position and, for publicly held corporations, that wealth position is measured by the price of the stock plus dividends paid. If there were perfect information, the real judge of an investment's worthiness would be the marketplace and how it would react to the news of the investment.

Business managers have a preference for easily understood, intuitively appealing, decision rules. The use of the weighted average cost of capital to evaluate investments is such a rule. If capital has a given cost (the weighted average cost of capital), then it would seem reasonable that an investment should be accepted if its return is higher than this cost. If the cost of capital reflects the risk of the asset being considered, it can be used as a hurdle rate in capital budgeting decisions. However, it combines in one measure time value considerations and risk attitudes, and this one measure is used for the cash flows of all periods. Using one risk-adjusted discount rate or certainty equivalents to compute present value equivalents are not reliable solutions to the problems of time value and risk, but they are usable approximations.

The President and Risk Analysis

The president of the _____ Company had an opportunity to make a major investment. It had a large net present value using the expected cash flows and the firm's weighted average cost of capital. In addition, the investment had a very low beta; that is, it had less risk using that measure than did the firm's normal assets.

The president rejected the investment. The reason for the rejection was the fact that it was perceived that there was .4 probability that the investment would have a negative net present value of $500 million.

Conclusions

The concept of probability was introduced as a means of describing the likelihood of the different possible outcomes. If the outcomes are described in numerical terms, whether as cash flows, net present values, internal rates of return, or some other measure, the expected value, variance, and standard deviation can be used to help summarize the possible outcomes.

Using these concepts, two main strategies for summarizing the possible outcomes of an uncertain investment were presented. One strategy is based on looking at the cash flows on a period-by-period basis. The cash flows may represent a guess at the expected cash flows or an estimate conditional on a particular scenario occurring. A sensitivity analysis is frequently used to supplement the period-by-period cash flow estimate. To produce a sensitivity analysis, the assumed value of one factor is varied, and the resulting variations in estimated cash flows are recorded. A second strategy is to simulate the possible cash flows and summarize the results. This is called a risk analysis using simulation or the Monte Carlo method. The term Monte Carlo applies since outcomes are selected randomly.

Some investments available to a corporation may be more risky than other investments; that is, there is a higher degree of uncertainty. The introduction of uncertainty opens up the possibility of losses, which in turn forces us to measure the relative importance of the possibility of large profits compared with the possibility of large losses.

It is suggested that management should consciously consider the possibility of not realizing the forecasted results and should incorporate this into the analysis. There remains the question of the psychological impact on business managers and investors of losses and gains. This area of analysis is still in its infancy. Finally, consideration must be given to the alternatives that are available to investors and how these alternatives affect the investment decisions of the firm.

When cash flows are discounted at a default-free interest rate, the resulting net present values adjust the cash flows for differences in timing, but not for risk. The net present value must be adjusted for risk. If a higher discount rate is used, there is an implicit risk allowance, and decision makers must ask themselves whether the appropriate risk allowance has been made. Some firms may prefer to use the rate at which they can borrow long-term funds as a discount rate. If their credit rating is good, this rate will not be far above the default-free rate, and it may be easier to explain and justify to management.

While we advocate the use of a default rate to compute a present value of a cash flow (not risk adjusted), for purposes of practical operation decision making, the use of the borrowing rate has a good deal of merit. It represents one estimate of opportunity cost, since the outstanding bonds could be retired or new bonds could be avoided (thus saving their cost). For a set of certain cash flows, a firm would not want to invest using borrowed funds, unless the cost of the debt were less than the internal rate of return of the investment. With risky cash flows, the conclusion is much more complex.

Even more important than the choice of a specific discount rate is the recognition that, when cash flows are uncertain, some investments may be undesirable because of risk, even though their expected cash flows have a positive net present value, whereas other very safe investments may be desirable even with expected cash flows having a negative net present value using a weighted average cost of capital. Because the risk characteristics of the investment will greatly influence the investment decision and the present value calculation is viewed as only one information input, it is most important that good investments should not be rejected by lower levels of management based on the use of a high rate of discount, so that they drop from consideration.

Investor diversification helps to reduce the importance of the type of risk analysis described here; however, there are three important qualifications:

1. Not all investors in the corporation may have diversified portfolios; a risky decision may have a significant impact on the well-being of some of the stockholders. Management can not assume that all stockholders possess well-diversified portfolios.
2. Even with the stock widely held, the corporation may encounter investments that the individual investor would reject if given the opportunity to invest in a proportion of the investment equal to the proportion of his or her investment in the firm. This can occur when the variance of the outcomes is large and there is a large probability of undesirable outcomes.
3. The management, workers, controlling stockholders, and communities where the major units of the firm are located all have an interest in the well-being of the corporation, and they may not be able to diversify to the same extent as the average stockholder.

Capital budgeting under uncertainty does not lend itself to simple solutions.

Review Problem 10.1

Assume a time discount rate of .15 and an investment with the following projected cash flows (they are independent of each other):

Time	Expected Cash Flows	Variance	Standard Deviation
0	− $18,000	4×10^6	2×10^3
1	11,500	25×10^6	5×10^3
2	13,225	36×10^6	6×10^3

(a) Compute the mean of the net present value distribution.

(b) Compute the standard deviation of the net present value distribution.

Solution to Review Problem 10.1

(a) Expected net present value $= \dfrac{\$13,225}{(1.15)^2} + \dfrac{\$11,500}{(1.15)^1} - \$18,000 = \$2,000$

(b) Variance $= \left[\dfrac{36}{(1.15)^4} + \dfrac{25}{(1.15)^2} + \dfrac{4}{(1.15)^0} \right] 10^6 = \$43.49 \times 10^6$

Standard deviation $= \$6.59 \times 10^3 = \$6,594$

PROBLEMS

1. An investment has two equally likely possible outcomes, $0 and $400.
   (a) Compute the expected monetary value.
   (b) Compute the expected present value if outcomes occur at time 1 and there is a 10 percent time value factor.

2. Using Problem 1 as a guide, write a general formula for the expected present value of a cash flow received at time n. Let p_i be the probability of the X_i cash flow.

3. Compute the variance of outcomes of Problem 1(a).

4. Compute the variance of outcomes of Problem 1(b).

5. Based on research, your logic, or the results of Problems 2 and 3, write a formula for the variance of the present value of an uncertain cash flow to be received at time n.

6. A new product has been proposed. In terms of after-tax net present values, introducing the new product will require initial outlays of $600,000 for specialized production facilities and promotional expenses. Over the life-

time of the product, the after-tax net present value of the proceeds could be any of the following.

Present Value of Proceeds	Probability
$1,000,000	.8
400,000	.1
200,000	.05
100,000	.05
	1.00

Find the expected net present value and its standard deviation.

7. A propsed exploratory well for oil will cost $1 million to drill. A large oil deposit would be worth $20 million and a small oil deposit would be worth $2 million; the probabilities of these events are .04 and .10, respectively. If no oil is found, the drillers can collect $200,000 in dry hole money from the owners of nearby leases.

What is the expected profit from drilling and its standard deviation?

8. It has sometimes been argued that net present value is "more sensitive" than the internal rate of return of an investment to variations in the cash flow estimates. For example, suppose that an immediate outlay of $3.859 million produces proceeds of $1 million per year for 15 years and an additional end-of-life salvage value that might be from $0 to $4.4 million. With a discount rate of 9 percent, the net present values would range from $4.2 million to $5.4 million (a variation of about 25 percent). The internal rate of return would range from 25 percent, if there is no salvage, to 26 percent, if there is a maximum recovery of salvage (a variation of only 4 percent).

If sensitivity is measured by the percentage of variation in the measure of investment worth for a given range of variation in the cash flow estimates, would you agree that in general net present value is a more sensitive measure of investment worth than internal rate of return?

9. Assume that $1,000 is to be received 30 years from today.

Compare the present values obtained using .05 and .20 as rates of discount.

10. The ABC Company can borrow and lend funds at an interest rate of .08. It can invest $11 million in a risky project that on the average will lead to net cash flows of $1 million per year. A consultant has suggested that the firm use its cost of capital of .10 in computing the present value of the

investment. The investment's life is extremely long. Insurance can be purchased that will guarantee the $1 million per year.

Should the investment be undertaken? How much could the firm afford to pay for the insurance?

11. The ABC Company currently has outstanding $1 milion of .05 debt with a maturity of two years. The only way it can finance a $500,000 investment is to refinance the $1 million with $1.5 million of .08 debt also maturing in two years. The investment would pay $55,000 in year 1 and $555,000 in year 2 (the investment has an internal rate of return of .11). The firm has a cost of capital of .10. Debt costs and investment cash flows are on an after-tax basis.

$$\begin{aligned} \text{cost of equity} &= .12 \times .5 = .06 \\ \text{cost of debt} &= .08 \times .5 = \underline{.04} \\ & .10 \end{aligned}$$

Should the investment be accepted?

12. The ABC Company has issued a $1,000, .05 bond with a four-year life. The interest rate for default-free securities is now .05. Assume that the following probabilities of payment apply (the probability of collecting in a given year is statistically independent of whether or not a collection occurred in the previous year; missed collections are not made up):

Principal or Interest of Period	Probability of Collection	Probability of No Collection
1	1.0	.0
2	.9	.1
3	.6	.4
4	.5	.5

(a) Assume that you are willing to pay the expected present value; what amount would you pay for this bond?
(b) If the investor pays the amount in (a), what is the approximate cost to the firm issuing the bond?

13. The ABC Company issued $1,000 bonds with a coupon interest rate of .05 per year at a price to yield .06 (the price was $885.30 per bond). The life of the bonds is 20 years.

Give three different reasons as to why the bond yield is .06.

14. The ABC Company has been offered a certain investment that yields .05. It can borrow funds at .06, and the interest rate on government securities of a similar maturity is .04. There are no taxes.

    Should the investment be accepted?

15. The ABC Company wants to use its cost of capital in evaluating investments. By a secret process it has succeeded in obtaining the forecasts of future dividends used by investors who currently purchase the stock. By equating the present value of these dividends to the price of the stock, it has obtained a number that it considers to be an estimator of the cost of common stock funds.

    Comment on the suitability of the measure obtained.

16. Assume that you have the choice between the following two investments:

Investment A

Probability	Immediate Outcome
.5	$ 0
.5	1,000

The outcome of B will be known now, but the payoff is one year from now and consists of the following outcomes:

Investment B

Probability	Outcome
.5	$ 0
.5	1,100

Which investment do you prefer? What amount does B have to offer with .5 probability for you to be indifferent between the two investments?

17. (Problem 16 continued)   Assume that investment B after 10 years pays an amount of $2,594 with .5 probability or $0 with .5 probability. Do you prefer A or B?

18. Assume a discount rate of .10 and an investment with the following projected cash flows:

Year	Expected Cash Flows
0	($1,600)
1	1,500
2	1,000

Assuming that the firm is willing to use expected monetary values, should the investment be accepted?

19. Assume that the cash flows of Problem 18 have the following probability distributions:

Period	Mean	σ	Variance
0	($1,600)	$400	16×10^4
1	1,500	500	25×10^4
2	1,000	600	36×10^4

The distributions are assumed to be independent of each other.
(a) Compute the mean of the net present value distribution.
(b) Compute the standard deviation of the net present value distribution.

20. Assume a .10 discount rate and an investment with the following projected cash flows:

Year	Mean Cash Flow	σ of Cash Flow Distribution	Variance
0	($1,600)	$ 700	49×10^4
1	2,000	1,000	100×10^4
2	1,000	1,500	225×10^4

The distributions are assumed to be independent of each other.
(a) Compute the mean of the net present value distribution. Using just the mean value, would the investment be accepted?
(b) Compute the standard deviation of the net present value distribution.

21. Define C_t^* to be the certainty equivalent of the uncertain cash flows of period t with mean $\bar{C}_t$. If the certainty equivalents are discounted using

r_f, a default-free rate, and the expected values are discounted using r, a risk-adjusted discount rate, what value does C_t^* have to be (in terms of $\bar{C}_t$) for the certainty equivalent method and the risk ajdusted discount rate method to have the same present values?

REFERENCES

Arrow, K. J. *Essays in Risk Bearing*. Amsterdam: North Holland Press, 1970.

Baron, David P. "On the Utility Theoretic Foundation of Mean-Variance Analysis." *Journal of Finance*, December 1977, 1683–1698.

Borch, K. *The Economics of Uncertainty*. Princeton, N.J.: Princeton University Press, 1968.

Borch, K., and J. E. Mossin (eds). *Risk and Uncertainty*. London: Macmillan Company, 1968.

Edwards, W., and A. Tversky. *Decision Making*. Hammondsworth, England: Penguin, 1967.

Grayson, C. J., Jr. *Decisions Under Certainty: Drilling Decisions by Oil and Gas Operators*. Boston: Division of Research, Harvard Business School, 1960.

Hertz, D. B. "Risk Analysis in Capital Investment." *Harvard Business Review*, January–February 1964, 95–106.

Hillier, F. S. "The Derivation of Probabilistic Information for the Evaluation of Risky Investments." *Management Science*, April 1963, 443–457.

Lintner, J. "The Valuation of Risk Assets and the Selection of Risky Investments in Stock Portfolios and Capital Budgets." *Review of Economics and Statistics*, February 1965, 13–27.

Litzenberger, R. H., and A. P. Budd. "Corporate Investment Criteria and the Valuation of Risk Assets." *Journal of Financial and Quantitative Analysis*, December 1970, 395–419.

Raiffa, H. *Decision Analysis*. Reading, Mass.: Addison-Wesley Publishing Company, 1968.

Robichek, A., and S. C. Myers. *Optimal Financing Decisions*. Englewood Cliffs, N.J.: Prentice-Hall, Inc., 1965.

Rubinstein, M. E. "A Mean Variance Synthesis of Corporate Financial Theory." *Journal of Finance*, March 1973, 167–181.

Sharpe, W. F. "Capital Asset Prices: A Theory of Market Equilibrium." *Journal of Finance*, September 1964, 425–442.

Stapleton, R. C. "Portfolio Analysis, Stock Valuation and Capital Budgeting for Risky Projects." *Journal of Finance*, March 1971, 95–117.

Tversky, A., and D. Kahneman. "The Framing of Decisions and the Psychology of Choice." *Science*, January 1981, 453–458.

Cases: Part II

 Case 1. **The A Chemical Company**

The A Chemical Company makes a wide range of products. About 10 percent of its sales and profits are generated by one product that we will call Basic.

At the current price of $200 per ton, the total world market of Basic is 2 million tons. Currently, A Chemical and a foreign competitor, Nisson Chemical, share the world market.

The following price and cost information applies:

Price per ton	$200
Variable costs	150
Incremental profit	$ 50

Both firms use essentially the same production processes and have the same cost structures. Both firms sell 1 million tons per year.

A major consulting firm has recently studied the market for A Chemical Company and has concluded that the product is in a mature phase of its life cycle and that the demand curve is not apt to shift to the right allowing additional price increases.

A university professor has recently published a journal article that could lead to a new manufacturing process for Basic. The A Chemical Company has tested the new process, and management is convinced that the variable costs could be reduced from $150 per ton to $50 per ton.

The minimum capacity for the new process is 3 million tons per year and the process would cost $600 million.

The A Chemical Company has a large tax-loss carry-over and is not likely to be paying income taxes in the foreseeable future.

The A Chemical Company and Nisson have been competing for a number of years, and given similar cost structures, they have avoided any extreme forms of price competition. The $50 incremental profit per ton is deemed to be a fair return on the capital currently being employed.

The A Chemical Company has been borrowing long-term funds at a cost of .14 and has comuted its weighted average cost of capital to be .20. It knows that Nisson uses .10. It has been using .20 as a hurdle rate to evaluate efficiency-increasing investments in any mature activities with little chance of growth.

There is reason to think that there will be no new significant cost saving developments in the future and that the demand for the product will stay constant at 2 million tons per year, if the price of $200 per ton is not changed. The physical life of the investment is extremely long. It is reasonable to assume that the equipment will have an infinite life.

QUESTION: What do you recommend that the A Chemical Company do?

Case 2. The Detroit Tool Company (A)

The Detroit Tool Company has 30 divisions. One of its best operating divisions is the Auto Parts Division. This division has capital of $45,000,000 and is earning $15,000,000. This earning measure is equal to the free cash flow generated by the division and can be expected to be constant through time. The division is currently earning a return on investment (ROI) of .33.

The time has come for the president of the Tool Company to consider a major modernization program for the Auto Parts Division. This automation will need $55,000,000 of additional capital (which is available) and will cause earnings to be $26,000,000. The new ROI will be:

$$\text{ROI} = \frac{\$26,000,000}{\$100,000,000} = .26$$

The ROI of the division will decrease from .33 to .26. ROI is an extremely important measure to divisional management, being the basis for the annual bonus (approximately 30 percent of management's wages is in the form of a bonus; the higher the ROI, the higher the bonus).

The Tool Company has computed its weighted average cost of capital to be .15. It uses the internal rate of return method to evaluate investments combined with the requirement that investments have no more than a four-year payback.

There are no special risks associated with the modernization program. In fact, the risks have been determined to be less than the normal corporate risk.

Should the Tool Company proceed with the modernization program for the Auto Parts Division? There is no thought of selling the division.

Case 3. The Detroit Tool Company (B)

The Detroit Tool Company's Brake Division has the opportunity to invest in a new piece of equipment costing $10,000,000. The statutory corporate tax rate is .46.

Exhibit 1 shows the capital budgeting analysis for the $10,000,000 investment. The entire amount of investment is eligible for the .10 investment tax credit (ITC). The tax basis of the investment is $9,500,000 ($10,000,000 minus half of the ITC). The estimated life of the equipment is five years with zero salvage value at the end of that period of time. The firm uses an accelerated cost recovery system (ACRS) method of equipment write-off for taxes.

The equipment will save $3,000,000 of labor costs per year. It will have a capacity of 2,500,000 units per year. This cost and capacity information is based on solid information and can be relied on to be correct.

Exhibit 1

Year	Depreciation Tax Savings	Present Value Factors	PV
1	.15($9,500,000).46 = $655,500	1.15^{-1}	$ 570,000
2	.22($9,500,000).46 = $961,400	1.15^{-2}	726.957
3	.21($9,500,000).46 = $917,700	1.15^{-3}	603,403
4	.21($9,500,000).46 = $917,700	1.15^{-4}	524,698
5	.21($9,500,000).46 = $917,700	1.15^{-5}	456,259
		Total present value =	$2,881,317

$$\text{Net PV} = -\$10,000,000 + \$1,000,000 + \$3,000,000(1 - .46)B(5, .15)$$
$$+ \$2,881,317$$
$$= -\$10,000,000 + \$1,000,000 + \$1,620,000(3.3522)$$
$$+ \$2,881,317$$
$$= -\$9,000,000 + \$5,430,564 + \$2,881,317$$
$$= -\$688,119$$

Management accepts the cash flow assumptions that result in the $688,119 negative net present value as shown in Exhibit 1. But it is bothered by the long-run consequences of rejecting the investment. It knows that the firm must modernize if it is to stay competitive.

The analysis considers only the first five years after the investment. Now assume that a new generation of equipment will be available at time 5. This new equipment will build on to the old equipment, automate it, and extend its life. It will cost $10,000,000, have a life of five years, and will save an additional $5,000,000 per year (the total annual savings will be $8,000,000).

If management accepts the fact that this sequence of investments is available, should it invest in the first set of equipment?

Case 4.   The Detroit Tool Company (C)

The Detroit Tool Company uses a basic type of equipment in 5 of its 30 divisions. In total there are 40 units of this equipment in operation. There has been a technological breakthrough that might result in this equipment becoming obsolete.

The new equipment costs $10,000,000 per unit. There is .3 probability that the equipment will save $6,000,000 per year and .7 probability that it will perform no better than the present equipment. However, if one machine works (saves $6,000,000), all the machines will perform in an identical manner.

Exhibit 1 shows the computation of expected net present value of the depreciation tax shield for the machine being considered. The entire amount of investment is eligible for the .10 investment tax credit. The tax basis of the investment is $9,500,000 ($10,000,000 minus one half of the ITC). The estimated life of the equipment is five years with zero salvage value at the end of that period of time. The firm uses a ACRS method of equipment write-off for taxes and a .20 discount rate.

What actions are appropriate?

Exhibit 1

Year	Depreciation Tax Savings	Present Value Factors	PV
1	.15($9,500,000).46 = $655,500	1.2^{-1}	$ 546,250
2	.22($9,500,000).46 = $961,400	1.2^{-2}	667,639
3	.21($9,500,000).46 = $917,700	1.2^{-3}	531,076
4	.21($9,500,000).46 = $917,700	1.2^{-4}	442,564
5	.21($9,500,000).46 = $917,700	1.2^{-5}	366,803
		Total present value =	$2,554,332

Case 5. The A Company's Manual

The following is an extract from A Company's *Manual*. Read it and find those sections that you think should be revised.

Appendix: Time-Adjusting Return on Investment

This *Appropriation Request Handbook* uses and discusses an improved method for calculating the rate of return on an investment. This new method, called "time-adjusted return on investment" or "discounted cash flow" recognizes the principle that time has an economic value. You may also hear this new method referred to as the "present value" method.

This appendix will explain the theory behind using cash flows and discounting for the timing involved.

A. Why Discount Future Earning Power

There are two basic reasons for weighing current earnings or cash flows more heavily than those expected in the future:

1. *Uncertainty*. Promise of future potential is based on many things. If any one of a series of things happens, this potential will not be fulfilled. This could consist of labor trouble, unforeseen national disaster, and so on, any one of which could adversely affect earnings.

2. *Alternative Uses*. This is the only argument that applies to all capital investment decisions. Cash received in the business today can be reinvested in the operations to earn a profit. Cash expected to be received in the future should be discounted because it is not earning until received. This discount factor should be the *required earnings rate* or the rate at which all new capital is expected to generate profit.

B. Required Earning Rate

One method of selecting a required rate is to take the average earning rate expected on funds now invested in the Company's operations. This average rate can be adjusted to account for any special considerations that make an individual proposal different from historical averages.

The Company has an average cash flow rate of return of approximately 17 percent. This rate is calculated as net profit after taxes from manufacturing operations plus depreciation, divided by net plant and equipment plus inventories.

Because there will always be investments that tend to reduce this historical return, a 20 percent rate of return should be considered a minimum for most future capital requirements. Any capital investment yielding substantially less than a 20 percent return may have merit to the Company, but it will require a detailed justification.

C. The Cash Flow Concept

As described in Section III of this *Handbook*, the stream of liquid funds that flow into or out of the business will determine the return on investment. Only cash can be used to purchase personnel, earn interest, or pay dividends.

Net income figures understate actual cash flows from operations because of the depreciation factor. By including this item, we tend to retain funds in the company that would otherwise be distributed in taxes or dividends.

The amount of funds derived from operation of the business, therefore, would be the figure of net income after taxes but before depreciation. The "shortcut" method of calculating this figure is merely to add back the depreciation charge to net profit after taxes. The result is a very close approximation to the true cash flow.

The stream of liquid funds may now be calculated over the life of a project. The main component parts of this stream are

1. *The project investment.* This, in turn, consists of the original capital investment, any subsequent capital outlay expected, any working capital required, any precious metals to be employed, and so on.
2. *Net profit after tax.*
3. *Depreciation charges.*
4. *Asset recovery.* In some cases recovery of working capital, precious metals, or equipment can be predicted. When the timing of this recovery is known, the cash generated through trade-in or sale should be treated as a cash inflow. In most cases this timing will be unknown and the cash cannot be so treated.

The sum of all the foregoing components will be the net cash inflow or outflow from the operation.

D. Timing

As discussed, cash in hand at the present is worth more than is the promise of an equivalent amount in the future, since these present funds may be reemployed in some other phase of company operation. To compensate for this discrepancy, a series of "present value" tables have been drawn up.

These tables given the "present value" of $1.00 promised at any time in the future, given the expected earning rate of that money. In other words, the value of a promise to pay $1.00 to Company four years from now (in year 5) is the same as having $.44 in the treasury right now, if we assume we can earn 20 percent on our money. We, therefore, "discount" the promise of future earnings at the rates shown in the "present value" tables.

The cash inflows and outflows calculated should be tabulated for each year of any project's economic life. The net cash inflow (outflow) figure for each year should then be discounted at the appropriate rate of return to determine its total economic worth to the Company.

E. *Rate of Return Calculation*
Projects that are obviously undesirable or those on which rates of return are so low or so high as to require detailed examination may be weeded out through a one-shot procedure: discount the total annual net cash inflows (outflows) at 20 percent—the company's desired rate for new project investments. The sum of these discounted flows should total at least zero. If the resultant figure is negative, the earning rate on the new project is less than 20 percent. If the discounted sum is positive, the earning rate is greater than 20 percent. Any investment that shows a very large positive or negative discounted figure should be examined in detail.

Case 6.   The Big International Chemical Company

Frances Smith, the president and CEO of The Big International Chemical Company, had reason to be very pleased. The company had just finished a very successful year (see Exhibit A).

However, she did have one problem. A year ago the company's research team had submitted a proposal for an interesting new compound. She had asked Tony Rambo, the financial vice-president, to prepare the economic analysis for bringing the new compound to market. Now the report was sitting on her desk. Tony's report considered two alternatives.

The first alternative required an upfront investment of $900,000,000 for plant and equipment. While the .20 internal rate of return was larger than the firm's .15 hurdle rate (the weighted average cost of capital was estimated to be .12 and .03 was added for nonrevenue producing assets and contingencies), Frances was concerned with the fact that while the compound had been made in test tubes, the production process was untested. Also, although the compound was expected to be a big success in the market, until the product was actually used by the buyers, she could not be sure of the existence of a market. Frances could not see betting $900,000,000 of the firm's resources on the type of coin flip associated with producing and marketing the compound.

The second plan was much more attractive and seemed to deserve more study. With this plan the company would construct a pilot plant at an initial

EXHIBIT A   Consolidated Balance Sheet (dollars in millions)

December 31	1985	1984
Assets		
Current assets		
Cash and short-term securities and time deposits,		
at cost approximating market	$ 176	$ 181
Accounts and notes receivable	728	933
Inventories	647	841
Prepaid expenses and other current assets	73	56
Total current assets	$1,624	$2,011
Other investments and long-term receivables	1,570	226
Property, plant and equipment less accumulated		
depreciation, depletion and amortization		
(1985—$2,374; 1984—$2,063)	2,858	2,866
Other assets	220	241
Total assets	$6,272	$5,344
Liabilities		
Current liabilities		
Accounts payable	$ 769	$ 974
Short-term borrowings	38	53
Accrued liabilities	302	286
Other current liabilities	99	60
Total current liabilities	$1,208	$1,373
Long-term debt and capitalized lease obligations	700	857
Deferred income taxes	287	335
Accrued pension obligations	79	89
Other liabilities	205	199
Preferred redeemable stock (aggregate liquidation		
preference: 1985—$619; 1984—$625)	586	591
Adjustable rate cumulative preferred stock	$1,194	—
Common stock and other shareholders' equity		
Capital—common stock—authorized 100,000,000 shares		
(par value $1 per share); issued:		
1985—35,448,911 shares; 1984—34,127,879 shares	669	629
Common stock held in treasury, at cost: 1985—198,954		
shares; 1984—384,188 shares	(10)	(19)
Cumulative foreign exchange translation adjustment	(48)	—
Retained earnings	1,402	1,290
Total common stock and other shareholders' equity	2,013	1,900
Total liabilities and shareholders' equity	$6,272	$5,344

Consolidated Statement of Income
(dollars in millions except per share amounts)

Years ended December 31	1985	1984
Net sales	$6,167	$6,407
Cost of goods sold	4,361	4,445
Depreciation, depletion, and amortization	382	347
Selling, general, and administrative expenses	639	534
Total costs and expenses	$5,382	$5,336
Income from operations	785	1,071
Other income, net	89	21
Nonrecurring items	(11)	29
Interest and other financial charges	(84)	(88)
Income before taxes on income	$ 779	$1,033
Taxes on income	507	685
Net income	$ 272	$ 348
Preferred stock dividend requirment	(68)	(38)
Earnings applicable to common stock	$ 204	$ 310
Earnings per share of common stock[a]	$ 6.22	$ 9.17

[a] Earnings per share of common stock are based upon the weighted average number of shares outstanding during each year as follows: 1985, 32,810,044 shares, 1984, 33,840,648 shares. No dilution results from outstanding convertible preferred stock and stock options, the only common stock equivalents.

Consolidated Statement of Retained Earnings
(dollars in millions except per share amounts)

Years ended December 31	1985	1984
Balance at beginning of year	$1,290	$1,057
Net income	272	348
Other	(12)	1
Dividends		
Preferred redeemable stock	(69)	(37)
Common stock (1985—$2.40 per share; 1984—$2.35 per share)	(79)	(79)
Balance at end of year	$1,402	$1,290

cost of $40,000,000. The cash flows associated with the pilot plant and a successful product were as follows:

0	1	2
− $40,000,000	− $10,000,000	+ $15,000,000

If the product is not successful, the cash flows of period 2 would be increased to $18,000,000 because of the tax write-offs. If the product is successful, a production plant costing $980,000,000 would be built in year 3. Reducing the $980,000,000 plant cost by $25,000,000 of cash flow from the pilot plant would result in a net cash outlay of $955,000,000 at time 3. The plant can be expected to earn $270,000,000 per year for perpetuity starting at time 4. The pilot plant will be shut down at time 3.

The cash flows are

Time	Cash Flow
0	− $ 40,000,000
1	− 10,000,000
2	+ 15,000,000
3	− 955,000,000
4	270,000,000

The present value of the $270,000,000 at time 3 is

$$\frac{\$270,000,000}{.15} = \$1,800,000,000$$

The net present value of the cash flows using .15 is

Time	Cash Flow		Present Value (.15)
0	− $ 40,000,000		− $ 40,000,000
1	− 10,000,000		− 8,700,000
2	+ 15,000,000		+ 11,300,000
3	− 955,000,000 + 1,800,000,000 =	845,000,000	+ 555,600,000
		Net present value =	+ $535,600,000

The $535,600,000 net present value was very attractive. Changing the life of the plant from being infinitely long to 20 years would not change the conclusion that this was a very desirable investment using the basic economic analysis.

The more that Frances looked at the basic economic analysis, the more upset she became. In the 20 years she had been a top manager at the firm, the board of directors had never accepted an investment with a payback period of longer than five years. The cash flow of this investment leads to a payback of period of in excess of six years (see Exhibit B). And this occurs only if the product is good! If the product is bad, it never pays back.

In addition to the long payback period, return on investment and earnings per share will be depressed for approximately the same length of time.

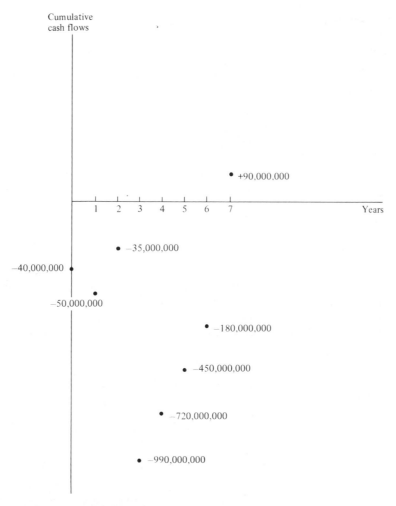

Exhibit B   Payback Period

Frances has received an inquiry from a competitor interested in acquiring the rights to the compound. The competitor has indicated that it would be willing to pay $100,000,000 in cash for the rights. This was a very tempting offer since she thought the $100,000,000 immediate gain would have a desirable positive effect on the firm's common stock price. She was much less sure of how the market would react to the news that the firm intended to spend over a billion dollars on new production facilities to produce a compound that has never been produced or sold before.

QUESTION: What should Frances do?

Case 7.   Jacobs Division*

Mr. Richard Soderberg, financial analyst for the Jacobs Division of MacFadden Chemical Company, was reviewing several complex issues relating to a new product introduction being considered for investment purposes in the ensuing year, 1974. The project, involving a specialty coating material, qualified for investment according to company guidelines. The Jacobs Division manager, Mr. Reynolds, was fearful, however, that the project might be too "risky." Moreover, Mr. Soderberg believed the only practical way to sell what he regarded as an attractive opportunity would place the product in a weak competitive position over the long run. Finally, he was concerned that the estimates employed in the probabilistic analysis were little better than educated guesses.

MacFadden Chemical Company was one of the 10 largest in the world with sales in excess of $1 billion. its volume had grown steady at the rate of 10 percent per year throughout the postwar period until 1957. Sales and earnings had grown more rapidly. Beginning in 1957, the chemical industry began to experience overcapacity, particularly in basic materials. Price cutting ensued. Also, more funds had to be spent in marketing and research to remain competitive. As a consequence, sales and profits were adversely affected. The company achieved only modest growth in sales of 4 percent in the 1960s and an overall decline in profits. Certain shortages began developing in the economy in 1972; by 1973, sales had risen 60 percent and profits over 100 percent as the result of price increases and near-capacity operations. Most observers believed that the "shortage boom" would be only a short respite from the intensively competitive conditions of the last decade.

There were 11 operating divisions of MacFadden, organized into three groups.

* Copyright © 1984 by The Colgate Darden Graduate Business School Sponsors, University of Virginia, and by Robert F. Vandell, The Charles C. Abbott Professor of Business Administration. This case was prepared by Professor Vandell and is used with his permission.

Each division had a multiplicity of products centered on one chemical, such as fluoride, sulphur, or petroleum. The Jacobs Division was an exception. It was the newest and smallest division with sales of $30 million. Second, its products were all specialty industrial products, such as dyes, adhesives, and finishes, purchased in relatively small lots by a great diversity of industrial customers. No single product had sales in excess of $5 million and many had only $100,000 or so in volume. There were 150 basic products in the division, each with several minor variations. Finally, it was one of the more rapidly growing divisions—12 percent per year prior to 1973—with a high return on total assets net of depreciation of 13 percent.

In capital budgeting analysis, there were some corporate wide guidelines for new investment opportunities: 8 percent for cost reduction projects, 12 percent for expansion of facilities, and 16 percent for new products or processes. Returns were measured in terms of discounted cash flows (internal rate). All calculations were estimated after taxes. Mr. Soderberg believed that these rates and methods were typical of the chemcial industry.

Mr. Reynolds, however, tended to demand higher rates for projects in his division, even though its earning's growth stability in the past marked it as one of the more reliable sectors of MacFadden's operations. Mr. Reynolds had three reasons for wanting to see better returns. First, one of the key variables used in appraising management performance of MacFadden was the growth of residual income (market share, profit margins, etc., were also considered). Residual income was the division's profits after allocated taxes minus a 10 percent capital charge on total net assets (assets after depreciation). Mr. Reynolds did not like the idea of investing in projects that were too close to the target rate of earnings imbedded in the residual income calculation. Next, many new projects had high start-up costs. Even though they made attractive returns over the long run, these projects hurt overall earnings performance in the short run. "Don't tell me what its (a project's) discounted rate of return is, tell me whether we're going to improve our return on total net assets within three years," Mr. Reynolds was known to say. Finally, Mr. Reynolds was skeptical of estimates. "I don't know what's going to happen here on this project, but I'll bet we overstate returns by 2 to 5 percent on average," was a typical comment by him. As a result, Mr. Reynolds tended to look for at least 4 percent in return more than the company standards before he became enthusiastic about the project. "You've got to be hardnosed about taking risk," he said, "By demanding a decent return for riskier opportunities, we've a better chance to grow and prosper."

Mr. Soderberg knew that Mr. Reynolds' views were reflected in actions at decision-making levels throughout the division. Projects that did not have fairly promising return prospects relative to Mr. Reynolds' standards tended to be dropped from analysis or shelved fairly early in the decision process. While this was hard to estimate, Mr. Soderberg guessed that almost as many projects with returns meeting the company hurdle rates were abandoned in this division as were ultimately approved. In fact, the projects submitted were usually so promising Mr. Reynolds rarely said no to a proposal. His capital budgets, in turn, were accepted virtually unchanged at higher management levels, unless top management happened to be unusually pessimistic about business and money prospects.

A new production process project was often under study for several years after research had developed a "test-tube" idea. The properties of the product had to be evaluated in relation to market needs, competition, and the like. A diversity of possible applications tended to complicate this analysis. At the same time, technological studies were under way examining material sources, plant location, manufacturing process alternatives, scale economics, and so on. Myriad feasible alternatives existed, only some of which could be actively explored. These activities often involved outlays in excess of several hundred thousand dollars before any real feel for the potential of the project could be ascertained realistically. A project manager was assigned to any major project to coordinate this work. "For every dollar of new capital approved, I bet we spent $.30 on business analysis of opportunities," observed Mr. Soderber, "and that doesn't count the money we spend on research."

The project that concerned Mr. Soderberg at the moment had been dubbed Silicone-X. The product was a special-purpose coating that added slipperiness to a surface. The coating would be used on a variety of products to reduce friction by increasing slide. The uniqueness lay in its hardness, adhesiveness (to the applied surface), and durability. It could be used in almost any application where lubricants might be imperfect in eliminating friction between moving parts. There were a great diversity of situations where Silicone-X might be useful. In terms of market, the product was likely to have a large number of buyers, each ordering small quantities. Only a few firms were likely to buy in yearly amounts larger than 5,000 pounds.

"Test-tube batches" of Silicone-X had been tested in a variety of applications inside and outside Jacobs. Comments were universally favorable, although an upper price limit of $2 per pound seemed likely to be the maximum possible. Lower prices were, of course, considered attractive, but this was unlikely to produce larger volume. For planning purposes a price of $1.90 per pound was used.

Demand was harder to estimate because of the variety of possible applications. Market research people had estimated a first-year demand of 1 million to 2 million pounds with 1 million cited as the most likely. Mr. Soderberg empathized with the problem of the market researchers. They had tried to do a systematic job of looking at the segments of most probable application, but the data were not good. "They could spend another year studying it, and state their opinions more confidently. But we wouldn't find them more believable. The estimates are educated guesses by smart people. However, they are also pretty wild stabs in the dark. They won't rule out the possibility of demand as low as 500,000 pounds and 2 million pounds is not a ceiling to possibility." Once the product was established, however, growth was considered to be pretty good.

Once the product became established, however, demand was likely to grow at a healthy rate—perhaps 10 percent per year. However, the industries served were likely to be cyclical with swings in volume requirements of plus or minus 20 percent depending on market conditions.

There was no patent protection on Silicone-X, and the technological know-how involved in the manufacturing process could be duplicated by others in time (perhaps months). "Someone is certainly going to get interested in this product when sales volume reaches $3 million and it's essentially a commodity," observed Mr. Soderberg.

"The product life is likely to be pretty good. We think demand should level off after 8 to 10 years, but the odds are very much against someone developing a cheaper or markedly superior substitute," claimed Mr. Vorst, the project manager. As most equipment required for the project was likely to wear out and need replacement after 15 years, give or take a few, this seemed like a natural point to terminate an analysis.

"Fortunately the cost estimates look pretty solid. Basic chemicals, of course, do fluctuate in purchase price, but we have a captive source with stable manufacturing costs. We can probably negotiate a long-term transfer price with Wilson (another MacFadden division), although this is not the time (sharply higher prices for an apparently temporary period) to do so," added Mr. Vorst.

In his preliminary analysis, Mr. Soderberg tended to use net present value calculations, and in this case the discount rate would be 20 percent. "We can always convert the data to a discounted cash flow rate when we have to do so," said he. "We also work with most likely estimates. Until we get down to the bitter end, there are too many alternatives to consider, and we can't afford probabilistic measures or fancy simulations. A conservative definition of most likely values is probably good enough for most of the subsidiary analyses. We've probably made over 200 present value calculations using our computer programs just to get to this decision point, and heaven knows how many quick and dirty paybacks," observed Mr. Soderberg.

Mr. Soderberg went on to say, "We've made a raft of pretty important decisions that affect the attractiveness of this project. Lord knows, some of them are bound to be wrong—I hope not critically so. In any case, these decisions are behind us. They're buried so deep in the assumptions, no one can find them, and top management wouldn't have time to look at them anyway."

Mr. Soderberg was down to two alternatives: a labor-intensive limited capacity solution and a capital-intensive solution. "The analysis all points in one direction," he said, "but I have the feeling it's going to be the worst one for the long run."

The labor-intensive method involved an initial plant and equipment outlay of $900,000. This alternative only had a capacity to service 1.5 million pounds. "Even if the project bombs out, we won't lose much. The equipment is very adaptable. We could find uses for about half of it. We could probably sell the balance for $200,000 and let our tax write-offs cover most of the rest. We should salvage the working capital part without trouble. It's the start-up costs and losses that we'll encounter until we decide that the project is no good that are our real risks," summarized Mr. Soderberg. "We can at least get this project on stream in one year's time. In the first year we'll be lucky to satisfy half the possible demand, and spending $50,000 debugging the process." Exhibit 1 shows Mr. Soderberg's analysis of the labor-intensive alternative. The calculations showed a small net present value when discounted at 20 percent. Mr. Soderberg noted, however, that there was a sizable net present value if an 8 percent discount rate was used. The positive present values when related to the negative present values looked particularly attractive.

The capital-intensive method involved a much more sizable outlay—$3 million—for plant and equipment. Manufacturing costs would, however, be reduced by $.35 per unit and fixed costs by $100,000, excluding depreciation, which would increase (depreciation would be over a longer period). The capital-intensive plant was designed to handle 2.0 million pounds, the lowest volume for which appropriate equipment could be acquired. The equipment was more specialized. Only $400,000 of this machinery might be redeployed to other company activities. The balance probably had a salvage value of $800,000. It would take two years to get the plant on stream, and the first operating year volume was likely going to be low—perhaps 700,000 pounds at the most. Debugging costs were likely to be $100,000.

Exhibit 2 presents Mr. Soderberg's analysis of the capital-intensive method. At 20 percent discount rate, the capital-intensive project had a sizable negative present value, and appeared much worse than the labor-intensive alternative. However, at an 8 percent discount rate it looked significantly better.

To gain some perspective, Mr. Soderberg estimated the internal rate on the incremental investment under the labor-intensive method in Exhibit 3. The internal rate was slightly above 14 percent. As a cost reduction opportunity, this rate was attractive, but partly because of the expanded capacity. As a part of a new product opportunity, it was unattractive. Mr. Soderberg was not sure how he should look at the project.

Several things concerned Mr. Soderberg about this analysis. Mr. Reynolds would only look at the total return. Thus, the capital-intensive project would not qualify. Yet it seemed the safest way to start the program based on a break-even analysis (see Exhibit 4): The capital-intensive alternative only needed a demand of 325,900 pounds to break even, whereas the labor-intensive method required 540,000 pounds of sales volume.

EXHIBIT 1 Jacobs Division: Analysis of Labor-Intensive Alternative Silicone-X

				Year			Terminal Year
	0	1	2	3	4	5–15	15
Investments							
Plant and equipment	$ 900,000						
Working capital		$ 140,000	$ 14,000	$ 15,000	$ 17,000	$ 20,000	$381,000
Demand (in pounds)		1,200,000	1,320,000	1,452,000	1,597,000	N.A.	
Capacity (in pounds)		600,000	1,500,000	1,500,000	1,500,000	1,500,000	
Units sold		600,000	1,320,000	1,452,000	1,500,000	1,500,000	
Sales price limit		1.90	1.90	1.90	1.90	1.90	
Variable costs per unit							
Manufacture		1.30	1.30	1.30	1.30	1.30	
Marketing		.10	.10	.10	.10	.10	
marketing total		1.40	1.40	1.40	1.40	1.40	
Contribution per unit		.50	.50	.50	.50	.50	
Contribution in dollars:		300,000	660,000	726,000	750,000	750,000	
Fixed costs		210,000	210,000	210,000	210,000	210,000	
Depreciation		60,000	60,000	60,000	60,000	60,000	
Start-up costs		50,000	0	0	0	0	
Total fixed costs		320,000	270,000	270,000	270,000	270,000	
Profit before tax		(20,000)	390,000	456,000	480,000	480,000	
Profit after tax at 50%		(10,000)	195,000	228,000	240,000	240,000	
Cash flow operations		50,000	255,000	288,000	300,000	300,000	
Total cash flow	$(900,000)	$ (90,000)	$ 241,000	$ 273,000	$ 283,000	$ 280,000	$381,000
Net PV at 20%	(900,000)	(75,000)	167,400	158,000	136,500	584,300	24,700
				Net present value $95,900 at 20%			
Net PV at 8%	(900,000)	(83,300)	206,600	216,700	208,000	1,469,300	120,100
				Net present value $1,237,400 at 8%			

N.A.–Not available.

311

EXHIBIT 2 Jacobs Division: Analysis of Capital-Intensive Alternative Silicone-X

					Year				Terminal Year
	0	1	2	3	4	5	6	7–15	15
Investments									
Plant and equipment	$1,900,000								$ (962,000)
Working capital		$1,400,000	$ 160,000	$ 11,000	$ 17,000	$ 20,000	$ 24,000	$ 30,000	(422,000)
Demand (in pounds)			1,320,000	1,452,000	1,597,000	1,757,000	1,933,000	2,125,000	
Capacity (in pounds)			700,000	2,000,000	2,000,000	2,000,000	2,000,000	2,000,000	
Units Sold			700,000	1,452,000	1,597,000	1,757,000	1,933,000	2,000,000	
Sales price/unit			1.90	1.90	1.90	1.90	1.90		
Variable costs per unit									
Manufacture			.95	.95	.95	.95	.95		
Selling			.10	.10	.10	.10	.10		
			1.05	1.05	1.05	1.05	1.05		
Contribution per unit			.85	.85	.85	.85	.85		
Contribution in dollars			595,000	1,234,200	1,357,500	1,493,500	1,643,100	1,700,000	
Fixed costs			110,000	110,000	110,000	110,000	110,000	110,000	
Depreciation			167,000	167,000	167,000	167,000	167,000	167,000	
Start-up costs			100,000	0	0	0	0	0	
Total fixed cost			377,000	277,000	277,000	277,000	277,000	277,000	
Profit before tax			218,000	957,200	1,080,500	1,216,500	1,366,100	1,423,000	
Profit after tax at 50%			109,000	478,600	540,200	608,200	683,000	711,500	
Cash flow operations			276,000	645,600	707,200	775,200	850,000	878,500	
Total cash flow	($1,900,000)	($1,400,000)	$ 116,000	$ 634,600	$ 690,200	$ 755,200	$ 826,000	$ 848,500	$1,384,000
Present value at 20%	($1,900,000)	($1,166,700)	80,600	366,900	332,900	303,500	276,600	1,144,800	89,800
					Net present value at 20% = ($471,600)				
Present value at 8%	($1,900,000)	($1,296,300)	99,500	503,300	507,300	514,000	520,500	3,338,200	436,300
					Net present value at 8% = $2,722,800				

EXHIBIT 3   Jacobs Division: Incremental Return on Investment Capital-Intensive Alternative

Year	Labor-Intensive Cash Flow	Capital-Intensive Cash Flow	Difference	PV at 14%
0	$(900,000)	$(1,900,000)	$(1,000,000)	$(1,000,000)
1	(90,000)	(1,400,000)	(1,310,000)	(1,149,100)
2	241,000	66,000	(175,000)	(134,700)
3	273,000	644,600	371,600	220,000
4	283,000	690,200	407,200	241,500
5	280,000	755,200	475,200	246,500
6	280,000	871,000	551,000	251,000
7–15	280,000	883,500	573,500	1,212,000
15	381,000	1,284,000	903,000	126,500
			Net present value = $	14,700

Mr. Soderberg was also concerned that competition might develop in the future and that price cutting would ensue. If the price per pound fell by $.20, the labor-intensive method would not break even unless 900,000 pounds were sold, and, of course, Jacobs would be sharing the market with a competitor. A competitor, of course, would—once the market was established—build a capital-intensive plant and be in a good position to cut prices by even more than $.20. In short, there was a risk, given the labor-intensive solution, that Jacobs could not remain competitive with Silicone-X. The better the demand proved to be, the more serious this risk would become.

Once the market was established, Jacobs could build a capital-intensive facility. Almost none of the labor-intensive equipment would be useful in the new plant. The new plant would still cost $3.3 million, and Jacobs would have to write off losses on the labor-intensive facility.

EXHIBIT 4   Break-even Analysis Silicone-X

Normal	Labor Intensive	Capital Intensive
Fixed costs		
Operations	$210,000	$110,000
Depreciation	60,000	167,000
Total	270,000	277.000
Contribution per unit	.50	.85
Units to break even	540,000	325,900
Price competitive		
Contribution per unit	.30	.65
Units to break even	900,000	426,200

The labor-intensive facility would be difficult to expand economically. It would cost $50,000 for each 100,000 pounds of additional capacity (only practical in 250,000 pound increments). An additional 100,000 pounds of capacity in the capital-intensive unit could be added for $25,000 in contrast.

Pricing strategy was also an element. At $1.90 a pound, Jacobs would invite competition. Competitors would be satisfied with a lower rate of return—perhaps 12 percent—in an established market. At somewhat lower prices, Jacobs might discourage competition. The project could not be "sold" at lower prices (that is, even the labor-intensive alternative would not provide a rate of return of 20 percent).

In short, it began to appear to Mr. Soderberg as if the use of a high discount rate forced the company to make riskier decisions and enhanced the prospects of realizing lower rates of return than forecast.

He was also concerned by the fact that the proposals did not consider expansion opportunities. The labor-intensive alternative would look better if 500,000 pounds of capacity were added as soon as demand warranted this aciton. In two years' time, expansion and, for that matter, cost reduction could be justified using lower rates of return.

ASSIGNMENT

As a financial analyst working for the vice-president of finance of McFadden Chemical, you have been assigned to review the guidelines the corporation uses to evaluate: (a) capital projects and (b) division managers. This assignment arose after one of the division managers complained that the two sets of guidelines were inconsistent.

Prepare a consistent set of guidelines and illustrate, by using the Silicone-X project as an example, that decisions that are in the best interests of the company are also in the best interests of the division manager.

QUESTIONS:

(a) What decision regarding Silicone-X is best for the McFadden Chemical Co.?

(b) What decision would Reynolds make given the existing corporate guidelines for evaluating investments and division managers?

(c) Would you recommend any changes in McFadden's policies and/or procedures?

Case 8.   The Modem Corporation

The Modem Corporation (MC) is considering opportunities to modernize (automate) its plant and equipment. Rachelle Brown, the president of the firm,

EXHIBIT 1

Year	Depreciation Tax Savings	Present Value Factors	PV
1	.15($9,500,000).46 = $655,500	1.2^{-1}	$ 546,250
2	.22($9,500,000).46 = $961,400	1.2^{-2}	667,639
3	.21($9,500,000).46 = $917,700	1.2^{-3}	531,076
4	.21($9,500,000).46 = $917,700	1.2^{-4}	442,564
5	.21($9,500,000).46 = $917,700	1.2^{-5}	366,803
		Total present value =	$2,554,332

$$
\begin{aligned}
\text{net PV} &= -\$10,000,000 + \$1,000,000 + \$3,000,000(1 - .46)B(5, .20) \\
&\quad + \$2,554,332 \\
&= -\$10,000,000 + \$1,000,000 + \$1,620,000(2.9906) \\
&\quad + \$2,554,332 \\
&= -\$9,000,000 + \$4,844,772 + \$2,554,332 \\
&= -\$1,600,896
\end{aligned}
$$

is enthusiastic about an automation strategy and sees it as essential if the firm is to stay competitive.

As a first step in the economic analysis of automated equipment, a cash flow net present value calculation was done for one of the more desirable pieces of equipment. The firm conventionally uses .20 to evaluate investment opportunities (debt currently costs .131, before tax). The statutory corporate tax rate is .46.

Exhibit 1 shows the capital budgeting analysis for the $10,000,000 investment. The entire amount of investment is eligible for the .10 investment tax credit. The tax basis of the investment is $9,500,000 ($10,000,000 minus half of the ITC). The estimated life of the equipment is five years with zero salvage value at the end of that period of time. The firm uses a ACRS method of equipment write-off for taxes.

The equipment will save $3,000,000 of labor costs per year. It will have a capacity of 2,500,000 units per year. This cost and capacity information is based on solid information and can be relied on to be correct.

Rachelle accepts the cash flow assumptions that result in the $1,600,896 negative net present value as shown in Exhibit 1. But she is bothered by the long-run consequences of rejecting the investment. She knows that the firm must modernize if it is to stay competitive. Rachelle also thinks it essential that any investment enhance the financial position of the stockholders. The negative net present value is disconcerting.

There are several other factors not directly incorporated into the cash flow analysis as well. The investment will increase the quality of the output. The product will be more consistent in its characteristics and thus more attractive to the purchasers. The economic value of this characteristic was thought to be too difficult to measure and was not included (its inclusion would have decreased the reliability of the cash flow measures used).

Moreover, the investment would increase the firm's productive capacity by 50 percent. With this increased capacity, the firm can react more rapidly to new orders and deliver goods straight from production rather than from inventory. It is estimated that the average inventory carried during a year could be reduced by $10,000,000. The annual after-tax cost of carrying inventory is estimated to be .25 of the investment.

A third advantage of the new equipment is that it is more reliable and has less down time than the present equipment. This would help to improve the ability to service customers as well as reduce inventories (this factor did affect the estimated inventory cost reduction).

The product line that the equipment would produce is currently earning $7,000,000 of cash flow per year.

The equipment being considered is a great departure from the equipment used in the past. While it is felt that the five-year life estimate is reasonable, it is also felt that a new generation of this type of equipment will be forthcoming after five years. It is estimated that even if the current investment is made, $15,000,000 of future cost savings per year is feasible with improved versions of the equipment.

QUESTION: What is your recommendation regarding the investment?

Case 9. The Continental Company (A)

Mr. Jeffrey Jones, the president and CEO of the Continental Company, felt a very strong obligation toward the firm's stockholders. In January 1984 he felt that, given the opportunity to earn high returns in fixed income securities, he had to earn .20 on stockholders' equity capital (long-term debt cost .12). Given a .6 stock/.4 debt capital structure and a .46 tax rate, this was a .146 weighted average cost of capital (WACC).

	Cost	Proportion	Weighted Cost
Debt	(1 − .46).12	.4	.026
Stock	.20	.6	.12
			WACC = .146

The Continental Company had six operating autonomous divisions. These divisions made their own decisions, and the division presidents were compensated using a residual income approach (a .146 capital charge was deducted in computing each unit's income).

Jeffrey had a definite policy of cutting the firm's losses. If a division was not earning a .146 return and there was no specific plan for turning the situation around, the division was sold to the highest bidder. The two most recent sales were to leverged buyout groups where the management of the divisions became the majority shareholders.

The Ultra Division was currently the worst performing division of the firm. The division used a large amount of plant and equipment, and inspection of the division's most recent balance sheet indicated that the total capital employed was $200,000,000, of which $180,000,000 was invested in plant and equipment.

For the past three years the division's reported accounting earnings were $10,000,000. The ROI was .05

$$\frac{\$10,000,000}{\$200,000,000} = .05$$

and the residual income was

Accounting income	$10,000,000
Capital charge,	
.146 ($200,000,000)	29,200,000
Operating loss	$19,200,000

While Jeffrey placed a great deal of faith in the accounting reports, he was a convert to price-level–adjusted accounting information. He realized that conventional accounting failed to consider price-level changes, and he considered this omission to be the major deficiency of generally accepted accounting principles. To rectify this failure, he had his controller prepare a price-level–adjusted income statement. The $18,000,000 of book depreciation expense was adjusted to $36,000,000 using an average of GNP price deflators, the consumer price index, and the wholesale price index. Capital was adjusted to $400,000,000 using the same price-level adjustors. And the $10,000,000 of accounting income reported now became an operating loss of $8,000,000.

Jeffrey was not willing to forecast an upward surge in sales and profits; on the other hand, he accepted an assumption that the present profit situation would continue into the future.

Ultra's industry is technologically mature, and there is excess capacity both in the industry and in the division. No significant capital expenditures are planned for the next 10 years, but normal maintenance type of capital expenditures would be $2,000,000 per year.

Given the inadequate accounting ROI and, more important, the loss resulting from the use of price-level–adjusted accounting figures, Jeffrey is inclined to sell the Ultra Division to the highest bidder. Feelers have been sent out to likely buyers, and the best cash purchase offer has been $50,000,000. If the division is sold, there will be a $150,000,000 tax loss on divestment, and this loss is worth $150,000,000 × .46 = $69,000,000 in immediate tax deductions; thus the Continental Company would net out $119,000,000 of cash flow.

Selling out appeared to be much more desirable than continuing to operate at a loss (using the residual income or the price-level–adjusted measure).

QUESTION: You have been hired as a consultant. What do you recommend?

Case 10.　The Continental Company (B)

Having recently reviewed the Ultra Division's performance very intensively, Jeffrey Jones, the president and CEO of the Continental Company, decided that it was desirable to review all six divisions as potential candidates for divesture. The following summary was prepared.

Division	Capital	Operating Income	ROI	Best Offer Price
Ultra	$200,000,000	$10,000,000	.05	$ 50,000,000
B	300,000,000	30,000,000	.10	200,000,000
C	100,000,000	15,000,000	.15	90,000,000
D	250,000,000	50,000,000	.20	300,000,000
E	80,000,000	20,000,000	.25	130,000,000
F	50,000,000	15,000,000	.30	120,000,000

To simplify an otherwise more complex problem, we shall assume that the operating income is equal to the net cash flow and that we can expect this cash flow to be constant (a perpetuity).

QUESTION: If a division is to be divested, which division should it be? Assume that the corporation is not currently paying income taxes and does not expect to in the future.

Part III

Long-Term Financing

In Part II we considered how decisions concerning long-term assets are made. In this section we will consider the different financing decisions. A corporation has the choice of pure debt or common stock and a wide range of securities that are variations of debt or common stock. Chapter 11 deals with debt and Chapter 12 with common stock. In Chapter 13, preferred stock, a security that is a mixture of debt and equity characteristics (though it is classified as equity), is introduced.

Chapters 14 and 15 discuss the financial structure, the cost of capital, and optimum capital structure. It is essential that the basic elements of financial mix be understood.

Chapter 16 is the mirror image of Chapters 11–15 that dealt with the obtaining of capital. That is, Chapter 16 deals with corporate dividend policy, the giving back of equity capital to investors.

Debt Financing

Major Topics

1. The cost of debt without and with taxes.
2. The term structure of interest rates and the concept of duration.
3. The factors affecting the cost of debt.
4. The bond refunding decision.
5. The capital asset pricing model and leverage effect.

The Cost of Debt

Long-Term Financing

The basic methods of long-term financing for U.S. corporations are the issuance of debt, common stock, and preferred stock and the use of retained earnings. Debt has become more widely used in the past 40 years as a result of tax factors and an optimism that severe business depressions will not occur in the future. If debt is used by a firm, it is desirable that the firm's financial officers be able to estimate the cost of the debt and understand the factors affecting the cost of debt and the pros and cons of debt as a source of capital.

It is commonly thought that debt is more risky to the issuing firm than other forms of capital, and while this is normally true, it is necessary to consider situations where the use of debt may actually decrease some types of risk to common stockholders. For example, if a risk-free investment having a .15 internal rate of return is financed with .10 debt, the risk of the firm is actually reduced by the investment financed with debt. Although financing the investment with stock would reduce the firm's risk even further, it is interesting that a safe investment financed with debt can reduce risk.

A "tombstone" advertisement in a newspaper or other publication announces a security issue and lists the brokers that are associated with the issue. An inspection of the tombstones on one day revealed the following new issues:

> Park Improvement Bonds of the Chicago Park District (a tax-exempt issue)
> Preference shares of Iowa-Illinois Gas and Electric Company
> Debentures of the Federal National Mortgage Association
> United States Government Guaranteed Ship Financing Bonds
> Shares of Inland Steel Company Common Stock

This list gives some indication of the variety of financing that takes place continuously in the capital market. Corporations and other types of economic enterprises frequently raise new debt capital and equity.

Exhibit 11.1 is a tombstone of a perpetual floating rate subordinated note issued by DnC. The note is a promise to pay interest at a variable rate tied to some index. The debt has no maturity date (it is a perpetual note), and it will be subordinate to other debt if there is financial difficulty. Morgan Stanley International is the lead investment banking firm for the transaction.

Bank Loans

Bank loans are a particularly advantageous type of debt financing because of the speed and flexibility with which funds can be obtained to meet both the firm's seasonal and longer-term demands for funds. Outstanding bank loans can be increased or decreased as the need for capital changes. It is not uncommon for a business to be almost continuously in debt to a bank, although the outstanding loans at a specific moment may be for a relatively short term. Although banks prefer seasonal loans (e.g., to finance inventories or accounts receivable) that are "self-liquidating" and backed by well-defined assets, they also enter regularly into short- (e.g., one-year or less) and intermediate- (one- to five-year) term loans and/or lines of credit with well-established customers based on overall creditworthiness of the firm. The interest rate on such loans is often stated as a given number of basis points over the prime rate, where the size of the differential depends on the creditworthiness of the customer and the maturity of the loan. A basis point is $\frac{1}{100}$ of a percent. Hence a "50 basis points over prime" rate is $\frac{1}{2}$ percent more than the prime rate. If the prime rate is .10, the 50 basis points over prime rate would be .105.

These Securities were offered and sold outside the United States. This announcement appears as a matter of record only.

U.S. $150,000,000

Den norske Creditbank

DnC

Perpetual Floating Rate Subordinated Notes

MORGAN STANLEY INTERNATIONAL

BANK OF TOKYO INTERNATIONAL Limited	NORDIC BANK PLC
ALGEMENE BANK NEDERLAND N.V.	BANKAMERICA CAPITAL MARKETS GROUP
BARCLAYS BANK GROUP	CREDIT LYONNAIS
DAI-ICHI KANGYO INTERNATIONAL Limited	DRESDNER BANK Aktiengesellschaft
GOLDMAN SACHS INTERNATIONAL CORP.	KREDIETBANK INTERNATIONAL GROUP
MERRILL LYNCH CAPITAL MARKETS	MORGAN GRENFELL & CO. Limited
NIPPON CREDIT INTERNATIONAL (HK) LTD.	SALOMON BROTHERS INTERNATIONAL Limited
UNION BANK OF SWITZERLAND (SECURITIES) Limited	S.G. WARBURG & CO. LTD.
BERGEN BANK A/S	CHRISTIANIA BANK OG KREDITKASSE
DEN NORSKE CREDITBANK (LUXEMBOURG) S.A.	ENSKILDA SECURITIES Skandinaviska Enskilda Limited
SPAREBANKEN OSLO AKERSHUS	SVENSKA HANDELSBANKEN GROUP

January 9, 1985

EXHIBIT 11.1

The prime rate is the rate that banks charge on short-term loans to credit-worthy customers. Each bank sets its own prime rate (although the rates tend to move together) at something greater than the interest rate currently earned on short-term U.S. government securities. A very strong firm may be able to borrow at less than prime, but a risky firm will pay a higher cost. Depending on credit conditions, some banks require the borrower to maintain a compensating balance equal to a percentage of the loan. Since compensating balances are funds on deposit that are not available for use, a requirement for compensating balances raises the effective cost of the firm's bank debt. For example, a bank loan at 8 percent interest with a 20 percent compensating balance has an effective interest rate of 10 percent, since only $80 of each $100 borrowed is usable and $8 of interest is paid per year.

$$\text{effective interest rate} = \frac{\text{nominal rate}}{1 - \text{compensatory balance percentage}}$$

$$= \frac{.08}{1 - .2} = .10$$

Trade Credit

There are several short-term liabilities that do not have explicit interest costs. Among these are taxes payable and wages payable. There are other short-term debts that may or may not have a cost if they are not paid promptly. For example, a trade creditor may offer terms of "2/10, n/30," which means that a 2 percent discount can be taken if the amount is paid within 10 days and the full (net) amount of the bill is due in 30 days. There is no cost for not paying the bill in the first 10 days, since the 2 percent discount may be taken at any time prior to the lapsing of 10 days. If the discount is allowed to lapse, there is a 2 percent penalty assessed for the use of the funds for a maximum of 20 days. If we assume a 360-day year, this is equivalent to an annual interest rate of approximately 44 percent:

$$98(1 + r)^{20/360} = 100$$

$$1 + r = 1.4386$$

$$r = .4386$$

With a 365-day year, we have

$$98(1 + r)^{20/365} = 100$$

$$1 + r = 1.4459$$

$$r = .4459$$

Some firms may allow the discount to lapse and then pay the bill some time after the 30-day period. This effectively lowers the cost of forgoing the discount, but it may also carry an implicit cost arising from the loss of credit standing, supplier ill will, and so on.

Commercial Paper

Large corporations with very good credit reputations can issue commercial paper. Commercial paper is a discount security. That is, the maturity amount and date are defined (less than a year) and the investor bids for the security. The highest bid sets the interest rate that the issuer pays.

The commercial paper is backed by the firm's line of credit with a bank. The purchaser requires the use of a line of credit since that is additional evidence of the issuer's creditworthiness.

There are two primary advantages of issuing commercial paper rather than arranging a bank loan. One is the fact that the commercial paper is likely to be cheaper. This is especially true in a market with falling short-term interest rates (bank rates tend to be more sticky coming down than commercial paper rates). Second, the commercial paper does not have to be paid until maturity unlike many bank loans that can be called prior to maturity under certain circumstances. This can also be a disadvantage of commercial paper since bank loans can be paid before they mature if the borrower no longer needs the funds. Commercial paper cannot be paid early.

Not all companies can issue commercial paper. The buyers of commercial paper insist that the firms issuing commercial paper be of the highest-quality credit standing. Buying the paper of a firm in shaky financial position is not desirable, since it is difficult to compensate the investor for high risk by paying a high interest rate for a short period of time. The interest rate would have to be so shockingly high that both the investor and the issuer would back off the deal (in many states, the usury laws would preclude the issuance of the paper).

Trading on the Equity (Financial Leverage)

One of the classical reasons for debt (independent of the tax law) is the fact that debt is a fixed income security. Any return earned from investing the borrowed money, in excess of the fixed contractual obligation to pay the debtholders, goes to the residual owners (in the case of a corporation, these are the stockholders).

EXAMPLE 11.1

This example is simplified, but it illustrates what is meant by trading on the equity. Assume that an investment costing $100,000 promises an internal rate of return of .10 with equal returns of $40,211 per year for three years and that the stockholders want a return of .12 if financed 100 percent by equity. If the investment were to be financed entirely with the capital obtained from common stockholders, the conventional response would be to reject the investment. But suppose that an .08 debt can be obtained for 90 percent of the investment and that the debt is to be repaid by three equal payments of $34,923. The cash flows are

	0	1	2	3
Investment	− $100,000	$40,211	$40,211	$40,211
Debt	+ 90,000	− 34,923	− 34,923	− 34,923
Stockholders' equity	− $ 10,000	$ 5,288	$ 5,288	$ 5,288

The bottom line can be interpreted to be an expected return of 27 percent on stockholders' equity funds, and this return could seem to be acceptable to stockholders who previously wanted 12 percent. But the 12 percent required return assumed 100 percent equity financing, and if the cash flows from the investment are uncertain, the variability of the rate of return on equity investment also increases as the amount of debt used increases. The firm may therefore reject the investment, even with the 27 percent expected return on the stockholders' equity associated with high financial leverage because of excessive risk.

Cost of Debt Without Taxes

The cost of debt is defined as the yield (internal rate of return) of the stream of contractual cash flows associated with the debt from the viewpoint of the firm. At the time of issuance, the cost of debt is determined by the cash received and the contractual cash payments to be made over time until the debt is retired. We assume zero taxes.

If new debt costs .10, it is difficult to justify undertaking an investment that earns a return that is less than .10. The cost of new debt sets a minimum required return.

After the debt has been issued, the implicit cost of outstanding debt is determined by the cash required to retire the debt at that moment in time (either the market price or the price that the firm has to pay the holders of the debt) and the cash flows associated with continuing the debt until maturity. One reason to concern ourselves with the cost of outstanding debt is that this cost establishes a minimum opportunity cost for a firm's funds. Other investments with certain cash flows must promise higher returns to be acceptable. That is, the firm with outstanding debt always has the opportunity to retire that debt, and, since the rate of return on that "investment" is certain, it is a floor on acceptable rates of return from other uses of the cash. If old debt can be retired at a cost of .08, it would not be desirable to invest funds in certain investments that earn .06. If we allow uncertainty, it is possible (though not likely) to have desirable investments that earn less than the return associated with retiring debt.

We wish to compute the cost of B dollars (face value) of debt paying an interest rate of k per period (the amount of interest to be paid is kB) currently selling at a price of B_0. Letting k_i denote the implicit cost or the yield to maturity of the debt (the internal rate of return) and n denote the number of years until maturity, the cost of debt is defined as that rate of discount that equates the present value of the cash flows associated with the future debt payments to the current market value of the debt; that is, k_i is such that

$$B_0 = \sum_{t=1}^{n} \frac{kB}{(1 + k_i)^t} + \frac{B}{(1 + k_i)^n} \tag{11.1}$$

We are assuming a balloon payment debt (principal paid at maturity). As shown in Appendix 11.1, if $B_0 = B$, then $k_i = k$. If B_0 is not equal to B, equation (11.1) must be solved (usually by search) for k_i.

EXAMPLE 11.2

Let

$B_0 = \$951.99$
$k = .10$ per year
$B = \$1,000$
$n = 3$ years

Assume that interest is paid annually and that the debt will be retired at the end of three years. Using equation (11.1),

$$\$951.99 = \sum_{t=1}^{3} \frac{\$100}{(1 + k_i)^t} + \frac{\$1,000}{(1 + k_i)^3}$$

and solving for k_i by trial and error, we find that $k_i = .12$ satisfies this equation. Typical calculations would be

		Rates of Discount (sequential trials)					
		First Trial (.14)		Second Trial (.08)		Third Trial (.12)	
Period	Cash Flow	PV Factor	PV	PV Factor	PV	PV Factor	PV
1	$ 100	.8772	$ 87.72	.9259	$ 92.59	.8229	$ 89.29
2	100	.7695	76.95	.8573	85.73	.7972	79.72
3	1,100	.6750	742.50	.7938	873.18	.7118	782.98
		Present value =	$907.17		$1,051.50		$951.99

It is important to understand that at the time of issue an appropriate measure of the value of the liability associated with a debt issue is its market price, although other measures are also likely to be of interest (for example, the debt may have a call provision that allows the firm to repurchase debt for some specified price more than the market price). With the debt as given in Example 11.2, the total cash flows to be paid sum to $1,300. However, the liability is not the $1,300 of total cash outlays to be paid over the life of the bond, since those cash flows have a net present value less than $1,300 as long as the discount rate is positive. Nor is the liability equal to the face value of $1,000 if the obligations can be discharged now by paying the market price of $951.99 and retiring the bond. The liability is reasonably measured by the market price of $951.99. If the bond had sold to yield .08 instead of .12, its market price would be $1,051.50, and that would be a measure of the value of the liability arising from the contractual obligations of the bond.

Equation (11.1) describes a bond with a maturity of n years paying kB interest annually issued at a price of B_0. When interest is paid periodically, but the principal is only paid at maturity, we say that the bond has a balloon payment or that it is balloon payment debt. We can generalize this by not assuming a balloon payment debt and by making the debt payment C_t for the year t. We then have

$$B_0 = \sum_{t=1}^{n} \frac{C_t}{(1 + k_i)^t} \tag{11.2}$$

where C_t includes both principal and interest.

The k_i that satisfies equations (11.1) and (11.2) is also known as the yield to maturity of the debt in question. Care must be taken to define what is meant by the terms "internal rate of return" or "yield." It is clear from equations (11.1) and (11.2) that the yield to maturity is a discounted cash flow concept. By contrast, the yield data published daily on the bond page of *The Wall Street Journal* is a "current" cash yield, that is, annual interest payment divided by current price. Only in the rare case where the current bonds are selling at par will the current cash yield be equal to the yield to maturity. A bond with a 10 percent nominal interest rate due in the year 1995 would be described as 10s 95 and would be selling at more than par if the current market interest rate were less than .10. The bonds are quoted in tens of dollars; thus a quote of $77 translates to a $770 price per $1,000 bond and a quote of 61⅞ translates to $618.75.

Exhibit 11.2 depicts an extract of the bond listing for December 30, 1983. Note that APL's 10¾ percent nominal interest rate bonds due in the year 1997 (10¾s 97) are selling less than par—$760 per bond with par value of $1,000— that and the current yield of 14 percent is less than the yield to maturity. Also note that Alabama Power's 7¾s due in 2002 are selling well below par with a current yield of approximately 13 percent (77.50/618.75 = .13).

50 THE WALL STREET JOURNAL, Tuesday, January 3, 1984

CORPORATION BONDS
Volume, $24,080,000

Bonds	Cur Yld	Vol	High	Low	Close	Net Chg.
APL 10¾97	14.	5	76	76	76	+1⅛
Advst 9s08	cv	60	94¼	94	94¼	+ ⅝
AetnLf 8⅛07	12.	25	69⅛	69⅛	69⅛	+1¼
AlaBn 10.65s99t	11.	20	99⅝	99⅝	99⅝	+ ⅛
AlaP 9s2000	13.	14	70½	70½	70½	− ¾
AlaP 8½s01	13.	5	67⅞	67⅞	67⅞	+ ¾
AlaP 7¾s02	13.	10	61⅞	61⅞	61⅞	+ ¼
AlaP 8⅞s03	13.	20	69	68⅞	68⅞	− ⅝
AlaP 8¼s03	13.	15	64¼	64¼	64¼	− ⅛
AlaP 9¾s04	13.	25	74⅜	74¼	74⅜	+ ¼
AlaP 10⅞05	13.	12	83⅛	83⅛	83⅛	+1⅜
AlaP 10½05	13.	25	80¾	79⅜	79⅜	+ ⅜
AlaP 8⅞06	13.	5	70¾	70¾	70¾	+1¾
AlaP 15¼10	14.	69	109¾	109¼	109¾	+ ¼
AlaP 17⅜11	16.	43	110½	110	110⅜	− ⅝
AlaP 18¼89	17.	64	111	110½	110½	+ ½
AlskH 18⅜01	16.	22	112¾	111	112¾	+ ¾
Alexn 5½96	cv	1	66	66	66	.....
AllgWt 4s98	9.9	5	40¼	40¼	40¼	.....
AlldC 7⅞96	11.	10	69⅛	69⅛	69⅛	+1⅛
AlldC zr92	..	22	36¼	35½	35½	− ½
AlldC zr98s	..	36	18⅛	18⅛	18⅛	.....
AlldC zr2000s	..	8	16½	16½	16½	+ ¼
AlldC 6s88	7.8	3	76½	76½	76½	− ⅝
AlldC 6s90	8.5	3	70¾	70¾	70¾	+1¼
AlldPd 7s84	7.4	5	94 9-32	94 9-32	94 9-32	− ¼
AlldSt 9½07	cv	26	126	125½	126	− ¾
AlsCha 16s91	15.	15	105⅞	105½	105½	+ ⅛
Alcoa 6s92	8.9	7	67¾	67⅝	67⅝	− ⅛
Alcoa 7.45s96	11.	10	69	69	69	+ ¼
AMAX 8s86	8.8	5	91⅜	91⅜	91⅜	.....
AMAX 8½96	13.	8	68	68	68	+1½
AForP 5s30	14.	11	36¾	36¾	36¾	+ ¼
AFor 5s30r	14.	18	37	36¾	36¾	.....
AAirl 4¼92	7.9	10	54⅛	54⅛	54⅛	.....
AAirl 10s89	11.	10	91	91	91	−1⅞
ABrnd 5⅞92	8.6	1	68⅛	68⅛	68⅛	+ ⅛
ABrnd 8⅛85	8.4	47	97⅝	97¼	97¼	.....
ABrnd 11⅛89	11.	16	97⅝	97¼	97¼	− ½
ACan 3¾88r	5.6	1	67⅜	67⅜	67⅜	.....
ACan 6s97	11.	5	54⅜	54⅜	54⅜	.....
ACan 7¾s01	12.	5	63½	63½	63½	.....
ACan 9¼84	9.3	10	99⅜	99⅜	99⅜	− ⅛
ACan 13¼93	13.	26	100¼	100	100¼	+ ¼
AExC 8½s86	9.1	35	94	93⅞	93⅞	− ¼
AExC 7.7s87	8.6	10	89⅝	89½	89½	.....
AHoist 5½93	cv	36	74½	74	74½	− ½
AInvt 8¾s89	12.	18	76	76	76	+1⅛
AmMed 9½01	cv	58	111	110½	110¾	− ¼
AmMed 8¼08	..	10	85⅝	85½	85⅝	− ⅛
AmMot 6s88	cv	31	92	91	91	− ½

New York Exchange Bonds

Friday, December 30, 1983

Total Volume $24,250,000

SALES SINCE JANUARY 1

1983	1982	1981
$7,572,315,000	$7,155,443,000	$5,733,071,000

	Domestic Fri.	Domestic Thu.	All Issues Fri.	All Issues Thu.
Issues traded	978	1052	983	1059
Advances	390	480	391	481
Declines	356	338	358	340
Unchanged	232	234	234	238
New highs	10	13	10	13
New lows	19	32	19	32

Dow Jones Bond Averages

−1981− High	−1981− Low	−1982− High	−1982− Low	−1983− High	−1983− Low		---Friday--- −1983−		−1982−		−1982−
65.78	54.99	71.52	55.67	77.84	69.35	20 Bonds	69.47	− .28	70.54	− .11	Closed
66.18	53.61	72.71	53.80	78.88	65.76	10 Utilities	65.93	− .54	69.86	− .22	Clos[illegible]
66.15	56.32	71.23	57.36	77.13	71.51	10 Industrial	73.02	− .01	71.22	− .01	Clos

Bonds	Cur Yld	Vol	High	Low	Close	Net Chg.
Boeing 8⅞06	cv	49	123	122	123	.....
BosE 9¼07	13.	1	68⅝	68⅝	68⅝	− ⅞
BrkUn 9⅛95	12.	9	78⅛	78⅛	78⅛	+ ⅝
BrkUn 9¾85	10.	5	97⅛	97⅛	97⅛	.....
BurlInd 11¼90	12.	10	95¾	95¾	95¾	− ⅛
BurNo 8.6s99	12.	1	73¼	73¼	73¼	.....
Burro 13½91	13.	1	105⅜	105⅜	105⅜	+ ⅞
Butte 10¼97	16.	47	66	65⅝	65⅝	−1⅜
CIGNA 8s07	cv	92	98	96½	96½	−1¼
Caesr 12½90	13.	7	96⅝	96⅝	96⅝	.....
Caesr 11¼97	13.	15	84⅛	84⅛	84⅛	− ⅛
CPc4s perp	11.	10	35¾	35¾	35¾	−1¼
CatTr 5½00	cv	5	100½	100½	100½	− ¼
Ceco 4.75s88	cv	26	96	96	96	−4
Celanse 4s90	cv	10	80	80	80	.....
Celanse 11⅞05	13.	10	92	92	92	+1
Celanse 9¾06	cv	21	109½	108	108	−2
Cenco 5s96	cv	21	68	68	68	−1⅛
Cenco 4¾97	cv	2	46⅝	46⅝	46⅝	+ ½
Centel 8.1s96	11.	3	71¾	71¾	71¾	+ ⅞
CtrlTel 8s96	11.	10	70½	70½	70½	− ⅜
Cent 7.85s97	12.	20	63¼	63¼	63¼	.....
CATS zr88	..	1	63	63	63	+ ⅛

Bonds	Cur Yld	Vol	High	Low	Close	Net Chg.
ColuG 9s94	11.	7	80⅝	80⅛	80⅛	− ⅛
ColuG 8¾95	11.	9	76⅞	76⅞	76⅞	− ⅛
ColuG 9⅛95	12.	6	78⅛	78⅛	78⅛	+1
ColuG 8⅜96	11.	5	73⅛	73⅛	73⅛	+ ½
ColuG 8¼96	11.	10	73⅜	73⅜	73⅜	.....
ColuG 7½97M	11.	1	66⅛	66⅛	66⅛	−1⅝
ColuG 7½97J	11.	3	69	69	69	+ ⅞
ColuG 9⅞99	13.	5	78½	78½	78½	−1⅞
ColuG 11¾99	13.	5	91¼	91¼	91¼	+ ¼
ColuG 12¾00	13.	15	100½	100	100	− ⅞
ColSO 4½87	5.9	15	76½	76½	76½	− ¼
ColSO 7⅝85	8.3	5	91⅝	91⅝	91⅝	+ ⅛
Cmdis 8s03	cv	231	74	73	74	+ ⅛
CmlCr 8¾91	11.	3	78	78	78	− ⅜
CmwE 7⅝03J	13.	12	60⅝	60⅝	60⅝	− ⅜
CmwE 8s03	13.	10	63⅜	63⅜	63⅜	− ¼
CmwE 9⅜04	13.	10	72	72	72	− ⅝
CmwE 8⅛07J	13.	30	63½	63	63	.....
CmwE 8⅛07D	13.	35	63¼	63¼	63¼	+ ¼
CmwE 8¼07	13.	55	64⅝	63⅞	64	.....
CmwE 9⅛08	13.	22	69⅝	69⅝	69⅝	+ ⅜
CmwE 12½86	12.	3	102	102	102	.....
CmwE 16¼89	15.	10	111¼	111¼	111¼	−1

EXHIBIT 11.2 **The *Wall Street Journal* New York Exchange Bond Listing (Source: Reprinted by permission of *The Wall Street Journal*, Dow Jones & Company, Inc., 1984. All rights reserved.)**

Floating Rate Loans

Bank loans may have fixed or floating interest rates. With fixed rate loans, the nominal interest rate is constant for the life of the loan; with floating rate loans, the interest rate is adjusted periodically depending on the level of some market-determined interest rate, such as the yield on treasury bills. Many banks have switched from fixed rate loans to floating rate loans. Banks tend to borrow money for short terms and loan it out for longer terms. They seek to profit by the spread between short- and long-term rates. When interest rates rise, banks that have made fixed rate loans may find that the money they are borrowing costs them more than the loan interest they are receiving on old fixed rate loans. Floating rate loans reduce this risk to the banks.

A corporate treasurer who has a floating rate loan has to allow for the possibility that the firm's interest cost will increase. The adjustment to the interest cost may be made daily, and the swings can be large.

Corporate Taxes and the After-Tax Cost of Debt

The introduction of a corporate tax into the analysis creates some problems in determining the cost of debt capital. Throughout, we assume that there is sufficient taxable income to take advantage of all tax savings arising from the deductibility of interest payments on the debt. We let t_c denote the corporate tax rate and assume, in the first case, that the debt issue is sold at par and that its current market value, B_0, is equal to par value, B. Appendix 11.2 shows that the after-tax cost of debt is $(1 - t_c)k$, where k is the contractual interest rate since $B_0 = B$.

EXAMPLE 11.3

$B = \$1,000 = B_0$

$k = .10 = k_i$

$n = 3$ years

$t_c = .40$

Assume that interest is paid annually and that the debt will be retired at the end of three years. The after-tax cost of debt is $(1 - t_c)k = (1 - .4).10 = .06$. This satisfies our definition of the cost of debt (after tax):

$$\sum_{t=1}^{3} \frac{\$100(1 - .4)}{(1 + .06)^t} + \frac{\$1,000}{(1 + .06)^3} = \$1,000 \tag{11.2}$$

There are two other situations that could be considered. One is where the existing issue, originally sold at par, now has a market price of B_0 not equal to the par value, B. As noted earlier, the cost of debt is an opportunity cost, the cost of continuing the debt rather than retiring it. In this situation, if the debt is retired, an ordinary gain (loss) of $B - B_0$ will be incurred and result in an increase (decrease) in taxes of $(B - B_0)t_c$. Hence, the net dollar cost of retirement is the market price plus the tax liability, $B_0 + (B - B_0)t_c$, and $(1 - t_c)k$ is no longer the after-tax cost of keeping the present debt outstanding.

A special case is where there is a new or existing issue, originally not sold at par. If the issue was originally sold at a discount, the difference between par and the issue price is accumulated over the life of the bond and treated as an interest expense for tax purposes, so that the total expenses deducted for tax purposes in each period are larger than the interest payments of that period. If sold at a premium, the amortized premium is treated as a return of capital. The expense deducted for taxes will then be less than the interest payments. As long as the interest expense for taxes is equal to the yield to maturity times the book value, the cost of the debt is $(1 - t_c)k_i$, where k_i is the yield to maturity. If the current market price is different from the book value, the effective cost of keeping the present debt outstanding will be different from $(1 - t_c)k_i$. The desirability of keeping the debt outstanding can be evaluated using the after-tax interest cost of issuing new debt.

The cost of continuing existing debt is unlikely to be equal to the cost of new debt for four reasons. First, if the current debt is selling at some price other than par, tax considerations associated with retirement are not present with new debt. Second, a new debt issue may have a different maturity date and thus may sell at a different yield. Third, the new debt may have a different payment priority or some other different economic characteristic. Fourth, there will be flotation costs with the new debt that will increase the effective cost of the debt.

The Level and Term Structure
of Interest Rates

The cost of debt for a particular firm depends (among other things) upon the overall level of interest rates that prevail in the economy at the time of cost determination, the maturity of the debt, and the default risk perceived by investors to be inherent in the debt obligations of the firm. In this section, we focus on the level and term structure of interest rates. In the next section, we examine default risk factors.

To focus on the level and term structure of interest rates, it is necessary to examine bonds that have no default risk. U.S. government bonds meet this test and, because of the importance of this data to the financial market, *The Wall Street Journal* reports the yields to maturity of most federal government securities daily. Bonds are quoted in tens of dollars and the decimals represent thirty-seconds. Hence, a bid price of 97.18 translates to $97\frac{18}{32} \times 10 = \$975.62$ per $1,000 par value, while a bid price of 97.8, is $97\frac{8}{32} \times 10 = \$972.50$.

THE WALL STREET JOURNAL
Tuesday, January 3, 1984

Treasury Issues

* * *

Bonds, Notes & Bills

Friday, December 30, 1983

Mid-afternoon Over-the-Counter quotations supplied by the Federal Reserve Bank of New York City.

Decimals in bid-and-asked and bid changes represent 32nds; 101.1 means 101 1/32. a-Plus 1/64. b-Yield to call date. d-Minus 1/64. n-Treasury notes.

Rate	Mat.	Date	Bid	Asked	Bid Chg.	Yld.
10½s,	1983	Dec n	99.30	100.2		0.00
13s,	1983	Dec n	99.30	100.2		0.00
15s,	1984	Jan n	100.14	100.18	– .1	6.85
7¼s,	1984	Feb n	99.22	99.26		8.67
15⅛s,	1984	Feb n	100.27	100.31	– .1	8.31
14⅛s,	1984	Mar n	100.31	101.3	– .1	9.09
14¼s,	1984	Mar n	101.1	101.5	– .1	8.95
13⅞s,	1984	Apr n	101.9	101.13	– .1	9.14
9¼s,	1984	May n	99.26	99.30		9.31
13¼s,	1984	May n	101.7	101.11	– .1	9.26
13¾s,	1984	May n	101.18	101.22		9.30
15¾s,	1984	May n	102.7	102.11	– .1	8.89
8⅞s,	1984	Jun n	99.18	99.22		9.53
14⅜s,	1984	Jun n	102.3	102.7	– .1	9.61
13⅛s,	1984	Jul	101.24	101.28		9.69
6⅜s,	1984	Aug	97.26	98.26		8.39
7¼s,	1984	Aug n	98.13	98.17	+ .1	9.77
11⅝s,	1984	Aug n	101	101.4		9.81
13¼s,	1984	Aug n	101.29	102.1	– .1	9.77
12⅛s,	1984	Sep n	101.14	101.18	– .1	9.89
9¾s,	1984	Oct	99.24	99.28		9.91
9⅞s,	1984	Nov n	99.25	99.29	– .1	9.99
14⅜s,	1984	Nov n	103.14	103.18	– .2	9.98
16s,	1984	Nov n	104.25	104.29	– .3	9.94
9⅜s,	1984	Dec n	99.10	99.14		9.99
14s,	1984	Dec n	103.19	103.27	– .1	9.83
9¼s,	1985	Jan n	99	99.4	– .1	10.13
8s,	1985	Feb n	97.28	98.4		9.81
9⅝s,	1985	Feb n	99.8	99.16		10.09
14⅝s,	1985	Feb n	104.14	104.22		10.08
9⅝s,	1985	Mar	99.4	99.12	+ .1	10.17
13⅜s,	1985	Mar n	103.10	103.18	– .1	10.24
9½s,	1985	Apr n	98.28	99	– .1	10.33
3¼s,	1985	May	92.11	93.11		8.52
4¼s,	1975-85	May	92.26	93.26		9.18
9⅞s,	1985	May n	99.6	99.10		10.41
10⅜s,	1985	May n	99.28	100.4		10.27
14⅛s,	1985	May n	104.15	104.23	– .1	10.33
14⅜s,	1985	May n	104.24	105	– .1	10.35
14s,	1985	Jun n	104.19	104.27	– .1	10.41
10s,	1985	Jun n	99.8	99.12		10.46
10⅝s,	1985	Jul n	99.31	100.7		10.47
8¼s,	1985	Aug n	96.29	97.5	+ .1	10.20
9⅝s,	1985	Aug n	98.18	98.26	– .2	10.44
10⅝s,	1985	Aug n	99.28	100	– .1	10.62
13⅛s,	1985	Aug n	103.17	103.21		10.60
10⅞s,	1985	Sep n	100.7	100.11		10.65
15⅞s,	1985	Sep n	107.28	108	– .2	10.72
10½s,	1985	Oct n	99.20	99.24		10.65
9¾s,	1985	Nov n	98.11	98.15		10.68
10½s,	1985	Nov n	99.17	99.21	– .1	10.70
11¾s,	1985	Nov n	101.19	101.27	– .1	10.63
10⅞s,	1985	Dec	100.2	100.4		10.80
14⅛s,	1985	Dec n	105.25	106.1		10.68
13½s,	1986	Feb n	104.24	105		10.80
9⅞s,	1986	Feb n	98.4	98.12		10.82
14s,	1986	Mar n	105.27	105.31	– .1	10.93
7⅞s,	1986	May n	93.24	94	– .2	10.82
9⅜s,	1986	May n	96.25	96.29		10.90
13¾s,	1986	May n	105.19	105.27	– .1	10.89
14⅞s,	1986	Jun n	108.8	108.12	– .1	10.94
8s,	1986	Aug n	93.10	93.18	– .1	10.90
11⅜s,	1986	Aug n	100.26	100.30		10.95
12¼s,	1986	Sep n	102.23	102.27	– .1	11.02
6⅛s,	1986	Nov	89.12	90.12		10.08
11s,	1986	Nov n	99.26	99.30	– .2	11.03
13⅞s,	1986	Nov n	106.21	106.29	– .2	11.00
16⅛s,	1986	Nov n	112.1	112.9	– .2	11.01
10s,	1986	Dec n	97.14	97.18	– .1	10.98
9s,	1987	Feb n	94.12	94.20	– .2	11.08
12¾s,	1987	Feb n	103.30	104.6	– .1	11.12
10¼s,	1987	Mar n	97.13	97.17	– .1	11.18
12s,	1987	May n	101.30	102.6	– .3	11.20
14s,	1987	May n	107.9	107.17	– .1	11.25
10½s,	1987	Jun n	97.24	97.28		11.25
13¾s,	1987	Aug n	106.25	107.1	– .1	11.33
11⅛s,	1987	Sep n	99.12	99.16	– .1	11.29
7⅝s,	1987	Nov n	89.2	89.10		11.10
12⅝s,	1987	Nov n	103.20	103.28	– .1	11.36
11¼s,	1987	Dec n	99.18	99.22	– .4	11.35
12⅜s,	1988	Jan n	102.29	103.5		11.38
10⅛s,	1988	Feb n	95.24	96	+ .1	11.37
13¼s,	1988	Apr n	105.25	106.1	+ .1	11.43
8¼s,	1988	May n	89.13	89.21	– .1	11.32
9⅞s,	1988	May n	94.17	94.21	– .1	11.47
14s,	1988	Jul n	108.14	108.22	– .2	11.49
10½s,	1988	Aug n	96.11	96.15	– .1	11.51
15⅜s,	1988	Oct n	113.22	113.30	– .1	11.51
8¾s,	1988	Nov n	90.3	90.11	– .1	11.39
11¾s,	1988	Nov n	100.19	100.23	– .2	11.56
14⅝s,	1989	Jan n	111.9	111.17	– .1	11.54
11⅜s,	1989	Feb n	99.7	99.11	– .3	11.55
14⅜s,	1989	Apr n	110.15	110.23	– .2	11.61
9¼s,	1989	May n	91.5	91.13	– .2	11.44
14½s,	1989	Jul n	111.9	111.17	– .1	11.62
11⅞s,	1989	Oct n	100.29	101.1	– .2	11.63
10¾s,	1989	Nov n	96.15	96.23	– .1	11.54
10½s,	1990	Jan n	94.24	95.5	– .8	11.64
3½s,	1990	Feb	89.30	90.30	– .2	5.25
10½s,	1990	Apr n	94.25	95.1		11.64
8¼s,	1990	May	86.3	86.19	– .1	11.26
10¾s,	1990	Jul n	95.17	95.21	– .2	11.72
10¾s,	1990	Aug n	95.18	95.26	– .2	11.68
11½s,	1990	Oct n	98.29	99.1	– .3	11.72
13s,	1990	Nov n	105.16	105.24	– .2	11.76
11¾s,	1991	Jan n	99.30	100.1		11.74
14½s,	1991	May n	112.24	113	– .3	11.81
14⅞s,	1991	Aug n	114.24	115	– .3	11.83
14¼s,	1991	Nov n	111.26	112.2	– .1	11.87
14⅝s,	1992	Feb n	113.25	114.1	– .7	11.89
13¾s,	1992	May n	109.19	109.27	– .3	11.87
4¼s,	1987-92	Aug	89.23	90.23	– .3	5.63
7¼s,	1992	Aug	77.1	77.17	– .2	11.42
10½s,	1992	Nov n	93.1	93.9	– .3	11.74
4s,	1988-93	Feb	89.24	90.24	– .3	5.30

EXHIBIT 11.3 **(Source: Reprinted by permission of *The Wall Street Journal,* Dow Jones & Company, Inc., 1984. All rights reserved.)**

The data for Friday, December 30, 1983, are reproduced in Exhibit 11.3. The bid price of 97.26 on the 6⅜% Treasury notes due in August 1984 translates to $97\frac{26}{32} \times 10 = \$978.125$ per $1,000 par value.

To determine the relationship between maturity and interest rate, we can plot this relationship. The curve fitted to the data points is called the yield to maturity curve. A security maturing in one year has a yield of .10, and a security maturing in three years has a yield of .12.

Figure 11.1 depicts what is thought to be the "normal" shape of the yield to maturity curve, that is, upward sloping to the right. This relationship reflects the basic biases of borrowers and lenders: borrowers prefer the maximum time before repaying and therefore are willing to pay a premium for longer maturities; lenders, with uncertain cash needs, prefer shorter-term securities to minimize the impact of interest rate changes on the value of their bonds, in case they must be sold to meet a cash need at a time when the general level of interest rates has risen. Investors, therefore, require a premium to be attached to longer-term securities. This factor is called liquidity preference.

Liquidity preferences, inflation expectations, and other supply and demand factors for securities of various maturities all interact to produce a given term structure. It is possible for these factors to be such that the resultant yield curve is "humped" or downward sloping. For example, the yield curve in the fall of 1978 was humped, probably because of the relatively low interest rates

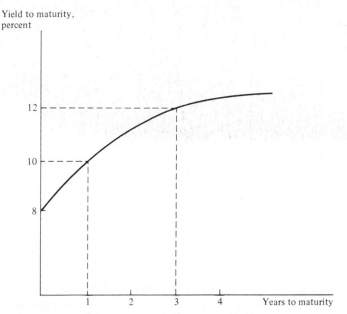

FIGURE 11.1   Term Structure of Interest Rates

in the short-term market and the expected high rates of inflation in the inter-mediate term but lower inflation rates in the long term.

To illustrate why a humped yield curve occurs, assume that the forecasted one period rates are

$$r_1 = .08 \text{ (at time 0)}$$

$$r_2 = .20 \text{ (at time 1)}$$

$$r_3 = .06 \text{ (at time 2)}$$

A person investing $100 at time 0 will have $108 at time 1, $108(1.20) = $129.60 at time 2, and 129.60(1.06) = $137.38 at time 3.

The average annual return earned will be .08 on a one-year security ($R_1 = 1.08 - 1$); .138 on a two-year security ($R_2 = (1.296)^{1/2} - 1$); and .112 on a three-year security ($R_3 = (1.37376)^{1/3} - 1$).

The nth-period return R_N is

$$R_N = [(1 + r_1)(1 + r_2) \cdots (1 + r_n)]^{1/n} - 1 \tag{11.3}$$

where r_i is the forecasted one-period rates for the ith period.

Note that the one-period security yields only .08, a two-period security yields .138, but then the three-period security yields only .112. To simplify the calculations, we are assuming single-payment types of securities.

Factors Affecting the Cost of Debt

The cost of debt is affected by the amount of risk associated with a particular issue as well as the overall level of interest rates. Among the factors affecting the risk of a particular issue are

1. The amount of operating and financial leverage, the financial position (liquidity), and the operating characteristics of the firm (business risk).
2. The relative size of debt payments and expected cash flows and other coverage ratios.
3. The longevity of the debt. Fixed or variable interest rates.
4. The amount of debt that is senior or can be senior (is the debt subor-dinate or can it be subordinated to future debt?).
5. The call and sinking fund provisions (terms for retiring the debt).
6. The asset security directly associated with the debt (does the debt have a mortgage on specific property?). Is the debt insured?

7. The safeguards against arbitrary action (such as a dividend payment in excess of that justified by financial position) by management that would harm the position of the debtholders.

8. The special provisions that make the debt part common stock (for example, detachable common stock warrants and conversion into common stock). A warrant allows the purchase of common stock at a given "exercise" price.

Bonds that are convertible into common stock or that have detachable warrants issued with them will be issued for yields that are less than bonds without such features, because of the value of the conversion privilege or warrants. The differential between the yields will depend on the characteristics of the conversion privilege or the warrants.

All the forgoing factors are evaluated by investors and also by experts who attempt to place a rating on bonds. The two major bond rating firms are Moody's Investor Service and Standard & Poor's Corporation. Standard & Poor's rating symbols for bonds are

AAA   prime securities (the highest quality)
AA   high grade
A   upper-medium grade
BBB   medium grade

BBB is the lowest "investment-grade" security rating. The equivalent grade used by Moody's Investor Service is Baa. Bonds graded below BBB (or Baa) are speculative with considerable risk of default over the life of the bond.

Although few firms default on their debt obligations, there are enough examples of default that cause investors to be wary. Some famous examples of default are Braniff Airlines, Penn Central Railroad, W. T. Grant, and Equity Funding. These are a few among the major well-known corporations that have gone bankrupt and only paid back to their debt investors a fraction of their investment. These rare occurrences are sufficient to make investors wary of lower-rated securities, especially in times of economic recession.

The spread of yields between rating groups is not constant over time. It tends to narrow in periods of economic prosperity and widen in times of recession. One finds the spread between a AAA and a Baa corporate security to be in excess of 100 basis points (1 percent) as in 1975 and as low as 50 basis points (as in 1977). The differentials between AAA and AA, and so on, are, of course, much smaller. It is generally true that the higher the bond rating, the lower the cost of debt. However, the interest savings from maintaining a higher bond rating by severely limiting the use of debt relative to equity financing or forgoing real investments may not be worth the cost of the lost opportunities. A very conservative financial structure leading to a AAA rating is not necessarily the best financial structure.

Basis Points

If one bond has a yield to maturity of 11.56 percent and a second bond has a yield to maturity of 12.716 percent, we can say that the second bond has a 1.156 percent higher yield. But this might be confusing since it can be said that the second bond has a 10 percent higher yield (that is, $12.716/11.56 = 1.10$). To remove the confusion, a bond expert would say that the second bond's yield is 115.6 basis points larger. One hundred basis points is equal to one percentage point of yield.

If the second bond had a yield of 11.89 percent, it would be 33 basis points larger than the bond with a 11.56 percent yield. The basis point terminology is very helpful in reducing confusion in talking about bond yields.

Semiannual Interest

In the United States most bonds pay interest semiannually. This creates a computational problem, since there is an effective semiannual interest rate and two annual interest rates, a nominal and an effective rate.

EXAMPLE 11.4

Assume that a $1,000 bond paying $200 interest (.20 per year) matures in one year. It pays $100 interest every six months. The bond is selling at par.

Using bond yield tables or the conventional method of calculation, we find that the annual yield of this bond is said to be .20. But this is a nominal return, not an effective interest rate. Using .10 as the effective semiannual interest rate, we have

$$\$100 \times (1.10)^{-1} = \$90.91$$
$$\$1,100 \times (1.10)^{-2} = \underline{\$909.09}$$
$$\text{present value} = \$1,000.00$$

The annual effective interest rate is

$$r = (1 + j)^2 - 1 = (1.10)^2 - 1 = .21$$

Using the annual effective interest rate to compute the present value, we have

$$\$100 \times (1.21)^{-1/2} = \$ \quad 90.91$$
$$\$1,100 \times (1.21)^{-1} = \underline{\$ \quad 909.09}$$
$$\text{present value} = \$1,000,00$$

The effective interest rates are .10 compounded every six months, or 21 compounded every year. To describe the return as being two times .10 or .20 is to understate the effective return being earned.

Consider a bond selling for $1,000 and paying $1,200 at time 1. This bond has a .20 yield to maturity. If instead of receiving $1,200 at time 1, the firm receives $100 at six months and $1,100 at one year, the effective return for the bond paying interest semiannually must logically be larger than .20. It is .21. For different nominal annual interest rates, we would have

Annual Nominal Interest Rate	Effective Semiannual Yield	Effective Annual Yield	Understatement of Effective Yield
.08	.04	.0816	.0016
.10	.05	.1025	.0025
.12	.06	.1236	.0036
.14	.07	.1449	.0049
.16	.08	.1664	.0064
.18	.09	.1881	.0081
.20	.10	.210	.0100

The use of the annual nominal interest rate understates the effective yield by 16 basis points if the annual nominal rate is .08 and by 100 basis points if the annual nominal rate is .20.

Serial Bonds

A bond issue may be composed of serial bonds where the bonds have different maturity dates. The advantage of this type of bond issue to the corporation is that serial bonds come due through time, this spreads the payments out and reduces the balloon payment that would otherwise be required at maturity. The bonds are to be retired on specified dates with the different dates of maturity being indicated on the bond. The disadvantage of serial bonds to the corporation is that they tend to reduce the duration (average life) of the debt, and this might result in the company repaying debt in periods when it has need for cash. Repayment occurs with any debt that is not a perpetuity, but the longer the time to repay, the more flexibility the company has in planning its cash needs.

It is possible for corporations to issue perpetual bonds (but currently it is likely that the Internal Revenue Service would not consider such securities to be debt). With a conventional finite-life bond, a corporation repays the debt coming due with funds from operations, with replacement debt (turn over the present debt), issues common stock, changes dividend policy, sells assets, or is willing to contract operations to reduce the need for capital.

Sinking Funds

A bond issue may contain a sinking fund provision. In conformance with this provision, funds are given to a trustee who invests them for future debt retirement. A sinking fund provision, like the serial bond characteristic, tends to reduce the duration of the debt if the provision requires that the corporation make a payment to the trustee of the bond issue so that outstanding bonds may be purchased either from the market or be called by the corporation (in which case, a call premium is frequently paid). The amount contributed to the sinking fund may be a fixed amount or a function of the earnings of the corporation. The advantage of having the sinking fund amount variable with earnings is that the provision does not then act as a factor contributing to the threat of the firm's bankruptcy during a bad year. A sinking fund reduces the effective duration of the available capital, and this feature tends to be attractive to investors because it reduces risk and thus may reduce the explicit interest cost to the firm.

A .08 bond issued at par will cost .08 with or without sinking fund payments if the bond is retired at a cost equal to par. If the bond is retired before maturity at a price different from par, the effective cost will differ from .08, but this is because of changing market interest rates and the retirement of the debt before maturity rather than because of the sinking fund per se.

EXAMPLE 11.5 ——————————————————————————————

Assume the issuance of two $1,000 bonds that promise to pay .08 and mature in two periods. The cash flows and the cost of debt would be

	0	1	2	Cost	
Interest		− $160	− $ 160		
Principal	+ $2,000		− 2,000		
Total	+ $2,000	− $160	− $2,160	.08	Yield of the net cash flows

Now assume that a $1,000 sinking fund payment is made at time 1 and that one of the bonds is repurchased at a cost of $1,000. The cash flows and the cost of the debt would be

	0	1	2	Cost
Interest		− $ 160	− $ 80	
Principal	+ $2,000	− 1,000	− 1,000	
Total	+ $2,000	− $1,160	− $1,080	.08 Yield of the net cash flows

The cost is again .08. If the bond was purchased in period 1 at a price different from $1,000, the .08 cost would change.

Protective Features

Bonds frequently contain restrictions on the actions of management in the areas of utilization of cash and issuance of more debt, especially with regard to issuing debt that is senior to the current debt. Restrictions on the use of cash and issuance of new debt are generally accomplished by a set of operating requirements, such as

1. Working capital must be at least a given amount, and the current or quick ratio must be in excess of some specified number.
2. Cash dividends must be limited in some manner (frequently a limit is set on the minimum amount of retained earnings).
3. Stock reacquisition (purchase by the corporation of its own shares) must be limited.
4. Capital expenditures and commitments to expend funds must be restricted.
5. New lease arrangements must be limited.

The objective of these features is to protect the interests of the debt holders by controlling the way that resources are used.

Debentures

Bonds are usually classified as either mortgage bonds or debentures. Mortgage bonds are backed by the security of specifically identified assets of the firm. If the firm goes into bankruptcy, the holders of the bond have first claim on those specific assets of the firm. Debentures are backed by the overall credit and debt-paying capability of the firm rather than by specific assets.

A debenture is subordinated if other debentures have payment priority if the firm has financial difficulties.

Other Types of Bonds

Characteristics of bonds are continuously changing to accommodate the needs of investors and borrowers. With high rates of inflation, lenders like bonds whose interest rates reflect the changes in the price level. A few bonds have been indexed to the price of commodities such as oil, silver, or gold.

At the other extreme, some corporations want to issue a bond that does not jeopardize the firm's continuity of existence. An "income bond" is not obligated to pay interest unless income is at least as large as the interest payments. This reduces the threat of bankruptcy arising from not paying interest.

Bonds can also be made convertible into stock in order to make them more attractive to investors (see Chapter 25). Although bells and whistles can be added to a bond, it must be remembered that a bond is no better than the company that issued the security.

Duration of Debt

Consider two companies with identical expected cash flows for the next year and both having debt/equity ratios of 40 percent. This information may lead us to believe that there is equal risk in granting a dollar of credit to either, but suppose that we now inform you that the former company has all its debt due in 1 year while the latter has no debt due for 10 years. Now, all other things being equal, the former is more risky, since its cash needs are greater in the first year. One measure of the immediacy of debt repayment is the average duration of the debt.

We define the duration of a series of debt payments to be the weighted average life of the cash flows, where the weights are the present values of the cash flows. Equation (11.4) is the mathematical expression for calculating duration, d:

$$ d = \frac{\sum_{t=1}^{n} t C_t (1 + k)^{-t}}{V} \tag{11.4} $$

where $C_t(1 + k)^{-t}$ is the present value of the debt cash flows of time t, V is the present value of all debt flows, and n is the time until maturity of the debt obligation in question. The duration of a single-payment debt coming due in 20 years is 20 years. The duration of a 2-year $1,000 bond paying $100 a year interest for 2 years, issued at par (the current market interest rate is 10 percent), is

$$d = \frac{1 \times \$100(1.10)^{-1} + 2 \times \$1,100(1.10)^{-2}}{\$1,000}$$

$$= \frac{\$90.91 + \$1,818.12}{\$1,000} = 1.91$$

(11.4)

The duration (or average life) of a conventional interest-paying bond is always less than its maturity. If the bond is a discount bond (such as a zero-coupon bond), the duration is equal to its maturity. A zero-coupon or discount bond is a bond that only promises a single payment at maturity. Discount bonds have no explicit interest payment. The difference between their purchase price and maturity (face) value is the interest earned.

In addition to measuring the average life of the debt, duration measures are useful for judging the sensitivity of the market value of a debt (or investment) to changes in prevailing interest rates. It can be shown, for example, that if two equal debts have the same duration, then a small change in the entire structure of interest rates will result in the same change in market values of the two debts.

It is frequently said that the longer the maturity, the more risk there is due to interest rate fluctuations. The value of a 20-year bond will change more than a 2-year bond for a given interest rate change. It is more accurate to say that the larger the duration, the more the value will change. The value change for small discrete changes in the interest rate is equal to $-d\Delta kV(1 + k)^{-1}$, where d is the duration, Δk is the change in the interest rate k, and V is the present value of the debt.

The Issue of Bonds

The pricing of bond issues poses an interesting set of problems. A corporation may have many different issues of bonds outstanding; but ordinarily each issue is unique in one or more respects, for example, the amount of collateral, coupon rate, maturity, sinking fund provisions, etc. To the extent that each issue is unique, the problems of pricing bonds are analogous to the problems of pricing a first public offering of stock. But while each bond issue is to some extent unique, there are other bonds that are similar in a great many ways and already have a public market. The comparable debt issues can be used as guides to pricing.

In some instances, the comparable issues will be other bonds issued by the same issuer. In other instances, they may be bonds that have been previously sold by other issuers whose credit standing, size, and other significant characteristics are very similar.

For most industrial corporations, the process of preparing for a public offering of bonds is similar to the process of preparing for a public offering of stock. An investment banker is chosen to help originate the issue and to manage its distribution; an underwriting syndicate is formed and the bonds are sold to the underwriters who subsequently resell them to final investors.

By federal law, public utility holding companies are required to sell bonds on the basis of competitive bids. Under special conditions, an exemption from this requirement can be obtained from the Securities and Exchange Commission (SEC). In this case, the corporation or a specially retained financial advisor will help to prepare the bond issue and advertise it among potential purchasers. Sealed bids are requested. Investment bankers who are interested in the issue may get together and form underwriting syndicates, each of which prepares a bid. The utility will sell its bonds to whichever syndicate has prepared the highest bid.

Competitive bidding is also used to sell most long-term bonds issued by states and local governments. Since the mide-1930s commercial banks have been prohibited from acting as underwriters for corporate bonds. However, they are allowed to participate as underwriters in "full faith and credit" bonds issued by state and local governments.

The Bond Refunding Decision

This section is concerned with the question of whether or not to refund an outstanding long-term debt (that is callable) now, assuming that refunding in the future will be less desirable than refunding now (implicitly, the possibility of future refunding is not considered). The primary objective is to reconcile different approaches to making this type of decision and to illustrate a procedure that resolves the question of which rate of discount to use in making the refunding decision. It will also be shown that alternative investment opportunities available to the firm are not relevant to its bond refunding decision.

Two alternative approaches to the bond refunding decision to be compared are

1. Assume that the liabilities before and after refunding are to be kept at the same present value.

2. Assume that the maturity amounts of the debt before and after refunding are the same (if the same par value bond is used, the same number of bonds will be issued as are currently outstanding).

Finally, it will be shown that the decision whether or not to call the present debt is independent of the amount of debt issued in the refunding process.

In recent years, corporations have been issuing debt with higher than normal historical interest rates. If the long-term interest rates were to decrease to levels close to historical averages, many firms would be faced with decisions of whether or not to refund outstanding callable long-term debt.

The bond refunding decision is one of the few business decisions for which the cash flows are known with reasonable certainty; nevertheless, it is a decision about which there has been a great deal of confusion, and there have been misleading recommendations.

Bond refunding is actually a combination of two decisions that can be separated in some circumstances. The first is the decision to retire the outstanding bonds before their normal maturity by exercising the call option. The second is the decision to sell new bonds. To justify a bond refunding, two separate determinations should be made: first, that it is desirable to call the existing debt; second, that it is desirable to issue new debt. If both decisions are made, there still remain the questions of how much new debt to issue, for what maturity, and with what other characteristics (callable, convertible, etc.). Sometimes one or the other of the two decisions may be desirable, but not both. Firms frequently issue new bonds without recalling existing debt (there may be none). It is also possible for a firm to call bonds without refunding if sufficient cash is on hand or can be raised in some other manner, for example by selling some assets.

We first consider the decision to retire the outstanding bonds by calling them. The first step is to compute the present value of the cash flows associated with calling the existing bond. Callable bonds usually provide that the issuer may call the bonds by paying the book value and a call premium. The call premium is usually large when the bonds are first issued and gradually approaches zero. Denote the book value by B_0 and the call premium and any additional costs associated with retiring the existing bonds by C_0. Then the cash outlay associated with calling the existing bonds is $(B_0 + C_0)$. The present value of the benefits from calling the bonds will be equal to the present value of the future interest and principal payments that will not be paid if the bonds are retired now. These should be discounted at the current cost of debt. If V_c represents the present value of these savings and B represents the present value of the outstanding bonds, then the net present value from calling the outstanding bonds now is

$$V_c = B - (C_0 + B_0) \tag{11.5}$$

There are other alternatives, e.g., calling the bonds later, that should be considered. But these are beyond the scope of an introductory book. We consider only two alternatives: call the bonds now or wait until they mature. Under these assumptions the bonds should be called if the present value of their future payments is greater than the immediate cash outlay and the other costs associated with retiring them now.

Suppose Equation (11.5) indicates that retiring the existing bond issue is desirable, but no excess cash is available. We now consider the second decision, to issue new bonds. The new bonds have a par value of B_1, pay an annual interest rate of I_1 (the coupon rate is I_1/B_1) and have a maturity of n years. The present value of the new bonds, will be B^*, where

$$B^* = I_1 B(n, k) + B_1 (1 + k)^{-n}$$

and where $B(n, k)$ is the present value factor for an n period annuity. If there are costs of C_1 associated with issuing new bonds, the net present value achieved from issuing new bonds will be

$$V_1 = [B^* - I_1 B(n, k) + B_1 (1 + k)^{-n}] - C_1 \tag{11.6}$$

Since the term in square brackets will equal zero if the bonds are sold for their current present value, it follows that

$$V_1 = -C_1 \tag{11.7}$$

If there are any costs associated with issuing new bonds, the net present value of issuing them taken by itself will be negative. This makes sense. It doesn't pay to borrow money unless the firm has some uses for the money that are more profitable than earning the current interest rate on the funds borrowed.

In the present context an obvious use for the money may be to retire the existing bonds. If the firm does not have the available cash and, thus, must borrow in order to retire, then the two decisions are not separable. It will pay to borrow money to retire the existing bonds if the combined present value of the two actions is positive, that is, if

$$V = V_c + V_1 = (B - B_0) - (C_0 + C_1) > 0$$

or alternatively, if

$$B - B_0 > C \quad \text{or} \quad B > B_0 + C \tag{11.8}$$

where $C = C_0 + C_1$ is the sum of the call premium and transaction costs of retiring the old debt and issuing the new. In other words, the old debt should be retired, in this case, if the difference between the market value of the old bonds and their book value is greater than the call premium and the transaction costs associated with retiring the old debt and issuing new debt.

EXAMPLE 11.6 ————————————————————————————————

There is presently outstanding $100,000,000 of bonds coming due in 20 years paying 10 percent interest per year. The current interest rate is 7 percent. The call premium and transactions costs associated with refunding would be $5,000,000. Management wants to keep the present value of the debt constant. Assume a zero tax rate.

  Should the debt be replaced with 7 percent debt? Using 7 percent discount factors, we obtain

present value of $100,000,000 = .2585 × $100,000,000   = $ 25,850,000
present value of $10,000,000 per year = 10.594 × $10,000,000 = $105,950,000
present value of currently outstanding debt   = $131,800,000

$$
\begin{aligned}
B &= \$131{,}800{,}000 \ \text{(present value of outstanding debt)} \\
B_0 + C_0 &= \underline{105{,}000{,}000} \ \text{(cash outlays at retirement)} \\
V_c &= \$ \ 26{,}800{,}000 \ \text{(net present value of refunding)}
\end{aligned}
$$

The net benefit from refunding is $26,800,000.

  The net present value of the savings from refunding is independent of the amount of debt issued in the refunding process. Since the present value of the new debt is assumed to be equal to the cash proceeds arising from its issuance, this conclusion is reasonable. The amount of the debt to be issued depends on the needs of the firm. The decision to call the present debt depends on the present value of the outstanding debt and the cash outlays of calling that debt. The value of refunding does not depend on the amount of new debt issued.

  If the transaction costs are made to be a function of the new debt issued, then the answer would be more complex, since the problem then becomes one of determining the optimum size of debt issued with a given rate of utilization of cash.

The Maturity Date

We made the maturity date of the new debt equal to the maturity date of the old. This was convenient, since it enabled us to compute the interest savings without explaining what happens if the lives of two debts differ. However, just as the amount of debt issued does not affect the desirability of refunding, neither does the maturity date of the new issue. The refunding depends only on the present value of the old debt and the dollar outlays of retiring that debt. A lengthening of the maturity can be considered to be a plus factor in the analysis.

Computation of the Relevant Cash Flows

Errors have been made in analyzing the bond refunding decision by incorporating sunk costs in the analysis. For example, consider the bond issue expenses discount associated with the currently outstanding bonds. Except as they might affect the income tax computation, these costs and discounts are not relevant to the decision. The call premiums and call expenses, the issue costs of the new bonds, duplicate interest payments during the period of issue (taking into account the return earned by investing the excess funds in short-term securities), and the savings in interest resulting from the new issue are relevant factors. The cash flows should be on an after-tax basis.

The Choice of the Rate of Interest

The choice of the rate of interest to be used in discounting the future cash flows has been an issue for many years. There are essentially three choices:

1. The weighted average cost of the capital
2. The rate of interest on the new securities
3. The rate of interest on default-free securities

Consider a situation in which the possible interest saving associated with refunding is $100,000 a year and the life of the current bonds is 10 years. If we use a .20 weighted average cost of capital as the rate of discount, the present value of this saving is $419,247. If we use a .10 discount rate (the interest rate of the new issue), the present value of the saving is $614,457. If the cost of the refunding is $500,000, should the refunding be made? Using the interest rate on default-free securities would make the present value of the saving even larger than $614,457.

Many firms would reject the refunding using the argument that the funds can earn more elsewhere in the firm. However, the risks associated with the refunding are much less than with the normal investment (the cash outlays for incremental interest on the present debt are certain from the viewpoint of the corporation's treasurer). Also, after refunding if the firm issues the same present value of debt, it will have more cash. The firm is better off accepting the investment. An accept decision is indicated if we take only the time value of money into account and leave out the risk premium incorporated in the cost of capital.

Most important, we have shown that if the debt is refunded with the same present value of debt being issued, the amount of cash on hand will actually increase if the refunding is economically desirable. The use of the cost of debt to discount the cash flows is consistent with this economic analysis.

Timing

An important problem having to do with bond refunding has not been solved in this chapter.

Let us assume that the ABC Company has issued a .10 bond. After issue, the treasurer may compute the interest rate that is required to make refunding desirable (a break-even interest rate). Each moment of time requires a different break-even rate, since the bond is continuously approaching maturity. Fortunately, the changes in the break-even rate will be slight, and for practical purposes the same rate may be used for several time periods. The treasurer of the firm will watch the bond market, and when the market rate of interest for bonds of comparable firms (or for its own bonds) reaches the break-even rate of interest, the firm has its first decision. Let us assume the current interest rate is a shade below the break-even rate. Should the refunding take place? If we ignore possible future decreases in interest rates, the analysis would indicate that it should. However, a more complete analysis suggests that we should be interested in the question as to whether the interest rate will soon be going lower than the current rate. If the rate is expected to decrease, then maybe we should wait for the reduction.

Obviously, the refunding problem has become complex. We must know not only what the future interest rates will be, but also when the changes in rates will occur. The present value of the saving that will occur if we refund at a given interest rate will be a function of when the refunding takes place, which, in turn, will be a function of when the interest rate that triggers the refunding is encountered.

The Call Provision

A call provision enables the corporation to refund a bond. Most corporate bonds have provisions that allow the corporation to "call" or retire the bond before maturity. The call price is generally above the face or maturity value at the time that the bonds may be first called. (The time of first call tends to be some reasonably long period, such as five years, after issue.) Corporations attach call provisions to bonds so that if interest rates fall, the bonds can be replaced with cheaper debt. It is because of the presence of call provisions that bond refunding can lead to an economic gain for the issuer. However, the presence of a call provision on new debt increases the interest rate that must be promised in order to sell the debt.

Pros and Cons of Debt

The primary disadvantage of debt is that it increases risk, both the probability of bankruptcy and the variability of the earnings of the stockholders. A second disadvantage is that there are generally restrictions placed on managerial actions when debt is issued. Third, each issue of debt makes it more expensive and more difficult to issue more debt; thus management loses some flexibility with each debt issue.

The advantages of debt as a method of raising capital are many. The following items are by no means independent of each other, and some of the items listed may be questioned, since they may be accompanied by disadvantages that outweigh the advantages.

1. Trading on the equity (this implies that debt has a lower cost than stock equity).
2. Tax savings arising because of the deductibility of interest expense in computing taxable income.
3. Retention of ownership control by stockholders (no dilution of the stockholders' voting position).
4. Flexibility (after the need for the cash is over, the size of the firm is easily shrunk if debt is used to meet the temporary cash need).
5. Ease and quickness of obtaining the capital (especially valid if the firm has a line of credit or credit agreement with a bank).
6. Hedge interest rate changes (if the debt payment coincides with certain investment cash flows from assets such as marketable securities, a perfect hedge against interest rate changes may be arranged).
7. Timing; if it is not a good time to issue stock because the market value of the stock is currently less than the value estimated by management, and if management expects the stock's market value to increase in the near future, then debt may be a desirable short-run substitute for stock equity.
8. Lower risk (the total exposure of stockholders to the loss of capital) because the total amount of the stockholders' investment is less than it would have been if no debt had been issued. This is related to the retention of control (item 3), trading on the equity (item 1), and the limited liability characteristics of a corporation.

Tax Savings from Interest Deductibility

A major reason for issuing debt is the tax savings that arise from the deductibility of interest payments as an expense of doing business in the calculation of the tax liability. To determine the size of the tax savings arising from debt, the following notation will be used:

$\bar{X}$ = expected earnings before interest and taxes
k = interest rate on the debt
B = amount of debt outstanding (the amount of interest is kB)
t_c = corporate tax rate
$\bar{C}$ = expected after-tax cash flow from operations

We assume that the investment necessary to maintain the income is equal to the depreciation expense. If only common stock is used, the expected after-tax cash flow available from operations accruing to capital suppliers (all common stockholders) is

$$\bar{C} = \bar{X}(1 - t_c) \tag{11.9}$$

With B of debt being used, we have

$$\bar{C} = (\bar{X} - kB)(1 - t_c) + kB = \bar{X}(1 - t_c) + kt_c B \tag{11.10}$$

From a comparison of equations (11.10) and (11.9), we can see that each dollar of debt creates a tax savings of kt_c. Thus with B dollars of debt, the firm has $kt_c B$ dollars of tax savings it can pay capital suppliers over and above what it could pay if only common stock was employed. This is an annual savings.

EXAMPLE 11.7

Suppose that a firm needs $80,000,000 of financing to undertake an investment promising to return $10,000,000 per annum before tax. Debt can be issued at a cost of 10 percent and the corporate tax rate is 40 percent. With no debt,

$$\bar{C} = \bar{X}(1 - t_c) = \$10,000,000(.6) = \$6,000,000 \tag{11.9}$$

is the amount of cash from operations available to pay capital suppliers or reinvest in the firm. If, instead of being all equity financed, the firm issued $30,000,000 of debt paying .10, then

$$\bar{C} = \bar{X}(1 - t_c) + kt_c B = \$6,000,000 + (.10)(.4)(\$30,000,000)$$
$$= \$7,200,000 \tag{11.10}$$

The $3,000,000 annual interest payment saves $1,200,000 in taxes per year that would be paid in the absence of the debt. With the use of debt, $7,200,000 is available for payment to capital suppliers, whereas only $6,000,000 is available if common stock is used.

The Capital Asset Pricing Model and Leverage Effects

It is generally agreed that the substitution of debt for common stock makes the stockholders' position more risky, thus increasing the expected return that stockholders require to buy or hold any common stock. The amount of the increase may be measured using the capital asset pricing model.

The CAPM model implies that for any security j

$$\bar{r}_J = r_f + (\bar{r}_m - r_f)\beta_j \tag{11.11}$$

where

$\bar{r}_J$ = the required expected return for jth security

r_f = the return on a default-free security

$\bar{r}_m$ = the expected return from investing in the market portfolio

β_j = cov (r_j, r_m)/var (r_m) and is defined as the firm's beta measure

Equation (11.11) states that in equilibrium the expected return for security j is equal to the default-free return plus an adjustment for risk. The adjustment for risk consists of $\bar{r}_m - r_f$, the difference between the expected return from investing in the market and the return from a default-free security, multiplied by

$$\beta_j = \frac{\text{cov }(r_j, r_m)}{\text{var }(r_m)}$$

where the covariance of the security's return, r_j, and the market return, r_m, are the crucial elements.

To consider the effects of leverage on the required return, let

$\bar{r}_B$ = the required expected return if B debt is outstanding

S = the amount of common stock with zero debt and

S_B = the amount of common stock with B debt

β_B = the value of the common stock's beta with B of debt where as shown in Appendix 11.3.*

$$\beta_B = \frac{S}{S_B}\,\beta_j$$

The analog of equation (11.11) with B debt outstanding is

$$\bar{r}_B = r_f + (\bar{r}_m - r_f)\beta_B \tag{11.12}$$

Since $\beta_B = \dfrac{S}{S_B}\,\beta$
we can rewrite (11.12) as

$$\bar{r}_B = r_f + (\bar{r}_m - r_f)\frac{S}{S_B}\,\beta_j \tag{11.13}$$

EXAMPLE 11.8 ─────────────────────────────

r_f = .06
$\bar{r}_m$ = .10
S = \$10,000,000
β_j = 1.2

Using this information

$$\bar{r}_j = r_f + (\bar{r}_m - r_f)\beta_j$$

$$= .06 + (.10 - .06)1.2 = .06 + .048 = .108$$

Now assume that instead of using \$10,000,000 of common stock, the firm uses \$6,000,000 of zero-coupon debt and \$4,000,000 of common stock. Using equation (11.13),

$$\bar{r}_B = r_f + (\bar{r}_m - r_f)\frac{S}{S_B}\,\beta_j \tag{11.13}$$

$$= .06 + (.10 - .06)\frac{10}{4}(1.2) = .06 + .12 = .18$$

*Also, see R. S. Hamada, "Portfolio Analysis, Market Equilibrium and Corporate Finance," *Journal of Finance*, March 1969, pp. 11–30.

The addition of the debt increases the expected return required by investors from .108 to .18.

Equation (11.13) can be rewritten to show the operating risk and the financial risk:

$$\bar{r}_B = \underset{\substack{\text{Default-}\\\text{free}\\\text{return}}}{r_f} + \underset{\text{operating risk}}{(\bar{r}_m - r_f)\beta_j} + \underset{\text{financial risk}}{(\bar{r}_m - r_f)\frac{B}{S_B}\beta_j} \tag{11.14}$$

Since the financial risk is

$$(\bar{r}_m - r_f)\frac{B}{S_B}\beta_j$$

we see that the amount that the required return is increased is affected by the debt/equity ratio and the value of the firm's beta.

For the example we would have

$$\bar{r}_B = .06 + (.10 - .06)1.2 + (.10 - .06)\frac{6}{4}1.2 \tag{11.14}$$

$$= .06 + .048 + .072 = .18$$

Debt/Equity Swaps

In the early 1980s many firms refunded their debts even though interest rates had gone up from the date of issue. The vehicle for refunding was a swap of common stock for debt selling at a discount. For example, in 1982 Procter & Gamble swapped 200,000 shares of common stock for $25 million of debentures, Exxon swapped common stock for $515 million of debentures, and GM swapped 1.2 million shares for $140 million of debentures.

There were two primary motivations for these transactions. First, the refunding increased income. Exxon increased income $203 million by the transaction (the face value of the debt exceeded market value). Second, the gain was not taxed as income because of a peculiarity in the tax law. The law was changed in 1984.

Conclusions

This chapter has considered the factors that affect the cost of debt and how to measure the explicit cost of new and outstanding debt. Debt also has implicit costs, such as restricting the actions of management by covenants that aim to protect the debtholders. Debt also increases the uncertainty of the return on the stockholders' investment and thus tends to increase the cost of equity capital. On the other hand, debt tends to be low in explicit cost because of tax deductibility of interest, and by allowing the firm to "trade on its equity," it provides the chance for larger stockholder profits. Most important, debt is a source of capital that enables a corporation to undertake investments that it would not otherwise be able to undertake. On balance, there seems to be sufficient rationale for most firms to issue some debt.

A bond refunding decision arises when there are callable bonds outstanding and interest rates fall. It is interesting that the amount of debt to be issued and its maturity date do not affect the present value of net benefits. However, different amounts of debt will be outstanding and different amounts of cash will be received now, depending on these amounts of debt issue.

Review Problem 11.1

The ABC Company has $100,000,000 of callable 10 percent debt outstanding. (Each bond is callable at a price of $1,080.) The firm can issue new debt at a cost of 8 percent. The transaction costs would be $3,500,000 (this is in addition to the call premium). The debt matures in 10 years (balloon payment). The firm has investment possibilities that are expected to yield 15 percent, and it has been using a weighted average cost of capital of 12 percent to evaluate investments. There are zero taxes.

(a) Should the firm refund? Assume that management expects interest rates to remain at 8 percent for the near and distant future. Explain your answer.
(b) Would the amount of the new debt issue quantitatively affect your decision? Yes _____ ? No _____ ? Explain.
(c) Would the maturity date of the new issue quantitatively affect your decision? Yes _____ ? No _____ ? Explain.

Solution to Review Problem 11.1

(a)
$$\$100{,}000{,}000(1.08)^{-10} = \$100{,}000{,}000(.4632) = \$\ 46{,}320{,}000$$
$$\$10{,}000{,}000B(10,\ .08) = \$10{,}000{,}000(6.7101) = \underline{\$\ 67{,}101{,}000}$$

$$\$113{,}421{,}000$$

$$\$108{,}000{,}000 + \$3{,}500{,}000 = \underline{\$111{,}500{,}000}$$

$$\text{Value of refunding} = \$\ \ \ 1{,}921{,}000$$

or

$$= (\$10{,}000{,}000 - \$8{,}000{,}000)6.7101 - \$11{,}500{,}000$$
$$= \$13{,}420{,}000 - \$11{,}500{,}000 = \$1{,}920{,}000$$

(b) No. The decision is invariant to the size or duration of the new issue.
(c) No. The present value of the new debt will equal the amount received regardless of the maturity date of the new debt.

PROBLEMS

1. A 20-year bond is issued at a price of $1,091.25. It pays $100 per year interest and $1,000 at maturity.

    Determine the yield to maturity of the bond.

2. (Problem 1 continued) If the issue price had been $687.03, what would the yield to maturity of the bond have been?

3. With a corporate tax rate of .4, what is the after-tax cost at the time of issue of a 10 percent 20-year $1,000 bond paying $100 a year if the bond is issued at par? Use the after-tax cost to obtain the present value of the after-tax cash flows of the debt.

4. A company is considering a $1,000 one-period investment that yields .09. It has heard of the advantages of using debt and "trading on the equity."

    What is the necessary condition for the firm to employ the principle in this case? Illustrate "trading on the equity."

5. A firm has a 40 percent marginal tax rate.

    How much annual tax savings will arise from interest deductions if a $1,000 investment is financed by 8 percent bonds rather than equity?

6. Assume that a debt of $1,000 is supposed to be paid two years from date of issue. The contractual rate is .10 ($1,210 will be paid at maturity). There is an .8 probability of full payment and a .2 probability of payment of $1,000.

What is the expected yield of this debt? What is the internal rate of return of the expected cash flows?

7. Suppose that a firm with a debt indenture that calls for a sinking fund payment of $500 per $1,000 bond one year prior to maturity expects to purchase the bonds at par to satisfy the requirement.

   Show that if the contractual interest is 10 percent and the corporate tax rate is 40 percent, the sinking fund provision is not expected to alter the cost of the debt. Assume that the bonds are currently selling at par, that two years remain to maturity, and that sinking fund obligations will be met at the end of the year.

8. (Problem 7 continued) Assume that the tax rate is zero (for simplicity) but that the expected price the firm will have to pay to retire a $1,000 par value bond is $1,030 with the sinking fund proceeds.

   Determine the cost with a sinking fund provision if $1,000 of the bonds are purchased at time 1 at a cost of $1,030.

9. The duration of Company A's debt is much shorter than that of Company B. All other characteristics of the firms are equal. It has been argued that the firms have an equal amount of risk.

   Which firm do you consider to have more risk? Explain.

10. An advertisement in *The Wall Street Journal* contained the following statement:

    A MORTGAGE CERTIFICATE

    HAS A 30-YEAR MATURITY

    BUT IS NOT A 30-YEAR INVESTMENT

    Why is the certificate described not a 30-year investment?

11. Suppose that the following debt structure is obtained from the footnotes of the balance sheets of two companies:

    Company A: Term loan for one year, 6 percent interest; principal of $23,365 and interest of $1,402 due at end of year.

    Company B: Term loan for two years, 6 percent interest; principal of $10,000 due at end of second year, interest payable at the end of each year. Mortgage, payable over three years, 6 percent interest, $5,000 payments at the end of each of the three years.

    (a) Compute the total amount owed by the two firms.
    (b) Compute the duration of Company A's debt.
    (c) Compute the duration of Company B's debt.

12. If a bond is selling above par, is its "current" yield greater than, equal to, or less than its "yield to maturity." Why?

13. Banks are charging .19 and commercial paper can be issued at a cost of .18. The bank's compensating balance requirement is .15 for such a loan.

Which source of borrowing should be chosen (make the decision based on the costs of borrowing)? The commerical paper requires a bank line of credit for which the bank requires a .10 compensatory balance.

14. The ABC Company has borrowed $10,000,000 at a cost of .10 to be repaid over 20 years in equal debt payments of $1,175,000. The company has a 40 percent tax rate. There is no risk.
    (a) What is the after-tax interest cost (in dollars) in year 1?
    (b) What is the after-tax present value of the debt at time 0?
    (c) What is the after-tax present value of the debt at time 1 (after payment of the interest)?

15. Assume that a company obtains capital (either debt or common stock) at a cost of .09. Its tax rate is .48.

    (a) What is the minimum cost of capital for a certain cash flow if 100 percent debt is used? (b) 100 percent common stock? (c) 40 percent debt and 60 percent stock equity?

16. The ABC Company has a debt of $30 million coming due in 20 years. It would like to have some investments with durations longer than 20 years.

    Describe the characteristics of an investment that will have a duration longer than 20 years.

17. The ABC Company is considering issuing a zero interest-paying debt security (also called a zero-coupon bond, original issue discount bond, or a money multiplier note) maturing in 10 years. Conventional 10-year bonds that are callable are currently being issued to yield .12.

    Would you expect the zero interest debt to yield more or less than .12?

18. The ABC Company has $100 million of callable 12 percent debt outstanding. (Each $1,000 bond is callable at a price of $1,080.) The firm can issue new debt at a cost of 10 percent. The transaction costs would be $3.5 million (this is in addition to the call premium). The debt matures in 10 years (a balloon payment). The firm has investment possibilities that are expected to yield 15 percent and it has been using an after tax weighted average cost of capital of 14 percent to evaluate investments.

    The tax rate is .46. Assume that call premium and transaction costs can be expensed immediately (this is an approximation, but use it).

    (a) The present value of the current debt is _____ .

    (b) Should the firm refund? Assume that management expects interest rates to remain at 10 percent for the near and distant future.

19. The York State Electric Corporation has $100 million of debentures outstanding that are currently paying interest of 5.5 percent ($5.5 million) per

year. The bonds mature in 24 years. It would be possible currently to issue 30-year debentures of like characteristics that would yield 5.0 percent. The firm considers its cost of capital to be 8.0 percent. The marginal tax rate is .4. The firm has other investment opportunities that yield .08 or higher. The following analysis has been prepared.

	Before Taxes	After Taxes
Cash outlays		
Premium @ $50 per $1,000	$5,000,000	$ 3,000,000
Duplicate interest for 30-day call period less interest received on principal @ 1.4% due to temporary investment	300,000	180,000
Refunding expense (80% of $250,000, total expense of new issue based on remaining life of old issue of 24 years)	200,000	120,000
Call expense	50,000	30,000
Less: Tax saving due to immediate write-off of unamortized debt discount and expense		(20,000)
Total cash outlay of refunding		$ 3,310,000
Interest calculations		
Annual interest of old issue @ 5.5%	$5,500,000	$ 3,300,000
Annual interest of new issue @ 5.0%	5,000,000	3,000,000
Total after-tax interest of old issue discounted @ 8.0% for 24 years (PV = 10.5288)		34,700,000
Total after-tax interest of new issue discounted @ 8.0% for 24 years (PV = 10.5288)		31,600,000
Total after-tax discounted interest		3,100,000
Total after-tax cash outlay of refunding		3,310,000
Net savings due to refunding at effective interest rate of 5%		$ (210,000)

ªThe remaining life of the old issue.

Should the firm refund? Explain briefly.

20. The ABC Company has $100 million of 12 percent debt outstanding that matures in 20 years. It could issue 20-year debt now for 10 percent. The bonds can be called at a price of $110 (that is, $1,100 per bond). There would be $8 million of transaction costs to accomplish the switch. The issue costs of the old bonds are recorded at $3 million (these costs have been expensed for taxes).

The ABC Company has an investment cutoff rate of 20 percent and a

WACC of 15 percent. There is a 40 percent tax rate. All the refunding costs of the new issue can be expensed for taxes.

Should the company refund?

REFERENCES

Barnea A., and H. Bierman, Jr. "The Use of Expected Short-Term Interest Rates in Bond Refunding." *Financial Management*, Spring 1974, 75–79

Barnea, A., R. Haugen, and L. W. Senbet. "A Rationale for Debt Maturity Structure and Call Provisions in the Agency Theoretic Framework." *Journal of Finance*, December 1980, 1223–1234.

Bierman, H., Jr. "The Bond Refunding Decision," *Financial Management*, Summer 1972, 27–29.

Bowlin, O.D. "The Refunding Decision: Another Special Case in Capital Budgeting." *Journal of Finance*, March 1966, 55–69.

Donaldson, G. *Corporate Debt Capacity*. Boston: Harvard Graduate School of Business, 1961.

Fisher, L. "Determinants of Risk Premiums on Corporate Bonds," *Journal of Political Economy*, June 1959, 217–237.

Hamada, R. S. "Portfolio Analysis, Market Equilibrium and Corporate Finance. "*Journal of Finance*, March 1969, 11–30.

Hess, A. P., Jr., and Winn, W. J., *The Value of the Call Privilege*. Philadelphia: University of Pennsylvania Press, 1962.

Ingersoll, Jonathan. "An Examination of Corporate Call Policies on Convertible Securities." *Journal of Finance*, May 1977, 463–478.

Jen, Frank C., and James E. Wert. "The Deferred Call Provision and Corporate Bond Yields." *Journal of Financial and Quantitative Analysis*, June 1968, 157–169.

Kalotay, A. J., "On the Advanced Refunding of Discounted Debt." *Financial Management*, Summer 1978, 14–18.

———. "On the Management of Sinking Funds." *Financial Management*, Summer 1981, 34–40.

Malkiel, Burton G. *The Term Structure of Interest Rates*. Princeton, N.J.: Princeton University Press, 1966.

Meiselman, David. *The Term Structure of Interest Rates*. Englewood Cliffs, N.J.: Prentice-Hall, Inc., 1962.

Modigliani, F., and M. H. Miller. "The Cost of Capital, Corporation Finance and the Theory of Investment." *American Economic Review*, June 1958, 261–277.

Pye, G. "The Value of the Call Option of a Bond." *The Journal of Political Economy*, April 1966, 200–205.

Schwartz, E. "The Refunding Decision." *Journal of Business*, October 1967, 448–449.

Weingartner, H. M. "Optimal Timing of Bond Refunding," *Management Science*, March 1967, 551–524.

Weinstein, Mark I. "The Seasoning Process of New Corporate Bond Issues," *Journal of Finance*, December 1978, 1343–1354.

Yawitz, Jess B., and James A. Anderson. "The Effect of Bond Refunding on Shareholder Wealth." *Journal of Finance*, December 1977, 1738–1746.

Appendix 11.1   A Sufficient Condition for the Yield of a Bond to Equal Its Coupon Rate

We want to show that if a bond sells at its face value ($B_0 = B$), its contractual rate is equal to the market rate ($k_i = k_0$). Setting $B_0 = B$ in equation (11.1) yields

$$B = \sum_{t=1}^{n} \frac{kB}{(1 + k_i)^t} + \frac{B}{(1 + k_i)^n}$$

Multiplying both sides by $1/B$, and factoring out the constant k, we obtain

$$1 = k \sum_{t=1}^{n} \frac{1}{(1 + k_i)^t} + \frac{1}{(1 + k_i)^n}$$

The first term on the right-hand side of the equation is a geometric series (the present value of an annuity). Substituting the closed form expression for the series, we find

$$1 = k \frac{1 - (1 + k_i)^{-n}}{k_i} + \frac{1}{(1 + k_i)^n}$$

Multiply both sides by k_i,

$$k_i = k[1 - (1 + k_i)^{-n}] + k_i(1 + k_i)^{-n}$$

Solving for k yields

$$k = \frac{k_i[1 - (1 + k_i)^{-n}]}{[1 - (1 + k_i)^{-n}]} = k_i$$

Appendix 11.2   The After-Tax Cost of Debt

Define r to be the after-tax cost of debt. We want to show that $r = (1 - t_c)k$ if $B_0 \doteq B$. The proof is analogous to that in Appendix 11.1. By definition, and a slight modification of equation (11.1) to include taxes,

$$B = \sum_{t=1}^{n} \frac{(1 - t_c)kB}{(1 + r)^t} + \frac{B}{(1 + r)^n}$$

Dividing both sides by B, and factoring out $(1 - t_c)k$, we find that

$$1 = (1 - t_c)k \sum_{t=1}^{n} \frac{1}{(1 + r)^t} + \frac{1}{(1 + r)^n}$$

and using the geometric series' closed form (the present value of an annuity) yields

$$1 = (1 - t_c)k \frac{1 - (1 + r)^{-n}}{r} + \frac{1}{(1 + r)^n}$$

Multiply both sides by $r(1 + r)^n$,

$$r(1 + r)^n = (1 - t_c)k[(1 + r)^n - 1] + r$$

Rearranging terms, we obtain

$$\frac{r[(1 + r)^n - 1]}{[(1 + r)^n - 1]} = (1 - t_c)k$$

Solving for r yields

$$r = (1 - t_c)k$$

Appendix 11.3   Beta with Debt

We wish to study how the introduction of debt affects the beta coefficient of the common stock. Let

S = the market value of a company's common stock if there were no debt outstanding.

S_B = the market value of the company's common stock with B of debt outstanding.

r = the rate of return on S,

r_B = the rate of return on S_B,

r_d = the rate of return on the debt,

r_m = the rate of return on the market portfolio, and

r_f = the rate of return on default free debt

We assume that replacing some stock with debt does not change the market value of the company, so that

$$S = S_B + B$$

or the total return available to capital suppliers, so that

$$rS = r_B S_B + r_d B$$

Dividing both sides of the above equation by S gives

$$r = r_B \left(\frac{S_B}{S}\right) + r_d \left(\frac{B}{S}\right)$$

Using the above relationship the covariance of r and r_m can be expressed as

$$\text{cov}\,(r,\, r_m) = \text{cov}\left[r_B \left(\frac{S_B}{S}\right) + r_d \left(\frac{B}{S}\right),\, r_m \right]$$

$$= \frac{S_B}{S}\,\text{cov}\,(r_B,\, r_m) + \frac{B}{S}\,\text{cov}\,(r_d,\, r_m)$$

Dividing both sides by var (r_m) we have

$$\beta = \frac{S_B}{S}\,\beta_B + \frac{B}{S}\,\beta_d$$

where β is the beta of the unlevered stock, and β_B and β_d are the betas of levered stock and new debt, respectively. If β_d is zero (this requires that cov $(r_d,\, r_m) = 0$), then $\beta = (S_B/S)\,\beta_B$ or

$$\beta_B = \frac{S}{S_B}\,\beta$$

which is the relationship used in the chapter.

Chapter 12

Common Stock

Major Topics

1. The cost of common stock equity capital using basic stock valuation models.
2. The cost of retained earnings and the cost of new capital.
3. Defining growth in dividends mathematically.
4. The price/earnings ratio and its relationship to the cost of equity.
5. The institutional factors associated with common stock.
6. The important concept of market efficiency.
7. The securities industry.

Cost of Equity Capital

There are several definitions of the cost of equity capital. The standard academic one is that the cost of equity capital is the rate of discount that equates the present value of all future expected dividends per share to the present price of the common stock. It is the return required by investors.

One of the simplest assumptions that can be made about expected dividend behavior is that dividends are expected to grow at a constant rate through time, so that $D_t = D_1(1 + g)^{t-1}$. If dividends grow at a rate g in perpetuity and if g is larger than k_e then (as shown in Chapter 3) we can obtain

$$P = \frac{D_1}{k_e - g} \tag{12.1}$$

where D_1 is the next period's expected dividend.

Solving equation (12.1) for the cost of equity capital, we find

$$k_e = \frac{D_1}{P} + g \qquad\qquad (12.2)$$

and this is a widely accepted measure of k_e, the cost of stock equity capital. Other methods of estimating the cost of equity capital involve the capital asset pricing model, but equations (12.1) and (12.2) are widely used because of their simplicity.

A critic of the dividend valuation model might argue that investors buy price appreciation, not future dividends. For many stocks, investors may expect the first n periods to have very small dividends (or zero dividends), and, nevertheless, the current market price may be very large. The current high price, however, is only justified in a rational market by the expectation of high future dividends, and the basic dividend valuation model can incorporate this increase in dividends. The summation of the present value of future dividends does not require that the near-term dividends be large. However, if there are several years of zero dividends and/or changing growth rates through time, then the mathematical formulation of P does not reduce to an expression as simple as $P = D_1/(k_e - g)$.

What would be the value of a stock that promised never to pay a dividend (including a liquidation dividend, purchase of its own stock, or payoffs arising from controlling the firm)? The value of these shares would be zero. There has to be the prospect of dividends (defined to be any cash distribution from the firm to its investors) for stock to have a positive value.

The constant growth rate dividend valuation model assumes that the dividend, D_1, is expected to grow at a constant rate g forever. It may be more realistic to assume that special investment opportunities allowing a high growth rate are available not in perpetuity but only over some finite interval of time, T, and after T the growth rate will be smaller. This two-stage model was discussed in Chapter 3.

Factors That Affect the Cost of Equity Capital

We have defined the cost of equity capital as that discount rate that equates the present value of the future expected dividend stream to the current market price of the stock. Thus, mathematically, the cost of equity capital is a function (usually implicit, but for some cases, it can be written explicitly) of the current price of the stock and the time path of expected dividends. A firm's cost of equity is determined by the time value of money for investors and the risk or uncertainty of the firm's future dividend stream as well as the correlation of the stock's returns and the market's returns.

Investors' time value of money can change over time, reflecting everything from a change in the basic investment/consumption decision (itself a function of a host of socioeconomic variables) to immediate conditions of tightness or easiness in the money markets. If specified in nominal terms, it will also reflect the current expectations regarding rates of inflation.

The variability of the future earnings depends on the business risk of the firm and the degree of financial leverage employed. The higher either of these factors, the greater the variability of earnings; but to evaluate the risk associated with a dividend stream is a difficult task. Investment decisions by capital suppliers are made in the context of portfolios of financial and real assets. Thus the risk of the stock from the viewpoint of a specific investor who is not perfectly diversified is determined not only by the variability of the dividend stream, but also by the covariability of the stream with the earning stream from the other assets in the investor's portfolio.

The Cost of Retained Earnings

The amount of common stock equity capital can be increased by retaining earnings or by issuing new common stock. The cost of retained earnings is not equal to the cost of new common stock equity capital. To be exact, when we speak of the cost of common stock equity, we should be speaking of either the cost of retention or the cost of issuing new common stock, and we should make clear which source is being used.

The two costs differ by transaction costs and tax consequences to investors. We initially assume a zero tax rate so that we can first concentrate on the transaction costs. Assume that common stockholders expect to earn 20 percent on new funds invested. Thus, if they invest $100 of new funds, investors expect to earn the equivalent of $20 per year. With zero transaction costs, we could say that these funds cost 20 percent. Now assume that $5 of each $100 raised by a corporation goes to pay investment bankers for arranging the financing so that the corporation nets out $95, on which there is a $20-per-year "cost." The percentage cost on new capital is now 20/95, or 21 percent.

Now we relax the assumption of zero taxes. With positive income taxes, the cost of both retention and new common stock funds become difficult to define exactly. A stockholder if asked should be able to describe the return required for retention and the return required for new common stock funds. For example, a stockholder might be satisfied with an 8 percent return for internally generated funds but require the corporation to earn a 20 percent return for new capital. The differential is explained by personal income taxes.

Assume that an investor can earn 8 percent after tax with alternative investments and will pay a 60 percent tax on dividends received. If $100.00 of earnings are retained, then the investor might be satisfied with the firm earning only $8.00 per year (8 percent) because the investor will net $3.20 after tax. If the $100.00 is paid to the investor immediately and then taxed at 60 percent, the investor will net $40.00 after tax and the $40.00 invested will again earn $3.20 after tax. Now if the firm wants the investor to buy $40.00 of new stock, the investor might well require more than the 8 percent return that was consistent with retained earnings and tax deferral. A return of 20 percent that must be earned by the corporation on the new $40.00 of common stock capital is required to lead to the $8.00 described earlier arising from retained earnings. It is difficult to quantify exactly the two returns required for equivalency since they will depend on personal investment opportunities, as well as on the way in which gains to investors are taxed.

The analysis can be made more complex by introducing capital gains and tax deferral, but it should be clear that retained earnings have a lower cost to a firm than new funds obtained from common stockholders who are subject to taxation.

Growth of Dividends

The anticipated growth rate of dividends for any given firm is not independent of the opportunities for investment and the financing strategies of the firm. In fact, the growth rate can be related systematically to the firm's return on investment and its rate of investment. To examine how these factors interact in determining earnings growth as well as the impact of financial leverage on the growth rate of a firm, consider the following model. Let

E = the net income in time period 0
ΔE = the change in earnings from period 0 to period 1
E_1 = the net income in period 1 ($E_1 = E + \Delta E$)
b = the net earnings retention rate maintained by the firm
r = the average rate of return after tax on new investment

Let us assume that the firm is all equity financed and uses no new external equity financing. The change in net income is equal to the product of the amount of earnings retained, bE, and the average after-tax return earned on the reinvestment, r:

$$\Delta E = rbE \tag{12.3}$$

or

$$E_1 = E + \Delta E = E + rbE = (1 + rb)E \tag{12.4}$$

If we define g to be the discrete growth rate of net income (and the growth in dividends if a constant retention rate is maintained), then

$$E_1 = (1 + g)E \tag{12.5}$$

and, by equating equations (12.4) and (12.5), we find

$$g = rb \tag{12.6}$$

The growth rate of net income for the period is equal to the product of the after-tax rate of return on reinvestment times the rate of earnings retention. Although this growth rate refers only to the one period in question, if b and r are constant for a number of periods, the g of equation (12.6) will apply to these periods. One of the most famous models of stock price behavior is the Gordon–Shapiro (1956) model, based on equations (12.1) and (12.6). When r and b are assumed constant throughout time,

$$P = \frac{D_1}{k_e - g} = \frac{(1 - b)E}{k_e - rb} \tag{12.7}$$

where the initial dividend is equal to the payout rate, $1 - b$, times the initial earnings rate, E.

If we relax the assumption that the firm is all equity financed by allowing the firm to adopt a constant debt/equity ratio, B/S, it can be shown (see Appendix 12.1) that

$$g = rb + b[r - k_i(1 - t_c)]\frac{B}{S} \tag{12.8}$$

which reduces to equation (12.6) when $B/S = 0$. If some financial leverage is employed ($B/S > 0$) and, for that degree of leverage, if $r > k_i(1 - t_c)$, then the second term of (12.8) is positive, implying that the use of this degree of leverage increases the growth rate of earnings and dividends over that which would have occurred without the use of debt. This follows since the average return on new investment, r, has been assumed to be constant, independent of the amount invested. Assuming $r > k_i (1 - t_c)$ is equivalent to assuming that the marginal (which equals average if the average is unchanging) return on new investment is greater than the after-tax cost of debt capital so that debt utilization creates residual equity earnings. Equation (12.8) could provide the basis for a discussion of the impact of financial leverage on the equity investment of the firm for the growing rather than the static firm.

EXAMPLE 12.1 ─────────────────────────────────

Suppose that a firm exhibits the following characteristics:

$$r = .15$$

$$t_c = .4$$

$$b = .6$$

If the firm is all equity financed, from equation (12.8) with $B/S = 0$,

$$g = rb = .15(.6) = .09 \tag{12.6}$$

If the firm were to adopt a debt/equity ratio of .8 at a debt cost of 8 percent, then

$$g = (.15)(.6) + .6[.15 - .08(1 - .4)](.8) \tag{12.8}$$
$$= .09 + .6(.102)(.8) = .09 + .049 = .139$$

so that the use of a debt/equity ratio of .8 increases the growth rate of earnings to about 1.54 times its previous level. The next step would be to assume that r is affected by the amount invested. That is, r should change as the amount invested changes.

Stock Prices and Inflation

Inflation, or the expectation of inflation, may affect the value of a company's stock. Let us assume that the market thinks that stock in Company X is a good hedge against inflation—that is, as a result of inflation, future dividends of Company X will increase more than the inflation (the real return will increase) while the dividends of most other firms will decrease in real terms. In this situation, it is possible that if the probability of inflation increases, the price of Company X's stock will rise. The cost of equity capital is unchanged, but higher future dividends are expected.

If the inflation expectation also changes the value of k_e (interest rates might be increasing as the inflation threat grows), the effect of the inflation on the stock price is more difficult to predict. The increase in the rate of discount might actually cause the stock price to decrease despite the forecasted increase in dividends.

For a decision maker attempting to determine a company's cost of capital, inflation makes it more difficult to forecast the growth in dividends anticipated by the market, because this growth rate is affected by the prospect of inflation and the amount of inflation is uncertain. There will be a wide range of expectations as to the amount of inflation and its effect on the future dividends. It is difficult for an observer to impute the growth rate the market is using in evaluating the stock.

The Price/Earnings Ratio and Its Determinants

A firm's P/E multiplier, that is, the ratio of the price of its common stock to the earnings per share of common stock, is a statistic often quoted by stock market analysts. High-growth-rate stocks are awarded high P/Es (say, greater than 15), whereas low-growth stocks have low P/Es (say, less than 10).

If we use the dividend growth rate stock price model, equation (12.1), it is possible to examine the factors that affect a firm's P/E. Again, letting E denote the current earnings, b denote the earnings retention rate, and D_1 denote the current dividend, the relationship between dividends and earnings is $D_1 = (1 - b)E$. If dividends are assumed to grow at a constant rate of g, we showed earlier that

$$P = \frac{D_1}{k_e - g} \tag{12.1}$$

Since $D_1 = (1 - b)E,$

$$P = \frac{(1 - b)E}{k_e - g} \tag{12.9}$$

so that dividing by E yields

$$\frac{P}{E} = \frac{1 - b}{k_e - g} \tag{12.10}$$

If we further assume, for simplicity, that the firm's earnings growth is financed solely by retained earnings, as we did in the derivation of equation (12.6), then $g = rb$ and

$$\frac{P}{E} = \frac{1 - b}{k_e - rb} \tag{12.11}$$

Thus we see that the *expected* ratio of price to earnings is determined by the return on the reinvested funds, the earning retention rate, and the market's required rate of return on the stock. The *actual* P/E is determined by observed price and earnings per share.

EXAMPLE 12.2 —————————————————————————

Suppose that an all-equity financed firm exhibits these characteristics:

$E = \$3$
$b = .4$ and $D_1 = (1 - b)E = \$1.80$
$r = .2$ and $g = rb = .08$
$k_e = .14$

Then, from equation (12.11), we expect that the firms' expected P/E would be

$$P/E = \frac{1 - .4}{.14 - .2(.4)} = \frac{.6}{.06} = 10$$

Suppose that the same firm were to reinvest a larger percentage of its earnings, say, 60 percent, and that r remained at .2. The resultant P/E should change to consider the new variables:

$$P/E = \frac{1 - .6}{.14 - .2(.6)} = \frac{.4}{.02} = 20$$

Since the present earnings are unchanged but the expected P/E has doubled, we would expect the price of the stock to double if the market used the same information. With the higher retention rate, the growth rate of earnings and dividends increases from 8 to 12 percent and the higher growth rate more than offsets the effect on the stock price of the reduction from $1.80 to $1.20 in the initial dividend.

E/P as an Estimator of the Cost of Equity Capital

Is the inverse of the P/E multiplier, E/P, a good measure of k_e, the cost of equity capital? By utilizing the constant growth rate model developed in this chapter, we develop the relationships between k_e and E/P for that model to show that the inverse of the price/earnings ratio is generally not a good estimator of the cost of equity capital, but it may be useful in some very special situations.

The inverse of the price/earnings ratio is, from equation (12.11),

$$E/P = \frac{k_e - rb}{1 - b} \tag{12.12}$$

Thus, if the earnings/price ratio is to be a good estimator of k_e, it is necessary that

$$E/P = k_e \tag{12.13}$$

Setting the right-hand sides of equations (12.12) and (12.13) equal and re-arranging terms, we have

$$k_e = \frac{k_e - rb}{1 - b} \tag{12.14}$$

We conclude that E/P will be a good estimator of the cost of equity capital if $b = 0$, or in case $b > 0$, if $k_e = r$.

Let us consider the two cases. First, if the firm is a nongrowth firm paying all its earnings as dividends ($b = g = 0$), then from equation (12.12), E/P = k_e and the earnings/price ratio is a good estimator of the cost of equity capital.

Second, assume that there is growth but that the funds are reinvested to earn a return of k_e and there is a zero debt so that $g = k_e b$; then

$$E/P = \frac{k_e - g}{1 - b} = \frac{k_e - k_e b}{1 - b} = k_e \tag{12.15}$$

If these assumptions do not hold, E/P will not be a good estimator of k_e.

If the firm also uses debt to finance its investments, then it is necessary that the average return on invested funds be equal to the firm's weighted average cost of capital for the E/P ratio to be a good estimator of the cost of equity.

Estimation of the Cost of Equity

Each method of estimating the cost of equity capital has severe limitations. We now briefly consider the following methods of determining the cost of equity.

1. Discounted cash flow (discounted dividend model)
2. Risk adjustment to cost of debt
3. Capital asset pricing model

The discounted cash flow model comes in different forms, but all involve finding the rate of time discount that equates the present value of future dividends to the current price of the common stock. For example, rearranging equation (12.1) we find that

$$k_e = \frac{D_1}{P} + g$$

The primary attractiveness of the model is its simplicity. If the annual dividend is expected to be $2, the stock price $20, and the growth rate .08, the cost of equity is estimated as

$$k_e = \frac{2}{20} + .08 = .18$$

Despite the seeming exactness of this formulation, there are several difficulties with its application:

1. The derivation assumes a constant growth rate that goes on forever (this also assumes that each year the firm can invest larger amounts that will continue to earn r).
2. There are difficulties in determining the exact values of D_1 and P that should be used (e.g., should P be an average or the price at a specific moment?).
3. The cost of newly raised capital and retained earnings should differ because of taxes and transaction costs.
4. The value of g can be determined in a variety of ways.

Let us consider the determination of g, since that is the most difficult measurement problem. One possibility is to determine the historical dividend growth rate and use it as a forecast of the future growth. But this estimate of the growth rate will be a function of the time period that is studied and is very much the result of relatively arbitrary dividend decisions by the firm.

A second possibility is to define the growth rate as $g = rb$, where r is the average return on new investment and b is the retention rate. Although b is reasonably exact (as long as the accounting income measure is accepted), there are apt to be differences of opinion about r. Also, growth in dividends and earnings can take place because of other reasons than investment, for example, increased efficiency and using more capacity. We want to use the market's expectation of growth, but we do not have that measure.

Thus we have an exact method of calculation that is based on many, somewhat hidden, assumptions. Unless we know the market's forecast of future dividends, the process will give us a rough approximation.

The yields to maturity on government bonds, AAA industrials, and so on are easily determined. We can take one of these yields and add an adjustment for risk to obtain a cost of equity. For example, if the risk adjustment is .03 and the government bond rate is .11, we would obtain a .14 cost of stock equity.

The problems are in determining the risk class of debt to be used, the maturity of debt to be used (or more exactly the duration), and the amount of risk adjustment to be added. Given the different tax treatments of debt and stock, it is possible that the cost of equity capital (before investor taxes) is less than the cost of debt. This statement would not be valid if the investors are all zero tax (e.g., pension funds), but it can be correct for high-tax investors. Thus we do not know that given the specific U.S. investor tax structure, the cost of equity will be larger than the cost of debt, and if it is larger, we do not know how much larger.

The capital asset pricing model has been offered as a method of estimating the cost of equity capital.

The major problems in implementing the CAPM are

1. The validity of the assumptions of the model (either quadratic utility functions or normal probability distribution of returns).
2. The determination of r_f, the risk-free rate (should the rate be long or short term?).
3. The determination of $(\bar{r}_m - r_f)$, the amount by which the expected market return exceeds the risk-free rate.
4. The determination of the value of the beta, where

$$\beta = \frac{\text{cov}(r_i, r_m)}{\text{var}(r_m)}$$

since the value will depend on the time period the calculation covers.

Thus we have a formula $\bar{r}_i = r_f + (\bar{r}_m - r_f)\beta$, but we do not know whether this relationship is valid, since the assumptions necessary for its derivation may not be valid. Even if the derivation is correct, we still have difficulties determining the values of r_f, $\bar{r}_m - r_f$, and the beta of the company being analyzed. We need to know the amount that the expected return of the market portfolio exceeds the risk-free rate, but this amount cannot be observed.

Managers want to know the cost of equity capital because it helps to guide their investment decisions. However, it should be realized that there are no ways to estimate exactly the cost of equity of a publicly owned firm.

Issuing Common Stock: Institutional Factors

Having discussed the factors that affect the cost of equity capital and how to measure it, we briefly turn to some fundamental elements in the issuance of new common stock. First we discuss the institutional factors and then the timing element.

Firms do not usually issue common stock on a regular basis. In fact, most firms issue common stock very infrequently, relying on debt and retained earnings for most of their new capital. In this sense, the reinvestment models discussed earlier in this chapter are reasonably realistic. This reluctance to issue common stock more frequently can be attributed to a number of factors.

First, there are tax avoidance reasons for using debt and retained earning rather than new equity capital. The use of debt helps to avoid corporate taxes, and retained earnings reduce the impact of personal taxes by means of tax deferral and offering a potential for the income to be taxed as a capital gain rather than as ordinary income. Second is the problem of paying flotation costs, which are higher on equity than on debt financing per dollar received. Third is the element of control. Selling new shares to new owners dilutes the existing owner's power to control the corporation. Having a firm that grows at a slower rate but under your control might be preferable to having a firm grow faster with someone else's money and subject to someone else's direction.

To provide some protection against unwanted dilution of ownership, many corporate charters require the firm first to offer any new equity securities to the existing shareholders on a privileged subscription basis (this is called preemptive rights). To ensure selling the issue, the price of the to-be-issued stock is set below its current market price, and each shareholder is given the right to purchase the new securities so as to maintain the proportion of ownership. For example, if the shareholder owns 500 shares and the firm is increasing its outstanding shares by 20 percent, then the owner would receive rights to 100 shares. In this situation the stockholder is said to have "preemptive rights." Stockholders can vote away preemptive rights so that shares can be issued directly to the public.

To determine the value of a right, let us examine the alternatives open to a potential purchaser of a share of stock when a rights offering is in process. The purchaser may do one of three things, as depicted in Figure 12.1, in order to end up with one share of stock: purchase the share "rights-on" and sell

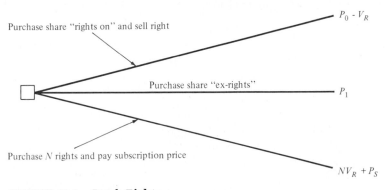

FIGURE 12.1   Stock Rights

the right, purchase the share "ex-rights," or purchase a right and pay the subscription price. We use the following notation:

N = the number of rights required to purchase one share

P_s = the subscription price

V_R = the value of a right

P_0 = the price of a share, rights-on

P_1 = the price of a share, rights-off

Aside from transaction costs, arbitrage should cause the three alternatives to have the same cost to the purchaser. Arbitrage is the process that ensures that in a perfect market two identical items cannot sell for a different price. We should logically expect the value of a share with rights on to be equal to the value of a share with rights off plus the value of a right, or

$$P_0 = P_1 + V_R \qquad (12.16)$$

or

$$V_R = P_0 - P_1 \qquad (12.17)$$

Also, the value of a share without the rights $(P_0 - V_R)$ should be equal to the cost of the rights necessary to purchase a share of stock plus the subscription price $(NV_R + P_s)$:

$$P_0 - V_R = NV_R + P_s \qquad (12.18)$$

or solving for V_R,

$$V_R = \frac{P_0 - P_s}{N + 1} \qquad (12.19)$$

Equation (12.19) gives the value of a right in terms of P_0, the price with rights-on, P_s the subscription price, and N, the number of rights required to subscribe to one share. Equating equations (12.17) and (12.19), we find

$$P_0 - P_1 = \frac{P_0 - P_s}{N + 1} \qquad (12.20)$$

or, solving for P_1, the ex-rights price,

$$P_1 = \frac{NP_0 + P_s}{N + 1} \qquad (12.21)$$

Equations (12.19) and (12.21) are the fundamental relationships that should hold during a rights offering. Equation (12.21) assumes that P_s dollars received are worth P_s and that the initial value of NP_0 is increased by P_s, where N rights are required to buy one share at a price of P_s.

EXAMPLE 12.3 ───

A stock is selling for \$50 immediately before the rights to purchase .25 share at a subscription price of \$40 are issued. The rights will go to the owner of the stock. Then

$$P_0 = \$50$$

$$P_s = \$40$$

$$N = 4$$

and so the value of a right from equation (12.19) is

$$V_R = \frac{50 - 40}{5} = \$2$$

and the expected price of the stock ex-rights is given by equation (12.21):

$$P_1 = \frac{4 \times 50 + 40}{4 + 1} = \frac{240}{5} = \$48$$

───

An investor holding 4 shares can exercise the 4 rights, sell them, or allow them to expire. If the rights are exercised, we have

Five shares of common stock, 5 × \$48	\$240
less: Additional investment	40
Net value	\$200

If the investor sells the 4 rights for \$2 each (\$8),

Four shares of common stock, 4 × \$48	\$192
Cash from sale of rights	8
Net value	\$200

If the investor allows the rights to lapse (a bad strategy), the investor will hold four shares worth \$192 in total and will lose \$8.

NYSE-Composite Transactions

Friday, December 30, 1983

Quotations include trades on the Midwest, Pacific, Philadelphia, Boston and Cincinnati stock exchanges and reported by the National Association of Securities Dealers and Instinet

60 THE WALL STREET JOURNAL Tuesday, January 3, 1984

Friday's Volume
86,722,230 Shares; 544,200 Warrants

TRADING BY MARKETS

	Shares	Warrants
New York Exchange	71,840,000	542,400
Midwest Exchange	6,496,900	....
Pacific Exchange	3,150,500	....
Nat'l Assoc. of Securities Dealers ...	2,300,330	1,800
Philadelphia Exchange	1,889,800	....
Boston Exchange	767,400	....
Cincinnati Exchange	163,700	....
Instinet System	113,600	....

NYSE – Composite

Volume since Jan. 1:	1983	1982	1981
Total shares-a ..	25,362,452,352	19,203,590,708	13,679,194,319
Total warrants .	158,281,300	57,342,050	40,155,100

New York Stock Exchange

Volume since Jan. 1:	1983	1982	1981
Total shares	21,589,576,997	16,458,036,768	11,853,740,659
Total warrants .	157,481,500	57,248,800	40,048,600

ACTIVE STOCKS

	Open	High	Low	Close	Chg.	Volume
Amer T&T wi....	17¾	18	17¾	17⅞	.....	1,827,200
LIL Co	10⅛	10⅝	10⅛	10⅜	+ ¼	1,346,500
Amer T&T	61¼	61⅝	61¼	61½	+ ⅜	1,335,600
GettyOil	97⅛	98½	96½	98⅛	+ ⅝	849,100
WarnrCom	25½	26⅞	24⅞	26⅞	+ 1⅛	760,500
AmExpress s.....	33⅛	33⅜	32⅛	32⅝	− ⅛	696,600
LTV Corp.........	18½	18⅝	18⅛	18⅜	− ⅜	627,800
PubSvc Ind......	11⅜	11⅞	11¼	11⅝	+ ⅛	584,100
Consu Pow......	14	14¼	13⅞	14⅛	+ ¼	580,400
Am Motors.......	6⅛	6¼	6	6¼	.....	565,300
StorgeTech	13¾	14	13½	13⅝	− ⅜	506,600
Pan Am..........	8	8⅛	7⅞	8⅛	+ ½	491,900
MerilLyn s......	31⅞	32¼	31⅝	32	+ ¼	490,400
Burrghs	50½	50⅝	50¼	50⅜	.....	471,800
Chrysler	27⅜	28⅛	27¼	27⅝	+ ½	460,900

52 Weeks High	Low	Stock	Div.	Yld %	P-E Ratio	Sales 100s	High	Low	Close	Net Chg.
		– A–A–A –								
17¾	8⅝	AAR	.44	2.6	21	183	17½	17⅛	17¼	.....
52⅜	30½	ACF	1.40	2.8	238	354	50	49⅛	50	+ ¾
22	18¼	AMCA n		..	..	1	21⅝	21⅝	21⅝	+ ⅛
18⅞	14¾	AMF	.50	3.1	..	714	16⅛	16	16	− ¼
39⅛	18½	AMR Cp		..	16	3985	36⅛	35½	36⅛	+ ¾
19½	15	AMR	pf 2.18	11.	..	123	u19¾	19	19¾	+ ¾
40¼	24⅞	AMR	pf2.13	5.6	..	278	38	37½	38	+ ½
16¼	3⅛	APL		..	21	91	14½	14⅛	14⅛	− ¼
55¼	33¾	ARA	2.05	4.0	11	37	51	50½	51	+ ⅜
79⅞	50¼	ASA	3a	5.4	..	298	55¾	55	55½	− ⅛
33¼	14	AVX s	.32	1.2	41	20	27⅝	27⅛	27⅛	− ¼
53⅜	36⅛	AbtLab	1	2.2	17	976	45¾	45⅛	45¼	− ⅛

52 Weeks High	Low	Stock	Div.	Yld %	P-E Ratio	Sales 100s	High	low	Close	Net Chg.
11⅞	8⅝	BncCtr	n.28e	3.2	..	1	8⅝	8⅝	8⅝	.....
7⅝	5½	BanTex	.20	3.3	43	1184	6	5⅝	6	+ ¼
59¾	38¾	Bandag	1	1.8	15	32	55½	54½	55½	+ ½
27¼	16¼	BangP	.80	2.9	..	376	u27⅜	27¼	27¼	.....
47⅝	32⅝	BkBos	2.32	5.7	5	64	40⅝	40⅛	40½	.....
33⅛	23⅝	BkNY	s 1.84	5.6	6	594	32¾	32¼	32¾	+ ¼
33⅜	21¼	BkofVa	1.52	4.6	6	17	33	32¾	32⅞	− ⅛
25½	18	BnkAm	1.52	7.3	8	1372	20⅞	20⅝	20⅞	+ ⅛
60½	48¼	BkAm	pf4.76e	9.5	..	245	50¼	49⅝	50¼	+ ¾
90	73½	BkAm	pf6.12e	7.7	..	10	79¾	79¾	79¾	.....
21¼	16	BkAm	pf2.88	14.	..	65	20⅛	20	20⅛	.....
28	20¾	BkARt	s1.92	7.6	13	25	25⅜	25⅛	25⅜	+ ⅛
49½	35⅝	BankTr	2.45	5.4	6	909	45¼	44¾	45⅛	+ ⅛
24⅝	21¼	BkTr	pf2.50	12.	..	2	21½	21¼	21¼	− ¼
41	35¼	BkTr	pf4.22	12.	..	3	35¾	35¾	35¾	− ⅛
12¾	6¾	Banner	.03e	.3	..	38	10⅞	10½	10¾	− ¼
46¾	27½	Bard	.40	1.2	16	220	34½	34	34½	+ ¼
26⅛	17⅛	BarnGp	.60	2.6	53	9	22¾	22⅜	22¾	+ ⅜
42½	26	Barnet	1.20	3.1	9	153	39¼	38⅝	39	− ⅛
45¼	30¾	Barnt	pf2.38	5.7	..	24	41⅜	41	41⅜	+ ⅜
33	18	BaryWr	.48	1.6	21	127	30	28⅞	30	+ ½
14½	6¾	BasRes	.10b	.8	14	268	12¼	12	12⅛	+ ⅛
30⅜	19⅜	Bausch	s.78	3.1	21	1938	25¼	24¾	25	− ½
31¼	20	BaxtTr	s.28	1.2	15	3212	23¼	22½	23¼	+ ¾
20½	11⅛	BayFin	.05e	.3	4	4	18	17¾	17⅞	+ ⅛
24⅜	20⅝	BayStG	2.48	12.	98	47	20⅞	20⅝	20⅝	− ⅛
33¼	21½	BeatFd	1.60	5.0	9	2591	31⅞	31⅝	31⅞	+ ¼
32	30⅞	BeatF	wd	..	..	526	31¾	31¾	31¾	.....
61½	41⅛	Beat	pf 3.38	5.7	..	21	59	58¾	59	+ ⅛
53½	34	BectnD	1.15	3.1	21	810	37	35⅝	36¾	+ ¾
12¼	5½	Beker		..	..	254	8¾	8½	8¾	.....
21⅛	8⅛	BeldnH	.40	2.0	13	53	20¼	20⅛	20¼	.....
28¾	12¾	BelHw	s .50	2.1	11	493	24	23⅜	24	+ ⅜
27¼	21⅝	BelHw	pf.60	2.5	..	132	23⅞	23¼	23⅞	+ ¼
71¼	65	BellAt	wi6.40	9.8	..	1962	65⅝	65⅛	65¼	− ¼
27⅛	18⅛	BelCd	g2.18	..	..	253	27⅛	26⅞	27	.....
39⅛	22	BellInd	.32	.9	21	11	35¼	35	35¼	+ ½
90½	83⅞	BellSo	wi7.80	9.3	..	1818	84⅝	84¼	84¼	− ⅛
40¾	36	Belo n	.72	1.9	12	89	39¼	38⅜	38⅜	− 1
43½	32¾	Bemis	1.60	3.9	15	18	41	40½	41	+ ½
86¾	59¼	Bndx	pf4.04	4.8	..	2	85	85	85	.....
35⅜	19⅝	BenfCp	2	5.9	11	490	33¾	33⅛	33¾	+ ⅝
37½	31⅛	Benef	pf4.30	13.	..	1	33⅝	33⅝	33⅝	.....
22½	18¼	Benef	pf2.50	13.	..	z330	19¾	19¾	19¾	+ ¼
11⅞	5¼	BengtB	.25e	4.2	8	723	6	5¾	6	.....
8⅜	4⅝	Berkey		..	40	111	8⅛	8	8	− ⅛
26⅜	15	BestP s		..	9	1286	18½	16⅞	17⅝	+ ⅝
28¼	18⅜	BethStl	.60	2.1	..	2526	u28½	27⅞	28½	+ ⅝
57¾	45	BethSt	pf 5	8.6	..	46	u58¼	57¾	58¼	+ ¾
28⅞	24⅞	BethSt	pf2.50	8.6	..	52	u29	28⅝	29	+ ¼
44¾	21¼	Bevrly	s .28	1.1	17	1521	25	24⅛	24¾	+ ⅜
28	18	BigThr	.80	3.7	17	680	21⅝	20¾	21½	+ 1
43½	30⅞	Binney	1.28	3.9	10	149	33½	33	33	− ⅜
27¼	17⅞	BlackD	.52	2.0	26	623	26½	26⅛	26⅜	+ ¼
24	15⅝	BlkHP	s1.36	6.1	7	14	22½	22¼	22⅜	− ⅛
46½	21⅝	BlairJ	s .56	1.9	13	162	29½	28⅝	29½	+ ⅞
49⅛	35½	BlckHR	2.08	4.3	14	367	48½	47½	48½	+ ¾
40	30⅛	BlueB	2	5.1	10	32	39⅜	39⅛	39⅛	.....
48¼	31⅞	Boeing	1.40	3.2	12	2327	44	43⅜	43¾	− ½
47⅜	34½	BoiseC	1.90	4.3	25	169	44⅛	43	43¾	− ¼
58¼	50⅝	BoiseC	pf 5	8.9	..	40	56	55½	56	.....
30⅝	10	BoltBr	s .10	.5	33	184	21¾	20¾	21⅝	+ ⅜
61	45¼	Borden	2.44	4.3	9	245	56⅞	56	56½	+ ¼
27⅝	18⅝	BrgWa s		..	13	394	25	24⅝	24¾	− ⅛
13¼	6¼	Bormns		..	..	81	7	6⅝	6⅝	− ⅜

EXHIBIT 12.1 (***Source:*** **Reprinted by permission of *The Wall Street Journal,* Dow Jones & Company, Inc., 1984. All rights reserved.)**

EXHIBIT 12.1 *(continued)*

EXPLANATORY NOTES

(For New York and American Exchange listed issues)

Sales figures are unofficial.

The 52-Week High and Low columns show the highest and the lowest price of the stock in consolidated trading during the preceding 52 weeks plus the current week, but not the current trading day.

u—Indicates a new 52-week high. d—Indicates a new 52-week low.

g—Dividend or earnings in Canadian money. Stock trades in U.S. dollars. No yield or PE shown unless stated in U.S. money. n—New issue in the past 52 weeks. The high-low range begins with the start of trading and does not cover the entire 52 week period. s—Split or stock dividend of 25 per cent or more in the past 52 weeks. The high-low range is adjusted from the old stock. Dividend begins with the date of split or stock dividend. v—Trading halted on primary market.

Unless otherwise noted, rates of dividends in the foregoing table are annual disbursements based on the last quarterly or semi-annual declaration. Special or extra dividends or payments not designated as regular are identified in the following footnotes.

a—Also extra or extras. b—Annual rate plus stock dividend. c—Liquidating dividend. e—Declared or paid in preceding 12 months. i—Declared or paid after stock dividend or split up. j—Paid this year, dividend omitted, deferred or no action taken at last dividend meeting. k—Declared or paid this year, an accumulative issue with dividends in arrears. r—Declared or paid in preceding 12 months plus stock dividend. t—Paid in stock in preceding 12 months, estimated cash value on ex-dividend or ex-distribution date.

x—Ex-dividend or ex-rights. y—Ex-dividend and sales in full. z—Sales in full.

wd—When distributed. wi—When issued. ww—With warrants. xw—Without warrants.

vi—In bankruptcy or receivership or being reorganized under the Bankruptcy Act, or securities assumed by such companies.

Stock Quotations

Exhibit 12.1 shows extracts from the Wall Street market quotations for the New York Stock Exchange. The first tables give the volume of trading by markets and a listing of the most active stocks. Some traders think that the volume of trading is an important indicator of the direction the market will be going in the near future. Immediately below the listing of most active stocks are the market quotations. Let us consider ACF. For the past 52 weeks the high has been $52\frac{3}{8}$ and the low $30\frac{1}{2}$ (the price of common stock is set in terms of eighths). The annual dividend based on the most recent quarterly (or semi-annual) declaration is $1.40. The dividend yield of 2.8 percent is obtained by dividing the $1.40 by the closing price of $50. The "P-E Ratio" is the price/earnings ratio, and the 238 is obtained by dividing the current price by the earnings per share. There were 35,400 shares traded during the day. The stock was traded at a high of $50 and a low of $49\frac{1}{8}$ and closed at its high of $50. The close was $\frac{3}{4}$ higher than the close of the previous market day.

Where there is a letter indicating a footnote, reference may be made to the "Explanatory Notes" at the end of the table. For example, with Borg-Warner (Brg Wa), the symbol "a" leads us to the footnotes. The footnote tells us that there was "split or stock dividend of 25 per cent or more in the past 52 weeks."

Speculative Bubbles

To this point we have assumed that expected dividends are the sole basis for stock valuation, but an equity valuation model should also incorporate the possibility of a short-run speculative bubble, that is, the possibility that the market price exceeds the intrinsic value of the stock. This involves explicitly considering the possibility of selling the stock in the future at a price P_T in excess of its intrinsic value. If the investor expects to hold the stock for T periods, the indifference price would be

$$P = \sum_{t=1}^{T} \frac{D_t}{(1 + k_e)^t} + \frac{P_T}{(1 + k_e)^T} \qquad (12.22)$$

where P_T is the investor's expected market price in period T. The maximum price the investor would be willing to pay today is the maximum P over all holding periods, T.

If the market is efficient, speculate bubbles do not exist.

Market Efficiency

It is frequently said that the stock market is "efficient." The term efficient in this context has a different meaning from the way the term efficient is normally used in a production activity context. This is not a reference to how effectively resources are used.

A market for securities is efficient if the risk-adjusted present value of each of the securities is equal to its market price. Secondly, with an efficient market, any information (e.g., newspapers and annual reports) that is available to the market has already affected the market prices. In an efficient market there are no good buys and no bad buys. You can throw darts at the set of companies and do as well as the most sophisticated analyst.

The efficient market theory comes in several forms. The weak form says that inspection of past prices gives you no information about the next price change. Knowing that the stock price is now $30 per share would lead to an estimate that the next price will be close to $30, but looking at the past pattern of price changes (the path the stock price took to arrive at $30) is no help in deciding whether the next price will be larger or smaller than $30. Price changes are random. A large group of stock market experts are called chartists. They inspect past patterns and conclude that the stock will go up or down. The weak form efficient market theory says they cannot do this. Future price changes are random.

With a semistrong efficient market, the market price intelligently reflects all publicly available information (newspapers, radio, publications of the firm, etc.). To say that a market is semistrong efficient is to make a stronger statement than it is to say that it is "weak form" efficient. The third form of efficiency is for the market to be "strong form" efficient. This would mean that the market price reflects all information, including inside information.

Intuitively, the weak form and the semistrong form are easier to accept than is the strong form. If we had inside information and could use it, we could probably make abnormal returns buying and selling based on that information. If you think that having inside information would *not* help you earn an abnormally high return, then you accept the strong form efficient market hypothesis.

If the capital markets are semistrong efficient, then why do so many investors spend so much money on investment analysis and financial analysts? The hope of beating the market causes investors to be willing to spend the resources. It is the expenditure of these resources by the nonbelievers that makes the market semistrong efficient.

There will always be anecdotes of investors who have a specific strategy that applied for a given time period has led to abnormally high profits. The question still remains as to how they will do in the next time period.

If we randomly divide the total market into 60 portfolios of 20 stocks each, approximately 30 of these portfolios will do better than average. We have 30 portfolio "managers" who are heros.

If we play the same game for another time period, we will have some of the same winners win again. But this does not mean that the probability of the two time winners winning again in the third time period is larger than that of the two-time losers.

Can we test the efficiency of markets? The answer is yes, but not so that we have decisive answers. The problem is that we need to use an equilibrium model of stock prices to test market efficiency. So any test will be implicitly testing the market model being used (say, the capital asset pricing model) and market efficiency. The market may be efficient, but the market model being used may not correctly capture the market process.

Thus we cannot rely on empirical tests to prove, without question, the extent of market efficiency. However, if we consider the size of the capital market and the number of sellers and number of potential buyers, it would be very surprising if the market were not very close to being semistrong efficient.

Even if we were to find some inefficiency (such as buying stock in January), publication that excess profits can be made by buying stock in January would tend to eliminate the opportunity to make profits by applying the strategy.

Certainly, for the investor who does not have inside information and cannot buy a high level of highly technical knowledge about a firm or an industry, it is safer to base an investment strategy on the assumption that the market is efficient than to assume that the market is inefficient with large profits to be made by trading.

The Securities Industry

If a manufacturer needed additional cash to finance working capital, it can go to its commercial bank. If it needed cash to buy some land or to construct a building, it can go to either the mortgage department of its commercial bank or a savings institution that specialized in handling mortgages. But suppose that the manufacturer needed additional funds on a long-term basis and had no mortgageable assets to use as collateral. There exists a diverse collection of firms that perform the function of bringing together the suppliers and demanders of long-term, nonmortgage capital. In addition to helping establish long-term relationships between suppliers and demanders of capital, these firms service various needs of both the suppliers and demanders for as long as the relationship is maintained. For example, investors who have committed a sum of money to a manufacturer on a long-term basis will probably want periodic progress reports from the borrower, or they may need cash before the term of the investment has expired and may want to sell the securities. The firms and other institutions, such as stock markets, that satisfy these needs are referred to as the securities industry. They are part of the *capital market*.

Life Cycle of a Firm

To get a better picture of the functions performed by the securities industry, it is helpful to take a hypothetical firm and follow it through its life history. Typically, a new firm is started by one or more owners using their personal savings and perhaps the savings of a few personal friends, or venture capitalists, and bank loans. Once profitable, many businesses are able to finance themselves on a long-term basis solely from retained earnings. However, if the business is successful and grows rapidly, it is very likely it will sometime have to choose between raising additional long-term funds externally or slowing down its rate of growth to what can be financed from retained earnings. If thousands or tens of thousands of dollars are needed, the firm may be able to raise the funds by itself. If hundreds of thousands or millions of dollars are needed, it is probable that specialized help will be required.

Individuals or firms that specialize in providing equity capital to small businesses are known as venture capitalists. The venture capitalist may be a wealthy individual, a partnership of a small number of wealthy individuals, a subsidiary of a one-bank holding company, a life insurance company, or some similar financial or nonfinancial institution. The business needing the funds may approach the venture capitalist directly, or it may operate through an investment banker. Investment banking is similar to commercial banking in that it involves arranging for a supply of funds. The commercial bank lends its own money (generally obtained by its own borrowing) at short term. The investment banker arranges for a placement of somebody else's money on a long-term basis.

An investment banker has access to a large number of venture capitalist firms. It knows the special requirements and objectives of each. Thus, if the business needing equity capital approaches the investment banker, the investment banker may be in a position to suggest whether or not this business could be attractive to one or more venture capitalist firms.

Other routes for raising capital are possible. If several millions of dollars are needed, the investment banker may inquire as to whether the owners of the firm would be willing to sell their business to a larger firm that could provide the necessary financing. The larger firm usually is already listed on a stock exchange, and it is large enough to provide the necessary funds to finance the rapid growth of a smaller firm. Most investment bankers and many commercial banks have the capability of acting as advisors to either an acquiring firm or the firm being acquired.

If the owners of the small firm are not willing to be acquired, the investment banker may suggest a public sale of the firm's stock. For example, if the firm needed $2 million, it might sell 1 million new shares at $2.20 each to investors with $.20 per share to cover the expenses of the sale, including the commission earned by the investment banker. In this situation, the investment bankers would sell blocks of 100 or more shares to the different investors.

When funds are obtained from a few acquaintances or from a venture capitalist, the owners of the business are in a position to discuss its prospects with the persons applying the funds. However, this is not possible when the number of fund suppliers reaches into the hundreds or thousands. A firm that has had a public sale of its stock needs to communicate by sending written documents from the company to its stockholders. The annual report is a primary example of such formal written communications. The firm has to conform to the information requirements of the Securities and Exchange Commission (SEC). This is discussed later in the chapter.

Another characteristic of a publicly owned firm is that it requires a secondary market for the company's stock. In a firm with a small number of stockholders who know each other, a stockholder wanting to sell stock can personally contact other stockholders who might buy it. However, once a company has had a public sale of its stock, there will be many stockholders who do not know each other. If one or more wishes to sell, they cannot personally contact other stockholders. However, the investment banking firm that handled the original sale of the stock to the public is in a strategic position because it is likely to know who owns stock and who might be interested in buying more. One service that investment bankers ordinarily provide for a company after it goes public is called market making. A market maker buys stock from stockholders who wish to sell it and keeps inventories on hand to sell to others who wish to buy. This market-making function is performed by investment bankers and by other specialized firms in the securities industry. When these firms operate outside the framework of an organized exchange, they are called over-the-counter market makers. (Really, the over-the-counter market for stock is an over-the-telephone market. The actual trades are arranged on the phone, although the stock certificates themselves may be delivered "over-the-counter.")

In the example described, stock was sold to the public by the issuing firm, which itself received the greatest part of the proceeds. A transaction in which stocks or bonds are sold by the issuer is called a primary transaction.

A transaction is also classified as a primary transaction if the stock is sold by an intermediary who had bought the stock from the company with the intention of promptly reselling it. Such intermediaries are called underwriters. In a public sale of the kind described in the text, the investment banker ordinarily acts as an underwriter, buying the stock from the issuing company and reselling it to the public. An advantage of this approach is that it guarantees that the company has the money. More rarely, stock may be sold on a "best efforts" basis. In this case, the investment banking firm merely guarantees that it will do its best to sell the stock as an agent. It incurs no liability if it is unable to do so.

Sometimes the occasion for the first public sale of a company's stock is that the owners need money, not the company. Suppose that a company has been started by its owner-managers and has grown to a substantial size solely through retained earning and additional capital contributions by the original owners and a few personal friends. Now, one or more of the stockholders needs additional cash for some reason. A common situation is that the primary stockholders are approaching retirement age or want to ensure that their estates will have sufficient funds to pay the estate taxes when they are due without a forced sale of the company's stock. In this case, the stockholders may approach an investment banker and arrange a public sale of part of their shares of the company's stock. The effect on the company is in some respects the same as if it has sold stock to the public. It must establish communications with the new stockholders, issue annual reports, and so on. The company's stock will now be bought and sold on a public market. This makes it easier to set a value on holdings of the stock and is one of the additional advantages of going public.

A first public offering occurs when stock is sold to the public for the first time. The offering may be a primary offering if the stock is sold by the company, or a secondary offering if the stock is sold by existing stockholders, or a combination of the two if some stock is being sold by the company and some by its stockholders. Secondary offerings also occur where the company's stock is already being traded but a major stockholder wants to sell a large number of shares.

Underwriting Syndicates

Four major functions are performed by the investment banker in arranging a public offering. The first is advising the corporation as to how it should raise money. If a public offering route has been accepted, the second function is helping the company with the various specialized tasks that are required.

These two functions are called origination. A third function performed in most, but not all, public offerings is underwriting, that is, buying a large block of the stock from the company (or a controlling stockholder) with the intention of reselling it to the public. This involves risks to the investment bankers since there can be no guarantee that the underwriters will be able to resell at a profit all of the stock they buy from the company. Underwriting is essentially a risk-taking function. The fourth function performed by the investment banker is the sale of the securities to investors who expect to hold them for a long period of time. This is called the distribution function.

Occasionally, for a very small issue, one investment banker may originate the issue, underwrite it, and then distribute it to the public. However, it is much more common for the investment banker that originates the issue to put together a temporary syndicate of firms who will share the underwriting risks and cooperate with the managing underwriter (originator) in distributing the issue. On very large issues, in addition to the underwriting syndicate, there may be a still third collection of firms, the selling group, who participate in distributing the issue but do not participate in underwriting it.

The investment banking firm that acts as the advisor to the issuer nearly always plays a role in managing the underwriting and distribution syndicate. If the originating investment banker is well known in the securities industry and is believed to be competent and experienced in this function, it may manage the syndicate by itself. Sometimes an investment banker that is not well known as an originator may be the chief financial advisor to the issuer. In these circumstances, the originator may request a more prestigious firm to work with it as co-manager in organizing the underwriting group and the distribution group. In effect, the more prestigious and experienced underwriter lends its prestige and experience to help make the issue a success.

A tombstone ad appears in the financial press at the time that a public offering is made. The tombstone ad lists the name of the issuer, the type of security being issued, and the names of the firms in the underwriting group from whom additional information can be obtained. The firms participating in the underwriting syndicate are listed in the tombstone ads in a precise style. The firms managing the offering are listed first. Next there are alphabetical listings of the other firms in the underwriting syndicate with more than one repetition of the alphabet. Each alphabetical repetition marks a different "class" of underwriters. Classes are ranked in prestige order, and it is a matter of great importance for firms to attempt to increase their prestige or standings in the industry. Within any class, firms are listed in strict alphabetical order. An investment banking firm's ranking depends on a great variety of factors, but generally it reflects the managing underwriter's appraisal of the firm's competence and its ability to fulfill its sales quota and thus contribute to the profitability of the underwriting syndicate. Firms that are higher in the ranking often will have larger sales quotas. Since firms are paid on a commission basis based on the proportion of the underwriting risks that they absorb and on the percentage of the issue that they sell, the higher a firm's ranking, the more profit opportunities are available to it.

Pricing a Public Offering

From the point of view of the issuing firm, a critical step in preparing for a public offering of common stock is to choose an investment banker who will become the firm's managing underwriter. If the firm has previously made a public offering and was satisfied with the managing underwriter at that time, it will probably return to the same investment banking firm. The firm making a first public offering that does not already have an established relationship with an investment banker may shop around to try to find the investment banking firm that can do the best job for it. Ordinarily, a primary interest of the issuing firm will be to sell its stock at the highest possible price per share, and this will probably be uppermost in its mind in selecting an investment banker. A problem is that the preparation of a public offering will take time. Since the price at which stock can be sold will depend very much on stock market conditions at the time of the sale, the investment banker who is approached by a firm is not going to promise an exact price. At best, the investment banker might indicate a range of prices within which it thinks the stock could be sold under the then existing market conditions. However, it is likely that market conditions will change before the stock is finally sold; in some cases, the issuing firm will find that it receives less than expected.

The decision about what price to charge for the stock is made just before the stock is actually sold, first to the underwriting group and then, almost immediately, to the public. From the time the managing underwriter is chosen until the underwriter and the issuer are ready to settle on the final offering price, several months will have passed, and the issuer will have committed and paid for a considerable amount of highly specialized legal accounting and printing work. This puts the issuing firm in a rather weak bargaining position at the time the price is set. If the issuer does not like the price suggested by the managing underwriter, it can select a new underwriter and start all over again. Although some of the legal work might still be useful in such a switch, a substantial portion of the accounting, and of course printing, would need to be repeated. Thus additional money would have to be expended, and the firm would have to wait several more months for its new capital, during which time market conditions could change for the worse.

The difference between the offering price at which members of the public can buy the stock from the underwriting group and the price at which the underwriting group bought the stock from the issuer is called the underwriting spread.

In the investment banking industry, an issue is said to be successful if the stock bought from the issuer is quickly sold at the offering price and subsequently increases in price in trading on the secondary market. An issue is described as unsuccessful if it takes a long time to sell or if it is not possible to sell all of it at the original offering price and it becomes necessary to sell the balance at a lower price or to incur more selling costs. In the latter case, the underwriting firms may suffer losses. An issue that is sold out at the offering price and neither rises nor falls in price in secondary trading is not considered to be as successful as one that increases modestly in price after the offering, but it is better than some of the alternatives.

To economists and, occasionally to issuers, defining a stock that increases in price to be a success seems somewhat a strange point of view. The fact that an issue rose in price in secondary market trading after the offering was completed suggests that the issue was sold at too low a price. With a higher price and the same spread, the issuer would receive more money if the same number of shares were sold or could sell fewer shares (a smaller interest in the company) to raise the same amount of money.

In the recent past, most issues have been successful; that is they sold out quickly and then increased in price in trading on the secondary market. Why is it in the best interest of the issue or of its underwriter to allow this to happen? At a higher price, the issue might be more difficult for the underwriter to sell and the risk of an unsuccessful offering would be greater. Both the firm and the underwriter want to avoid this appearance of failure. The underpricing provides potential buyers with an incentive to buy a relatively large amount of stock rapidly. If the underpricing of new issues continues, abnormal returns can be earned, and this is a form of semistrong market inefficiency.

The magnitude of the underpricing is greater than can easily be explained as a necessary inducement to potential buyers. The magnitude of the apparent underpricing of new issues seems to be greater for small companies than for larger ones, greater for primary issues than for secondary issues, and greater for companies that are unable to attract a prestigious underwriter than for companies that can.

A possible explanation has to do with the method of determining the investment banker's compensation. The National Association of Security Dealers, which regulates the over-the-counter market, has recommended that underwriters should not receive a cash compensation of more than 10 percent of the value of an issue. This is more than adequate for a large well-established company selling a large block of stock, but it is not adequate for smaller companies with less attractive records if the investment banker has to expend a lot of selling effort.

Underwriters are allowed to accept options to buy additional stock at the offering price as a part of their compensation. The value of these options is not included in the 10 percent, and the options ordinarily cannot be exercised until a year after the offering. In this situation, underpricing the stock increases the value of the options to the underwriters and, therefore, increases their compensation. The issuer might have been better off if it had been allowed to pay the underwriters a higher spread and then obtained a price closer to the aftermarket price.

Pricing a stock offering is particularly interesting when a company is going public for the first time because there is no past history of stock prices or price/earning ratios to use in predicting the market price. If a company is already public and wishes to sell additional stock, the pricing problem is much less severe.

Government Regulation

Before 1933, public offerings of primary issues of stock or bonds were regulated by the individual states. Most of the states had "blue-sky" laws to regulate the sale of securities (operators were selling everything, even the "sky"). These laws are not very effective, partly because it was so easy for the perpetrators of security frauds to move from one state to another. In 1933, the federal government passed the first of a series of major reform laws dealing with the securities markets. The Thirty-Three Act, as it is commonly called, deals mainly with primary issues of securities. It is an investor protection act whose philosophy is not to prevent people from making unwise choices but to be sure they have available to them the proper information for decision making. The act makes it a violation of federal law for an issuer or its officers or underwriters to sell a security without first disclosing all the relevant material facts that they know or should know. This provision can be enforced by government action and by private suits to recover damages.

Suppose that a company sells stock to the public but fails to disclose some material facts. If an investor buys the stock and subsequently it goes down in price, the investor can sue the issuer, its officers, and underwriters for fraud and for violating the SEC regulations for failing to disclose the adverse information.

Business firms selling stock or bonds to the public must register the securities with the SEC. Registration involves preparing a booklet called a prospectus that contains the information about a company that needs to be disclosed to satisfy the antifraud provisions. This booklet is submitted to the SEC staff that reviews it. The SEC does not certify that the information in the booklet is correct, but if the staff notices any material gaps, it may request the issuer to provide additional information before it recommends that the SEC allow the securities to be registered and sold. The act also provides that a copy of the booklet must be given to every purchaser before the sale becomes final.

As in many other social institutions, the system does not work the way its founders thought it would. Every neophyte securities lawyer quickly learns that it is absolutely vital to include in the prospectus all possible derogatory information in order to protect the issuer against the possibility of being sued if the value of the stock declines after the sale. However, there is no equal necessity to include favorable information. The courts have decided that if favorable information is omitted and the stock goes up, a potential purchaser who did not buy the stock because the favorable information was not available cannot sue the company for failing to disclose. According to the courts, a loss has not been suffered. (An economist might argue that there is an opportunity loss.) On the other hand, if a favorable statement later turns out to be false or misleading, someone who bought stock that goes down in price may sue. Therefore, the common practice is not to say anything optimistic in a prospectus but to make it a compendium of pessimistic comments and of accounting statements prepared in accordance with generally accepted accounting principles.

Prospectuses are carefully prepared by the issuer's lawyer, are carefully reviewed by the SEC's staff, and are printed and distributed to every purchaser, many of whom never read it. Few investors would buy a stock based only on the information in its prospectus. But securities analysts carefully read prospectuses for the statistical and background information they contain and occasionally become rich as a result. Average investors are likely to rely on their broker or investment advisor to give them a balanced view of the pros and cons of various new issues. Under current rules and practices, such a balanced view is not included in a prospectus.

One interesting disclosure in a prospectus several years ago involved an electronics firm (now bankrupt) that had one product and had just lost the right to sell that product, since its licensing arrangement with the patent owner had lapsed.

The saddest prospectus the authors have read involved a single-plant firm that was suffering operating losses and additionally felt that it had to disclose the fact its sole plant was sinking into a swamp.

A prospectus does not disclose all, but investors should take advantage of their existence and at least learn of the pitfalls (or swamps) that exist.

Private Placements

Complying with the registration requirements of the Thirty-Three Act is an expensive and time-consuming process that exposes the issuer and its lawyers, accountants, and underwriters to considerable potential risk. Therefore, business managers have sometimes sought ways to raise long-term funds that avoid these problems. The provisions of the Thirty-Three Act apply only to public sales of securities. Private placements are exempt. Even though a company has already sold stock to the public, it might wish to place an issue of its bonds privately. Someone who buys stock in a private sale cannot later resell it in a public sale without going through registration except under very special procedures.

Sometimes even additional stock can be sold without going through the public registration process if the stock is sold on a person-to-person basis so that the general public is not involved. Some stock bought in a private placement is "letter" stock. The name comes from the custom of requiring the purchaser to write a letter to the seller indicating that the purchaser intended to buy the stock for "investment" and not for resale. The purpose of the letter was to provide evidence that the purchaser was not a statutory underwriter. The buyer of letter stock may agree not to sell the stock for a given period of time. Letter stock generally has voting rights.

Stock that is sold privately is often priced 30 percent below identical shares that are registered. This is an impressive differential in two ways. It is impressive that buyers consider the lack of liquidity so important that it reduces the value of stock by 30 percent. If buyers felt that the stock was worth more than this reduced amount, the competition between potential buyers would allow the company to sell the stock at a higher price. It is impressive that a seller may be willing to accept 30 percent less for its stock in order to avoid the hassles of the Thirty-Three Act registration.

Although nonregistered privately placed stock of publicly held companies sells at a substantial discount, the same is not true with respect to bonds. The interest rate that corporations pay on privately placed bonds is slightly more than what they would have had to pay on publicly traded bonds, but the differences are relatively modest.

Secondary Markets

There are 15,000 or 20,000 firms in the United States that have sold stock to the public and are still in existence as separate firms having neither failed nor been acquired. About 1,500 of these companies have stock that is listed and traded on the New York Stock Exchange. About another 1,000 are listed and traded on the American Stock Exchange.

A few dozen companies that are not listed or either of these exchanges are listed on one of the regional exchanges. The main regional exchanges in operation today are the Boston Stock Exchange, the Philadelphia Stock Exchange, the Midwest Stock Exchange (Chicago), and the Pacific Coast Stock Exchange (Los Angeles and San Francisco).

Over 4,000 companies are traded on NASDAQ, a computerized trading system developed and maintained by the National Association of Security Dealers.

The Investor Populations

Who owns the stock issued by these publicly held corporations? The investor population is ordinarily divided into two broad categories: individuals and institutions. Both are very diverse collections. Nearly half of all the stock is managed by institutions, about half is owned and managed by individuals directly. There is considerable variation from year to year, mostly because of changes in stock prices.

Commercial banks are not allowed to own common stock directly. However, the trust departments of commercial banks are allowed to serve as executors and administrators and investment managers for trusts and estates. Typically wealthy individuals prepare wills so that on death, property will be transferred to the bank to be held "in trust" for the benefit of spouses and children or grandchildren. The bank is to manage the assets and uses the proceeds for those purposes. The beneficiaries do not directly control the assets. There are tens of thousands of personal trust accounts in the 50 or so banks that have the largest trust departments and do most of the trust business. Personal trust business is relatively stable since once a trust is established and assigned to a particular bank, it is rare that it will be transferred to some other institution. Trustees are typically compensated by being paid a certain percentage of the value of the assets.

The next most important type of account within the bank trust department is the corporate pension fund account. Corporate pension funds can be managed directly by banks, insurance companies, and independent investment advisors, or in other ways. However, bank trust departments have become leaders in this field, and they manage a large fraction of these funds.

Another important category of financial institutions consists of investment companies. An investment company is a corporation that sells its stock and invests the proceeds in the stocks and bonds of other companies. Investment companies that pay out their earnings and capital gains in the same year that they receive them are exempt from corporate income tax. (The shareholders in the investment company pay ordinary income or capital gain taxes on the dividends and capital gains that they receive, but the investment company itself does not have to pay the tax.) Some investment companies are like ordinary corporations in that they sell their own stock to the public only occasionally; at other times, someone wishing to buy shares must find a stockholder who is willing to sell. Investment companies who operate in this way are called closed-end investment companies. If the company is large enough, its shares may be traded on stock exchanges just like other companies' shares.

Most investment companies are mutual funds. A mutual fund is an open-end investment company. At any time a mutual fund will sell additional shares or buy its own shares from its stockholders. The shares are bought and sold on the basis of the market value of the assets of the mutual fund. If a mutual

---

Valuation of Teledyne

An attempt to value the common stock of Teledyne highlights all the difficulties of applying any of the dividend valuation models.

In 1961 Teledyne had *sales* of $4.5 million. In 1983 it had *income* of $304.6 million ($14.87 per share). The annual growth rate in earnings per share for the 22-year period was 39 percent.

The company does not pay a cash dividend and never has and will not in the foreseeable future.

During 1983, it sold as low as $123 per share and as high as $173 per share.

The market is betting that cash will be distributed in some form to investors some time in the future.

---

fund needs cash to buy (redeem) its stock, the funds are obtained by selling some of its assets. Since the assets of a mutual fund are the stocks and bonds, it is relatively easy to determine their market value. Most mutual funds calculate the market value of their assets daily.

Conclusions

Measuring the cost of equity capital requires a theory of stock price determination. We explored a model of price behavior based on expected future dividends and defined the cost of equity capital to be the discount rate that equates the present value of the expected dividend stream to the current market price, normalized to adjust for speculative bubbles or temporary market imbalances.

It is one thing to measure the cost of equity capital and another to determine the factors that affect it. We can suppose that the cost of equity capital is determined by the market's time value of money and a compensation for risk, but obtaining reliable estimates of the cost of equity is difficult.

The bringing together of people (and organizations) with funds to invest and organizations (both profit and not-for-profit) that need capital is a major industry unique to capitalist economics. The organizations that successfully present their cases obtain capital, and those that fail to present an attractive case must do without until they can modify their situation.

The arrangement is perfectly democratic in the sense that people vote freely with their dollars. The vote, it is hoped, is a reasonably informed one, with government regulations being aimed at improving the quality of information.

An efficient allocation of capital is extremely important to the well-being of the members of society. Has the system described in this chapter worked? Can it be improved? These are questions that will be asked not only by the citizens of the United States but also by citizens of many other countries throughout the world.

Review Problem 12.1

It is shown in the appendix to the chapter that the growth rate for a company using debt is

$$g = rb + b[r - k_i(1 - t_c)]\frac{B}{S}$$

The RST Company currently has a debt-to-common stock ratio of .6 and expects to maintain the ratio. Its after-tax borrowing rate is .08, and it can earn .13 after tax on new investments. The dividend payout rate is .3.

(a) Compute the growth rate.
(b) What would be the growth rate if the firm were to issue no additional debt?
(c) If the dividend for the next year is expected to be $2.40 and if investors want a .12 return from investment in this common stock, what is the value of a share? Assume that the debt/equity ratio is .6.
(d) What will be the value of the common stock after one year?

Solution to Review Problem 12.1

(a) The retention rate is .7.
$$g = .13 \times .7 + .7(.13 - .08).6$$
$$= .091 + .021 = .112$$

(b) $g = rb = .091$

(c) $P = \dfrac{D_1}{k_e - g} = \dfrac{\$2.40}{.12 - .112} = \$300$

(d) $P_1 = \$300(1.112) = \$333.60$

or

$$P = \frac{\$2.6688}{.12 - .112} = \$333.60$$

where $2.40(1.112) = 2.6688$.

PROBLEMS

1. The ABC Company is retaining .4 of its earnings and is able to earn an average of .15 on these retentions. It can borrow funds at .09 and has a debt/equity ratio of .5. Earnings are currently $10 million. There are zero taxes.
  (a) What is the current growth rate? What will be the next year's earnings?
  (b) What would be the growth rate if no debt were used at all?
  (c) Assume that the average return on new funds invested goes to .13 if the retention rate goes to .6. What would be the new growth rate? The new earnings?
  (d) Would you recommend the policy implied by (a) or (c)?

2. Assume the relationship $P = D_1/(k_e - g)$ applies and

$$D_1 = \$1 \qquad k_e = .15$$

  (a) What is P if $g = .14$?
  (b) What is P if $g = .05$?
  (c) What is P if $g = -.05$?
  (d) What is P if $g = .25$?

3. Assume that a firm currently earns $1,000. It invests (retains, with zero debt) .4 of its earnings on which it earns a .25 return and has a .10 growth rate. Present a table showing:
  (a) Earnings
  (b) Dividends
  (c) Retention
  (d) Change in earnings for the next three years

4. The president of ABC Company in discussing the future of his firm indicated that there would be no change in dividend policy (currently it employs a payout rate of .4 of earnings) or profit rate on investments (investment opportunities were expected to earn .12 on the average). He forecasted a growth rate in earnings of .10 per year. The firm has used no long-term debt to date and is expected to continue this policy.
  Discuss the comments of the president.

5. Assume that the firm in Problem 4 has a normal capital structure of $1 debt for every $2 of stock. Debt costs .04 (after taxes).
  How does this change your answer?

6. Derive $P = D_1/(k_e - g)$ using discrete compounding by assuming that D_1 is the first dividend to be received, one period from now, and that further dividends grow at rate g. That is, show that

$$P = \frac{D_1}{(1 + k_e)^1} + \frac{D_1(1 + g)^1}{(1 + k_e)^2} + \frac{D_1(1 + g)^2}{(1 + k_e)^3} + \cdots$$

reduces to

$$P = \frac{D_1}{k_e - g}, \quad \text{if } k_e > g$$

Hint: If $0 < x < 1$, then

$$\sum_{i=0}^{\infty} x^i = \frac{1}{1 - x}$$

7. (Problem 6 continued) If the dividend in period 1 is $D_0(1 + g)$ instead of D_1, what value do you get for P?

   What is the formula for k_e in this case?

8. Mr. Jones thinks that the dividends of the ABC Company will stay constant at $1 per year. Mr. Smith thinks the dividend will grow at a constant rate of .15 per year forever. Both think the stock is a reasonable but marginal buy at a price of $20.

   What is the implicit cost of equity capital for each of the investors?

9. Mr. Jones thinks that the $1 dividend of the ABC Company will increase at a rate of .15 per year. Mr. Smith thinks that the $1 dividend will decrease at a rate of .04 per year. Both investors require a .16 return per year on their funds. The ABC Company will pay a $1 cash dividend at year end.

   What would you expect each of the two investors to be willing to pay for a share of common stock?

10. Now assume for Problem 9 that Jones thinks that the .15 increase will continue for two years and then the rate of growth will be zero.

    What value would you expect Jones to place on a share? **Hint:** Rather than seek a formula write out the dividends for each year and compute the present value.

11. It can be shown that if

    $$g = bk_e$$

    then

    $$E/P = k_e$$

    (that is, E/P can be used as estimator of k_e).

If a firm has zero debt and retains some earnings, what will the average yield on investments have to be for E/P to be a good estimate of the cost of equity capital?

12. Under certain conditions the growth rate for a company using debt is

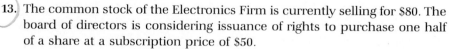

$$g = rb + b[r - k_i(1 - t_c)]\frac{B}{S}$$

The ABC Company currently has a debt-to-common stock ratio of .4, but with future retained earnings, it expects to use $1 of debt for each additional $1 of retained earnings. Its after-tax borrowing rate is .05, and it can earn .12 on new investments. The dividend payout rate is .3.
   (a) Compute the growth rate.
   (b) What would be the growth rate if the firm were to issue no additional debt?

13. The common stock of the Electronics Firm is currently selling for $80. The board of directors is considering issuance of rights to purchase one half of a share at a subscription price of $50.
   (a) What would be the value of a right?
   (b) What would you expect the price of the common stock to be after the rights are separated from the stock?
   (c) Verify your answer to (b), assuming that 1 million shares were outstanding prior to the offering. What is the value of the firm prior to the offering and after? What is the value per share before and after the rights offering?

14. Mr. Jones expects the dividend of ABC Company to be $2 at the end of this year and further expects it to grow at a 4 percent rate thereafter. He believes that a yield of 14 percent would adequately compensate him for the time value of money and the uncertainties associated with the dividend stream. The stock is currently selling at $22 per share.
   (a) If Mr. Jones expects to hold the stock indefinitely, should he purchase it?
   (b) If Mr. Jones plans to hold the stock only for two years but anticipates that the market price will adjust to reflect his expectations and yield requirements by the end of the holding period, should he purchase the stock?
   (c) If, for "technical reasons," Jones expects the stock price to rise to $25 by the end of the second year, should he purchase the stock?

15. Assume that a company is currently paying dividends of $1 per share. The stockholders expect a return of .12 (they apply this discount factor to future cash flows).
    (a) If an investor expects the dividends to grow at a rate of .08 per year per share, how much would the investor pay for a share of the stock?
    (b) If an investor were willing to pay $100 for a share of the stock, what dividend growth rate would this imply?

16. Mrs. Smith has a time value of money of .16. She has just bought for $101 a stock that is paying a $1-per-share dividend at the end of the year.
    At what price does Mrs. Smith expect the stock to be selling one period from now? Assume that she expects to earn .16.

17. A company is currently paying a year-end dividend of $10 and the stock is selling for $100. Investors think the dividend growth will be at a rate of .06 per year.
    What is the implied cost of equity capital?

18. The XYZ Company is retaining .4 of its earnings and is able to earn an average of .20 on these retentions. Earnings are currently $1,000,000.
    (a) There are zero taxes. What is the growth rate if no debt is used?
    (b) What is the growth rate if a debt/equity ratio of .8 is maintained? Assume that with the use of debt the average return on new investments is .15. The cost of debt is .12.
    (c) (Problem 18(b) continued)   What will the earnings be in the next year?
    (d) (Problem 18(a) continued)   If the retention rate is increased to .65, it is expected that .15 will be earned on new investments. No debt is used. What will be the new growth rate? Should the retention rate be .4 or .65? Explain.

19. Give True or False answers and explain.
    (a) Since $k_e = D/P + g$, if g were to increase, k_e would increase.
    (b) If a firm is growing at a rate of .25, this implies that $k_e \geq .25$.
    (c) The relationship $P = D_0/(k_e - g)$, where $g = rb$, implicitly assumes that in each successive year more dollars may be invested to earn r.

20. A company intends to retain .6 of its earnings. The marginal return on the invested funds will be .20, and the average return will be .15. The firm on the average earns .12. There will be $1 of debt added for every $4 of common stock, but the firm's overall debt/equity ratio (total debt/total stock) will be 1. New funds can be borrowed at a cost of .10, but the average cost of all borrowed capital by the firm will be .07.
    New funds can be borrowed at a cost of .10, but the average cost of all borrowed capital by the firm will be .07.

The statutory income tax rate is .46. The average tax rate for the firm will be .30. The new investments will be taxed at .46.

(a) The growth rate in dividends for the firm is _____ .

(b) The growth rate in earnings for the firm is _____ .

(c) If the firm used zero debt, the growth rate in dividends would be

_____ .

21. The ABC Company has an average cost of debt of .08, but the next debt borrowed will cost .12. It is currently earning .15 on investment, but it will earn .18 on the average on the next period's investments (the marginal return on new investment will be .0648).

For every $1 of common stock, the firm has used $1 of debt, but in the future (this period), $2 of debt will be used for every dollar.

The statutory corporate tax rate is .46. Because of investment tax credits, the average tax rate is .30.

The company pays out .4 of its earnings as dividends.

If growth is going to occur only because of investment, what growth rate do you expect the firm to have for the next period?

REFERENCES

Barnea, A., R. A. Haugen, and L. W. Senbet. *Agency Problems and Financial Contracting.* Englewood Cliffs, N.J.: Prentice Hall, Inc., 1985.

Bauman, W. Scott. "Investment Returns and Present Values." *Financial Analysts Journal,* November–December 1969, 107–120.

Bierman, H., Jr., and J. Hass. "Normative Stock Price Models." *Journal of Financial and Quantitative Analysis,* September 1971. 1135–1144.

Bierman, H., Jr., D. H. Downes, and J. Hass. "Closed Form Stock Price Models." *Journal of Financial and Quantitative Analysis,* June 1972, 1797–1808.

Brigham, Eugene F., and James L. Pappas. "Duration of Growth, Change in Growth Rates, and Corporate Share Prices." *Financial Analysts Journal,* May–June 1966, 157–162.

Clendenin, John C., and Maurice Van Cleave. "Growth and Common Stock Values." *Journal of Finance,* December 1954, 365–376.

Durand, David. "Growth Stocks and the St. Petersburg Paradox." *Journal of Finance,* September 1957, 348–363.

Eiteman, David. "A Computer Program for Common Stock Valuation." *Financial Analysts Journal,* July–August 1968, 107–111.

Fama, Eugene F. "Efficient Capital Markets: A Review of Theory and Empirical Work." *Journal of Finance,* May 1970, 383–417.

———. "Components of Investment Performance." *Journal of Finance,* June 1972, 551–567.

———. *Foundations of Finance.* New York: Basic Books, Inc., 1976.

————, and James D. Macbeth. "Risk, Return and Equilibrium: Empirical Tests." *Journal of Political Economy*, May–June 1973, 607–36.

————, Merton H. Miller. *The Theory of Finance*. New York: Holt, Rinehart and Winston, 1972.

Francis, Jack Clark. "Intertemporal Differences in Systematic Stock Price Movements." *Journal of Financial and Quantitative Analysis*, June 1975, 205–20.

Friend, Irwin, Yoram Landskroner, and Etienne Losq. "The Demand for Risky Assets Under Uncertain Inflation." *Journal of Finance*, December 1976, 1287–1298.

Gordon, Myron J., and E. Shapiro. "Capital Equipment Analysis: The Required Rate of Profit." *Management Science*, October 1956, 102–110.

Holt, Charles C. "The Influence of Growth Duration on Share Prices." *Journal of Finance*, September 1963, 465–475.

Lerner, E. M., and W. T. Carleton, *A Theory of Financial Analysis*. New York: Harcourt, Brace and World, 1966.

Lorie, J. H., P. Dodd, and M. H. Hamilton. *The Stock Market Theories and Evidence*. Homewood, Ill.: Richard D. Irwin, Inc., second edition 1983.

Malkiel, Burton G. "Equity Yields, Growth, and the Structure of Share Prices." *American Economic Review*, December 1963, 1004–1031.

Modigliani, Franco and Gerald A. Pogue. "An Introduction to Risk and Return." *Financial Analysts Journal*, March–April 1974, 68–80, and May–June 1974, 68–86.

Mossin, Jan. *Theory of Financial Markets*. Englewood Cliff, N.J.: Prentice-Hall, Inc., 1973.

Pogue, Gerald A., and Kishore Lall. "Corporate Finance: An Overview," *Sloan Management Review*, Spring 1974, 19–38.

Roll, Richard. "A Critique of the Asset Pricing Theory Tests, Part I: On Past and Potential Testability of the Theory." *Journal of Financial Economics*, March 1977, 129–76.

————. "Performance Evaluation and Benchmark Errors." *Journal of Portfolio Management*, Summer 1980, 5–12.

————. "Orthogonal Portfolios." *Journal of Financial and Quantitative Analysis*, December 1980, 1005–1011.

Soldofsky, Robert M. "The History of Bond Tables and Stock Valuation Models." *Journal of Finance*, March 1966, 103–111.

Solomon, Ezra. *The Theory of Financial Management*. New York: Columbia University Press, 1963.

Walters, James E. "Dividend Policies and Common Stock Prices." *Journal of Finance*, March 1956, 29–41.

Wendt, Paul F. "Current Growth Stock Valuation Models." *Financial Analysts Journal*, March–April 1965, 91–103.

Williams, John Burr. *The Theory of Investment Values*. Cambridge, Mass.: Harvard University Press, 1938.

Appendix 12.1   Calculation of g with Leverage

We assume that the firm employs debt and desires to maintain a constant debt/equity ratio of B/S and that each dollar invested will earn a return of r.

If the change in the value of the stock is ΔS and the firm maintains its current debt/equity ratio, B/S, then the change in debt must be such that

$$\frac{B + \Delta B}{S + \Delta S} = \frac{B}{S}$$

or

$$B + \Delta B = \frac{B(S + \Delta S)}{S}$$

or

$$\Delta B = \frac{BS + \Delta SB - BS}{S} = \frac{B}{S} \Delta S$$

The change in common stock capital is

$$\Delta S = bE$$

where bE is the amount of retained earnings. Then it follows that

$$\Delta B = \frac{B}{S} \Delta S = \frac{B}{S} bE$$

is the additional debt issued to maintain the current debt/equity ratio, and the total investment is the sum of debt issued plus retained earnings:

$$I = \Delta B + bE = \frac{B}{S} bE + bE$$

If each dollar of investment earns r, the additional earnings net of debt interest are

$$\Delta E = rI - \text{interest on debt}$$

$$= rbE + r\frac{B}{S}bE - k_i(1 - t_c)\frac{B}{S}bE$$

$$= rbE + [r - k_i(1 - t_c)]bE\frac{B}{S}$$

Dividing both sides by E yields

$$\frac{\Delta E}{E} = rb + [r - k_i(1 - t_c)]b\frac{B}{S}$$

Letting g denote the growth rate in earnings, we obtain

$$E(1 + g) = E + \Delta E$$

$$1 + g = 1 + \frac{\Delta E}{E}$$

so that subtracting 1 from both sides,

$$g = \frac{\Delta E}{E} = rb + [r - k_i(1 - t_c)]b\frac{B}{S}$$

This is the general case. If $B = 0$, then

$$g = rb$$

Chapter 13

Preferred Stock

Major Topics

1. Preferred stock, its uses and cost.
2. Preferred stock versus debt.
3. Institutional factors (the tax laws) and the relative desirability of preferred stock compared with other capital sources.
4. Convertible exchangeable perferred stock.
5. Variable rate preferred stock.

Preferred Stock: A Hybrid

Preferred stock is a security that, similar to debt, promises a well-defined (specified) but not necessarily a constant contractual dividend to the holders of the security. Unlike debt, it does not cause the firm to be subject to bankruptcy if the dividends are not paid. The term *preferred stock* implies that this security is in a more favorable position than the common stock. This conclusion is not likely to be valid for an individual investor paying taxes at a high rate. A corporate investor might like preferred stock because of a "dividend received credit" (in the United States only .15 of the dividend income received by a corporation is subject to tax).

Although preferred stock once played a major role in financing business firms, its role today is substantially less than it was before corporate taxes increased to a level of approximately 50 percent. The corporate tax savings associated with interest on debt make it difficult for preferred stock to compete with debt in the nonregulated sector of corporate activity. The capital gains possibilities for individual investors of common stock give common stock an advantage over preferred stock tied to a contractual dividend.

Preferred stock has historically been important to public utilities, and it is likely to be approximately 10 percent of a typical public utility's capital structure.

Preferred stock is a hybrid form of capital, possessing a mixture of debt and common stock characteristics. Like the interest on debt, its dividends may be fixed over time. However, "participating" preferred stock shares income with common stock according to some prearranged formula, and other preferred stock may pay a dividend that is linked to some independent measure such as the yield on government bonds. Like common stock, preferred stock is generally treated as equity capital for corporate tax purposes, so its dividends are paid from corporate earnings that have been taxed. Preferred stock generally has a perpetual life, although it may have a finite life, and it may have a call price specified and even a sinking fund where stock is to be repurchased by the firm in the open market. It is important to the issuing firm and to the investor that nonpayment of the preferred stock dividend does not trigger bankruptcy (preferred frequently has an accumulation provision and common stock dividends cannot be paid until all past due preferred dividends have been paid or the preferred stockholders have been compensated by some other means), and preferred stock dividends have to be approved by the board of directors before they become a legal liability of the corporation. Preferred stock generally does not have voting rights, but if a preferred stock dividend is passed over, the preferred stockholders sometimes have the right to select one or more members of the board of directors.

Although the dividends on some preferred stock are allowed as a tax deduction (these securities were all issued over 40 years ago), currently in the United States dividends of preferred stock are not deductible for taxes by a corporation (unlike the interest payment of debt). This is a major drawback, and it tends to limit the use of preferred stock by corporations. However, in some parts of the world preferred stock dividends are treated in the same manner for taxes as interest; thus in those areas this drawback would not apply. We can expect to see hybrids of preferred stock in the future and also changes in the tax laws encouraging the use of such securities. It is logical to have securities that bridge the gap between debt, where failure to pay interest results in bankruptcy, and common stock, where there is no stated commitment to pay dividends. From the investors' viewpoint, compared to common stock, preferred stock reduces somewhat the amount of uncertainty associated with future dividend payments.

Measuring the Cost of Preferred Stock

The cost of preferred stock is defined as the discount rate that equates the future expected preferred dividends (and call price if callable) to the present market price. Let P denote the current price of a share of preferred, D the annual constant dividend payment, and k_p the return required by investors or cost of the preferred stock. The current price of a share, if noncallable, may be defined in terms of D and k_p. The dividend is assumed to be a perpetuity with first payment one year from now:

$$P = \frac{D}{k_p} \qquad\qquad (13.1)$$

Solving for k_p, we obtain

$$k_p = \frac{D}{P} \qquad\qquad (13.2)$$

under the assumption that the issuing firm expects to pay the dividend for perpetuity. So the current cost of noncallable preferred stock to the issuing corporation is the stock's dividend yield.

Many recent issues of preferred stock have call provisions to provide protection to the issuing firm against decreases in k_p. If interest rates and stock yields should fall after selling a new issue and the issue is not callable, the issuing firm is stuck with perpetual financing at a high cost. For example, if the interest rate on a $100 preferred stock were 10 percent at time of issue (a $10 per year cash dividend) and if the market required a .08 return, the stock would have to be repurchased in the open market for

$$P = \frac{10}{.08} = \$125$$

if the firm wished to retire the obligation. If, on the other hand, a call provision were specified at, say, $110, the firm could call the $10 obligation per annum for $110 and replace it with a $110 par value, 8 percent issue paying only $8.80 per annum and issued at par. The company replaces a security promising to pay $10.00 a year with a security paying $8.80 a year. This is a saving of $1.20 per year. The $110 issue price is just enough to retire the outstanding preferred stock.

If there were no call provision and the company paid $125 to retire a share, the new security issued at $125 with a par of $125 and paying .08 would have an annual dividend of $10 and the company's financial position is not improved.

Investors prefer the preferred stock to be noncallable so that if interest rates fall, they may continue to earn a high return. Thus investors will require a higher yield on the callable preferred stock issue than on the noncallable issue. For example, if a noncallable issue is selling for 10 percent, an otherwise comparable callable issue would have to promise to pay somewhat more than 10 percent if the investor is to pay the same price for both issues.

In the example, if the 10 percent preferred stock were noncallable and if the fall in interest rates to .08 occurred in the first year, the investor who sells would receive $10 of dividends and $25 of capital gains for a total return on investment of 35 percent. With the preferred stock callable at $110, there would be only $10 of capital gains and the return on investment would be 20 percent.

If the call is expected to take place some time in the future, the expected return from holding the security until the call can be computed.

EXAMPLE 13.1

XYZ Corporation has decided to issue preferred stock even though current interest rates are thought to be abnormally high and are expected to fall. The preferred stock will carry a $10 dividend and will be sold for $105 with a call price of $110. The firm expects lower interest rates (say, 8 percent) in approximately two years and therefore expects to call the issue at that time. We can solve by trial and error for the cost of this preferred stock issue or equivalently the return earned by the investor):

$$105 = \sum_{t=1}^{2} \frac{10}{(1 + k_p)^t} + \frac{110}{(1 + k_p)^2}$$

In this case, k_p is approximately 12 percent while the nominal dividend yield of 10/105 is approximately 9.5 percent. The call provision seems to make the cost of the preferred stock greater than the nominal dividend yield, but this is misleading. Assume that after two years the stock price goes up to 125. Without a call provision, the two-period economic cost is

$$105 = \sum_{t=1}^{2} \frac{10}{(1 + k_p)^t} + \frac{125}{(1 + k_p)^2}$$

Solving for k_p (by trial and error), we find that k_p is now 18.25 percent. In this example the call provision reduces the cost of the preferred stock as long as the issue price of $105 is assumed to be independent of the call provision.

We could also compute the cost if the stock is called after period 2, and we would find that the cost is between .12 and .095, depending on when the security is called.

Factors Affecting the Cost of Preferred Stock

Preferred stock is similar to debt, and the factors affecting the cost of debt are also important here. There is, however, one additional factor that has to be discussed: the dividend received credit. If a corporation purchases equity capital (preferred or common stock) of another corporation, 85 percent of the dividends it receives on that stock is nontaxable income for the receiving corporation. On the other hand, all interest the corporation receives on taxable debt securities held is taxable. Insurance companies in particular find that the dividend received credit plus the relative predictability of the dividend flow makes preferred stock a desirable form of investment.

Not as risky as common stock and offering a high after-tax yield on the investment, a substantial amount of preferred stock is held by insurance companies. In fact, the demand for preferred stock by these companies is so great that the before-tax yield on preferred stock is sometimes below that of the before-tax yield on the debt of the same issuing firm, despite the fact that the preferred stock is obviously more risky, insofar as the debt has first claim to earnings and prior claim on assets in case of liquidation.

To explain why preferred stock may yield less than debt, let us examine the after-tax yield of debt. The effective after-tax yield on debt of a corporation being taxed at a rate of t_c is

$$k_i(1 - t_c)$$

if the debt yields k_i before tax to the holder. The after-tax yield on the preferred stock with the 85 percent dividend received tax credit (only 15 percent of the income is taxed) is

$$(k_p - .15k_p t_c) = k_p(1 - .15t_c) \tag{13.3}$$

if the preferred yields k_p before tax to the holder. If both debt and preferred stock securities yielded the same before-tax return, the after-tax yield on the preferred stock would be greater than that on the debt since $(1 - t_c)$ is less than $(1 - .15t_c)$. For example if $t_c = .46$ and $100 of interest is received, the investing corporation nets $54 after tax. If $100 of dividends are received, the tax is $6.90 and the corporation nets $93.10.

If the preferred stock is only slightly more risky than the debt, then it could yield less than debt before tax and still return enough in excess of the yield on debt after tax to compensate a corporate investor for the additional risk.

Preferred Stock Versus Debt

Suppose that a corporation can buy either a corporate debt instrument that is yielding 10 percent at present or a comparable (in risk) preferred stock that pays 8 percent. If the corporate tax rate is 46 percent, which security should the company buy?

$$\text{after-tax yield on debt} = k_i(1 - t_c)$$

$$= .10(1 - .46)$$

$$= .054$$

$$\text{after-tax yield on preferred stock} = k_p(1 - .15t_c)$$

$$= .08(1 - .069)$$

$$= .07448$$

The "lower-yielding" preferred stock is the better of the two investments using contractual return as the criterion.

A $100.00 investment in debt will earn $10, and this will net to $5.40 after the $4.60 tax.

A $100.00 investment in preferred stock will earn $8.00. Only .15 of $8.00, or $1.20, will be subject to tax and the tax will be $.552. The corporate investor will net out $7.448, which is larger than the $5.40 after-tax net with an investment in debt.

Is it preferable for a corporation to issue debt or preferred stock? If both securities promise the same before-tax return, the preferred stock offers a higher after-tax yield to a corporate investor.

However, if we just consider the after-tax cost to the issuing corporation, the debt has an edge because of the tax deductibility of interest. Thus, although the dividend received credit gives preferred stock a tax advantage over debt for the corporate investor, it does not follow that the cost of preferred stock is less than that of debt. Since interest on debt is treated as an expense of doing business for tax purposes, it is tax deductible. If a debt issue is priced to yield k_i, it has an after-tax cost to the issuing firm of $k_i(1 - t_c)$, where t_c is the corporate tax rate. Dividends on preferred stock are treated as a return to equity for tax purposes and are not deductible in computing taxable income; thus the after-tax cost is k_p.

Consider a firm that is contemplating the issuance of either debt to yield k_i or preferred stock to yield k_p. If the market considers the two perfect substitutes (i.e., the preferred dividends have the same risk as the debt cash flows) and corporate investors are dominant in the market, k_p will be set such that the after-tax yields on both are the same to the corporate investors

$$k_p(1 - .15t_c) = k_i(1 - t_c) \tag{13.4}$$

or, solving for k_p,

$$k_p = k_i \frac{1 - t_c}{1 - .15t_c} = k_i(1 - t_c)\left(\frac{1}{1 - .15t_c}\right) \tag{13.5}$$

Since $(1 - t_c)$ is less than $(1 - .15t_c)$, for t_c greater than zero it follows that k_p is less than k_i. But comparing the after-tax cost of both types of capital, the after-tax cost of debt is $k_i(1 - t_c)$ and the after-tax cost of preferred stock is k_p. Equation (13.5) can be used to determine the cost of preferred stock that gives the same after-tax return to investors as a bond yielding k_i before tax. Since the factor $1/(1 - .15t_c)$ is greater than 1, k_p is larger than $k_i(1 - t_c)$; therefore, preferred stock still has a higher after-tax cost to the issuing firm than does debt if the after-tax returns to the corporate investor are equal.

EXAMPLE 13.2

Assume that debt costs 10 percent before tax and that the tax rate is 46 percent. The after-tax cost of debt to the issuer is .054. What does k_p have to be for a corporate investor to be indifferent between the debt and preferred stock?

$$k_p = k_i(1 - t_c)\left(\frac{1}{1 - .15t_c}\right) = .10(.54)\frac{1}{1 - .069} = .058 \tag{13.5}$$

With debt paying 10 percent, the corporate investor buying $100.00 of debt ends up with $5.40 after-tax interest. Buying $100.00 of preferred stock yielding .058 leads to a dividend of $5.80 of which 15 percent or $.87 is subject to tax. There is a $.40 tax, and the corporate investor again nets $5.40. Thus, with equal probability of payment, there is indifference for the corporate investor between the debt yielding 10 percent and the preferred stock yielding 5.8 percent. The preferred stock costs the issuing firm .058 and the debt costs .054. Debt is less costly to the corporate issuer if the corporate investor is indifferent.

In arriving at the conclusion that generally preferred stock costs the issuing firm more than debt, two assumptions were made. First, we assumed that the risk of the two types of securities was identical. In fact, to an investor, preferred stock dividends are the more risky set of cash flows, so k_p has to be greater than that specified in equation (13.5) for investors to be interested in buying the security. Second, we assumed that corporate investors were the dominating force in the market so that the dividend received credit was instrumental in determining the yield required on preferred stock. If this assumption is relaxed and noncorporate market forces are present, the required yield on preferred stock will again be higher than that implied by equation (13.5), reflecting the fact that the preferred dividend has essentially the same tax status as interest earned for noncorporate investors. Thus relaxing both assumptions merely strengthens the conclusion that debt is likely to cost the issuing firm less than preferred stock.

Another assumption being made is that the issuing firm is currently paying taxes at a reasonably high rate and will pay taxes in the future, and thus has need of the interest deduction. If this assumption is not valid (the company is not paying taxes or is paying at a low rate), preferred stock becomes more attractive compared with debt.

Given current tax laws, there should be a strong preference to issue debt rather than preferred stock if the issuing firm has taxable income. Although both securities provide financial leverage that allows the common stock investment to earn a higher rate of return (at a higher risk), debt costs the issuing firm less after taxes than does preferred stock. Several factors, however, contribute to the explanation why some firms still issue preferred stock.

It can be argued that if the corporation has reached its limit of debt capacity, preferred stock may be the only feasible alternative. It is likely that this so-called "debt capacity" is thought to be a limiting factor more often than it is in fact.

Management may regard preferred stock as being less risky for the common stockholders, for there is no question that a given amount of debt imposes more risk on a corporation than does an equal amount of preferred stock at the moment of issue. Preferred stock dividends may be passed over by a corporation with much less severe consequences than the passing over of bond interest. Despite this fact, the question of whether preferred stock or bonds impose more risk on stockholders of the issuing corporation is not clear cut. A complicating factor arises because the two securities may not be outstanding for the same period of time. Let us assume that the difference between the bond interest and preferred stock dividends (both on an after-tax basis) is used to retire the bonds. In this situation, assuming that the yields required by investors of the two securities are reasonably close and that the after-tax interest cost is less than the after-tax preferred stock dividend cost, in a finite number of years the bonds will be completely retired using only the after-tax savings in interest compared with preferred stock dividends to accomplish the retirements.

EXAMPLE 13.3

Z Company is considering issuing $10 million of 40-year bonds or perpetual preferred stock. Assume that the tax rate is .4. The bonds can be issued to yield 10 percent and the preferred stock to yield 9 percent.

We want to compute the number of years to retire the bonds if the bonds are retired using the savings from issuing debt and paying interest rather than issuing preferred stock and paying dividends.

	Preferred Stock	*Bonds*
Dividends (or interest)	$900,000	$1,000,000
Tax savings		400,000
Net cost per year	$900,000	$ 600,000

The net savings of bonds over preferred stock is $300,000 per year.

We want to determine the number of years, n, such that the present value of $300,000 per year for n years is equal to the present value of the bonds, $10,000,000. Let $B(n, r)$ be the present value an annuity (first payment one period from now) for n periods with r rate of interest. Assume that r is equal to .06. We want to determine the value of n for which

$$\$300,000B(n, r) = \$10,000,000(1 + r)^{-n}$$

This can be simplified (see Appendix 13.1) to

$$n = \frac{\ln\left[\dfrac{r(\text{principal})}{\text{savings}} + 1\right]}{\ln(1 + r)} = \frac{\ln\left[\dfrac{.06(\$10,000,000)}{\$300,000} + 1\right]}{\ln 1.06}$$

$$= \frac{\ln 3}{\ln 1.06} = \frac{1.098}{.058} = 18.9 \text{ years}$$

(13.6)

Thus, if $r = .06$, the bonds could be retired in 18.9 years (or the bonds could be retired as the savings are realized), and this would take no more of a cash outlay than if preferred stock were issued and not retired (even though the preferred stock can be issued at a lower yield than the bonds). If debt is used, after 19 years, the return to the common stockholders is less risky than if preferred stock is used, but this requires that the firm survive the first 19 years. The financial risk is reduced through time, since the $300,000 could be used to retire debt annually. It is possible that the preferred stock would be riskier than the debt before year 19, at least according to some definitions of risk, because of the larger amount outstanding (some of the debt having been retired).

In recent years preferred stock has frequently been issued in connection with mergers and acquisitions. Often the preferred stock is issued with a conversion freature, so in the long run, there is a probability it will become common stock capital. Preferred stock allows the acquired firm's owners a prior claim relative to common stock and reasonably defnite dividends while simultaneously giving the acquiring firm a form of leverage without strapping it with the rigid obligations of debt.

These reasons provide some justification for the fact that some firms do issue preferred stock. However, on a pure explicit cost comparison with debt, preferred stock tends to be inferior (have a higher after-tax cost). This helps to explain why so little preferred stock compared with debt is used by non-regulated firms.

A firm not making sufficient taxable income to use the tax shield of the debt may have incentive to use preferred stock, as will a firm close to its debt capacity.

Variable Rate Preferred Stock

Treasurers of corporations would like to invest in preferred stock having before-tax yields about the same as (or somewhat less than) short-term debt if some of the risk of preferred stock can be removed.

One risk that investors would like to see removed is the risk that the price of preferred stock will fall because the market's required return went up.

In 1983 variable rate preferred stocks became very popular. Rather than paying a fixed dividend, this type of security paid a dividend that was frequently a fixed fraction of the highest of three government bond yields (e.g., the T-bill rate, the U.S. Treasury 10-year constant maturity rate, and the U.S. Treasury 20-year constant maturity rate). The advantage of a variable rate preferred stock is that its market price should always be close to its face value. If the payment risk does not change, it will differ only because the linkage to the U.S. Treasury securities does not perfectly reflect the market's required return on preferred stock. If it reflects the market's required return perfectly in one period, it is not likely to reflect it in all periods.

To protect the issuing firm against very large cash outlay commitments, a maximum dividend rate is established. To protect the investor against very low dividends, a minimum dividend rate is established. While not necessary to the basic concept of the security, these provisions are generally present, but the levels of maximum and minimums vary greatly. Also, the differential between the maximum of the three U.S. Treasury returns and the preferred stock dividend also differ from issue to issue. These factors are set by market conditions (supply and demand) for this particular type of security.

Preferred Stock Versus Common Stock

Now we compare the issuance of preferred stock and the issuance of common stock. It is easy to confound the question being studied by comparing preferred stock and the retention of earnings. When the latter is done, there are two decisions being considered: (1) whether to pay dividends or retain the earnings and (2) whether it is more desirable to finance the investments with common stock or preferred stock. We only want to consider the second question here.

The primary advantage to an investor of holding preferred stock compared with common stock is that the preferred stock return is somewhat more predictable (more certain). But in recent years, more preferred stock issues have variable dividends. The dividend may be tied to an external factor (such as the yield on government securities or the firm's operations or dividends on common stock).

The company will generally make a real effort to try to avoid defaulting on the preferred stock dividend. Since the return to preferred stock is reasonably well defined and since the preferred stockholders precede the common stockholders (the preferred dividends are paid before the common dividends), preferred stock is a popular type of security for mergers and acquisitions (perhaps debt would be an even more desirable type of security).

From the point of view of an issuing corporation's common stockholders, preferred stock offers the opportunity to introduce a form of leverage (the preferred stockholders generally have a maximum dividend return) that could benefit the common stockholders if the corporation does very well in the future. The preferred stockholders do not participate in any bonanza that might occur since their dividend rate is either fixed or if variable generally has a set maximum.

It is wrong to assume that preferred stock fills a unique demand for an investment security in the market that other securities cannot fill. Dividends from common stock are as eligible for the 85 percent dividend received credit available to corporations as preferred stock. Second, a portfolio of a firm's debt and common stock can be constructed to have a return that behaves in essentially the same manner as the return on preferred stock. Although preferred stock may appear to be more desirable than common stock because of its financial leverage characteristics, this advantage is likely to be illusory. With the present tax law, preferred stock has no special attributes for which an efficient market would be willing to pay a premium; thus its cost is not likely to be cheaper than other forms of financing.

If the types of risks associated with an investment in common stock and preferred stock purchased individually (not a mixture) are what the market desires and if the risks and returns could not be exactly duplicated in any other way, then it would be possible for a firm with preferred stock outstanding to sell at a premium. As a theoretical as well as a practical matter, it is unlikely that the investors need the preferred stock to accomplish their investment objectives. If an explanation is to be found for the issurance of preferred stock, it is likely to be found in institutional considerations.

The issuing corporation does not have a tax shield with either preferred stock or common stock so there is no advantage for the issuing corporation to be found in the tax laws. The common stock can give rise to retained earnings (deferring taxes to the investor) and the prospect of capital gains from these retained earnings. The preferred stock does not offer these possibilities; thus it is at a disadvantage. For zero-tax investors, neither preferred stock or common stock have any specific advantage for the investor. Debt is likely to be more desirable than either security because of the tax shield provided to the issuer by the interest expense.

With a public utility, preferred stock offers the investor some protection against arbitrary actions by the regulatory commission in regard to the return to be allowed on common stock equity. The preferred stock dividend is contractual, whereas the common stock dividend is a combined result of the judgments and actions of the regulatory commission and the corporation's board of directors. In the case of zero-tax investors, it would be difficult to argue that preferred stock is inferior to common stock. We could still argue that preferred stock is inferior to debt from the point of view of consumers (the common stockholders might be indifferent if the preferred stock cost is merely passed through to the consumers).

Convertible Exchangeable Preferred Stock

Let us assume that a corporation is operating at a level that leads to zero taxes. There are no current tax benefits associated with the issuance of debt. If exchangeable (into debt at the option of the issuing firm) preferred stock can be issued at a lower before-tax yield than debt, it will have a lower cost than debt.

But what if the corporation starts earning sufficient income to start paying taxes? The corporation would then prefer to have outstanding debt rather than preferred stock. The "exchangeable" feature of the security allows the corporation to force the investors to accept debt for the preferred stock. If both the preferred stock and debt cost .15 before tax, with a .46 tax rate, the after-tax cost of debt becomes .081. This is a significant saving compared with the .15 cost of the preferred stock.

The corporate investor that purchased the preferred stock with its 85 percent dividend received credit will not be pleased with the forced exchange into a debenture. The corporate investor can sell, convert into common stock, or merely accept the exchange. The interest rate on the bond is likely to be at least as large as the preferred stock dividend, and will be somewhat safer. Zero-taxed investors, such as pension funds, are likely to find the debentures of more value than will a corporation taxed at a marginal rate of .46.

The fact that the security is exchangeable at the option of the issuing corporation reduces the expected overall cost to that corporation, but it does decrease the attractiveness of the security to the normally taxed corporate investor.

The individual investor or the zero-taxed institutional investor would welcome the exchange, since the bond interest is safer than the preferred stock dividend. The investor cannot initiate the exchange and thus has to wait until the corporate issuer finds it advantageous to force the exchange.

The conversion feature is valuable to the investor since the investor can convert into common stock at any time. If the conversion value is $1,900 at the time of maturity of the exchangeable debenture, and the maturity value is $1,000, the value of the conversion right at that time will have a value of approximately $900. If the issuing corporation can call the bond prior to maturity, the value of the conversion feature may be cut off before it reaches $900, but it is likely to have some positive value.

The investor is not likely to opt for conversion prior to call or maturity unless the common stock dividend exceeds the preferred stock dividend or the debenture interest (the relative safety to the debenture interest and principal should also be considered), and even then there are strong reasons (risk avoidance) for not converting. The corporation is likely to call the convertible security if it can call and if the conversion value exceeds the call price.

The corporation can move the security from being preferred stock to being a debenture (desirable if the corporation changes from having zero taxable income to needing tax deductions). It can also call the security if the conversion value is larger than the call price and change the security into common stock.

The convertible exchangeable preferred stock is a sensible security, and we would expect the corporate and personal tax laws as written to encourage further flexibility in the definition of securities. As long as the tax law distinguishes between securities that are essentially the same, we can expect corporate financial officers to exploit this fact.

Money Market Preferred

In 1984 the American Express Company issued a "Money Market Preferred Shares." Each quarter, the dividend rate is to be established by auction. The objective is to reduce greatly interest rate risk.

This security issue illustrates the imagination shown by the investment community in designing new securities.

PROSPECTUS

®

American Express Company

Money Market Preferred Shares

American Express Company (the "Company") from time to time may issue in one or more series up to 600 shares of its Money Market Preferred™ Shares (the "MMP™"). Each series of MMP will be offered on terms determined at the time of sale. The specific designation, number of shares, redemption terms or other specific terms of the series of MMP in respect of which this Prospectus is being delivered are set forth in the accompanying Prospectus Supplement.

Dividends on the shares of MMP of each series are cumulative from the Date of Original Issue of such series and are payable commencing on the Wednesday that is the 49th day after the Date of Original Issue and on each Wednesday that is the last day of successive 49-day periods thereafter, subject to certain exceptions. The dividend rate on the MMP of each series for the Initial Dividend Period will be as set forth in the Prospectus Supplement relating to such series. For each Dividend Period thereafter, the dividend rate for such series will be the Applicable Rate per annum in effect from time to time. The Applicable Rate for each series for each such Dividend Period will be determined on the basis of Orders placed in an Auction conducted on the Business Day preceding the commencement of such Dividend Period. In each Auction, each Existing Holder will indicate its desire to (i) continue to hold shares of such series without regard to the Applicable Rate that results from the Auction, (ii) continue to hold shares of such series if the Applicable Rate that results from such Auction is equal to or greater than the rate bid by such Existing Holder, and/or (iii) sell shares of such series without regard to the Applicable Rate that results from the Auction. Potential Holders will offer to purchase shares of such series if the Applicable Rate that results from such Auction is equal to or greater than the rate bid by such Potential Holders. The Applicable Rate for any series that results from an Auction for any Dividend Period will not be greater than 110% of the 60-day "AA" Composite Commercial Paper Rate. If the Company fails to deposit funds timely to pay any dividend on or redeem shares of MMP, the Applicable Rate for such series shall be equal to two-month LIBOR plus the additional rate per annum, if any, set forth in the Prospectus Supplement relating to such series.

Prospective purchasers should carefully review the Auction Procedures described in this Prospectus, including its Appendices, and should note that (i) an Order constitutes a commitment to purchase or sell shares of MMP based upon the results of an Auction, (ii) the Auctions will be conducted through telephone communications and (iii) settlement for purchases and sales will be on the Business Day following the Auction.

The shares of MMP of each series are redeemable at any time, as a whole or in part, at the option of the Company, at $515,000 per share if redeemed on or before the first anniversary of the Date of Original Issue of such series and at declining prices thereafter, plus accrued dividends. The shares of MMP of each series are also redeemable at the option of the Company on any Dividend Payment Date, as a whole, at a redemption price of $500,000 per share, plus accrued dividends, if the Applicable Rate for such series for the Dividend Period ending on such Dividend Payment Date is equal to or greater than the 60-day "AA" Composite Commercial Paper Rate on the date of determination of such Applicable Rate.

Shares of MMP may be transferred only pursuant to a Bid or a Sell Order placed in an Auction or to or through a Broker-Dealer or to a person that has delivered a signed Purchaser's Letter to the Trust Company.

THESE SECURITIES HAVE NOT BEEN APPROVED OR DISAPPROVED BY THE SECURITIES AND EXCHANGE COMMISSION NOR HAS THE COMMISSION PASSED UPON THE ACCURACY OR ADEQUACY OF THIS PROSPECTUS. ANY REPRESENTATION TO THE CONTRARY IS A CRIMINAL OFFENSE.

The MMP will be offered by Shearson Lehman/American Express Inc. as Underwriter.

Lehman Brothers
Shearson Lehman/American Express Inc.

Preferred Stock as an Investment

Corporations have the dividend received credit that acts as an incentive for them to invest in preferred stock (but the use of debt to finance preferred stock investments is limited). Individuals and zero-taxed investors do not have that incentive and normally should not hold straight preferred stock in their portfolios. Straight debt with its tax deductibility for interest at the corporate issuer level is apt to be lower cost to the issuing corporation and should have a better risk-return relationship for the noncorporate investor than preferred stock.

Unless the tax laws are changed, preferred stock tends to be dominated for the noncorporate investor by straight debt and by common stock. A change in the tax laws could change this conclusion.

Conclusions

It is not at all obvious that a firm's common stockholders benefit from the issuance of preferred stock over other financial instruments, if the issuing firm is paying income taxes. Like debt, preferred stock provides leverage that is likely to increase the rate of return on common stock investment as well as increase the riskiness of that return. Since debt also provides leverage at a lower after-tax cost, unless the firm does not wish to run the short-run risk associated with debt, has reached its institutionally acceptable debt ceiling, or does not have taxable income, the stockholders would be better off with the issuance of debt to achieve financial leverage.

Tax considerations play a predominant role in the financing decision. It is almost a paradox that preferred stock can be a more risky form of financing than debt. Since all earnings before interest and taxes are available to pay interest on debt, and taxes must be paid prior to paying any income out as preferred dividends, the tax savings from debt can be used to retire the debt, while a lower-yielding preferred stock's dividend can continue as a claim perpetually. Thus, in a sense from a long-run perspective, preferred stock is more risky.

If debt capacity is available, debt has tax advantages compared to preferred stock. If the firm does not wish to issue debt (or cannot issue debt because of institutional barriers or restrictive covenants in its existing debt instruments), then the choice of whether to issue preferred stock or common stock is relevant and the risks and returns of each alternative must be weighed.

Review Problem 13.1

The AB Company is attempting to decide whether to issue $10 million of .12 debt or an equal amount of .10 preferred stock. The firm's tax rate is .46. It is confident that it can earn .15 after tax on any marginal investment funds.

First, formulate the basic equation that must be solved to determine the length of time at which time any manager would agree that debt was more desirable; then determine that length of time.

Solution to Review Problem 13.1

	Interest	Dividend
Tax savings	1,200,000 − 552,000 $ 648,000	$1,000,000 1,000,000 648,000 $ 352,000 Savings per year

The basic equation is

$$\$352,000B(n, .15) = \$10,000,000(1.15)^{-n}$$

The solution is

$$n = \frac{\ln\left[\dfrac{.15(\$10,000,000)}{\$352,000} + 1\right]}{\ln (1.15)}$$

$$= \frac{\ln 5.26136}{\ln 1.15} = \frac{1.66039}{.13976} = 11.88 \text{ years}$$

Note:

$$\$352,000B(11.88, .15) = \$1,901,000$$
$$\$10,000,000(1.15)^{-11.88} = \$1,901,000$$

This is a check.

PROBLEMS

For all problems, assume there is a 85 percent dividend received credit for a corporate investor (15 percent of the dividend is taxed).

1. Assume that there is a corporate investor wanting to invest $10 million in your firm. Debt or preferred stock can be issued at a cost of .10. The firm needs $10 million of capital. Assume a .4 corporate tax rate.
   (a) On a straight cash flow basis, should you issue debt or preferred stock.
   (b) If $1 million of earnings before interest and taxes (EBIT) is available, on a cash flow basis, are the firms better off with debt or preferred stock? $1,000,000
   (c) What amount does the firm have to earn to pay $1 million of interest? To pay $1 million of preferred stock dividends? $1,670,000
   (d) What is the before-tax percentage cost of debt? Of preferred stock? .10 .167
   (e) What is the after-tax cost of each? .06 .10
   (f) What does an investment have to earn *after tax* to be financed by debt? By preferred stock? Assume a break-even objective for the firm.

2. How much does a corporate investor net out (after tax) from $100 of interest? $100 of preferred stock dividends?

3. What are the risks to a corporation buying preferred stock?

4. If callable preferred stock is issued at a price of $100 and promises to pay $9 per annum, what is the cost (as a percentage) of the issue after tax to the issuing firm if the call provision is expected to be exercised two years from now at a price of $105?

5. If the dividend received credit was 100 percent rather than its current 85 percent, at what preferred stock yield, k_p, would a corporate investor be indifferent between holding preferred stock and debt of equal risk yielding k_i?

6. If the net savings from issuing a 10 percent debt $10 million issue rather than a 13 percent preferred stock issue are used to retire the debt over time, in how many years can the debt be retired? Assume a 40 percent corporate tax rate.

7. If the firm of Problem 6 takes the after-tax savings of $700,000 per year and places them in a savings account in a bank that pays 10 percent on them, in how many years will the savings account amount to $10 million

8. Assume that a firm can issue $100 million of debt at .10 or preferred stock at .08. The tax rate is .52.

   How long will it take for the debt to be retired using the savings from paying interest rather than dividends?

9. A corporation has earned $100 (before tax) and is paying the after-tax residual to its stockholders. Assume

$$k_i = k_p = .10$$

The tax rate on all securities is .4, but there is an .85 dividend received credit for corporations.

To a corporate stockholder, what is the after-tax dollar return if the security is a debt? A preferred stock? A common stock?

10. Assume a .4 tax rate. To pay .10, a company must earn what percentage return (before tax) if the security is
    (a) Debt?
    (b) Preferred stock?
    (c) Common stock?

11. Assume a .4 tax rate. What after-tax return must an investment earn to supply sufficient cash flows to pay a before-tax (personal) .10 to
    (a) Debtholders?
    (b) Preferred stockholders?
    (c) Common stockholders?

12. Assume that a corporation can issue $10 million debt at .08 or preferred stock at .10. The tax rate is .5.

    How many years will it take for the "savings" from issuing debt to retire the debt compared with having the preferred stock outstanding?

13. Describe the economic consequences of a corporation issuing .08 debt to finance an investment of $1 million in .08 preferred stock. The corporate tax rate is .4.

14. An advertisement in the financial section of *The New York Times* (November 4, 1970) said

WHY A LOT

OF SMART MONEY BUYS

PREFERRED STOCKS AT $7\frac{1}{2}\%$

INSTEAD OF

CORPORATE BONDS AT $8\frac{1}{2}\%$

In fact, there are three very good reasons.
First of all, many discount preferred stocks offer a greater current *percentage return than do discount corporate bonds. To some investors, this immediate high return on their capital is all important.*
Second, preferreds offer a unique advantage to corporations and mutual holders such as insurance companies. They are only required to pay taxes on 15% of the income they receive from most preferred stock

dividends. So, depending on their particular tax situation, company treasurers might well find that preferreds give them higher aftertax income.

Third, many high-quality preferreds are now selling at substantial discounts. With an easing in interest rates, they could show a worthwhile price appreciation.

Don't get us wrong. We're not suggesting that everyone rush right out and buy preferred stocks. But we do think they deserve serious consideration by income-oriented individual and corporate investors.

Discuss the advantages of preferred stock that are listed.

15. The holders of Amerada Hess Corporation $3.50 cumulative convertible preferred stock received the following notification:

> *You are hereby notified, pursuant to Paragraph 9 of the Amerada Hess Corporation (the "Corporation") Certificate of Incorporation, that the Board of Directors of the Corporation has declared a $2\frac{1}{2}$% stock dividend on shares of its Common Stock payable on July 27, 1973 to holders of record of such common stock at the close of business on June 15, 1973.*
>
> *As provided in the Certificate of Incorporation, the conversion rate of the $3.50 Cumulative Convertible Preferred Stock is not subject to adjustment with respect to annual stock dividends of $2\frac{1}{2}$% or less paid on the Corporation's Common Stock. Accordingly, no adjustment will be made in said conversion rate and each share of $3.50 Cumulative Convertible Preferred Stock will remain convertible, at the option of the holder thereof, into 2.2 shares of the Corporation's Common Stock.*
>
> *Amerada Hess Corporation*

Would you convert?

REFERENCES

Bildersee, John S., "Some Aspects of the Performance of Non-Convertible Preferred Stocks." *Journal of Finance* December 1973, 1187–1202.

Donaldson, Gordon. "In Defense of Preferred Stock." *Harvard Business Review*, July–August 1962, 123–136.

Elsaid, Hussein H. "The Function of Preferred Stock in the Corporate Financial Plan." *Financial Analysts Journal*, July–August 1969, 112–117.

Fisher, Donald E., and Glen A. Wilt, Jr. "Nonconvertible Preferred Stock as a Financing Instrument, 1950–1965." *Journal of Finance*, September 1968, 611–624.

Pinches, George E. "Financing with Convertible Preferred Stock, 1960–1967." *Journal of Finance*, March 1970, 53–63.

Soldofsky, Robert M. "Convertible Preferred Stock: Renewed Life in an Old Form." *The Business Lawyer*, April 1968, 899–902.

Stevenson, R. A. "Retirement of Non-Callable Preferred Stock." *Journal of Finance*, December 1970, 1143–1152.

Appendix 13.1   Determining Time Until Retirement of Debt

We want to determine the length of time for the after-tax savings of interest to retire the outstanding debt.

Let

> sav = the after-tax savings of interest compared to preferred stock dividends
> prin = the principal of the debt
> r = the earnings rate on invested funds
> n = the length of time

We want

$$\text{sav } B(n, r) = \text{prin } (1 + r)^{-n}$$

$$\frac{1 - (1 + r)^{-n}}{r} \times (1 + r)^n = \frac{\text{prin}}{\text{sav}}$$

$$(1 + r)^n - 1 = \frac{r \text{ prin}}{\text{sav}}$$

$$n \ln (1 + r) = \ln \left(\frac{r \text{ prin}}{\text{sav}} + 1 \right)$$

$$n = \frac{\ln \left(\dfrac{r \text{ prin}}{\text{sav}} + 1 \right)}{\ln (1 + r)}$$

Chapter 14

Cost of Capital and Capital Structure

Major Topics

1. Definition of weighted average cost of capital.
2. Discussion of whether there is an optimum capital structure.
3. The effect of corporate and personal taxes on capital structure decisions.
4. Delevering a firm.

The Weighted Average Cost of Capital

Later in this chapter we shall show that an investor can delever a highly levered firm; thus capital structure is not an important consideration unless taxes and bankruptcy costs are considered. The value of the firm would not be affected by leverage if there were no taxes and no transaction costs.

When capital budgeting with time discounting was first introduced in the business finance literature in the early 1950s, the common recommendation was that an investment was acceptable if the net present value was positive using the weighted average cost of capital (WACC) as the discount rate (or, equivalently, if the investment's internal rate of return was greater than the weighted average cost of capital). Even today, more business firms are using the weighted average cost of capital as the hurdle rate than any other capital budgeting decision required return. This utilization makes the cost of capital calculation of great importance. Although we do not endorse the general use of the cost of capital in the capital budgeting process as a single hurdle rate, it nevertheless is used; thus we should compute it in a reasonable manner.

There is also the question of how the firm's value is affected by the financial mix decision. Four theories deserve consideration.

1. The value of a firm and the consequent wealth position of the stockholders is not affected by the type of financing.
2. There is an optimum capital structure and the utilization of this structure will maximize the value of the firm.
3. Given the present corporate tax laws, a firm should use as much debt as possible to maximize its value and the wealth position of its stockholders who either do not pay taxes or can effectively eliminate the tax on the common stock dividends.
4. Given the presence of personal taxes as well as corporate taxes, common stock may have tax advantages compared to debt by means of tax deferral as well as preferential treatment of capital gains.

In this chapter we examine and evaluate each of these theories and the role the weighted average cost of capital plays in the capital structure decision. The key symbols to be used are

k_0 = the weighted average after-tax cost of capital
k_i = the before-tax average cost of debt, $k_i(1 - t_c)$ the after-tax cost of debt
k_e = the after-tax average cost of equity capital
B = the market value of the debt in the capital structure
S = the market value of the stock equity in the capital structure
V = the total market value of the firm: V_U is the value of an unlevered firm; V_L is the value of a levered firm
t_c = the corporate tax rate

Definition

The weighted average cost of capital (k_0 or WACC) is defined as the sum of the weighted costs of debt (k_i) and equity capital (k_e), where the weights are the relative importance of each in the firm's capital structure and the k_i and k_e costs are the expected average returns required by investors as an inducement to commit funds. For simplicity, we initially consider only one class of debt and common stock. Multiple classes of debt and preferred stock could be include without altering the logic, but the notation becomes difficult to handle.

The market value of the firm is the sum of the market values of the outstanding debt and equity:

$$V = B + S \tag{14.1}$$

The measure of relative importance of debt and equity in the capital structure are the ratios B/V and S/V, respectively. If we use these measures as weights, the after-tax WACC is defined to be

$$k_0 = k_i(1 - t_c)\frac{B}{V} + k_e\frac{S}{V} \tag{14.2}$$

In equation (14.2), we have $k_i(1 - t_c)$, the after-tax cost of borrowing, and k_e, the cost of common stock capital, weighted, respectively, by the percentages of debt and common stock capital being used to obtain a weighted average cost of capital.

The WACC of a firm can be interpreted as being the cost of both current capital and an additional dollar of new capital if the existing capital structure is maintained. This is inexact, but it simplifies the analysis.

EXAMPLE 14.1 ———————————————————————

Suppose that the market value of a company's common stock is estimated at $42 million. The market value of its interest-bearing debt is estimated at $28 million, and the average before-tax yield on these liabilities is 10 percent per year, which is equivalent on an ofter-tax basis to 6 percent per year (equal to 10 percent times .60, assuming a 40 percent tax rate).

Assume that the company just described is currently paying a dividend of $8 per year and that the stock is selling at a price of $100. The rate of growth of the dividend is projected to be 12 percent per year. One estimate of the cost of the common stock equity is

$$k_e = \frac{D}{P} + g \tag{14.3}$$

$$= \frac{\$8}{\$100} + .12$$

$$= .08 + .12$$

$$= .20, \text{ or } 20\%$$

The weighted average cost of capital for the company as a whole is estimated in Table 14.1:

TABLE 14.1   Estimate of the Cost of Capital

Capital Source	Proportion of Total Capital	After-Tax Cost	After-Tax Weighted Cost
Common stock	.60	.20	.120
Debt, interest bearing	.40	.06	.024
		Weighted average cost of capital =	.144

Example 14.1 is expressed in terms of the expected return required for present debt and the present common stock. If we were considering the raising of new capital to finance additional investments, it would be more accurate to speak in terms of the return that would be required if a mixture of additional debt and common stock were to be issued. The word *average* that is used in the term weighted *average cost of capital* refers to the average of the different types of capital. For decisions we want a weighted average of marginal costs for debt and stock. In situations where the issuance of the debt and common stock will not change the firm's capital structure, the marginal costs may equal the average costs. If the capital structure were to change, but the weighted average cost of capital does not change, the marginal cost of capital is again equal to the average cost.

Shareholders are exposed to the risk of bankruptcy as soon as debt in some form (e.g., accounts payable or a bank loan) is acquired. With debt, it is possible that equityholders will lose their interest in a company that may again become a profitable operation. With a well-managed profitable company in a safe industry, the introduction of a small amount of nonequity capital presumably will increase the risks of bankruptcy only a small amount. In practice, the legal possibility of bankruptcy is nearly always present, because a company will always have at least some accounts payable outstanding. However, as the amount of debt rises, the risks of bankruptcy become greater. Every dollar of debt increases risk. The amount of the increase depends upon the activities in which a company is engaged.

One advantage of debt capital comes from the financial leverage it provides for the remaining equity capital. However, increases in the debt equity ratio will increase the year-to-year variability of earnings per share (including negative earnings arising from bankruptcy or near bankruptcy) compared to the use of common stock capital. Taken by itself, this is likely to decrease the price per share that investors are willing to pay. However, the issuance of debt will also tend to increase the expected earnings per share, and this will counterbalance the increased risk.

Another important advantage of debt is that interest expense is deductible by the corporation for purposes of computing taxable income, whereas dividends on common stock are not deductible. With corporate tax rates at approximately .46, there is a very real incentive for firms to use debt as a major component of their capital structure.

It is impossible to give any simple rules for determining in advance the optimum capital structure for a particular firm. Theoretically, the optimum structure is reached when any change in the debt-equity ratio will result in a decrease in the price per share of the common stock. The capital structure just prior to the issue of that debt is the optimum capital structure. Unfortunately, we do not know how much debt is the correct amount of debt. In determining whether a company's capital structure is optimum, management must to a large extent rely on the intuitive judgment of well-informed persons. Optimum capital structure is a "judgment call."

The Weights

We weight the cost of each type of capital by the percentage that the type of capital is to the total capital. There is a difference of opinion as to whether book values or market values should be used. Those of an academic bent tend to prefer the use of market values. The logic is that the weights should reflect the economic importance of the capital and not the historical amounts of debt and common stock as recorded by the accountants. Practitioners tend to favor the book values since they are objective and tend to be used by other managers (e.g., bankers and bond analysts).

Since the issue is unresolved, a safe position for an analyst is to make calculations using both market and book values and let the user of the information decide which calculation is more useful. If only one calculation is being made, we would prefer the use of market value.

Depreciation Accruals Are Not Capital

The accounting process includes entries to expense accounts that result in credit entries to accumulated depreciation and tax deferral accounts. Since these entries can affect the calculation of cash flow from operations, it is easy to slip into the error that accumulated depreciation and tax deferral accounts give rise to capital.

EXAMPLE 14.2 ————————————————————————

Assume that a firm has the following balance sheet:

Plant $1,000   Common stock $1,000

During the next period sales are $200 and depreciation expense is $200. The income is zero. The balance sheet after these transactions is

Cash		$ 200		
Plant	$1,000			
Less: accumulated depreciation	200	800	Common stock	$1,000
		$1,000		

Note that the capital consists of $1,000 common stock. The accumulated depreciation is not capital. We could revise the balance sheet and not change the conclusion that the capital is not affected by the accumulated depreciation.

Cash	$ 200	Accumulated depreciation	$ 200
Plant	1,000	Common stock	1,000
	$1,200		$1,200

The location of the accumulated depreciation account on the balance sheet does not change the conclusion that it is properly a subtraction from the plant asset account.

Existence of a Unique Optimal Financial Structure

A controversy has arisen concerning the existence of a minimum cost of capital structure for a given firm; that is, it is difficult to determine the behavior of k_0, where

$$k_0 = k_i(1 - t_c)\frac{B}{V} + k_e \frac{S}{V} \qquad (14.2)$$

as a function of the degree of financial leverage.

Let us consider how the two cost components of the cost of capital, k_i and k_e, react to an increase in financial leverage, that is, a substitution of debt for equity financing. Assuming that investors demand more return if their investment is subject to greater risk, we conclude that k_i will increase as more debt is substituted for equity because the payment stream to debtholders becomes more risky. The same logic leads to the conclusion that k_e will also increase as debt is substituted for equity since the dividend stream accruing to equity becomes more risky as debt obligations increase in size relative to the amount of equity. Furthermore, if investors are adverse to risk for any given degree of financial leverage, k_i is less than k_e since debtholders (as prior claimers) are subject to less risk than are equityholders. Finally, as B/V approaches 1, k_i approaches the cost of equity for zero leverage. This is true, since the most risky position a debtholder could be in is equivalent to that of an equityholder of an all-equity–financed firm. As B/V approaches 1, debtholders in fact become implicit equityholders. Figure 14.1 depicts this assumed behavior of k_i and k_e.

The shape of the k_0 curve will depend on the shapes of the k_i and k_e curves. The traditional or classical position assumes that k_i and k_e are shaped such that the resultant k_0 curve is U- or saucer-shaped, implying that there exists a unique minimum cost of capital structure, as depicted in Figure 14.2. Starting from the observation that most firms in any given industry (firms with roughly the same degree of business risk) tend to have roughly the same capital structure, the traditionalist might argue that k_e rises at an ever-increasing rate with increased leverage while k_i begins to rise significantly only after a significant degree of leverage. The weighted average cost of capital thus initially falls as the leverage is increased, since the rise in k_e is more than offset by the utilization of cheaper debt. At some point, however, the WACC begins to rise as k_e rises at a faster and faster rate, and k_i also rises more rapidly in response to the increased leverage. It is assumed that there is either a single value or a range of values of B/V that minimizes k_0. It should be remembered that we

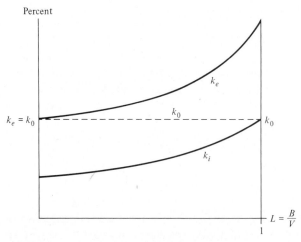

FIGURE 14.1   A Constant Weighted Average Cost of Capital

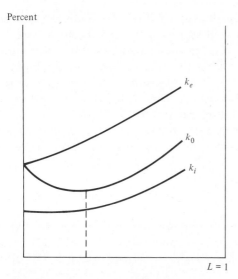

Percent

k_e

k_0

k_i

$L = 1$

FIGURE 14.2   The Classical View of an Optimum Capital Structure

are currently considering a zero-tax situation. With zero taxes, the classical position is not appealing because it is not consistent with theory.

A comprehensive theory for k_0 was formulated by Modigliani and Miller (hereafter M & M) in their famous 1958 *American Economic Review* article. With a well-formulated set of assumptions, including no corporate taxes, k_0 is a constant, independent of capital structure, and it follows that any capital structure is equally desirable. A constant k_0 is illustrated in Figure 14.1.

The M & M position is based on the set of assumptions that (1) markets are perfect, (2) transaction costs are negligible, (3) market behavior is rational, and (4) taxes are zero. With these assumptions all capital structures are equally desirable.

When corporate taxes (but no personal taxes) are considered, it can be argued that k_0 is a monotonically decreasing function of B/V, implying that the minimum cost of capital structure consists of nearly 100 percent tax-shielding debt financing and a minimum of equity financing.

No Taxes

Let us consider the M & M arguments for the no-corporate-tax case. The perfect market assumption implies that with zero taxes, two nongrowth firms, which pay all net income as dividends and are identical in every respect except for capital structure, should have the same market value. The market, as a whole, is purchasing the same future stream of net operating income (EBIT) from both. How that EBIT stream is divided into interest and dividend payments is immaterial in a perfect market, and the total value of the firm will not be affected by the firm's capital structure. Two identical commodities (in this case the future net operating income streams) cannot sell for two different prices (market values). The law of one price is assumed to hold. If a value disparity exists, the arbitrage process will remove it. Thus, the value of the firm (V) is independent of the amount of debt, and we can write

$$V = \frac{\text{EBIT}}{k_0} \tag{14.4}$$

where EBIT is a perpetual earnings stream (earnings before interest and taxes). Solving for k_0,

$$k_0 = \frac{\text{EBIT}}{V} \tag{14.5}$$

Given the assumptions, we cannot determine *the* optimal financial structure, for any amount of leverage is equally desirable.

The zero-tax M & M position is depicted in Figures 14.1 and 14.3. Given the M & M assumptions, k_0 is a constant. If we wish to assume some functional

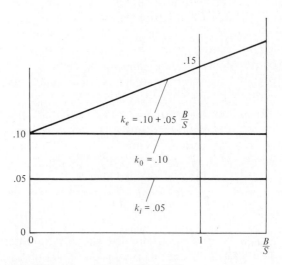

FIGURE 14.3   Costs of Capital

form for k_i, we can explore the behavior of k_e. For example, we can solve equation (14.2) for k_e (with $t_c = 0$):

$$k_0 = k_i \frac{B}{V} + k_e \frac{S}{V} \qquad (14.2)$$

$$k_0 + k_0 \frac{B}{S} - k_i \frac{B}{S}$$

$$k_e = k_0 + (k_0 - k_i)\frac{B}{S} \qquad (14.6)$$

Equation (14.6) indicates that the cost of equity capital is larger than the overall cost of capital by an adjustment factor that is a function of the amount of debt compared to the amount of common stock. If k_i is a constant, then k_e will be a linear function of B/S (it is not a linear function of B/V). This is illustrated in Figure 14.3. Note the X axis of Figure 14.3 is B/S, not B/V.

EXAMPLE 14.3

Assume that $k_0 = .10$ and $k_i = .05$ and that these values are not a function of the amount of leverage. The value of the firm is $10,000,000 and the firm currently has $2,000,000 of debt and $8,000,000 of stock. The cost of equity capital implied by these facts is

$$k_e = k_0 + (k_0 - k_i)\left(\frac{B}{S}\right) \qquad (14.6)$$

$$= .10 + (.10 - .05)\frac{B}{S} = .10 + .05\frac{B}{S}$$

Since $B = \$2,000,000$ and $S = \$8,000,000$, then

$$k_e = .10 + .05(\tfrac{2}{8}) = .10 + .0125 = .1125 \qquad (14.6)$$

The values of k_i and k_e for different degrees of leverage are plotted in Figure 14.3 from B/S equal to 0 to B/S equal to 1. In this case, k_e rises linearly with respect to B/S.

If the firm substituted $6,000,000 of debt for $6,000,000 of stock with k_i unchanged, we would have

$$k_e = .10 + (.05)\frac{\$8,000,000}{\$2,000,000} = .30 \qquad (14.6)$$

While k_e increases, the value of k_0 remains .10:

$$k_0 = \tfrac{2}{10}(.30) + \tfrac{8}{10}(.05) = .10 \tag{14.2}$$

Other functional forms for k_i lead to different functional forms for k_e. Normally, we expect the k_e to be everywhere increasing but not linear since we would not expect k_i to be a constant with respect to changes in B/S.

A Constant WACC

Let us assume that a substitution of debt for equity will increase the cost of both debt and common stock. Can the substitution be desirable? Surprisingly, the answer is yes. Even if both costs go up, the substitution of the lower-cost debt can cause the average cost to stay constant or decrease.

EXAMPLE 14.4

Assume that

$$k_i = .05 + .10\frac{B}{V}$$

and that

$$k_e = .15 + (.15 - k_i)\frac{B}{S}$$

Assume that the firm has $B = S$ so that $B/S = 1$, $B/V = \tfrac{1}{2}$, $k_i = .10$, $k_e = .20$. Then $k_0 = .15$:

$$k_0 = .10(\tfrac{1}{2}) + .20(\tfrac{1}{2}) = .15$$

Now assume that $B/V = \tfrac{2}{3}$, $S/V = \tfrac{1}{3}$, and $B/S = 2$:

$$k_i = .05 + .10\frac{B}{V} = .05 + .10(\tfrac{2}{3}) = .1167$$

$$k_e = .15 + (.15 - k_i)\frac{B}{S}$$

$$= .15 + (.15 - .1167)\,2 = .2167$$

The value of k_i was .10, and the value of k_e was .20, so the increase in the leverage increases both costs. But the WACC is unchanged. The WACC is

$$k_0 = (.1167)\tfrac{2}{3} + .2167(\tfrac{1}{3})$$

$$= \tfrac{1}{3}(.2333 + .2167) = \tfrac{1}{3}(.45) = .15$$

Just because debt costs less than common stock does not mean that substituting debt for common stock will reduce the average cost of capital. This is a surprising and very important observation.

Buying a Combination of Stocks and Bonds to Delever the Firm: No Taxes

Assume two firms i and j. We want to show that we can buy the stock and bonds of firm j so that the return and risk are identical to that of investing in the stock of firm i, where the firms are identical in every respect except that firm j has more debt outstanding than firm i.

Assume that both firms are of the same size, are earning the same dollar return, X, and are paying the same rate of interest, k_i, and have the same market value, V. The assumption that k_i does not change is not realistic since we would expect firm j with more debt to pay a higher borrowing cost than firm i. If we allow the borrowing rate of firm j to be different from k_i, the analysis is more complex and the conclusions less definite. We want to find the proportion of the investment (α) to be placed in the stock of j and the proportion to be invested in the firm's debt $(1 - \alpha)$ so that the weighted average return per dollar invested in firm j is equal to the average return per dollar invested in the stock of firm i.

It is shown in Appendix 14.1 that if we invest α in the stock of firm j and $(1 - \alpha)$ in the bonds of firm j, we have an equivalent investment as investing in the stock of firm i, if

$$\alpha = \frac{S_j}{S_i} \tag{14.7}$$

and

$$(1 - \alpha) = \frac{S_i - S_j}{S_i} \tag{14.8}$$

EXAMPLE 14.5

	Firm	
	i	*j*
Debt (*B*)	$ 6,000,000	$ 7,000,000
Stock (*S*)	4,000,000	3,000,000
Total market value (*V*)	$10,000,000	$10,000,000

Assume that the EBIT is $1,000,000:

$$k_i = .08, \quad \alpha = \tfrac{3}{4}, \quad 1 - \alpha = \tfrac{1}{4}$$

The return from investment in the stock of *i* is

$$r_i = \frac{X - k_i B_i}{S_i} = \frac{\$1{,}000{,}000 - .08(\$6{,}000{,}000)}{\$4{,}000{,}000} = .13 \qquad (14.9)$$

The return from investment in the stock of *j* is

$$r_j = \frac{X - k_i B_j}{S_j} = \frac{\$1{,}000{,}000 - .08(\$7{,}000{,}000)}{\$3{,}000{,}000} = \frac{\$44}{\$300} = .147 \qquad (14.10)$$

The expected return of investment in the stock and bonds of *j* is

$$r_p = \alpha(r_j) + (1 - \alpha)k_i = \tfrac{3}{4} \times \tfrac{44}{300} + \tfrac{1}{4} \times .08 = .13 \qquad (14.11)$$

which is equal to r_i. No matter what the value of EBIT, this equality will hold.

Example 14.5 shows how a firm with too much debt may be "delevered." It can also be shown that an investment in a firm with too little debt may be "levered" by personal borrowing. Thus, if markets are perfect, the markets can lever or delever any firm to the degree they choose, making the market value of the firm (and, consequently, the stockholders' wealth position) invariant to the financial leverage employed by the firm. Tax and bankruptcy cost considerations could nullify this conclusion.

We can also delever a firm to a zero-debt level. That is, an investment in the highly levered firm *j* can be made equivalent to an investment in the common stock of a zero-debt firm. The return on investment for a zero-debt firm with the same operating characteristics of *j* is

$$r = \frac{X}{S} = \frac{\$1,000,000}{\$10,000,000} = .10 \tag{14.12}$$

To obtain this same return on investment with the levered firm, the investor will buy a vertical slice of all the firm's securities. If the investor is buying p fraction of the firm, the investor will buy p of all securities. The investment will be split with S/V of the total investment invested in the firm's common stock and B/V of the total investment invested in the firm's debt.

If the total investment is Q, then the investor will buy $(B/V)Q$ of debt and $(S/V)Q$ of stock.

Since $p = Q/V$, the foregoing amounts are equivalent to buying pB of debt (since $pB = (Q/V)B = (B/V)Q$) and pS of stock.

For this example $B/V = .7$ and $S/V = .3$. Since r_j has been determined to be $\frac{44}{300}$, the investor's return will be

$$r_p = .3(\tfrac{44}{300}) + .7(.08) = .044 + .056 = .10 \tag{14.11}$$

which is the same as the return from investing in the zero-debt firm per dollar of investment.

The implications of these examples are extensive. Firm j, highly levered, cannot sell at a discount compared to a firm with a smaller amount of debt since an investor can always delever the highly levered firm by buying B/V of debt and S/V of stock. An equivalent statement is that the 100 percent common stock firm cannot sell at a premium compared to the highly levered firm j since j can always be purchased in such a way as to delever it.

The delevering illustrated is a perfect delevering in the sense that whatever return is earned by the zero-debt firm will also be earned by the investment in the highly levered firm.

For example, assume that both firms earn \$600,000 (EBIT) instead of \$1,000,000. The zero-debt firm will now earn per dollar of equity investment:

$$r_i = \frac{\$600,000}{\$10,000,000} = .06 \tag{14.9}$$

The investment in the bonds and stock of j will also earn .06:

$$r_p = .3\left(\frac{\$600,000 - \$560,000}{\$3,000,000}\right) + .7(.08) \tag{14.11}$$

$$= \frac{\$40,000}{\$10,000,000} + .056 = .004 + .056 = .06$$

The returns from the investment in both the debt and common stock of firm j in the appropriate proportions will always be identically equal to the return from the investment in the common stock of the zero-debt firm, assuming that the operating results are identical.

Levering a Firm

The previous section showed how a firm can be delevered by the investor buying stocks and bonds of the same firm. A firm with too little leverage can also be levered by the use of personal borrowing. Investors substitute their own borrowing capacity for that of the firm to attain the amount of total leverage that is desired.

A third possible way of changing the amount of leverage of a firm is to purchase a combination of firms (one firm with too low and one firm with too high leverage) to obtain a mixture of investment that is equivalent to a medium levered firm. Thus, if the stock of the medium levered firm is priced high compared to the other two firms, a mixture of the underpriced securities can be purchased at a lower cost to obtain an investment equivalent to the medium levered firm. The only limitations of this procedure is the difficulty of finding firms that differ only by capital structure. In practice, a mixture of the extreme firms (very high or very low financial leverage) will not exactly duplicate the medium firm.

Taxes

Before- and After-Tax Costs

We want to illustrate the before- and after-tax costs to the issuer of debt, preferred stock, and common stock.

EXAMPLE 14.6 ———————————————

Let us assume that the corporate tax rate is .48, and that investors require the following returns:

.10 with debt
.12 with preferred stock
.18 with common stock

Remember that preferred stock dividends offer no tax shield to the corporate issuer.

The following table shows the before-tax costs and the after-tax costs of the three different types of capital:

	Returns	Before-Tax Costs	Tax	Tax Savings	After-Tax Cost
Debt	.10	.10		.048	.052
Preferred stock	.12	.231	.111		.120
Common stock	.18	.346	.166		.180

Assume that the firm is financed with .4 debt, .1 preferred stock, and .5 common stock. The before- and after-tax costs of capital are

before-tax WACC $= .4(.10) + .1(.231) + .5(.346) = .236$

after-tax WACC $= .4(.052) + .1(.12) + .5(.18) = .123$

To pay preferred stockholders .12, the firm must earn

$$(1 - .48)k_p = .12$$

$$k_p = .231$$

For common stockholders to earn .18, the firm must earn

$$(1 - .48)k_e = .18$$

$$k_e = .346$$

An investor who buys a vertical slice of the firm's securities would earn

return to investor $= .4(.10) + .1(.12) + .5(.18) = .142$

Implications of Example 14.6

The previous example has a very important message. With zero taxes, a highly leveraged firm can be converted into a lower leveraged firm by an investment strategy that consists of buying both common stock and debt of the levered firm. This means that a highly leveraged firm cannot sell at a discount compared to a firm with a smaller amount of debt. It can also be shown that a firm with a small amount of debt cannot sell at a discount compared to a high-debt firm. All of this translates to a conclusion that in the absence of taxes, capital structure does not affect the value of a firm. If we are to argue that capital structure makes a difference, then we must turn to institutional reasons. One important reason is the tax law. A second reason for capital structure being important is the cost of bankruptcy.

Bankruptcy has costs arising from the court's administration of the corporation's affairs as well as the costs arising from other companies being reluctant to offer credit. Bankruptcy has costs that are not built into the basic model illustrated in Example 14.6.

A Tax Deduction for Dividends

A tax revision proposal made by President Reagan in May of 1985 was to allow 10 percent of the cash dividends on stock to be a tax deduction for the issuing corporation. This provision would reduce the cost of common stock capital.

Let us assume that the cost of equity capital has been computed to be .20. This is the return that stockholders want for common stock investment in the firm and it is the after-tax cost of equity capital. If the corporate tax rate is .46 and if 10 percent of the dividends are allowed as a deduction, then the after-tax cost of equity capital is

$$\text{After-tax cost of equity} = (1 - .1(.46))k_e = .954k_e$$

$$= .954(.20) = .1908$$

The proposed provision would reduce the cost of equity capital if the company pays dividends. It also tends to encourage cash dividends compared to retained earnings. If a company did not pay cash dividends, and never intended to pay a dividend, the provision would not affect the cost of equity. If cash dividends and other forms of cash distributions are made to investors, the calculation for cost of equity capital would be more complex than illustrated.

Valuing a Firm: Capital Structure and Corporate Taxes

Let us define X to be equal to EBIT. Then we have

$$(X - k_iB)(1 - t_c) = \text{the after-tax return to stockholders (assume that it is all paid as dividends to stockholders)}$$
$$k_iB = \text{the interest paid to debtholders}$$

The total cash flows accruing to capital suppliers will be the sum of the dividends plus interest payments:

$$(X - k_i B)(1 - t_c) + k_i B$$

This sum can be written as

$$X(1 - t_c) + (k_i B)t_c$$

The return to stockholders with zero debt is

$$X(1 - t_c)$$

Thus a levered firm $(B > 0)$ has cash flows each period that are larger than those of the unlevered firm $(B = 0)$ by $k_i B t_c$. Leverage creates an annual corporate tax saving of $k_i B t_c$.

Let us define the present value of the cash flows of an unlevered firm to be V_u and equal to the present value of $X(1 - t_c)$ per period. The value of the levered firm V_L has been shown (with some assumptions) to be

$$V_L = V_U + Bt_c \qquad (14.13)$$

If a theoretical maximum amount of debt is used so that B equals V_U, then

$$V_L = \frac{V_U}{1 - t_c} \qquad (14.14)$$

If with a corporate tax rate of .4 an unlevered firm had a value of $60,000,000, then with maximum debt, the value of the levered firm would be

$$V_L = \frac{\$60,000,000}{1 - .4} = \$100,000,000 \qquad (14.14)$$

Thus, with corporate taxes included in the analysis but without considering personal taxes, the value of the zero-growth firm is maximized by utilizing as much debt as is legally permissible.

An alternative approach to equation (14.14) would be to state that the value of the firm is equal to the discounted value of the expected cash flows accruing to the capital suppliers, where the discount rate used is the borrowing rate, k_i and risk is accounted for by a dollar risk adjustment factor, R. Then for the unlevered firm, the value is

$$V_U = \frac{X(1 - t_c)}{k_i} - R \qquad (14.15)$$

and, if debt is issued to the existing stockholders, no change in the dollar risk compensation will occur, and the expected cash flows will be

$$V_L = \frac{X(1 - t_c) + k_i B t_c}{k_i} - R = V_U + B t_c \qquad (14.16)$$

Thus, again, maximum debt should be issued to maximize the value of the firm. However, the determination of the value of R would not be an easy well-defined exercise.

Personal Taxes

The conclusion that the optimal capital structure decision is for the corporation to issue as much debt as is permissible must be modified when we allow the firm to retain earnings and to include personal tax considerations in examining the wealth position of stockholders. This position was strongly argued by M. H. Miller in 1977.

Assume that the primary objective of a corporation is to maximize the wealth position of its stockholders. Dividends received by shareholders are taxed as ordinary income. If the firm retains the earnings instead of paying them as immediate dividends and reinvests the earnings to earn a competitive return, payment of personal taxes on the dividend is deferred (so the entire earnings rather than the after-tax dividend is reinvested). Furthermore, when the shareholders wish to obtain cash, they can sell stock and pay the capital gains tax on the present value of the reinvestment as viewed by the market rather than having dividends taxed now at ordinary income rates. Thus personal tax considerations for stockholders in high tax brackets exert some pressure for a corporation to use retained earnings to finance growth.

With finite investment possibilities and personal tax implications considered, stockholders with high personal tax rates might be better off having the firm use retained earnings rather than debt to finance investment opportunities.* While the debt financing would save corporate taxes, the personal tax savings from the use of retained earnings might be greater than the corporate tax savings resulting from the use of debt.

If the debtholders and equityholders are identical groups, tax avoidance by labeling "dividends" as "interest" is in the owners' best interest. Although

---

* The "accumulated earnings tax" is intended to keep firms from retaining earnings expressly to avoid dividend payments. To be exempt from this onerous tax, the retained earnings must be used to finance active (plant and equipment, working capital) investments rather than passive (marketable securities, real estate) investments. This provision of the tax code has been administered in an inconsistent manner, so it is not always possible to compute the effects of corporate investment decisions on the accumulated earnings tax.

there are not exact rules, beyond some ill-defined degree of leverage, interest payments may be treated as dividends by the Internal Revenue Service and their deductibility for tax purposes disallowed.

The optimal financial structure depends in part on the tax circumstances of the shareholders and the dividend policy of the firm and in part on the corporate tax saving associated with debt financing. No single strategy is optimal for all firms. A "zero-tax-investor"–oriented firm might pay out a large fraction of its income as dividends and employ a high degree of financial leverage (any public utility?) to meet its capital needs, whereas a "growth" firm (IBM?) might plow most of its earnings back and maintain a low degree of financial leverage.

There follows a valuation model that considers the taxes paid by investors. We first compute the cash flows to investors with a levered firm (X_L) and then the cash flows without any leverage (X_U).

The after-tax cash flow to the stockholders is

$$(X - k_i B)(1 - t_c)(1 - t_s)$$

and the after-tax cash flow to the debtholders is

$$k_i B(1 - t_p)$$

Thus X_L is

$$X_L = (X - k_i B)(1 - t_c)(1 - t_s) + k_i B(1 - t_p)$$

or

$$X_L = X(1 - t_c)(1 - t_s) + k_i B[(1 - t_p) - (1 - t_c)(1 - t_s)] \qquad (14.17)$$

where

t_c = the corporate tax rate
t_p = the ordinary personal tax rate
t_s = the tax rate on stock earnings (an average of the tax on dividends and capital gains)

With zero leverage, the cash flow to the stockholders is

$$X_U = X(1 - t_c)(1 - t_s) \qquad (14.18)$$

Therefore,

$$X_L = X_U + k_i B[(1 - t_p) - (1 - t_c)(1 - t_s)] \tag{14.19}$$

If

1. $t_s = t_p$, then $X_L = X_U + k_i B(1 - t_p t_c)$.
2. $(1 - t_p) = (1 - t_c)(1 - t_s)$, then $X_L = X_U$.
3. $t_s = 0$ and $t_c = t_p$, then $X_L = X_U$.
4. $(1 - t_c)(1 - t_s) > (1 - t_p)$, then $X_L < X_U$.

Now we cannot say that debt is more desirable than common stock without defining the values of t_c, t_s, and t_p.

To compute the value of the levered firm (V_L), we need a rate of discount. Assume that the investor's time value factor is $(1 - t_p)k_i$. Then the value of the unlevered firm is

$$V_U = \frac{X(1 - t_c)(1 - t_s)}{k_i(1 - t_p)} \tag{14.20}$$

and the value of the levered firm is

$$V_L = V_U + \frac{k_i B}{k_i(1 - t_p)} [(1 - t_p) - (1 - t_c)(1 - t_s)]$$

$$V_L = V_U + B\left[1 - \frac{(1 - t_c)(1 - t_s)}{(1 - t_p)}\right] \tag{14.21}$$

New York City and Con Edison

In 1985 Mayor Koch asked the state government to order the Consolidated Edison Company to reduce its percentage of equity. The public service commission had recommended a reduction from 54 percent to 40 to 45 percent equity. It was said that the customers could save $277 million a year in electricity bills.

The Con Edison spokesman said, "The way we are structured now is financially beneficial to our customers."*

* See *The New York Times*, January 3, 1985, p. B5.

If $t_s = t_p$, then

$$V_L = V_U + t_c B \tag{14.22}$$

The value of the levered firm is equal to the value of the unlevered firm (V_u) plus the tax rate times the amount of added debt ($t_c B$).

Conclusions

Presumably, one amount of debt leverage is preferred to another if moving to that leverage will improve the stockholders' wealth position. But to determine the degree of financial leverage that leads to a weighted average cost of capital that maximizes stockholders' wealth is no easy task.

Although the traditional (classical) position states that a judicious amount of debt is to be employed, the Modigliani and Miller position* states that with well-defined assumptions, any degree of financial leverage is equally desirable (with no corporate taxes). When corporate taxes are considered, it can be argued that the theoretical minimum cost of capital structure is virtually all debt. But when personal taxes are considered, the conclusion changes again.

Care must be used in taking sides on this controversy. The traditionalists argue their position by noting that firms adopt capital structures substantially less than 100 percent debt and substantially more than 0 percent debt. The Modigliani and Miller zero-tax argument for a value that is independent of capital structure, on the other hand, is clearly spelled out in terms of their assumptions and models. While the latter are correct given their assumptions, their assumptions are worth reconsidering. The extent to which (1) markets are imperfect and (2) equity suppliers discriminate between dividends and capital gains (treated differently for tax purposes) and (3) the fact that there are both corporate and personal taxes makes it difficult to make the definitive exact statements as to the exact optimum capital structure. Most important, there is general agreement the different tax treatment awarded interest and stockholder's earnings affect the relative desirability of debt and stock.

If there were no personal taxes, the use of debt in the capital structure of a corporation would enable a firm to reduce its cost of raising capital since the interest payments are deductible for corporate tax purposes. The desirability of debt compared to common stock is dramatized when the debt is purchased by the common stockholders, since in this situation there is no increase in the risk to the investors. One could be led to the conclusion that

---

* Franco Modigliani and M. H. Miller, "Cost of Capital, Corporation Finance and the Theory of Investments," *American Economic Review*, June 1958, pp. 261–297.

a firm should issue as much debt as possible, with zero-tax stockholders purchasing the debt if they fear an excessive increase in risk arising from the highly levered capital structure. However, the Internal Revenue Service might limit the amount of this type of debt that a corporation may issue and too much debt may result in the cash distribution being relabeled as dividends.

The addition of debt, even where the debt is a relatively cheap source of capital because of the tax structure, does add risk to the stockholders if the debt is sold to nonstockholders. If there is no taxable income, the full cost of the interest falls on the corporation and ultimately on the stockholders. Thus we can conclude that the present tax structure offers strong incentives to issue debt but that there are forces (the risk of bankruptcy and the conventions of the investment banking community) that restrain the corporation considering the issuance of unusually large amounts of debt compared to common stock.

Finally, if we consider personal taxes as well as corporate taxes, we are led to conclude that the optimum amount of debt is not clearly defined. There are tax advantages to common stock (tax deferral and capital gains) that may outweigh the advantages to the corporation of the tax deductibility of interest.

Business managers quite properly want to know how different capital structures affect the cost of obtaining capital to reduce the cost of using the firm's present capital or to reduce the cost to the firm of obtaining new capital. Although managers may also want to use the weighted average cost of capital as the discount rate (the hurdle rate) in evaluating all investments, we are not enthusiastic about this usage. If the risk of the asset is different from the risk of the firm's other assets, or if the timing of the cash flows is different, using the one risk-adjusted discount rate (the cost of capital) to evaluate all the investments is not likely to lead to correct decisions.

Review Problem 14.1

(a) The corporate tax rate is .46. Complete the following table.

	Required Returns	Before-Tax Costs	Tax	Tax Savings	After-Tax Cost
Debt		.12			
Preferred stock	.11				
Common stock	.14				

(b) The after-tax weighted average cost of capital (.45 debt, .15 preferred stock, .40 common stock) is

WACC =

(c) An investor buying a vertical slice of the firm will earn how large a return if the required returns are earned?

Solution to Review Problem 14.1

(a) The corporate tax rate is .46.

	Required Returns	Before-Tax Costs	Tax	Tax Savings	After-Tax Cost
Debt	.12	.12		.0552	.0648
Preferred stock	.11	.2037	.0937		.11
Common stock	.14	.25926	.11926		.14

(b) The after-tax weighted average cost of capital (.45 debt, .15 preferred stock, .40 common stock) is

$$\text{WACC} = .45(.0648) + .15(.11) + .40(.14) = .1017$$

(c) An investor buying a vertical slice of the firm will earn a return of .1265 if the required returns are earned.

$$r = .45(.12) + .15(.11) + .40(.14) = .1265$$

PROBLEMS

1. Assume a .46 tax rate. To pay .10 to investors, a company must earn what return (before tax) if the security is
   (a) Debt?
   (b) Preferred stock?
   (c) Common stock?

What after-tax internal rate of return must an investment earn for a corporation to supply sufficient cash flows to pay a before-tax (personal) .10 to

(d) Debtholders?

(e) Preferred stockholders?

(f) Common stockholders?

2. (Problem 1 continued)

(a) Assuming .5 common stock, .4 debt, and .1 preferred stock, the after-tax WACC of the firm is _____ .

(b) An zero-tax investor holding the proportion of securities given in (a) would earn _____ .

3. Assume that a firm has earned $100 of before-tax income. The corporate tax rate is 48 percent.

(a) If the security used to finance the investment is $1,000 of 10 percent debt, the firm holding the debt (supplying the debt capital) will have _____ after tax.

(b) If the security used to finance the investment is $1,000 of 10 percent preferred stock, the corporation holding the preferred stock (supplying the capital) will have _____ after tax.

(c) If the security used to finance the investment is $1,000 of common stock and if the entire tax amount of income is paid as a dividend, the corporation holding the common stock will have _____ after tax.

If the investor is a zero tax entity, the answers to the preceding questions for the *investor* are:

(d) _____

(e) _____

(f) _____

4. Assume that a company borrows at a cost of .14. Its tax rate is .46. What is the minimum after-tax cost of capital for a certain cash flow if

(a) 100 percent debt is used? _____

(b) 100 percent common stock? _____ (assume that the stockholders will accept .14)

(c) 40 percent debt? _____

5. Assume that the return on tax-exempt securities is .09 and that $t_p = .3$, $t_g = .20$, and $t_c = .46$, where t_g is the rate on capital gains, t_c is the corporate tax rate, and t_p is the personal tax rate on dividends and interest. Equilibrium conditions exist.

   (a) The return to investors on taxable bonds raised as new capital can be expected to be _____ .

   (b) The return to investors on common stock (all capital gains) raised as new capital can be expected to be _____ .

   (c), (d) If taxable debt is issued, the company will have to earn _____ before tax, and if common stock is issued, the firm will have to earn _____ before tax.

6. The tax rate for the Gas Corporation is .46. The following table has been prepared for the president of the firm. The 1985 U.S. Internal Revenue Code applies.

	Before-Tax Cost	After-Tax Cost	Capital Structure
Bonds	.14	.0756	.4
Preferred stock	.2407	.1300	.1
Common stock	.3333	.18	.5

   (a) Compute the weighted average after-tax cost of capital of the firm, with the given capital structure.
   (b) Compute the return before tax for an investor who splits the investment in the company in the same proportion as the sources of capital.
   (c) If $1,000 of each type of capital were raised, the capital would have to earn before tax

   Bonds $_____

   Preferred stocks   _____

   Common stock   _____

7. For a company with zero debt, the cost of the first dollar of debt is .10, and the cost of common stock is .18 (these are returns required by investors). We have determined that the cost of debt is

$$k_i = .10 + .08\frac{B}{V}$$

and that there are no taxes and no bankruptcy costs. The capital market is rational and well informed.

(a) What is the weighted average cost of capital? _____

(b) Should the next issue of the company be common stock or debt if the objective is to minimize the cost of the capital? _____

(c) What will be the cost of equity if the capital structure has equal amounts of debt and equity? _____

8. The following facts apply to the XYZ Company:
   Bonds can be issued to yield .10.
   Preferred stock can be issued to yield .08.
   Common stock can be issued with an expected yield to stockholders of .18.
   The tax rates are .4 for all sections of this problem.
   (a) Compute the before-tax *cash flows* that have to be earned to compensate investors for $1,000 of capital:
       (1) Debt. (2) Preferred stock. (3) Common Stock.
   (b) Compute the WACC (after tax) if the capital structure is .5 debt, .1 preferred stock, and .4 common stock.
   (c) Compute the weighted average return for an investor who invests in the same proportion (for different securities) as the capital structure.

9. Assume the M & M zero-tax model, where $k_0 = .14$ and $k_i = .10$ for all capital structures (both k_0 and k_i are constants).
   (a) Give the equation for k_e.
   (b) What is the value of k_e if $B = 4 million and $S = 8 million.

10. Assume that tax-exempt bonds are being issued at a cost of .12 and risk-equivalent taxables at .18.

    (a) What is the personal tax rate of the marginal investor? _____

    (b) An investor in tax exempts in the 58 percent tax bracket would earn the equivalent of what before-tax return? _____

    (c) If $10 billion of tax-exempt securities are issued, the annual interest savings to the issuing authorities are _____ .

11.

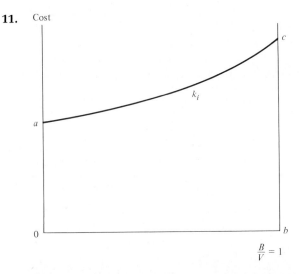

Assume that the k_i curve is correctly drawn. Comment on the following statements or complete them. (There are zero taxes.)

(a) The k_e curve may be below the k_i curve at some point.

(b) The weighted average cost of capital is approximately equal to

_____ .

(c) If the shape of the k_0 curve is a horizontal straight line, then logically

the k_e curve will have a _____ slope.

(d) If the k_e curve has a positive slope, then the k_0 curve must also slope upward.

12. A firm has $10 million of assets to be financed with $6,000,000 debt and $4 million of equity. You have $2 million to invest in the firm. There are zero taxes.

How would you invest so that your investment is equivalent to investing in an identical firm with 100 percent common stock?

13. Company A's bank requires a 10 percent compensating balance for a loan. The company is borrowing $10,000,000 at a stated cost of .09. The company has computed its WACC as follows:

		Cost	*Weights*	
Debt	$10,000,000	.09	.2	.018
Common stock	40,000,000	.15	.8	.120
				.138

(a) Assume that the .15 is correct and a zero tax rate, evaluate the WACC calculation.

(b) What is the effective cost of the bank debt?

(c) If Company A is a regulated firm allowed to earn its WACC, how much should it be allowed to earn?

14. Assume a zero-tax situation and three identical firms except for capital structure.

	A	B	C
Assets	$10,000,000	$10,000,000	$10,000,000
Preferred stock	2,000,000	6,000,000	
Common stock	8,000,000	4,000,000	10,000,000

All three firms have 200,000 shares of common stock outstanding. A sells for $40 per share, B for $20 per share, and C for $50.

(a) An investor intends to invest $1,000,000 in the common stock of C. Develop an alternative investment strategy involving the securities of Firm B where the objective is to have an identical return to that of C's common stock.

(b) An investor intends to invest $1,000,000 in the common stock of A. Develop an alternative investment strategy involving the securities of Firm B where the objective is to have an identical return to that of A's common stock.

(c) If the market is upset about the excessive preferred stock used by Firm B so that the market values are

Preferred stock $5,000,000
Common stock   3,000,000

describe a strategy that is better than an investment of $1,000,000 in Firm C's common stock.

15. A firm is being organized that requires an initial investment of $20 million. You have $200,000 and will buy .01 of the common stock if it is 100 percent financed with common stock. The use of $8 million of 10 percent preferred stock and $12 million of common stock is being considered.

(a) If this capital structure is chosen, what investment strategy should you choose to have the same identical outcomes as investing in the common stock at the 100 percent common stock–financed firm?

(b) If the firm earns $900,000, what will you earn if the common stock financing is chosen? _____ What will you earn if the preferred stock financing is chosen and you invest as described in (a)? _____

16. For a company with zero debt, the cost of the first dollar of debt is .12 and the cost of common stock is .18 (these are returns required by investors). We have determined that

$$k_i = .12 + .06\frac{B}{V}$$

and there are no taxes and no bankruptcy costs. The capital market is rational and well informed.

(a) What is the WACC? _____

(b) Should the next issue of the company be common stock or debt if the objective is to minimize the cost of the capital? _____

(c) What will be the cost of equity if the capital structure has equal amounts of debt and equity? _____

17. Encircle one numeral for the correct statement.
   (a) If with a substitution of debt for common stock the cost of both common stock and debt increase, then the WACC will
      (1) Increase.
      (2) Decrease.
      (3) Stay the same.
      (4) Increase, decrease, or stay the same.
   (b) If debt is substituted for common stock, one would logically expect the cost of stock equity to
      (1) Increase.
      (2) Decrease.
      (3) Stay the same.
      (4) Increase, decrease, or stay the same.
   (c) In the absence of bankruptcy costs and corporate taxes, a firm with more debt than the market thinks is rational will sell
      (1) At the same value as an identical firm properly financed (as viewed by the market).
      (2) At less than a firm properly financed.
      (3) At more than a firm properly financed.
      (4) The same value, or less than, or more than, depending on risk preferences.

18. Assume that for a public utility the following facts and estimates apply and are accepted:

$$k_i = .10$$

$$k_e = .15$$

$$\frac{B}{V} = .2$$

$$t_c = .46$$

The rate commission thinks that the capital structure should be $B/V = .6$ and has made the following calculation for WACC:

$$k_0 = (1 - .46)\ .10(.6) + .15(.4)$$

$$= (.054)(.6) + .06$$

$$= .0324 + .06 = .0924$$

Briefly evaluate the calculation.

19. The earnings of firms X and Y are identically distributed (they are the same firm except for capital structure). Other facts are

	Market Values	
	Firm X	Firm Y
Debt	$0	$75,000,000
Common stock	110,000,000	25,000,000

The cost of the debt is .10.

(a) Assume that you are going to invest $1,000,000 in one of the firms. What would be your investment plan *if* you want your strategy to dominate the alternative of investing in the equity of the other firm?

(b) Explain why your plan is desirable.

20. The planning team of the ABC Insurance Company is trying to organize the capital structure of an acquisition. Both firms are paying income taxes. You are given the choice of two capital structures:

	Structure[1]	Structure[2]
10% Debt	60%	
10% Preferred stock		60%
Common stock	40%	40%

ABC will own .40 of all securities. The 1985 U.S. tax laws apply.

Which capital structure should the firm prefer? _____ Explain.

21. The ABC Insurance Co. follows a policy of buying the same percentage of common stock as debt. That is, if it buys .20 of a company's debt, it will buy .20 of the company's common stock.

The Metro Insurance Co. will only buy common stock in companies that have zero long-term debt. All the companies being invested in have the same operating risk.

Assume that there are zero taxes.

Which insurance company has a more risky investment strategy? Explain.

22. The A Company is going to issue $100 million of securities. The corporate tax rate is .46. The debt can be issued to yield .10 and the preferred stock to yield .095.

(a) The after-tax annual dollar cost of issuing all debt is $ _____ ?

(b) The after-tax annual dollar cost of issuing all preferred stock is

$ _____ ?

(c) How long would it take for there to be zero debt outstanding if the savings from issuing debt were used to retire debt? _____ years.

23. Company D has the following balance sheet:

Assets	$1,000,000	Debt	$500,000 (book and market value)
		Preferred stock	200,000 (book and market value)
		Common stock (150,000 shares)	300,000

Company E is an identical firm (same earnings before interest), but it uses only common stock for capital. Company E has 500,000 shares outstanding selling for $2 per share.

Company D's common stock is selling for $1.50 per share.

You have $500,000 to invest. You are going to invest the $500,000 in either D or E. The operations are risky, and you want your investment to be no more risky than an investment in E's common stock, and you want to earn at least as much as you can earn by investing in E's common stock. There are zero taxes.

What investment strategy do you recommend? Be specific and justify your answer.

24. Debtholders and stockholders will both accept a .16 return if there is zero operating risk. Assume that a corporation has .35 debt and .65 common stock.

    (a) If an investment is to be financed by that mixture of debt and common stock, what after-tax rate of return will it have to earn? The corporate tax rate is .46.

    (b) Assume a $1,000 investment with a one-year life. Show the total income at time 1, the taxes, and the distributions to debt and common stock. All investors earn the exact required return.

25. It has been shown that

$$g = rb + b[r - k_i(1 - t_c)]\frac{B}{S}$$

Compute the growth rate for a company, where

    (a) The average return on all assets after the investment will be .16 and on the new investments undertaken as a result of the earnings retention will be .18, and the marginal return on the last dollar invested will be .15. The relevant value for r is

        $r = $ _____

    (b) The earnings will be $2 per share, and the cash dividend will be $1.20.

        $b = $ _____

    (c) The average cost of presently outstanding debt is .10, the average cost of new debt will be .17, and the marginal cost of the last dollar of debt is .19.

        $k_i = $ _____

    (d) The law states that the corporate tax rate is .46, but because of provisions in the law (e.g., ITC), the average tax rate .30.

        $t_c = $ _____

    (e) The company has been using all common stock. During the next period, the investment will be financed with equal amounts of debt and common stock. At the end of the period, the capital structure will be $\frac{1}{9}$ debt and $\frac{8}{9}$ common stock.

$$\frac{B}{S} = \underline{\hspace{3cm}}$$

$$g = \underline{\hspace{3cm}}$$

26. Assume that a company borrows at a cost of .09. Its tax rate is .48.
    (a) What is the minimum cost of capital for a certain cash flow if 100 percent debt is used? _____
    (b) 100 percent common stock? _____
    (c) 40 percent debt? _____

27. A corporation financed completely with common stock is expected to earn $100,000 of cash flow a year before tax for perpetuity. The corporate tax rate is .46.
    (a) If the capital structure could not be changed, a zero-tax investor with a borrowing and lending rate of .12 would place a value of _____ on the firm.
    (b) If the capital structure can be changed, the maximum value to the investor would be _____ .
    (c) If the debt of the corporation could be issued at a cost of .12, the maximum amount of debt that could be issued is _____ .
    (d) If only common stock is used, the after-tax cash flow each year will be _____ . With maximum debt the after-tax cash flow each year is _____ .

28. (a) The ABC Company has a simple capital structure. Management wants to substitute $100 million of .12 debt for common stock. What effect will the change have on the value of the firm to a zero-tax investor? The corporate tax rate is .46.
    (b) The XYZ Company is thinking of acquiring a firm that is earning before-tax $100,000 a year. XYZ's borrowing rate is .10, and its tax rate is .46. Thus, its after-tax borrowing rate is .054. The investment in the firm will be financed with sufficient debt to cause the amount of income taxes paid to be zero on this investment.
    What is the maximum amount that XYZ could afford to pay for the firm?

29. The ABC Company has an average cost of debt of .08, but the next debt borrowed will cost .12. It is currently earning .15 on investment, but it will earn .18 on the average on the next period's investments.

    For every $1 of common stock the firm has used $1 of debt, but in the future (this period), there will be $2 of debt used for every dollar.

    The statutory corporate tax rate is .46. Because of investment tax credits the average tax rate is .30 for the company. The company pays out .4 of its earnings as dividends.

    If growth is going to occur only because of investment, what growth rate do you expect the firm to have for the next period?

30. The tax rate for the Tompkins Corporation is .46.

	Before-Corporate Tax Cost	After-Tax Cost
Bonds	.15	
Preferred stock	.26	
Common stock	.30	

The firm has a capital structure of .4 debt, .1 preferred stock, and .5 common stock.

(a) Complete the table assuming that the "Before-Corporate-Tax Cost" column is correct.

(b) Compute the after-tax weighted average cost of capital of the firm, with the given capital structure.

(c) Compute the return for a zero-tax investor who splits the investment in the company in the same proportion as the sources of capital.

31. Assume that the corporate tax rate is .46 and that there is a .85 dividend received credit. You are the corporate treasurer of a firm investing $1 million in Firm B. B agrees to pay you $200,000 of its earnings *before its income tax* (if B pays taxes, you will receive $200,000 less the taxes paid). The security can be classified as either debt or preferred stock with essentially the same protection in case of bankruptcy.

    Prepare the necessary numerical analysis to reach a decision.

32. The tax rate for The Ithaca Corporation is .4. The following table has been prepared for the president of the firm.

	Before-Tax Cost	After-Tax Cost
Bonds	.10	.06
Preferred stock	.12	.072
Common stock	.20	.12

Only bond interest is deductible for income taxes. The firm has a capital structure of .4 debt, .1 preferred stock, and .5 common stock. Assume that the U.S. Internal Revenue Code applies.

(a) Compute the weighted average cost of capital of the firm, with the given capital structure.

(b) Compute the before-tax return for an investor who splits her investment in the company in the same proportion as the sources of capital.

REFERENCES

Barnea, A., R. A. Haugen, and L. W. Senbet, *Agency Problems and Financial Contracting*, Englewood Cliffs, N.J.: Prentice-Hall, Inc., 1985.

Baumol, William, and Burton G. Malkiel. "The Firm's Optimal Debt-Equity Combination and the Cost of Capital." *Quarterly Journal of Economics*, November 1967, 547–578.

Fama, Eugene, and Merton Miller, *The Theory of Finance*. New York: Holt, Rinehart and Winston, 1972.

Masulis, Ronald. "The Effects of Capital Structure Change on Security Prices: A Study of Exchange Offers." *Journal of Financial Economics*, June 1980, 139–178.

Miller, M. H. "Debt and Taxes." *Journal of Finance*, May 1977, 261–275.

———, and Franco Modigliani. "Cost of Capital to Electric Utility Industry." *American Economic Review*, June 1966, 333–391.

Modigliani, Franco, and M. H. Miller. "The Cost of Capital, Corporation Finance and the Theory of Investment." *American Economic Review*, June 1958, 261–297.

———, and ———. "The Cost of Capital, Corporation Finance and the Theory of Investment: Reply," *American Economic Review*, September 1958, 655–669; "Taxes and the Cost of Capital: A Correction." *American Economic Review*, June 1963, 433–443; "Reply." *American Economic Review*, June 1965, 524–527; "Reply to Heins and Sprenkle," *American Economic Review*, September 1969, 592–595.

Robichek, Alexander A., and Stewart D. Myers. *Optimal Financing Decisions*. Englewood Cliffs, N.J.: Prentice-Hall, Inc., 1965.

Scott, James. "A Theory of Optimal Capital Structure." *Bell Journal of Economics and Management Science*, Spring 1976, 33–54.

Solomon, E. "Leverage and the Cost of Capital." *The Journal of Finance*, May, 1963, 273–279.

———. *The Theory of Financial Management*. New York: Columbia University Press, 1963.

Vickers, Douglas. "The Cost of Capital and the Structure of the Firm." *Journal of Finance*, March 1970, 35–46.

Appendix 14.1   Determining $\alpha = S_j/S_i$

We want to show that $\alpha = S_j/S_i$.

By buying the common stock of i, a return of $(X - k_iB_i)/S_i$ is earned. Buying α of common stock of j and $(1 - \alpha)$ of the debt of j earns a return of

$$\alpha \frac{X - k_iB_j}{S_j} + (1 - \alpha)k_i$$

Equating the two returns, we obtain

$$\frac{X - k_iB_i}{S_i} = \alpha \frac{X - k_iB_j}{S_j} + (1 - \alpha)k_i$$

$$\alpha = \frac{(X - k_iB_i)S_j - k_iS_iS_j}{(X - k_iB_j)S_i - k_iS_iS_j}$$

Since $B_i = V - S_i$ and $B_j = V - S_j$,

$$\alpha = \frac{(X - V)S_j + k_iS_jS_i - k_iS_iS_j}{(X - V)S_i + k_iS_jS_i - k_iS_iS_j}$$

$$\alpha = \frac{S_j}{S_i} \qquad \text{and} \qquad 1 - \alpha = \frac{S_i - S_j}{S_i}$$

Chapter 15

Capital Structure: A Managerial Perspective

Major Topics

1. The risk consequences of substituting debt for stock equity (leverage)
2. Operating and financial leverage.
3. The amount of earnings (EBIT) that results in indifference as to the amount of debt.
4. Degree of operating leverage, degree of financial leverage, degree of total leverage.

Leverage

A firm can employ two types of leverage: operating leverage and financial leverage. Operating leverage refers to the effect that fluctuations in sales will have on operating earnings before interest and taxes (EBIT); financial leverage refers to the effect that fluctuations in operating earnings before interest and taxes will have on the (after-tax and after-interest expense) earnings available for common stockholders. An increase in either operating or financial leverage means that the corresponding measure of after-tax income will exhibit greater fluctuations for a given change in unit sales.

A firm has some control over the amounts of operating and financial leverage that it wishes to employ. In general, substituting fixed costs (such as equipment) for variable costs (such as hourly labor) increases operating leverage. The methods of production employed, which are reflected in the asset structure of the firm, influence its operating leverage. For example, substituting machinery for labor usually increases operating leverage. The capital sources employed, which are reflected in the capital structure of the firm, influence its financial leverage. For example, substituting debt for common stockholders' equity increases financial leverage.

There are many ways in which to measure risk. Although there may be disagreements about which measure of risk is best in a given situation, there is little disagreement about the relationship between leverage and risk. Under almost all circumstances, increasing leverage increases risk, and for a business enterprise, risk is generally considered to be an undesirable characteristic. Therefore, an increase in leverage will be undesirable unless accompanied by an increase in potential returns to stockholders. If there is an increase in potential returns, leverage decisions involve evaluating a risk-return trade-off.

Operating Leverage

Operating leverage may be illustrated using break-even charts. The top panel of Figure 15.1 shows the total expenses and total revenues for different levels of sales. The bottom panel of Figure 15.1 shows the same situation, but now only operating income (revenues minus expenses) is shown. Since we are interested in operating leverage at this point, income is measured as operating earnings before interest expense and taxes.

The basic relationships may be shown algebraically. Let

$$
\begin{aligned}
R &= \text{the total revenues (dollars per period)} \\
EXP &= \text{the total operating expenses (dollars per period)} \\
F &= \text{the fixed operating costs (dollars per period)} \\
X &= \text{the operating income (dollars per period)} \\
P &= \text{the price per unit (dollars per unit)} \\
Q &= \text{the unit sales (units per period)} \\
b &= \text{the variable costs per unit (dollars per unit)}
\end{aligned}
$$

In the top panel of Figure 15.1, the two straight lines drawn are total revenue

$$R = PQ \tag{15.1}$$

and total expenses:

$$EXP = F + bQ \tag{15.2}$$

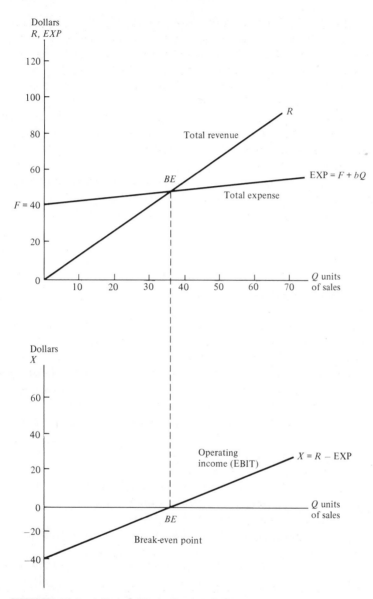

FIGURE 15.1   A Break-Even Presentation

Operating income is measured as the vertical difference between these two lines. A one-unit increase in sales will increase revenue by P, expenses by b, and operating income by $(P - b)$, which is a convenient measure of operating leverage. The difference between the slopes of the two lines in the top panel of Figure 15.1 is a measure of operating leverage. The difference is plotted in the bottom panel.

In Figure 15.1 the equation for EBIT is

$$X = R - EXP \tag{15.3a}$$

Equation (15.3a) is used to show the relation between sales and income directly. Substituting PQ for R and $F + bQ$ for EXP, the equation for the EBIT line in the bottom panel of Figure 15.1 is

$$X = -F + (P - b)Q \tag{15.3b}$$

F is the measure of fixed costs, and $-F$ is the intercept with the Y axis (the income with zero sales).

Operating Leverage and Break-Even Analysis

The traditional use of a break-even chart is to measure the level of sales needed to breakeven. Each additional unit of sales results in an additional b dollars of variable expenses and produces a contribution of $(P - b)$ dollars toward covering fixed costs and profits. The break-even point is $F/(P - b)$ units of sales. At the break-even level of sales, the operating earnings before interest and taxes (EBIT) will equal zero. Thus this level of sales may be designated as the break-even point. It is denoted by the point BE in Figure 15.1.

The measure of F conventionally leaves out the interest cost on the capital utilized. Assuming that the amount of the investment was V and that the cost of obtaining funds was k_i, then it would be necessary to earn (revenues minus variable costs) an amount of k_iV plus the fixed costs F in order to break even economically.

In Figure 15.2 the operating leverages associated with two different cost structures are compared. The amount of sales A^* at which the lines intersect indicates the level of sales at which the two cost structures would produce the same income.

In this chapter we shall assume that the fixed costs, F, are easily measured unambiguous periodic out-of-pocket costs (say, unavoidable lease payments). If an investment type of outlay is involved, the analysis should shift to a capital budgeting analysis with the added dimension of considering what happens

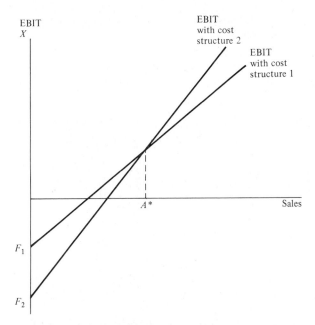

FIGURE 15.2   Comparison of Operating Leverage with Two Cost Structures

if sales are different than the expected level of sales (this is called sensitivity analysis). The different cost structures would be mutually exclusive investments.

Financial Leverage

Financial leverage refers to the effects that the capital structure combined with the fluctuations in operating income will have on the earnings available to common stockholders (after taxes and interest expense). Changes in operating leverage are brought about by changing the asset composition and thus the cost structure of the firm. Changes in financial leverage are brought about by changing the mix of equity and debt. For present purposes we assume that there are only two sources of long-term capital, common stock and long-term debt. As a general rule it is easier and quicker to change the financial structure of a firm than it is to change its asset structure. In a later section we shall consider the combined effects of operating and financial leverage on the variability of earnings.

Algebraic Analysis: Financial Leverage

Financial leverage can be demonstrated by building a simple mathematical model of a firm and exploring the impact of debt utilization on the return on the stockholders' investment. We use the following notation:

X = the EBIT, a random variable with mean $E(X)$
Y = the net income to common stockholders after interest and taxes
t_c = the corporate tax rate
S = the amount of stockholders' equity
ROE = the return on stockholders' equity investment
k_i = the cost of debt capital
B = the amount of debt

The after-tax net income to common stockholders is EBIT less interest and taxes:

$$Y = (X - k_i B)(1 - t_c) \qquad (15.4)$$

Rearranging the equation into a form analogous to the straight-line equation $Y = a + mX$, where a is the intercept and m is the slope of the line, we obtain

$$Y = -(1 - t_c)k_i B + (1 - t_c)X \qquad (15.5)$$

Note that the intersection with the Y axis is equal to the amount of after-tax interest cost but that the slope is equal to $(1 - t_c)$.

The return on stock equity is

$$\text{ROE} = \frac{Y}{S} = \frac{(X - k_i B)(1 - t_c)}{S} = \frac{-(1 - t_c)k_i B}{S} + \frac{(1 - t_c)X}{S} \qquad (15.6)$$

where $[-(1 - t_c)k_i B]/S$ is the Y axis intercept and $(1 - t_c)/S$ is the slope.

Graphic Analysis

The relationship between before-tax operating income (EBIT) and the income available to common stockholders is illustrated graphically in Figure 15.3. EBIT is measured on the horizontal axis and Y, the amount of income available to common stockholders after interest and taxes, is measured on the vertical axis. The line labeled Y_1 illustrates the situation in which there is no financial leverage. With zero debt, the relation between Y and X will be a straight line through the origin with a slope determined by the income tax rate and equal to $(1 - t_c)$. If the corporate income tax rate were zero, the line would have a slope of 1. With a corporate income tax rate of .4 the slope of the line is .6;

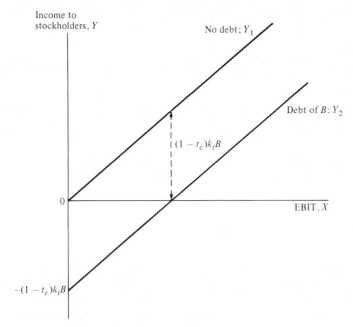

FIGURE 15.3 **Financial Leverage:** $Y = -(1 - t_c) k_i B + (1 - t_c) X$

each dollar of before-tax operating income is converted to $0.60 of after-tax income. The line Y_1 goes through the origin because there are no fixed financial charges.

Suppose that $1,000 of debt is outstanding with an interest cost of 10 percent before taxes. This case is illustrated by the line labeled Y_2. There are fixed financial charges of $60 per year after taxes, and $100 of before-tax operating income is required to break even. The line for Y_2 is parallel to that for Y_1 because the same tax rate is assumed for both. For every level of X, Y_2 is $60 below Y_1 because of the existence of $1,000 of debt. This difference is equal to $-(1 - t_c)k_i B$.

The Indifference Point

Return on Equity

Figure 15.4 shows the returns on stockholders' equity that will result from using two different capital structures for different values of EBIT. If we assume that the interest rate is not a function of the amount of debt, then all the lines

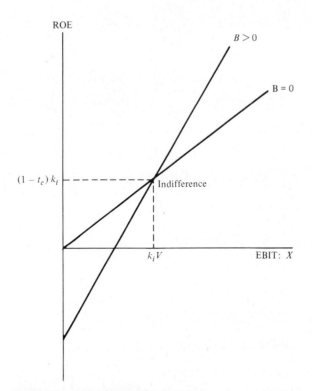

FIGURE 15.4   Financial Leverage

plotting the returns of investment for the different capital structures (and the same cost structure) must go through the same point. We call this point the indifference return on equity investment.

If we know that the actual value of X will be to the right of the indifference point, the more financial leverage the firm has, the better off stockholders are (the ROE is increased by more debt). When the actual value of X is to the left of the indifference point, the more financial leverage, the worse off stockholders are. Unfortunately, in the real world, we do not know the value of the next period's X.

It is shown in Appendix 15.1 that the indifference ROE has the following coordinates:

Y axis: $\text{ROE} = (1 - t_c)k_i$ (15.7)

X axis: $X = k_i V$ (15.8)

where V is the amount of capital (debt plus stock equity) employed by the firm.

TABLE 15.1 Assume $X = \$80{,}000$, $V = \$1{,}000{,}000$, $k_i = .08$, $t_c = .4$

Amount of Debt: B	Amount of Common Stock: S	$X - k_iB$	$(X - k_iB)(1 - t_c)$	ROE
$ 0	$1,000,000	$80,000	$48,000	.048
500,000	500,000	40,000	24,000	.048
900,000	100,000	8,000	4,800	.048

In the example, let

$V = \$1{,}000{,}000$

$t_c = .4$

$k_i = .08$

The indifference point is $80,000 of EBIT and .048 of ROE:

$$\text{ROE} = (1 - .4)(.08) = .048 \tag{15.7}$$

$$X = .08(\$1{,}000{,}000) = \$80{,}000 \tag{15.8}$$

If EBIT $= \$80{,}000$ and with the facts given, the capital structure makes no difference; the return on investment will be .048. Table 15.1 shows the values of ROE for different capital structures and $X = \$80{,}000$. All the ROEs are equal to .048 for $X = \$80{,}000$. The ROE is not affected by the amount of debt if $X = \$80{,}000$.

Earnings per Share

Instead of finding the leverage indifference point for return on stock equity, we could determine the leverage indifference point for earnings per share (EPS). Remember, the investor is indifferent only if the actual EBIT is the one amount that results in indifference. With the amount of EBIT uncertain, the investor in common stock will not be indifferent as to different amounts of debt.

Let S be the amount of common stock equity, N be the number of shares, and S/N be the amount of equity employed per share of common stock. The indifferent value of EBIT (the amount of EBIT that causes the firm to be indifferent to the amount of debt) will again be

$$X = k_iV \tag{15.8}$$

TABLE 15.2   Assume $X = \$80{,}000$

Amount of Debt: B	Amount of Stock: S	$(X - k_iB)(1 - t_c)$	Number of Shares	Earnings per Share
0	$1,000,000	$48,000	100,000	$.48
$500,000	500,000	24,000	50,000	.48
900,000	100,000	4,800	10,000	.48

and now the corresponding earnings per share for indifference is

$$\text{EPS} = (1 - t_c)\, k_i \frac{S}{N} \tag{15.9}$$

We will assume that the S/N is $10 and that the number of shares, N, will be 100,000 with zero debt, 50,000 with $500,000 of debt, and 10,000 with $900,000 of debt. The value of V is $1,000,000.

Table 15.2 shows that, for the example with $k_i = .08$ if $X = \$80{,}000$, the EPS is independent of the amount of debt.

The EPS indifference point can be determined directly using equations (15.8) and (15.9):

$$X = k_iV = .08(\$1{,}000{,}000) = \$80{,}000 \tag{15.8}$$

$$\text{EPS} = \frac{(1 - t_c)k_iS}{N} = (1 - .4)(.08)(10) = .48 \tag{15.9}$$

If we could predict with 100 percent certainty that the EBIT would be greater than $80,000, then we could maximize both the return on stock equity and earnings per share by issuing as much .08 debt as the market would take.

Since we never know the future with certainty, the fear that the EBIT will be less than $80,000 limits the amount of debt that is issued. With earnings before interest less than $80,000, the presence of debt will reduce both the return on stock investment and earnings per share.

Allowing interest to be a function of the amount of debt would result in an analogous but more complex set of calculations. The lines for return on investment and EPS for different capital structures with EBIT measured on the X axis would not all go through one indifference point.

Operating Risk

The degree of risk in a firm's operating earnings is determined by the demand for its product, by its cost structure, and by the probablity distribution of its sales. If the firm's cost structure is dominated by fixed costs, total expenses will be not very responsive to sales fluctuations; in this case income is greatly affected by changes in sales and if sales fluctuate widely the firm may be relatively risky.

The concept of operating leverage risk can be expressed mathematically using the standard deviation as a measure of risk. Although it is undoubtedly true that price, volume, fixed costs, and unit variable cost may all be random variables, we shall make the simplifying assumptions that only the quantity sold is a random variable and that price, unit variable cost, and fixed costs are known with certainty.

Using equation (15.3b), we have

$$X = -F + (P - b)Q \tag{15.3b}$$

Figure 15.5 shows the plot of X as a function of Q. The slope of the operating leverage line is $(P - b)$.

The larger the difference between the price and variable costs, the larger the sensitivity of X to changes in units sold. This does not mean that one would prefer a small difference to a large difference between price and variable costs. It merely means that X will change more with a given change in Q if $(P - b)$ is large.

Table 15.3 shows the effect on EBIT of changes in Q for different values of $(P - b)$ and two different levels of sales.

If $(P - b) = \$1$ and 50 units are currently being sold, \$40 of EBIT will be lost if sales decrease to 10. But if $(P - b) = \$10$, the loss will be \$400 if sales decrease from 50 units to 10 units.

Business risk arises because unit sales are uncertain; thus there is uncer-

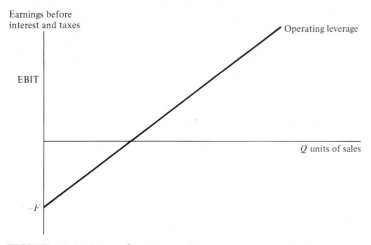

FIGURE 15.5 Operating Leverage

TABLE 15.3   EBIT for Different $(P - b)$

$(P - b)$	Units Sold: 10	Units Sold: 50
$ 1	10	50
5	50	250
10	100	500

tainty as to the earnings before interest and taxes. Operating leverage determines the extent to which fluctuations in sales get amplified through the operating cost structure. Insofar as cost structures can be altered, operating leverage can be changed and business risk can be altered.

Financial Risk

Financial risk arises from the variability in EBIT (business risk), which is then amplified through the use of fixed claim securities. Figure 15.6 shows the financial risk for two different capital structures.

We next want to combine operating and financial leverage. Figure 15.7 shows Figure 15.6 rotated 90 degrees counterclockwise. Figure 15.8 shows the combination of Figure 15.5 and 15.7. For a given level of sales, we can now determine the amount of stockholders' equity income and the ROE.

The amount of sales is converted to a given EBIT in the upper right-hand quadrant by the operating leverage line. The EBIT is converted to stockholders' ROE by the amount of financial leverage in the upper left-hand quadrant of

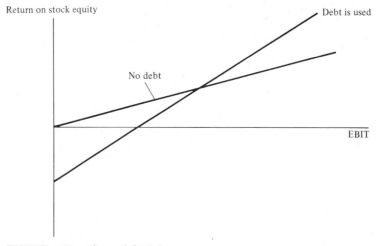

FIGURE 15.6   Financial Risk

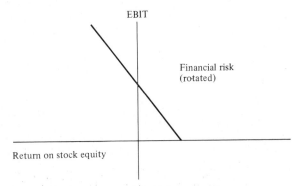

FIGURE 15.7   Financial Risk Rotated

Figure 15.8. The amount of fluctuation in return on stockholders' equity for a given change in sales will depend on the operating leverage and the amount of financial leverage.

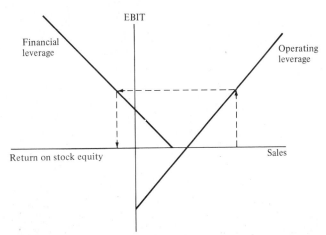

FIGURE   15.8   Operating   and   Financial   Leverage Combined

Degree of Operating Leverage

The degree of operating leverage (DOL) gives the percentage change in earnings before interest for a percentage change in sales. Mathematically it is equal to

$$DOL = \frac{C}{C - F}$$

where C is the total contribution to profits (sales minus variable costs) and F is the total fixed costs.

EXAMPLE 15.1 ————————————————————————————

Assume that sales are $10,000,000 and that variable costs are $4,000,000 so that the contribution to profits is $6,000,000 and the fixed costs are $1,000,000. The earnings are $5,000,000. The DOL is

$$\text{DOL} = \frac{C}{C - F} = \frac{\$6,000,000}{\$6,000,000 - \$1,000,000} = \frac{6}{5} = 1.2$$

If sales increase by 10 percent, the contribution goes up by $.10 \times 1.2 = .12$, or 12 percent.

Assume that sales go from $10,000,000 to $11,000,000. The income goes from $5,000,000 to $5,600,000, a 12 percent increase.

Sales	$11,000,000
Variable costs	4,400,000
Fixed costs	1,000,000
Income	$ 5,600,000

With less operating leverage, the change in income would be less. Assume that the variable costs are $5,000,000 with $10,000,000 of sales but that the fixed costs are zero so that the initial income is again $5,000,000. The DOL is

$$\text{DOL} = \frac{C}{C} = 1$$

Now when sales increase by 10 percent, the income increases by only 10 percent to $5,500,000.

With more operating leverage, a sales increase will increase income more than in the previous two examples. Assume that variable costs are only $.10 per dollar of sales and that fixed costs are $4,000,000 so that the initial income is again $5,000,000.

Now with $10,000,000 of sales, the degree of operating leverage is

$$\text{DOL} = \frac{C}{C - F} = \frac{\$9,000,000}{\$9,000,000 - \$4,000,000} = \frac{9}{5} = 1.8$$

When sales go up 10 percent, the income of $5,000,000 will go up 18 percent:

Sales	$11,000,000
Variable costs	1,100,000
Fixed costs	4,000,000
Income	$ 5,900,000

Income increased from $5,000,000 to $5,900,000. This is a 18 percent increase.

The DOL is a function of both C and F; thus the level of sales will affect the DOL, as will the method of production being used.

Usually the type of production process will be determined by the cash flow analysis that feeds into a discounted cash flow model. The degree of operating leverage does not normally enter the analysis. However, after the production process is in place, management will want to know how incremental decisions will affect profits. The DOL measure is a useful summary measure for that purpose.

Degree of Financial Leverage

The degree of financial leverage (DFL) gives the percentage change in earnings after interest for a given percentage change in earnings before interest.

$$DFL = \frac{X}{X - I}$$

where X is the earnings before interest (EBIT) and I is the amount of interest. The degree of financial leverage is for a given level of X and a given amount of debt.

EXAMPLE 15.2

Assume that EBIT is $5,000,000 and that the interest expense on $30,000,000 of debt is $3,000,000. The degree of financial leverage is

$$DFL = \frac{X}{X - I} = \frac{\$5,000,000}{\$2,000,000} = 2.5$$

If EBIT changes to \$6,000,000 (a 20 percent increase), the earnings after interest will increase 2.5 × .20 = .50, or 50 percent from \$2,000,000 to \$3,000,000.

Degree of Total Leverage

The third leverage measure is the degree of total leverage (DTL). The degree of total leverage is equal to the product of DOL and DFL.

Since $X = C - F$, we have

$$DTL = DOL \times DFL$$

$$= \frac{C}{C - F} \times \frac{X}{X - I}$$

$$= \frac{C}{C - F} \times \frac{C - F}{C - F - I} = \frac{C}{C - F - I}$$

The DTL will give the percentage change in earnings after interest for a given percentage change in sales, reflecting both operating and financial leverage.

EXAMPLE 15.3 ————————————————————————————————

Assume that sales are \$10,000,000, that variable costs are \$.40 per dollar of sales, and that fixed costs are \$1,000,000. The interest is \$3,000,000. We have

$$DOL = \frac{C}{C - F} = \frac{6}{6 - 1} = 1.2$$

$$DFL = \frac{X}{X - I} = \frac{5}{5 - 3} = 2.5$$

$$DTL = DOL \times DFL = 1.2 \times 2.5 = 3.0$$

or

$$DTL = \frac{C}{C - F - I} = \frac{6}{6 - 1 - 3} = \frac{6}{2} = 3.0$$

If sales increase by 10 percent the earnings after interest will increase by 30 percent.

	Before Increase	After Increase	Percentage Increase
Sales	$10,000,000	$11,000,000	10%
Variable costs	4,000,000	4,400,000	
Fixed costs	1,000,000	1,000,000	
Income before interest (EBIT)	$ 5,000,000	$ 5,600,000	12
Interest	3,000,000	3,000,000	
Income	$ 2,000,000	$ 2,600,000	30

These calculations do not tell us what type of production facilities should be obtained or how much debt to use, but they do give insights as to the effects of such decisions on earnings before and after interest for changes in sales.

Risk and the Cost of Debt

We want to illustrate why the cost of debt (and cost of stock) increases as the percentage of debt increases.

EXAMPLE 15.4

Assume that a firm with zero taxes faces the following five equally likely outcomes:

Earnings Before Interest: X	Probability	Probability Distribution Prob. (earnings) Being Larger than X
$1,000,000	.2	1.00
2,000,000	.2	.80
3,000,000	.2	.60
4,000,000	.2	.40
5,000,000	.2	.20
6,000,000	0	0

If the firm is financed completely with common stock, there is a probability of 1 that the stockholders will earn some income.

Now assume that the firm substitutes $10,000,000 of debt costing .12 for $10,000,000 of common stock. With $1,200,000 of annual interest, there is now .2 probability that the interest will not be earned. This event increases the likelihood of bankruptcy and increases the expected return required by stockholders (if they are risk averse).

If $20,000,000 of debt is issued paying $2,400,000 per year of interest, there is now .4 probability that the interest will not be earned. The increased probability of default will result in a higher interest rate being required to sell the debt securities. If the interest rate goes up from .12 to .16, the interest payments will be $3,200,000, and there will be .6 probability that the interest will not be earned. With a smaller probability of earning the interest, the contractual interest amount will have to increase to attract investors.

If instead of only having five possible events, we had a continuous probability density function, then each dollar of debt increases the probability of not earning the interest. Figure 15.9 shows the probability density of earnings before interest. The area under the curve sums to 1 and is equal to the probability.

Assume areas $A = .35$, $B = .25$, and $C = .40$. With zero debt, there is .35 probability of a loss. If interest equals $1,000,000, there is a .60 probability that the firm will not earn the interest. If more debt is added, the probability of the actual earnings being less than the earnings required to break even will increase. This increased probability of not earning the interest will lead investors to require a larger contractual return.

We have focused on the probability of not earning the interest in a given year. We could also compute the probability of not earning the interest in one or more of a given number of years.

For example, if the probability of being able to pay the interest in a given year is .8, and if each year's operations are independent, the probability of earning the interest in each of five years is $.8^5 = .33$ and the probability of not earning the interest in at least one year is $1 - .33$ or .67.

The conclusion is that each dollar of debt increases the probability of financial crisis and thus increases the cost of both debt and common stock.

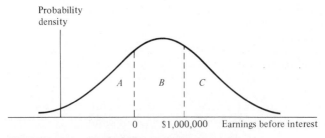

FIGURE 15.9   Probability Density Function

Leverage: Crystal Oil

In 1984 the common stock of Crystal Oil Corporation, an oil refiner with a large amount of debt, went from a high of $17 to a low of $2⅞. As an oil refiner, it had a large operating leverage. It was financed with a large amount of debt. The large total leverage combined with a decrease in oil prices and overcapacity in the oil refinery industry led to a large decrease in profits and a large decrease in stock price.

The liabilities and stockholders' equity section of the 1982 balance sheet follows.

Crystal Oil Company and Subsidiaries
Consolidated Balance Sheets
(in thousands)

	December 31	
	1982	1981
Liabilities and Stockholders' Equity		
Current liabilities		
Trade accounts payable	$ 55,951	$ 56,754
Accrued expenses (primarily interest and taxes)	9,342	11,316
Income taxes payable	120	2,027
Current installments on long-term debt	591	1,282
Total current liabilities	$ 66,004	$ 71,379
Long-term liabilities		
Senior long-term debt	76,495	42,808
Debentures, subordinated	137,784	134,787
Debentures, convertible subordinated	68,062	67,846
Total long-term liabilities	$282,341	$245,441
Deferred income taxes	14,848	20,145
Total liabilities	$363,193	$336,965
Commitments and contingencies		
Stockholders' equity		
Preferred stock, par value $5 per share	—	—
Common stock, par value $1 per share	20,937	20,937
Additional paid-in capital	38,017	38,017
Retained earnings	442	10,837
Total stockholders' equity	$ 59,396	$ 69,791
	$422,589	$406,756

Business Risk

The term *business risk* is often used to characterize the variability of EBIT and is therefore linked directly to operating leverage. More precisely, this risk depends on the variability in sales and the responsiveness of total cost to these variations as characterized by the variable cost per dollar of sales. Both the expected EBIT and its variability are important to the suppliers of debt capital, since they rely heavily on the firm's income-generating ability to meet debt obligations. These factors also affect the uncertainty of the return received by equity suppliers. The variability of the earnings per dollar of equity investment depends in part on business risk as measured by the standard deviation of EBIT. Insofar as the market is adverse to risk, we can state that, all other things being held equal, the higher the degree of business risk, the higher is the rate of return demanded by both debt and equity suppliers of capital.

The term *financial risk* is often used to characterize the impact of the financial structure on the uncertainties faced by capital suppliers. The total risk faced by the firm's capital suppliers is the firm's business risk. Although the firm cannot alter that risk by changing its financial structure, it can reallocate this risk among various claim groups by altering the degree of financial leverage employed. All other things being equal, the higher the degree of debt utilization, and its consequent fixed obligations, the higher the degree of risk faced by debt suppliers. Also, as more debt is utilized, with a given business risk, the greater the uncertainties faced by equity suppliers. Thus, all other things being held equal, the fixed obligation of debt will lead the suppliers of both debt and equity capital to demand higher rates of return as debt utilization increases.

Conclusions

This chapter explores the relationships between operating leverage and financial leverage. We have not yet reached the stage in our understanding at which we can attempt to analyze the more difficult problem of choosing an optimal amount of financial and operating leverage. An increase in the amount of either kind of leverage will increase the amount of risk per dollar of equity capital. Under favorable circumstances it may increase the expected return. Clearly a trade-off is required. If the firm were owned entirely by the managers, their personal preferences might be the determining factor. More commonly, managers are, in theory at least, representatives of the absentee equity owner. Before attempting a normative approach to the questions of the optimal amount and type of leverage, we must understand how the market values the securities of a firm when there is risk.

Review Problem 15.1

A manufacturing process has the following characteristics:

Fixed costs per year	$4,000,000
Variable costs per unit	$10
Selling price	$30
Units sold	1,000,000
Interest per year	$2,000,000

(a) Compute the EBIT.
(b) Compute the income.
(c) Compute the degree of operating leverage.
(d) Compute the degree of financial leverage.
(e) Compute the degree of total leverage.

Solution to Review Problem 15.1

(a) EBIT = $1,000,000(30 − 10) − $4,000,000 = $16,000,000
(b) Income = $16,000,000 − $2,000,000 = $14,000,000

(c) $DOL = \dfrac{C}{C - F} = \dfrac{\$20,000,000}{\$20,000,000 - \$4,000,000} = \dfrac{20}{16} = 1\frac{1}{4}$ or 1.25

(d) $DFL = \dfrac{X}{X - I} = \dfrac{16}{16 - 2} = 1.14$

(e) $DTL = DOL \times DFL = \dfrac{20}{16} \times \dfrac{16}{14} = 1.43$

$DTL = \dfrac{C}{C - F - I} = \dfrac{20}{20 - 4 - 2} = 1.43$

PROBLEMS

1. A company has the choice of two different processes with the following cost structures:

	Process 1	Process 2
Fixed costs per month	$500,000	$800,000
Variable cost per unit	$20	$15

   The expected sales per month are 100,000 units. The sales price is $30 per unit.

   Compute the expected EBITs for the two processes.

2. Assume that it is decided to manufacture a product using a process where X is the EBIT and $E(X) = \$700,000$. The total investment required is $6,000,000. The tax rate is .4. The life of the investment is infinite.
   (a) Assuming all common stock financing, compute the expectation of earnings after tax per dollar of common stock investment.
   (b) Repeat (a) assuming that debt is used to finance 50 percent of the investment at a cost of .08. Is it desirable to use debt in this situation?

3. (Problem 2 continued) Determine the linear relationship of return on equity with respect to EBIT for a given amount of debt B for the facts as given in (b).

   For $3,000,000 of debt, compute the return on equity for EBIT equal to

   $ 0
     480,000
   1,000,000
   3,000,000

   If EBIT were known with certainty, which of two debt levels ($3,000,000 or $5,000,000) is preferred?

4. Suppose that a firm has two possible cost structures and is considering three alternative financing strategies. Under one technology, fixed costs would be $1,000,000 and variable costs are $8 per unit; under the other technology, fixed costs would be $2,200,000 and variable costs would be cut to $6 per unit sold. Sales (quantity) have a mean of 800,000 units and the price of the product is $10. The corporate tax rate is 40 percent. If the low fixed cost technology is used and no debt is employed, the firm's equity investment is estimated at $2,400,000, while it is estimated at $3,000,000 if the high fixed cost technology is employed and no debt is used.

Fill in the following table for both levels of debt and the two cost structures.

	Low Fixed Cost		High Fixed Cost	
	k_i	*E(ROE)*	*k_i*	*E(ROE)*
Debt				
$0				
2,000,000	12%		15%	

Which cost structure is preferred if $E(ROE)$ is used as the basis of making the decision?

5. The ABC Company makes one type of product that it sells for $180 per unit. The variable costs per unit are $80, and the fixed costs are $40,000 per year. The firm has a capacity of 900 units per year.
   (a) Draw the total revenue and total expense curves on a graph. Indicate the break-even point.
   (b) Below the graph drawn for (a) draw the income (EBIT) curve.

6. (Problem 5 continued) Assume that the XYZ Company makes the same product as ABC Company but has a different cost structure. It has fixed costs per year of $10,000 and variable costs of $130 per unit. The firm has a capacity of 900 units per year.
   (a) Plot the cost information for both firms.
   (b) Which (if either) firm is in the better competitive position?

7. The ABC Company makes one type of product that it sells for $180 per unit. The variable costs per unit are $80, and the fixed costs are $40,000 per year. The firm has a capacity of 900 units per year.
   The total capital used is $100,000. Debt costs .15 per year, and the income tax rate is .46. The firm uses $30,000 of debt.
   (a) Write the equation for return on stock equity.
   (b) Plot return on stock equity as a function of units sold. How many units must be sold to break even?
   (c) What is the ROI if $Q = 900$?

8. (Problem 7 continued) Assume that the ABC Company is thinking of substituting $50,000 of additional debt for common stock. The total debt will be $80,000 and common stock will be $20,000. Debt still costs .15.
   Recompute (a), (b), and (c) of Problem 7, and draw several conclusions.

9. (Problems 7 and 8 continued)
   (a) How many units have to be sold for the firm to be indifferent between $30,000 and $80,000 of debt?

(b) What will be the return on the stock equity investment at that level of sales?

(c) Compute the ROE for $30,000 and for $80,000 of debt.

10. (Problems 7 and 8 continued) Assume that with $30,000 of debt ABC would have 7,000 shares of common stock and with $80,000 of debt it would 2,000 shares.

(a) How many units have to be sold for the stockholders to have the same EPS regardless of the capital structure?

(b) What will be the EPS at the indifference number of units?

11. Assume that the following table applies to the R Company.

EBIT	Probability
− $1,000,000	.10
0	.20
1,000,000	.30
2,000,000	.20
3,000,000	.15
4,000,000	.05

Compute the probability of a deficit for the following amounts of debt if debt costs .10:

(a) $0 of debt.

(b) $15,000,000 of debt.

(c) $35,000,000 of debt.

(d) $45,000,000 of debt.

12. The following facts apply for the next year:

Sales	$20,000,000
Units sold	1,000,000
Variable costs	$ 5,000,000
Fixed costs	$ 7,500,000
Interest costs	$ 2,500,000

Compute the DOL, DFL, and DTL.

REFERENCES

Bierman, H., Jr. "Risk and the Addition of Debt to the Capital Structure." *Journal of Financial and Quantitative Analysis*, December 1968, 415–426.

Borch, K. "A Note on Uncertainty and Indifference Curves." *Review of Economic Studies*, January 1969, 337–343.

Brigham, E. F. *Financial Management, Theory and Practice*, 3rd ed. Chicago: The Dryden Press, Division of CBS College Publishing, 1982.

Feldstein, M. S. "Mean-Variance Analysis in the Theory of Liquidity Preference and Portfolio Selection." *Review of Economic Studies*, January 1969, 5–12.

Fisher, Lawrence. "Determinants of Risk Premiums on Corporate Bonds." *Journal of Political Economy*, June 1959, 217–237.

Hong, Hai, and Alfred Rappaport, "Debt Capacity, Optimal Capital Structure, and Capital Budgeting." *Financial Management*, Autumn 1978, 7–11.

Jaedicke, Robert K., and A. A. Robichek. "Cost-Volume-Profit Analysis Under Conditions of Uncertainty." *The Accounting Review*, October 1964, 917–926.

Litzenberger, Robert H., and Howard B. Soosin. "A Comparison of Capital Structure Decisions of Regulated and Non-regulated Firms." *Financial Management*, Autumn 1979, 17–21.

Melnyk, Z. Lew. "Cost of Capital as a Function of Financial Leverage." *Decision Sciences*, July–October 1970, 372–386.

Schwartz, Eli, and J. Richard Aronson. "Some Surrogate Evidence in Support of the Concept of Optimal Capital Structure." *Journal of Finance*, March 1967, 10–18.

Scott, David F., Jr., and John D. Martin. "Industry Influence on Financial Structure." *Financial Management*, Spring 1975, 67–73.

Stone, Bernell K. *Risk, Return and Equilibrium*. Cambridge, Mass.: M.I.T. Press, 1970.

Tobin, James. "Liquidity Preference as Behavior Towards Risk." *Review of Economic Studies*, February 1958, 65–86.

Vickers, D. *The Theory of the Firm: Production, Capital, and Finance*. New York: McGraw-Hill, Inc., 1968.

Appendix 15.1 Determining the Indifference Point for the Amount of Leverage

We want to show that the ROE will be the same for any capital structure and will equal $r = k_i(1 - t_c)$ if

$$X = k_i V$$

where

k_i = the cost of borrowing
V = the total capital
X = the earnings before interest and taxes
t_c = the tax rate
r = the return on capital

We want to find the value of X for which the returns on capital are equal for debt of B_1 and B_2:

$$\frac{(X - k_i B_1)(1 - t_c)}{V - B_1} = \frac{(X - k_i B_2)(1 - t_c)}{V - B_2}$$

$$X(V - B_2) - k_i B_1(V - B_2) = X(V - B_1) - k_i B_2(V - B_1)$$

$$X(B_1 - B_2) = k_i(B_1 V - B_2 V)$$

$$= k_i V(B_1 - B_2)$$

$$X = k_i V$$

If $X = k_i V$, then

$$r = \frac{(k_i V - k_i B_1)(1 - t_c)}{V - B_1} = k_i(1 - t_c)$$

Thus, for indifference we need

$$X = k_i V$$

At that level of X

$$r = k_i(1 - t_c)$$

Chapter 16

Corporate Dividend Policy

Major Topics

1. Stock dividends as an alternative to cash dividends.
2. The relevance of dividend policy in a world with taxes.
3. The advantage of tax deferral and capital gains.
4. The cost of retained earnings.
5. Dividends: the clientele effect.
6. Reacquisition of shares as an alternative to cash dividends.

Dividends

For some time the question of how a firm's dividend policy can be expected to influence the value of its shares has been of interest to managers, investors, and economists. In recent years, many theories of the relationship between dividend policy and share valuation have been put forward including the work of Modigliani and Miller, Gordon, Lintner, and others. In addition, a number of empirical studies have attempted to isolate the effect of dividend policies on the market value of equity.

Miller and Modigliani argue that with no income taxes and with other well-defined assumptions (such as perfect knowledge and certainty), a dollar retained is equal in value to a dollar distributed; thus dividend policy is not a relevant factor in determining the value of a corporation. However, when taxes are allowed in the analysis, dividend policy affects the value of the stockholders' equity. In practice, corporations appear to be influenced in setting dividend policy by the behavior of their competitors and by a desire to have a relatively stable dividend.

In this chapter we shall investigate the institutional and economic considerations that should be taken into account by a publicly held corporation in setting common stock dividend policy. The considerations that determine dividend payments on preferred stock are somewhat different and will not be discussed here.

A common stock dividend is a distribution of a portion of the assets of a corporation to its common stock shareholders. The amount received by each investor is proportional to the number of shares held by the investor. In most cases, cash is distributed. On rare occasions, a publicly held corporation may pay a dividend in a form other than cash. Thus the owners of shares in a distillery might receive a bottle of whiskey as a dividend. In practice, this event is so rare as to be only a curiosity. A corporation may distribute, as a dividend, the shares it owns in another corporation. The Owens-Illinois Corporation did this as a means of complying with a court decree that required it to reduce its holdings of common stock in Owens-Corning Fiberglass.

When a corporation pays a dividend, its assets are reduced by the amount of the dividend. In publicly traded stock, the price per share declines by a fraction of the amount of the dividend on the day that the stock goes "ex-dividend." A person who buys the stock on or after the ex-dividend date will not receive the dividend. Because of other factors affecting the stock price, as well as tax considerations, the decline in the share price will not be exactly equal to the amount of dividend paid. The change will be a percentage of that amount.

Stock Dividends

Stock dividends are not dividends in a real sense. With a so-called stock dividend, the corporation distributes additional shares of its common stock on a pro rata basis to existing shareholders. This increases the number of shares outstanding but leaves the assets of the corporation unchanged (except for transaction costs). The amount of a cash dividend is usually expressed (in the United States) in terms of dollars and cents per share. The amount of a stock dividend is usually expressed as a percentage or a ratio. With a 4 percent stock dividend, the holder of 100 shares of stock receives an additional 4 shares.

The so-called stock dividend, from an economic standpoint, is actually a stock split. Thus, a 100 percent stock dividend and a 2-for-1 stock split are the same thing so far as shareholders are concerned. When a stock dividend is declared and becomes effective, the new price of the shares must reflect the additional shares outstanding. The actual percentage decline depends on the amount of the stock dividend.

When a 10 percent stock dividend is paid, all things being equal, the new price per share will be $1/1.1$ of the old price. For example, if shares were selling for $100 before the dividend, each share would tend to sell for about $90.91 after the 10 percent stock dividend. If there were N shares outstanding before the stock dividend, there would be $1.1N$ shares after the stock dividend. The total value of the stock equity was $100N$ before and $90.91(1.1N) = $100N$ after. The total value is unchanged.

As an additional explanation as to why a stock dividend is not comparable to a cash dividend, imagine the following situation. You are sitting in a restaurant and have just ordered a piece of cherry pie. When it arrives, it looks so good that you tell the waitress that you want two pieces. She picks up the plate with the piece of cherry pie on it, cuts the piece of pie into two, and hands both pieces back to you. The original piece of pie on the plate corresponds to your interest in the company (your share of the total pie) before the stock dividend. The two pieces on your plate after the waitress has cut the original piece in half indicates how your ownership interest would change after a 100 percent stock dividend.

In the example, an investor holding 10 shares would have a total investment of $1,000 before the stock dividend. After the stock dividend, the investor would own 11 shares and the stock would have a value of $90.91 per share. Again, the value of the investment is $1,000. Logically, stock dividends should not be taxed as income, and they are not.

Stock dividends are a way of increasing the total cash dividends that are paid, while the per share dividend amount stays constant. For example, if the cash dividend is $1 per share before a 10 percent stock dividend, where there are N shares outstanding, the total dividends will be N. After the 10 percent stock dividend, if the per share cash dividend stays at $1 but the number of shares increase to $1.1N$, the total dividend is $1.1N$ after the stock dividend, compared to N before.

Dividend Policy

A corporation is not legally obligated to declare a dividend of any specific amount. Thus a firm's board of directors actually has made a specific decision every time a dividend is declared. However, once the board declares a dividend, the corporation is legally obligated to make the payments. Therefore, a dividend should not be declared unless a corporation is in a financial position to make the payment. On January 31, 1973, Ancorp National Services Incorporated announced that it would pay its usual dividend of $.02 a share to holders of record on March 20. The corporation, which previously had been known as the American News Company, operated 1,200 Union News outlets and the Savarin restaurant chain. It had paid a dividend every year since 1864. That record was broken on March 20, 1973. The company went into receivership the day the dividend was payable, since cash necessary to pay its liabilities, including the dividend that had been declared, was not available.

The expectation of receiving dividends (broadly defined as any distribution of value) ultimately determines the market value of the common stock. By declaring a dividend, the board of directors is not only turning over some of the assets of the corporation to its stockholders, but it may be influencing the expectations that stockholders have about the future dividends they can expect from the corporation. If expectations are affected, the dividend decision and the underlying dividend policy will have an impact on the value that the market places on the common stock of the corporation.

Many financial experts believe that a highly stable dividend is advantageous to a company. The most common reason stated for this belief is that stockholders prefer a steady income from their investments. There is at least one other important reason for thinking that a highly variable dividend rate may not be in the best interest of a company. In the long run, the value of a share of stock tends to be determined by the discounted value of the expected dividends. Insofar as this is the case, a widely fluctuating dividend rate will tend to make it difficult for current or prospective stockholders to determine the value of the stock to them, and as a result, the stock is likely to sell at a somewhat lower price than comparable stocks paying the same average dividend through time but making the payments at a steady rate. This conclusion assumes that investors are risk averse and have incomplete information about the company.

Factors Affecting Investor Reaction to Dividends

Traditional concepts about the distinction between income and capital, some of which have been embodied into laws that control the behavior of certain financial institutions, are important considerations in understanding how these investors react to corporate dividend decisions and policies.

The more recent and sophisticated thinking about financial matters tends to emphasize the total return received from an asset and to ignore distinctions between capital gains and other forms of income except insofar as they affect taxes.

EXAMPLE 16.1 ——————————————————————————————————

Suppose that an investor held 100 shares of Company A and 100 shares of Company B. At the beginning of the year, the shares in both of the companies were selling for $50, and the total investment was $10,000. During the year, Company A paid a dividend of $3 per share, and the stock was selling for $52 a share at the end of the year. Company B paid a dividend of $1 per share, but the stock in that company was selling for $56 per share at the end of the year.

The total return approach considers that the stockholder had received a return of $5 per share from Company A and $7 a share from Company B. The total return from this portfolio would be $1,200. This equals 12 percent of the initial $10,000 value of the investment. The total return approach would focus on the fact that the investor had a total of $11,200 in liquid assets available at the end of the year, which could be divided between consumption and investment. If the investor chose to consume 10 percent of the initial capital or $1,000, this could be done by using the $400 in dividends and liquidating $600 of the stock. Similarly, if the investor chose to consume only 2 percent or $200 of the initial holdings, $200 of the dividends could be applied to consumption expenditures and the remaining $200 reinvested.

The total return approach treats the market value of the securities held and dividends received as one pool of liquid assets that can be divided up at each decision point into consumption and further investment. The fact that some of the liquid assets available have come from dividends and others from a change in the value of the investment is of secondary importance.

There are many investors who approach these same events with a very different point of view. For some investors, there is an important distinction between income and capital gains. Income is typically defined as dividends and interest. Investors who think in these terms often are quite comfortable in consuming part or all of their dividend or interest "income" but are very uncomfortable about having to dispose of some of their securities in order to pay for living expenses. Such an investor would consider that the portfolio described previously has provided an income of $400 during the year. If consumption requirements are in excess of $400, the investor might switch to the higher dividend paying stock (Company A). An investment of $10,000 in Company A will give $600 of dividends and the stock at the end of the year would be worth $10,400. With the switch and with only the dividends defined to be income, income has increased from $400 to $600. But the total return from the $10,000 investment has decreased from $1,200 to $1,000.

If dividends are considered to be the only income from common stock, and if this concept is embodied in legal documents, then the amount of cash dividends will tend to influence the likelihood of a company's shares being purchased by this segment of the market.

EXAMPLE 16.2 —————————————————————————————————

A wealthy individual wishes to give a gift to a university to provide scholarships to deservng individuals who would not otherwise be able to pay tuition. The donor specifies as a condition of the gift that only the "income" is to be used to make scholarship payments and that the capital is to be preserved. Universities have tended to interpret language such as this as meaning that the university can apply only the funds received from dividends and interest to scholarship payments. Thus, if the university wished to increase the scholarship disbursements in a particular year, it would have to rearrange the portfolio in such a way as to acquire more stocks that paid high dividends even though they earned a lower total return than other securities.

A somewhat similar situation frequently occurs with respect to wills. For example, suppose that a wealthy man specifies in his will that the income from his estate is to go to his wife during her lifetime but that the capital is to be preserved and applied for the benefit of their children after his wife passes away. If the estate is large, a bank trust department will frequently be appointed as trustee to carry out the intentions of the person creating the will. There are billions of dollars of assets managed by bank trust departments under the terms of trust agreements that are basically similar to the one described. In most of these cases, only dividends and interest are considered to be income.

The distinction between dividends and capital gains is also reinforced by tax laws that define the receipt of dividends or interest as a taxable event. By contrast, changes in the value of common stock are not taxable events unless, and until, the securities are actually sold.

One further institutional factor that should be mentioned in connection with dividends is the so-called trust legal list. Banks, insurance companies, and other financial institutions, as well as individual trustees, often manage substantial sums for the benefit of others. Over the years, many states have passed laws designed to ensure that the beneficiaries of these assets do not incur losses because trustees have purchased excessively risky investments for the trust. Various controls have been designed to accomplish this end. One is to restrict the kinds of assets that are eligible for consideration as investments by a particular kind of trustee or financial institution. Such a list of eligible assets is called a trust legal list. The laws do not specify the particular securities that are eligible for inclusion on the legal list but rather the characteristics that a security must possess in order to be eligible. A state official is responsible for determining which securities have the necessary characteristics. To be eligible for inclusion on a legal list, a common stock may need to have paid dividends without interruption for a given length of time. A consequence of this procedure is that if a company fails to pay dividends in one quarter, it may substantially reduce the population of investors who are eligible to buy or hold its common stock.

Corporate Dividend Practice

There have been a number of important studies dealing with the actual behavior of corporations in setting dividend policy. A classic one was conducted by Harvard economist John Lintner.* Lintner found that two considerations account for a large part of the actual behavior of corporations. One consideration was the desire to have a relatively stable dividend; the second was the desire to pay out, in the long run, a given fraction of earnings. This fraction is usually referred to as the payout target. These objectives may be conflicting. Earnings tend to fluctuate substantially from year to year. If a corporation routinely paid out a given fraction of those earnings as dividends, then the dividend itself would tend to fluctuate drastically from year to year or quarter to quarter. These fluctuations would conflict with the objective of maintaining a stable dividend policy. On the other hand, if the dividend is a constant amount, then it will be a fluctuating proportion of earnings.

Assume that a corporation starts with a dividend amount. If earnings are stable, then the dividend is unlikely to be changed. However, if earnings are increasing, then, with a constant dividend, the payout ratio will gradually decrease. If the increase in earnings is expected to be temporary, for example, as a result of some extraordinary event or unusually good business conditions, then it is unlikely that the company will change its dividend. However, if management believes that earnings are likely to be maintained at their new level or to increase even farther, then it is likely that the dividend will be increased. The increase will be in the direction of approaching the amount that the board of directors has set as a target payout ratio. Companies vary the payout ratio they select, and the speed with which they adjust the dividend of a period to changes in earnings, but they do tend to adhere to a target payout ratio. Over long periods of time, this policy tends to result in a dividend payout that is approximately equal to the payout target, but dividends will tend to be more stable from year to year than earnings. Another important consequence of this process is that dividend decisions tend to

* John Lintner, "Distribution of Incomes of Corporations Among Dividends, Retained Earnings, and Taxes," *American Economic Review*, May 1956, pp. 97–113.

proivde information to stockholders about management's forecasts of future earnings. This will be considered in a later section.

Assume that a firm has a large amount of desirable investments and that these investments require more funds than are available internally after dividend commitments have been met. In such circumstances, one or two major alternatives must be chosen if the alternative of changing the dividend policy is not thought to be available. The company must either forgo some profitable investments or seek additional funds. On the other hand, if the payout ratio is set too low, relative to the level of earnings and the quantity of profitable investments available to it, the company may either find itself accumulating an unwarranted amount of liquid assets or be tempted to accept investments that are not truly consistent with the objective of maximizing the economic well-being of the stockholders. A company that consistently follows either of these policies is likely to become a target for a takeover bid since its stock will be depressed compared to its potential value. The disadvantages of too low a dividend payout, relative to the profitable investments available to the company, are more serious from the point of view of the shareholders if the funds are being reinvested at less than competitive rates.

The Setting of Dividend Policy

Dividend policy is likely to be set in the form of a goal rather than a rigid rule, even though a definite policy has the advantage of providing the investor, or potential investor, a clear basis of choice. Investors knowing the dividend policy of the alternative companies can choose the type of company that best fits their individual investment goals. This is desirable, because stockholders differ in the extent to which they prefer dividends rather than opportunities for capital appreciation. One must remember that, while one group might well prefer capital gains, a second group of zero-tax investors may be primarily interested in dividends. This second group of investors includes universities, foundations, and private pension funds, all of which accrue no special tax advantages from capital gains as distinct from dividends.

Sometimes a company will distinguish between a "regular" dividend and an "extra" dividend. Although this distinction does not have any cash flow significance, it is an important means by which the directors can signal their intentions to stockholders. By labeling part of a dividend payment as an "extra," the directors are indicating that they did not necessarily expect to continue those payments in future years. By declaring the remainder of the dividend payment as a regular payment, the directors indicate an intention to maintain this dividend for the foreseeable future. Extras often occur in the fourth quarter of a good earnings year.

Dividend Changes and Earnings Forecasts

When a dividend increase is logical for a company, given its earnings and its traditional payout target, then the mere fact that an increase has not been declared may sometimes be interpreted as evidence that management does not expect the current level of earnings to be maintained. Thus failure to increase a dividend in such a circumstance might be interpreted as evidence that management does not expect the current level of earnings to be maintained. On the other hand, if a dividend increase takes place at a time when it is not expected on the basis of the company's historical behavior, the financial community may interpret this as evidence that management is more bullish about future prospects for the company than had previously been expected.

The stock price effect that can occur when a dividend change is unexpected is dramatically indicated by the history of the Consolidated Edison Corporation. Consolidated Edison's regular dividend in 1973 was $.45 per share per quarter. In the spring of 1974, the board of directors decided not to declare a dividend. This took place in a context in which the earnings of public utilities were being adversely affected in a dramatic way by a combination of large increases in the cost of fuel, reduction in consumption of electricity, and increases in the cost of new additions to plant and equipment. Since Consolidated Edison is one of the largest utilities in the United States and was considered a very safe common stock investment, its announcement of no dividend had a dramatic impact on the share prices of almost all privately owned electric utility companies in the United States. Consolidated Edison shares dropped from a preannouncement level of around $21.00 to a postannouncement low of about $6.00 per share. The market took the elimination of the dividend by Con Ed to be a forecast by management that the industry faced severe financial difficulties and introduced a level of risk into the investors' analysis that in their view previously did not exist.

Dividend Policy, Investment Policy, and Financing Policy

The dividend policy of a firm cannot be considered in isolation from its other financial policies. In particular, dividend policy is intimately connected with investment policy and financing policy. When a firm changes its dividend amount, it may, at the same time, have to change one or the other of these other polices. To illustrate the relationships between these policies, Table 16.1 will be helpful. This table is a simplified source and use of cash projection for a company in a particular year on the assumption that the company

**TABLE 16.1   Simplified Cash Flow Statement Projection
if the Current Dividend Is Maintained**

Sources		Uses	
From Operations	$200,000	Dividends	$130,000
New securities sold	50,000	New plant, equipment, and working capital	120,000
Total sources	$250,000	Total uses	$250,000

continues its existing dividend. The cash flows from all sources are expected to total $250,000, of which $200,000 would be from operations and $50,000 would be from the sale of newly issued securities. To maintain the current dividend rate would use $130,000 of the total cash flow. The remaining $120,000 is allocated for new plant, equipment, and working capital.

Suppose, in these circumstances, that the firm is considering increasing its dividend by $25,000. If the firm increased its dividend, it would be necessary for it, at the same time, to generate more cash flow from operations, to sell more securities, or to reduce its expenditures on new plant, equipment, and working capital or some combination of the above.

The simplified statement of Table 16.1 emphasizes the relationships among dividend policy, financing policy, and investment policy. When the dividend amount changes, it may be necessary to change either the firm's investment policy or its financing policies.

In reading the various approaches described in this chapter, you should keep in mind the assumptions that are being made with respect to policy or policies to which dividend policy is linked.

A framework for visualizing the long-run policy-setting process for dividends is shown in Figure 16.1. It will be helpful to interpret this figure as representing the firm's estimate of its long-run position.

The II curve of Figure 16.1 shows the investment opportunities expected to be available to the firm. The vertical axis measures the cost of equity to the firm. The horizontal axis measures the number of dollars that would be profitably invested at each possible cost of capital. The II curve is downward sloping because additional investment opportunities will be less profitable than the best alternatives. The II curve can be considered to represent the firm's demand for investable stockholders' equity capital. The investment opportunities measured by the II curve includes the necessary investments in working capital.

The solid horizontal line labeled k_e represents the firm's cost of equity given its present investment, financing, and dividend policies. We assume the cost of equity is not a function of the amount invested.

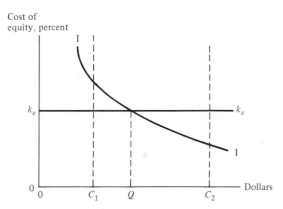

FIGURE 16.1   An Investment Schedule

If the firm wishes to invest up to the point at which the marginal rate of return on stockholders' equity investment equals the cost of equity, then the firm will invest Q dollars.

If the firm anticipates that its cash flows from operations will equal C_2 dollars and is willing to vary its dividend, then it will pay a dividend of $C_2 - Q$ dollars and still invest Q dollars. If, with Q investment, the firm anticipates that its cash flows from operations will be C_1 dollars, the firm will need to plan on raising new equity capital. The amount needed for investment will be $Q - C_1$ dollars if the firm chooses to pay no dividends. If the firm chooses to pay a dividend of D dollars when the cash flow is C_1, the amount of external equity capital required will be $(Q + D) - C_1$.

In any particular year it would be surprising if the amount of cash generated internally and the schedule of available investment opportunities were exactly as anticipated. Thus some temporary adjustments are needed. The firm can adjust its dividend policy, its financing policy, or its investment policy. It will try to make the adjustments that are least costly to its long-term objectives.

Except as a last resort, a firm will not reduce a well-established dividend as a means of coping with a temporary shortage of cash. On the other hand, a one-time special dividend might be used to cope with a temporary surplus of funds if a dividend increase could be labeled as an "extra."

For industrial firms, changes in the amount of investment are the most common method of adjustment. In some cases this can be done at relatively low cost by delaying the start of new long-term investment projects. Another alternative is temporarily to increase or decrease working capital. The various policy adjustments are summarized in Table 16.2.

TABLE 16.2   Summary of Policy Adjustment to a Temporary Deviation from Long-Run Position

	Type of Temporary Situation	
Policy	*Cash Shortage*	*Cash Surplus*
Dividend	Reduce previous dividend (used as last resort)	Declare extra dividend
Financing	Increase size of a new issue	Decrease size of optimal new issue
Investment	Reduce working capital or delay start of long-term projects	Increase working capital, accelerate start of long-term projects, and seek new projects

Irrelevance of Dividend Policy

Dividend policy is not relevant in determining the value of a firm if some well-defined conditions are met. The conditions are

1. Prefect capital markets (including rational investors, perfect information available to all, certainty).
2. No transaction costs.
3. No personal taxes.
4. The investment policy of the firm is set and is determined in accordance with the basic logic of Figure 16.1. The amount invested is not affected by the dividend policy but rather is Q, determined by the intersection of II and k_e.

Later we shall consider the consequences of relaxing some of these assumptions. First, we examine the impact of dividend policy on valuation assuming that these conditions hold. Let S_t denote the market value of the common stock (after the investment) at time t, k_e denote the cost of equity capital, C denote actual cash generated internally over the next period, and Q denote the amount of financing required to meet cash needs for the investment program. If Q is larger than C and no dividends are paid, $Q - C$ will have to be raised by a new equity issue. The current market value of the common stock will be

$$S_0 = \frac{S_1}{(1 + k_e)} - \frac{(Q - C)}{(1 + k_e)} = \frac{S_1 - Q + C}{(1 + k_e)} \tag{16.1}$$

where the term $S_1/(1 + k_e)$ is the present value of next period's market value and $(Q - C)/(1 + k_e)$ is that portion of $S_1/(1 + k_e)$ that will require new equity funds. We interpret $(Q - C)/(1 + k_e)$ to be the present value of the new capital that will have to be supplied by the common stockholders as a group. It is immaterial to the analysis whether existing or new equityholders provide $(Q - C)$ of financing.

Now consider the impact of a cash dividend of D paid one period from now to the existing stockholders; if D is paid, $Q - C + D$ will have to be raised by a new issue of common stock in order to undertake the desired investments, and

$$S_0 = \frac{S_1 + D}{(1 + k_e)} - \frac{Q - C + D}{(1 + k_e)} = \frac{S_1 - Q + C}{(1 + k_e)} \qquad (16.2)$$

which is identical to the present value obtained with zero dividend. We have assumed that the real assets of the firm are not affected by the dividend.

Figure 16.2 shows a no-tax situation where the dividend policy is not relevant. Q, the amount of funds invested by the firm, is the same whether or not a dividend is paid. The amount of newly issued stock is a function of the amount of dividends.

With no dividends (see Figure 16.2a), the stockholders supply $Q - C$ of new funds. With dividends of D (see Figure 16.2b), stock buyers must supply $Q - C + D$. The net change in the stockholders' cash is again $Q - C$ since the stockholders receive D in dividends and pay D back to the firm. With a dividend, stockholders receive D dollars more from the firm, for certain, and the firm must raise D dollars more from stockholders, for certain. The value of the firm is not changed.

However, if some of the assumptions stated are relaxed, the conclusion that the amount of earnings paid as dividends is irrelevant in determining the present value of the common stock may not be true. For example,

1. If transaction costs paid by the firm in raising new capital are substantial, the firm will incur larger transaction costs if dividends are paid, since more capital must be raised; also, investors in need of funds would prefer the dividend to selling the appreciated stock and paying transaction costs on the sale.
2. Since capital gains are not taxed until realized by stockholders, and in addition the tax rate on capital gains is less than or equal to the tax rate on ordinary (dividend) income, tax-paying stockholders who do not need funds or who can obtain the funds they need by selling securities may prefer smaller dividends and more retained earnings; in this respect, earnings retention can be viewed as a method of tax deferment. If the market views frequent new equity offerings as a sign of weakness, the firm may base its investment (and, hence, its dividend) policy on its ability to generate cash internally and through debt instruments.

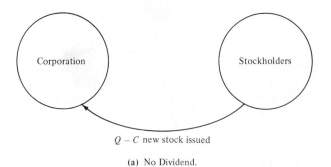

$Q - C$ new stock issued

(a) No Dividend.

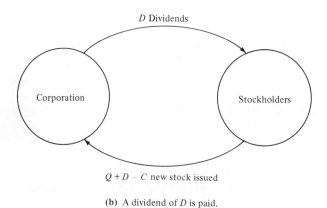

D Dividends

$Q + D - C$ new stock issued

(b) A dividend of D is paid.

FIGURE 16.2   No Taxes: Dividend Policy

We shall now explore the effect of personal tax considerations on dividend policy and then examine some models of stock pricing based on particular dividend policies.

Income Taxes and Dividend Policy

The income taxes of stockholders should affect the dividend policy of a firm. To help understand these tax implications, we shall first examine the importance of tax deferral and then show the impact of having two different tax rates, one for ordinary income and one for capital gains.

Rational stockholders should value a stock based on the after-tax returns they expect to receive from owning it. The tax status of the return depends on the form in which it is received. Investors can sometimes exclude from their taxable income some of the dividends received each year. For a high-tax stockholder, the marginal tax rate on such income could exceed 50 percent when both state and federal income taxes are considered. High-tax individuals are the beneficial owners of a large fraction of all stock outstanding, but the stock may be owned indirectly through mutual funds or trusts.

The returns received by pension funds and by other nontaxable entities are not subject to either ordinary income or capital gains taxes. Payments made by the pension funds to pensioners may be taxable to the pensioner, but the amount of the tax on the distribution will not depend on whether the pension fund received its return in the form of dividends or capital gains. Thus managers of pension funds can and should value stocks based on the before-tax returns they expect to receive from them.

The provisions of the U.S. tax code tend to lead to a situation that, among a group of securities with similar risks and other characteristics, high-tax individuals should prefer stocks whose returns are in the form of capital gains. Also, by comparative advantage, pension funds should find that they can do better by holding stocks whose returns are in the form of dividends. There is some evidence that this occurs in practice. Pension funds managed by bank trust departments have stocks with a higher average dividend payout ratio than do personal trust funds (whose beneficiaries tend to have relatively high marginal tax rates) managed by the same banks.*

Tax Deferral Advantage

Consider the effect on the stockholders' wealth at the end of one period if a company, instead of paying D dollars of dividends, retains D dollars and reinvests D to earn a return of r after corporate taxes and then pays a cash dividend of $D(1 + r)$ at time 1. This policy will be compared to a policy of paying a dividend of D to the stockholders, having it taxed at a rate of t_p, and then having the stockholders invest $D(1 - t_p)$ to earn a taxable return of r for one period or an after-tax return of $(1 - t_p)r$ in a second company. After one period with reinvestment by the corporation earning r and then a cash dividend, the stockholders will have $D(1 + r)(1 - t_p)$. With a cash dividend and then investment to earn $(1 - t_p)r$, the stockholders will have after one period

$$D(1 - t_p) + rD(1 - t_p)(1 - t_p) \quad \text{or} \quad D(1 - t_p)[1 + r(1 - t_p)]$$

* U.S. Securities and Exchange Commission, *Institutional Investor Study Report*, Chapter IX, "Distribution and Characteristics of Holdings in Institutional Portfolios" (Washington, D.C., Government Printing Office, 1971), pp. 1330–1331.

The relative advantage of retention and tax deferral for one period compared to a dividend is

$$\text{deferral advantage} = D(1 + r)(1 - t_p)/D(1 - t_p)[1 + r(1 - t_p)] \qquad (16.3)$$

$$= (1 + r)/[1 + r(1 - t_p)] \qquad (16.4)$$

Since $t_p < 1$, the advantage is in favor of retention and deferral of the tax. As long as r is positive and applies to both internal and external investments, and the personal tax rate, t_p, is greater than zero and less than one, the advantage is in favor of retention. On a dollar of potential dividend, the deferral advantage is $(1 - t_p)rt_p$ per period. This calculation is relevant for stockholders who do not need funds during the current period.

If the internal reinvestment rate differed from the investment rate external to the firm, a minimum required return of internal investments could be computed.

A somewhat different calculation is relevant for tax-paying stockholders who do not earn $(1 - t_p)r$ on reinvested funds but who have an after-tax opportunity cost of k, where k is the personal after-tax borrowing and lending rate. In this case, the advantage to the stockholder of corporate retention and tax deferral for one period is

$$\text{deferral advantage} = D(1 + r)(1 - t_p)/D(1 - t_p)(1 + k)$$
$$= (1 + r)/(1 + k) \qquad (16.5)$$

For such stockholders, tax deferral is advantageous only if the rate of return the corporation can earn on the funds it retains is greater than the stockholders' after-tax opportunity cost, that is, if $r > k$.

A typical corporation is faced with the fact that it has stockholders with widely different tax rates. Both pension funds (with zero tax rates) and high-tax investors will own the common stock of the same corporation. This makes it impossible to determine the one value of t for the common stockholders for a specific firm. Nevertheless, we can determine the gain or loss to an investor of different dividend policies using the models of this chapter.

Capital Gains and Tax Deferral Advantages

We shall now assume not only the possibility of tax deferral, but also a capital gains tax rate of t_g, where $t_g < t_p$. The assumption is made that if D dollars are retained per share instead of being paid as a dividend and are reinvested to earn r after one period, the value of a share will increase by $D(1 + r)$. Also, it is assumed that this gain is taxed at a rate of t_g (implying a sale of the stock) at the end of the one period. After one period with reinvestment by the corporation earning r, the stockholder has $D(1 + r)(1 - t_g)$ after the capital gains tax. After one period with an immediate cash dividend and then reinvestment to earn $(1 - t_p)r$, the stockholder will have

$$D(1 - t_p)[1 + r(1 - t_p)]$$

after tax if the dividend and the earnings on the after-tax dividend are both taxed at the ordinary income tax rate. The advantage of retention taxed at a capital gains rate compared to dividends taxed at ordinary income rates is now

deferral and capital gains advantage $\hspace{5em}$ (16.6)

$$= D(1 + r)(1 - t_g)/D(1 - t_p)[1 + r(1 - t_p)]$$

$$= [(1 + r)(1 - t_g)/(1 - t_p)(1 + r - rt_p)]$$

$$= \left(\frac{1 - t_g}{1 - t_p}\right) \frac{(1 + r)}{[1 + r(1 - t_p)]} \hspace{5em} (16.7)$$

Equation (16.7) reduces to equation (16.4) if the capital gains tax advantage is eliminated by setting $t_g = t_p$. This comparison is valid for stockholders who do not need funds during the current period or borrow at a rate of r.

EXAMPLE 16.3

Let us compute the deferral advantage of a corporation reinvesting $10 for one year to earn .10 compared to paying a dividend of $10. The stockholders can also earn .10 on external investments and do not need current funds. Assume that the personal marginal tax rate on ordinary income is .60. Using equation (16.4), the advantage of retaining for one period, compared to an immediate dividend, is

relative advantage $= (1.1)/[1 + (.1)(.4)] = 1.0577$

The retention alternative yields $4.40 to the stockholders at the end of the year compared to $4.16 if the dividend is paid. Multiplying $4.16 by the relative advantage ratio, 1.0577, gives $4.40. If we had assumed that the reinvestment earning rate, r, was not equal to the external earnings rate, we could not have used equation (16.4).

If capital gains are taxed at .25 and if the retention of D leads to a capital gain of $D(1 + r)$, we would have an advantage of retaining for one period as given by equation (16.7):

$$\text{relative advantage} = \left(\frac{1 - t_g}{1 - t_p}\right)\frac{(1 + r)}{[1 + r(1 - t_p)]}$$

$$= \left(\frac{.75}{.40}\right)\left(\frac{1.1}{1.04}\right) = (1.875)(1.0577) = 1.9832$$

with the retention alternative yielding $8.25 to the stockholders at the end of the year compared to $3.09 if the dividend is paid. Multiplying $4.16 by the relative advantage ratio, 1.9832, gives $8.25.

Cost of Retained Earnings

Because of taxes, the cost of retained earnings is less than the cost of new equity capital. The cost of retained earnings is the return that retained earnings would have to earn on reinvestment in order for stockholders to be indifferent between the immediate receipt of the funds as a dividend and their retention. We assume zero transaction costs.

To calculate the cost of retained earnings, we examine the change in stockholders' wealth under the assumption that if reinvestment takes place at an after-corporate-tax ROE of r leading to a price of $(1 + r)$, the entire proceeds to the investor are taxed as ordinary income. The after-tax change in stockholders' wealth after one time period will be

$$(1 + r)(1 - t_p)$$

per dollar of reinvested funds.

If the dividend payment were to take place immediately and, after payment of ordinary income taxes on it at rate t_p, the residual funds were reinvested in another security of equivalent risk earning k after personal tax, the net change in stockholders' wealth per dollar of dividend paid is

$$(1 - t_p)(1 + k)$$

where k is the after-investor-tax return on the invested funds.

Define the cost of retained earnings, r, to be the rate of return that the firm must earn on reinvested funds for stockholder indifference between a dividend and retention. Let us equate the after-tax change in stockholder wealth per dollar of funds under the two alternatives:

$$(1 + r)(1 - t_p) = (1 - t_p)(1 + k)$$

Solving for r we find that $r = k$. It can be shown that this result is independent of the number of time periods. If the firm can earn the same return as stockholders can earn after tax, stockholders would be indifferent between having the firm pay a dividend and reinvest the funds, and this is the definition of the cost of retained earnings.

If new capital is being obtained, the investor has a choice between having $1 in hand or investing in a firm that will earn r and pay r dividends with an after-tax present value of $r(1 - t_p)/k$. Equating the two alternatives and solving for r, we now have

$$1 = \frac{r(1 - t_p)}{k}$$

$$r = \frac{k}{1 - t_p}$$

(16.8)

With retained earnings, the cost of stockholders' equity capital was k. With new capital being obtained, the cost of stockholders' equity is now increased to $k/1 - t_p$.

Having established the fact that the cost of stockholders' equity depends on whether the firm is retaining earnings, $r = k$, or whether the firm is obtaining new capital, $r = k/(1 - t_p)$, we could next introduce capital gains taxes and the decision by the investor to hold or sell. These factors will also affect the cost of equity capital. Thus the cost of equity capital, rather than being one easily determined number, is a function of the tax law and the decisions of investors.

The solution offered by equation (16.8) is an approximate solution since corporations will typically pay dividends and retain earnings simultaneously. More complex models would have to be used to obtain measures applicable to specific situations. However, equation (16.8) does illustrate the fact that the cost of stockholders' equity funds depend on the source of the capital as well as on the dividend policy of the firm.

Dividends: The Clientele Effect

Theory says that zero-tax investors will prefer high-dividend-yield stocks and the high-tax investors will prefer zero- or low-dividend-yield stocks. This implies that dividend policy will affect the types of investors (the clientele) who will own a company's stock. Researchers have attempted to estimate the effects of dividends on stock prices.

Litzenberger and Ramaswamy (1979 and 1982) find that higher-dividend-yielding stocks tend to have higher expected returns. However, Black and

Scholes (1974) and Miller and Scholes (1981) do not find that dividends have any effect on the stocks' expected return. Thus the empirical evidence is not definitive. One thing is certain: no one has proved that dividend policy does not affect stock prices. It is useful to think about the prospective economic consequences of different dividend policies.

Reasons for Dividends

There are several good reasons for a firm to pay dividends. Some of these have been illustrated in the models of the preceding sections. These reasons include

1. The firm generates more cash internally than can be profitably reinvested.
2. Dividends provide stable "income" to investors (they can plan assuming the dividends will be paid).*
3. The Internal Revenue Service penalizes unnecessarily retained earnings.
4. Transaction costs associated with an investor selling stock make dividends less costly if the investor needs cash income.
5. Changes in dividends have information for investors.
6. Legal lists (eligible securities for trusts) require a record of dividend payments.
7. Some investors pay zero taxes, and there is no tax advantage in deferred income taxes to this group.
8. If a firm is currently paying a dividend, it is difficult to stop without hurting some stockholders.
9. Nonpayment of dividends may encourage "raiders."
10. A market that heavily discounts the risky future (reflecting a high degree of uncertainty) will value current dividend payments more than future dividend payments.

The primary arguments against dividends are that retained earnings save flotation costs compared to a new issue, and in addition, the payment of a dividend causes the stockholder to be taxed at ordinary rates on the amount

---

* If dividends were not paid and investors needed money, they would have to sell stock. In the short run, many factors outside the firm's control can affect the price of the stock, such as a depressed economy and tight money. A stable dividend policy allows investors to bypass the risk of a temporary depression in the market price of the stock when they need funds.

of cash received.* Since some investors prefer to defer taxes, one way to do so is to have the firm retain and reinvest earnings. Furthermore, there is a distinct tax advantage in taking capital gains rather than ordinary income.

In addition to cash dividends, there are also

1. Stock dividends (more shares are issued to each shareholder in proportion to holdings).
2. Repurchases of stock (a distribution to a self-selected group of stockholders).
3. Liquidating dividends (this may include a return of capital).

Stock dividends are not actually dividends; rather, they represent a change the description of the ownership (a change in the number of shares). The repurchase of stock by a corporation differs from a cash dividend in terms of the tax consequences and in that the cash is not distributed equally to all stockholders (it only goes to those stockholders who sell their stock).

Reacquisition of Shares

In the past two decades, major U.S. corporations have increasingly repurchased significant amounts of their own common shares. The reasons for this development and its implications for the theory of share valuation and for public policy, however, have been subject to numerous, and often conflicting, interpretations. This chapter presents a theoretical analysis of the economics of share repurchasing, which leads to some fairly definite conclusions concerning the questions of share valuation.

The reacquisition of shares is not legal under all codes of law, but in the countries where it is legal, it opens up a variety of opportunities for gains to stockholders. In many situations, the motivation will be perfectly legitimate (a desire to shrink the size of the firm, with desirable consequences as to who receives the cash distribution), but it is also possible for one group to use this device to take advantage of information that is not available to the remainder of the investing public.

The reacquisition of shares is not uncommon and, barring changes in legislation, is likely to accelerate in the future. For example, during 1973 Gulf Oil Corporation acquired 10 million of its shares at a price of $26 per share. It

---

* Flotation costs are twofold. First are the out-of-pocket expenses: legal fees, underwriters' commission, and so on. Second is the discount that must be offered to ensure that the issue is sold. Existing shareholders suffer some dilution from the second type of expense, unless the stock is sold to them.

acquired an additional 10 million of its shares in 1981 and another 10 million in 1982.

During the past 20 years corporations have acquired significant amounts of their own shares of common stock. The reacquisition of common stock has been said to have been motivated by many factors. Among these are

1. Repurchased stock is used by the corporation for such reasons as mergers and acquisitions of firms, stock options and stock purchase plans, and so on.
2. Stock repurchase is a form of investment.
3. Repurchasing stock increases the amount of financial leverage employed by the firm.
4. Stock acquisition is a form of dividend, and, as a form of dividend payment, stock acquisition has favorable tax consequences compared with ordinary dividends.
5. Stock acquisition can lead to a change in ownership proportions (maintenance of control being the objective).
6. By taking advantage of special information, stock acquisition can improve the wealth position of certain stockholders.
7. Stock acquisition is a method of shrinking the size of the firm (a form of liquidating dividend).
8. Reacquiring stock compared to a cash dividend may improve financial measures such as earnings per share and, consequently, the price of the stock.
9. Different expectations held by the firm and the market can lead, through reacquisition, to improving the wealth position of certain stockholders.

We shall consider each of these reasons separately, even though several of them are interrelated.

Acquisition of Stock for Use by the Corporation

Corporations use shares of their own stock for several purposes, including the acquisition of other corporations. However, this is not a complete explanation as to why a corporation reacquires its own shares, since a corporation is generally able to issue new shares for the types of purposes for which the shares are acquired.

There may be valid reasons why a corporation does not want to issue additional shares, and so it reacquires shares for reissue. But it is these other reasons that are relevant, not the fact that the shares are going to be used by the corporation.

Stock Reacquisition as an Investment

A corporation cannot "invest" in its own shares. With the normal investment, cash is converted into working assets. Profitable investments increase the size of the firm, and they may be accompanied by increases in the debt or equity accounts; they are never accompanied by decreases in these accounts. However, if a firm repurchases its own shares, there is disinvestment by the corporation. With the firm's acquisition of its own shares, the assets decrease as cash is used, and the stockholders' equity also decreases. The corporate entity does not make an investment when shares are acquired.

It is possible for one group of stockholders to benefit and one group to be harmed by the acquisition of shares. The group not selling may increase the size of its investment in the firm compared to the investment of selling group, but this is not the same as saying that the firm is investing. The term *invest* must be reserved for situations where the firm is actually committing resources to productive activities rather than a situation where the firm is becoming smaller as the result of an action.

The fact that the process of stock reacquisition is not "investing" does not mean that the utilization of funds to purchase (retire) outstanding stock may not be the best use of the funds from the viewpoint of some or all of the stockholders. This point will be considered in later sections.

Increases in Financial Leverage

It is true that reacquisition of shares will lead to an increase in the ratio of debt to total stockholders' equity employed and thus will increase the amount of financial leverage. However, this cannot be the sole explanation of the stock acquisition process, since a cash dividend of the same amount would have an identical leverage effect. The explanation of stock reacquisition must be found elsewhere.

A Form of Dividend

Stock acquisition is a special type of dividend. If there were no separate tax treatment between ordinary income and capital gains, and if a proportionate number of the shares are acquired from all stockholders, the economic effects would be almost identical for stock reacquisition as for a cash dividend (the number of shares outstanding would change, and this would be the only difference).

If the stock is not acquired proportionately from all investors, stock reacquisition is a special type of dividend, since it goes only to those stockholders preferring cash compared to increased ownership. Those stockholders preferring to increase their investment compared to receiving cash do not sell. The self-selectivity of the process is an advantage for the stockholders as a group. One disadvantage is that a stockholder wanting cash usually incurs some transaction costs.

The foregoing conclusion assumes zero taxes. Once taxes are considered, stock reacquisition has real advantages. The tax savings to stockholders of a stock reacquisition compared to a cash dividend may be sizable. Suppose that an investor owns and sells stock for $1,200 that has a tax base of $1,000. The marginal tax rate for ordinary income is 60 percent and for capital gains is 30 percent. With a $1,200 cash dividend, the stockholder would net out $480 (the tax would be $720). With the $1,200 disbursed in the form of a stock acquisition the stockholder would net out $1,140 (the tax would be $60 on a capital gain of $200). Models have been developed showing the great power of stock acquisition as a tax saver.[*] One example follows.

Assume that a firm has stable earnings that it intends to distribute annually by repurchasing stock rather than paying cash dividends on the stock. For ease in developing the effects of the policy, we assume that all the present stockholders will sell a portion of their holdings to the company each period to keep their percentage ownership interest constant and that the firm declares a stock dividend each period to maintain a constant number of shares outstanding.

Let

D = the annual cash distribution
S_0 = the value of the common stock
t_g = the stockholders' capital gains tax rate
k_e = the required return of stockholders

The present value of the common stock is equal to the discounted after-tax cash flows accruing to the stockholders. After summing infinite series and simplification, we obtain

$$S_0 = \frac{D}{2}\left[\left(1 + \frac{4(1 + k_e - t_g)}{k_e^2}\right)^{1/2} - 1\right]$$

where D is the amount of cash distributed annually.

---

[*] For example, see H. Bierman, Jr., and R. West. "The Acquisition of Common Stock by the Corporate Issuer," *Journal of Finance*, December 1966, pp. 687–696; or E. Elton and M. Gruber, "The Effect of Share Repurchase on the Value of the Firm," *Journal of Finance*, March 1968, pp. 135–149; H. Bierman, Jr., *Financial Policy Decisions* (New York: Macmillan Publishing Company, 1970), pp. 166–169, for a more complete description of this model. The derivation of the equation assumes that the tax base at time 0 is the repurchase price.

EXAMPLE 16.4

D = $10,000,000 = annual cash distribution
k_e = .10 = required return of stockholders
t_g = .30 = capital gains tax rate

$$S_0 = \frac{D}{2}\left[\left(1 + \frac{4(1 + .10 - .30)}{.10 \times .10}\right)^{1/2} - 1\right]$$

$$= \frac{\$10,000,000}{2}\left[\left(1 + \frac{4(.80)}{.01}\right)^{1/2} - 1\right]$$

$$= \$5,000,000[(321)^{1/2} - 1] = \$5,000,000[(17.9 - 1)]$$

$$= \$5,000,000(16.9)$$

$$= \$84,500,000$$

If cash dividends had been paid subject to an ordinary income tax rate of t_p = .6, we would have, using a basic dividend valuation model,

$$S_0 = \frac{D(1 - t_p)}{k_e} = \frac{\$10,000,000 \times .4}{.10} = \$40,000,000$$

Thus the stock reacquisition method of cash distribution will result in an intrinsic value for common stock in excess of that found using a cash dividend method of distribution, if tax rate differentials exist.

The advantage of repurchase over ordinary dividend distribution occurs for two reasons. First is the difference in the two tax rates. If $t_p = t_g = .30$, the present value of dividends would lead to an intrinsic value of S_0 = ($10,000,000 × .7)/.10 = $70,000,000, which is still less than the value under the repurchase plan. Different tax rates are not the only reason for the difference. This leads us to the second reason: under the repurchase plan, part of the payment is considered a repayment of principal for tax purposes and so is not taxed at all. Although systematic repurchase over time would eventually drive the cost base to zero, the present value methodology weights the early tax savings high and so the difference between systematic repurchase and ordinary dividend is still consequential when both capital gains and ordinary income are taxed at the same rate. If both personal and corporate tax rates were zero, either method of income distribution would lead to the same intrinsic value. As Miller and Modigliani observed years ago, "There are no financial illusions in a rational and perfect economic environment. Values are determined solely by real considerations . . . and not by how the fruits of the (firm *i*) earning power are 'packaged' for distribution."* The introduction of tax considerations, however, can affect the value of different "packages."

The current tax laws provide powerful incentives for firms with liquid assets available for distribution to purchase shares rather than pay dividends. Under present federal and state tax structures, many persons prefer capital gains to ordinary income. The reason for their preference is that the marginal rate of taxation on ordinary income can be over 50 percent while the rate on long-term capital gains is no larger than 20 percent.

Consider now a corporation with excess liquid assets that it desires to pay out in the form most attractive from its shareholders' point of view. If it distributes them as dividends, they will represent ordinary income to shareholders and will be taxed accordingly. If, on the other hand, the corporation buys back shares, a portion of its distribution will be regarded as a return to the shareholders' capital and will not be taxed at all, while that portion of the return that is taxed, namely, the capital gain, will be subject to a lower rate than ordinary income. In addition, the investors who merely want to reinvest are not taxed at all since they do not sell their stock.

Given these incentives for returning cash to stockholders by repurchasing shares, a relevant question would seem to be: Why do firms ever pay dividends? An important reason is that there are significant investors who pay zero taxes. A second explanation is related to the attitude of the Internal Revenue Service toward share repurchasing. The current Internal Revenue Code clearly seeks to prohibit firms from disguising dividends in the form of share repurchases. Proportional repurchases, for example, are treated the same as dividends for tax purposes. Also, if all firms began to make distributions in the form of the share repurchases, they could bring forth a response from Congress.

Control

It is not clear that reacquisition will facilitate the retention of control. For instance, if two competing groups each owned 40 percent of the stock before the reacquisition, they might well own 45 percent after the company acquires 10 percent of the shares, but their proportion of ownership compared to each other would stay the same (each would own 45 percent). Now if one of the competing groups sold its stock to the corporation, this would alter the situation. But, in general, stock acquisition will not be an effective means of beating off a raider unless the stock is actually purchased from the raider,

---

* Merton H. Miller, and Franco Modigliani, "Dividend Policy, Growth, and the Valuation of Shares," *Journal of Business*, October 1961, p. 413.

from those stockholders most likely to sell to the raider, or from those stockholders most likely to support the raider rather than the incumbent group. In fact, the decrease in the number of the shares outstanding might make it easier for the raider to negotiate with the remaining stockholders. Thus the control factor is not likely to be significant with a large corporation, unless the firm can identify those parties likely to sell. However, debt issuance combined with stock acquisition can discourage a raider. For example, in 1985, CBS discouraged Ted Turner by borrowing up to its debt capacity and acquiring its own shares with the proceeds.

Special Information

If there is one group of stockholders that has special information (say, they are closely associated with management), then this group could have the corporation buy stock at the expense of the group that did not have the information and would, consequently, be willing to sell at a low price. Using special information in this manner would seem to be, at a minimum unethical, and is likely to be illegal. If stock is to be acquired, this information should be made known to the stockholders as well as the reasons why the stock is to be acquired. One group of stockholders should not be free to take advantage of another less well-informed group.

Shrinking the Size of the Firm

If the objective is to shrink the size of the firm, the tax-effect rationale for using stock acquisition compared to cash dividends holds. Although shrinkage can be accomplished by a cash dividend, stock acquisition leads to part of the return being treated as a tax-free return of capital and the residual taxed at capital gain rather than ordinary income tax rates.

Improving Financial Measures

The effect of stock acquisition on financial measures and the stock price are obviously of interest to the stockholders. We shall attempt to determine the conditions under which changes in the measures take place and how the stock price is affected.

1. *Book value*: If the market price paid for the common stock is less than the current book value, the book value per share will increase for the remaining shares. However, if the market price is more than the book

value, the book value will decrease. It would be surprising if such book value changes are sufficient justification for acquiring shares.

2. *Earnings per share and market price of stock*: Earnings per share will change if the firm reacquires shares rather than pays a cash dividend. Consider a firm that currently has D dollars available for distribution either in the form of a cash dividend or stock reacquisition. If n is the number of shares outstanding prior to the reacquisition and the firm pays p dollars per share to purchase the shares, the number of shares after acquisition will be $(n - D/p)$ rather than n if a cash dividend is paid. Since D is going to be distributed in either case, the firm's future earning stream is unaffected and consequent earnings per share will be higher if the repurchase strategy is followed. Although the earnings per share will be higher under repurchase, fewer shares will be outstanding, and one would expect the total value of the common stock to be the same under either strategy. If the value of the firm and the earnings are both unaffected, then the firm's price/earnings multiple is unaffected. Applying the same price/earnings multiple to the higher earnings per share, however, leads to a higher market price per share.

EXAMPLE 16.5 ————————————————————————————

Assume that a company currently earning (and expecting to continue to earn) $1,000,000 per year net income now has 1,000,000 shares outstanding. Further, assume that the price/earnings multiplier is 10 and that the firm has excess cash of $2,000,000 that can be used to pay a cash dividend or reacquire stock. The earnings component of the stock is worth $10 ($1 per share with a multiple of 10), and the excess cash adds $2 to that value. If a dividend is paid the stock will be worth $10 ex-dividend, but if the stock is reacquired, it must

TABLE 16.3   Comparing a Cash Dividend and Stock Reacquisition

	Cash Dividend	*Reacquisition*
Earnings	$1,000,000	$1,000,000
Number of shares	1,000,000	833,333
EPS	$1.00	$1.20
Price/earnings multiplier	10	10
Price per share	$10.00	$12.00
Market value of stock[a]	$10,000,000	$10,000,000

[a]Number of shares times price per share.

be repurchased at $12 per share. If stock is reacquired, the firm can purchase ($2 $\times$ 10^6)/$12 = 166,667 shares. Table 16.3 shows the earnings per share, price per share, and market value of the firm under the two alternatives.

Consider an investor who owns one share of stock. If a $2 cash dividend is paid, the wealth position is $2 in dividends plus $10 in stock or $12 total. If stock is reacquired, the investor who sells receives $12; the investor who does not sell has a share of stock worth $12. Thus, with no personal tax considerations, either tax alternative is acceptable to an investor. Existing tax legislation favors reacquisition.

In the context of the Example 16.5, it is worthwhile to comment on the tax-related rationale for reacquisition. Although the Internal Revenue Service will not allow the distribution to be treated as ordinary income if the firm repurchases stock pro rata (so that ownership proportions do not change), it will evidently allow less structured forms of reacquisition (e.g., open market purchases or tendering) to be so treated.

There is also another factor that may influence the method of distributing cash. Suppose that you are the manager of the firm in Example 16.5 and that you have a stock option to buy the stock at $15 and the current market price is $12 (this is the expected price before the cash distribution). If the $2 cash dividend is paid, it can be expected that the price of the stock will fall to about $10 (the EPS are $1 and the price/earnings multiple is 10). If the stock is acquired, the number of shares will decrease, the EPS will be $1.20, and the price will be $12. A series of stock acquisitions will tend to drive the price of the common stock upward compared to the price with a cash dividend and make it easier for the stock option to be exercised under favorable circumstances. Thus stock acquisition is a logical strategy for firms whose policies are administered by managers holding stock options. Retaining earnings rather than paying cash dividends is still another desirable strategy tending to increase the price of a share of stock higher than it would be if the cash were distributed.

Different Expectations

A situation may arise in which the market assesses the value of the stock differently from management's assessment, not because of different information but rather because of different expectations. If management thinks that the stock is underpriced, repurchase of the stock will benefit those who continue to hold the stock if management's assessment is proved correct.

EXAMPLE 16.4 ——————————————————————————————

Suppose that the following facts apply:

Earnings	$1,000,000
Number of shares	1,000,000
Extra cash available for distribution to stockholders	$2,000,000
Current market price	$8
Management's projected price/earnings ratio	10
Management's intrinsic value	$12 ($10 of capitalized earnings plus $2 excess cash)

If the firm is able to repurchase at $8 per share, 250,000 shares will be repurchased. Assuming that everyone had the same information, but only the conclusions (the expectations and the analyses) differ, then the persons selling are not harmed since they sell at a price at least as high as they would have received if the company had not been buying. The nonselling stockholders will benefit if the management is correct since there will be fewer shares outstanding. After acquisition the remaining stockholders would have earnings per share of

$$\text{EPS} = \frac{\$1,000,000}{750,000} = \$1.33$$

If management is correct and a price/earning ratio of 10 applies to the basic earning stream, the market value of a share after the acquisition will be

projected market value = 10 × $1.33 = $13.30 per share

However, if the current price/earnings ratio of 6 continues to apply, the market value will be $8.00 per share, and those who sell and those who hold will be in equivalent financial positions (ignoring taxes and transactions costs).

If $12 a share is paid for 166,667 shares, there will be 833,333 shares outstanding and the revised earnings per share will be

$$\text{EPS} = \frac{\$1,000,000}{833,333} = \$1.20$$

If the price/earnings ratio increases from its current value of 6 to 10, the market price per share would be $12 per share, and those selling their stock and those holding are in equivalent financial position.* However, if the ratio

---

* The current P/E ratio is 6 so that the capitalized earnings component of the $8 stock price is $6; the remaining $2 per share is the prorated value of the cash to be distributed.

remains at a value of 6, the price per share would be $7.20 per share and the persons selling their common stock would be better off financially than those holding the stock.

Thus, if management is correct, the firm can repurchase stock at any price less than what it believes to be the intrinsic value without harming the financial position of those who do not sell. If management is incorrect (overly optimistic) and a smaller price/earnings ratio prevails, the extent to which the stockholders who do not sell are harmed is determined by the spread between the repurchase price and the market price.

A Flexible Dividend

One real advantage of stock acquisitions in lieu of cash dividends is that investors who do not want to convert their investments into cash do not sell their stock back to the corporation. By not selling they avoid realization of the capital gain, and they do not have any taxation on the increment to the value of their wealth (they also avoid transaction costs).

The investors who want to receive cash sell a portion of their holdings, and even though they pay tax on their gains, this is apt to be less than if the cash distribution were taxed as ordinary income. By using stock acquisition as the means of the cash distribution, the company tends to direct the cash to those investors who want the cash and bypass the investors who do not need cash at the present time.

Western Union Omits Its Dividend

During 1984 a share of Western Union's common stock sold for as high as 39¾. The stock reached a low of 8⅛ after Western Union announced that it would cease paying a dividend on its common stock.

Was the 76 percent decrease in stock price caused by the stopping of the dividend?

The company was in the midst of introducing an electronic mail system and was incurring large losses in the introduction.

What caused the price decline? Probably it was the fact that the dividend elimination acted to verify for the market the bad news of the operating losses.

The Biggest Buybacks

Exhibit 16.1 from the *The New York Times* highlights the stock buyback situation in 1984:

The Biggest Stock
Buybacks of 1984*

COMPANY	COMMON SHARES	VALUE
Exxon Corp.	48,397,000	$1.98 billion[1]
Teledyne Inc.	8,700,000	1.74 billion
Standard Oil Co. (Indiana)	30,000,000	1.7 billion[2]
Atlantic Richfield Co.	25,000,000	1.18 billion[2]
U S West Inc.	12,000,000	800 million[3]
R.J. Reynolds Industries Inc.	10,000,000	735 million
Chrysler Corp.	25,000,000	719 million[4]
General Dynamics Corp.	9,800,000	532 million
Dart & Kraft Inc.	7,200,000	531 million[5]
Standard Oil Co. (Ohio)	11,000,000	522.5 million
Santa Fe Southern Pacific	20,000,000	492 million[2]
Ford Motor Co.	10,000,000	427 million[2]

[1] First nine months 1984
[2] Estimated
[3] Purchases at market over next three years
[4] Purchases at market over next two years
[5] Includes 2.2 million-share repurchase from Teledyne
* Excludes "greenmail"

EXHIBIT 16.1   The Biggest Stock Buybacks of 1984* (*Source: The New York Times*, **January 2, 1985.**)

Conclusions

Two public policy questions concerning corporate share repurchasing become apparent. First, should firms be allowed to buy back their own shares, and, if so, should they be required to give stockholders advance notice of their intentions for the future?

We have shown that repurchasing shares can have a significant impact on the after-tax returns of stockholders. Should the form of the firm's distribution, rather than its substance, influence the amount of taxes paid by stockholders? It seems clear that as more and more firms become aware of the advantages of repurchasing shares compared with paying dividends, this issue will have to be faced.

Should corporations that decide to repurchase shares be required to notify stockholders of their intention? We have shown that the value of the firm's stock is a function of the form of its cash distributions. Thus it seems reasonable that shareholders should be advised of a company's distribution policy and of changes in that policy. The corporation that repurchases shares without giving its stockholders advance notice is implicitly penalizing those investors who sell their shares without this information.

Corporations have offered many reasons for acquiring their own common stock. At the beginning of the chapter we listed a number of reasons and then proceeded to examine each of those reasons in turn. Two factors were of prime importance: tax effects and expectational differences between the market and management. The other explanations offered for reacquisition are relatively weak.

It is very easy for a situation to develop where one group of stockholders benefits at the expense of another group; thus a stock acquisition program must be administered with care if it is desired to attain a position where all stockholders are treated fairly.

For an all-equity–financed firm that does not use external funds, we examined the relevancy of a dividend policy (with investment being affected). These policies did affect the value of the stock. We then relaxed the restriction on external funds and found that under very special conditions, which are not likely to hold in the real world, the market value of a firm's stock was shown to be independent of its dividend policy. Next, we relaxed some of these assumptions and examined the institutional factors and investor characteristics that determine the effect of dividend policy on the market value of the stock. It seems that different firms might wish to adopt different dividend policies depending on the economic and behavioral characteristics of their stockholders.

Review Problem 16.1

The real investment strategy of the ABC Company is set. The company will invest an extra $100,000,000 on which it expects to earn .15 after corporate income taxes. At issue is whether it retains the $100,000,000 or pays the $100,000,000 as dividends to investors who pay taxes on dividends at a .52 rate and on capital gains at a .20 rate. If the dividend is paid, the investors will supply an equal amount of new capital to the firm. The investor has a .15 alternative use discount rate for before-tax money. At time 1 the investor will sell.

$$t = .52, \quad t_g = .20, \quad t_c = .46.$$

What is the value of a retention policy compared to a cash dividend policy?

Solution to Review Problem 16.1

The relative tax advantage of capital gains revenues versus dividends in this case is given by equation (16.7).

$$\frac{(1 - .2)}{(1 - .52)} \times \frac{(1.15)}{[1 + (.48)(.15)]} = \frac{(.8)}{(.48)} \times \frac{(1.15)}{(1.072)}$$

$$= (1.67)(1.07) = 1.79$$

If a dividend is paid, stockholders will have in one year ($100,000,000)(.48)(1.072) = $51,460,000. If the money is retained and stockholders realize a capital gain the next year, they will have ($100,000,000)(1.15)(.8) = $92,000,000. The ratio of these amounts is (92/51.46) = 1.79.

PROBLEMS

1. Assume that the ABC Company is earning $2 currently, is paying an $.80 dividend and will continue to have a 40 percent dividend payout policy in the future. All reinvested funds will earn .08. The stockholders require a .10 return on their investment and are not taxed.
   (a) What is the value of a share of common stock?
   (b) What would the value be if the optimal dividend strategy was followed and a $2 dividend can be maintained?

(c) If reinvested funds could earn .15 what would be the value of a share *$90.00* of common stock with the 40 percent payout policy?

(d) What would you expect to happen to *r* if more funds were reinvested? *decrease*

2. On a "per dollar of potential dividend per period" basis, calculate the advantage of (a) deferring one period and (b) deferring one period and taxing at capital gain rather than ordinary rate if the yield on reinvested funds is 20 percent, the personal tax rate on ordinary income is 60 percent and the capital gains tax rate is 25 percent.

3. Suppose that you did not know the tax situation of the holders of your common stock but were able to ascertain that the average personal tax rate was about 40 percent. Assume that the cost of equity for comparable common stocks is .12 ($k_e = .12$).

   What could you conclude to be the cost of retained earnings?

4. In discussing a policy of issuing annual stock dividends, a corporate public utility manager stated:

   > The stock dividend plan has done a good job for us, helping to finance our expansion, eliminating public offerings of our common stock, and enabling us to retire our preferred stock. It also made debt financing unnecessary.

   Evaluate the manager's statements.

5. The ABC Company could pay out all its earnings as dividends; however, it wants to choose between a policy of paying out dividends as the income is earned (now and for the next three years) or alternatively reinvesting all its earnings and paying one dividend three years from now. With no additional retained earnings, the firm can maintain a dividend of $100 per share.

   Stockholders can earn .10 by investing any dividends received. These earnings are subject to tax.

   Assume that capital gains and ordinary income are both taxed at a rate of .6.

   (a) ABC has many one-period investments that yield .08. Should the firm invest or pay a current dividend? Find the future value of stockholder's wealth three years from now. *180.25*

   (b) How low a yield can an investment have and still be acceptable to the firm? *.04*

   (c) Assume the firm has investments yielding .10. What is the improvement in value arising from retaining for one year compared with a $100 dividend? *2.40*

6. It has been argued that it makes no difference whether or not a firm pays dividends or retains the earnings, since the value to the stockholders is the same for both.

For example, assuming a .4 tax rate and an ability to find a stock that is growing at a before-tax rate of .10, if $100 is paid as a dividend, the investor will have after one period:

$100(.6)(1.10) = $66 $39.60

If the funds are retained and invested internally to earn .10, and then paid as a dividend after one period, the investor will again have

$100(1.10)(.6) = $66.

Comment on the illustration.

7. The Tax Court decided several years ago that increases in the value of endowment policies under certain circumstances are income. The court drew a distinction between endowment policies and other assets such as stock whose appreciation reflects price changes over time. The gain in value of an endowment policy results from the annual addition to the investment fund of the earnings on the investments and the gain is not directly related to price changes.
Comment on the distinction.

8. The Big Oil Company's treasurer explained his company's dividend policy (a low dividend compared to earnings) by stating that "the stockholders did nothing to earn the money." And that "if the stockholders did not like the present policy, they could sell the stock."
Discuss the statements.

9. A public utility announced a new plan whereby the full amount of earnings would be paid to the stockholders, the current cash dividend per share would be kept constant, and the remainder of the dividend would be in the form of a stock dividend. This policy would enable the firm to "retain and reinvest in the business a higher percentage of our earnings than we would retain under our past dividend policy and help us to finance our expansion program and cut down, if not eliminate, the need for periodic offerings of additional common stock."
Evaluate the policy.

10. The report of the annual meeting of the Boise Cascade Corporation (dated May 5, 1977) contained the following item:

Boise Cascade Corporation's achievements of the past five years were reflected in the company's good earnings in 1976 ($97,300,000 or $3.30

*per share), John B. Fery, president and chief executive officer, said in
his presentation at the Annual Meeting of Shareholders held May 5, 1977,
in Boise, Idaho. The meeting was presided over by Stephen B. Moser,
chairman of the board. Fery pointed out that this summer, five years
will have passed since management embarked on a program that would
return the company to its basic building materials and paper businesses,
restore its financial strength, and build a solid earnings record. Fery
listed five accomplishments that have helped the company achieve the
three objectives set forth in the program. He said:*

1. *We have sold or liquidated virtually all of those businesses not
   related to our building materials and paper operations. Latin American investments unrelated to our forest products businesses have
   all been sold. We are essentially out of the real estate business.
   Although portions still remain, today they are a small factor in our
   overall picture. As they are sold, they will provide an additional
   source of cash for the company.*
2. *We have strengthened our balance sheet. Initially, proceeds from
   the sale or liquidation of unrelated businesses went to reduce debt.
   Today, Boise Cascade has one of the stronger balance sheets in the
   forest products industry.*
3. *We have reestablished a strong flow of earnings. Earnings have
   improved substantially since 1972 and are on a positive trend. We
   have demonstrated our ability to capitalize on a good economy and
   to weather successfully a tough business year like 1975.*
4. *We initiated a five-year, $1.1 billion capital program in 1974 de-
   signed to improve and expand our building materials and paper
   businesses. The program is the largest in the company's history
   and one of the larger in the forest products industry.*
5. *We have increased our cash dividend on the company's common
   stock in each of the last four years. It was 25¢ a share in 1974 and
   is now at an annualized rate of $1.10 per share.*

Evaluate Mr. Fery's statement.

11. Jane Doe (zero tax) expects ABC Company to begin paying dividends on
    an annual basis at the end of two years. She expects the first annual
    dividend to be one dollar and further expects dividends to grow contin-
    uously at a rate of 4 percent thereafter. What is the maximum price she
    would be willing to pay for the stock today if she wants to earn at least
    12 percent on her investment?

12. (a) If an investor can earn .08 by investing in tax-exempt bonds, a cor-
    poration investing in comparable risk investments would have to earn
    what minimum return(s) after corporate tax to justify retention? As-
    sume that the investor is in a .55 tax bracket for ordinary income and
    that all income from the corporation will be received in the form of
    cash dividends.

(b) (Problem 13(a) continued)   If new capital is raised and if the investment banker takes .10 of the price paid by the investors, the investment

made by the corporation must earn _____ after corporate tax.

13. Company XYZ has found itself with $5 million of unneeded cash, and the firm's president has indicated that he will suggest the board of directors declare an "extra" dividend of $5 per share on the million shares outstanding. The current stock price is $45 per share and current annual earnings are about $8 per share (excluding interest income on the $5 million held currently in the form of a certificate of deposit).

The market price of $45 appears to be comprised of a basic P/E of 5 on the current earnings plus the anticipated extra $5 dividend. The corporate treasurer suggested the firm use the $5 million to repurchase stock. The firm's investment banker indicates that a purchase price of $50 per share on a tender offer would be sufficient to attract 100,000 shares for repurchase.

Assume that the P/E ratio that would be adopted by the market after the reacquisition is again 5. *Assume a zero-tax, zero-transaction-cost world.*
(a) Which of the two plans (stock acquisition or dividends) should the stockholders prefer? Why?
(b) If you, the corporate president, held stock options, which of the two plans would you prefer? Why?

14. The ABC Company has earned $10. It is thinking of paying a cash dividend of $10 per share. Its stockholders would be taxed at a .55 rate on ordinary income and .20 on capital gains. The stockholders can earn a .05 return after tax per year.

The alternative to the cash dividend is to retain for 10 years, and then pay a cash dividend. The firm can reinvest for 10 years and earn .12 per year after corporate taxes.
(a) How much will an investor have after 10 years with a cash dividend now?
(b) How much will an investor have after 10 years if the first dividend is at time 10?
(c) How much will an investor have after 10 years if the first dividend is at time 10 and if the investor sells before the stock goes ex-dividend? (The dividend goes to the buyer of the stock.) Assume that a dollar of retained earnings results in a dollar of stock price increase.
(d) Assume that the corporate tax rate is .46.

If the capital had been classified as debt and if the $18.52 of before-tax income were paid as interest, how much would the investor have after 10 years?

15. Investors can earn .12 after personal tax (e.g., investing in tax-exempt bonds). Their marginal tax rate on ordinary income is .55.

 (a) What return (after corporate tax) does a corporation have to earn so that the investors are indifferent to receiving a cash dividend now and a cash dividend at time 1. _____

 (b) Answer (a) if the deferred dividend will be deferred and will be paid 10 years hence. _____

 (c) If the corporation wants to invest new capital obtained from the investors, it has to earn at least _____ . Assume that a dividend will be paid at time 1.

REFERENCES

Bierman, H., Jr., and R. West. "The Acquisition of Common Stock by the Corporate Issuer." *Journal of Finance*, December 1966, 687–696.

———. "The Effect of Share Repurchase on the Value of the Firm: Some Further Comments." *Journal of Finance*, December 1968, 865–869.

Black, Fischer, and Myron Scholes. "The Effects of Dividend Yield and Dividend Policy on Common Stock Prices and Returns." *Journal of Financial Economics*, May 1974, 1–22.

Brigham, Eugene. "The Profitability of a Firm's Repurchase of Its Own Common Stock." *California Management Review*, Winter 1964, 69–75.

Brittain, J. A. *Corporate Dividend Policy*. Washington, D.C.: The Brookings Institution, 1966.

Donaldson, Gordon. "From the Thoughtful Businessman." *Harvard Business Review*, July–Auguest 1965, 31.

Durand, David. "Growth Stocks and the St. Petersburg Paradox." *Journal of Finance*, September 1957, 348–363.

Ellis, Charles. "Repurchase Shares to Revitalize Equity." *Harvard Business Review*, July–August 1965, 119–128.

Elton, E., and M. Gruber. "The Effects of Share Repurchase on the Value of the Firm." *Journal of Finance*, March 1968, 135–149.

Farrar, Donald E., and Lee L. Selwyn. "Taxes, Corporate Financial Policy and Return to Investors." *National Tax Journal*, December 1967, 444–454.

Friend, I., and M. Puckett. "Dividends and Stock Prices." *American Economic Review*, September 1964, 535–561.

Gordon, M. J. "Dividend, Earnings, and Stock Prices." *Review of Economics and Statistics*, May 1959, 99–105.

———. *The Investment, Financing, and Valuation of the Corporation*. Homewood, Ill.: Richard D. Irwin, Inc. 1962.

Kalay, Avner. "The Ex-Dividend Day Behavior of Stock Prices: A Re-examination of the Clientele Effect." *Journal of Finance*, September 1982, 1059–1070.

———. "The Ex-Dividend Day Behavior of Stock Prices: A Re-Examination of the Clientele Effect: A Reply." *Journal of Finance*, June 1984, 557–661.

Lakonishok, J., and T. Vermaelen. "Tax Reform and Ex-Dividend Day Behavior." *Journal of Finance*, September 1983, 1157–1179.

Lerner, Eugene M., and Willard T. Carleton. *A Theory of Financial Analysis*. New York: Harcourt, Brace and World, 1966.

Linter, J. "Dividends, Earnings, Leverage, Stock Prices, and the Supply of Capital to Corporations." *Review of Economics and Statistics*, August 1962, 243–270.

Litzenberger, R., and K. Ramaswamy. "The Effect of Personal Taxes and Dividends on Capital Asset Prices: Theory and Empirical Evidence." *Journal of Financial Economics*, June 1979, 163–196.

Miller, M., and M. Scholes. "Dividends and Taxes: Some Empirical Evidence." *Journal of Political Economy*, December 1982, 1118–1141.

———. "The Effects of Dividends on Common Stock Prices: Tax Effects or Information Effects." *Journal of Finance*, May 1982, 429–443.

Modigliani, Franco, and Merton Miller. "Corporate Income Taxes and the Cost of Capital: A Correction." *American Economic Reivew*, June 1963, 433–443.

———. "Dividend Policy, Growth, and the Valuation of Shares," *Journal of Business*, October 1961, 411–434.

Walter, J. "Dividend Policies and Common Stock Prices." *Journal of Finance*, March 1956, 29–41.

———. *Dividend Policy and Enterprise Valuation*. Belmont, Calif.: F. W. Wadsworth, Inc., 1967.

West, R. R., and H. Bierman, Jr., "Corporate Dividend Policy and Preemptive Security Issues." *Journal of Business*, January 1968, 71–75.

Young Allen. "Financial, Operating, and Security Market Parameters of Repurchasing." *Financial Analysts Journal*, July–August 1969, 123–128.

Cases: Part III

Case 1. The Problems of a Treasurer

The treasurer of a large public corporation must fund a capital expenditure program and working capital needs amounting to $50 million next year. He has narrowed his alternatives down to two types of debt issues. One bond issue would involve borrowing $50 million at 6 percent with level payments over 20 years that would cover principal and interest payments. Alternatively, he may obtain $50 million in a private placement at 6.1 percent with a $50 million balloon payment at the end of 20 years. The cost of issuing the two pieces of debt are equal at 1 percent of the face amount of the debt.

ASSUMPTIONS

1. The treasurer believes that *on the average* he will be able to borrow at 6 percent in future years. The company's cost of capital is 10 percent after tax. The 90-day Treasury bill rate is 4.5 percent and the 15- to 20-year U.S. government bond rate is 5.0 percent. The company has also been financing pollution control expenditures with tax-exempt industrial revenue bonds at 5.0 percent. The company has a 40 percent tax rate.

QUESTION: Which means of debt financing do you prefer?

2. In another situation the treasurer was faced with refinancing $50 million in debt at 6 percent in a bond issue that had a level amortization over 20 years.

Alternatively, the treasurer could borrow $50 million in a private placement with a single balloon payment at the end of 20 years at a rate of 5.8 percent. Use the same assumptions already given, including issue costs.

QUESTION: Which debt instrument do you prefer?

3. In another situation the treasurer was faced with varying amortization schedules on two tax-exempt industrial revenue bond proposals. The first proposal involved level payments of principal and interest over 20 years. This carried a coupon of 5.0 percent. Alternatively, the corporation could issue tax-exempt bonds with a balloon payment at 5.5 percent. The company's cost of capital is 10 percent, its average borrowing costs in the future are expected to be 6 percent, the 90-day Treasury bill rate is 4 percent, and the 15- to 20-year government bond rate is 4.5 percent.

QUESTION: Which tax-exempt issue would you prefer?

Case 2.   The Cost of Common Stockholders' Equity

Choose a public utility and compute its cost of common stockholders' equity.

QUESTION: What are the weak points of your analysis?

Case 3.   Western Union

In 1977 Western Union Corporation issued $75 million of preferred stock.

The shares were issued through a "Depositary" because, while $100 preferred stock had been authorized by the common stockholders, $12.50 preferred had not been. The desire for the cheaper shares resulted from the fact that the shares would be sold to individuals ($1,250 for a round lot of 100 shares was more feasible than was $10,000).

Extracts from the prospectus follows.

QUESTIONS:

(a) Evaluate the issurance of the preferred stock. Would you have changed any aspect of the transaction?
(b) Evaluate the preferred stock from the point of view of an investor. Assume that you are a salesperson of securities. Describe the characteristics of the investor who might be interested in purchasing the stock.

western union

Western Union Corporation

6,000,000 Depositary Preferred Shares

each representing ⅛th share of

9.50% Cumulative Preferred Stock

Preferred Stock—*Par Value:* $100. *Sinking Fund:* 2% of the issue annually, beginning April 1, 1982, through redemption at par plus accrued dividends or purchases of Preferred Stock or Depositary Preferred Shares. *Optional Redemption:* Redeemable by the Corporation through March 31, 1978 at $109.50 per share and at decreasing prices thereafter, plus accrued dividends. Non-refundable at a lower effective dividend or interest cost through March 31, 1982. See "Description of Preferred Stock".

Depositary Preferred Shares—The Depositary Preferred Shares represent ownership of 750,000 shares of Preferred Stock ($100 par value) deposited with Morgan Guaranty Trust Company of New York, and entitle their holders to all rights and preferences of such underlying Preferred Stock. Holders of Depositary Preferred Shares may obtain the underlying Preferred Stock at any time by surrendering Depositary Preferred Shares to the Depositary on an eight for one basis. See "The Offering".

Application has been made to list the Depositary Preferred Shares and Preferred Stock on the New York Stock Exchange.

THESE SECURITIES HAVE NOT BEEN APPROVED OR DISAPPROVED BY THE SECURITIES AND EXCHANGE COMMISSION NOR HAS THE COMMISSION PASSED UPON THE ACCURACY OR ADEQUACY OF THIS PROSPECTUS. ANY REPRESENTATION TO THE CONTRARY IS A CRIMINAL OFFENSE.

	Initial Public Offering Price(1)	Underwriting Commission(2)	Proceeds to Company(1)(3)
Per Depositary Preferred Share ...	$12.50	$.56	$11.94
Total	$75,000,000	$3,360,000	$71,640,000

(1) Plus accrued dividends, if any, from February 24, 1977.
(2) See "Underwriting" for indemnification arrangements.
(3) Before estimated expenses of $375,000.

E. F. Hutton & Company Inc.

February 16, 1977

SUMMARY

The Corporation

Western Union Corporation provides telecommunication systems and services to business, the government and the public at large through nationwide, interconnected communication networks. The Corporation also provides a variety of information processing services and rents and maintains data communications terminals. During the past decade Western Union has expended over $1 billion to expand and modernize its telecommunications plant. Approximately 50% of 1976 consolidated operating revenues was derived from services added over the previous ten years.

Operating Results

(millions)	1972	1973	1974	1975	1976
Operating Revenues	$456.2	$493.3	$534.6	$572.2	$607.3
Operating Income	49.2	51.2	71.9	74.7	77.1
Income from Continuing Operations	32.2	26.9	35.0	33.1	34.0
Net Income	32.2	26.9	6.5	33.1	34.0
Ratio of Earnings to Combined Fixed Charges and Preferred Dividends:					
Based on Net Income	1.78	1.50	1.07	1.47	1.47*
Based on Income from Continuing Operations	1.78	1.50	1.51	1.47	1.47*

* See Note 6 to Consolidated Statement of Income for pro forma ratio.

Summary Statement of Financial Position at December 31, 1976

(millions)				As Adjusted†
Net Plant and Equipment	$1,306.3	Stockholders' Equity	$ 601.9	$ 676.9
Current Assets	167.5	Subsidiary Preferred Stock	104.3	104.3
Other Assets	33.9	Long-Term Debt	643.2	568.2
		Current Liabilities	133.6	133.6
		Deferred Credits	24.7	24.7
Total	$1,507.7	Total	$1,507.7	$1,507.7

† As adjusted to reflect the issuance of $75.0 million of Preferred Stock and the prepayment of $75.0 million of long-term debt. See "Capitalization."

Issue: Depositary Preferred Shares, each representing ⅛th share of 9.50% Cumulative Preferred Stock ($100 par value).

Offering Price .... $12.50 per Depositary Preferred Share.

Annual Dividend ...... $1.18¾ per Depositary Preferred Share; payable April 1, July 1, October 1 and January 1; cumulative.

Sinking Fund .... 2% of the initial issue of Depositary Preferred Shares annually, beginning April 1, 1982 at par plus accrued dividends or open market purchases.

Optional Redemption ... Redeemable through March 31, 1978 at $13.68¾ per Depositary Preferred Share and at decreasing prices thereafter, plus accrued dividends. Non-refundable at lower effective dividend or interest cost through March 31, 1982.

Use of Proceeds .... To prepay bank debt.

Withdrawal .... Holders of Depositary Preferred Shares may obtain the underlying Preferred Stock at any time by surrendering Depositary Preferred Shares to the Depositary on an eight for one basis.

CONSOLIDATED STATEMENT OF INCOME

The following statement has been examined by Price Waterhouse & Co., independent accountants, whose report thereon appears elsewhere herein. Results for 1972-1975 have been restated for a 1976 pooling of interests as described in Note B. This statement should be read in conjunction with the other financial statements and notes thereto included elsewhere herein.

	Year Ended December 31,				
(dollars and shares in thousands)	1972	1973	1974	1975	1976
Operating revenues:					
Teletypewriter networks	$157,468	$186,678	$203,910	$210,239	$220,138
Leased systems and related services	127,366	134,055	141,917	154,644	170,359
Telegram message services	99,872	86,119	82,144	76,574	68,245
Money order services	38,724	39,517	44,410	46,099	46,822
Mailgram services	6,433	13,395	23,501	32,124	40,963
Other services	26,368	33,546	38,689	52,503	60,781
Total	456,231	493,310	534,571	572,183	607,308
Operating expenses:					
Operating, administrative and general	228,059	239,479	253,354	274,833	295,523
Maintenance	51,714	56,452	59,321	60,319	60,703
Depreciation and amortization	77,490	85,745	91,188	100,233	111,072
Pensions and other employee benefits (Notes 1 and C)	37,112	47,423	45,443	47,939	47,783
Property and other taxes	12,673	12,994	13,411	14,149	15,110
Total	407,048	442,093	462,717	497,473	530,191
Operating income	49,183	51,217	71,854	74,710	77,117
Other income (deductions):					
Allowance for funds used during construction (Note 2)	10,098	9,117	13,338	11,385	9,008
Gain on repurchase and exchange of debentures (Note I)	1,161	22,566	1,661	3,197	3,661
Interest expense	(28,552)	(39,122)	(54,763)	(57,501)	(54,743)
Preferred dividends of subsidiary company (Note 1)	(3,033)	(2,953)	(2,873)	(2,804)	(5,409)
Write-off of deferred severance (Note 1)	—	(10,397)	—	—	—
Other, net	2,464	(4,371)	4,961	3,260	3,526
Total	(17,862)	(25,160)	(37,676)	(42,463)	(43,957)
Income from continuing operations before federal income tax	31,321	26,057	34,178	32,247	33,160
Deferred federal income tax (credit) (Note E)	(840)	(840)	(840)	(840)	(840)
Income from continuing operations	32,161	26,897	35,018	33,087	34,000
Loss on disposal of discontinued business (Note 4)	—	—	(28,500)	—	—
Net income	32,161	26,897	6,518	33,087	34,000
Dividends on preferred stock	2,302	2,143	2,143	2,143	2,143
Net income applicable to common stock	$ 29,859	$ 24,754	$ 4,375	$ 30,944	$ 31,857
Weighted average number of common and common equivalent shares (Note 5)	13,734	14,596	14,751	14,976	15,200
Net income per common and common equivalent share:					
Income from continuing operations	$2.17	$1.70	$2.23	$2.07	$2.10
Loss on disposal of discontinued business	—	—	(1.93)	—	—
Net income	$2.17	$1.70	$ .30	$2.07	$2.10
Dividends declared per common share	$1.40	$1.40	$1.40	$1.40	$1.40
Ratio of earnings to combined fixed charges and preferred dividends (Note 6): Based on Net Income	1.78	1.50	1.07	1.47	1.47
Based on Income from continuing operations	1.78	1.50	1.51	1.47	1.47

Lettered notes refer to Notes to Consolidated Financial Statements.

Case 4. Arkansas Petroleum Company*

In May 1974, Mr. Warren Edwards, financial vice-president of the Arkansas Petroleum Company, was concerned with a number of issues that had been raised recently about the company's capital budgeting policies and prcedures. His task was to develop new methods of capital budgeting more appropriate to emerging circumstances.

Arkansas Petroleum Company was a significant domestic oil company with sales of approximately $2.0 billion. The Arkansas Company brand was well known in the Midwest, where 90 percent of its sales were concentrated. Arkansas was diversified outside oil (mostly petrochemicals and coal) and fully integrated. However, crude production represented only 15 percent of refinery needs, and refined products (about 10 percent) were purchased. Its strength lay at the marketing end of the process, where it enjoyed a strong 12 percent market share in its limited regional markets.

Up until 1974, top management determined an overall corporate hurdle rate, based upon the firm's estimated historic average cost of capital, and applied this rate as a minimum return on investment criteria for all operating divisions.

In evaluating an investment opportunity, an operating unit would discount cash inflows and outflows at the hurdle rate. Projects with present value ratios greater than 1 (present value of inflows divided by present value of outflows) were given further consideration. A number of projects could not be evaluated exclusively on economic grounds (e.g., office buildings, antipollution devices, security systems), and some projects with inadequate net present value ratios were submitted and approved. Most projects were, however, justified on economic grounds. Riskier projects might not be approved even if their present value ratio, based on expected value calculations, was above 1. While there were no firm guidelines, management tended to use a net present value ratio of 1 only for very low-risk projects. Moderate-risk projects tended to be evaluated against a standard of a 1.2 present value ratio, and high-risk project usually required a ratio of 1.5. These guidelines were rather fuzzily applied, because of different views about risk. In any case, project economics was only one factor considered in any evaluation.

Capital availability had never been a problem prior to 1974. Arkansas benefited from high cash flows, as the result of depletion allowances. Dividend payouts were low relative to earnings so that retained earnings were favorable. Additional needs had been financed by long-term borrowings. No new equity

financings were necessary. However, the debt proportion in the capital structure had risen steadily from 18.2 percent in 1960 to 46.8 percent at the end of
1973. Lenders had begun signaling management that the present debt equity
ratio was about as high as the firm could go without seriously jeopardizing
bond ratings, or their equivalent, for new issues. Indeed, with the increase in
interest costs, coverage ratios were considered very low, already, and the debt
proportions might have to be further reduced. Mr. Edwards had decided to
have a moratorium on new debt issues for at least one year to allow the equity
proportion of the capital structure to grow.

In the period 1960 to 1973, financings had been achieved as follows (dollar
figures in milliions):

Sources		Applications	
Depletion/depreciation	$ 489	New plant	$1,359
Retained earnings	307	Working capital	210
Net debt financing	773	Total	$1,569
Total	$1,569		

The major sources of capital had all come under pressure recently. As the
result of changes in the law with regard to depletion, the percentage of noncash charges divided by gross plant had been declining. Congress was considering even more restrictive depletion allowances, and Mr. Edwards was
fearful some adverse decisions might lie ahead. Profits after taxes but before
interest as a percentage of capital structure had until recently been declining,
whereas interest and dividends had been rising. As a result, retained earnings
were squeezed (relative to the dollar value of the capital structure). While price
increases, relating to the oil crisis, had reversed this trend, Mr. Edwards was
fearful this situation might be temporary. The moratorium on borrowing removed an important source of capital.

At the same time demand for capital was rising as a percentage of gross
plant. Some needs related to environment requirements. Inflation had increased the cost of new investments. And the present energy shortage was
expected to increase pressures for new investment. Arkansas thus expected
to need to raise sizable amounts of new capital externally to finance its growth.
Equity funds would have to be raised for the first time. However, equity markets for Arkansas' stock, as measured by the ratio of market price to estimated
12 months of future earnings, were at their lowest postwar levels. Capital from
this source was certainly not attractive.

The funds forecast for the next three years (1975–1977) was as follows (in millions of dollars):

Sources		Applications	
Depletion/depreciation	$ 216	Capital expenditures	$1,620
Retained earnings	163	Working capital	214
Total	$ 379	Total	$1,834
Short fall	$1,455		

The shortage of funds was large compared with Arkansas' net worth at the end of 1973 of $1,019 million.

During the period, Arkansas' cost of capital had declined until 1970. In part this reflected the increased use of debt financing and in part a rise in the price earnings ratio helped. By 1973, however, a precipitous decline in the price earnings ratio, coupled with a higher average of cost of interest, had increased the capital charge as shown in Exhibit 1.

	Weight	Cost After Tax	Weighted Cost
1960			
Debt	.182	4.3%	.78%
Common stock	.818	8.5%	6.95
		Weighted average	7.73%
1965			
Debt	.325	4.8%	1.56%
Common stock	.675	7.1%	4.79
		Weighted average	6.35%
1970			
Debt	.436	5.7%	2.49%
Common stock	.564	5.5%	3.10
		Weighted average	5.59%
1973			
Debt	.468	6.0%	2.81%
Common stock	.532	11.1%	5.91
		Weighted average	8.72%

Note: The after-tax cost of debt funds represented the average interest of outstanding long-term debt, stated on an after-tax basis. Tax rates averaged about 30 percent of reported income over the period.

Equity cost was determined by dividing a trend line measure of earnings per share for the year by the average of monthly closing prices for the common stock.

EXHIBIT 1   Arkansas Petroleum Company: Cost of Capital Calculations, Representative Years

Management believed that these costs understated the real cost of money to the firm, because historically Arkansas' growth rate was about 3 percent above the average for all firms. Management added 3 percent to the capital cost to recognize the performance superior expected by creditors and stock-holders. Some individuals believed that the 3 percent should apply only to equity capital.

Management did not adjust its hurdle rates, year by year, to recognize changes in the cost of capital. However, the hurdle rate had declined from 11 percent in 1960 to 9 percent in 1970. Under 1973 conditions, a 12 percent hurdle rate seemed more appropriate to Mr. Edwards, although the effective rate was still 9 percent.

Mr. Edwards was not, however, satisfied with this conclusion. The price earnings ratio for Arkansas stock had since fallen to 6.9 times earnings per share, suggesting an equity cost of 14.4 percent. Moreover, equity funds would be the main source of capital in the next year or so. He wondered perhaps if this implied that a 17 to 18 percent hurdle rate might be more appropriate. Clearly the choice of the hurdle rate would affect the amount of expenditures considered attractive, and perhaps their mix as well.

Mr. Edwards was further troubled by the comment made by Arkansas' primary investment banker to the effect, new equity issues would be very difficult to place in the depressed market conditions and prevailing mood, and might be impossible. It seemed to Mr. Edwards that cost of capital measures were pretty meaningless if capital was unavailable or restricted in quantity. In any case, his measure did not consider the underpricing and issuing costs of raising equity funds, a figure that might be 6 to 7 percent of the issue in today's market.

The weighted average cost calculation in Mr. Edwards' mind was backward looking. He wondered whether he should be projecting future capital mixes and their related costs in determining an appropriate hurdle rate. For instance, new debt funds might cost 9.5 percent to 10.0 percent at the moment, and if any refinancing were required, the marginal cost of the incremental debt funds would be higher. Weighted average debt costs still reflected some financings in the early 1950s when interest rates were 4 percent.

Related to this question was how far in the future to project. Forecasting market prices for common equities for six months was problematic enough, let alone trying to anticipate what these prices might become in several years' time. The present moratorium on debt would drastically affect capital costs this year, but over time, the impact would diminish. He was uncertain what sort of planning horizon was appropriate, especially given the firm's current unique circumstances.

In recent years Mr. Edwards was concerned by the growth in importance of "nonproductive investments," that is, the necessary investments that did not add to earning power or avoid erosion of earning power directly. In the early 1960s these nonproductive investments amounted to about 10 percent of the total new fund commitments. Today, largely as a result of environmental laws and pressures, they had increased to 20 percent. Mr. Edwards believed that in order to earn 12 percent on all new capital investments, Arkansas now had to earn at least 15 percent (12% ÷ .8) on its productive investments. This issue needed resolution.

At the time the present value ratio had been adopted for evaluating projects, management was completely satisfied with the intellectual relevance of a hurdle rate, as an expression of the opportunity cost of money. While the notion that the average cost of capital represented this opportunity cost had been debated and its measurement was never considered wholly scientific, it had been accepted. Circumstances had now changed, however. It looked to be difficult, if not impossible, to fund all desirable expenditures in the future because of the prevailing capital scarcity. Mr. Edwards wondered what the relevant notion of hurdle rate should be during periods of capital scarcity and internal fund rationing.

Recently, one of his assistants, Robert Drew, had raised a question about how the hurdle rate should be used. Two years ago, in recognition of inflation, Arkansas had adjusted its methods of present value calculations. In effect, future cash flows were adjusted to reflect the effects of inflation. Estimates of the rates of inflation for various items (e.g., labor costs, prices, construction costs) were supplied by the firm's economic department and plugged into future cash flows. The net cash flows in future years were then deflated by an estimate of the cost of living index to put them in current (common dollar) terms. The common dollar cash flows were then discounted at the hurdle rate to determine the net present value ratio for the project. Mr. Drew argued that the last step was wrong. Cost of capital had risen to reflect investors' views of inflation. (That is, the investor was seeking the same common dollar rate of return as in the past and to do so had to add to this basic rate, roughly, the rate of inflation to determine satisfactory return on investment opportunities.) If this was so, the double step of deflating the value of future cash flows and discounting at a hurdle rate, reflecting inflation expectations, overcompensated for inflation. Mr. Edwards believed that Mr. Drew was right in part, but doubted if money costs yet fully considered inflation expectations. In one sense, this was troublesome, for considering inflationary effects was certainly appropriate in evaluating investment opportunities, yet a procedure that dealt with them incorrectly would only increase confusion and misinformation. To the extent that inflation did in fact influence money costs, it also meant that capital would remain expensive, or could become more costly.

Even if the apropriate hurdle rate was clear cut, how the rate should be used within the company in evaluating projects was not. As noted, Arkansas historically had used one rate to discount all projects in all phases of its operations. This practice had come under increasing attack.

Perhaps, Robert Charles, president of the pipeline company presented these views most vigorously:

Each phase of our business is different, must compete differently, and must draw on capital differently. Pipelines are a regulated industry, and the return on our total capital is limited to about 7 percent. In most cases, this return is highly certain. The throughput and the profit margins are contracted for on a long-term basis to assure a satisfactory rate of return (by major oil companies who depend on the suppliers). We are not as deeply into pipelines as our competitors, primarily because it is almost impossible to justify an investment with our present single hurdle rate system. This unique constraint adds to our production costs and in the end weakens our profit margins on sales and our long-run competitive position.

Given the recognized safety of the investment, many independent pipeline companies can raise most of the capital needed from the debt markets. In projects comparable to the ones we would consider, 85 to 90 percent of the necessary capital is raised through the debt markets at interest rates reflecting at least A quality. If we could do the same, notice what this would do to our capital costs (using 1973 data):

	Weight	Cost	Weighted Cost
Debt	.85	6.0%	5.10%
Equity	.15	11.1%	1.67
Total			6.77%

Even at today's high capital costs, pipeline projects develop favorable present value ratios. I contrast this with the exploratory drilling division where risks are high and where independents are financed primarily by equity funds (i.e., 11.1 percent). In my book, their hurdle rate should reflect the cost of equity funds.

There is another subtlety. Our corporate tax rate is 30 percent on average because of heavy write-offs on exploratory drilling. However, the tax savings are heavily concentrated in one or two operating divisions. The rest of us pay about 50 percent of our income in taxes. The firm's interest costs before taxes are 8.7 percent. This should mean that the after-tax cost of interest is only 4.35 percent for pipelines. Considering taxes properly materially reduces our division's weighted cost of capital (to 5.37 percent).

In short, I believe that we are really rationing equity funds. We should be seeking a constant rate of return on equity. Those of us who benefit from lower risk, and, hence, can trade on our equity more extensively, should not be penalized because our ability to earn on our assets is restricted in ways not detrimental to very favorable capacity to achieve high returns on our equity, when stated comparably to our competition.

Implicit in Mr. Charles' arguments, as Mr. Edwards understood it, each division in the company would have a different hurdle rate. The costs of the various forms of capital would remain the same (except perhaps for the tax element). However, the mix of capital used would change in the calculation. Low-risk operations would use leverage more extensively, while the high-risk divisions would have little or no debt funds. Thus, lower-risk divisions would have lower hurdle rates.

Mr. Charles' views were supported by several other division managers. Opposition was just as strong, however, particularly from the divisions whose hurdle rate might be increased. George Pritchett, division manager of the Exploratory Drilling Division, expressed his opinion as follows:

> *Money is all green. We should be putting our money where the returns are best. A single hurdle rate may deprive the underprofitable divisions of investments in order to channel more funds into profitable divisions. But isn't this the aim of the process?*
>
> *We don't finance each division separately. The corporation raises capital based on its overall prospects and record. The diversification of the company probably helps keep our capital costs down and enables us to borrow more in total than the sum of the capabilities of each division separately. As a result, developing separate hurdle rates in both unrealistic and misleading. All our stockholders want from us is to invest our funds wisely in order to increase the value of their stock. This happens when we pick the most promising projects, irrespective of their source.*
>
> *Several years ago we installed probability calculations in our project evaluations in order to determine the expected value of projects. I thought the purpose of this calculation was to take risk and uncertainties fully into account. Multiple hurdle rates will only confuse things by adding a second dimension to our risk appraisals in a way that will obscure the meaning of the basic calculation.*

Mr. Charles countered these arguments as follows:

> *In considering how much to loan us, lenders will consider the composition of risks. If money flows into safer investments over time, their willingness to lend us funds will tend to increase. While multiple hurdle rates may not reflect capital structure changes on a day-to-day basis, over time they will reflect prospects more realistically.*
>
> *Our stockholders are just as much concerned with risk. If they perceive our business as being more risky than other companies, they will not pay as high a price for our earnings. Perhaps this is why our price/earnings ratio is below the industry average most of the time.*
>
> *Probability calculations leading to expected value measures of the return potential of projects measure average prospects. They do not consider the*

dispersion around the expected value. Projects with high dispersion should be less attractive.

It is not a question of whether we adjust for risk—we already do. We look for higher present value ratios before we fund riskier projects. The only question in my mind is whether we make these adjustments systematically or not. If we attribute a capital structure to a division or, for that matter, to a project so that the rate of return on equity represents equivalent risks, then we are in a position to pick the projects with the best returns on imputed equity.

At the moment, as I understand it, our real problem is an inadequate and very costly supply of equity funds. If we are really rationing equity capital, then we should be striving for the best returns on equity for the risk. Multiple hurdle rates achieve this objective.

As he listened to these and several similar arguments over the course of several months, Mr. Edwards became increasingly concerned with several other considerations. First, the corporate strategy directed the company toward increasing its integration, particularly toward developing strong crude oil production. One effect of using multiple hurdle rates would be making it more difficult to justify exploratory drilling proposals, since the required rate of return would be increased. In contrast, pipeline investments had a relatively low priority, since they were more in the nature of cost reduction. Drilling and marketing investments tended to build the overall strength of the firm more. Perhaps multiple hurdle rates were the right idea, but the notion that they should be based on capital costs rather than strategic considerations was wrong. On the other hand, perhaps multiple rates based on capital costs should be used, but, in allocating funds, higher net present value ratios should be used for screening projects in divisions that were less strategically important. (Theory was certainly not clear on how to achieve strategic objectives when allocating capital, in Mr. Edwards' mind.)

When the present value ratio replaced the discounted rate of return as the primary economic screening tool, it has been adopted because it was considered an ideal tool for the economic rationing of capital. Capital rationing was now a more material problem for Arkansas. Using a single measure of the cost of money (hurdle rate or discount factor) made the present value ratio results consistent at least in economic terms. If Arkansas adopted multiple rates for discounting cash flows, Mr. Edwards was afraid the calculation would lose its meaning. A present value ratio of 1.2 to 1 would not mean the same thing from division to division. To him, a screening criterion had to be consistent and understandable, or its usefulness would decrease.

Finally, Mr. Edwards was concerned with the problems of attributing capital structures to divisions. In the marketing division, for example, a new gas station might be 100 percent financed either by lease or debt arrangement.

This was feasible only because the corporation guaranteed the debt. New gas stations, in Mr. Edwards' mind, were fairly risky, perhaps warranting only a 20 percent debt structure on average. The financing conventions in this division would make this point difficult to sell. And, in any case, Mr. Edwards considered debt capacity decisions very difficult to make for the corporation as a whole, let alone for each of its divisions. At best, judgments would be very crude.

Mr. Edwards had two bright young MBAs working for him, and he had discussed the problem of multiple hurdle rates at length with them. Their views differed.

William Lombard stressed that he had learned at his school that the investment decision should never be mixed with the financing decision. A firm should decide what its investments should be, and then how to finance them most efficiently. If leverage were added to a present value calculation, it would distort the results. Use of multiple hurdle rates was simply a way of mixing financings with investment analysis. He also believed that a single rate left the risk decision clear-cut. Management could simply adjust its standard (demanded present value ratio) as risks increased.

Thomas Gamble, in contrast, noted that the weighted average cost of capital calculation tended to represent an average market reaction to a mixture of risks. Lower than average risk projects should probably be accepted even though they did not meet a weighted average criterion. Higher than normal risk projects should provide a return premium. While the mutliple hurdle rate system was a crude way of achieving this end, it at least was a step in the right direction. Moreover, he believed that the objective of a firm should be to maximize return on equity funds. Since equity funds were and would remain the chief scarce resource being allocated in the foreseeable future, a multiple-rate system would tend to maximize returns to stockholders better than a single-rate system. The company in effect was still using a single rate, and that was its desired rate of return (e.g., 11.1 percent) on equity funds allocated to divisions and projects.

Mr. Edwards had one further factor to consider. A recently concluded study, reviewing the actual results against forecasts for new investments made 5 to 10 years ago, produced disturbing results. Although the methodology might be debatable, the results nevertheless seemed consistent with his impressions. The real returns on projects, according to the study, were running about three percentage points less than originally forecast on average. In certain divisions and for certain types of projects, results were much worse.

In particular, prices, either for purchased items like foreign crude (30 percent of Arkansas' total) or for finished products like gasoline had been difficult to estimate, with serious repercussions on the accuracy of forecasts. The recent Arab oil embargo, related price increases, and so on, would only make these forecasts more uncertain in the future.

Mr. Edwards wondered whether this evidence should be used to penalize projects from certain divisions with persisting estimating problems, and if so, how penalties might be put into force without distorting the usefulness of economic evaluating activities.

Mr. Edwards had no hope that all the issues before him could be resolved systematically. He did want, however, to institute a pragmatic system of appropriate hurdle rates (or one rate) that would tend to facilitate better judgments under the new circumstances faced by Arkansas. He knew that his final resolutions of these issues would not only have to be convincing to himself but understandable and convincing to top management, the division managers, and the individual analysts in the operating divisions.

There were sufficient funds on hand to fund the 1974 capital budget. The capital budgeting process for 1975 would begin with the submission of plans and expenditure proposals in September 1974, by division managers. Some divisions had already begun the planning process. If any changes were to be made in the budgeting analysis, the screening criteria, and so on, the announcements would have to be made very shortly.

Case 5. Emerson Electric Co.

Selected extracts from the company's 1983 annual report follow.

QUESTION: Would you change its dividend policy? If not, why not?

Financial Highlights

Fiscal Years Ended September 30	1983	1982	Percentage Change
Net sales	$3,475,709,000	$3,502,327,000	(0.8%)
Net earnings	302,927,000	300,105,000	0.9
As a % of net sales	8.7%	8.6%	
Earnings per common share	4.42	4.37	1.1
Dividends per common share	2.10	2.00	5.0
Return on average stockholders' equity	18.6%	20.1%	
Return on average total operating capital	17.7%	18.2%	
Total assets	$2,493,041,000	$2,319,799,000	7.5
Capital expenditures	$128,042,000	$139,451,000	(8.2)
Stockholders' equity	1,701,745,000	1,558,715,000	9.2
Long-term debt/total capitalization	7.9%	8.2%	

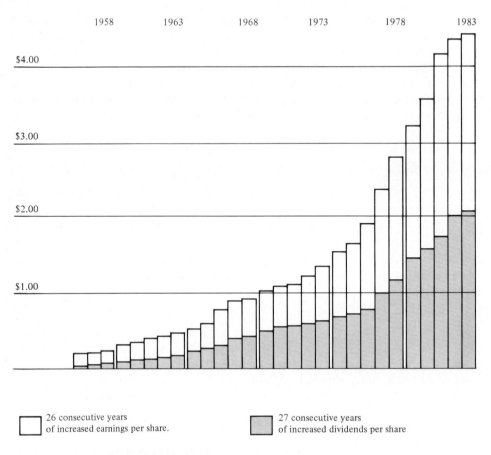

26 consecutive years
of increased earnings per share.

27 consecutive years
of increased dividends per share

To Our Stockholders

Fiscal 1983 represented Emerson Electric's 26th consecutive year of increased net earnings and earnings per share despite one of the most challenging economic environments in the Company's history. Both net earnings and earnings per share reached record levels despite a sales decline of approximately one per cent. Net earnings improved 0.9 per cent to $302.9 million and earnings per share gained 1.1 percent to $4.42.

Sales in Emerson's consumer spending related businesses—appliance components, tools and residential construction products, with the exception of air moving products—were ahead of the prior year's levels. The capital goods related businesses—process control, motors and drives, professional tools, and nonresidential construction products—were in aggregate down from prior-year sales levels. International sales moved ahead modestly despite the lagging international economy and impact of the strong dollar on exports. Government and defense sales and orders continued strong with backlogs reaching a record $715 million at year end. New product sales increased 12.9 percent, to reach a record level of $402 million in 1983. In support of these programs, expenditures for product engineering and development increased to $93 million. At 2.7 percent of sales, this represents the highest level of engineering and development expenditures in the Company's history.

Profitability continued at high levels, with return on average equity at 18.6 percent and return on average operating capital at 17.7 per cent. In 1983 cost reductions totaled $176 million, exceeding the cost reduction target of $165 million. Cost reductions were an important part of Emerson's effort to offset competitive pricing in many of our markets. Capital spending for cost reduction and productivity programs was the highest ever at $53 million and contributed to a domestic productivity increase of 6.5 percent. During the year, Emerson initiated a facilities consolidation program. The costs associated with this consolidation program are approximately $20 million, most of which were written off during the year. The annualized savings from this program are estimated at approximately $30 million.

The fiscal 1983 dividend of $2.10 per share represented the 27th consecutive year of increased cash dividend payout. Emerson Directors have voted to increase the quarterly dividend 9.5 percent effective with the December payment to an annual rate of $2.30. Emerson's financial position at the close of 1983 was the strongest in its recent history. Long-term debt at year end stood at only 7.9 percent of total capitalization. The Company is in an excellent position to fund its future growth.

The Company continued to diversify through the acquisitions of Morse Industrial Products, a manufacturer of mechanical power transmission products, and Southwest, a defense contractor. Subsequent to year end, Emerson acquired Vacco Industries, a manufacturer of high technology fluid flow components for the energy, space, electronics, process and defense industries.

R. H. McRoberts will retire as Secretary, General Counsel and a Director after 45 years with the Company. In honor of the significant contribution he has made to the Company over the past four and one-half decades, Mr. McRoberts will be elected Director Emeritus. A special tribute to him is included in this report. During the year, there was a realignment of senior management responsibilities. William A. Rutledge, Vice Chairman, assumed responsibility for all of Emerson's operating divisions, and E. Lawrence Keyes, Jr., President, assumed responsibility for all of the Company's administrative functions. Four new Executive Vice Presidents were also elected.

James F. Hardymon, Robert W. Staley and Albert E. Suter were given expanded operating responsibilities and J. Joseph Adorjan increased his responsibilities in the areas of corporate development, acquisitions and finance.

For 1984, we are optimistic about the continued recovery of the economy and believe that the Company is well postured to participate in the economic recovery.

We appreciate the continuing support of Emerson's stockholders and Directors. It is especially important to comment at the close of this challenging year on the contribution of Emerson's employees. The dedication of people at every level in the organization made it possible to sustain the Company's continuing record performance. To emphasize this point, the body of this year's annual report is dedicated to the people of Emerson.

On behalf of the Office of the Chief Executive,

> Charles F. Knight
> Chairman of the Board
> and Chief Executive Officer

November 1, 1983

1973–1983: Ten Years in Review

A review of Emerson's performance over the past ten years puts into perspective the basic elements of the Company's growth and operations strategy. During the ten-year period, 1973–1983, the size and scope of the Company's operations has changed. Sales have grown to approximately three times their former size and net earnings are now approximately three and one-half times those of 1973.

The corporate strategic planning framework consists of a growth strategy that can be broken down into Emerson's fundamental sources of growth;

> Domestic core business.
> New products.
> International.
> Government and defense.
> New partners.

and an operations strategy based on being the low-cost producer in the major markets served by the Company.

The plans and programs required to meet the Company's growth and profit targets are developed in detail at annual division planning conferences. During the past ten years, the plans and programs identified and implemented in support of the growth and profit targets required a gross investment of $1.6 billion and provided an incremental rate of return on total operating capital of 18.6 percent.

Emerson Performance

(Dollars in Thousands Except Per Share Amounts)	1973	1983	10-Year Growth Rate
Net sales	$1,192,790	$3,475,709	11.3%
Net earnings	88,137	302,927	13.1
Earnings per share	1.32	4.42	12.8
Dividends per share	0.625	2.10	12.9
Stockholders' equity	536,600	1,701,745	12.2
Return on average stockholders' equity	17.4%	18.6%	
Return on average total operating capital	15.8%	17.7%	
Long-term debt/total capitalization	13.7%	7.9%	

The performance of Emerson Electric against its strategic objectives over the past ten years can be summarized as follows:

- Achieved consistent, above-average sales and earnings growth.
- Repostured Emerson's core businesses for stronger market leadership, faster growth and better diversification through acquisitions and divestitures.
- Successfully blended short-term performance with a commitment to sustained new product and technology development.
- Managed a period of profitable international growth.
- Built a major defense supplier.
- Improved the profitability of the Company.
- Financed above-average growth and maintained a AAA balance sheet.

Case 6. A House Mortgage

A marketing professor has built a house and now is the time to arrange long-term financing. She has rejected the terms of a fixed rate mortgage and narrowed the alternatives to two.

ALTERNATIVE 1

A 30-year variable rate mortgage can be obtained from her savings bank. When the rate changes, the monthly payment changes.

The mortgage interest rate is tied to an average of medium- and long-term Treasury securities. Three hundred basis points are added to the index to determine the mortgage cost.

ALTERNATIVE 2

A 30-year variable rate mortgage can be obtained from her credit union. When the rate changes, the monthly payment stay the same, but the maturity date changes. If it is impossible to lengthen the maturity date further, the amount of the debt is increased.

The mortgage interest rate is tied to an index of 90-day Treasury bills. Three hundred basis points are added to the index to determine the mortgage cost.

Help the marketing professor to make this financial decision.

Part IV

Short-Term Financial Management Topics

This part of the book deals with short-term financial management. The importance of working capital decisions tends to be underrated by corporations. Proposals to invest capital in long-lived assets are carefully reviewed by layers of management. Proposals to invest or not to invest capital in working capital (cash, accounts receivable, and inventory) are frequently made at a much lower level with much less structure and careful consideration. We find that there are useful models that can be used to structure and improve the decisions involving working capital.

Chapter 17 presents the basic tools of financial analysis with special attention to the measurement of liquidity. Chapters 18 and 19 review the managerial decisions involving cash, accounts receivable, and inventory. Chapter 20, Financial Planning and Forecasting, gives very useful techniques for preparing cash flow forecasts as well as the preparation of pro forma financial statements.

Financial Analysis

Major Topics

1. Analysis of financial statements and the need for adjustments.
2. Measuring financial liquidity with ratios (the use of stock, flow, and mixed ratios).
3. Long-term financial measures.
4. Before- and after-tax cash flows and their use in ratios.

Analysis of Financial Statements

Imagine that you are a loan officer of a major commercial bank and that the president of a railroad has invited you to lunch. During the conversation, the president tells you that your bank is going to have the opportunity to lend the railroad a $100 million, two-year loan. The senior vice-president to whom you report has been after you to get more "business," but the memory of Penn Central and its financial difficulties are still on both of your minds.

> What questions do you ask the president of the railroad?
> What information would you like to have?

This chapter attempts to answer these and similar types of questions.

Financial statements are used for many different purposes, and each different use requires somewhat different information. A bank officer approving a three-month loan is interested in different information from an investor considering the purchase or sale of common stock or long-term debt. An economist measuring the contribution of the firm to society would require a third set of data.

It should be recognized that financial analysis is an inexact art that at best leads to reasoned judgments. The accountant presents some indicators of financial position and the direction from which the firm has come. However, the major question we would all like the answer to is, "What is going to happen in the future?" Unfortunately, this answer is not provided directly by the accountant (even if the accountant attempts to provide it, the information is uncertain).

After a firm goes bankrupt, there is no shortage of experts who are then able to "predict" the event. Before the immediate events leading to the bankruptcy occur, however, it would be extremely difficult to predict the fact that the firm is going to have financial difficulties. Very few firms operate with large amounts of liquid assets readily convertible into cash (in fact, in many economies, it is normal practice to operate with negative cash amounts; i.e., the firm normally has zero cash and is in debt to one or more banks). Thus any change for the worse in the firm's economic affairs could be extremely unsettling. To a large extent firms rely on lines of credit with banks to supply resources in such situations, but even such arrangements cannot be expected to save a firm in major difficulty. Line-of-credit information for a firm is not generally presented to the public by accounting reports.

A firm can be presenting reasonably good statements of financial affairs, but if there are basic changes in the firm's competitive position taking place, disaster may be looming and the financial reports will give little or no indication of the storm clouds. The change that is of crucial importance to the firm may be taking place in another company in another country (a new product that makes the product of the firm being analyzed obsolete or noncompetitive). Or the change may be a legislative change (such as the requirement of installing pollution control devices), which may make it impossible for a firm to operate profitably; in fact, it might well cause immediate bankruptcy.

The primary point being made is that accounting information tends to be backward looking rather than incorporate guesses about the future. Because of this characteristic, even the best available conventional accounting information must be adjusted to take into consideration future events that might occur or even events that are now occurring.

Despite the foregoing disclaimers about usefulness, given the absence of crystal balls, there are many accounting measures that are useful to a person making a credit decision or an investment decision. An investor in common stock wants to know that the earnings of a firm are $2.50 per share compared with those of another firm (otherwise essentially identical) where the earnings are a deficit of $.80 per share. Also, any purchaser of common stock should want to know the amount of debt that is outstanding and its characteristics. Debt purchasers would also want to know the amount of debt as well as coverage ratios (e.g., earnings divided by interest) to gain an impression of the amount of safety (or risk) that is present.

Although the analysis of financial statements is more of an art than a science, several steps can be taken that will lead to better information:

1. The reports for the several years being reviewed should be made comparable. This may require adjusting the reports of several time periods so that the accounting methods will be consistent through time.
2. The accounting reports of the several companies (or operating units) being analyzed and compared should be placed on as comparable a basis as possible (the same accounting methods).
3. Ratios, percentages, and key totals should be computed.
4. The several quantitative measures should be appraised, intangible or nonquantitative factors should be introduced into the analysis, and a final decision should be made.

The first step in the analysis of financial statements is to place the reports of different companies (or operating units) and of different time periods on as comparable a basis as possible. This will frequently require adjustment of both balance sheets and income statements.

The nature of the adjustments required will vary considerably. It may be that a change in the accounting procedure was made (such as changing the method of computing depreciation expense), for a wide variety of accounting procedures are generally accepted and thus likely to be found in accounting reports. While the procedures may be generally acceptable to the accounting profession, it may still be necessary for the analyst to adjust the circulated reports in order to obtain more useful information for the decision being made.

Measuring Financial Liquidity

Liquidity measures are needed by external observers to estimate the likelihood that a firm will have problems in being able to meet its fixed financial obligations. One of the first indications of such problems is that the firm is not making payments to creditors within the allowed time period for taking discounts for prompt payment. Since the loss of a trade discount is expensive, this type of financing is an early warning signal that the firm is having difficulties.

Liquidity measures of a firm are also of interest to the managers of the firm.

The manager is interested in knowing whether the firm has an actual or a potential liquidity problem, since decisions currently being made might relieve or accentuate the problem.

It might be possible to manage a firm so that there was little or no risk of a future liquidity problem. But, usually, this is possible only at the cost of a reduction in the amount of investment and a resulting reduction in the future profits, or the underutilization of current assets so that there is a larger amount of current assets on hand than normal optimization practices would require.

Financial problems tend to create additional financial difficulties. A potential liquidity problem for a firm will tend to be made worse if all the potential lenders are aware of the problem or think that the firm is worse off then it actually is. Similarly, the potential liquidity problem of a firm will nearly always be easier to handle, at least in the short run, if lenders and trade creditors are not fully aware of the extent of the problem. However, both ethics and the law dictate full disclosure, since failure to disclose the known facts is likely to be considered fraud. A firm concerned about a potential liquidity problem should take steps to rectify the situation rather than hide it. It wants to maintain its credit rating and to avoid, to the extent possible, the existence of a liquidity problem by taking anticipatory actions.

Since well-known financial ratios are customarily used to identify and diagnose potential liquidity problems, a manager must take into account how decisions might affect these ratios, as well as the benefits and costs of the decisions. The financial analyst in turn must distinguish actions that lead to window dressing with no real substance, from steps that actually improve the underlying liquidity situation.

A continually unprofitable firm is almost certain to encounter liquidity problems. Sometimes the occurrence of the liquidity problem can be delayed by selling off fixed assets, by borrowing, or by contracting the business at a sufficiently rapid rate and converting accounts receivable and inventory into cash. On the other hand, a business that is profitable and expanding rapidly may face a temporary liquidity problem if the nature of the business is such that rapid expansion tends to require more cash than is generated by sales.

In the first situation, a firm may be a poor credit risk even though the ordinary static liquidity measures look extremely favorable; in the second, a firm may be a much better risk than its unfavorable static liquidity measures might suggest. Liquidity measures need to be interpreted with caution, intelligence, and some skepticism and with an eye to the long-run profitability of the firm.

In measuring the ability of a firm to generate cash, we shall use the term *liquidity*, although some analysts would prefer the term *solvency* when the analysis is measuring the long-run survival ability of the firm.

Financial reports are frequently relied on by both managers and external observers of a corporation to judge the liquidity of the firm. For example, a bank officer considering a loan request will use financial statements in an attempt to measure a corporation's financial liquidity to determine the likelihood of the firm being able to repay the loan when it comes due. Since bank loans are generally for short periods of time, the bank officer will primarily be interested in the firm's short-term survival prospects. But even a long-term investor, such as a bond buyer or an investor in common stock, should determine the firm's short-run liquidity, since the firm must survive in the short run for it to prosper in the long run. Thus the measures of financial liquidity of a corporation are important information inputs for all persons evaluating the financial affairs of a corporation.

Elements of Financial Liquidity

There are several elements of financial liquidity that deserve consideration. These include

1. Availability of additional resources externally from banks (this may be in the form of a "line of credit" or "credit agreement") or other sources.
2. The current stock of liquid or nearly liquid assets compared to the firm's current liabilities.
3. The timing of near-term payments required on long-term debt and of the near-term receipts from long-term investments.
4. The rate at which funds are being generated internally or payment commitments are coming due.
5. The current profitability and the expected future profitability.

In the following sections we consider several ways of quantifying aspects 2, 3, and 4. However, the measurement of liquidity is an art, and exact defensible conclusions are difficult if not impossible to achieve.

Liquidity Ratios

Measuring liquidity is no easy task. It requires the development of a set of measures that summarize financial information in a manner consistent with the decision to be reached as well as an understanding of these measures so that an unambiguous interpretation can be rendered.

The two most common financial position measures of liquidity are the acid-test or quick ratio (liquid assets divided by current liabilities) and the current ratio (current assets divided by current liabilities). The two ratios differ in the degree of liquidity that they indicate. They are both useful indicators of the short-term ability of a corporation to meet its obligations.

The two ratios have several weaknesses. For one, they ignore the rate at which funds are being used or generated by the firm. More important, the numerical values of the ratios can be changed by canceling assets against liabilities or by paying off current liabilities at the end of the accounting period.

The quick ratio includes in the numerator only the most liquid of assets such as cash, bank deposits, readily marketable securities, and good short-term accounts receivable. Inventories are excluded, since the items in inventory must be sold to be converted into cash and the sale transaction is still an uncertain event. The liquid assets are compared to current liabilities (liabilities coming due within a year) to obtain a measure of liquidity. A quick ratio of approximately 1.0 is considered to be reasonable:

$$\text{quick ratio} = \frac{\text{liquid assets}}{\text{current liabilities}}$$

The second widely used balance sheet ratio used to measure liquidity is the current ratio:

$$\text{current ratio} = \frac{\text{current assets}}{\text{current liabilities}}$$

Most business finance experts suggest the computation of the two ratios in appraising the financial health of a firm. However, there are difficulties in applying the measures: They are imperfect as measures of financial strength. For example, assume that a firm applying for credit has a low current ratio. If the potential customer is a shrewd profit maximizer, such a low ratio may be a result of extraordinary managerial capabilities rather than reflect financial weakness. The customer may have small cash balances, using the funds generated by operations to meet liabilities as they come due. It may sell for cash and consequently have no receivables, have good inventory controls (the goods to be sold arrive just as they are needed), and in general not find it profitable to hold a large amount of current assets. While a high current ratio is usually an indicator of a firm's ability to meet short-term liabilities, a low current ratio does not necessarily imply financial weakness. To have a high current ratio requires tying up cash in working capital when it could be earning a competitive return in other assets. If the current assets are relatively low-earning assets compared to other possible uses of cash, the firm may justifiably be reluctant to pay the cost of a high current ratio.

What is a "good" current ratio? From the point of view of a creditor, the higher the current ratio, the better the creditor's position because a strong current ratio tends to increase the probability of the creditor being paid at the maturity of the debt. However, a good current ratio from the point of view of a present stockholder is much more difficult to define. A low current ratio is relatively more risky than is a high ratio, but it may mean that management is efficient in controlling its current assets and is working them more effectively than is a company with a high current ratio. It may be that idle balances of cash are minimized and inventory controls are being used to reduce the amount of money tied up in inventory (consistent with a profit maximization objective). The opposite condition—namely, a high current ratio—reduces financial risk, but it may also indicate that management is not exercising sufficient control over working capital items.

There is no completely correct or simple answer to the question of what is a good current ratio. A banker or a bondholder may require a strong current position and high current ratio. A current stockholder may prefer that the resources be worked more intensively, even at the cost of increasing the financial risk. They may both be correct in the sense that their wishes are consistent with their attitudes toward risk and the nature of their relationships with the firm.

Whatever their shortcomings, liquidity ratios are used in practice by creditors to judge a firm's ability to repay short-term obligations. It follows that, other things being equal, a lending firm would prefer that the borrower have a larger liquidity ratio. But other things may not be equal. There are various ways in which a firm can act to improve its liquidity ratios. They differ both in their economic implications and their cost.

EXAMPLE 17.1

Suppose that a firm has the following simplified balance sheet:

Current assets	$ 30,000	Current liabilities	$ 20,000
Fixed assets	70,000	Long-term liabilities	55,000
		Stockholders' equity	25,000
Total assets	$100,000	Total liabilties and stockholders' equity	$100,000

Under these conditions the firm's current ratio can be computed as follows:

$$\text{Current ratio} = \frac{\text{current assets}}{\text{current liabilities}} = \frac{\$30,000}{\$20,000} = 1.5$$

Assume that a current ratio of 2.0 is conventionally believed to be desirable. To improve its image as a short-term creditor, the firm in question may wish to consider steps to improve its current ratio. An analysis of this policy should proceed in four steps. First, what actions are possible? Second, what effect will the actions have on the current ratio? Third, what is the cost of the action (in terms of forgone profits or otherwise)? Fourth, are the benefits worth the cost?

Suppose that the firm sells $10,000 of fixed assets for $10,000. (For simplicity, we assume that the change in book value corresponds to the amount of cash received.) If the cash is used to increase current assets, the balance sheet will be

Current assets	$ 40,000	Current liabilities	$ 20,000
Fixed assets	60,000	Long-term liabilities	55,000
		Stockholders' equity	25,000
Total assets	$100,000	Total liabilities and stockholders' equity	$100,000

The current ratio will now be

$$\text{current ratio} = \frac{\$40,000}{\$20,000} = 2.0$$

If the $10,000 of cash received from selling the fixed assets is used to reduce the firm's current liabilities, the resulting balance sheet will be

Current assets	$30,000	Current liabilities	$10,000
Fixed assets	60,000	Long-term liabilities	55,000
		Stockholders' equity	25,000
Total assets	$90,000	Total liabilities and stockholders' equity	$90,000

and its current ratio will be increased to 3.0:

$$\text{current ratio} = \frac{\$30,000}{\$10,000} = 3.0$$

Long-Term Financial Measures

Instead of current liquidity, we can focus attention on the long-term financial health of the firm. Noncurrent items would now be included in the analysis.

The first step is to relate the debt to the total equities (or total assets) or to relate the stockholders' equity to the total equities (a variation is to relate the stockholders' equity directly to the total debt).

$$\text{debt-asset ratio} = \frac{\text{total debt}}{\text{total assets}}$$

$$\text{stockholders' equity/asset ratio} = \frac{\text{stockholders' equity}}{\text{total assets}}$$

$$\text{stockholders' equity/debt ratio} = \frac{\text{stockholders' equity}}{\text{debt}}$$

$$\begin{array}{l}\text{long-term debt to total} \\ \text{capitalization}\end{array} = \frac{\text{long-term debt}}{\begin{array}{c}\text{long-term debt and} \\ \text{stockholders' equity}\end{array}}$$

All these ratios accomplish the objective of indicating the long-run financial structure of the firm and give an indication of the firm's ability to withstand adversity over the long run (all other things being equal). But they are all ratios of "stocks" of assets and equities and ignore the flow of funds and earnings. They also ignore the market value of the securities. Instead of using the book figures, for some purposes an analyst might want to use market quotations to compute the value of the stockholders' equity and the debt.

Return on Investment

The term *return on investment* (ROI) refers to several different performance measures as well as a method of making investment decisions. The term is used here to mean a measure of performance equal to income divided by investment. The investment measure can be either before or after the deduction of accumulated depreciation.

There are several difficulties with using this measure effectively. Most important, there are the problems of measuring income and investment. In addition, there is the fact that we are measuring a percentage (or ratio) that eliminates from consideration the size of the investment; thus, the measure may be misleading when we form an opinion of "goodness."

There is another important difficulty with use of return on investment that arises in a variety of industries: the problem of assets not currently generating revenues. This problem is typified by firms that grow timber. Assume that a timber company is growing 30 different stands of timber and that it wants to compute its return on investment. The investment of the company is in mills, roads, equipment, and timber. The operating income of the company is relatively easily determined except for the cost of the timber, but let us assume that this cost has been determined. Assume that 29 of the timber stands are being grown for future harvesting. Should the cost (or the value) of these stands be included in computing the return on investment of the company (or of a division)? It can be argued that growing timber should be excluded from the investment base in computing the return on investment of such a company. Each timber stand is an independent investment and will have its own return on investment as it grows and when it is harvested.

Do the growing timber stands have a return during a year prior to cutting? In accordance with generally accepted accounting procedures, they do not have returns because no income is realized. However, it would be possible to consider the increase in value of each stand to be income and divide this increase in value by the beginning-of-the-period value to obtain the return on investment during the period. Most accountants would consider this gain to be unrealized and thus not to be reported. However, if the value of the growing timber is to be included in the return on investment computation, it is also necessary to include the increment in value of the timber. The common procedure is to divide the operating income by the total investment in the denominator, including assets that are not expected to earn any realized income for a number of years.

The same type of adjustment as that described may have to be made for an oil company that owns a large oil reserve it does not intend to pump out for a number of years. Including this oil in the investment base would distort the return on investment of the operating assets.

Income Statement Ratios

Previous ratios illustrated in this chapter have all made use of some measure of financial position. It is also possible to obtain significant information from income statement ratios. These are frequently called operating ratios. The term *operating rate* may refer to the ratio of total expenses to total revenues or to the ratio of income to total revenues (profit per dollar of sales). The most meaningful procedure is to compute all items in the income statement as a percentage of sales and make comparisons to the percentages of previous periods or to the percentages of competitive firms. Where there has been a large change in the level of activity, the ratios may be expected to change because of the fixed nature of certain costs, but the analysis is frequently helpful in revealing causes of changes in operating income.

Although the ratios of the income and expense to sales are important, the absolute amount of income is probably the most significant single figure presented. A large profit per dollar of sales may be desirable, but a smaller profit per dollar of sale, and a large amount of sales and income may be even more desirable. The following relationship is a useful summary of this conclusion:

$$\frac{sales}{investment} \times \frac{income}{sales} = \frac{income}{investment} = ROI$$

Many firms will focus on the gross margin percentage (sales less costs of goods sold divided by sales) as the most important single measure of operating results. As important as it is, we prefer to look at it as one of many inputs into a very complex analysis.

Primary Financial Statements

There are three financial statements that form the basis of a great deal of financial analysis: the income statement, the balance sheet, and the statement of changes in financial position. The following sections illustrate how to take information from these three statements and transform it into meaningful measures of the ability of a firm to meet financial obligations, both short and long term.

Statement of Changes in Financial Position

In recent years, financial analysts have tended to focus attention on the income statement and to pay less attention to the balance sheet. Accounting conventions have implicitly encouraged this point of view by producing a balance sheet that is a residual of accounting procedures rather than a meaningful statement of financial position that interested parties can use for decision making. In addition, distrust of accounting conventions relative to measuring expenses such as depreciation and pension expenses has led to the use of a funds from operations measure. However, the exact use of funds from operations in financial analysis has not been well defined. In this section we shall investigate the combined use of balance sheet and funds generated by operations to measure the financial liquidity of a firm.

The term *funds* means different things to different people, but funds are ordinarily defined as working capital. Working capital is used here to mean the difference between current assets and current liabilities. A statement of changes in financial position is either a statement of sources and applications of working capital as well as the changes in each working capital account or a statement of changes in cash. For internal management purposes, a cash flow statement may be more useful than a statement explaining the changes of working capital. However, for general financial reporting purposes, the statement reporting the changes in working capital is more widely utilized because it is somewhat less subject to manipulation. For example, the cash balance may be temporarily increased by deferring the payment of accounts payable, but this action does not change the net working capital.

There are two pieces of information of primary interest that can be derived from a statement of changes in financial position. The first is the change in working capital (or cash); the second is the amount of funds generated by operations. The change in working capital is a measure of the change in the liquidity position of the firm.

The ability of a firm to meet financial obligations ultimately rests not only upon the firm's current financial position but also upon the firm's ability to generate cash from future operations. In most cases, this ability to closely approximated by the measure "funds from operations." Funds from operations can be defined as either the sum of net income plus nonfund-utilizing expenses such as depreciation or as revenue less fund-utilizing expenses. A fund-utilizing expense would be any expense that resulted in a decrease in a current asset or an increase in a current liability. Although we could estimate funds from operations for the coming year by a careful and detailed analysis of all accounts, the funds from operations obtained by adding depreciation (and other noncash utilizing expenses) to income is a good estimator of funds from normal operations. In fact, the use of funds from operations as an estimator of cash from operations avoids some short-run distortions.

EXAMPLE 17.2 ──────────────────────────────

The following information applies to the coming period's operations (depreciation expense for taxes is $400):

Sales		$10,000
Tax expense	$3,000	
Cost of goods sold expense	2,100	
Depreciation expense	1,500	6,600
Income		$ 3,400

The funds flow from operations is

Sales		$10,000	or	Income	$3,400
Less:				Plus:	
Tax expenses	$3,000			Depreciation	1,500
Cost of goods sold	2,100	5,100			
Funds flow		$ 4,900		Funds flow	$4,900

The calculation of the tax expense (with a .4 tax rate) is

Revenues	$10,000
Cost of goods sold	$ 2,100
Depreciation	400
Total expenses	$ 2,500
Income for tax	$ 7,500

The tax on $7,500 of taxable income is $3,000. The income statement as reported by the accountant might show an income of $3,400.

The tax calculations uses the $400 of "tax depreciation," and the accounting income uses the $1,500 of accounting or book depreciation. Frequently, the accountant will make entries for "deferred taxes" that tie together the accounting and tax depreciation expenses. This "normalization" practice is likely to be changed in the future, and more important, the entries do not affect fund flow or financial decisions, unless the firm is a public utility.

Short-Term Liquidity and Flow Measures

We shall utilize funds from operations as a proxy for cash generated from normal operations and combine this measure with balance sheet data to derive dynamic measures of a firm's liquidity and consequent ability to meet financial obligations.

In the short run, a firm has at its disposal current assets and cash from operations to meet current liabilities. If a firm's current liabilities *exceed* its current assets and the firm has generated funds from operations over the past year, then the ratio

$$\frac{\text{current liabilities} - \text{current assets}}{\text{funds per day}} = \begin{array}{l}\text{number of days required} \\ \text{to obtain funds sufficient} \\ \text{to pay net current liabilities}\end{array}$$

is the dynamic equivalent of a static current ratio. Thus two firms with current assets of $100 and current liabilities of $200, but one generating $2 funds per day and the other $4 funds per day, are not equally liquid, since the latter can generate funds sufficient to cover all its liabilities (assuming current assets can be transformed into cash to pay current liabilities) in 25 days, whereas the former would require 50 days.

Like most ratios, the foregoing measure has its limitations. For example, it may not be feasible for the firm to sell inventories to pay off short-term liabilities without having to cease operations. Thus a more relevant measure might employ liquid (or disposable) assets rather than current assets. If we define liquid assets as the sum of cash, marketable securities, and accounts receivable, the ratio

$$\frac{\text{current liabilities} - \text{liquid assets}}{\text{funds per day}} = \begin{array}{l}\text{number of days required to} \\ \text{obtain funds sufficient to} \\ \text{pay current liabilities net} \\ \text{of liquid assets}\end{array}$$

is a measure of the number of days of operations required to obtain sufficient funds to pay off current liabilities net of liquid assets (without liquidating inventories). This measure is the dynamic equivalent of the "quick" or "acid-test" ratio. Both measures, of course, have meaning and can be used jointly to determine upper and lower limits on days of operations required to meet short-term financial obligations. For this meaning to hold, it is necessary that current liabilities be greater than the asset measure (current assets or liquid assets).

EXAMPLE 17.3 ————————————————————

As of December 31, the current liabilities of the Motor Company exceeded the $417 million of liquid assets (cash, government securities, and receivables) by $239 million. The income for the year was $283 million, and the funds generated by operations was $669 million.

Dividing $669 by 365 gives $1.83, the funds generated per day. Dividing $237 by $1.83 gives 130 days. This tells us that the excess of current liabilities over liquid assets is equivalent to 130 days of generated funds, based on the rate of fund generation during the past year. This would seem to be more meaningful than the absolute amount of $239 million or a quick ratio of 64 percent. If the generation of funds had been at a slower rate, the impact of an excess of current liabilities over liquid assets on liquidity would be greater.

A Limitation

The ratios just introduced are economically meaningful only under some conditions. If current assets or liquid assets are greater than current liabilities, then to divide the excess working or liquid capital by the funds generated by operations is meaningless. A high ratio may indicate a large excess of liquid assets over current liabilities (indicating high liquidity) or a small generation of funds (indicating low liquidity). On the other hand, if a firm has been losing funds instead of generating funds, then a division of the net current assets or net liquid asset by the loss of funds multiplied by 365 gives the number of days' supply of short-term assets on hand. Here again, the stock of resources is related to a flow measure in order to increase its significance.

$$\text{supply of current assets, in days} = \frac{\text{current assets} - \text{current liabilities}}{\text{funds per day}}$$

if the funds flow is negative and current assets are greater than current liabilities.

Instead of using the difference between current assets and liabilities (which requires that current assets be greater than current liabilities and funds flow negative or current liabilities be greater than current assets and funds flow positive), we can use the following formulation:

$$\text{current liability coverage} = \frac{\text{current assets and funds generation}}{\text{current liabilities}}$$

If the funds generation is for a year, the formulation gives the number of times the current liabilities are covered by the stock of current assets plus the expected funds generation.

EXAMPLE 17.4 ──

Assume that funds generation is $669,000,000, that current liabilities are $656,000,000, and that current assets are $417,000,000, we thus obtain

$$\text{current liability coverage} = \frac{\$417,000,000 + \$669,000,000}{\$656,000,000} = 1.66$$

Variations of the formulation would use total liabilities and/or liquid assets.

Total Liabilities and Flow Measures

Some of the effects of long-term debt on the financial well-being of a firm may be of a qualitative nature, including the restriction of management action; in this chapter we focus attention only on the quantitative measures. Long-term debt generally requires current interest payments (which affect the flow of funds from operations) and will require principal payments as the debt matures.

Because of the consequences of failure to meet interest or principal payments (failure to pay may lead to bankruptcy), it is important to determine how well the long-term debt payments are protected.

Frequently, it is implicitly assumed that the bonds will not have to be repaid, since additional bonds can be issued. This ability to refund should not be taken for granted. The financial ability of a firm to meet its long-term obligations should be taken into consideration. First, we will do this using the total funds from operations and the balance sheet. Assume that the total liabilities exceed the total liquid assets. This assumption is necessary because if liquid assets exceed the total liabilities, in the presence of funds being generated by operations, then a ratio relating the two would not be meaningful.

The excess of total liabilities over current or liquid assets, divided by the funds generated by operations, gives an indication of the impact of the total debt on the company. It is more meaningful than just balance sheet ratios, since it relates the static picture of the balance sheet to the flow of funds from operations into the firm. The magnitude of the net debt has little meaning unless it is related to the expected generation of funds. The measure using total liabilities and liquid assets would be

$$\frac{\text{total liabilities} - \text{liquid assets}}{\text{funds per day}} = \frac{\text{days of operations required to pay}}{\text{of all debt, net of liquid assets}}$$

EXAMPLE 17.5

As of December 31, the Steel Company had long-term debt of $448 million and liabilities of $457 million in excess of liquid assets. The generation of funds from operations during the year was $506 million; the company generated more than enough funds in one year of operations (in fact, it took 330 days) to pay off the entire debt net of liquid assets.

These computations implicitly assume that the funds from operations were all available for debt servicing; however, there may be capital expenditures that are necessary for maintaining the fund flow at its current level even in the short run. It may be desirable to estimate these necessary capital expenditures and deduct them from the forecasted funds from operations in computing the available flow of funds.

Coverage Ratios

Coverage ratios can be used to obtain a measure of a firm's ability to meet cash outlay requirements imposed by interest-bearing debts. The two most commonly recommended coverage ratios are the income-interest coverage ratio and the cash flow coverage ratio. Both measures have their place in financial analysis. The following sections of this chapter contain a discussion of the advantages and limitations of each ratio, a reconciliation of the two ratios, and a method of relating these ratios to a form of break-even analysis.

Income-Interest Coverage Ratio

The income-interest coverage ratio is generally defined as income before interest and taxes as divided by interest payments:

$$\text{income-interest coverage ratio} = \frac{\text{EBIT}}{\text{interest}}$$

This ratio is sometimes labeled times interest earned or the overall coverage ratio. The measure is intended to provide a basis for estimating the probability of interest being paid. If a firm's earnings before interest and taxes (EBIT) are 20 times interest, presumably there is a smaller likelihood that this firm will not be able to meet the interest payments than a firm with the same business risk characteristics whose EBIT is 2 times interest.

There are two difficulties with the income-interest coverage ratio. To be accurate, it depends on having a reasonable, but rather unusual, depreciation calculation that leads to a sensible income measure. Second, the measure does not take the principal payment of the debt explicitly into account. The after-tax cash flow from operations differs from EBIT not only by taxes but also by noncash expenses such as depreciation expense. To the extent, however, that principal repayments are approximately equal to depreciation and other noncash expenses deducted in computing EBIT, the income-interest coverage ratio implicitly takes into account principal repayments. Under well-defined conditions, the income-interest coverage ratio can take principal payments into account (depreciation must be computed in a special manner). Thus, while the conventional income-interest coverage ratio is not an exact measure of ability to meet financial obligations, it is a good practical estimator.

EXAMPLE 17.6

Net revenues (after out-of-pocket expenses)	$100
Depreciation expenses	60
Earnings before taxes (EBIT)	$ 40
Interest	10
Taxable income	$ 30
Taxes (at the rate of 40%)	12
Income	$ 18

The income-interest coverage ratio is

$$\frac{\text{EBIT}}{\text{interest}} = \frac{\$40}{\$10} = 4$$

Instead of EBIT as the numerator, we can have EBIT minus interest. The ratio of income after interest to interest, then, is

$$\frac{\text{EBIT} - \text{interest}}{\text{Interest}} = \frac{\$40 - \$10}{\$10} = \frac{\$30}{\$10} = 3$$

If income after interest and taxes is used, we have

$$\frac{\text{income}}{\text{interest}} = \frac{\$18}{\$10} = 1.8$$

Before- and After-Tax Cash Flows

Frequently, there is a need to convert after-tax cash needs into required before-tax earnings. That is, given an after-tax cash need and an income tax rate of t_c, what will before-tax earnings have to be in order to have enough cash after tax?

The basic formulation is

$$\text{after-tax earnings} = (1 - t_c) \cdot \text{before-tax earnings}$$

or, equivalently,

$$\text{before-tax earnings} = \frac{\text{after-tax earnings}}{(1 - t_c)}$$

EXAMPLE 17.7 ————————————————————

The firm needs \$60 of after-tax funds and the tax rate is 40 percent. It will need to generate earnings before tax of

$$\text{before-tax earnings} = \frac{\$60}{1 - .4} = \$100$$

Depreciation for Taxes

With principal payments of a debt not equal to tax depreciation, the after-tax cash needs for the amount of debt payment in excess of tax depreciation is

principal payment − depreciation for taxes

and the before-tax earnings are

$$\frac{\text{principal} - \text{depreciation for taxes}}{(1 - t_c)}$$

EXAMPLE 17.8

Assume that a firm has a debt principal payment of $94, that depreciation taken for taxes is $70, and that the tax rate is .40. Applying the preceding formulation, we have

$$\text{before-tax earnings} = \frac{\$94 - \$70}{1 - .4} = \frac{\$24}{.6} = \$40$$

If before-tax earnings are $40, the tax will be $16 and the after-tax earnings will be $24. The after-tax earnings plus the $70 of depreciation taken for taxes equals $94, which is the amount of cash needed to meet the principal payment. Equivalently, the before-tax cash flow or revenue will be $40 plus $70, or $110. Subtracting the $16 of income tax from $110 leaves $94, which is enough to pay the $94 of principal payment.

Cash Flow Coverage Ratio

The cash flow coverage ratio differs from the income-interest coverage ratio, since it relates both principal and interest payments on debt to the firm's ability to generate cash. The analysis will be done on a before-tax basis, but an after-tax analysis would be equally useful.

The purpose of the cash flow coverage ratio is to related the cash coming in from operations to the cash that will be required to service the debt. A ratio less than 1 indicates that the debt coming due next period cannot be serviced from cash flows from operations.

The cash flow coverage ratio is the ratio of cash flows arising from operations to the cash requirements arising from debt obligations (adjusted to a before-tax basis):

$$\text{cash flow coverage} = \frac{\text{cash flow from operations before tax}}{\text{cash requirements to service debt}}$$

The cash flowing from operations before taxes to meet debt obligations is the sum of earnings before interest and taxes plus accounting depreciation and other noncash-utilizing expenses. These noncash-utilizing expenses are added back to income since they should not be deducted from revenues (they did not use cash). Adding these items back has the effect of making the cash flow independent of the method of accounting depreciation since depreciation was already deducted in computing the value of EBIT. We obtain the before-tax cash flows from operations.

If we let t_c denote the firm's tax rate, the cash requirements before taxes arising from debt obligations is the sum of interest plus the before-tax cash flows necessary to meet the principal repayments. If the depreciation expense for taxes is larger than the principal payment (thus the debt payment is tax shielded), we have for the cash requirements to pay the debt

interest + principal

If the principal payment is larger than the depreciation tax expense, the before-tax cash flows needed are

$$\text{interest} + \text{depreciation for taxes} + \frac{\text{principal} - \text{depreciation for taxes}}{(1 - t_c)}$$

The depreciation deduction shields from taxes an amount of cash flow equal to the depreciation tax expense, since depreciation is an allowable deduction in computing taxes. If the depreciation deduction is not large enough, then some of the cash flow necessary to pay the debt will be taxed and we must compute a before-tax equivalent.

EXAMPLE 17.9 ——————————————————————————————

Let

cash flow from operations before taxes = $120
depreciation expense for taxes = $20
principal payment = $50
interest = $10
corporate tax rate = .4

Since the principal payment is larger than the depreciation expense for taxes, we have for the cash requirements to pay the interest and principal:

$$\$10 + \$20 + \frac{\$50 - \$20}{1 - .4} = \$80$$

The cash being generated by operations is $120, and the cash flow coverage is

$$\text{cash flow coverage} = \frac{\$120}{\$80} = 1.5$$

The cash flow from operations is 1.5 times as large as the cash flows needed to service the debt. If the cash flow from operations were equal to $80 and all other things are held constant,

$$\text{cash flow coverage} = \frac{\$80}{\$80} = 1$$

As the following income statement shows with an earnings before interest, taxes, and depreciation of $80, with interest payments of $10, and tax depreciation of $20, taxes would be $20 (40 percent of $50), leaving net income after interest and taxes of $30:

Net revenue		$80
Less: Interest	$10	
Depreciation for taxes	20	30
Taxable income		$50
Income taxes (.4)		20
Net income		$30

We are now ready to show that $80 of before-tax cash flows is just sufficient to pay the interest and principal.

Subtracting the $20 of taxes from the cash flows of $80 gives $60, which is sufficient to pay the interest of $10 and the principal of $50. After deducting all out-of-pocket expenses including interest, the cash generated is precisely equal to the $50 required to pay the debt principal. The coverage ratio is properly 1.0 when the cash flows (before interest and taxes) are $80.

Leases

Lease payments are frequently analogous to debt and should be part of the cash flow coverage ratio when the lease contract is not readily cancellable. Basically, the cash flow ratio consists of the cash flow entering the firm divided by the cash flow commitment (before tax) necessary to service the debt. Since lease payments are deductible for taxes, a lease payment of L would only require L dollars of cash generation to service the lease. Thus, if leases are to be taken into consideration, the lease payment should be added to the denominator, and the numerator should be before the deduction of the lease expense (if the lease expense has already been deducted, then leases would be added back).

The Present or Future

We have computed several ratios using income or funds from operations. For practical purposes, these amounts will probably be the actual funds or income of the most recent period. If possible, an additional computation should be made using the forecasted income or funds of the coming period. If we could rely on the forecasts, the forecasted amounts are actually the relevant amounts, since we are concerned with the financial liquidity of the firm in the future time periods, starting with the present amount of assets and liabilities.

Because we are interested in financial data of the future, we will be interested in the trend of the financial affairs of the firm, and this leads to the use of comparative income statements and balance sheets. By looking at the reports for two or more years, you can obtain some feel for the direction in which the firm is going. It is common for firms to include 10-year financial summaries of operations that are very helpful in gauging the trend. It is important to keep in mind the fact that while we can plot the historical data, obtain trends, and extend the trend line and use the extensions for purposes of prediction, we can never be sure when the trend line becomes a curve that has reached its maximum or minimum point.

An Evaluation

The major criticism that can be raised against the cash flow coverage ratio is that it is a nearsighted measure, incapable of seeing beyond one period. If, for example, there are no principal payments in this period, but large principal payments are due during other periods in the future, the cash flow coverage ratio of this period may be misleading. This nearsightedness requires that due care be taken in interpreting the ratio of a single period. It would probably be wise to estimate the ratios for future periods where principal payments are high.

Frequently in this chapter, we have used measures of income and cash flows. The relevant flows for all liquidity measures are future (forecasted) incomes and cash flows, since we are trying to relate the present (or proposed) stock of debt to the ability to repay the obligations arising from it. The past measures of flows are relevant only to the extent that they offer a basis that we can use for estimating the future. In addition to being the basis of estimating the expected amount of income or cash flow, the variability of the flows in the past may offer an insight as to the reliability of the forecasts that are being made. Thus, using past fluctuations of the cash flows, an insight may be gained as to the magnitude of operating and financial risk.

An Analysis by an Investment Banking Firm

The following analysis was done by a major investment banking firm.

	As of December 31, 1979
Shares outstanding	8,681,730
Where traded (symbol)	ASE
Current price (4/1/80)	$28⅛
52-Week range	$34¾–$9⅛
Lastest 12 months discretionary cash flow (000's)	$39.971
Per share	$4.60
Estimated future net revenue (000's)	$279.550
Per share	$32.20
Latest 12 months' net income (000's)	$10,233
Per share	$1.18
Stock price multiples (based on current prices)	
To cash flow per share	6.11x
To estimated future net revenue per share	.87x
To net income per share	23.83x
Annual compound growth rates (1975–1979)	
Revenues	16.2%
Net income	15.8
Cash flow	51.3
Capital expenditures	44.4

Conclusions

A number of factors should be taken into account in analyzing financial statements. One of the basic rules to observe in utilizing financial information is to be sure to know the rules under which the information was prepared. Also the statements must be interpreted. The use of standard ratios, especially comparing them to industry norms, can be very revealing. An analyst can develop and use a wide range of ratios (and other diagnostic devices) that have economic meaning.

It is also important to recognize that in the long run the most important factor determining the firm's financial health will be the firm's ability to make profits. Profits will result in positive fund flows from operations and favorable credit ratings from potential investors. A sound financial position will enable the firm to absorb temporary setbacks and will allow it to attain its long-run profit potential. Thus the analyst must look at financial position, as well as the results of operations, for a more complete appraisal of the financial health of an organization.

Determining the financial health of a firm is no simple task. In the long run, the firm's well-being may depend on the profitability of the firm, but whether the stockholders will survive to reach the long run will depend to some extent on the firm's financial structure. It is necessary for both management and investors to make comprehensive computations indicating the financial strength of a firm.

Accounting information is based on transactions or events that have already occurred. However, the value of a firm is based on the expectations of future events. It is the task of the financial analyst to take the past accounting data and project it into the future, using not only the accounting information but also knowledge about the firm, the structure of the industry in which the firm is operating, and overall trends of the economy. The material in this chapter may be considered a first step in the analysis of a firm—an important first step because the future of a firm is not independent of its past.

Review Problem 17.1

The ABC Company has to pay off $10,000,000 of debt (principal) and $800,000 of interest. It has taxable income and is paying taxes at a .46 rate. Its depreciation for taxes next period will be $7,000,000 and for accounting will be $5,000,000.

(a) What minimum revenue will it have to earn to pay its debt obligations?

(b) What minimum EBIT (computed using accounting depreciation) will it have to earn to pay its debt obligations?

Solution to Review Problem 17.1

(a)

10,000,000	Principal		
7,000,000	Tax depreciation		
$ 3,000,000	Not shielded		

$$\frac{\$3,000,000}{1 - .46} = \$ 5,556,000 \quad \text{Before tax}$$

7,000,000

800,000

$13,356,000

(b)

Revenue	$13,356,000	$13,356,000
Interest	800,000	
Depreciation	5,000,000	5,000,000
Taxes	2,556,000	
Expenses	$ 8,356,000	8,356,000 EBIT
Net income	$ 5,000,000	

Taxes = ($13,356,000 − $7,800,000).46 = $2,556,000

PROBLEMS

1. As of the end of December the current liabilities of the Large Steel Company are $800 million and its liquid assets are $600 million. The funds generated by operations in the past year were $1 billion, and it is expected that this rate will continue in the future.

    How many days of funds generation would be needed to pay the amount of current liabilities in excess of liquid assets?

2. (Problem 1 continued)   The Large Steel Company also has $1 billion of long-term debt.

    How many days of fund generation would be needed to pay the amount of total liabilities in excess of liquid assets?

3. The Large Steel Company has $1.5 billion of current assets, $.8 billion of current liabilities, and $1 billion of long-term debt. It generates $1 billion of funds per year.

    Compute some meaningful measures relating assets, debt, and funds generation.

4. An investment with a rate of return of 20 percent is to be financed with the debt costing 10 percent. The investment and debt cash flows are as follows:

	Time		
	0	*1*	*2*
Investment	− $15,278	$10,000	$10,000
Debt	+ 15,278	− 16,806	

Compute the cash flow coverage ratios for periods 1 and 2.

5. The following information applies to the ABC Company for the coming year:

Earnings before interest and taxes	$3,000,000
Interest	300,000
Principal repayment	1,200,000
Depreciation (for taxes and accounting)	800,000
Tax rate	.40

(a) What before-tax cash flow has to be earned to meet the debt requirements in the coming year?
(b) What is the cash flow coverage ratio?

6. An investment with a rate of return of 20 percent is to be financed with the debt costing 20 percent. The investment's cash flows (net income before depreciation and interest) and debt payments are as follows:

	Time		
	0	*1*	*2*
Investment	− $15,278	$10,000	$10,000
Debt	+ 15,278	− 10,000	− 10,000

The depreciation expense of year 1 is $6,945 and of year 2 is $8,333.
   Compute both the income-interest and the cash coverage ratios for years 1 and 2.

7. Does the use of inventory necessarily affect the amount of cash that is held by a corporation?

8. The ABC Company has $100 million of total liabilities and $20 million of liquid assets. It generates funds flow at the rate of $40 million per year.

(a) Compute the number of days of funds flow that would be required to pay off the total liabilities net of liquid assets.

(b) What other information would you like? *avail. funds flow disposible assets*

9. Why is EBIT generally used in the interest coverage ratio rather than income after taxes?

10. A bank loan officer is considering lending $2 million on a 60-day note to a corporation.

What quantitative measures should the loan officer compute? If the loan is for 20 years, how should the analysis differ?

11. The following facts apply to two companies for the year ending December 31 of the same year:

	Company A	Company B
Income	$10,000,000	$10,000,000
Funds flow	16,000,000	16,000,000
Interest payments	4,000,000	3,000,000

No long-term debt (principal) payments are due for either firm for 10 years.

Before evaluating the liquidity of the two firms, what additional information would you desire?

12. The basic defensive interval (BDI) is defined as

$$\frac{\text{total defensive assets}}{\text{forecasted daily operating expenditures}}$$

limited usefulness

The defensive assets include those assets that can readily be turned into cash (liquid assets) such as cash, marketable securities, and accounts receivables. Sorter and Benston originated this computation in their 1960 article.*

Evaluate the usefulness of the BDI.

13. An analyst wants a cash flow coverage ratio prepared from the point of view of the common stockholders of a firm. The firm has a long-term debt and preferred stock outstanding.

Prepare a useful ratio for the analyst.

14. An analyst wants a cash flow coverage ratio prepared from the point of view of the common stockholders of a firm. The firm has a long-term debt and preferred stock outstanding and makes annual lease payments of L.

Prepare a useful ratio for the analyst. *Add $L to cash requirements — handle like interest*

* See G. H. Sorter and G. Benston, "Appraising the Defensive Position of a Firm: The Internal Measure," *Accounting Review*, October 1960, pp. 633–640.

15. To earn $78 after tax, how much has to be earned before tax? The tax rate is .4.

16. The depreciation expense for taxes is $80 and the debt principal payment is $110.

    With a tax rate of .4, what do the before-tax earnings have to be in order to have sufficient cash to pay the debt principal?

REFERENCES

Altman, Edward I. "Financial Ratios, Discriminant Analysis and the Prediction of Corporate Bankruptcy." *Journal of Finance*, September 1968, 589–609.
———, and Arnold W. Sametz (eds). *Financial Crises*. New York: John Wiley & Sons, Inc., 1977.
Beaver, W. H. "Financial Ratios as Predictors of Failure." *Empirical Research in Accounting, Selected Studies, 1966.* Chicago Institute of Professional Accounting, January 1967, pp. 71–110.
———. "Market Prices, Financial Ratios, and the Prediction of Failure." *Journal of Accounting Research*, Autumn 1968, 179–192.
Edmister, Robert O. "An Empirical Test of Financial Ratio Analysis for Small Business Failure Predictions." *Journal of Financial and Quantitative Analysis*, March 1972, 1477–1493.
Findlay, M. Chapman, III, and Edward E. Williams. "Toward More Adequate Debt Service Coverage Ratios." *Financial Analysts Journal*, November–December 1975, 58–61.
Foster, George. *Financial Statement Analysis*. Englewood Cliffs, N.J.: Prentice-Hall, Inc., 1978.
Helfert, Erich A., *Techniques of Financial Analysis*. Homewood, Ill., Richard D. Irwin, Inc., 1977.
Jaedicke, R. K., and R. T. Sprouse. *Accounting Flows: Income, Funds, and Cash*. Englewood Cliffs, N.J.: Prentice-Hall, Inc., 1965.
Lemke, Kenneth W. "The Evaluation of Liquidity: An Analytical Study." *Journal of Accounting Research*, Spring 1970, 47–77.
Lev, Baruch. *Financial Statement Analysis: A New Approach*. Englewood Cliffs, N.J.: Prentice-Hall, Inc., 1974.
O'Connor, Melvin C. "On the Usefulness of Financial Ratios to Investors in Common Stock." *Accounting Review*, April 1973, 1–18.
Pinches, George E., and Kent A. Mingo. "A Multivariate Analysis of Industrial Bond Ratings." *Journal of Finance*, March 1973, 1–18.
Revsine, Lawrence. *Accounting in an Inflationary Environment*. New York: Laventhol and Horwath, 1977.
West, Richard R. "An Alternative Approach to Predicting Corporate Bond Ratings." *Journal of Accounting Research*, Spring 1970, 118–125.

Chapter 18

Managing Accounts Receivable and Inventory

Major Topics

1. Structuring the credit-granting decision using the relevant costs and the probability of collection.
2. The multiperiod credit decision; revision of probabilities.
3. Inventory decisions and finance.

The Credit-Granting Decision

A major chemical company found itself producing so much of a by-product that it ran out of storage capacity and had to pump the material into a settling pond. A large New York bank during a credit squeeze found itself desperately attempting to increase its deposits to meet the borrowing needs of its customers. Should the production situation of the chemical company or the deposit situation of the bank influence these firms' credit policies? We shall argue very strongly in this chapter that credit policy should be influenced by these types of factors and shall present decision models that incorporate these factors for determining whether or not to offer credit.

Credit granting is an important decision in most firms, and changes in credit policy can quickly affect the economic well-being of the firm. In this chapter we consider methods of correctly structuring credit policy decisions. Like many financial decisions, they can be viewed as a capital budgeting problem. Viewed in this fashion, the problem becomes one of first ascertaining the relevant incremental cash flows and then subjecting these flows to the appropriate economic analysis, ranging from a straightforward application of discounted cash flows (using the expected cash flows) to a more complete risk analysis.

For expository purposes we shall assume that the firm makes its decisions on the basis of expected net present value, deciding to grant credit in those cases where the decision carries a positive expected net present value. This assumption means that for any decision, we can weight the dollar outcomes (in present value) that can occur with that decision by the probability of their occurring to obtain an expected net present value, and we assume that with the customer credit decision we do not have to be concerned with risk aversion that normally accompanies decision making under uncertainty. For a firm operating with a wide range of types of customers, where no one customer is receiving an extremely large amount of credit, the assumption that we can ignore risk-aversion considerations is a reasonable first approximation to risk. The more diversified the customers, the smaller the credit risk. Unfortunately, changes in business conditions and in money market conditions tend to affect nearly all customers in the same way, and therefore, diversification may be of limited help in reducing total risk.

We shall consider a basic credit decision involving a one-shot sale and known costs where either the entire amount will be paid or nothing will. Complications can be readily introduced, but they would merely distract from major components of the decision. Let the probability of collection be p and the amount to be collected be R and the incremental cost of making the sale be C. Then it is desirable to offer credit if the expected revenue, pR, is greater than the cost, C. Offer credit if

$$pR > C$$

A firm should offer credit if the expected revenues are greater than the relevant costs of making the sale.

Let us consider a grocery store where for a $1 of sales the incremental cost, C, is equal to $.80. If the revenues are collected a relatively short time after the sale, then

$$p > \frac{C}{R} = \frac{.80}{1} = .80$$

Credit should only be offered if the probability of the collection is in excess of .80.

Let us assume that a credit sale may be made today, that the cash to be collected in the very near future is R, and that the incremental cost of the

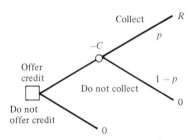

FIGURE 18.1   Tree Diagram for Credit Decision

goods or service sold is C. Let us assume further that either of two events may happen; either the entire amount of R is collected with probability p or nothing is collected. Figure 18.1 shows a tree diagram for the basic situation. We assume that the time value of money may be ignored because the time period is very small. Credit should be offered if $(pR - C)$ is greater than zero or equivalently if p is greater than C/R.

In some situations, C is a reasonably large percentage of R and p is large. This is true with some types of retailing operations such as food distribution. In other situations, C is a small percentage of R and p is small. A beach motel with a large number of empty rooms at 11 P.M. on a weekday has a relatively small C for a given R.

A tree diagram shows the possible decisions, the possible events with each decision and their probabilities of occurrence, and the outcomes associated with these events. The box at the left-hand node in Figure 18.1 indicates a decision is being made. Should credit be offered?

Moving to the right, the circle at the node indicates that a stochastic event occurs (two or more outcomes may occur with their probabilities summing to one). During the credit cycle, either a "collect" event occurs with p probability or a "no-collect" event occurs with $(1 - p)$ probability. If the "no-collect" occurs, the firm loses C associated with the credit offering. If "collect" occurs, the firm receives R.

Calculation of Costs

The incremental cost of the goods or services sold is C. For an airline with empty seats, it would be the cost of an additional meal and free drinks. For an airline with no empty seats, it would be the opportunity cost (full fare lost by accepting a credit-risk customer).

For a bank considering making a loan, the value of C is equal to the number of dollars being loaned. An alternative (equivalent) calculation would use the dollars the bank could have earned by rejecting the risky loan and investing in a riskless security.

A manufacturing firm would want to compute the incremental costs of manufacturing the product, unless the plant is operating at capacity, in which case the relevant cost becomes the lost revenues of rejecting riskless customers in favor of risky customers.

One-Period Case with Time Discounting

We now consider a one-period credit-granting situation (after the sale the customer will not do repeat business with the firm), and so we are only concerned with the profitability of the one transaction. If we let R denote the revenue from the transaction to be collected one period after the sale, C the incremental cost of the goods or services sold, r the time value of money, and p the probability of collection, the transaction should take place if the present value of the expected revenue exceeds the incremental outlays associated with the transaction, that is, if

$$\frac{pR}{(1 + r)} - C > 0 \quad \text{or} \quad p > \frac{C(1 + r)}{R}$$

To illustrate, consider a bank officer deciding whether or not to lend $1,000 to a customer at 8 percent with an expected probability of repayment equal to .9; the bank could invest the $1,000 in the government bond market to earn 6 percent for certain. Solving for the critical probability, p, we have

$$p = \frac{C(1 + r)}{R} = \frac{\$1,000(1 + .06)}{\$1,080} = \frac{\$1,060}{\$1,080} = .98$$

Since the .9 probability of collection is less than $C(1 + r)/R$, the loan should not be undertaken. This example helps to explain why bankers tend to be conservative when they are considering a loan application. Banks work with a very slim margin.

The expected net present value of the transaction for the bank is a negative $83, and again the loan is not acceptable.

Gross Outcomes	Present Value Using .06	Present Value Net of $1,000 Outlay	Probability	Expectation
$1,080	$1,019	$ 19	.9	$17
0	0	− 1,000	.1	− 100
			Expected net present value =	− $83

The example could be made more realistic by assuming that other events are possible, but this would not change the basic analysis.

The same customer who wanted a bank loan might ask a manufacturing firm to sell it $1,000 worth of goods on credit. If the incremental cost of the goods to the firm is $600 and the firm's time value of money is 6 percent and if p still equals .9, then the transaction should be approved by the manufacturer. We have

$$p = \frac{C(1 + r)}{R} = \frac{\$600(1 + .06)}{\$1,000} = \frac{\$636}{\$1,000} = .64$$

Since the probability of collection, .9, is greater than .64, the goods should be sold on credit to the firm. The desirability of offering credit in this instance can be illustrated by computing the manufacturer's expected net present value. Either of two events can occur. The events and their associated payoffs are

Event	Present Value of Cash Flows	Probability	Expectation
No collection	− $600	.1	− $60
Collection	343[a]	.9	309
		Expected net present value =	$249

*$1,000/$1.06 − $600 = $343, assuming that collection is one period after payment of expenses.

The manufacturing firm's accept decision differs from the bank's reject decision because the outcomes for both the favorable and unfavorable events are different, with a lower possible loss and a greater potential profit for the manufacturer. Thus, the size of the profit margin greatly affects the credit decision.

The foregoing illustration highlights the relevant characteristics of the credit-granting decision. The decision depends on the economic affairs of both the potential customer and the seller. The economic health of the customer determines the probability of collection, and the economic situation of the seller sets the critical probability that determines whether the sale is expected to be profitable. If, in the manufacturing example, the plant was at near capacity, so that the relevant cost was the opportunity cost of a lost sale, a reject decision might have been reached. The conclusion is that credit policy cannot be determined independent of operations; credit policy should reflect the incremental costs of production, including any opportunity costs incurred.

Multiperiod Case

Although these models have restrictive assumptions, they can be easily relaxed to increase their usefulness. Our first step is to allow for more than one time period.

Consider the manufacturer's decision but with the modification that, instead of a single period of operation, there will be a second period after the first. In addition, let us assume that the initial probability of collection is .6 so that considering just a single period would lead to a reject decision. However, now add the information that if credit is extended and if collection is made, another sale will be possible with a .9 probability of collection. If a collection takes place, the probability of collection increases. The tree diagram is shown in Figure 18.2.

The three possible outcomes and their probabilities are

Event	× Probability	= Expectations
$667.36	(.6 × .9) =	$360.37
−222.64	(.6 × .1) =	− 13.36
−600.00	.4 =	−240.00
	Expected value =	$107.01

The expected value of offering credit is positive, and thus credit should be offered even though the expected value of the first period's operations is negative. From this illustration, we can conclude that the credit-granting decision must be based on an analysis of the full long-term impact of the decision on the firm and not on its immediate, short-run effects.

Another lesson can also be drawn from the illustration. Note that the table indicates a .4 probability of losing $600 present value, so there is obviously some risk involved here, and we can question the use of the expected net present value criterion being applied. Yet, if what we are determining is whether or not to extend credit to a relatively diverse group of customers, the expected

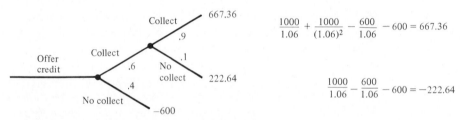

FIGURE 18.2 A Two-Period Credit Decision

net present value criterion applied to one customer may be deemed appropriate when portfolio effects are considered, that is, when we examine how the group behaves in the aggregate. If the outcomes (collect or no collect) are independent between customers of the group, the amount by which the group's actual outcome will differ from the group's expected outcome is smaller than when the outcomes are positively correlated. The choice of a credit policy toward a class of customers will depend on the correlation between customers' repayment patterns as well as the expected monetary value. In the example, it was assumed that the probability of collection in the second credit cycle changed, given a collection in the first cycle. If it is assumed that the probability does not change with collection, then the analysis can be made using only one credit cycle since the decision will not be affected by the sequence of cycles or the duration of the analysis.

Systematic Revision of Probabilities

In the above example the probability of collection in the second time period, given collection in the first period, was arrived at in a nonsystematic manner. Now we shall assume that the probability of collection for the first time period can be defined as x/n. The ratio x/n is the value of the probability of collection that the decision maker believes is applicable for the first time period. The relative size of x and n reflects the strength of belief (small values of x and n indicate considerable uncertainty; i.e., the probability is not believed with strong convictions). After the first period, the decision maker believes the probability of collection is x''/n'', where

$$x'' = x + x'$$
$$n'' = n + n'$$

and n' is the number of times credit is offered and x' is the number of times the credit is collected. For simplicity, we shall assume that if collection is not made in a period, no further credit is offered.

For example, assume that the probability of collection for the first time period is .5 but that we have considerable uncertainty about the estimate so that $x = 1$ and $n = 2$. Thus, $x/n = \frac{1}{2} = .5$. If collection is made in the first cycle, the probability of collecting in period 2 is $\frac{2}{3}$:

$$x'' = 1 + 1 = 2$$
$$n'' = 2 + 1 = 3$$

and

$$\frac{x''}{n''} = \frac{2}{3}$$

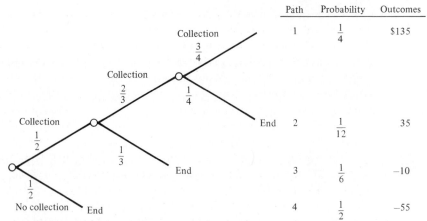

FIGURE 18.3   A Three-Period Credit Decision

Figure 18.3 shows the decision tree for three cycles. We assume a zero time value factor.

Assume that each credit cycle is for $100 where the incremental costs are $55, so that for one time period, the critical p is $55/$100 = .55 and credit would not be offered if we considered only one cycle with a first period probability of collection of only .5.

Each cycle, with collection, leads to a net profit of $45. Each failure to collect results in a loss of $55. The expected value of offering credit is

Path	Outcome	Probability	Expectation
1	$135	.25	$33.75
2	35	.083	2.92
3	−10	.167	−1.67
4	−55	.5	−27.50
		Expected value =	$ 7.50

The expected value is positive, and credit should be offered. Considering more than three periods would further enhance the offering of credit. Adding time value would decrease the present value of the benefits of future periods and tend to make the offering of credit less desirable.

If we had felt confident that the initial probability of collection was .5 then we might have chosen initial values of x = 50 and n = 100. Now the probability of collection would revise very slowly and the offering of credit would not be desirable.

We used a simple method of revising probabilities. Bayes' theorem can be applied in more complex situations to revise probabilities in a much more complicated manner. This type of revision is beyond the scope of this chapter. The important conclusion is that collection experience affects the probability of collection.

Calculation of Outcomes

$45 + $45 + $45 =	$135
$45 + $45 − $55 =	$ 35
$45 − $55 =	− $ 10
− $55 =	− $ 55

Problems in Application

The use of sales price and incremental costs implies that each product being sold having a different incremental profit per dollar of sales theoretically will require a different credit policy.

The prior probability of collection should be adjusted whenever we obtain additional information. Prompt adjustment is desirable to avoid mounting losses. Any information about the financial affairs of the customer (or the customer's customers) may affect the probability of collection.

The suggestions made here lead to a control of the level of all receivables by controlling the individual accounts. We would not say that the total accounts receivable were too large if each individual account was at a proper level. Inspection of the total receivables may give a hint that control of the specific accounts has lapsed, but the total accounts receivable balance (even if related to sales) cannot be definitive evidence in judging how well credit is being managed.

Similarly, the amount of uncollectibles for the period, in total or as a percentage of receivables or sales, cannot be the sole criterion for judging the credit function. A smart credit manager can always reduce uncollectibles by increasing the quality of the customers being serviced, but an elimination of marginal customers may have an undesirable effect on profits. One of the problems of credit management is to ensure that the decision maker adopts the point of view of the firm rather than try to make the credit operation "look good." In many situations, there is a conflict in goals.

The degree of statistical independence of the economic affairs of the customers is another consideration in evaluating the amount of risk associated with the outstanding credit. If the customers are separated geographically and involve relatively different types of industries, then we can assume there is relatively little risk. Selling exclusively to a housing project in Dearborn,

Michigan, is an example of a relatively large amount of dependence (Ford Motor Company contributes heavily to the economics of the area) and a relatively large amount of risk. If automobile production slacked off, a large percentage of the residents might find it difficult to pay their bills. The credit-granting decision could be considered to be a "portfolio" type of investment problem. We have assumed that expected monetary value is a reasonable guide to action; thus we only had to determine the probability of collection for each customer. If we were to consider the portfolio effect, we would have to determine how the probabilities of collection of the customers were related to each other (the covariances).

Other Considerations

We now show how an overall credit policy can be analyzed, using conventional terms and capital budgeting procedures. Suppose that the current credit policy yields these results:

Sales	$200,000 per month
Accounts receivable balance	$200,000
Average collection period	1 month

A modified credit policy is being considered that is expected to generate the following characteristics:

Sales	$210,000 per month
Accounts receivable balance	$420,000
Average collection period	2 months

We want to determine if the change in credit policy is profitable for a company that requires a return of 1 percent per month on its funds.

Suppose that the incremental cost of an additional dollar of sales is $.80. Then sales of $210,000 per month will result in immediate costs of $168,000. The collection of the $210,000 will take place at time 2. With the present credit policy, there is an immediate outlay of $160,000 followed by the collection of $200,000 at time 1.

We can compare the incremental cash flows associated with the two credit policies. This is done in Table 18.1, which is based on the convention that the goods are produced and sold in period 0 and that the sales revenues are collected either one or two periods later (one with the present policy and two with the proposed policy). The discount rate used is 1 percent per month, the company's required return.

The cash flow analysis provides a relatively easily understood approach to the

TABLE 18.1   Comparison of Two Credit Policies

	Cash Flow of Month			
	0	*1*	*2*	*Net Present Value*
Proposed	− $168,000		+ $210,000	$37,862
Present	− 160,000	+ $200,000		38,020
Incremental:				
Proposed less present	− $8,000	− $200,000	+ $210,000	− $158

solution. In this case the increase in sales resulting from the change in policy is not large enough to justify the proposed relaxation of credit terms.

Although the analysis is only for one credit cycle, the results are consistent with those that would be obtained if the period of analysis were to be enlarged.

Aging of Accounts Receivable

In judging a credit-granting collection policy, several sets of calculations can be made. One of the more important of these is an aging of accounts receivable. This is a calculation of the average age of the accounts receivable. Each accounts receivable is weighted by the time since sale, all these weighted receivables are summed, and then an average is computed by dividing the total by the total receivables.

EXAMPLE 18.1 ───

It is now December 31 and the accounts receivable account reveals the following information:

Customer	Amount	Date of Sale
A	$10,000	Dec. 1
B	20,000	Oct. 1
C	5,000	July 1

The aging calculation in terms of months would be

Customer	Amount	Age (in months)	Weighted Receivable
A	$10,000	1	$ 10,000
B	20,000	3	60,000
C	5,000	6	30,000
	$35,000		$100,000

The average age is 2.86 months:

$$\text{average age} = \frac{\$100{,}000}{\$35{,}000} = 2.86 \text{ months}$$

If customer C had paid, the average age would have been 2.33 months:

$$\text{average age} = \frac{\$70{,}000}{\$30{,}000} = 2.33 \text{ months}$$

Other Measures

There are several other measures associated with receivables. For example, one can compute a turnover of the receivable account, by dividing the sales by the average accounts receivable:

$$\text{AR turnover} = \frac{\text{sales}}{\text{average AR}}$$

All things being equal, a firm would want a higher accounts receivable turnover. Unfortunately, improving the turnover by decreasing the average accounts receivable is apt to affect sales adversely. A second calculation is to compute the number of days sales that are on hand at the end of the time period. Dividing annual sales by 365 gives the daily sales, and dividing that number into the accounts receivable balance gives the number of days' sales on hand in the form of receivables:

$$\text{number of days' receivables} = \frac{\text{accounts receivable}}{\text{sales per day}}$$

These measures of performance have to be used very carefully. Conclusions as to goodness or badness are difficult to make since an improvement in any of these measures can have second-order effects on profits that may be negative. For example, we know that the smaller the number of days' receivables on hand the better, but we do not know if it is desirable to shorten the terms of credit to reduce this measure. The effect on sales and profits may be too adverse.

Inventory and Finance

There are two relevant financial aspects of inventory. First, the accounting measures of inventory stocks and flows affects both the income statement and balance sheet. Second, the level of inventory held affects the amount of capital needed as well as the income of the period. The availability of inventory affects the likelihood of making a sale as well as the costs of carrying inventory.

The determination of the optimum level of inventory under conditions of certainty is the result of balancing the costs of ordering with the costs of carrying inventory. With uncertainty, the firm also has to balance the costs of having too much inventory with the costs of having too little. Inadequate inventory levels lead to disruptions in production and lost sales opportunities. Excessive inventories tie up capital in assets that are not earning an adequate return. Excessive and leftover inventory can lose value through obsolescence and cause excessive storage cost.

Inventory Models Versus "Just in Time"

The competitive success of Japanese industry has given an aura of correctness to everything that is done by Japanese management, just as in the post–World War II era, U.S. management could do no wrong.

One managerial technique that has been exported from Japan to the United States is the "just in time" inventory model. Rather than having excessively large safety stocks, the next shipment arrives just as the last unit is used. This reduction in inventory levels results in increased profits. Also, by reducing set-up costs (including set-up time), the order size (or production run) is further reduced, again resulting in less inventory.

Despite the great appeal of a zero inventory decision model, we will take the position that the optimum level of inventory will depend on the facts and must be determined. A "just in time" inventory procedure may be just right where the instantaneous supply is certain or when there is zero cost of being short of inventory. With other facts, a just in time policy may not be attractive. Imagine flying across the Atlantic Ocean in a Boeing 747 that had just enough fuel to reach the other side of the ocean if the tail wind is a constant 40 miles per hour. Most of us would prefer a margin for error arising from carrying extra fuel.

An Inventory Model

Although inventories are held for speculation (the price is expected to increase or a strike is anticipated), we shall only consider the situation when inventories are held for transactions (either for production or for sales).

First, we assume that the rate of usage (demand) and all other factors are known with certainty.

The economic order quantity model (EOQ) is the most simple and most widely used of all the formal mathematical inventory models. It gives exact answers that are correct if the assumptions are valid. This model will be used in the next chapter to solve the cash problem.

Let

K = the order cost (per order)
r = the carrying cost (per unit per time period)
D = the total expected demand (during the time period)

If we define Q to be the optimal order size (the EOQ), then the average inventory on hand is $Q/2$. Total carrying costs for the period can now be defined to be $r(Q/2)$. The number of orders required is D/Q, and, hence, purchase order costs are $K(D/Q)$. Total cost, TC, for the period considering holding and ordering costs is given by

$$TC = r\left(\frac{Q}{2}\right) + K\left(\frac{D}{Q}\right)$$

As Q increases, the carrying cost, $r(Q/2)$, increases. But as Q increases, the cost of ordering, $K(D/Q)$, decreases.

To minimize this expression requires that its derivative be taken, set equal to zero, and solved for Q.*

$$Q = \left(\frac{2KD}{r}\right)^{1/2}$$

Assumptions implicit in the EOQ model are

1. A known, constant demand over the period and known delivery times
2. No change in holding costs per unit or order costs
3. No change in prices through time and no quantity discounts

If K (order costs) is equal to or close to zero, then Q will be equal to or close to zero. If set-up or order costs are very small, then the amount ordered will

* $$\frac{dTC}{dQ} = \frac{r}{2} - \frac{DK}{Q^2} = 0$$

The optimum order size is.

$$\frac{r}{2} = \frac{DK}{Q^2} \qquad \text{and} \qquad \frac{rQ}{2} = \frac{DK}{Q}$$

or

$$Q = \left(\frac{2KD}{r}\right)^{1/2}$$

The two components of total cost are equal if Q is the optimum order size.

be very small and the resulting inventory, which is $Q/2$, will be very small. The "just in time" rule would be effective with small amounts of inventory arriving each time.

The Value of Inventory Reductions

What is it worth to a firm to reduce its average inventory by $1 million? The answer is $1 million plus any reductions in costs such as insurance, storage, taxes, and so on. The economic incentive to have a theoretically correct inventory policy is very large.

Inventory Levels and Uncertainty

If we relax the assumption of certainty, then the firm will want to have inventory to prevent stockouts.

Let:

k_u = the cost per unit of not having enough inventory (cost of underage)

k_o = the cost per unit of having excess inventory (cost of overage)

Define p to be the probability that the next unit of inventory is demanded and $(1 - p)$ that it is not demanded. We assume that if the unit has not been ordered, it cannot be reordered when the actual demand is established.

We want the expected cost of underage to be equal to the expected cost of overage:

pk_u = the expected cost of having an unit demanded and not having it

$(1 - p)k_o$ = the expected cost of not having an unit demanded but having it in inventory

At the margin,

$$pk_u = (1 - p)k_o$$

Solving for p yields

$$p = \frac{k_o}{k_o + k_u}$$

EXAMPLE 18.2

Assume that

$$k_o = \$20$$
$$k_u = \$80$$

since each unit costing $20 can be sold for $100. A leftover unit is worthless. The probability of demand is

Units Demand D	Probability	Probability of Demand Being at Least as Large as D
0	.10	1.00
1	.20	.90
2	.30	.70
3	.20	.40
4	.10	.20
5	.10	.10
6	0	0

Solving for p, we obtain

$$p = \frac{k_o}{k_o + k_u} = \frac{20}{20 + 80} = .2$$

The number of units that should be obtained is 3 or 4 (the fourth unit does not add to profit). The expected profit of ordering three or four units is $140:

Order 4 Units

Demanded	Units Sold	Profits on Units Sold	Leftover Units	Cost of Leftover Units	Net Profit	Probability
0	0	0	4	$80	− $ 80	.10
1	1	$ 80	3	60	20	.20
2	2	160	2	40	120	.30
3	3	240	1	20	220	.20
4	4	320	0	0	320	.10
5	4	320	0	0	320	.10
					Expected profit = $140	

Order 3 Units

Demanded	Units Sold	Profits on Units Sold	Leftover Units	Cost of Leftover Units	Net Profit	Probability
0	0	0	3	$60	− $ 60	.10
1	1	$ 80	2	40	40	.20
2	2	160	1	20	140	.30
3	3	240	0	0	240	.20
4	3	240	0	0	240	.10
5	3	240	0	0	240	.10
					Expected profit = $140	

The expected profit calculation for ordering two units is $120:

Order 2 Units

Demanded	Units Sold	Profits on Units Sold	Leftover Units	Cost of Leftover Units	Net Profit	Probability
0	0	0	2	$40	− $ 40	.10
1	1	$ 80	1	20	60	.20
2	2	160	0	0	160	.30
3	2	160	0	0	160	.20
4	2	160	0	0	160	.10
5	2	160	0	0	160	.10
					Expected profit = $120	

If we allow reordering but the time to replenish inventory is not known, then there will be need for safety stock.

From a finance point of view, every dollar that is released from inventory saves a dollar of capital. Unfortunately, we cannot then conclude that it is desirable to reduce inventory. Management must balance the costs and benefits of inventory reduction. Carrying inventory has a cost, but so does excessive reordering or being caught short.

In some cases it might be feasible to reduce the ordering costs or the downtime associated with production changeovers. Uncertainty as to timing of replacement can also be reduced with good management. Thus the inventory models and the values of the variables should not be taken as given, but rather the possibility of changing them to improve efficiency should be investigated.

Saxon Industries

The 10-year financial review of Saxon Industries, a company listed on the NYSE, showed 9 consecutive years of profits (from 1972 to 1980). The profit in 1980 was $5,373,000 on sales of $709,601,000.

In 1981 the company filed for bankruptcy under Chapter XI (seeking protection of the court from its creditors).

On February 23, 1983, Saxon Industries reported the final results of operations for 1981. There was a $322 million net operating loss before tax ($299 million after tax) and a stockholders' deficit of $174 million.

The reported profits had been acheived by understating the cost of goods sold and overstating the inventories. The auditors checking the inventory were fooled by management.

In the real world things are not always as they seem.

Conclusions

The credit-granting decision can be made in the context of the risks and returns of the incremental cash flows arising from alternative courses of action. Since our major objective is to highlight this basic methodology, we have not considered the difficult task of determining the input data that the models require. We have found that the credit granting decisions rests very heavily on (1) the firm's time value of money, (2) the incremental profits arising from the sale, (3) the extent to which the risk associated with a single creditor is mitigated by the degree to which one creditor's paying behavior is correlated with other creditors' behavior, and (4) the extent to which the analysis considers the total (long-run) impact of granting credit rather than its immediate (one-time period) impact. Finally, we note that since the credit granting or the change in credit policy decision can be characterized in terms of incremental cash flows, its desirability can be ascertained using capital budgeting techniques.

Credit management requires balancing the expected gains from sales against the possible loss if the account receivable is not collected. A good credit policy will result in some uncollectible accounts, but it should also result in sales that increase profits despite the fact that the collection might be a risky operation. We have offered here a set of models that quantify the expected value of future credit opportunities, thereby reflecting an important factor in the credit decision. If credit is not granted today, we not only lose this period's sales but also the sales of future periods.

Implicit in any credit decision is a probability of making the collection. We have suggested that it might be appropriate to use an a priori probability distribution on p, the estimated probability of collection, and then revise this distribution as new information about collections or defaults becomes available.

Although our a priori probabilities are subjective, we can use information regarding the financial affairs of the customer in selecting these probabilities. The use of the method presented here could then alter the decision from being entirely subjective to one that effectively incorporates projections of the future and revises these projections as additional information concerning collection is obtained.

Credit decisions are interesting since they give us an opportunity to consider the interrelationships of finance and other areas of operations such as marketing and production. There is evidence that the top-level managers of corporations neglect credit decisions, with the result that in many situations, credit policy decisions are made by the wrong managers with the wrong objectives in mind, based on the wrong set of information. Credit decisions are frequently made by a relatively low level of management and are only reviewed when some major event occurs such as when it becomes obvious that uncollectible accounts have reached disastrous proportions or when the marketing manager complains about the number of customers who have been refused credit. Credit policy decisions deserve more attention.

We have investigated some basic inventory models that illustrate the fact that a zero inventory level is not likely to be optimum.

The basic lesson to be learned is that each working capital item requires its own optimization level, depending on the economic facts affecting it. If the general level of working capital resulting from optimizing the subcomponents is not optimum, then additional adjustments may be necessary.

In 1985 the "liquidification of current assets" (selling current assets or using them as loan collateral) expanded rapidly. For example, banks sold car loans which were then used as the basis of a new security (appropriately called "cars") which was issued by financial intermediaries with the car loans as the underlying asset.

Banks that accept unusual assets as collateral face some special problems. They must verify the existence of the assets (quantity and quality) and be concerned about possible changes in their market value. Banks accepting salad oil, gemstones, and oil reserves as collateral have become famous because of the problems they subsequently encountered.

For example, Swiss banks made $45 million of loans backed, they thought, by $90 million of collateral in the form of rubies, emeralds, sapphires, etc. In 1982, when the loans were not paid, the bankers discovered that their collateral had a market value of only $5 million.

Review Problem 18.1

The Morris Company has applied to the Great Manufacturing Company for $10,000 of credit. A careful evaluation of the Morris Company's financial statements leads to the following conclusions:

Event	Probability
Payment within 30 days	.00
Payment 12 months from sale	.70
No payment	.30

The following information applies to the product for which Morris wants the credit line:

Cost of goods sold	$.70 per dollar of sale (gross price)
Variable selling costs	$.05 per dollar of sale (gross price)

The manufacturing of the product consists of $.15 fixed costs and $.55 variable costs per dollar of sales. The cost of money of the firm is .10 per year.

(a) Should $10,000 of credit be offered to Morris, assuming that there is significant excess productive capacity? Show calculations.
(b) Should credit be offered if there are alternative customers and there is very little excess capacity and capacity is fixed over the relevant time period? Explain.

Solution to Review Problem 18.1

(a) The cost of goods sold includes variable costs of $.55 and variable selling costs of $.05 for total variable cost of $.60.

$$\$10,000 \, p = \$6,000(1.10)$$
$$p = .66$$

Offer credit since the probability of collection is .70, and this is larger than .66.

(b) The opportunity cost becomes $10,000 if the other customers pay cash.

PROBLEMS

1. A decision has to be made for a one-shot credit situation. The product sells for $100 per unit. The incremental cost of the product is $40. There is only a .6 probability of collection. The collection will take place one period after manufacture. The time value of the money is .10.
   (a) Assuming that there is excess productive capacity, should the credit be offered for one unit of product? *yes*
   (b) At what probability of collection would you be indifferent to offering credit? *, 44*

2. (Problem 1 continued) The productive capacity could be used to make another product that will realize an incremental profit of $50 for certain in the amount of time that the product being considered in Problem 1 will take to be manufactured. There is no excess capacity.
   Should the credit be granted? *no*

3. A decision has to be made in a one-shot credit situation. The product sells for $100 per unit, and the incremental cost of the product is $40 per unit. There is a .3 probability of collection. The collection and production will take place close enough together so that time value consideration can be ignored.
   (a) Assuming that there is excess productive capacity, should credit be offered for one unit of product?
   (b) Assume that if credit is offered and if collection is made, the customer will purchase a second unit. For the second unit, given collection on the first, the probability of collection is .9. Now would you offer credit for the first unit? Assume that the two transactions occur so close to one another that the time value of money can be ignored.

4. Kreskie's financial vice-president has suggested that the firm (a retailer) might be better off terminating its own credit system and accepting bank credit cards. As a financial staff analyst, he has asked you to determine all the factors that should be taken into account in reaching a decision.
   List these factors.

5. List the following categories of businesses in terms of the tightness of their credit policies and explain why: banker, food wholesaler, food retailer, novelty manufacturer, dress shop operator.

6. The credit manager of the ABC Company regularly ages his accounts receivable. Each account is aged by computing a weighted average duration:

$$\text{age of account} = \frac{\sum\limits_{t=1}^{\infty} tC_t}{\sum\limits_{t=1}^{\infty} C_t}$$

where C_t is the amount of the receivable originating in the tth month measured from the present. The following calculations were made for two customers:

Time Since Sale	Amount Due	
(Months)	Customer X	Customer Y
1	20,000	10,000
3		30,000
12	2,000	
	22,000	40,000

$$\text{Age (X)} = \frac{1 \times 20{,}000 + 12 \times 2{,}000}{22{,}000} = \frac{44{,}000}{22{,}000} = 2 \text{ months}$$

$$\text{Age (Y)} = \frac{1 \times 10{,}000 + 3 \times 30{,}000}{40{,}000} = \frac{100{,}000}{40{,}000} = 2.5 \text{ months}$$

The credit manager concluded that X was a better risk than Y, since the age of the X account was 2 months while the age of the Y account was 2.5 months.

The credit terms offered by ABC are that the full amount has to be paid within 90 days.

Comment on the manner in which the results of the computations were used.

7. Assume that a decision has to be made for a one-shot credit situation. The product sells for $1000 per unit. The average cost of the product is $800 and the incremental cost is $300. Analysis indicates that there is a .55 probability of collection.

   Should the credit be offered for the one unit assuming the plant has excess capacity? What would the probability of collection have to be to change your decision?

8. (Problem 7 continued)   Assume that the probability of collection is .25 but that, if collection is made, the probability of collection on a second sale is .6. If collection is not made, the probability of collection is .1 on the second sale. Only two sales (in sequence) can be made.

   Should the credit be offered? Draw a decision tree illustrating the decision. Assume that if credit is offered, the second sale is made after information is obtained about the first collection.

9. (Problem 7 continued)   Assume that the probability of collection is .25 and that we have a beta prior distribution with parameters x equal to 1 and n equal to 4. Ignore the time value of money. Also, if no collection occurs, no further credit is offered.

Prepare an analysis that shows how we might arrive at a decision assuming the period of analysis is

(a) One period.

(b) Two periods.

(c) Four periods.

10. (Problem 7 continued)   Assume that the time value of money is .04 and that each transaction will be separated by one time period.

For the four-period case, determine whether credit should be offered. Assume that the first credit and collection occurs instantaneously.

11. The Mini Department Store sells to a middle-class clientele. Because of the competitive situation in its area and aggressive effective marketing strategies, it has enjoyed a somewhat larger markup than the average department store. The markup of most items is 40 percent of retail, and some are 50 percent. It has traditionally handled its own credit arrangements, deciding who should receive credit. Generally, it has adopted a lenient credit policy, and at times top management has thought credit has been lax. Bad-debt losses have been significant, especially when local industry has been adversely affected by economic events. Credit sales are generally collected within 60 days.

The Mini Department Store has been approached by a major bank that has a credit card organization. The bank would handle the credit arrangements for the department store by issuing its credit card to eligible customers. Payments would then be made directly by store customers to the bank just as any other credit card holder. The bank would pay the store 95 percent of the sale within 30 days of the sale and would aim to collect the balance within 60 days.

Currently, customers buying $800,000 of merchandise (retail value) per year apply for credit and receive it. The bank would take as its charge a fixed percentage (5 percent) of the total credit sales and would be responsible for making collections. The store has computed that the payment to the bank for credit service would be less than the costs ($150,000 per year) of administering the credit department. Credit sales are running at $2 million per year. The store has a cost of money of 12 percent per year.

(a) What factors should the store consider in making its decision?

(b) What decision should it make?

12. The ABC Company uses a multiperiod credit model when a prior probability of $p = x/n$ is established and the probability is revised based on credit sales that are paid. Assume that a collection increases x and n by 1. Assume that the prior distribution on p has parameters $x = 3, n = 5$. The expected probability of collection is $x/n = 3/5 = .6$. The selling price R equals $10,000$, and the incremental cost is $7,000$ per unit.

(a) Considering one cycle, should credit be offered? *Reject*

(b) Considering four cycles (a zero time value factor), should credit be offered? Assume that credit stops if a failure occurs. *Reject*

13. (Problem 12 continued)   Now assume that p is again .6 but that $x = 1.2$ and $n = 2$. We are less certain about the initial probability of collection.

(a) What is the expected value of offering credit?

(b) Do the analysis for four periods. Assume that a collection increases both x and n by 1.

REFERENCES

Barzman, Sol. *Everyday Credit Checking: A Practical Guide*, rev. ed. New York: National Association of Credit Management, 1980.

Beranek, W. *Analysis for Finanical Decision*. Homewood, Ill.: Richard D. Irwin, Inc., 1963, Chap. 10.

Bierman, H., Jr., C. P. Bonini, and W. H. Hausman. *Quantitative Analysis for Business Decisions*, (7th ed. Homewood, Ill.: Richard D. Irwin, Inc., 1986).

Cyert, R. M., H. J. Davidson, and G. L. Thompson. "Estimation of the Allowance for Doubtful Accounts by Markov Chains." *Management Science*, April 1962, 287–303.

Cyert, R. M., and G. L. Thompson. "Selecting a Portfolio of Credit Risks by Markov Chains." *Journal of Businesss*, January 1968, 39–46.

Dyl, Edward A., "Another Look at the Evaluation of Investment in Accounts Receivable," *Financial Management*, Winter 1977, 67–70.

Edmister, Rober O., and Gary G. Schlarbaum, "Credit Policy in Lending Institutions," *Journal of Financial and Quantitative Analysis*, June 1974, 335–356.

Eisenbeis, Robert A., "Pitfalls in the Application of Discriminant Analysis in Business, Finance and Economics." *Journal of Finance*, June 1977, 875–900.

Greer, C. C. "The Optimal Credit Acceptance Policy." *Journal of Financial and Quantitative Analysis*, December 1967, 399–415.

Herbst, Anthony F. "Some Empirical Evidence on the Determinants of Trade Credit at the Industry Level of Aggregation." *Journal of Financial and Quantitative Analysis*. June 1974, 377–394.

Hill, Ned C., and Kenneth D. Riener. "Determining the Cash Discount in the Firm's Credit Policy." *Financial Management*, Spring 1979, 68–73.

Joy, Maurice O., and John O. Tollefson. "On the Financial Applications of Discriminant Analysis." *Journal of Financial and Quantitative Analysis*, December 1975, 723–740.

Kim, Yong H., and Joseph C. Atkins, "Evaluating Investments in Accounts Receivable: A Wealth Maximization Framework," *Journal of Finance*, May 1978, 403–412.

Lewellen, W. G., and R. W. Johnson. "Better Ways to Monitor Accounts Receivable." *Harvard Business Review*, May–June 1972), 101–109.

Mehta, D. "The Formulation of Credit Policy Models." *Management Science*, October 1968, 30–50.

Weingartner, H. M. "Concepts and Utilization of Credit-Scoring Techniques." *Banking*, February 1966, 51–58.

Weston, J. Fred, and Pham D. Tuan. "Comment on Analysis of Credit Policy Changes." *Financial Management*, Winter 1980, 59–63.

Chapter 19

Managing Working Capital: The Cash Position

Major Topics

1. Working capital as a safety stock.
2. Cash decisions and decisions affecting cash.
3. The line of credit decision.

Working Capital

The management of working capital is based on two conflicting objectives. The first is the desire to have a safety stock of liquid assets that will enable the firm to survive unforeseen difficulties. When a very large Mexican corporation sold its accounts receivables to finance long-term investments, it removed a possible source of immediate cash. This lack of flexibility helped lead to its bankruptcy. The second objective is to apply a series of optimizing models with the objective of minimizing the costs of carrying working capital and maximizing the firm's profits.

A Safety Stock of Working Capital

Every firm faces the possibility of one or more bad years where operating losses lead to a net drain on assets and capital. Usually, the period of red ink is short enough, or the necessary credit is available, so that the firm avoids bankruptcy.

The advantage of having working capital that can be readily converted into cash is that this is another way by which the firm can gain the liquidity necessary to survive the period of unprofitable operations. If you are willing to make the necessary assumptions, you can prepare a mathematical model showing how different levels of working capital will affect the probability of bankruptcy. Unfortunately, having more working capital than is needed for operations has a cost (capital is being used, thus there is an interest cost). In this and the next chapter we shall consider models for optimizing the amount of working capital held for operations.

Managing Cash

When AT&T raises $400 million in the bond market or U.S. Steel issues $150 million of debentures, how does management arrive at these particular amounts? Although the advice of investment bankers may set limits, management has the responsibility for determining how much cash will be raised and how that cash will be invested until needed. The formulations of this chapter, even the models based on the most simplifying assumptions, are practical, easily applied tools that are useful in managing the cash position of an enterprise. Given the rate of need for financial resources, the cost of raising funds, and the net borrowing cost, there is an exact answer to the question as to how much capital should be raised at a particular moment. The appropriate mathematical model gives this answer.

Decisions Affecting Cash

Decisions affecting cash and short-term marketable securities are influenced by an interesting mixture of facts and subjective judgments. The treasurer of a corporation may know the cost of borrowing from a bank, but these facts (the explicit terms of the loan) are only part of the information required. There are also the implicit costs associated with issuing more debt; there are also subjective benefits arising from having more cash on deposit in the bank (thus being in a safer position).

The treasurer may decide to buy some insurance against financial illiquidity by arranging and paying for a credit agreement committing a bank to lend up to an agreed-upon sum. The value of this insurance is difficult to measure, since the benefit consists of an increase in the probability of being able to obtain cash if it is needed. What would be the cost to the firm if the funds were not obtained? These values and costs may be difficult to measure.

The decisions affecting cash and readily marketable securities may be classified as follows:

1. Bank relation decisions.
2. Cash decisions (the term *cash* includes demand deposits).
3. Marketable security (near-cash) decisions.

Bank Relation Decisions

The terminology used in discussing the arrangements between borrower and bank for future borrowings is confusing. Among the terms encountered are *line of credit*, *credit agreement*, and *committed line of credit*. We define a line of credit as an arrangement whereby the bank agrees to consider in a favorable manner a loan application but does not make a legally binding commitment to lend the funds. The company may pay for the line of credit by agreeing to leave compensating balances (idle deposits) in the bank. If the financial affairs of the firm deteriorate, or if the bank does not have the lending capacity, the bank may refuse to lend, but it would make efforts to act in a manner consistent with the credit agreement. The firm benefits from a credit agreement by having established preliminary relations with the bank and indicating an intention to borrow in the near future. A sudden attempt to borrow might be unsettling to the banker, who might think that the borrowing was being made from a position of weakness. The bank benefits by having a customer indicate a desire to borrow (this increases the probability that the borrower will obtain the funds from the bank), and the information will help the bank's planning.

A credit agreement or a committed line of credit implies a firm commitment by the bank to lend the funds. This commitment cannot be dropped by the bank during the term of the agreement just because the financial affairs of the corporation seeking to borrow are not as good as the bank would like. To obtain this firm commitment, the corporation will have to pay, either by keeping larger compensating balances or by paying an explicit dollar amount. The fee paid is frequently a percentage of the total commitment, which has not yet been taken down (borrowed) by the firm.

The terms of loan are not necessarily affected by the presence or absence of an agreement between the corporation and the bank. Generally, the terms of the loan will be established at the time of the borrowing, but this can be modified by agreement between the parties.

In making the credit agreement decision, the corporation cannot be sure of

1. How much it will want to borrow.
2. Whether it could have obtained the funds anyway and did not need a formal agreement with the bank.

Thus we have all the elements of decision making under uncertainty. We do not know which state of nature will prevail. How much will be needed and could it be obtained without an agreement? In addition, we do not know for sure the consequences of not being able to obtain the funds when they are needed. In fact, we may find it difficult to determine the costs of a particular agreement if the agreement is paid for by leaving more funds on deposit. The compensating balances may be required in return for more than one bank service, and the valid measure of the cost is the opportunity cost for the cash.

Cash Decisions

The basic cash decisions made by a corporation are (1) determining when cash should be obtained and how much new cash should be obtained from sources outside the firm, and (2) determining whether marketable securities should be purchased or sold.

A corporation will hold cash (including bank balances) for three reasons:

1. To conform with the bank's request that balances be carried. These compensating balances serve to pay the bank for account activity, services, a line of credit, and bank loans outstanding and in compensation for the float arising from the corporation's account. The float arises because the bank has credited the account for a deposited check but has not yet collected from the party paying the check.
2. To finance transactions involving normal operations or capital asset acquisitions.
3. To prepare for contingencies.

The amount to be held to satisfy the banks with which the company does business is determined either by meeting all the requests of the bank, since they seem fair, or by negotiating with the bank. The corporation will attempt to minimize the amount sitting idle in the banks but must recognize that the bank's desire to be compensated for its services is natural. The bank will use the average account balance in computing the profitability of the account and in effect gives the corporation "credit" for the amount of cash sitting in the account.

If we assume that the firm is reasonably large, the amount of cash held to provide for transactions should be no more than the amount necessary to pay today's bills. The remainder of the near-cash assets should be in the form of interest-earning, readily marketable securities. A firm can enter and leave the marketable securities market with great ease and low cost. An assistant treasurer can be given the task of selling the amount of securities necessary to meet the day's bills or investing the amount of excess cash.

The third reason offered for holding cash is to anticipate an unusual event. We argue that a firm should not hold cash for contingencies. It may want to hold near-cash assets such as marketable securities (or investment-type securities) for minor cash needs that may arise. It is more difficult for a corporation to provide for major cash shortfalls by holding liquid assets. For example, corporations would find it difficult to hold enough liquid assets to provide for the survival of the firm during a major depression or war. The amount of liquid assets held for minor surprise cash needs will depend on the desires of the owners and managers to be safe compared with their desire to invest the funds in higher-earning but less liquid assets.

We conclude that a firm should hold cash to satisfy its banks (the compensating balance amount may be determined in negotiation with the bank) and for transactions (an amount equal to the most immediate payments coming due). Excess cash should be invested in marketable securities until it can be used to finance operations or the acquisition of long-lived assets. The desire for liquidity should lead to the holding of readily marketable securities; it should not lead to the holding of cash.

Timing Strategies

One of the prime responsibilities of a corporate financial officer is to ensure the availability of cash for maintaining operations and executing the budgeted investment plans of the corporation. Growth companies must often turn to sources of outside financing (e.g., banks, insurance companies, and debt or equity markets) to acquire sufficient cash to meet needs created by capital expenditures and increases in net working capital.

Given a projected time pattern of cash needs, the financial officer can meet these cash needs in a number of ways. At one extreme, the firm may obtain funds by borrowing short term (e.g., drawing upon its lines of credit) until the balance warrants a long-term issue to pay it off, as illustrated in Figure 19.1. At the other extreme, the firm may obtain long-term capital in advance of its cash needs, placing the idle balances in marketable securities until needed, as illustrated in Figure 19.2. The best strategy is likely to be a combination of the two, as depicted in Figure 19.3. In all cases, the transaction costs of obtaining the long-term funds must be offset against the net interest expense incurred in obtaining long-term funds prior to their use. Figure 19.2 illustrates the strategy in which acquisition of the cash precedes the need for the cash. This is the easiest strategy to formulate mathematically. Since we have decided to follow a strategy of obtaining long-term funds before the time of usage, two decisions must be reached. First, how much cash shall be raised per issue of new securities? Second, once this cash has been raised, what should be done with it until it is needed? In answering these questions, we shall assume that

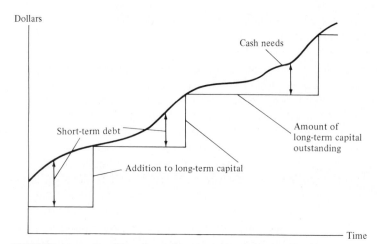

FIGURE 19.1   Need Cash and Issue Long-Term Debt

the firm has a constant usage rate of cash and that management expects future interest rates to equal present interest rates; we shall also assume that the alternative to holding cash is to hold a single type of marketable security paying a known interest rate and that future cash needs are known with certainty. Although these assumptions are somewhat restrictive, they allow us to deal with the essence of the problem in a relatively understandable manner. Extensions are easy to imagine, and books have been written on the topic.*

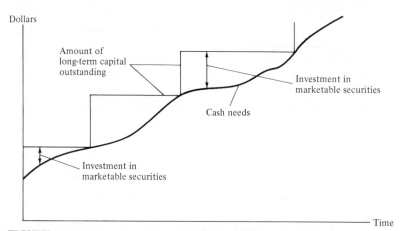

FIGURE 19.2   Issue Long-Term Debt and Then Have Need

* For example, see Yair E. Orgler, *Cash Management* (Belmont, Calif.: F. W. Wadsworth, Inc., 1970); Robert F. Calman, *Linear Programming and Cash Management/CASH ALPHA* (Cambridge, Mass.: M.I.T. Press, 1968); and K. V. Smith, *Guide to Working Capital Management* (New York: McGraw-Hill Book Company, 1979).

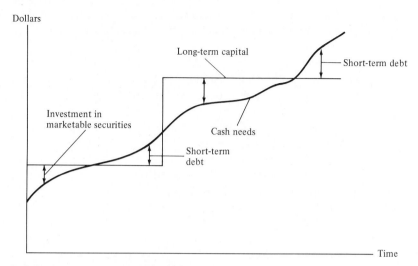

FIGURE 19.3   A Mixed Strategy

These extensions employ the same basic logic and economic rationale that we will utilize here.

Where the cash needs of a firm are seasonal, the firm has another related decision. This decision is illustrated in Figure 19.4. Strategy 1 of Figure 19.4 leads to sufficient permanent capital, so that the seasonal cash needs are met by internal resources. When there is slack, the excess cash is invested in short-term securities. Strategy 2 has a minimum of long-term capital, and the short-term seasonal cash needs are satisfied by short-term borrowing.

Short-term borrowing has three basic uses. It may serve as a substitute for a buffer stock of working capital against financial crises, it may be used in sequence with long-term debt to supply the cash needed to finance the growth of a firm, and it can be used to supply the temporary (seasonal) cash needs of a firm.

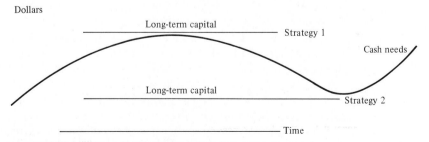

FIGURE 19.4   Two Cash Strategies

Acquiring the Cash from Long-Term Sources

We want to develop a strategy for acquiring cash from long-term sources. Suppose that the firm has decided to finance its cash needs over the planning period by using long-term debt. We use the following notation

C = the amount of cash to be raised over the planning period by issuing debt instruments (dollars per year).

r = the difference between the interest cost of long-term debt capital, k_i, and return earned in idle funds, i.

K = the fixed cost of raising debt (e.g., legal fees); this cost is independent of the size of an issue and is a cost per issue.

b = the variable cost per dollar of issuing debt other than interest charges (for example, underwriting fees); this cost is a function of the size of the issue (dollars of expense per dollar of debt issued).

Q = the size of each separate debt issue.

T = the total cost of acquiring cash (flotation costs plus interest charges) over the planning period (dollars per year).

The total cost of acquiring cash over the planning period is the sum of acquisition costs plus interest charges minus the interest earned on idle balances:

$$T = K \frac{C}{Q} + bC + k_i \frac{C + Q}{2} - i \frac{Q}{2} \tag{19.1}$$

where $K(C/Q)$ is the fixed costs incurred with C/Q flotations per year, bC is the total variable flotation cost, $k_i(C + Q)/2$ is the total annual interest expense, and $i(Q/2)$ is the total interest earned on the idle cash (Q is received and $Q/2$ is the average balance). The initial debt is Q, and the final debt level is C, so the average debt level is $(C + Q)/2$ and the total interest cost is $k_i(C + Q)/2$.

Since the amount of cash to be raised, C, is assumed to be given by the operating and capital requirements of the business, the only decision the finance officer has to make is to determine the size of each debt issue.

It is important to look behind the arithmetic to the logic of the model. Two basic types of costs are being incurred: the cost of acquiring the funds and the cost of holding idle funds. The optimal decision strikes a balance between these two costs. If Q is small, we will approach the market often; this means that we will not pay a great deal of interest on idle funds, but we will pay substantial transaction charges. If Q is large, the total cost of acquiring the funds will be small, since only a few flotations will occur, but idle cash will be sitting around and interest will have to be paid on it. In Figure 19.5 we

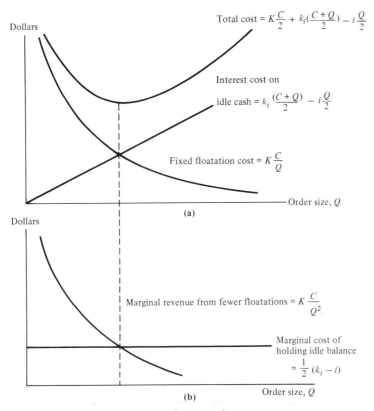

Dollars

$$\text{Total cost} = K\frac{C}{2} + k_i(\frac{C+Q}{2}) - i\frac{Q}{2}$$

$$\text{Interest cost on idle cash} = k_i\frac{(C+Q)}{2} - i\frac{Q}{2}$$

$$\text{Fixed floatation cost} = K\frac{C}{Q}$$

Order size, Q

(a)

Dollars

$$\text{Marginal revenue from fewer floatations} = K\frac{C}{Q^2}$$

$$\text{Marginal cost of holding idle balance} = \frac{1}{2}(k_i - i)$$

Order size, Q

(b)

FIGURE 19.5   Optimum Bond Issue Size

have graphed the components of the cost function that vary with Q, the interest cost on idle cash, and the fixed flotation cost. Note that the optimal Q falls precisely at the point where the two cost curves cross (this results because of the functional form of the cost curves). At the optimum, the marginal "revenue" of less frequent flotation (fewer dollars spent on flotation costs) is balanced against the marginal cost of holding idle balances, as shown in Figure 19.5b. The factor bC is omitted since it is independent of Q and is not needed to solve for the optimum amount. At the optimum issue size, the two relevant cost components will be equal. The two cost curves intersect at the optimum amount of debt issue size.

A Reformulation

A shift in the definitions of terms gives us an alternative formulation that may be easier to comprehend than the previous model. Now let TC be the total

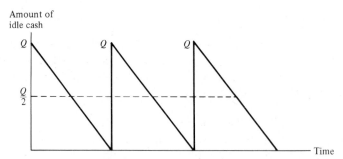

FIGURE 19.6   Amount of Idle Cash

relevant cost of carrying the "inventory" of cash (net of interest earned) and "ordering" the cash (the fixed costs of issuing). Figure 19.6 shows that the average amount of idle (extra) cash through time is $Q/2$. The firm starts with Q dollars after the first debt issue and then uses the excess cash until there is zero cash, and the firm again obtains Q from the issue of a new set of securities. The average amount of cash is $Q/2$, and the net cost per dollar per year is r. There are C/Q cycles and the fixed cost of ordering for each cycle is K. The sum of these two relevant costs are the total controllable cost, TC.

The total controllable relevant costs for a year are now

$$TC = K\frac{C}{Q} + r\frac{Q}{2} \tag{19.2}$$

where $r(Q/2)$ is the net cost of the excess of cash for one year (cost of borrowing minus the earnings on the investment of the idle cash).

Focusing on the controlled cost, TC, enables us to simplify the total cost equation. The value of Q that minimizes the total cost is*

$$Q = \sqrt{\frac{2KC}{r}} \tag{19.3}$$

---

* Let $r = k_i - i$. To determine the Q that minimizes the total cost of meeting the cash needs, we take the derivative of equation (19.1) with respect to Q, equate the derivative to zero, and solve for the Q that satisfies this relationship (the second-order conditions necessary for a minimum of total cost should be checked):

$$\frac{dT}{dQ} = -\frac{KC}{Q^2} + \frac{r}{2} = 0 \quad \text{or} \quad Q^2 = \frac{2KC}{r}$$

so that

$$Q = \sqrt{\frac{2KC}{r}}$$

is optimal.

See W. J. Baumol, "The Transactions Demand for Cash: An Inventory Theoretic Approach," *Quarterly Journal of Economics*, November 1952, pp. 545–556, for the initial presentation of this model.

EXAMPLE 19.1

Suppose that the total cash needs over the next two years are $2,000,000 per year with usage at a constant rate, the fixed cost of each debt issue is $20,000, and the interest rate on the debt is 14 percent and that 6 percent can be earned on idle cash balances:

C = $2,000,000 per year, or 2×10^6
r = 8 percent per year, or 8×10^{-2}
K = $20,000, or 2×10^4

$.08 = 8 \times 10^{-2}$

and the optimal Q from equation (19.2) is

$$Q = \sqrt{\frac{2 \times 2 \times 10^4 \times 2 \times 10^6}{8 \times 10^{-2}}} = \sqrt{\frac{8 \times 10^{10}}{8 \times 10^{-2}}} = 10^6 = \$1,000,000$$

We obtain for Q = $1,000,000 a total controllable cost of

$$TC = \$20,000(2) + .08(\$500,000) = \$80,000$$

For Q = $2,000,000, we would have

$$TC = \$20,000(1) + .08(\$1,000,000) = \$100,000$$

For Q = $500,000, we would have

$$TC = \$20,000(4) + .08(\$250,000) = \$100,000$$

As we would expect, having determined that Q = $1,000,000 is optimum, the total costs for Q = $2,000,000 and Q = $500,000 are larger than the total costs that results from using Q = $1,000,000.

This model assumes zero transaction costs for investing or disinvesting excess cash. Relatively complex models can be developed where these costs are not zero. Fortunately, the real-world costs of these transactions tend to be low; thus the solution obtained by ignoring these costs is generally a reasonable solution.

The foregoing solution indicates that we should make two flotations per year for $1 million each to minimize the total cost of obtaining the $2 million cash needed annually. After the first issue of long-term debt at the beginning of the period, $1 million in cashlike assets will be on hand. This amount will be reduced with time as funds are used. When the amount held in marketable securities just equals the amount that will be used during the time necessary to prepare and float the new loan, the reorder process should be begun. It should be noted that the optimum order size of the amount of borrowing is affected by the square root of demand (the amount of cash needed). If the expected need for cash increased fourfold to \$8 million per year, the optimum size of borrowing would double.

$$Q = \sqrt{\frac{2 \times 2 \times 10^4 \times 8 \times 10^6}{8 \times 10^{-2}}} = \sqrt{\frac{32 \times 10^{10}}{8 \times 10^{-2}}} = \sqrt{4 \times 10^{12}} = \$2,000,000$$

Explaining the Average Amount of Debt

The use of $(C + Q)/2$ for the average amount of debt requires explanation. Figure 19.7 shows the total amount of debt for the time period and Figure 19.8 shows the continuous counterpart.

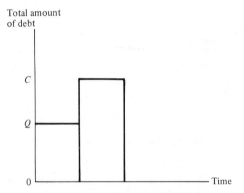

FIGURE 19.7   Total Amount of Debt

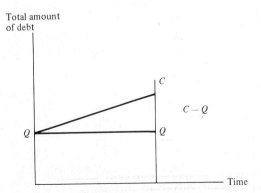

FIGURE 19.8   Total Amount of Debt

Using Figure 19.7 or Figure 19.8, we see that the average amount of debt is

$$\left(Q + \frac{C - Q}{2}\right) \qquad \text{or} \qquad \frac{Q + C}{2}$$

If we multiply $(Q + C)/2$ by k_i, we obtain the interest cost of a strategy of issuing Q of debt each time debt is issued.

Other Uses

Although we developed the models here in the context of the long-term debt issuance decision, they are appropriate for determining the size of transactions for bank debt, the issuance of common stock, or any other single source of financing. They are not, however, appropriate for determining the type of capital (debt or stock) to be obtained.

The decisions all assumed that the long-term borrowing rate was larger than the short-term lending rate. If the short-term rate is larger, there are economic incentives for issuing large amounts of long-term debt and investing the proceeds in short-term securities.

Timing Considerations

In the previous models, the size of a debt issue was determined by balancing the costs of carrying inventory and the fixed costs of issuing debt. Another factor that a financial officer may try to take into account is anticipated changes in the level of interest rates. In the earlier example, when the cash needed for the year was $2 million, the model recommended issuing $1 million debt at one time. This would be enough to supply cash requirements for six months. However, if the corporate treasurer expected interest rates to decline in the next three months, the firm may consider borrowing less now. For example, suppose that the treasurer expects that three months from now, the long-term rate will decline by one half a percentage point (50 basis points) from 14.0 percent to 13.5 percent. In consequence, the firm may wish to consider the possibility of borrowing short term now (enough cash for three months) and then issuing an optimal-sized debt at the lower rate that is expected to be in effect after three months. (Note that if k_i and i both decline by .5 percent, the optimal size debt will not change.)

Caution is advisable when attempting to gain an advantage by forecasting interest rate changes. If the treasurer correctly anticipates the change in interest rate levels, and if other borrowers and lenders in the market have not anticipated the change, then a real advantage for the firm may be achieved.

On the other hand, if the change in interest rates is generally expected to occur, it will be difficult to profit from it. If the treasurer's expectations were widely shared, borrowers would be reluctant to borrow now (it will be cheaper later), but lenders will be anxious to lend now (their return will be lower later). The structure of interest rates will tend to adjust so that there is no special advantage to borrowing or lending now rather than later. In general, to beat the market, one needs better information or better judgment than most market participants. This is difficult to achieve.

Techniques for Managing Cash

The basic objectives in cash management are to collect cash as rapidly as possible and pay it as slowly as possible. To collect money as rapidly as possible, firms use a wire transfer system. Regional banks where funds are deposited are directed automatically to wire the funds to other banks acting as collection points. This enables the firm to invest the funds more quickly in higher-yielding securities than would be earned with the funds on deposit.

A second technique is to use *lock boxes*. Creditor firms are directed to send payments to a post office box. The firm's bank takes the mail from the box, records the cash received, and only then transmits the remaining contents to the firm. This process accelerates the receipt of cash.

To slow down the outlay of cash, firms will pay their bills as late as is feasible, consistent with being able to take any trade discounts.

A practice that is sometimes used (but not endorsed by all) is to write a check on a distant, not accessible, bank. Thus, if a firm in Seattle is being paid, the check will be written on a bank in South Carolina whose airport service is spotty because of bad weather. The business community, as a whole, is not likely to approve of such artificial ways of slowing payment. Certainly, society is not benefited (it is harmful to the extent additional effort is expended on such activities).

Management of "float" has long been of interest, but the interest in 1985 increased greatly when E. F. Hutton was caught using an illegal form of float. Float occurs because of the time lag between the time a check is written and the time the funds are withdrawn from the writer's account.

Near-Cash Securities

We have spoken generically about near-cash securities that earn a known interest rate without being specific about the kind of securities we are considering. A number of securities meet this definition, and any of them can be used as the near-cash security. Among them we would include savings deposits, certificates of deposit (savings deposits with a maturity), marketable certificates of deposit (savings deposits with a specific maturity that can be purchased or sold in the open market), U.S. government bills and notes, and prime commercial paper. If issuers are carefully screened these securities may be subject to virtually no risk of default and transaction costs are extremely low.

Two other popular securities are variable rate preferred stock and short-term tax-exempt securities because of their tax advantages. Other securities such as long-term state and local government bonds, corporate long-term debt instruments, and common stock are not usually considered near-cash securities either because of the default risks associated with them or interest rate risk or because transaction costs are too high.*

There is some risk associated with holding a marketable security if the timing of the firm's cash needs does not coincide with the maturity of the security. That is, if market interest rates change over the holding period, the price of the security will change so as to earn the current market rate. To avoid this risk of change in interest rates, it is possible to "hedge" the securities by buying securities that mature when a known cash need is forecasted to occur, since the securities can then be redeemed at their face value. By holding to maturity, the yield on near-cash securities can be determined with certainty.

The decisions that will be encountered by a firm willing to invest in marketable securities (rather than leaving the cash in the bank) are

1. The amount of cash to be invested in securities.
2. The types of securities to be purchased (nature of the issuing body and the characteristics of the securities and their maturity).
3. The timing of the security purchases.

The amount of cash to be invested has already been discussed.

Essentially, the purchase of securities is a residual decision resulting from previous decisions that brought the cash into the firm and resulted in excess cash being available. Most of the securities that are conventionally used as short-term investments have low levels of risk. The probability that IBM will default on its commercial paper is probably not much greater than the prob-

---

* The largest component of transaction costs is the dealer's spread, the difference between the price at which a security can be bought and the price at which it can be sold. Money market instruments normally trade in units of $1 million of face value. The spread on a very short-term Treasury bill might be as little as $20 per million. On less active issues, the spread could amount to several thousands of dollars per million of face value. The main determinant of spreads is the volume of trading. See *Handbook of Securities of the United States Government and Federal Agencies and Related Money Market Instruments* (New York: The First Boston Corporation, 1976), p. 179. The volume of trading in U.S. Treasury bills amounts to billions of dollars per day.

ability that the U.S. government will become insolvent. Nevertheless, there are significant risk and yield differences among the various near-cash securities. For each kind of security, yields normally are higher with increases in time till maturity because of the possibility that interest rates may arise, thus decreasing the market value of a security if it has to be sold before maturity (this is an interest rate risk). Yield differences between securities with similar maturities mainly reflect differences in the volume of trading and the level of risk.

Tax-exempt securities have the advantage of offering higher after-tax returns due to their tax-exemption status (the before-tax return is generally lower than securities with comparable risk). However, tax regulations prevent a corporation from exploiting the full possibility of investment in these securities (temporary excess cash may be so invested, but the interest on debt borrowed for the purpose of investing in tax-exempt securities may not be tax deductible). There are times where it is institutionally feasible for a corporation to buy these securities, but a corporation should check the current Treasury regulations before doing so.

The timing of purchase of securities is not an important consideration unless you are a superior forecaster of interest rates. Without this skill, securities should be purchased as soon as the excess cash is on hand. The timing aspect might seem to be important since we could conclude that a firm expecting interest rates to increase should postpone investment. We would answer this by suggesting that investment should still be made but that the expectation of higher interest rates should lead a firm to invest in short-term securities so that the firm will be in cash or near-cash when the interest rate change takes place. Thus rather than facing a timing of purchase problem, a firm has a maturity determination problem. There is no question that a firm investing its excess cash in marketable securities has an opportunity to speculate and profit from prospective interest rate changes, but it can also lose from changes that are not anticipated.

The safest procedure is for the firm to invest in securities that mature when the cash is needed, since this will result in the firm having an amount of cash equal to the amount invested plus the interest expected to be earned. In any other investment policy, there is a possibility that the amount of cash held at the time of need will be different from the amount expected to be held.

Line of Credit Decision

Up to this point, we have been treating the cash management decision as though it had no element of uncertainty. Of course, the uncertainty of cash needs is real. One method of reducing the consequences of uncertainty is to buy insurance, and in the cash management area, the usual insurance is a line of credit with a bank. Although a firm without a line of credit is likely to be charged the same rate of interest for bank loans as a comparable firm with a line of credit, a line of credit makes funds readily accessible during periods when it may be otherwise difficult to obtain loans. Once a line of credit is approved by the bank's officers for the coming period of time (say, a year), it may not be necessary for the bank to consider each borrowing request as a new item, thus facilitating borrowing. On the other hand, unless there is a firm credit agreement, the bank has not committed itself to making the loan. Generally, lines of credit (or credit agreements) are only made by banks for corporations with good credit standing (firms with profitable records and in good financial condition).

We shall illustrate one possible method for determining how large a line of credit a firm should purchase. The numbers used in the analysis that follows do not apply to any specific situation but illustrate the general principle that may be applicable in many cases.

EXAMPLE 19.2

Assume that the cost of a line of credit is .5 percent of the unborrowed portion of funds available under the arrangement, or $5,000 per million dollars per year. This is the cost of the line of credit, not the cost of funds borrowed. We also have to make some assumption about the cost to the corporation if the demand for cash exceeds the line of credit, for if no cost were involved, a line of credit would not be necessary. The cost from the viewpoint of the corporation is the additional cost of requesting a loan at short notice without any preparation or the cost of forgone opportunities. We shall assume a cost of $6,000 for each million dollars of funds needed in excess of the line of credit. Frequently, a corporation will compensate a bank for a line of credit by keeping a compensating balance of an agreed-upon size in the bank.

To simplify the computations, we shall further assume that if the money is borrowed at all, it is borrowed immediately and for an entire year. We shall also assume that there are five possible events: the amount needed during the year may be $0 million, $1 million, $2 million, $3 million, or $4 million. There are five possible (and reasonable) acts: negotiate a line of credit of $0 million, $1 million, $2 million, $3 million, or $4 million. The conditional costs associated with each of the acts and each event are shown in Table 19.1. Since the maximum demand is $4 million, it would not be reasonable to have a line of credit of $5 million (the probability of cash demand being greater than $4 million is equal to zero).

Taking the situation in which the demand for cash is $2 million, there is a conditional cost for each of the possible lines of credit (the possible acts). If the line of credit were zero (i.e., $2 million less than the amount needed), the corporation would experience a cost of $12,000, or two times the unit cost of

TABLE 19.1   Conditional Costs

Act: Line of Credit (in millions of dollars)	Event: Maximum Demand for Cash (in millions of dollars)				
	0	*1*	*2*	*3*	*4*
$0	0	$ 6,000	$12,000	$18,000	$24,000
1	$ 5,000	0	6,000	12,000	18,000
2	10,000	5,000	0	6,000	12,000
3	15,000	10,000	5,000	0	6,000
4	20,000	15,000	10,000	5,000	0

$6,000; if the line were for $1 million, the cost is $6,000; if the line were for $2 million, the cost is zero; if the line of credit were larger than the need, then the cost would be the $5,000 commitment fee for each million dollars of un-used credit.

We define the optimal act to be that act with the minimum expected cost. To find the optimal act, it is necessary to determine the probability of occurrence of each event. Let us assume that the probability of occurrence of a given demand (or event) is as shown in Table 19.2. By multiplying the conditional costs of each event for each act by the probability of the event, we can compute the expected cost of the act. For example, the act of obtaining a line of credit of $2 million has an expected cost of $5,000. As Table 19.3 indicates, this expected cost is derived by summing the products of the probability of occurrence for each outcome and the dollar cost of each outcome.

TABLE 19.2   Probability of Demand

Event: Demand for cash (millions of dollars)	$0	$1	$2	$3	$4
Probability of event	.10	.20	.30	.30	.10

TABLE 19.3   Calculation of Expected Cost of Obtaining a Line of Credit for $2 million

Event: Demand for Cash (millions of dollars)	Conditional Cost	Probability	Expected Cost
$0	$10,000	.10	$1,000
1	5,000	.20	1,000
2	0	.30	0
3	6,000	.30	1,800
4	12,000	.10	1,200
		1.00	$5,000

TABLE 19.4   Expected Cost of Different Lines of Credit

Act: Line of credit (millions of dollars)	$0	$1	$2	$3	$4
Expected cost (dollars)	$12,600	$7,700	$5,000	$5,600	$9,500

Repeating this computation for each act gives the expected cost of each act as shown in Table 19.4. Based on expected cost, the optimum line of credit is $2 million, since this act has the lowest expected cost.

If management has a strong aversion to borrowing money without a line of credit, then it could place a higher cost on those situations for which demand for cash was greater than the line of credit. This would tend to change the decision toward a larger line of credit. Similarly, if management thought it could go to the market and do just about as well without a line of credit, then a low cost would be associated with those situations where the demand exceeded the line of credit, and this would lead toward a decision that indicated a smaller line of credit. Consequently, the basic procedure is applicable to any management attitude. It will lead to decisions that are consistent with the subjective preferences of the management, since their preferences are incorporated into the decision process.

The probabilities assigned to the several events (the possible demands for cash) may be based on past experience, or they can be a combination of past experience and the feelings of management about what is going to happen in the future. The number of events possible and strategies allowable can be easily expanded.

The cost estimates of needing more cash than the line of credit are an important element of the decision. If these costs are zero, there is no need for a line of credit. Although the example used a straight-line cost function, it is probable that the function is not linear. It may be very desirable to avoid situations where the cash needs greatly exceed the line of credit, in which case very high costs should be placed on these situations. On the other hand, where the cash needs are only slightly in excess of the line of credit, there may be no cost.

Emerson Electric: Cash Management

As of September 30, 1983, the end of its fiscal year, Emerson Electric had total assets of $2,493,041,000, of which $5,898,000 were short-term investments. Less than .24 percent of the assets were in the form of cash. Marketable securities were 42 times as large as cash.

Conclusions

One of the prime responsibilities of a financial officer is to ensure the availability of cash to meet operational and investment needs. This requires forecasting cash flows from operations and nonoperational sources and then determining how to obtain needed funds or how to invest excess funds. Firms use many sources of funds, ranging from bank lines of credit and commercial paper to long-term debt and equity. They invest temporary excess balances in marketable securities of many types. A trade-off must be made among costs, returns, and risk: If the firm is willing to hold substantial excess balances in low-yielding marketable securities and/or pay compensation for a large line of credit, it will be able to meet almost any cash need facing it; if, however, it does not choose to pay the high costs of such insurance, it must be prepared to bear the costs of not having sufficient cash to do all it desires.

This chapter has introduced the decisions encountered by a corporation treasurer in administering cash and near-cash assets. A corporation must first decide on the nature of its relationships with its banks and may attempt to formalize these relationships by establishing lines of credit (the banks are not committed to make a loan) or a credit agreement (a bank commits itself to lend up to a set amount). The next decision is to determine the amount of cash that will be obtained from sources external to the firm. Once the cash has been obtained and the corporation finds that it has excess cash, the firm is then faced with decisions involving marketable securities. These decisions involve determination of the nature of securities (type and maturity), the amount to be purchased, and the timing of purchase.

A manager of cash may be able to hide an inability to administer liquid resources efficiently behind a policy of having a large amount of excess cash on deposit (thus satisfying the banker and ensuring no difficulty in paying bills) and investing only in very safe government securities maturing when the cash is needed (thus ensuring that there is no risk of default or loss arising from fluctuating interest rates). This set of policies will tend to bypass most of the controls established to indicate inefficiency. There will be no complaints from bankers or other creditors, and there is little or no risk that a security that is purchased will default or that less cash will be obtained from the sale of the security than was invested. However, the failure of the system to report the opportunities that are lost should not prevent us from realizing that such opportunities exist. In the management of cash and near-cash, there are opportunities for taking risk, for being efficient, and for increasing the profit of the firm.

The models of this chapter can readily be made more useful by assuming a wider range of decision alternatives. Frequently, in this book we present models using stringent assumptions (such as a constant rate of cash utilization). It should be recognized that the basic model can readily be made more realistic but that the level of mathematical difficulty will also increase. The benefits from the increased accuracy of a more complex model must be balanced against the cost of calculations and information gathering associated with the increased complexity.

In this chapter we have examined the basic elements of a cash management system and have used several models to illustrate basic relationships. Although sophisticated models can handle more complex cash flow patterns (both certain and uncertain), allow for many forms of near-cash securities, and permit the firm to both borrow and lend short term, the basic principles remain unchanged from those presented in this chapter.

Review Problem 19.1

The ABC Company needs \$600,000,000 of new cash in the coming 12 months. Debt will cost .10. The issue costs of a debt issue are

  Variable costs of issuance: \$2 per \$1,000 of debt
  Fixed costs of issuance: \$300,000 per bond issue

(a) What size debt issue do you recommend? Cash will be used at a constant rate.

(b) What size issue do you recommend if funds can be invested short term, when they are not used, to earn .096 (there are no transactions costs associated with investing short-term excess funds).

Solution to Review Problem 19.1

(a) $Q = \left(\dfrac{2KC}{r}\right)^{1/2} = \left(\dfrac{2 \times (3 \times 10^5) \times (6 \times 10^8)}{.10}\right)^{1/2}$

  $= \$60,000,000,\ \text{or}\ 6 \times 10^7$

(b) $Q = \left(\dfrac{6^2 \times 10^{13}}{.004}\right)^{1/2}$

  $= 3 \times 10^8,\ \text{or}\ \$300,000,000$

PROBLEMS

1. The ABC Company has cash needs of \$4 million in the next year in excess of the cash to be generated internally. The fixed costs associated with a new issue of long-term securities are \$8,000 and the variable costs are \$2

per $1,000. The new securities will cost .10 per year. Temporary excess cash will earn no return (it cannot be invested in short-term securities). Determine the optimum size of the security issue. $800,000$

2. (Problem 1 continued)   Excess cash can be invested to earn .09 in relatively riskless short-term securities.

Now, what is the optimum size of issue if there are no transaction costs for buying or selling short-term securities? $2,529,822$

3. (Problems 1 and 2 continued)   Assume that the company has decided to issue the long-term securities in a block of $4 million because of the advice of an investment banker. The fixed cost per short-term security transaction is $100. There are no variable costs. Assume that the $4 million is invested in short-term securities.

When the company sells short-term securities (assuming that cash needs are constant), how much should the company sell at once?

4. CASHCO, Inc., uses cash at a steady rate and employs the following strategy to meet its cash needs: it borrows Q of short-term debt from its banking group (at zero transaction costs) until it "pays" to replace this short-term debt by floating an amount of long-term debt (at a lower interest rate) equal to the short-term debt owed.

(a) Draw a graph that depicts CASHCO's strategy.

(b) Use the following notation to write the total cost function CASHCO wishes to minimize: $T = i(Q/2) + k_i(C-Q)/2 + K(C/Q) + bC$

  T = the total cost of cash acquisition for the period
  K = the fixed costs of arranging a long-term debt issue
  b = the variable cost of arranging a long-term debt issue (per dollar)
  k_i = the interest rate on long-term debt
  i = the interest rate on short-term investments and debt
  Q = the amount of long-term debt issued by CASHCO each time it floats long-term debt
  C = the total cash needed over the period

  Hint: $Q of short-term debt is accumulated before the first long-term debt issue of $Q occurs, and the long-term debt proceeds are just sufficient to repay the short-term debt. If a total of $C is issued in long-term debt over the period, the average long-term debt outstanding is $(C - Q)/2$.

(c) Is there possibly a better strategy than the one being used?   borrow more long term than owed shout pm

5. The ABC Company needs $100 million of additional cash during the coming 12 months. It can borrow long-term funds at .09 and lend short term

at .07. The "fixed" costs of issuing securities is $90,000 (these costs are incremental to the number of issues).

(a) How much debt should the firm issue at once? What is the total relevant cost of this policy?

(b) What is the total relevant cost of obtaining the entire $100 million at once?

6. If you were a corporate treasurer, would you wait until interest rates were "right" before investing your excess funds?

7. As a corporate officer would you prefer for a bank to require compensating balances or charge a direct fee?

8. The ABC Company must make a decision relative to the amount of the credit agreement it carries with its bank. The cost of the credit agreement is .005 of the unused credit. There is an implicit psychological cost of $9,000 per million dollars for funds needed in excess of the credit agreement.

To simplify the computations, assume that if the money is borrowed at all, it is borrowed immediately for the entire period. Management has determined the following probabilities of possible events:

Event: The Demand for Cash Is		Probability of Event
0	millions of dollars	.20
1	millions of dollars	.30
2	millions of dollars	.40
3	millions of dollars	.10
4	millions of dollars	.00
		1.00

Determine the size of the credit agreement the ABC Company should establish.   2,000,000

9. The FGH Company must make a decision relative to the amount of cash credit agreement it carries with its bank. The cost of the credit agreement is .004 of the unused credit. Management has determined the following probabilities of possible events:

Event: The Demand for Cash Is		Probability of Event
0	millions of dollars	.20
1	millions of dollars	.50
2	millions of dollars	.30

There is a $10,000 cost of being short per million dollars of shortage. If there is no credit agreement, the firm has a .6 probability of being able to arrange the financing.

Determine the size of the credit agreement the FGH Company should establish.

10. If a company paying a borrowing rate of .06 maintains a minimum compensating balance of $10 million to reward the bank, which has lent it $80 million in total, what is the effective interest rate on the loan?

11. The GHI Company currently has $100 million invested in marketable securities that are earning .04. The firm expects to use the $100 million over the coming 12 months to finance an expansion program. The fixed costs associated with a security transaction are estimated to be $50 per transaction.

    (a) Assuming that the cash will be needed evenly throughout the year, at what rate should the securities be sold?

    (b) How many days supply of cash will be obtained each time a batch of securities is sold?

REFERENCES

Batlin, C. A., and Susan Hinko. "Lockbox Management and Value Maximization." *Financial Management*, Winter 1981, 39–44.

Baumol, William J. "The Transactions Demand for Cash: An Inventory Theoretic Approach." *Quarterly Journal of Economics*, November 1952, 545–556.

Bierman, Harold, Jr., and Alan K. McAdams. *Management Decisions for Cash and Marketable Securities*. Ithaca, N.Y.: Graduate School of Business and Public Administration, Cornell University, 1962.

Calman, Robert F. *Linear Programming and Cash Management/CASH ALPHA*. Cambridge, Mass.: M.I.T. Press, 1968.

Carleton, Willard T., Charles L. Dick, Jr. and David H. Downes. "Financial Policy Models: Theory and Practice. *Journal of Financial and Quantitative Analysis*, December 1973, 691–710.

Gale, Bradley T., and Ben Branch. "Cash Flow Analysis: More Important than Ever." *Harvard Business Review*, July–August 1981, 131–136.

Gitman, Lawrence J., D Keith Forrester, and John R. Forrester, Jr., "Maximizing Cash Disbursement Float." *Financial Management*, Summer 1976, 15–24.

———. Edward A. Moses, and I. Thomas White. "An Assessment of Corporate Cash Management Practices." *Financial Management*, Spring 1979, 32–41.

Hartley, W. C. F., and Yale L. Meltzer, *Cash Management*. Englewood Cliffs, N.J.: Prentice-Hall, Inc., 1979.

King, Alfred M. *Increasing the Productivity of Company Cash*. Englewood Cliffs, N.J.: Prentice-Hall, Inc., 1969.

Mehta, Dileep R. *Working Capital Management*. Englewood Cliffs, N.J.: Prentice-Hall, Inc., 1974.

Miller, M. H., and Daniel Orr. "A Model of the Demand for Money by Firms." *Quarterly Journal of Economics*, August 1966, 413–435.

Mullins, David W., Jr., and Richard B. Homonof. "Applications of Inventory Cash Management Models." In Stewart C. Myers (ed), *Modern Developments in Financial Management*. New York: Praeger Publishers, Inc., 1976.

Nauss, Robert M., and Robert E. Markland. "Solving Lock Box Location Problems." *Financial Management*, Spring 1979, 21–31.

Orgler, Yair E. *Cash Management: Methods and Models*. Belmont, Calif.: F. W. Wadsworth, Inc., 1970.

Stone, Bernell K. "The Use of Forecasts and Smoothing in Control-Limit Models for Cash Management." *Financial Management*, Spring 1972, 72–84.

———. "Cash Planning and Credit-Line Determination with a Financial Statement Simulator." *Journal of Financial and Quantitative Analysis*, December 1973, 711–729.

———. "Allocating Credit Lines, Planned Borrowing, and Tangible Services over a Company's Banking System." *Financial Management*, Summer 1975, 65–78.

———, and Ned C. Hill. "Cash Transfer Scheduling for Efficient Cash Concentration." *Financial Management*, Autumn 1980, 35–43.

———. "The Design of a Cash Concentration System." *Journal of Financial and Quantitative Analysis*, September 1981, 301–322.

———, and Robert A. Wood. "Daily Cash Forecasting: A Simple Method for Implementing the Distribution Approach." *Financial Management*, Fall 1977, 40–50.

Van Horne, James C., *Financial Market Rates and Flows*. Englewood Cliffs, N.J.: Prentice-Hall, Inc., 1978.

Chapter 20

Financial Planning and Forecasting

Major Topics

1. Basic nature of financial planning.
2. Preparing proforma financial statements.
3. Preparation of cash flow statements.
4. Forecasting of cash flows from operations.
5. Forecasting of cash flows.
6. Interest rate forecasting.

Basic Nature of Financial Planning

Financial planning and forecasting take a variety of forms. At one extreme is a procedure for structuring the financial statements that are expected if a given set of decisions are made through time. At the other is forecasting a specific item (such as cash) or a special variable (such as interest rates).

Financial planning is an integral part of financial management. Since cash is a primary means of fulfilling financial obligations, forecasting the cash flows of the firm is an important part of financial planning. Coupling forecasted cash flows with pro forma financial statements complements this planning effort and provides a consistency check on the forecasting procedure as well.

Too often financial planning is merely equated with the projection of financial statements. We shall attempt to broaden the definition to make clear decisions that are being made.

Pro Forma Financial Statements

Since the basic financial statements are interrelated by virtue of the double-entry accounting conventions, if independent forecasts are made for each item in the accounts, the income and balance sheet statements are not likely to reconcile.

The preparation of a consistent set of pro forma statements is a powerful tool for the financial manager. One reason for the nearly universal use of the approach is its flexibility. The preparation process can be relatively simple, as when the summary statements are prepared one period ahead for one set of conditions. Complexities may be added if the statements are projected ahead for several periods (for example, quarterly statements for two years), if separate statements are prepared for major segments of the business, or if projections are made under different assumptions about important factors such as the level of sales or the proportion of overdue accounts receivable. Complexities should be introduced only to the extent that they are really needed.

Specialized computer programs, called financial statement simulators, are often employed when the relationships become sufficiently complicated. Spread sheet programs (such as Lotus 1, 2, 3) are very useful for allowing us to prepare future financial statements rapidly for a wide range of assumptions. The assumptions can be changed by typing in a few numbers and an entirely new set of statements obtained in a matter of seconds.

Successful implementation of a financial statement projection, whether manual or computerized, requires a careful analysis of the interrelations among the various accounts, for example, between sales and accounts receivable, and an understanding of how they might be affected by company policies, such as credit terms and economic conditions. Sometimes a subset of these relationships can be usefully isolated and studied in terms of a simplified quantitative model. This will be illustrated later in the chapter with a simple model of the main factors that might determine the rate at which cash is generated from current operations. The following example illustrates the preparation of a simple set of pro forma accounting statements.

EXAMPLE 20.1 ——————————————————————

Suppose that the Brake Company has the following balance sheet at the beginning of the year:

Brake Co.
Balance Sheet, January 1
(milions of dollars)

Cash		$ 90	Accounts payable	$171
Accounts receivable		231	Long-term debt	80
Inventory		30	Common stock	120
Plant and equipment	$200		Retained earnings	100
Less: Accumulated				
depreciation	80	120		
Total assets		$471	Total liabilities and	
			stockholders' equity	$471

Further, suppose that the following transactions were forecast to take place during the first quarter of the next year:

1. Purchase $360 million of goods, 70 percent payable in the first quarter and 30 percent in the second quarter.
2. Sell merchandise that cost $320 million for $400 million; 40 percent of sales will be collected this quarter, 60 percent the next quarter.
3. Collect the current outstanding accounts receivable.
4. Pay current accounts payable.
5. Pay quarterly interest of $2 million on long-term debt.
6. Depreciation for accounting and taxes on plant and equipment for the quarter is $3 million.
7. Taxes, 40 percent of taxable income, are paid.
8. Pay dividends of $15 million.

From this information it is possible to develop a pro forma income statement and balance sheet as well as a cash flow forecast. Since the amount of taxes paid depends on taxable income, we begin with the income statement for the calculation of taxes:

Brake Co.
Pro Forma Income Statement:
January 1 to March 31
(millions of dollars)

Sales	$400
Cost of goods sold	320
Gross margin	$ 80
Depreciation	3
Earnings before interest and taxes	$ 77
Interest	2
Earnings before taxes	$ 75
Taxes (40%)	30
Net income	$ 45

The Brake Company is forecasted to be profitable in the first quarter, with net income equal to .1125 of sales.

The pro forma end-of-the-quarter balance sheet is

Brake Co.
Pro Forma Balance Sheet, March 31
(millions of dollars)

Cash		$ 11	Accounts payable	$108
Accounts receivable		240	Long-term debt	80
Inventories		70	Common stock	120
Plant and equipment:	$200		Retained earnings	130
Less: Accumulated				
depreciation	83	117		
Total assets		$488	Total liabilities and	
			retained earnings	$488

This balance sheet is obtained from the beginning balance sheet and the given transactions by either

1. Using basic accounting transactions (debits and credits) to record the economic events.
2. Computing the balance of each account using the transactions and intelligence.

For example, the retained earnings started at $100 million, the company earned $45 million, and it paid dividends of $15 million, for a balance of $130 million.

The use of basic accounting illustrates the systematic process. The following T accounts are keyed to the foregoing transactions. Note that the balances in all accounts agree with the ending pro forma balance sheet.

Transactions for the Brake Company

Cash		Accounts Payable	
Additions	Subtractions	Subtractions	Additions
√ 90	(1) 252		√ 171
(2) 160	(4) 171	(4) 171	(1) 108
(3) 231	(5) 2		
	(7) 30		
	(8) 15		

Accounts Receivable		Long-Term Debt	
√ 231			√ 80
(2) 240	(3) 231		

Inventories			*Common Stock*	
√ 30				√ 120
(1) 360	(2) 320			

Plant and Equipment		*Retained Earnings*	
√ 200		(5) 2	√ 100
		(6) 3	(2) 80
		(7) 30	
		(8) 15	

Accumulated Depreciation	
	√ 80
	(6) 3

An accountant would use revenue and expense accounts instead of recording the income items directly to retained earnings. But that is a device to facilitate the bookkeeping and is not a substantive change. It would not affect the end results or their use.

Preparation of the Cash Flow Statement

All firms want to know the cash flow forecast. The forecast for the Brake Company can be obtained from the cash T account ("cash in" entries are on the left and "cash out" on the right). The resulting cash forecast statement follows.

The Brake Company
Cash Flow Forecast, January 1 to March 31
(millions of dollars)

Beginning cash, January 1			$90
Cash in			
Accounts receivable collection	$231		
Sales collected during period	160	$391	
Cash out			
Accounts payable	$171		
Purchase paid	252		
Interest	2		
Dividends	15		
Taxes	30	470	
Net cash outflow			79
Ending cash, March 31			$11

The firm is anticipating a $79 million net cash outflow for the quarter.

Note the ease with which the cash flow forecast is prepared from the cash flow account if the pro forma entries are recorded. Accountants will sometimes prepare a "funds statement" (called a "changes in financial position" statement) that shows the sources and uses of working capital. For managerial purposes, the cash flow forecast will be more useful than a funds statement.

The balance sheet, income statement, and cash flow statement provide basic information for financial planning. For example, on January 1, the firm may wish to purchase some commercial paper or certificates of deposit with its idle cash balances. At the end of March, the company might plan to raise new funds since idle cash balances have dwindled to $11 million.

This example illustrates the process of detailed cash flow forecasting. This process can be used for even much more complex transactions, for example, the sale of plant assets; also, the same technique can be used to determine the cash flows for use in capital budgeting, but adjustments would have to be made in the tax calculation, the debt flows, and working capital changes.

Forecasting Cash Flows from Operations

The primary objective of this section is to stress the relevant variables affecting the cash flow of a firm and how the magnitude of these variables affects the cash flow.

Many of the parameters that determine cash flows are well specified, such as the rate of collection and payments (credit policies), bad-debt rates, and direct, out-of-pocket expenses as a percentage of sales. However, the rate at which sales will grow is often less certain. It may turn out that, given the basic parameters of the cash flow process, normal operations will generate positive flows if sales grow slowly but negative cash flows if they grow rapidly.

We shall develop a simple analytic model of the cash flow process considering only direct out-of-pocket costs (those that vary in proportion to sales), leaving indirect out-of-pocket costs to be analyzed separately. Such a model will indicate the ability of the firm to generate cash under the given conditions. Such information will indicate whether the firm has financing needs and, if so, whether its financing needs are long or short term. Also, if financing the cash needs is not feasible, the model will enable us to consider other solutions to the cash shortage.

The effect of changes in sales on cash needs would be easy to determine if all sales were for cash and if all expenses of a period were accompanied by cash expenditures in that period. In this very special situation, if sales were profitable (revenues greater than cash expenses), a dollar of sales would increase cash, and if sales were increased by any amount, cash on hand would also be increased.

On the other hand, if either the timing of cash receipts did not coincide with the timing of sales or cash expenditures did not coincide with expenses, then the analysis would be more complex, and we could not predict the effect on cash of a change in sales without more information.

We are going to construct a simple model of the cash flows accruing from operations, a model that reflects the timing of receipts arising from sales and outlays arising from the out-of-pocket component of the cost of goods sold.

The primary purpose of the mathematical model will be to establish the basic relationships between the cash flow of the period and several variables such as the contribution margin per dollar of sales, the rate of collecting accounts receivable, and rate of growth in sales. The model will be extremely useful in explaining why strange events occur. For example, why might increased sales and income lead to a decrease in cash for a large number of periods? Although this can be explained in words, it is helpful to have an explicit and specific model that explains why a given change will take place. With the additional understanding of the relationships provided by the model, we might be better able to make decisions that modify the relationships and eliminate cash flow problems. It should be remembered that the model is a simplification of the real world. More inclusive models can readily be prepared, but they do add to the complexity of presentation.

Let

C_t = the cash flows of the t period.

R_t = the sales revenue of the t period.

p = the out-of-pocket cost percentage such that the out-of-pocket expense and cash outlay of period t is pR_t.

q = the proportion of the tth period's sales that are collected in the tth period. The parameter q is determined by the percentage of sales that are cash sales and the percentage of credit sales collected in the current period.

g = the growth rate in sales such that $R_t = R_{t-1}(1 + g)$ and $R_t = R_0(1 + g)^t$, where the period of g is the same as the period of q.

Assume that q is the proportion of the tth period's sales that are collected in the tth period and $(1 - q)$ is the proportion collected in period $t + 1$. The cash flows of the tth period are equal to the sum of this period's sales times the percentage collected and the last period's sales times the percentage collected less the expenses associated with this period's sales:

$$C_t = qR_t + (1 - q)R_{t-1} - pR_t \tag{20.1}$$

Since $R_t = (1 + g)R_{t-1}$, we can rewrite equation (20.1), making the net cash flows from operations in period t a function of sales in period $t - 1$, the growth rate of sales, g, and the collection and out-of-pocket cost parameters q and p:

$$C_t = q(1 + g)R_{t-1} + (1 - q)R_{t-1} - p(1 + g)R_{t-1} \qquad (20.2)$$

or more simply

$$C_t = [(1 - p) + (q - p)g]R_{t-1} \qquad (20.3)$$

To ascertain whether the normal net cash flow from operations is positive, we must ascertain that

$$(1 - p) + (q - p)g > 0 \qquad (20.4)$$

for if it is, $C_t > 0$, since last period's sales will always be nonnegative. Note that when the collection rate and out-of-pocket cost parameters (q and p) are assumed fixed, the rate at which cash is generated or absorbed by operations is a function of the growth rate of sales, g.

Before proceeding to illustrate the use of this model, let us highlight two aspects of it. First, the model assumes that all cash expenses are paid in the period of analysis, a highly restrictive assumption. Second, the collection of sales is assumed to be made in either period t or $t + 1$; the parameter q thus depends on the length of the time period chosen for the analysis.

EXAMPLE 20.2 ───────────────────────────────────

The Able Company has a normal out-of-pocket cost of goods sold rate of 80 percent, collects 40 percent of its sales in the year of their occurrence and 60 percent in the following year, and forecasts sales to grow at a rate of 4 percent per year. Thus, if the Able Company paid all its out-of-pocket expenses in the year of sale,

$$p = .8$$
$$q = .4$$
$$g = .04$$

From equation (20.3),

$$C_t = [(1 - .8) + (.4 - .8)(.04)]R_{t-1}$$
$$= (.20 - .016)R_{t-1}$$
$$= .184R_{t-1}$$

so that for each dollar of sales in year $t - 1$, the net cash flows from operations will be \$.184 in year t.

Suppose, however, that sales were forecast to grow at the rate of 60 percent per year. Then the normal net cash flow from operations would be negative:

$$C_t = [(1 - .8) + (.4 - .8)(.6)]R_{t-1}$$
$$= -.04R_{t-1}$$

This illustration sheds light on the paradox of growth: How is it possible for an extremely profitable firm to need cash continually? If the firm's sales are growing at a fast rate, if collections are delayed, and if out-of-pocket costs must be paid promptly, then it is possible that cash flows from operations may be negative.

A more precise answer can be given by examining a modification of equation (20.3). If we divide both sides of equation (20.3) by R_{t-1}, we find that the rate of net cash flow in period t per dollar of sales in period $t - 1$ is*

$$\frac{C_t}{R_{t-1}} = (1 - p) + (q - p)g \qquad (20.5)$$

that is, it is a linear function of g, the sales growth rate

$$\frac{C_t}{R_{t-1}} = a + mg \qquad (20.6)$$

where $a = (1 - p)$ is the Y axis intercept and $m = (q - p)$ is the slope of the line. If $q > p$, then as the sales growth rate increases, the rate of net cash flows increases, as illustrated in Figure 20.1. On the other hand, if $q < p$, any

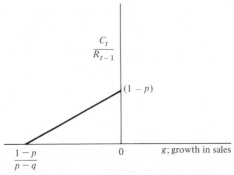

FIGURE 20.1   Cash Flow and Growth in Sales

* Equation (20.5) could be written in the form of cash flow per dollar of current sales by substituting $R_{t-1} = (1 + g)^{-1} R_t$, but the relationship between g and C_t/R_t is nonlinear:

$$\frac{C_t}{R_t} = \frac{(1 - p) + (q - p)g}{(1 + g)}$$

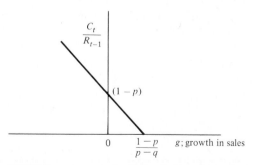

FIGURE 20.2   Cash Flow and Growth in Sales

increase in sales growth will lower the rate of net cash flow, since the expenses for period t are greater than the collections of sales revenues, as illustrated in Figure 20.2. Finally, note that as p increases or q decreases, the rate of cash generation (utilization) decreases (increases) for a given growth rate in sales.

EXAMPLE 20.3 ——————————————————————————————————

For the Able Company, with $p = .8$ and $q = .4$, $q < p$, Figure 20.2 is the correct depiction. Using equation (20.5), the rate of net cash flow per dollar of last period's sales is

$$\frac{C_t}{R_{t-1}} = (1 - p) + (q - p)g \tag{20.5}$$

$$\frac{C_t}{R_{t-1}} = .2 - .4g \tag{20.6}$$

so that with $g = .04$, $C_t/R_{t-1} = \$.184$ is positive but would decrease with an increased growth rate. If the Able Company were to tighten its credit policy, speeding up the rate on collections until $q = .9$, then

$$q > p \quad \text{and} \quad \frac{C_t}{R_{t-1}} = .2 + .1g$$

so that the rate of cash flow would increase with an increase in the sales growth rate.

——

The rates at which sales are collected and disbursements are made are as important in determining the net cash flows from operations in the growing firm as the basic profitability of the operations itself.

We could next allow the cash outlays associated with expenses to take place in a different time period than that in which the expense is recognized as well as allow the collection of revenues to lag behind the period of sale. Conceptually, this is not difficult, but the formulations are involved. Also, if desired, different assumptions can be made for growth rates in sales for different time periods. If this is done, care must be taken in using the equations that have been presented, since many of them only apply if the cash flows have been growing at a rate of g for several periods.

The Choice of Time Period

In the examples of this chapter, we have assumed that the period of analysis in a year. Any other time period could have been chosen as long as the variables q, g, and R_{t-1} were all measured consistently with the choice of time period.

If the data are given in terms of a year, it is a nontrivial task to convert that data to quarterly or monthly data. It is not obvious, but the measures of q, g, and R_{t-1} all must be changed when we change the length of the time period.

Limitations of the Models

The models presented in this chapter are illustrative of the types of models of cash flows that can be produced, but they are not operational in their present form. They can indicate the relationship of cash flow and contribution margin (i.e., $1 - p$) and rate of collection, but they cannot generally be used to predict the cash flow of the period. Too much else is left out. For example, the out-of-pocket fixed cost expenses are not included in any of the equations.

Another important consideration that is omitted is the cash necessary to finance the increase in inventories accompanying an increase in sales. Do inventories increase linearly with sales, or would some other relationship be more appropriate? This should be built into an operational equation. There may be a need to maintain a given current or quick ratio or a minimum net working capital, and these considerations must be included.

The analysis has been on a before-tax basis, and before the model becomes operational taxes must be included in the analysis. The model presents an estimate of operational cash flows and leaves out the cash necessary to restructure the balance sheet. For example, it may be necessary to reduce accounts payable or to expand long-lived assets. These transactions will generate or use cash flows, but they have not been included.

In summary, we have explored a relatively simple model of estimating the cash flows of a period associated with changes in sales. We could add another complication by assuming that cash expenditures precede cash sales as well as follow them and that sales are collected over more than two periods. We might wish to extend the model to include a desired relationship between sales levels and inventories or any of the other complications described earlier. These alterations would add to the complexity of the model but would not change the method of analysis or the nature of the conclusions drawn.

The fact that the sales of the next period will increase or decrease is relevant information (this determines the size of the g), but until we know the cost percentage and the timing of both the cash receipts and the cash disbursements, we cannot predict whether the cash flows of the coming period will be positive or negative. Once we have established the relationships of the sales to receipts and expenditures, we should be able to predict the effect on the cash flows of a change in the level of sales.

There are more sophisticated mathematical models of the effects on the firm's cash position of different rates of change in sales. These models can readily incorporate more realistic assumptions than we used in this chapter. It is true that anything a mathematical model can do an analyst can also accomplish by producing pro forma statements showing the forecasted cash positions. But the advantage of the mathematical model is that we can rapidly test the effect of changing assumptions. Thus we can determine the sensitivity of the cash position to these assumptions and to decisions that can be made (such as increasing or decreasing the rate of sales).

Three Cash Flow Strategies

One of the major problems facing a profitable, but growing, firm is meeting its cash needs. If cash flow forecasts indicate the need for continual financing for a long period, three strategies should be considered.

First, if the firm has a debt capacity and a solid financial reputation, short-term funds may be available on a revolving basis (borrowing again shortly after the repayment) from numerous sources. For example, if the firm is large enough to operate in the commercial paper market, it may meet some of its recurrent cash needs by repeatedly issuing and then refunding commercial paper. In some cases, a revolving bank loan or line of credit might be taken down on a permanent basis. But since prudent banking principles stress that the best bank loan is a self-liquidating loan (short term to cover seasonal or other temporary increases in inventories or accounts receivable), banks may be unwilling to participate in a scheme that uses short-term financing to meet long-term needs. This reluctance may be in the customer's best interest, for such a strategy involves not only the risk of higher interest costs at a later date but also the risk of a pull-out by the supplier of credit before the firm is able to pay the debt, leaving the firm in a serious predicament.

The second strategy would be to turn to the long-term capital markets, selling either long-term debt or equity to obtain the needed funds and investing the excess funds in marketable securities or alternatively using a mixture of short-term and long-term capital.

The third strategy would be to change some of the operating characteristics of the firm, altering the profitability, collection rate, disbursement rate, or growth rate of the firm in such a way as to meet cash needs from internal sources. In this regard, the models developed in this chapter (or more detailed and complicated versions) are of value in examining alternative strategies. For example, offering a discount for prompt payment will increase the collection rate (q) but decrease the profit margin ($1 - p$). Since these two effects have opposite impacts on cash flows, we cannot predict the net effect on the firm's cash position without some numerical values. An alternative might be to raise prices, thereby increasing the profit margin; this, by itself, would improve cash flow. Both strategies will most likely also affect the growth rate in sales, and this effect must also be included in the analysis. The models developed in this chapter are good bases for this type of "sensitivity analysis."

In addition to changing terms of sale or price, cash collection and disbursement procedures can be modified to improve cash availability. Regional collection centers or lock boxes with wire transfers of cash will enable the firm to make the cash available more readily once the customer has written a check; also being willing to play the float (to take note of the delay in checks clearing to your account) will reduce necessary bank balances. Some of these kinds of procedural devices can be used with little cost; others are not without cost, and the value of the incremental cash they supply must be weighted against the incremental cost of modifying the receipts or disbursement procedures.

A combination of these strategies is the most likely solution. For example, if the firm gets some external long-term financing, short-term suppliers may be willing to make up the difference. In choosing a strategy to follow, the cash flow forecasts of the firm play a crucial role, since creditors can be expected to request them prior to making any commitments.

Forecasting of Cash Flows

In Part II of this book we discussed several discounted cash flow capital budgeting techniques. They all required an input of cash flows. The biggest operating difficulty of project analysis is to forecast the cash flows to be used in computing the net present value and internal rate of return.

In the models discussed, we assumed a growth rate of g and did not limit the sales growth that could take place. Once sales reach some level, more productive capacity will be needed, and the model shifts from a sales–cash forecast model to a capital budgeting model. There is a discontinuity in the amount of cash flows that take place when new plant and equipment have to be acquired. Costs previously considered to be fixed jump up with new plant and equipment.

The single most difficult item to estimate in estimating cash flows is the sales revenue (price and quantity) to be received. It is very easy to be excessively optimistic.

Interest Rate Forecasting

Assume that a firm is about to issue $500,000,000 of 30-year, zero-coupon debt at a cost of .14 (the price would be $9,814,000). An expert financial forecaster, however, has suggested that the issuance of the debt be delayed one year since the expected long-term rate will then be .130. The saving of 100 basis points (.01 interest rate) will result in a price of $14,444,000 at time 1 if a 29-year zero-coupon $500,000,000 security is issued. By giving up $9,814,000 at time 0, and getting $14,444,000 at time 1, the company earns a rate of .472 for the one period.

If interest rates could be forecast with a .472 return resulting, a firm would pay a great deal for the information. Unfortunately, forecasting interest rates is very difficult. On the other hand, the market is constantly forecasting the future and incorporating these forecasts into the interest rates.

EXAMPLE 20.4 ───────────────────────

Let

r_1 = the spot rate for one period
r_{30} = .140, the spot rate for a 30-period zero-coupon debt
$_1r_{29}$ = .130, the forward rate at time 1 for a 29-year zero-coupon security

$$(1 + r_{30})^{30} = (1 + r_1)(1 + {_1r_{29}})^{29}$$

$$(1.14)^{30} = (1 + r_1)(1.13)^{29}$$

$$1 + r_1 = \frac{50.950}{34.616} = 1.472$$

$$r_1 = .472$$

If a 30-year security yields .14 and if at time 1 a 29-year security will yield .13, then the one-period interest rate must be .472 or an issuer can make money. For example, if the one-period rate is .10, a borrower can issue

$14,444,000/1.10 = $13,131,000 of one-period debt at time 0, pay the $14,444,000 owed with the issuance of $14,444,000 of 29-year debt at time 1. The amount payable in 29 more years will be $500,000,000. This is better than issuing $9,814,000 of .14 debt at time 0 and paying $500,000,000 at time 30 years.

If the one-period spot rate is .472 and the 30-year rate is .14, then we would expect to issue 29-year debt at time 1 at a rate of .13. We could borrow short term at .472 and then wait for one period until we could borrow long term at .13. But the cost would be the same as borrowing immediately at .14.

Thus long-term rates are in a sense forecasts of future long-term rates. At time 1, the 29-year forward rate may actually be different from the .13 rate that we expect at time 0 to be in effect at time 1. However, the issuing firm can lock in the .13 cost by issuing .14 debt at time 0 for 30 years. An investor can lock in a .14 return for 30 years by buying the 30-year security.

The examples used zero-coupon debt because the mathematics are easier than with interest paying balloon payment debt.

Conclusions

Some types of forecasting are very exact. A cash forecast for the next period will be exact if the assumptions about cash in and cash out are valid. This was illustrated in the cash forecast pro forma statement example of the chapter.

Some types of forecasting are very inexact. In the example of the previous section, we can use the values r_1 and r_{30} to estimate the interest rate for 29 periods at time 1. If a forecaster predicts a higher or lower rate, the forecaster is betting that the market's expectations are faulty.

The Lombard-Wall, Inc., Bankruptcy

In August 1982 the security firm of Lombard-Wall, Inc., filed for bankruptcy under Chapter XI of the federal bankruptcy act. It had assets of $2.06 billion in 1982.

The head of Lombard-Wall, Inc., stated, "If interest rates had not gone up we would have been walking away fat city."

Forecasting interest rates and betting on the forecast is dangerous.

The New York Times, August 19, 1982, p. D4.

Review Problem 20.1

Assume that the following market rates of interest can be observed for zero-coupon debt:

1-year security	.20
2-year security	.19
30-year security	.15

(a) What rate is the market "forecasting" for a 1-year security issued at time 1?

(b) What rate is the market "forecasting" for a 29-year security issued at time 1?

(c) What rate is the market "forecasting" for a 28-year security issued at time 2?

Solution to Review Problem 20.1

(a) $(1.19)^2 = (1.20)(1 + {}_1r_1)$

$_1r_1 = .18$, where $_1r_1$ is the 1-period rate at time 1.

(b) $(1.15)^{30} = 1.20(1 + {}_1r_{29})^{29}$

$(1 + {}_1r_{29})^{29} = 55.176$

$_1r_{29} = .148$, where $_1r_{29}$ is the 29-period rate at time 1.

(c) $(1.15)^{30} = (1.19)^2(1 + {}_2r_{28})^{28}$

$(1 + {}_2r_{28})^{28} = 46.756$

$_2r_{28} = .147$, where $_2r_{28}$ is the 28-period rate at time 2.

PROBLEMS

1. Assume that a two-year zero-coupon $1 million note can be issued at a price of $826,400.

   If one-year debt can be issued at a cost of .16, what one-period interest rate is the market forecasting to be in effect at time 1? As an investor interested in investing for two years, how can you win?

.043

2. Assume that a one-period security can be issued to yield a .10 return, that a two-period zero-coupon security can be issued to yield .243 per year, and that a 30-year zero-coupon security will yield .14 per year.
   (a) What return is the market "forecasting" for a 29-year zero-coupon security issued at time 1?
   (b) What return is the market "forecasting" for a 28-year zero-coupon security issued at time 2?
   (c) What return is the market "forecasting" for a 1-year security issued at time 1?

3. The following facts apply to The Tire Company.

The Tire Company
Balance Sheet
January 1

Cash	$ 30,000	Current liabilities	$ 35,000
Accounts receivable	25,000	Long-term liabilities	60,000
Inventory	45,000	Capital stock	15,000
Plant	120,000	Retained earnings	90,000
Accumulated depreciation	(20,000)	Total liabilities	
Total assets	$200,000	and stockholders' equity	$200,000

The following forecasts are made for the next year:
   (1) Credit sales are $400,000. Collections are $225,000 of accounts receivable.
   (2) Purchases of inventories are $200,000 on credit.
   (3) Cost of inventories sold is $160,000.
   (4) Payments of accounts payable are $215,000.
   (5) Depreciation expense is $10,000.
   (6) Income taxes to be paid are $12,000.
   (7) Interest payments are to be $6,000.
   (a) Forecast all the end-of-period balance sheet items.
  −(b) Prepare a cash forecast for the coming year.
   (c) Prepare a cash flow to be used for conventional investment evaluation purposes. Assume that the interest expenses saved $2,760 of taxes.

4. The ABC Company has sales in January of $100,000 and sales are growing at a rate of .10 per month. Variable costs are $.40 per dollar of sales and are paid for at the time of sale. For each dollar of sales, $.30 is collected in the month of sale and $.70 is collected in the month following sale.
   (a) Estimate the cash receipts for February.
   (b) Estimate the cash receipts for February if the sales growth rate is .50 and the variable costs are $.90 per dollar of sales. Plot the cash receipts

per dollar for the previous period's sales as a function of the growth rate in sales.

5. The XYZ Company has sales of $1 million in January. Variable costs are $.60 per dollar of sales and are paid for at the time of sale. For each dollar of sales, $.70 is collected in the month of sale and $.30 is collected in the month following sale.

Plot the cash receipts per dollar of the previous period's sales as a function of the growth rate in sales. At what growth rate are the cash receipts equal to zero?

6. (Problem 5 continued)   Now assume that $.40 is collected in the month of sale and that $.60 is collected in the next month.

Plot the cash receipts per dollar of the previous period's sales as a function of the growth in sales.

7. The ABC Company had December sales of $100,000 and sales are growing at the rate of .20 per month. Variable costs are $.90 per dollar of sales and all are paid for at the time of sale. For each dollar of sales, $.30 is collected in the month of sale and $.70 is collected in the month following sale.

What are the cash needs to finance the expanding sales during the first quarter of the year? Assuming that the foregoing information applies to the entire year and beyond, what type of financing would you seek to finance the working capital needs associated with the increased sales?

8. Suppose that 30 percent of total sales are for cash and that 40 percent of credit sales are collected in the current period. What percentage of total sales is collected in the current period?

9. The ABC Company has made the following forecasts:

	Year	
	19X4	19X5
Sales	$9,091	$10,000
Variable costs	6,364	7,000
Income	$2,727	$ 3,000

All sales are on account. In the year of sale, 45 percent of the accounts are collected. All expenses are paid currently.

What is the forecasted cash flow for 19X5?

10. The sales of last year were $1,000. The variable costs are .7, the collection rate is .838 in the year of sale, the growth rate of sales is .21. Expenses are paid currently.

What is the operational cash flow of the next period?

11. (Problem 10 continued)   Assume that the analysis of Problem 10 is conducted on a six-month rather than an annual basis. The sales of the past six months were $523.81 (they were $1,000 for the year).
    (a) What is the growth rate in sales for six months if it is .21 for the year?
    (b) What are the projected sales for the first six months of next year? The second six months? For the year?

REFERENCES

Carleton, W. T., C. L. Dick, Jr., and D. H. Downes. "Financial Policy Models: Theory and Practice." *Journal of Finance*, December 1973, 691–709.

Chambers, John C., Satinder K. Mullick, and Donald D. Smith. "How to Choose the Right Forecasting Technique." *Harvard Business Review*, July–August 1971, 45–74.

Francis, Jack Clark, and Dexter R. Rowell. "A Simultaneous Equation Model of the Firm for Financial Analysis and Planning." *Financial Management*, Spring 1978, 29–44.

Grinyer, P. H., and J. Wooller. *Corporate Models Today—A New Tool for Financial Management*. (London: Institute of Chartered Accountants, 1978.

Helfert, Erich A. *Techniques of Financial Analysis*, 4th ed. Homewood, Ill.: Richard D. Irwin, Inc., 1977.

Jaedicke, Robert K., and Robert T. Sprouse. *Accounting Flows: Income, Funds, and Cash*. Englewood Cliffs, N.J.: Prentice-Hall, Inc., 1965.

Pan, Judy, Donald R. Nichols, and O. Maurice Joy. "Sales Forecasting Practices of Large U.S. Industrial Firms." *Financial Management*, Fall 1977, 72–77.

Pappas, James L., and George P. Huber. "Probabilistic Short-Term Financial Planning." *Financial Management*, Autumn 1973, pp. 36–44.

Parker, George G. C., and Edilberto L. Segura. "How to Get a Better Forecast." *Harvard Business Review*, March–April 1971, 99–109.

Traenkle, J. W., E. G. Cox, and J. A. Bullard. *The Use of Financial Models in Business*. New York: Financial Executives' Research Foundation, 1975.

Weston J. Fred. "Forecasting Financial Requirements." *The Accounting Review*, July 1958, 427–440.

Cases: Part IV

Case 1. The X Company

Assume that you are a bank officer and that on February 1, 1973 you have been given the opportunity to lend the X Company $50 million at prime plus 100 basis points. Your bank has been having trouble placing loans at prime. The X Company is a very large retailer with a long history of profitability.

QUESTION: What is your decision?

The X Company Financial Summary

	1973	1972
Sales	$1,849,802,346	$1,644,747,319
Net earnings	$8,429,473	$37,787,066
Per common share	$ .59	$2.70
Average number of common shares		
outstanding	13,885,813	13,882,138
Dividends paid per preferred share	$3.75	$3.75
Dividends paid per common share	$1.50	$1.50
Total dividends paid	$21,122,043	$ 21,141,362
Increase (decrease) in earnings retained		
for use in the business	$(12,692,570)	$ 16,645,704
Depreciation and amortization of		
properties	$13,579,083	$12,004,268
Capital expenditures	$23,537,000	$26,983,000
Employee compensation and benefits	$434,368,156	$397,133,721
Cents per sales dollar	23.5¢	24.1¢
Merchandise inventories	$450,636,556	$399,532,793
Store properties, fixtures, and		
improvements	$100,983,800	$91,419,748
Long-term debt	$220,336,000	$126,672,000
Book value common stock, per share	$22.43	$23.25
Number of preferred stockholders	511	625
Number of common stockholders	30,174	20,211
Number of stores	1,189	1,208

Year	Number of New Stores Opened	Number of Stores Enlarged	Capital Expenditures
1973	77	4	$ 23,537,000
1972	92	5	26,983,000
1971	83	5	26,476,000
1970	65	8	15,995,000
1969	52	3	13,668,000
Total	369	25	$106,659,000

1515 BROADWAY
NEW YORK, N.Y. 10036

To Our Stockholders

During the last six years your Company opened 410 large stores of over 50,000 square feet, enlarged 36 successful stores, and closed 307 smaller units. In view of the decline in earnings in 1973, you might well ask. . .WHY?

Retailing is synonymous with change. Selling methods, size and types of stores, and lines or departments of merchandise change as the demands of the American Consumer dictate. The Management of your Company recognized this inevitable shift from smaller, limited stores to larger "full-line" stores and committed itself to the complete restructuring of the Company.

In this Letter to Stockholders we will cover more fully the factors influencing operations in 1973 and our prospects for the future.

—In 1946, the Company first introduced a credit service to aid its customers to purchase wanted merchandise and pay on an installment plan. The stores were small and stocked with merchandise limited in lines and price. The credit coupon book was selected as the most practical method as these coupons could be used as cash and the customer did not have to wait for individual sales slips on each item purchased. It gave us a method of granting credit without incurring the expense of a sophisticated credit system to keep customer credit limits under control. For smaller stores, this type was not only popular with customers—but it was tailor-made for the simplified operation of this small unit. However, as the Company developed new full-line stores, customers indicated a preference for the revolving credit charge plan. In addition, governmental regulations have made it increasingly difficult and expensive to administer the coupon-type credit plan. Primarily, in recognition of the customer preference for revolving credit charge accounts, this plan was promoted in 1973, and this emphasis will be continued in the future. This change from the credit coupon book plan produces less service charge revenue and is more expensive to operate. During 1973, although credit sales were $45,000,000 higher, service charge revenues were down by over $7,000,000. On the other hand, our experience in the past year indicates that customers prefer the revolving credit charge and will purchase more merchandise with this plan.

—Every corporation is financed with a mixture of stockholders' equity and debt (both long and short term). Our rapid store expansion during the last six years, coupled with the necessary service facilities to support the new stores, required substantial investments in inventories and customer credit receivables.

At the beginning of 1973, the Company had outstanding three long-term debt issues totalling $126,672,000, with interest rates of 4 percent and 4¾ percent. In July 1973, the Company concluded a loan arrangement, with eight of the largest banks in the United States, for $100,000,000 for five years, with interest at the minimum commercial lending rate of the Guaranty Trust Company of New York that ranged between 8 percent and 10 percent during the balance of 1973.

The balance of Company financing, as in previous years, was done in the short-term commercial paper market—with bank lines of credit always in effect for more than the total short term borrowings. These short-term borrowings were always less than customer account receivables, which at year end totaled $602,000,000 and are made up of 2,900,000 individual accounts, located in all sections of the country.

Interest rates in the United States, which reached record levels in the second half of 1973, directly affected the cost of a substantial portion of our borrowings. For the year, total interest costs were $30,000,000 greater than for the year 1972.

—At midyear, Management decided that the levels of inventory were higher than desirable. A planned program was instituted to reduce inventories, and this program was implemented on a progressive basis throughout the remainder of the year. At year end, inventories were in satisfactory condition. The additional $51,000,000 of merchandise, represented an increase that was equal to the sales increase of 12.5 percent and included the inventory investment necessary to stock the 5,606,000 square feet of new stores opened in 1973. The planned inventory reduction had an adverse effect on the sales trend in the fourth quarter.

—In 1973 the Company opened 77 new stores and enlarged 4 existing units, for an additional 5,606,000 square feet of new store space. In addition, construction of the new 475,000 square foot Distribution Center in Windsor, Connecticut, was completed in late fall 1973.

In 1974, we will open approximately 45 new stores and enlarge 1 unit for approximately 3,000,000 square feet. The reduction, both in number of stores and square footage from 1973 levels, is due to developers encountering difficulty in securing necessary materials to complete centers on schedule, inability to start some projects because of the high cost of interim financing, and the increased time required to be spent before beginning a project in satisfying environmental control requirements. It is our estimate at this time that the 1975 program will be of the same magnitude as 1974, or smaller, and management feels that this is a more workable program in view of present conditions. This will, of course, reduce preopening costs and the additional funds required for investment in capital expenditures, and inventories and to carry customer receivables, from the peaks of the last few years.

—Dividends of $1.50 per share on the common stock and $3.75 per share on the preferred stock were paid in 1973. Based on fiscal 1973 earnings, your Directors felt that prudent financial management dictated a reduction in the dividend payout. At the February 26, 1974 meeting of the Board, a quarterly dividend of $.15 per share was declared on the common stock, payable April 1, 1974. The new dividend will reduce the cash payout, with a consequent conservation of the Company's cash resources.

—Every organization is judged not only by its physical plants and the products marketed, but by the personnel making up its organization. The organization consists of over 85,000 men and women working in stores, offices, distribution centers, and foreign buying offices. The average age of the officers of the company is 48, and they have an average length of service of 20 years. We are confident that this dedicated group will provide the necessary leadership in producing sales and profit in 1974 and the years beyond.

The Management of the Company takes this opportunity to express appreciation to its stockholders for the cooperation, support, and loyalty they have shown over the years. We are proud of the fact that the number of common stockholders last year increased by 10,000, from 20,000 to over 30,000.

The growth in numbers and the support of our stockholders reflect, in good measure, the effects of the Employees' Stock Purchase Plan instituted 24 years ago to put Company ownership within the reach of thousands of employees. Over the years employees have paid for and been issued over 3,000,000 shares of stock.

Balance Sheet Comparisons

	January 31,	
	1974	*1973**
Current Assets		
Cash, Note D	$ 45,951,301	$ 30,943,099
Accounts receivable (Note H)		
Customers' installment accounts	602,305,130	556,091,352
Less: Allowance for doubtful accounts and unearned credit insurance premiums	22,989,598	24,538,014
	$ 579,315,532	$ 531,553,338
Other accounts receivable, refundable taxes, claims, etc.	19,483,020	11,198,027
Total accounts receivable, net	$ 598,798,552	$ 542,751,365
Merchandise inventories (including merchandise in transit), at the lower of cost or market determined principally by the retail inventory method	450,636,556	399,532,793
Prepaid rents, supplies, etc.	7,299,440	6,648,311
Total current assets	$1,102,685,849	$ 979,875,568
Other assets		
Investment in Y Limited, at equity, Note B	30,239,218	26,948,675
Investment in Z Jewelers & Distributors, Inc., at equity, Note B	2,360,388	2,081,319
Investment in debentures of unconsolidated subsidiaries, at cost, Note B	11,651,109	5,951,109
Other	1,200,000	600,000
Total other assets	$ 45,450,715	$ 35,581,103
Common stock of the X Company Held for Deferred Contingent Compensation Plan, at cost, 155,400 and 145,400 shares, respectively	2,499,538	2,381,044
Store properties, fixtures, and improvements, on the basis of cost		
Buildings	1,474,765	1,295,488
Furniture and fixtures	138,827,493	126,670,880
Improvements to leased properties	12,619,744	10,640,270
	$ 152,922,002	$ 138,606,638
Less: Allowance for depreciation and amortization	52,546,310	47,926,186
	$ 100,375,692	$ 90,680,452
Land	608,108	739,296
Total store properties, fixtures and improvements	$ 100,983,800	$ 91,419,748
Unamortized debt expenses, Note A	1,362,782	1,440,144
	$1,252,982,684	$1,110,697,607

Balance Sheet Comparisons (continued)

	January 31,	
	1974	1973*
Current liabilities		
Short-term commercial notes, Note I	$ 453,096,715	$ 380,033,500
Bank loans, Note I	—	10,000,000
Accounts payable for merchandise	58,191,731	60,973,283
Salaries, wages, and bonuses	14,677,793	18,999,960
Other accrued expenses	13,199,372	9,267,297
Taxes withheld from employees	4,411,758	2,194,696
Sales and other taxes	13,429,292	12,981,337
Federal income taxes payable	—	8,480,036
Deferred credits, principally income taxes related to installment sales, Note A	133,057,084	130,137,144
Total current liabilities	$ 690,063,745	$ 633,067,253
Other liabilities		
Long-term debt, Note D	220,336,000	126,672,000
Deferred federal income taxes, Note A	14,649,141	11,925,657
Deferred contingent compensation	2,395,367	2,394,131
Other	1,800,000	2,300,000
Total other liabilities	$ 239,180,508	$ 143,291,788
Capital, Notes A, D, and F		
Capital stock		
Cumulative preferred, $100 par value Authorized 250,000 shares Issued 74,645 and 85,998 shares, respectively, of 3¾% series	7,464,500	8,599,800
Common, $1.25 par value Authorized 22,500,000 shares Issued 14,879,554 and 14,870,198 shares, respectively	18,599,443	18,587,748
Paid-in capital	84,271,469	84,717,986
Amounts paid by employees under purchase contracts for common stock	1,638,359	1,429,077
Earnings retained for use in the business	248,460,873	261,153,443
	$ 360,434,644	$ 374,488,054
Less 808,054 and 876,794 shares, respectively, of treasury common stock, at cost	36,696,213	40,149,488
Total capital	$ 323,738,431	$ 334,338,566
Leases, Note G		
	$1,252,982,684	$1,110,697,607

*Reclassified to conform to current year presentation. (See notes to financial statements.)

Statement of Operations

	Year Ended January 31,	
	1974	*1973**
Sales	$1,849,802,346	$1,644,747,319
Income from concessions	3,970,745	3,752,866
	$1,853,773,091	$1,648,500,185
Cost of merchandise sold, buying and occupancy costs	1,282,944,615	1,125,261,115
	$ 570,828,476	$ 523,239,070
Selling, general, and administrative expenses, Note H	518,278,977	442,211,192
Interest expense, Note H	51,047,481	21,127,084
	569,326,458	463,338,276
	$ 1,502,018	$ 59,900,794
Other income		
Interest earned, Note H	1,035,384	602,218
Miscellaneous, Note D	2,027,121	585,766
	$ 3,062,505	$ 1,187,984
Earnings before income taxes and equity in net earnings of unconsolidated subsidiaries	4,564,523	61,088,778
Provision for federal, state, and local income taxes, Notes A and E		
Current	(6,020,906)	11,255,373
Deferred	6,807,350	17,161,946
	$ 786,444	$ 28,417,319
Earnings before unconsolidated subsidiaries	3,778,079	32,671,459
Equity in net earnings of unconsolidated subsidiaries, Notes A and B.		
Y Limited	4,372,325	5,074,288
Z Jewelers & Distributors, Inc.	279,069	41,319
	$ 4,651,394	$ 5,115,607
Net earnings	$ 8,429,473	$ 37,787,066
Net earnings per common share, Note A	$.59	$2.70

*Reclassified to conform to current year presentation. (See notes to financial statements.)

Stock Equity Accounts

For the Two Years Ended January 31, 1974

	Cumulative Preferred Stock	Common Stock	Paid-in Capital	Amounts Paid by Employees Under Stock Purchase Contracts	Earnings Retained for Use in the Business	Treasury Common Stock
Balance at February 1, 1972	$9,053,000	$18,529,243	$83,963,834	$1,231,674	$244,507,739	($31,540,394)
Purchase of 284,140 shares of treasury common stock						(11,466,195)
Purchase and cancellation of 4,532 shares of cumulative preferred stock	(453,200)		201,609			
Receipts from employees under stock purchase contracts				3,491,518		
Issuance of 40,525 shares of unissued common stock and 62,355 shares of treasury common stock under employee's stock purchase plans		50,656	386,353	(3,294,115)		2,857,101
Conversion of 4% convertible subordinated debentures into 6,279 shares of common stock		7,849	166,190			
Net earnings for the year					37,787,066	
Cash dividends						
3¾% cumulative preferred stock, four quarterly dividends of 93¾¢ each per share					(334,709)	
Common stock, four quarterly dividends of 37½¢ each per share					(20,806,653)	
Balance at January 31, 1973	$8,599,800	$18,587,748	$84,717,986	$1,429,077	$261,153,443	$(40,149,488)

Purchase of 4,600 shares of treasury common stock						(133,316)
Purchase and cancellation of 11,353 shares of cumulative preferred stock	(1,135,300)					
Receipts from employees under stock purchase contracts			517,513			
Issuance of 73,340 shares of treasury common stock under employees' stock purchase plans			(1,211,874)	2,583,998		3,586,593
Conversion of 4% convertible subordinated debentures into 9,356 shares of common stock		11,695	247,844	(2,374,716)		
Net earnings for the year					8,429,473	
Cash dividends						
3¾% cumulative preferred stock, four quarterly dividends of 93¾¢ each per share					(293,054)	
Common stock, four quarterly dividends of 37½¢ each per share					(20,828,989)	
Balance at January 31, 1974	$7,464,500	$18,599,443	$84,271,469	$1,638,359	$248,460,873	($36,696,213)

Sources and Applications of Funds

	Year ended January 31,	
	1974	*1973**
Source of funds		
From operations:		
Net earnings	$ 8,429,473	$ 37,787,066
Less: Increase in the undistributed equity		
in unconsolidated subsidiaries	3,569,612	3,402,785
	$ 4,859,861	$ 34,384,281
Plus: Charges to income not affecting		
working capital		
Depreciation and amortization of		
properties	13,579,083	12,004,268
Increase in deferred federal income taxes	2,723,484	2,262,127
Decrease in other liabilities	(498,764)	(558,404)
Total from operations	$ 20,663,664	$ 48,092,272
Notes payable to banks	100,000,000	—
Receipts from employees under stock		
purchase contracts	2,583,998	3,491,518
Common stock issued upon conversion of		
4% debentures	259,539	174,039
Decrease (increase) in other assets	(600,000)	2,228,645
Total funds provided	$122,907,201	$ 53,986,474
Application of funds		
Dividends to stockholders	21,122,043	21,141,362
Investment in properties, fixtures, and		
improvements	23,143,135	26,250,518
Retirement of long-term debt	6,074,000	1,584,000
Investment Z Jewelers & Distributors, Inc.		
Convertible notes	5,700,000	—
Common stock	—	2,040,000
Purchase of cumulative preferred stock, for		
cancellation	617,787	251,591
Purchase of treasury common stock	133,315	11,466,198
Conversion of 4% convertible subordinated		
debentures	262,000	176,000
Increase (decrease) in sundry accounts, net	41,132	(79,436)
Total funds applied	$ 57,093,412	$ 62,830,233
Working capital increase (decrease)	$ 65,813,789	$ (8,843,759)
Current assets increase (decrease)		
Cash and short-term securities	$ 15,008,202	$ (18,907,685)
Total accounts receivable, net	56,047,187	65,427,296
Merchandise inventories	51,103,763	100,856,623
Other current assets	651,129	1,270,676
	$122,810,281	$148,646,910

Sources and Applications of Funds (continued)

	Year ended January 31,	
	1974	1973*
Current liabilities increase (decrease)		
Short-term commercial notes and bank loans	63,063,215	152,292,800
Accounts payable for merchandise	(2,781,552)	(15,147,075)
Salaries, wages and bonuses	(4,322,167)	3,325,227
Other accrued expenses	3,932,075	(2,835,989)
Taxes withheld from employees	2,217,062	726,479
Sales and other taxes	447,955	2,835,611
Federal income taxes payable	(8,480,036)	(997,220)
Deferred credits, principally income taxes related to installment sales	2,919,940	17,290,836
	$ 56,996,492	$157,490,669
Working capital increase (decrease)	$ 65,813,789	$ (8,843,759)

*Reclassified to conform to current year presentation.

Notes to Stockholders' Reports January 31, 1974

NOTE A—SUMMARY OF SIGNIFICANT ACCOUNTING POLICIES

The financial statements include the accounts of the X Company and its two wholly owned subsidiaries, Financial Corporation and B Studios, Inc.

The Company carries its investments in Y Limited (a 50.2%-owned Canadian subsidiary, cost $8,893,326) and Z Jewelers & Distributors, Inc. (51%-owned, cost $2,040,000), at equity and has included in net earnings its equity in net earnings of such subsidiaries. Y Limited has consistently followed the policy of distributing approximately 40 to 50 percent of current earnings and permanently reinvesting the remainder. In any event, no U.S. deferred income taxes or Canadian withholding taxes have been provided on such undistributed earnings, as such taxes would be substantially offset by available foreign tax credits. No deferred income taxes have been provided on the equity in net earnings of Z Jewelers & Distributors, Inc., as it is intended that such earnings be reinvested in the business.

Gross profits on sales on the installment basis are reflected in the financial statements when the sales are made, whereas for federal income tax purposes, such gross profits are reported as income as collections are received. The resulting difference between taxes accrued and taxes actually payable is included as "Deferred credits, principally income taxes related to installment sales."

At January 31, 1974 accumulated depreciation of approximately $30,094,500 has been deducted for tax purposes in excess of the amount (using the straight-line method) reflected in the financial statements. The resulting tax difference is included in "Deferred federal income taxes."

Investment credits (using the flowthrough method) totaling approximately $1,509,000 have been added to refundable federal income taxes for the year ended January 31, 1974 and $1,750,000 has been deducted from the provision for federal income taxes for the year ended January 31, 1973.

The Company has an Employees' Retirement Plan available to all its employees. The amounts charged to operations for the years ended January 31, 1974 and 1973 for this plan were $1,247,202 and $1,261,018, respectively. The Company funds pension costs accrued.

Expenses associated with the opening of new stores are written off in the year of store opening.

Unamortized debt expenses are being amortized over the lives of the debentures by the "bonds outstanding method."

Net earnings per share of common stock (equivalent to fully diluted), after deduction of dividends on preferred stock, have been determined based upon the average number of shares outstanding during each year.

NOTE B—INVESTMENT IN UNCONSOLIDATED SUBSIDIARIES

Investment in debentures of unconsolidated subsidiaries includes $5,951,109 at January 31, 1974 and 1973 of 5½% convertible debentures of Y Limited and $5,700,000 at January 31, 1974 of convertible notes of Z Jewelers & Distributors, Inc., bearing interest at 125% of the minimum commercial lending rate of the Guaranty Trust Company of New York.

Equity in net earnings of Y Limited includes dividends received of $2,080,782 and $1,712,822 for the years ended January 31, 1974 and 1973, respectively, less in the year ended Janaury 31, 1974, applicable federal income taxes of $999,000 as a result of the inability of the Company to utilize available foreign tax credits due to a net operating loss incurred for federal income tax purposes.

Certain financial information for the years ended January 31, 1974 and 1973, with respect to these unconsolidated subsidiaries is presented below:

| | Y Limited (Canadian $ = U.S. $) | | Z Jewelers & Distributors, Inc. | |
	1974	1973	1974	1973
Assets	$138,671,137	$122,050,661	$30,289,673	$5,480,568
Liabilities	76,680,003	65,756,394	25,661,461	1,399,551
Capital	61,991,134	56,294,267	4,628,212	4,081,017
Sales	$287,016,728	$252,701,343	$30,813,348	$1,366,325
Net earnings	10,304,894	10,257,820	547,195	81,017

NOTE C—DEFERRED CONTINGENT COMPENSATION AND EXECUTIVE BONUS PLANS

The amount charged to operations for the deferred contingent compensation plan was $560,000 and $650,000 for the years ended January 31, 1974 and 1973, respectively.

The amount charged to operations for the executive bonus plan, in which all executives participate, was $1,552,523 and $4,803,365 for the years ended January 31, 1974 and 1973, respectively.

NOTE G—LEASES

Total rental expenses for all leases amounted to

	Year Ended January 31,	
	1974	1973
Financing leases		
Minimum rentals	$101,236,977	$87,659,988
Contingent rentals	2,300,195	2,176,237
Other leases		
Minimum rentals	3,577,735	2,227,950
Less: Rentals from subleases	1,747,848	1,821,251
	$105,367,059	$90,242,924

The contingent rentals are based upon various percentages of sales in excess of specified minimums.

The future minimum rental commitments as of January 31, 1974 for all noncancellable leases (as defined by ASR No. 147) are as follows, (in thousands):

Years Ended January 31,	Financing Leases		Other Leases	Less: Rental from Subleases	Total
	Real Estate	Equipment	Real Estate	of Real Estate	
1975	$ 95,512	$8,522	$ 3,162	$1,539	$105,657
1976	94,013	8,522	3,090	1,240	104,385
1977	91,292	8,522	3,021	1,077	101,758
1978	88,087	7,272	2,993	916	97,436
1979	85,546	7,272	2,993	844	94,967
1980–1984	385,846	1,859	12,522	2,777	397,450
1985–1989	319,693	1,859	12,522	1,379	332,695
1990–1994	167,626	681	12,522	731	180,098
1995 and subsequent	8,391	—	8,139	113	16,417

The estimated present value of the next fixed minimum rental commitments for noncapitalized financing leases and the estimated impact on net earnings had such leases been capitalized is not currently available and will be included in the Company's Form 10-K annual report filed with the Securities and Exchange Commission. A copy of this information will be mailed to all stockholders.

NOTE H—ACCOUNTS RECEIVABLE AND INTEREST

Unearned credit insurance premiums amounted to $4,922,700 and $8,768,405 at January 31, 1974 and 1973, respectively.

Finance charges on customers' installment accounts, included as a reduction of selling, general, and administrative expenses, amounted to approximately $69,756,000 and $76,826,000 for the years ended January 31, 1974 and 1973, respectively. Pro forma interest expense and operating expenses related to the credit operations exceeded finance charges to customers.

Customers' installment accounts range in maturities up to 36 months, with finance charges, where appropriate, ranging up to an annual percentage rate of approximately 18 percent.

Interest earned for the years ended January 31, 1974 and 1973 includes $777,339 and $267,281, respectively, on investments in debentures of unconsolidated subsidiaries. For the years ended January 31, 1974 and 1973, interest expense on long-term debt amounted to $11,300,900 and $6,070,375, respectively.

NOTE I—SHORT-TERM BORROWING

Maturities on short-term commercial notes range from 1 to 270 days from the date of issuance.

The average interest rate on short-term commercial notes outstanding at January 31, 1974 and 1973, was approximately 9.6 percent and 5.7 percent, respectively. The average interest rate on bank loans at January 31, 1973 was approximately 6.0 percent and in connection with such bank loans, the Company agreed to maintain compensating balances that amounted to $705,000 at such date.

The following relates to aggregate short-term borrowings for the years ended:

	January 31,	
	1974	*1973*
Maximum amount outstanding at any month end	$518,871,000	$407,661,000
Average daily amount outstanding	465,204,000	314,101,000
Weighted average daily interest rate	8.55%	4.76%

The Company's line of credit arrangements for short-term borrowings with banks amounted to $493,182,500 and $509,532,500 at January 31, 1974 and 1973, respectively, upon such terms as the Company and the banks may mutually agree. The arrangements do not have termination dates but are reviewed annually for renewal. At January 31, 1974 and 1973, the unused portion of such credit lines were $493,182,500 and $499,532,500, respectively, providing coverage for commercial paper outstanding. The Company maintained cash balances at such banks amounting to $597,000 and $369,000 at January 31, 1974 and 1973, respectively. Subsequent to January 31, 1974 the Company has felt it prudent to reduce its borrowing in the commercial paper field and place a greater reliance on its banks for short-term loans.

Compensating balances are not restricted as to withdrawal, serve as compensation to the banks for their account handling function and other services, and additionally serve as part of the Company's minimum operating cash balances.

Case 2. Bi-State Gas and Electric Company

QUESTION: How much debt capital should Bi-State raise at one time?

The Treasurer of the Bi-State Gas and Electric Company had to decide on the size of a new issue of debentures that would be marketed in the near future. The usual considerations that influenced the size of such an issue by the firm were several.

1. The projection of cash needed over the next several years.
2. The limitations on capital structure proportions desired by management.
3. The general state of the securities market.
4. The potential reaction of the financial community to the particular type of security.
5. The interest costs. The current interest rate on comparable debentures is .155 and short-term marketable securities are yielding .135.
6. The limitations on borrowing put into effect by various indentures of previous bonds and of the preferred stock.
7. The expected reaction of regulatory bodies.

The pattern of Bi-State's cash generation was seasonal, influenced quite heavily by residential sales of gas for space heating purposes. Heavy cash outflow resulted from the firm's construction activities, which were normally carried out during the summer and fall months. The recent rate of construction had been at about $30 million a year, two thirds of which was being supplied from internal sources. The sum of depreciation charges and income in excess of dividends in a normal year were about $20 million. The usual financial pattern was to meet cash needs from internal sources to the degree possible and then borrow the amount necessary to finance construction. When the company did go to the market for funds, it usually borrowed an amount large enough to carry it for about one year. The total sum borrowed would always include funds for the repayment of bank loans and sufficient fund in addition to carry the company through the rest of the year. On the average, financing took place in the capital markets at slightly more than annual intervals. it is estimated that $10 million of debt capital will be needed in the coming 12 months and $20 million in 24 months.

There were several reasons for the company borrowing for one year. In the first place, regulatory agencies tend to frown on excessive idle cash held by a utility; thus the issue was not made larger. It was not smaller than a year's needs since there was a general feeling in the treasurer's office that the market would look askance at a company that had not planned ahead sufficiently to get enough funds for a full year when it went to the market and had to return to the market within 12 months. The specific timing of a security issue was dependent upon the calendar of marketings by corporations published by an investment banking house, the interest rates that were effective in the market, and the degree to which the company had flexibility in relation to the limitations set by indentures, bank loans, and so on. Another important factor was the demand for the particular securities of the company. It often became known to the corporation through various informal communication channels that specific large investors were interested in an offering by Bi-State. This information could often influence the timing of the issue.

The company has an excellent reputation in the financial community, and the history of recent offerings has been that they have "gone out the window" within a few hours of the offering. This reputation is highly valued by financial executives of the company.

The company policy is to make its offerings to the public through competitive bidding. The corporation itself selects the attorney for the offering (whose fees are paid by the low-bidding syndicate). There are a number of fixed charges to a security offering, which must be assumed by the seller. The major expenses are

1. Cost of legal fees (exclusive of the fees described above).
2. Cost of printing of the security issue itself and all the documents that accompany it. (The Trust Indenture Act, applicable SEC regulations for public offerings, and the requirements of the State Public Service Commission are the major causes for the extensive documentation.)
3. Various taxes: state mortgage tax and federal original issue tax.

The treasurer and one other person in her office plus three or four people from the controller's office are ordinarily tied up extensively for a period of approximately 60 days from the time of the decision to make an offering, until the offering has been completed in the market. There is a considerable investment of management time, energy, and emotion in this activity. This results in a considerable aversion to the possibility of frequent offerings in the security market.

The usual types of securities that the corporation offers are unsecured debentures, secured first mortgage bonds, preferred stock, and common stock. The company attempts to maintain a predetermined "target" proportion of these types of securities. The rule of thumb that is ordinarily applied is that the mortgage bonds will not be more than 50 percent of the total value of the property of the firm. The common stock is kept somewhere between 35 and 40 percent of total capital and the preferred stock is usually somewhere around 10 percent. There is an upper limit (60 percent of the value of its property) on the amount of the mortgage bonds that the company can issue. The limit is an enforceable requirement of the trust indenture.

The treasurer states that the general order of desirability of sources of financing is (1) moderate short-term bank borrowings, (2) mortgage bonds, (3) debenture bonds, and (4) common stock issues. Preferred stock is regarded as something of a costly hybrid and is generally not offered except under unusual circumstances (the fact that insurance companies like preferred stock influences the thinking of the treasurer). The bonds of the corporation are usually rated AA. The market has come to expect high quality in the securities of Bi-State, an expectation that the company has tried to live up to.

In its dealings with its banks, management likes to have a margin of safety; it does not want to be "under the gun" by being very near its unsecured financing limit when borrowing from the banks. If management allowed the company to be put in this position, it would also find itself at a disadvantage in the competitive bidding of various investment bankers when it went to the market to refund the bank financing. The margin of safety between the maximum bank indebtedness limit and the amount that the company has borrowed from the banks ensures it a reasonable bargaining position with the banks and gives the firm the ability to turn down all bids on a security offering if they are deemed to be unsatisfactory.

A limit on total borrowings is placed on the company by the indenture covering two series of debentures, which includes a clause binding the company on the amount of interest that may be paid during a 12-month period. The annual earnings before taxes of the company must be at least twice all annual interest charges and long-term rental payments (on leases of five or more years) before additional long-term indebtedness (over one year) of any type may be incurred.

Annual interest charges at this time are about $7,800,000 and long-term rental obligations are $51,000; the total is $7,851,000. Annual earning must be at least $15,702,000 before new debt can be issued. Earnings available for fixed charges are currently $67,600,000.

In a recent issue of $25 million of mortgage bonds, the total recorded out-of-pocket expenses came to about $225,000. Of this amount, $125,000 was the 50-cents-per-hundred mortgage tax and $100,000 was made up of printing costs, legal, and accounting fees, and so on.

Special Topics in Financial Management

Part V contains topics that are of importance to a financial manager, but are not as high in priority for an introduction to managerial finance as are the subjects discussed in the other chapters of this book. For example, two of the chapters deal with types of financing: (in Chapter 21, it is leases; in Chapter 25, it is convertible bonds). We have also included the topic of international finance (Chapter 22) in this part, since this subject is too important to be excluded from a study of basic managerial finance.

Because inflation considerations and inflation forecasts affect long-term capital decisions, we also have to consider how to incorporate inflation in the decision process in a correct manner (Chapter 23). Then Chapter 24 discusses the causes and benefits of mergers and acquisitions. The analysis is consistent with the stock valuation and leverage models discussed in Part III. Finally, the valuation of options (Chapter 26) is included both because options are an important type of security and because option valuation theory is likely to be used in a wide range of applications other than the valuation of an option security.

Chapter 21

Financing by Lease

Major Topics

1. Accounting for leases.
2. The lease calculation and the rate of discount—a simple solution using the after-tax borrowing rate.
3. The complexities arising from taxes, using a risk-adjusted discount rate and the presence of residual value.

Leasing

Leasing is one of the most popular means of financing equipment. You name it, you can lease it—atomic fuel for nuclear power plants, hospital equipment, truck fleets, helicopters and 747s—the list is long. The total value of leased equipment in the United States has been growing at a rate of more than 15 percent per year.

While all this leasing activity has been going on, numerous "buy versus lease" articles have appeared in both trade and academic publications. Although one would expect some sort of consensus to have evolved by now regarding the basic buy versus lease analysis, fundamental misunderstandings about the relative merits of the two modes of financing continue to persist.

For example, it has been argued that

1. The leasing of land has a large tax advantage over outright purchase since land, if owned, cannot be depreciated for tax purposes whereas lease payments are tax deductible.

2. If one were indifferent between buying and leasing without considering taxes, the addition of tax considerations would drive the decision in the direction of leasing.

If you said "yes" to these rules of thumb without qualifications, you have something to learn. Although differential tax rates may have been a prime motivator for the increase in leasing, improper lease versus buy analysis has probably been somewhat responsible for the tremendous popularity of leasing.

The confusion regarding the lease decision is not helped by the fact that the tax laws keep changing dramatically. The 1981, 1982, and 1984 tax acts greatly affected what is allowed and not allowed in the general area of leasing. Not only is it necessary to be familiar with the specifics of the current tax acts, but it is also necessary to be familiar with the Treasury Department regulations that interpret the tax laws passed by Congress.

There are two very important characteristics of leases that should be carefully distinguished and understood. The more important is the way in which a lease will affect the firm's tax situation. The second is the way in which a lease will affect the accounting reports.

Accounting for Leases

The accounting for leases is currently defined by Financial Accounting Standards Board statement No. 13 and the supplementary statements issued to explain FASB (Financial Accounting Standards Board) No. 13.

For the lessee (the user of the asset), there are two types of leases. The lease may be a capital lease or an operating lease. If any one of several criteria is satisfied, the lease is a capital lease. Among the criteria are the longevity of the lease (the lease is a capital lease if the lease term is equal to or greater than 75 percent of the useful life of the asset) and the amount of the lease payments (the lease is a capital lease if the present value of the lease payments is equal to or larger than 90 percent of the fair value or normal selling price of the asset at the beginning of the lease term). With a capital asset, the financial statements of the lessee must show an asset and liability equal to the present value of the payments as well as report in a note the minimum payments for the next five years. A capital lease is analogous (for reporting purposes) to a purchase of an asset.

With an operating lease, the lessee does not include the present value of the payments on the balance sheet, but the payments for the next five years as well as the total payments for the entire life of the lease are shown in a note to the financial statements.

If the lease is a capital lease, the expense shown for a period is not the actual cash paid but will be equal to an interest expense on the liability and a depreciation expense associated with the asset. The total of these two revenue deductions is not likely to be equal to the actual lease payment made during the period, which would be the expense if the lease were an operating lease. They are likely to be larger in the early years of asset life than the expense of an operating lease if the payments are the same for both types of leases.

If there is predictable collectibility and no cost uncertainty and if the lease has the characteristic of a capital lease, it is treated by the lessor as a sales-type or direct financing lease. If the lease is not a financing lease, it is an operating lease. With a sales-type lease, the present value of the lease payments is treated as revenue at the time of the lease signing. With an operating lease, the revenue of a period is equal to the cash received.

A capital or sales-type lease is sometimes referred to as a "full-payout" lease (the present value of the lease is approximately equal to the cost of the asset). With such a lease, the full profit (except for interest) earned by the lessor is recorded at the time of the lease signing. Since a consistent earning stream is considered to be an important attribute for a firm to display in the financial markets, equipment manufacturers have found leasing and the operating method of accounting for leases to be a vehicle for smoothing earnings. As a general business activity rises and falls, the amount of new leases may also rise and fall, but reported earnings are much more stable since income is recorded as payment is received from the old leases as well as the new. The sales method of reporting results in more volatile earnings.

This section has dealt with accounting issues. Accounting practice has nothing to do with taxes in dealing with leases.

Lessors and Lessees

Any business entity can be a lessee. The biggest leasing category, real estate aside, is transportation equipment—oil tankers, railroad rolling stock, airplanes, trucks, and autos. Other major groups of assets that are leased are computers and other data processing devices, copiers, and specialized machinery.

Lessors fall into two major categories. First are high-income, high-tax individuals and the financial institutions with large cash flows (the insurance companies, banks, and finance and investment companies with large taxable incomes "requiring" tax sheltering). With little by way of depreciable assets, these individuals and institutions have a strong incentive to buy equipment and then lease it to equipment users who cannot take advantage of such tax benefits as accelerated depreciation and investment tax credits because they do not have taxable income. In some cases, the plant or equipment purchased by the lessor is financed by loans made to the lessor, thereby creating a situation known as leveraged leasing.

The second type of lessor is the manufacturer-lessor. These companies use leases and rental agreements as key tools in the marketing of their products, enabling them to attract customers who might not be able to finance an outright purchase.

The Pros and Cons of Leasing

Table 21.1 shows in summary form many of the arguments offered in favor of and against leasing. It can be seen that frequently a "pro" argument is canceled by a "con" argument, leaving the decision maker to evaluate subjectively how the factor is to be brought into the decision.

TABLE 21.1   Ten Pros and Cons of Leasing

Pro	*Con*
1. It is 100 percent debt financing.	1. A lease may preclude other debt financing if it is a firm obligation to pay.
2. With a short-term lease, there is less risk of being "stuck" with a bad asset if the useful life is less than expected; there is no argument about life with IRS.	2. No residual value if life is longer than expected.
3. The short-term lease gives flexibility.	3. Lease terms may be adjusted upward at the end of the lease.
4. Maintenance may be cheaper than if you did it yourself.	4. The same maintenance contract can probably be purchased if you buy.
5. An operating lease is off-balance-sheet financing.	5. Many experts reconstruct financial statements to include operating leases.
6. With a lease it is easier to justify investments (higher return on investment since there is zero or a small investment.	6. It does not fool as many as it used to. The lease should be capitalized.
7. A lease is easy and quick to obtain.	7. Not always. Some lease arrangements are very complex.
8. Higher book income is generated in early years.	8. This is a result of accounting convention; also later incomes will be less.
9. Lower property taxes are paid.	9. Property taxes are likely to be built into lease payments.
10. There are tax savings.	10. There are tax dissavings.

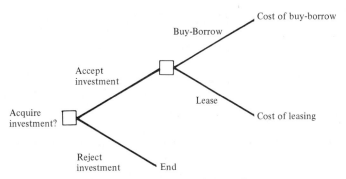

FIGURE 21.1   Buy-Borrow Versus Lease: Lessee

We do not expand on all these items in this chapter; rather, we stick to basic economic analysis using the cash flows associated with the two alternatives (buy and lease) under well-defined conditions. We will consistently compare leasing with conventional debt accompanying the buy alternative.

Figure 21.1 shows the basic buy versus lease analysis. First, it must be decided whether or not the investment is acceptable. Second, the annual cost of buying the asset with borrowed funds must be compared with the annual cost of leasing. If the cost of buy and borrow is less than the cost of leasing, then the third and final step is to consider whether it is desirable to finance the investment with debt or with a mixture of debt and stock equity.

The Fundamental Misunderstanding

The fundamental misunderstanding about the lease analysis lies in how to evaluate the financial aspect of leasing and to separate the financing and investment elements. Throughout this chapter, we shall assume that we are discussing a lease that is highly similar to a purchase with the borrowing of the purchase price. The lease contract being considered has all the characteristics of a long-term legal debt obligation. The lessee must pay the specified sum to the lessor at the specified times of payment or suffer legal consequences. Any lease that can be broken within 30 days notice by the lessee without substantial penalty is not the type of lease being discussed in this section.

The key to putting leasing in proper perspective is to realize that committing one's company to a set of lease payments is equivalent to committing the company to a set of comparable debt service payments in the eyes of the financial community. Any knowledgeable financial analyst immediately capitalizes financial leases even if they are technically operating leases. For example, if it is disclosed that a given company is obliged to pay, say, $36,829 per year for three years to a leasing firm, the present value of those lease obligations at the existing opportunity cost of debt, say, 10 percent, would be

$$\$36,289 \times B(3, .10) = \$36,829 \times 2.4869 = \$91,590$$

The analyst would modify the existing balance sheet data by adding $91,590 worth of lease-equivalent assets to the firm and $91,590 worth of debt-equivalent liabilities. The relevant comparison for decision purposes is not buy versus lease, but buy and borrow versus lease.

The Basic Problem

We shall try to isolate the basic components of the buy versus lease decision. Consider the following set of situations:

EXAMPLE 21.1   BUY-BORROW VERSUS ─────────────── LEASE

The Setting

1. No tax considerations
2. No uncertainty regarding cash flows
3. The investment has no salvage value

The Problem

It is time to acquire equipment that will permit you to turn a currently useless by-product of your production process into a marketable product (scrap reclamation). The economic life of such equipment is three years. You have already decided to proceed with the project, but the problem is whether to buy the machine at a cost of $90,000 or lease it from the manufacturer at an annual lease fee of $36,829 for three years. The lease is "net, net" meaning that you provide all the maintenance and insurance.

The Analysis

A quick call to your local banker reveals that the bank is willing to lend the firm the $90,000 at an interest rate of 10 percent. This, the bank lending officer informs you, will require annual payments at $36,190. The bank credit officer did the following calculations to obtain the annual payments.

Let R be the annual payment; then

$$R \times B \ (3, .10) = \$90,000 \qquad \text{or} \qquad R = \frac{\$90,000}{2.4869} = \$36,190$$

The Decision
Since buy-borrow is cheaper than lease by $639 per year for the three years, you arrange for the loan and purchase the equipment. The firm would rather pay $36,190 to the bank than $36,829 to the lessor. It can be shown that the lease has an implicit cost of 11 percent.

Given these facts, we see that buy-borrow is preferred to lease if it is already decided that we need the equipment. Thus our decision at the second node of the decision tree depicted in Figure 21.2 is to buy-borrow. Now consider the first decision—the acquisition decision.

EXAMPLE 21.2   ACQUIRE THE NEW EQUIPMENT?

The Setting
No tax considerations

The Problem
The incremental cash flows associated with an equipment acquisition would be $38,000 per year (estimated annual revenue from sale of product less cost of production excluding equipment cost). The Equipment Costs $90,000.

The Analysis
The firm normally uses the weighted average cost of capital (WACC) as its "hurdle rate" in investment analysis. The WACC is estimated to be 14 percent.

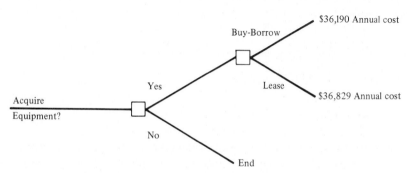

FIGURE 21.2   Buy-Borrow Versus Lease: Lessee

Method of Financing	Cost	Weighted in Capital Structure	Weighted Cost
Debt	.10	.5	.05
Equity	.18	.5	.09
			.14 = WACC

If we use 14 percent as a discount rate, the net present value analysis for acquiring the equipment is

Time	Cash Flow	Present Value Factor @ 14%	Present Value @ 14%
0	− $90,000	1.0000	− $90,000
1–3	38,000	2.3216	88,221
		Net present value @ 14% =	− $ 1,779

The net present value of acquiring the equipment is negative using the WACC as a discount rate. But, if we lease the equipment, the net present value is clearly positive at any discount rate since leasing provides an expected net benefit of $38,000 − $36,829 = $1,171 per year.

At 14 percent, these benefits have a net present value of $2,719.

The Decision

This analysis would seem to indicate that the firm should reject the buy alternative, but that leasing is acceptable (leasing has a positive net present value with any positive rate of discount). But the work in Example 21.1 already showed that if the equipment is acceptable, the firm should buy-borrow not lease!

The Proper Perspective

The analysis in Example 21.2 leading to the acceptance of leasing and the rejection of the buy alternative is faulty. We cannot logically compare "buy" and "lease"; rather, we compare "buy-borrow" and "lease" or compare buy with a lease alternative that is placed on a basis that is comparable to buy. The lease alternative implicitly includes debt financing flows while the buy alternative has no such flows. A comparison of the net present values as structured above is likely to be faulty.

With an optimal capital structure, there is no reason to think that one type of capital (e.g., debt) costs less than other types of capital (e.g., stock), if all costs are considered. Substituting debt for common stock increases the average cost of debt and the average cost of stock, and theory indicates that at the margin debt costs the same as stock. If the use of 14 percent properly leads to a reject decision for the buy and borrow analysis, the lease analysis must be placed on a comparable basis.

The analysis of Example 21.2 with a consequent decision to lease is a common error in financial decision making. Using the WACC, or any other other rate larger than the borrowing rate, as a discount rate in comparing buy and lease alternatives builds a bias toward leasing into the analysis. Since there are implicitly debt-equivalent flows in the lease cash flows, discounting these cash flows at a discount rate (WACC) greater than the cost of debt will increase the net present value of leasing compared to the buy alternative that excluded debt flows.

A Proper Comparison

Assume an investment analysis that uses cash flows with debt flows subtracted from the basic investment flows (stock equity flows are being used). Any conventional investment with an internal rate of return greater than the cost of debt can be made to appear better (a greater net present value) by including the debt flows in the analysis or by increasing the debt used to finance the investment and focusing on the net present value of the residual cash flows. Since lease payments are effectively debt service, it is important that comparability be established between the lease and buy alternatives in acquisition analysis. There are essentially three methods of neutralizing the financial differences between the two alternatives.

The first method would be to recognize the lease payments as debt service and discount these payments at the cost of debt, thereby comparing the cost of buying with debt against acquiring with lease. In the illustration, the debt equivalent of leasing (the present value of the lease payments at 10 percent) is

$$\$36,829 \times B(3, .10) = \$36,829 \times 2.4869 = \$91,590$$

If funds are borrowed and the equipment is purchased, the present value of the debt service and flows is $90,000 and buy-borrow is preferred to leasing that costs $91,590.

The second method of comparing buy-borrow and lease is to include the debt flows in the buy analysis. The net of debt flows of buying are $38,000 − $36,190 = $1,810 per year. The net benefits from leasing are $1,171 per year, which is less than the buy-borrow net benefits of $1,810.

The third method is comparable to the second. We contend that the decision tree approach of Figure 21.1 is an appropriate approach. If acquisition is desirable and leasing is an alternative, we can compare the annual equivalent costs of financing the acquisition by debt and by leasing. Since the benefit stream of cash flows from acquisition is the same under either acquisition strategy, the differential cash flows between buy-borrow and lease arise solely from the differences in the contractual obligation of the two alternatives. Debt financing costs $36,190, and the lease costs $36,829; therefore, buy-borrow is more desirable than leasing.

These three procedures tell us what to do if we have decided to accept the equipment. They do not tell us whether or not the equipment is desirable. With no uncertainty, the investment is desirable. With uncertainty, both buying and leasing may not be acceptable.

The Effect of Taxes

Let us assume that the equipment acquisition is deemed desirable and that the method of acquisition is the only question. Taxes exert substantial influence and must be considered. With respect to income taxes, the total lease payments are tax deductible, whereas depreciation and interest payments on debt are deductible under the buy-borrow alternative. Either the lessor or lessee may take any current investment tax credit offered.

How do these tax factors affect the decision? Let us proceed with our previous illustration, assuming that there is no investment tax credit. Now assume that the lessor offers to lease at $36,190 per year, the same as the debt service payments to the bank if the $90,000 were borrowed. This would result in indifference if there were zero taxes. Do taxes force the analysis toward lease or buy-borrow in this case?

Suppose that the tax rate is 40 percent. If the $90,000 is borrowed the debt repayment schedule would be

Period	Amount Owed Beginning of Period	Interest at 10%	Principal Payment	Total Payment
1	$90,000	$ 9,000	$27,190	$ 36,190
2	62,810	6,280	29,910	36,190
3	32,900	3,290	32,900	36,190
		$18,570	$90,000	$108,570

If straight-line depreciation is used by the firm for taxes, the total tax deductions resulting from buy-borrow and leasing would be

Period	Interest	Straight-Line Depreciation	Buy-Borrow Total Tax Deductions	Lease Tax Deductions
1	$ 9,000	$30,000	$ 39,000	$ 36,190
2	6,280	30,000	36,280	36,190
3	3,290	30,000	33,290	36,190
	$18,570	$90,000	$108,570	$108,570

The tax deduction each year with leasing is $36,190 or $108,570 for three years. The sums of the deductions arising from both buy-borrow and leasing are $108,570, but the timing of the cash flows clearly favor the buy-borrow alternative, even if straight-line depreciation expense is used for taxes rather than accelerated depreciation.

Note that if the firm used accelerated depreciation, as it normally would for tax purposes, the buy-borrow alternative would be even more preferable. Total tax deductions would again be the same, but the timing would be even more favorable in the early years to buy-borrow. In this situation where there was initially indifference and zero taxes, the inclusion of taxes moved the decision toward buy-borrow.

A Method of Solution

If we use straight-line tax depreciation and the after-tax borrowing rate of .06, the net cost of buy-borrow is

$$\$90,000 - .4(\$30,000)2.673 = \$90,000 - \$32,076 = \$57,924$$

The $32,076 is the present value of the tax savings resulting from the use of straight-line tax depreciation.

Let

$$r = \text{the after-tax borrowing rate}$$
$$t_c = \text{the corporate tax rate}$$
$$L = \text{the annual lease payment}$$
$$B(n, r) = \text{the present value of an annuity for } n \text{ periods discounted}$$
$$\text{at } r \text{ interest rate}$$

The after-tax present value cost of leasing is

$$(1 - t_c)LB(n, r) = \$36,190 (1 - .4)B(3, .06) = \$58,042$$

Buy has a smaller after-tax present value cost than does leasing. We can use $(1 - t_c)LB(n, r)$ to compute the present value of leasing since the after-tax borrowing rate is being used as the discount rate.

This calculation is a reasonable solution to the problem of determining whether leasing or buying with borrowing is more desirable. This very easy method of solution is possible, since the firm is willing to use the after-tax borrowing rate to discount all the cash flows. If any other discount rate is used, we must use a more complex method of solution. The use of the after-tax borrowing rate has the advantage of causing the after-tax present value of the debt flows associated with borrowing to be equal to zero. This makes the buy-borrow and the lease calculations equivalent.

You should not be lulled into the belief that if there is indifference between buy-borrow and lease on a before-tax basis, the after-tax analysis will always demonstrate that buy-borrow is less costly. Suppose that the lessor offered the equipment at $32,901 per year, with payment due at the beginning of the year rather than at the end. The present value of the lease payments at the before-tax cost of debt is again $90,000,

$$\$32,901 + \$32,901 \times B(2, .10) = \$90,000$$

which is the same as the present value of the debt service cash flows, and there is before-tax indifference. But the present value of the after-tax cash flows of leasing discounted at the after-tax cost of debt,

$$(1 - .4)(\$32,901)\,[1 + B(2, .06)] = \$55,933$$

is in this case less than the present value of the after-tax cash flows from buy-borrow with straight-line depreciation ($57,924). Leasing is now less costly than buy-borrowing. Changing the timing of the lease payments and the tax deductions affects the relative desirability of buy-borrow and lease, even though the before-tax present values are not changed.

There are no easily applied consistently correct rules of thumb in buy versus lease analysis—a complete after-tax discounted cash flow analysis is the safest way of making the decision.

The After-Tax Borrowing Rate Model

We want to analyze the lease versus buy-borrowing decision using the after-tax borrowing rate.

t_c = the corporate tax rate

PVD = the present value of the depreciation deductions for taxes using the after-tax cost of debt (obtained from tables or by calculation) per dollar of investment

C = the initial cost (tax basis) of the investment
L = the annual lease payment
r = the after-tax borrowing rate
$B(n, r)$ = the present value of an n period annuity discounted at r

The net present value cost of buy-borrow is

$$C - (\text{PVD})\, t_c C$$

Here we are not ignoring the after-tax debt cash flows but are recognizing that their net present value is zero if they are discounted at the after-tax borrowing rate.

Since the after-tax borrowing rate is being used, the net present cost of leasing is the present value of the after-tax lease payments:

$$L(1 - t_c)B(n, r)$$

For this example, the depreciation expense each year is $.333 per dollar and the present value is .891. The net present value of the net of tax cost of buying using straight-line depreciation and a .06 rate of discount is

$$C - (\text{PVD})t_c C = \$90{,}000 - (.891).4(\$90{,}000) = \$90{,}000 - \$32{,}076 = \$57{,}924$$

If lease payments are $36,190, the net present value of the cost of leasing using a .06 rate of discount is

$$L(1 - t_c)B(n, r) = \$36{,}190\,(1 - .4)2.673 = \$58{,}042$$

Buy-borrow is preferred to leasing, since $57,924 is the lower net present value cost.

This solution takes advantage of the fact that the benefits are common to both alternatives and we are only considering the choice between buy-borrow and leasing; thus the benefits can be omitted from the analysis. The simplified calculations are feasible since the after-tax borrowing rate is being used to discount all the cash flows.

Any residual value at time 3 would further reduce the cost of buying.

Risk-Adjusted Discount Rate

In the previous section we used the after-tax borrowing rate as the discount rate. We shall now assume that management is willing to discount debt flows using the borrowing rate but wants to use a "risk-adjusted rate" for other cash flows. These "other" cash flows include (1) depreciation tax savings (or the equivalent) and (2) residual value.

EXAMPLE 21.3

Assume that both the lease payments and debt payments with buy-borrow are $36,190. The firm evaluates investments using a risk-adjusted rate (j) of .20.

The total annual tax deduction with leasing is $36,190, but we have to break that down into "interest" and "depreciation." For leasing, the "depreciation" equivalent is equal to the "principal" portion of the lease payment.

Using the before-tax borrowing rate of .10, we obtain a present value (debt equivalent) of lease payments of

$$\$36,190B(3, .10) = \$36,190(2.4869) = \$90,000$$

The implicit debt amortization schedule for the lease is

Period	Beginning Liability	Interest (.10)	Principal Payment
1	$90,000	$9,000	$27,190
2	62,810	6,280	29,910
3	32,900	3,290	32,900
			$90,000

The tax savings associated with the investment like aspects of the lease are

Period	Lease Outlay	Interest	"Depreciation" or Principal	Tax Rate .4	Cash Flow (tax savings)	Preset Value of Tax Savings (j = .20)
1	$36,190	$9,000	$27,190	.4	$10,876	$ 9,063
2	36,190	6,280	29,910	.4	11,964	8,308
3	36,190	3,290	32,900	.4	13,160	7,616
			$90,000		$36,000	$24,987

For the buy alternative using straight-line depreciation, we have

Period	Buy		Cash Flow (tax savings)	Present Value of Tax Savings (j = .20)
1	$30,000	× .4 =	$12,000	$10,000
2	30,000	× .4 =	12,000	8,333
3	30,000	× .4 =	12,000	6,944
			$36,000	$25,277

The depreciation tax savings of buy are larger than the depreciation equivalent tax savings of leasing. Since all other things are equal, buy is better than leasing.

These depreciation tax savings are the only cash flows for both alternatives that are not debt types of flows, and it can be argued that only these flows and not the financing-type flows should be discounted at a risk-adjusted rate.

Inspection of the tax saving numbers reveals that at any positive rate of interest, the buy stream (even with zero residual value) is to be preferred to the leasing stream. A decrease in the lease payments from $36,190 is necessary to increase the relative desirability of lease compared to buy-borrow. Using $j = .20$, the after-tax present value cost of buying is $90,000 - $25,277 = $64,723.

If we had incorrectly used $j = .20$ to discount all the after-tax cash flows of leasing, we have

$$(1 - t_c)LB(3, .20) = (1 - .4)\$36,190(2.1065) = \$45,741$$

This calculation indicates that leasing has a smaller net cost than does buying. It is an incorrect calculation because it implicitly includes the debt component in the lease cash flows that are being discounted at .20. If we included the debt flows in the buy analysis and discounted at .20 the net cost would be $45,451. The cost is reduced since .10 debt is being discounted at .20.

Debt Calculations Using .20

Period	Interest	$(1 - .4)$ Interest	Principal Payment	After-Tax Cash Flows	Present Value Using .20
1	$9,000	$5,400	$27,190	$32,590	$27,158
2	6,280	3,768	29,910	33,678	23,388
3	3,290	1,974	32,900	34,874	20,182
				Present value of outlays =	$70,728

net present value of debt = $90,000 − $70,728 = $19,272

net cost of buying = $64,723 − $19,272 = $45,451

or

net cost of buying = $70,728 − $25,277 = $45,451

where $70,728 is the present value of the debt outlays, and the $25,277 is the present value of the tax savings from depreciation.

Lease Payments Less than Debt Payments

If the lease payments are less than the debt payments of the buy-borrow alternative, the method of analysis is analogous to the foregoing calculations. The first step is to compute the present value of the before-tax lease flows using the before-tax borrowing rate associated with straight debt. This is the before-tax debt equivalent of leasing. We then compute the amount of the excess of the cost if the asset were purchased over the present value of the lease. It is necessary to split the lease payments into "interest" and "principal" as was done earlier but now the total amount of principal will not be $90,000. We can compute the annual tax savings from the principal payments (the depreciation equivalent of leasing).

EXAMPLE 21.4

Assume the lease payments are $35,555 per period rather than $36,190. This is an implicit before-tax cost of 9 percent.

$$RB(3, .09) = \$90,000$$
$$2.5313R = \$90,000$$
$$R = \$35,555$$

The present value of the lease payments using 10 percent the before-tax borrowing rate is

$$\$35,555(2.4869) = \$88,422$$

The amortization of the $88,422 using .10 as the interest rate is

Period	Implicit Lease Debt	Interest (.10)	Principal Payment or "Depreciation"	Payment
1	$88,422	$8,842	$26,713	$35,555
2	61,709	6,171	29,384	35,555
3	32,325	3,232	32,323	35,555
			$88,420	

The tax savings associated with the lease depreciation deductions (the deduction will actually be a lease payment) are

Period	Principal Payment	Tax Rate	Tax Savings	Present Value (.06)
1	$26,713	.4	$10,685	$10,080
2	29,384	.4	11,754	10,461
3	32,323	.4	12,929	10,855
				$31,396

The final step is to compute the present value of the tax savings. If .06 is used as the discount rate, the present value is $31,396.

The complexity of the Example 21.4 calculations arises because of a desire to separate the debt cash flows from the other flows of buy-borrow and leasing. If the after-tax borrowing rate is being used as the discount rate for all flows, the separation is not necessary. Using any risk-adjusted rate for a discount rate necessitates a separation of the cash flows into debt and nondebt cash flows.

Using .06, we have

	Buy	Lease
Value of depreciation tax saving	$32,076	$31,396
Cost difference ($90,000 − $88,422)		1,578
Total savings	$32,076	$32,974

The total savings of buying are $32,076 and with leasing are $32,974. Leasing is more desirable. The net costs are

net cost of buying $= \$90,000 - \$32,076 = \$57,924$
net cost of leasing $= \$88,422 - \$31,396 = \$57,026$

Since the after-tax borrowing rate is being used, we can take a shortcut in the calculations and use

$(1 - t_c)LB(n, r) = (1 - .4)\$35,555(2.673) = \$57,023$

Except for a rounding error, we obtain the same net cost as the longer procedure.

Residual Value

Assume that .06 is the correct interest rate and that the same facts apply as earlier when the lease payments are $35,555 per year, except that the expected residual value is $1,070 if the firm buys. The present value of depreciation tax savings $32,076 plus the present value of residual value ($898) is $32,974 for buy-borrow using .06. This is equal to the present value of the tax shield of the noninterest portion of the lease payments ($31,396) plus the $1,578 of savings because the present value of before-tax lease payments ($88,422) are less than the present value of debt flows of buying ($90,000). Figure 21.3 shows that if the appropriate discount rate is greater than .06 leasing is more desirable than buy-borrow.

Instead of plotting the present value of the nondebt flows as in Figure 21.3, we could plot the net cost of the two alternatives as in Figure 21.4.

With a zero rate of discount the net cost of buying is

$$\$90,000 - .4(\$90,000) - \$1,070 = \$52,930$$

and the net cost of leasing is

$$\$88,422 - .4(\$88,422) = \$53,053$$

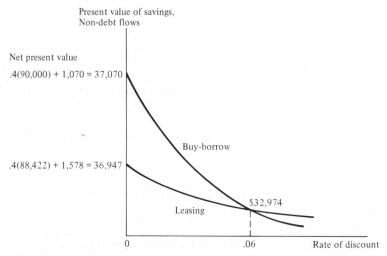

FIGURE 21.3   Buy Versus Lease with $1,070 of Residual Value (Present Value of Savings)

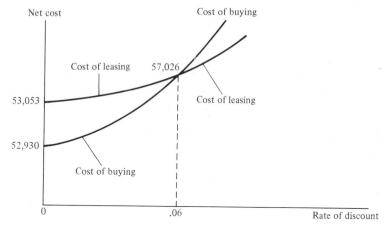

FIGURE 21.4   Net Costs (Residual Value = $1,070)

Note that $88,422 is obtained using .06 as the rate of discount. If we use .06 to discount the tax savings, the net cost of leasing is

$$
\begin{aligned}
\text{PV of lease (before tax)} &= \$88,422 \\
\text{PV of tax savings} &= \underline{\;31,396\;} \\
\text{net cost of leasing} &= \$57,026
\end{aligned}
$$

The net cost of buying with residual value of $1,070 is also $57,026 using .06:

$$\$90,000 - \$32,076 - \$898 = \$57,026$$

With a lower interest rate than .06 buy-borrow is more desirable than leasing and with a higher interest rate leasing wins (has a lower cost). At .06 there is indifference.

The Issues

We have illustrated a procedure that allows the use of any rate of discount for computing the present value of the tax savings from depreciation (or the depreciation equivalent of leasing) and the present value of the residual value.

Some analysts will want to discount depreciation tax savings using a risk-free rate since these cash flows are nearly certain. Others will prefer the after-tax borrowing rate since it avoids certain types of error and is consistent with the opportunity cost of new debt capital. Finally, some will prefer to include an adjustment for risk in computing the present value of depreciation tax savings and residual value (or for one of them).

We do not want to reach a final decision on this issue since there is not one correct answer. However, if an interest rate larger than the after-tax borrowing rate is used, care must be taken to place the buy-borrow analysis on a comparable basis to the lease analysis. The lease analysis tends to include debt flows, and if a high interest rate is used, this creates a bias for leasing. The solution recommended is to compute a debt equivalent of leasing and analyze separately the investment characteristics of leasing so that leasing and buying are comparable.

K Mart Corporation

As of January 25, 1984, K Mart showed as a noncurrent liability on its balance sheet "Obligations under capital leases" of $1,822,300,000. The notes to the statement included the following:*

Future minimum lease payments with respect to capital and operating leases are

Fiscal Year	Minimum Lease Payments Capital (million)	Operating
1984	$ 341.4	$ 214.5
1985	337.4	211.3
1986	331.6	207.0
1987	325.4	203.0
1988	320.4	196.3
Later years	4,175.9	2,430.6
Total minimum lease payments	5,832.1	$3,462.7
Less: Minimum sublease rental income		(160.5)
Net minimum lease payments	5,832.1	$3,302.2
Less: Amount representing estimated executory costs	(1,591.7)	
Amount representing interest	(2,347.5)	
Obligations under capital leases, of which $70.6 is due within one year	$1,892.9	

* Leases are an important type of financing.

Conclusions

Leasing is an important financial device. For smaller firms without access to debt money, it may be the only way of acquiring equipment. But for many potential lessees, the option to buy is available, and, with ready access to the debt-capital market, the relevant decision is to compare buy-borrow and lease since firm lease commitments are, in effect, debt-type obligations. Furthermore, in focusing on the incremental cash flows of buy-borrow and lease, the use of the after-tax borrowing rate enables us to choose the form of the debt. The use of a conventional investment hurdle rate (j) or WACC to discount total lease flows with the formula $(1 - t_c)LB(n, j)$ is in error.

Many firms have made the wrong financing decision by not following these principles. Comparing buy (without including debt flows) with lease flows using a high discount rate and cash flows of $(1 - t_c)L$ creates an inherent bias toward the leasing alternative, and we suspect that the phenomenal growth rate in leasing witnessed in the past few years is, in part, the result of faulty analysis.

There are no easy rules of thumb to help decide which alternative is preferable even when the intangibles are ignored. Calculating and comparing the net present after-tax cash flows of the two alternatives will provide a guideline with respect to these factors if the correct discount rate and correct cash flows are employed.

Review Problem 21.1

Assume that the A Corporation can obtain a 10-year noncancellable lease of $12,500 per year for an asset that it wants. The lease payment is due at the end of each year. The asset will have zero value at the end of 10 years.

The asset would cost $70,000 if purchased. It will earn gross cash flows of $13,500 per year.

Corporate taxes are .46. The asset fits in the 5-year accelerated cost recovery system (ACRS) class life. If the .10 investment tax credit (ITC) is taken, the depreciation base for taxes is .95 of the cost.

The corporation can borrow money repayable in equal installments at a before-tax cost of .13. It has a weighted average cost of capital of .15 and a cost of equity capital of .20. Round the discount rate to three decimals.

Assume that the firm has decided to acquire the asset. Assume that the firm is willing to use the borrowing rate (before or after tax, as is appropriate). If the asset is leased the lessor will take the ITC.

The net of tax cost of buying is _____ .

The net of tax cost of leasing is _____ .

Present Value of Depreciation of $1,000,000 of Assets Under ACRS

Discount Rate	Class Life			
	3 Years	5 Years	10 Years	15 Years
01	979156	969618	949194	928486
02	959001	940615	902132	864282
03	939507	912912	858479	806496
04	920645	886436	817933	754358
05	902386	861118	780223	707203
06	884707	836893	745105	664453
07	867582	813701	712360	625607
08	850988	791487	681788	590226
09	834904	770198	653211	557930
10	819309	749784	626466	528385
11	804183	730201	601407	501299
12	789507	711404	577900	476415
13	775263	693353	555825	453508
14	761435	676010	535071	432377
15	748007	659340	515539	412848
16	734962	643309	497136	394764
18	709968	613040	463395	362398
20	686343	584973	433263	334347

Solution to Review Problem 21.1

net cost of buying = $70,000 − .46($70,000)(.813701).95 − $7,000 = $38,109

net cost of leasing = $12,500(1 − .46)$B(10, .07)$ = $47,409

Review Problem 21.2 (Problem 1 continued)

The A Corporation wants to use its WACC of .15 to evaluate all investment types of alternatives. Prepare an analysis using .15 to evaluate investment flows.

(a) What is the net of tax cost of buying?
(b) What is net after-tax cost of leasing (round off to nearest dollar in calculating)?
(c) What is the present value of the "depreciation equivalents" with leasing
   if .07 is used as the discount rate?

Solution to Review Problem 21.2

(a) $70,000 − .46($70,000)(.95)(.65934) − $7,000 = $42,831 = net cost of
   buying.
(b) $12,500(5.42624) − .46($29,630) = $54,198 = net cost of leasing
(c) $44,532 and the tax savings are $44,532 × .46 = $20,485.

   The $44,532 is obtained by discounting the "principal payments" using .07.

Amount Owed	Interest (.13)	Principal
1. $67,828	$8,818	$ 3,682
2. 64,146	8,339	4,161
3. 59,985	7,798	4,702
4. 55,283	7,187	5,313
5. 49,970	6,496	6,004
6. 43,966	5,716	6,784
7. 37,182	4,834	7,666
8. 29,516	3,837	8,663
9. 20,853	2,711	9,789
10. 11,064	1,438	11,062
	Present value (.15) =	$29,630
	Present value (.07) =	$44,523

PROBLEMS

1. Assume zero taxes. Equipment can be leased at $10,000 per year (first
   payment 1 year hence) for 10 years or purchased at a cost of $64,177. The
   company has a weighted average cost of capital of 15 percent. A bank has
   indicated that it would be willing to make the loan of $64,177 at a cost of
   10 percent.
      Should the company buy or lease? There are no uncertainties. The
   equipment will be used for 10 years. There is zero salvage value.

2. (Problem 1 continued)   If the bank was willing to lend funds at 9 percent, should the company buy or lease?

3. (Problem 2 continued)   If the company pays $64,177 for the equipment, it will save $10,000 a year lease payments for 10 years.
   What internal rate of return will it earn on its "investment?"

4. (Problem 1 continued)   Now assume a marginal tax rate of .4. Assume that the funds can be obtained for .10 at a bank. The company uses sum-of-the-years' digits depreciation for taxes.
   Should the firm buy or lease? (Assume that the present value of the depreciation deductions is .79997 per dollar of depreciable assets using .06 as the discount rate.)

5. (Problem 1 continued) Now assume a marginal tax rate of .4 and that a loan can be obtained from the bank at a cost of 9 percent.
   Should the firm buy or lease? Using .054, the present value of depreciation is .811. Use .054 as the discount rate.

6. (Problem 5 continued)   Assume that the lease payments of $10,000 start immediately and that they are paid at the end of each year. There are 10 payments.
   Compute the present value of leasing; compare the present value with that obtained for Problem 5.

7. Assume that there is a .4 marginal tax rate. An asset with a life of three years can be bought for $25,313 or leased for $10,000 per year. Funds can be borrowed at a cost of .09 (payments of $10,000 per year).
   (a) What is the present value of the debt (the liability) if the funds are borrowed at a cost of 9 percent? Assume that the payments to the bank are $10,000 per year.
   (b) What is the present value of the lease payments of $10,000 (the liability).

8. (Problem 5 continued)
   (a) Include the borrowing cash flows in the buy analysis. Assume equal payments of debt. How does this change the net cost?
   (b) Assume that the net cost of buying was computed using the cost of capital of 15 percent. Now include the borrowing cash flows. How will this change the net cost of buying (you do not have to compute the present value)?

9. What factors might make a lessor's expected cost of acquiring and disposing of equipment less than the lessee's expected cost.

10. Why are leasing companies (lessors) so highly levered?

11. Consider the following investment:

Cash Flows at Time			
0	1	2	Internal Rate of Return
−$1,000	$576	$576	10%

If debt can be obtained at a cost of 5 percent, determine the net present value of the equity cash flows discounted at 15 percent if
(a) No debt is used to finance the investment.
(b) $500 of debt is used to finance the investment.
(c) $900 of debt is used to finance the investment.
   Repeat the calculations using 5 percent as the discount rate.

12. Suppose that $100,000 is borrowed at 8 percent and is to be repaid in three equal annual installments. Prepare a debt amortization table and show that the net present value of the after-tax cash flows of the debt is zero using the after-tax cost of debt as the discount rate. The tax rate is 40 percent.

13. Suppose that a firm has substantial taxable income and a small amount of depreciable assets.
   (a) What are the after-tax equity cash flows if it buys a machine for $800,000, takes a 10 percent investment tax credit, and leases the machine to a user for $120,000 per year for eight years payable at the beginning of each year? Further, suppose that the firm borrows $700,000 at 10 percent to help finance the purchase of the machine and that the bank is to be repaid in three equal installments. Assume a 40 percent tax rate. It is expected that the machine will be worth $160,000 (after tax) at the end of eight years. The entire $800,000 of cost can be depreciated using straight-line depreciation for tax purposes over a five-year life.
   (b) If the next best alternative is to earn 15 percent after tax, is this a good investment?

14. (a) MBI has offered to sell or lease computing equipment to Cornell University that has an expected life of three years. If purchased, the initial cost would be $2 million. If leased, the annual lease payments would be $800,000 per year. Cornell can borrow money at about 7 percent on its endowment and pays no taxes. Ignoring salvage value, what should Cornell do?
   (b) MBI has offered the same deal to EXNOX Corporation, If EXNOX can borrow money at 10 percent, has a weighted average cost of capital of 11 percent, and has a 40 percent marginal tax rate, what should EXNOX do? Assume straight-line depreciation with a life of six years, a 7 percent investment tax credit, and no salvage value.

15. The ABC Company can purchase a new data processing machine for $35,460 or rent it for four years at a cost of $10,000 per year. The estimated life is four years. The machine will result in a saving in clerical help of $11,000 compared with the present manual procedure. The corporation has a cost of capital of .10 and a cost of available short-term debt of .05. The incremental tax rate is .52. Assume that the investment tax credit does not apply. The following analysis was prepared for the two alternatives:

Buy Analysis

		0	1	2	3	4
1.	Outlay	− $35,460				
2.	Savings before tax		$11,000	$11,000	$11,000	$11,000
3.	Depreciation[a]	—	17,730	8,865	4,432	4,432
4.	Taxable income (2 − 3)		(6,730)	2,135	6,568	6,568
5.	Tax on savings (.52 of income)		(3,500)	1,100	3,415	3,415
6.	Net cash flow (2 − 5)		$14,500	$ 9,890	7,585	$ 7,585
7.	Present value factor using .10)		.9091	.8264	.7513	.6830
8.	Present values (6 × 7)	− $35,460	$13,182	$ 8,173	$ 5,699	$ 5,181

[a]Assume that the depreciation of each year for tax purposes is computed using the twice straight-line method of depreciation with a life of four years.

The net present value is − $3,255, using .10 as the discount rate.

Lease Analysis

Gross savings	$11,000	$11,000	$11,000	$11,000
Lease payments	− 10,000	− 10,000	− 10,000	− 10,000
Savings before taxes	$ 1,000	$ 1,000	$ 1,000	$ 1,000
Income tax	520	520	520	520
Net savings	$ 480	$ 480	$ 480	$ 480

   "Buy" was rejected since the net present value was minus $3,225. The lease alternative was accepted since the present value of the savings is positive for any positive rate of discount.
   Comment on the decision to lease.

16. The assistant treasurer of the ABC Company has argued that the firm should use the after-tax borrowing rate to compare the lease alternative to the buy-borrow alternative for an asset when the firm has already decided to proceed with the asset.

The treasurer is unimpressed with the position, stating that "Just this past summer we issued preferred stock, common stock, and long-term debt. Why should we use the after-tax debt rate to discount for time when we know that capital has a higher cost than that to the firm? We will have to enter the market again this winter. The debt rate does not measure the average cost of obtaining capital."

Evaluate the position of the treasurer.

REFERENCES

Beechy, T. H. "Quasi-Debt Analysis of Financial Leases." *Accounting Review,* April 1969, 375–381.

Bierman, H., Jr. "Analysis of the Buy-Lease Decision: Comment." *Journal of Finance,* September 1973, 1019–1021.

Bower, R. S. "Issues in Lease Financing." *Financial Management,* Winter 1973, 25–34.

———, F. C. Herringer, and J. P. Williamson. "Lease Evaluation." *Accounting Review,* April 1966, 257–262.

Brealey, R. A., and C. M. Young. "Debt, Taxes, and Leasing—A Note." *Journal of Finance,* December 1980, 1245–1250.

Childs, C. R., and W. G. Gridley. "Leverage Leasing and the Reinvestment Rate Fallacy." *The Bankers Magazine,* Winter 1973, 53–61.

Crawford, P. J., C. P. Harper, and J. J. McConnell. "Further Evidence on the Terms of Financial Leases." *Financial Management,* Autumn 1981, 7–14.

Financial Accounting Standards Board (FASB). FASB No. 13. Stamford, Conn., 1976.

Myers, S. C., D. A. Dill, and A. J. Bautista. "Valuation of Financial Lease Contracts." *Journal of Finance,* June 1976, 799–820.

Offer, A. R. "The Evaluation of the Lease Versus Purchase Alternatives." *Financial Management,* Summer 1976, 67–74.

Roenfeldt, R. L., and J. S. Osteryoung. "Analysis of Financial Leases." *Financial Management,* Spring 1973, 74–87.

Schall, L. D. "The Lease-or-Buy and Asset Acquisition Decisions." *Journal of Finance,* September 1974, 1203–1214.

Vanderwickin, P. "The Powerful Logic of the Leasing Boom." *Fortune,* November 1973, 132–194.

Chapter *22*

International Finance

Major Topics

1. Definition of international finance and balance of trade.
2. The theory of comparative advantage.
3. Currency exchange rates and their relationship to interest rates and inflation rates.
4. The effective cost of debt.
5. Accounting for international transactions.

Components of International Finance

The subject of international finance may be described as consisting of an understanding of

1. Balance-of-trade data and information and international trade theory.
2. Currency exchange rate theory and institutions.
3. The impact of currency exchange rate changes (actual or expected) on debt and investment decisions and on accounting measures.
4. Tax considerations.

In this era of the multinational corporation and mutual economic dependency of countries on each other, it is necessary for finance managers to have a basic understanding of international finance. Although there are more similarities than differences between international and domestic finance, one should understand the differences that exist.

Balance of Trade

For a country as large as the United States, the attempt to have a positive balance of trade represents a paradox. Although the leaders and the press would prefer to have a positive balance of trade, if the U.S. balance of trade is large and positive, portions of the rest of the world will have negative balances and will tend to run into liquidity problems since the dollar is the medium of exchange in many international transactions (the story goes that if the United States sneezes, the rest of the world catches cold).

The relevant trade measure is difficult to define since the definition should depend on the use to which the measure is being put. On the one hand, the net cash flows are of interest since they give an indication of what is likely to happen to the strength of the country's currency (if not in the short run, then in the long run). But cash flows would include short-term investment flows and are greatly affected by the level of a country's interest rates and thus are not by themselves a good measure of the change in a country's competitive position in international trade.

The difference between imports and exports of goods and services is also of interest since again it gives a measure of the amount that is going to have to be made up by disbursement of accumulated wealth or other sources of foreign currencies. Also, it gives an indication of the capability of the economy to sustain its current level of consumption. There is a limit to how long a country can import more consumption goods than it exports.

A short-run problem with comparing imports and exports is that the measure omits the purpose of the imports. The importing of caviar and furs has different economic significance than does the importation of machine tools or turbines to be used in the production of exports. For one thing, the lives of the different products will differ. But the primary distinction is analogous to the difference between importing fishing equipment or importing fish. To evaluate the economic significance of a balance of trade, it is necessary to know what is being imported.

If a country has a large negative balance of trade caused by importing consumption goods and if its creditors think that the country is living beyond its means, sooner or later the country will use up its credit. It will have to reduce consumption or increase the amount of its exports or accept its dependence on a permanent subsidy. Cuba and Israel both face these alternatives.

A persistently large negative balance of trade over long periods of time is apt to mean a shift in the ownership rights of the country's factors of production. The claims of external lenders may be in the form of government bonds, bank time deposits, corporate debt, ownership of real estate, or common stock. These claims will tend to increase in a situation when a country is running large negative balances of trade over long periods of time.

A complete statement of international activities for a country should include

1. The amount and nature of imports and exports.
2. The amount of investments by the country and by other countries in the country, including the incomes from these investments.
3. Gifts and loans (not likely to be repaid) made and received.

A loan made to finance a dam to be used for electricity generation and irrigation in a developing country is different from a loan made to finance the purchase of sophisticated fighter planes by the same country. Only the former has it within itself the ability to generate economic resources that can be used to repay the loan.

The Principle of Comparative Advantage

The principle of comparative advantage is one of the more important economic principles. It helps to explain a great deal of foreign trade, and it is useful in a wide range of other contexts.

Comparative advantage refers to the fact that one party may be better than a second party in everything, but it is still desirable that the chores be split between the two parties. A seven-foot center of a basketball team may be both the best leaper and the best dribbler on the team, but it may still be desirable to concentrate the center's activities on the court to leaping and minimize the amount of dribbling. The second best dribbler and the best leaper may be a better combination for the team than the one player trying to do everything. In the area of international trade, one country may produce everything cheaper than a second country, but it may still be desirable that the countries trade.

EXAMPLE 22.2 ───

Assume that Countries A and B can produce bananas and automobiles with the following costs. Note that A is the low-cost producer for both products.

	Bananas	*Automobiles*
Country A's costs	$200/ton	$3,200 per car
Country B's costs	$600/ton	$3,300 per car

Assume that each country needs 75 tons of bananas and 5 cars. Either country can produce 150 tons of bananas or 10 cars (producing 1 car is equivalent to producing 15 tons of bananas) or smaller amounts. Country A can produce both bananas and cars cheaper than Country B, but it has a comparative advantage with bananas. Country A can produce the 75 tons of bananas it needs and the 5 cars it needs at a total cost of $31,000, or it can produce 150 tons of bananas at a cost of $30,000 and trade 75 tons of bananas to Country B for the 5 cars. Or it can produce 10 cars and trade for the 75 tons of bananas. What should it do?

The total costs to A for 75 tons of bananas and 5 cars are

$$75(\$200) + 5(\$3,200) = \$15,000 + \$16,000 = \$31,000$$

If it produces 150 tons of bananas, its total costs are

$$150(\$200) = \$30,000$$

If it produces 10 cars its total costs are

$$10(\$3,200) = \$32,000$$

Country A saves $1,000 by only producing bananas and allowing country B to make its cars. The worst arrangement would be for A to produce 10 cars.

It would cost B $33,000 to produce 10 cars and $90,000 to produce 150 tons of bananas. Country B should produce 10 cars and trade 5 of them to A for 75 tons of bananas. The relative cost of producing in the two countries as well as the trade-offs that are possible between bananas and cars in Country A affect the extent of the trading possibilities. Even though A can make cars cheaper than B, comparative advantage dictates that it sticks to bananas and that B stick to cars.

Currency Exchange Rates

Institutions exist for trading currencies at moments in time as well as through time. The spot rate of exchange is the current price for a currency. When a current "spot" rate is quoted, we obtain the current rate at which two currencies may be exchanged immediately. Exhibit 22.1 shows that on Tuesday, November 22, 1983, a British pound could have been purchased for $1.4755. Equivalently, a dollar cost $1.00/1.4755 = £.6777. A "forward" rate refers to the rate associated with a contract bought now that sets the price at which two currencies will be traded at a future moment in time. Thus a pound purchased for delivery 30 days hence cost $1.4761 on November 22, 1983.

Tuesday, November 22, 1983
The New York foreign exchange selling rates below apply to trading among banks in amounts of $1 million and more, as quoted at 3 p.m. Eastern time by Bankers Trust Co. Retail transactions provide fewer units of foreign currency per dollar.

Country	U.S. $ equiv. Tues	U.S. $ equiv. Mon	Currency per U.S. $ Tues	Currency per U.S. $ Mon
Argentina (Peso)	.0605	.0605	16.537	16.537
Australia (Dollar)	.9219	.9204	1.0847	1.0865
Austria (Schilling)	.0528	.0527	18.93	18.97
Belgium (Franc)				
Commercial rate	.01824	.01821	54.815	54.9200
Financial rate	.01807	.01809	55.35	55.290
Brazil (Cruzeiro)	.00119	.00119	840.	840.
Britain (Pound)	1.4755	1.4668	.6777	.6817
30-Day Forward	1.4761	1.4674	.6775	.6815
90-Day Forward	1.4779	1.4694	.6766	.6805
180-Day Forward	1.4802	1.4721	.6756	.6793
Canada (Dollar)	.8086	.8081	1.2367	1.2374
30-Day Forward	.8088	.8083	1.2364	1.2371
90-Day Forward	.8096	.8092	1.2352	1.2358
180-Day Forward	.8105	.8100	1.2338	1.2345
Chile (Official rate) ...	.01181	.01181	84.64	84.64
China (Yuan)	.5040	.5040	1.984	1.984
Colombia (Peso)	.01174	.01174	85.15	85.15
Denmark (Krone)	.1031	.1029	9.7005	9.7150
Ecuador (Sucre)				
Official rate	.01926	.01926	51.92	51.92
Floating rate	.01201	.01201	83.25	83.25
Finland (Markka)	.1735	.1732	5.765	5.7740
France (Franc)	.1220	.1220	8.1975	8.1975
30-Day Forward	.1217	.1217	8.2175	8.2155
90-Day Forward	.1210	.1210	8.2675	8.2615
180-Day Forward	.1197	.1197	8.3575	8.3525
Greece (Drachma)	.0104	.0103	96.55	96.80
Hong Kong (Dollar) ...	.1280	.12796	7.8155	7.8150
India (Rupee)	.0960	.0956	10.42	10.460
Indonesia (Rupiah)	.001015	.001015	985.50	985.50
Ireland (Punt)	1.1535	1.1520	.8669	.8681
Israel (Shekel)	.01206	.01206	82.90	82.90
Italy (Lira)	.0006143	.000611	1628.	1636.75
Japan (Yen)	.004266	.004258	234.43	234.85
30-Day Forward	.004278	.004270	233.75	234.14
90-Day Forward	.004302	.004311	232.43	231.96
180-Day Forward	.004339	.004333	230.49	230.80
Lebanon (Pound)	.1910	.1910	5.235	5.235
Malaysia (Ringgit)	.4267	.4266	2.3437	2.3442
Mexico (Peso)				
Floating rate	.006116	.00612	163.50	163.50
Netherlands (Guilder) .	.3313	.3310	3.0185	3.0215
New Zealand (Dollar) .	.6590	.6583	1.5175	1.519
Norway (Krone)	.1337	.1338	7.4800	7.4725
Pakistan (Rupee)	.0763	.0763	13.10	13.10
Peru (Sol)	.0004680	.0004680	2136.83	2136.83
Philippines (Peso)	.07139	.07139	14.008	14.008
Portugal (Escudo)	.00779	.0078	128.40	128.60
Saudi Arabia (Riyal) .	.2873	.2874	3.4805	3.48
Singapore (Dollar)	.4692	.4691	2.1315	2.1318
South Africa (Rand) ..	.8315	.8270	1.2026	1.209
South Korea (Won) ...	.00127	.00127	789.70	789.70
Spain (Peseta)	.00646	.00643	154.75	155.45
Sweden (Krona)	.1261	.1259	7.9300	7.94
Switzerland (Franc) ...	.4607	.4598	2.1705	2.1750
30-Day Forward	.4632	.4622	2.1588	2.1637
90-Day Forward	.4674	.4665	2.1393	2.1437
180-Day Forward	.4736	.4731	2.1115	2.1139
Taiwan (Dollar)	.02491	.02491	40.15	40.15
Thailand (Baht)	.04350	.04350	22.99	22.99
Uruguay (New Peso)				
Financial	.02662	.02662	37.57	37.57
Venezuela (Bolivar)				
Official rate	.19417	.19417	5.15	5.15
Floating rate	.08026	.08026	12.46	12.46
W. Germany (Mark) ..	.3717	.3712	2.6900	2.6940
30-Day Forward	.3730	.3724	2.6812	2.6856
90-Day Forward	.3753	.3747	2.6648	2.6686
180-Day Forward	.3787	.3787	2.6407	2.6435
SDR	1.04967	1.04870	.952682	.953558

Special Drawing Rights are based on exchange rates for the U.S., West German, British, French and Japanese currencies. Source: International Monetary Fund.
z-Not quoted.

EXHIBIT 22.1 *Source:* Reprinted by permission of *The Wall Street Journal,* © Dow Jones & Company, Inc., 1983. All Rights Reserved.

If a U.S. company was going to receive £100,000 (100,000 English pounds) in 30 days and preferred to eliminate the exchange rate risk, the company could have sold on November 22 for $147,610 the £100,000 for delivery in 30 days. This transaction would set the amount of dollars to be received from the receipt of the £100,000 30 days hence.

In like manner, if the firm had to pay £100,000 30 days hence and wanted to eliminate exchange rate risk, it could have purchased £100,000 for delivery 30 days hence for $147,610.

If £1 costs $1.4755 now, we say that the spot rate for a pound is $1.4755. If £1 can be purchased for delivery 180 days from today for $1.4802, the forward rate is $1.4802 for 180 days (see Exhibit 22.1).

The Effective Cost of Debt to Multinational Firms

Large corporations are becoming more and more willing to cross national boundaries to borrow funds. An important reason why firms like to borrow in foreign lands to finance local investment is that such foreign borrowing reduces the amount of the parent's investment. Other reasons for using foreign debt are that the debt of a subsidiary may not appear on the consolidated financial statement, that there may be national restrictions on the importation (or exportation) of capital, and finally that there are advantages in establishing good relations with local banking institutions.

This section will consider the effective cost of borrowing "foreign" funds. If we assume away exchange restrictions and tax differences, then the problem of analyzing the different costs of debt becomes a matter of correctly combining the nominal cost of borrowing in the different countries and the exchange rate changes that are expected to take place.

In the real world, a decision arises when the management of a firm sees the possibility of borrowing funds at a lower stated cost in a foreign country than it can borrow in its own country. For example, a Mexican firm might find local banks asking a 16 percent rate of interest at the same time that a German bank will lend funds at 10 percent. One explanation for this difference in nominal interest rates is that the 16 percent loan is payable in pesos and the 10 percent loan is payable in marks. The true effective cost of borrowing must take into consideration the expected exchange rate changes and risks that accompany the interest rates. The interest rates reflect the expected inflation in each country, and the exchange rates can be expected to change in a manner more or less consistent with the rate of inflation.

We shall assume the management is willing to make the decision about where to borrow on the basis of an effective cost that incorporates both the nominal interest rate and the expected rate changes. In addition, it will be assumed that there are no possibilities for hedging or that management does not want to hedge, so that the decision can be made on an expected value basis.

Interest Rate Parity

We want to consider the interrelationships among the real interest rate, inflation rates, and the nominal interest rate for a given country. Let

k = the nominal interest rate
r = the real interest rate
j = the country's inflation rate

In equilibrium,

$$1 + r = \frac{1 + k}{1 + j} \tag{22.1}$$

or solving for k yields

$$k = r + j + rj \tag{22.2}$$

and solving for r,

$$r = \frac{k - j}{1 + j} \tag{22.3}$$

Assume that there is a second country where

$$r' = \frac{k' - j'}{1 + j'}$$

The primes identify the information as pertaining to the second country. If we assume that the real interest rate is the same for both economies (there is interest rate parity), $r = r'$, and therefore

$$\frac{k - j}{1 + j} = \frac{k' - j'}{1 + j'} \tag{22.4}$$

Solving for $k - k'$ using equation (22.2) yields

$$k - k' = r + j + rj - (r' + j' + r'j')$$

If $r = r'$, then

$$k - k' = (j - j') + r(j - j') = (1 + r)(j - j') \tag{22.5}$$

This equality holds when there is interest rate parity $(r = r')$.

EXAMPLE 22.2

Assume that two countries have different rates of inflation but the same real interest rate, where

$$r = .05, \quad j = .12$$
$$r' = .05, \quad j' = .20$$

The nominal interest rates for the two countries are

$$k = .05 + .12 + .05(.12) = \quad .176$$
$$k' = .05 + .20 + .05(.20) = \quad \underline{.260}$$
$$k - k' = -.084$$

Also, we obtain the same results using the formula for the interest rate differential:

$$k - k' = (1 + r)(j - j') \tag{22.5}$$
$$= 1.05(.12 - .20) = -.084$$

With a difference in the rates of inflation of .08, there is to be expected a difference of .084 in interest rates if both countries have the same real interest rate of .05.

In equation (22.5), we can substitute $(k' - j')/(1 + j')$ for r and obtain the important relationship between the nominal interest rates and the inflation rates:

$$\frac{k - k'}{1 + k'} = \frac{j - j'}{1 + j'} \tag{22.6}$$

This is purchasing power parity.

The importance of this relationship is that it highlights the linkage between the interest rates and the inflation rates of the two countries. In explaining the difference in interest rates, this calculation bypasses the exchange rates and focuses on the inflation rates of the two countries.

Forward and Spot Rates for Currency

We want to relate the forward and spot rates for currency to the interest rates. We shall assume that the forward rate F and the expected spot rate one period from now are equal.

Let

F = the forward rate for one unit of foreign currency one period from now expressed in dollars

S = the spot price for one unit of foreign currency expressed in dollars

If $1 is invested in the U.S. market, the investor will have $(1 + k)$ at time 1.

If the $1 is invested in the foreign market, then $1/S$ will be invested at time 0, and this investment will have a value of $(1/S)(1 + k')$ in terms of the local currency at time 1 and $(F/S)(1 + k')$ in terms of the expected number of dollars. For equilibrium to exist between the two markets, we need the two dollar returns (in the two markets) to be equal:

$$\frac{F}{S}(1 + k') = (1 + k)$$

or dividing both sides by $(1 + k')$:

$$\frac{F}{S} = \frac{1 + k}{1 + k'}$$

Subtracting 1 from both sides, we obtain

$$\frac{F - S}{S} = \frac{k - k'}{1 + k'} \tag{22.7}$$

The spot and forward rates are linked together by the interest rates in the respective countries.

EXAMPLE 22.3

Assume that the U.S. interest rate is .32 and that the following facts apply:

$$k = .32, \qquad k' = .10, \qquad S = \$1, \qquad F = \$1.20$$

$$\frac{F - S}{S} = \frac{1.20 - 1}{1} = .20 \tag{22.7}$$

$$\frac{k - k'}{1 + k'} = \frac{.32 - .10}{1.10} = .20$$

If there is equilibrium between the two markets the equality must hold.

An investment of \$100 will result in \$100(1.32) = \$132 in the U.S. money market. The \$100 converted into 100 units of the foreign currency ($S = 1$ at the beginning of the year) will earn .10, and at the end of a year the investor will have

$$\$100(1.10) = \$110$$

and this \$110 will be worth \$110(1.20) = \$132 in terms of dollars. The investor is indifferent (there is equilibrium) as to which country in which to invest. With the given spot and forward exchange rates, if more than .10 could be earned in the foreign country, the investor would prefer to invest in the foreign market.

We now have

$$\frac{F - S}{S} = \frac{k - k'}{1 + k'} \tag{22.7}$$

which is one form of interest rate parity, and

$$\frac{k - k'}{1 + k'} = \frac{j - j'}{1 + j'} \tag{22.6}$$

which is purchasing power parity; therefore,

$$\frac{F - S}{S} = \frac{k - k'}{1 + k'} = \frac{j - j'}{1 + j'} \tag{22.8}$$

We can conclude that spot and forward prices, interest rates, and inflation rates are all linked together in very exact ways, if the markets are in equilibrium. There is both interest rate and purchasing power parity.

We can add 1 to both sides of

$$\frac{F - S}{S} = \frac{j - j'}{1 + j'}$$

and obtain

$$\frac{F}{S} = \frac{1 + j}{1 + j'} \qquad \text{or} \qquad F = \frac{1 + j}{1 + j'}(S) \tag{22.9}$$

For example, if $j' = .30$, $j = .10$, and $S = \$.65$, then in equilibrium,

$$F = \frac{1 + j}{1 + j'}(S) = \frac{\$1.10}{\$1.30}(.65) = \$.55. \tag{22.9}$$

The .30 inflation in the second country compared to a .10 inflation rate in the United States leads to a decrease in the spot rate now of $.65 to a forward rate of $.55.

Continuing the example, we assume that the inflation rate in the United States is still .10 and in the foreign country is .30. Currently, the price level is 100 in the United States and 154 in the foreign country.

Consistent with the foregoing facts, we have

	Price Levels for the Coming Two Periods			Expected Inflation Rate
	0	1	2	
U.S.	100	110	121	.10
Foreign	154	200	260	.30
Rate of prices				
U.S./foreign	.65	.55	.47	
Spot and forward prices	$.65	$.55	$.47	

These facts are in line with the derivation of $F = .55$ for time 1 forward rate at time 0.

If the inflation rate in both countries had been .10, we would have

	0	1	2
U.S.	100	110	121
Foreign	154	169	186
Rate of prices			
Local/foreign	.65	.65	.65
Spot and forward prices	$.65	$.65	$.65

If $j = j'$, the exchange rate does not change and $F = S$. If both countries have the same inflation rates, we can expect the exchange rate not to change.

Effective Cost of Money

We want to compute the effective cost of borrowing funds in one currency when the investment will earn funds in a second currency and there is no opportunity to hedge.
Let

k = the annual nominal cost of borrowing expressed in the currency of the lending country

i = the annual effective borrowing cost taking into into consideration exchange rate changes

B_n = the present value of the debt coming due at time n of amount
$(1 + k)^n B_n$

Assume that B_n is borrowed in the United States and that $(1 + k)^n B_n$ of dollars will be repaid in the nth period. If B_n is borrowed in U.S. currency, this will translate into B_n/S of the foreign currency. If $(1 + k)^n B_n$ must be repaid then $[(1 + k)^n B_n]/F_n$ of the foreign currency will be required for repayment of the dollars, where $F_n = [(1 + j)/(1 + j')]^n S$ is the forward rate at time n. We assume that the forward rate, F_n, and the expected spot rate at that time are equal.
In terms of local (foreign) currency, we have an effective borrowing cost of i, where

$$\frac{B_n}{S} = (1 + i)^{-n} \frac{(1 + k)^n B_n}{F_n}$$

Since $F_n = [(1 + j)/(1 + j')]^n S$,

$$\frac{B_n}{S}\left(\frac{1 + j}{1 + j'}\right)^n S = (1 + i)^{-n}(1 + k)^n B_n$$

Simplifying yields

$$\frac{1 + j}{1 + j'} = \frac{1 + k}{1 + i} \tag{22.10}$$

or

$$i = \frac{(1 + k)(1 + j')}{1 + j} - 1 \tag{22.11}$$

EXAMPLE 22.4

$$S = \$.65, \quad F = \$.55, \quad k = .166, \quad j' = .30, \quad j = .10$$

Assume that the cost of the foreign company borrowing locally is .26. Should the firm borrow in the United States at a cost of .166 or locally at a cost of .26?

$$i = \frac{(1 + k)(1 + j')}{1 + j} - 1 = \frac{(1.166)(1.30)}{1.10} - 1 = .378 \tag{22.11}$$

The effective cost of borrowing in the United States is .378, even though the nominal cost is only .166.

If the firm borrows \$1,000 in the United States, it will owe \$1,166 at time 1. But to pay the \$1,166 will require 2,120 units of foreign currency. This is a .378 cost. The calculations are

	0	1	
Dollars	+1,000	−1,166	.166 Cost
Spot rate	.65	.55	
Foreign currency	+1,538	−2,120	.378 Cost
Calculations of foreign currency needed	$\dfrac{1,000}{.65} = 1,538$	$\dfrac{1,166}{.55} = 2,120$	

A unit of foreign currency now costs $.65. To buy $1,000 costs $1,000/.65 = 1,538 in terms of the foreign currency.

In deciding where to borrow, a firm must consider more than nominal costs of borrowing. The effective cost of borrowing that includes changes in the exchange rates that are expected to take place may differ greatly from the nominal borrowing costs.

Capital Budgeting

Two interesting capital budgeting problems arise when a firm invests in a foreign subsidiary. One involves the exchange rate risk; the second is the method of evaluating the return on funds employed. We will assume that the U.S. parent is investing funds in a foreign subsidiary and requires a 10 percent return on its U.S. investments.

First, we consider the exchange rate problem. Assume that the spot rate is expected to decrease by 20 percent. The spot rate is now $1.00 for the foreign currency, and after one year the spot rate is expected to be $.80 (the forward rate is $.80). To earn 10 percent in terms of dollars on an investment of $1,000 in the foreign country, it is necessary to earn 37.5 percent. Since $F/S = (1 + k)/(1 + k')$ or $(1 + k') = (S/F)(1 + k)$, solving for k' we find that

$$\text{required return} = \frac{S}{F}(1 + k) - 1$$

$$= \frac{1}{.8}(1.10) - 1 = .375$$

(22.12)

where k is the basic U.S. required return and k' is the amount that has to be earned in the foreign country.

For example, if the $1,000 investment earned 1,375 of the foreign currency at the end of the year, this would convert to 1,375(.8) = $1,100 U.S. This is a 10 percent return on the $1,000 initial investment.

The second problem arises when the foreign subsidiary uses debt as well as the funds from the parent (the same problem can exist with a domestic subsidiary or even without a subsidiary, but it is very likely to appear with a foreign subsidiary).

EXAMPLE 22.5

Consider a situation in which no exchange rate change is expected. A foreign subsidiary has requested a $1,000 investment from the parent that requires a

10 percent return. The subsidiary promises a 20 percent return on the $1,000 investment.

At the level of the subsidiary the analysis indicates the following results:

	0	1	Internal Rate of Return
Investment	− $10,000	+ $10,920	.092
Debt (8%)	+ 9,000	− 9,720	
Equity needed	− $1,000	+ $1,200	.200

Although the investment returns 20 percent to the parent, the method of analysis requires explanation. The 20 percent return is on a highly levered investment. The basic investment (unlevered) has a 9.2 percent return. It is only by introducing the debt that the investment is made to seem to be acceptable (i.e., have a return larger than 10 percent). A return earned on the stockholders' equity is not the same as a return earned on the basic investment.

It is not sufficient for a foreign subsidiary to "promise" an acceptable return on a parent's investment. The basic underlying characteristics of the investment must also be analyzed. This implies a more systematic method of risk analysis than is illustrated in Example 22.5.

Tax Considerations

The tax laws in the area of international trade change rapidly and are apt to be aimed at accomplishing social and political objectives. For example, when the U.S. government wants to encourage investment in developing foreign countries, it offers insurance to cover the investments of the U.S. companies operating overseas. It also allows a wide range of foreign taxes to be deductible against U.S. taxes as a tax credit (a tax credit is more powerful than a tax deduction, since a dollar of foreign taxes reduces U.S. taxes by $1 rather than by $.46, as would be the case if the foreign tax expenses were a tax deduction rather than a tax credit with a tax rate of .46).

When the dollar was under pressure, Congress passed a provision that encouraged companies to increase exports. This provision allowed the setting up of separate corporations (Domestic International Sales Corporations or DISCs). A portion of the income earned by engaging in foreign trade could then be protected from U.S. income taxes by a series of real and artificial maneuvers.

There are other provisions in the federal tax code that offer special advantages (such as Western Hemisphere Trade Corporations), but the important thing to realize is that countries will frequently arrange their tax laws to facilitate international trade and to encourage the trade to go in a given direction. For example, the European Common Market countries have used the value added tax (a type of sales tax) very adroitly to accomplish trade goals. To make intelligent international finance decisions, the tax laws of the countries concerned must be well understood, or faulty corporate decision making is going to take place.

Accounting for International Transactions

*FASB No. 8**

Multinational corporations do business all over the globe, but they report their financial affairs in one currency. The translation of the financial affairs of foreign subsidiaries leads to two primary accounting issues: (1) What rate (or rates) should be used to accomplish the translation of accounts into the currency of the reporting firm, and (2) should the gain or loss on exchange rate changes affect the parent's income for the period? There are also a large number of subsidiary issues, but we shall focus on the two primary issues.

In 1975 the Financial Accounting Standards Board (FASB) issued Financial Accounting Standards Board statement No. 8, titled "Accounting for the Translation of Foreign Currency Transactions and Foreign Currency Financial Statements." While FASB No. 8 has been supplemented by FASB No. 52, elements of FASB No. 8 are still in effect; thus you should understand it. FASB No. 8 accomplished two primary objectives:

1. It placed the accounting for foreign transactions on a "temporal" basis.
2. It required the recording of gains and losses as they occurred (rather than allowing their deferral).

The temporal method refers to the use of two exchange rates: a current rate and an historical rate. The current rate was used for cash, accounts

---

* Although FASB No. 52 has to a great extent replaced FASB No. 8, a knowledge of FASB No. 8 is still desirable, since there are still times when it can be used.

receivables, real assets carried at market values, and all payables (including long-term debt). The historical rate was used for real assets recorded at cost as well as prepayments (such as prepaid rent).

EXAMPLE 22.6

Assume that the foreign subsidiary of a U.S. company acquired a plant in a foreign country at a cost of 20,000,000 yen when the exchange rate was $.05 ($1 for 20 yen). The asset was recorded on the books of the foreign company at 20,000,000 yen. Assume that the plant was financed by long-term debt paying 10 percent interest payable in yen and that the life of the plant was infinite so that there was no depreciation expense. In the first year, the plant earned just enough to pay the interest. At the end of the year, the exchange rate changed to $.0667 so that a dollar was then worth 15 yen. The balance sheet of the company for the beginning and end of the year was as follows:

	In Yen		In Dollars	
	Beginning of Year	*End of Year*	*Beginning of Year*	*End of Year*
Plant	20,000,000¥	20,000,000¥	$1,000,000	$1,000,000
Long-term debt	20,000,000	20,000,000	1,000,000	1,333,333
Stockholders' equity	0	0	0	−333,333

At both moments in time the plant is converted at the historical rate of 20 yen to a dollar. The end-of-year debt was converted at the current rate of 15 yen to a dollar. The increase in the debt stated in dollars resulted in a loss of $333,333. The loss was caused by the use of the current exchange rate in converting the long-term debt.

The possibility of having a firm's income statement affected by the types of losses illustrated in Example 22.6 caused much concern among the managers of international firms. The financing of plant assets with long-term debt denominated in foreign currencies resulted in large gains and losses from period to period. This risk of fluctuating income was said to act as a depressing effect in considering the undertaking of foreign investments financed by debt.

There were several theoretical difficulties with FASB No. 8. It is possible that the firm has entered into a long-term contract to supply product produced in the plant so that the payment obligations of the debt are essentially balanced by net revenues to be earned in the same currency. If these facts are valid, it is possible that the plant is worth $1,333,333 (in terms of dollars) at the end of the year; thus there was not actually a loss of $333,333. Following FASB No. 8, the loss would be recorded despite the existence of a contract that tended to provide the cash flows necessary to pay the debt or despite a change in the value of the asset. As long as period-to-period gains or losses associated with long-term debt affected operating incomes (while long-term assets were not changed), management was concerned with the magnitude of the accounting exposure that existed. The accounting exposure and the economic exposure were not necessarily identical. A firm could be perfectly hedged economically and still have accounting exposure.

FASB No. 52

Using Financial Accounting Standard Board No. 52, the translation method and the disposition of the translation adjustments for each foreign operation depends on the choice of the "functional currency." If the foreign entity's functional currency is the local currency when the parent's reporting currency is the dollar, then the foreign entity's financial statements should be translated into U.S. dollars using the current exchange rate. Revenues and expenses are translated at a weighted average of the period's current exchange rate.

The translation adjustment is made to a stockholders' equity account and does not affect the period's income. This is an important departure from the requirement of FASB No. 8 that income be affected currently by exchange rate gains and losses.

EXAMPLE 22.7

Assume that the functional currency is the pesos. The beginning- and end-of-period balance sheets (in pesos) are

	Beginning	*Ending*		*Beginning*	*Ending*
Assets	4,500	4,375	Liabilities	2,050	1,750
			Stockholders' equity	2,450	2,625

The income statement (in pesos) is

Revenues	875
Expenses	700
Income	175

The relevant exchange rates for the period are

January 1	75.0 pesos for $1
December 31	100.0 pesos for $1
Average	87.5 pesos for $1

If we assume that sales and expenses took place evenly throughout the year, the translated income statement using the average exchange rate is

Revenues	$\dfrac{875}{87.5}$	$= \$10$
Expenses	$\dfrac{700}{87.5}$	$= \underline{8}$
Income	$\dfrac{175}{87.5}$	$= \$\ 2$

The adjusted end-of-period balance sheet using the December 31 exchange rate is

Assets	$\dfrac{4,375}{100} = 43.75$	Liabilities	$\dfrac{1,750}{100} = 17.50$
		Stockholders' equity	$\dfrac{2,625}{100} = 26.25$

The beginning translated balance sheet using the January 1 exchange rate is

Assets	$\dfrac{4,500}{75} = 60$	Liabilities	$\dfrac{2,050}{75} = 27.33$
		Stockholders' equity	$\dfrac{2,450}{75} = 32.67$

If the firm starts operations on January 1, the stockholders' equity is 2,450 pesos. With income of 175 pesos, the ending stockholders equity is 2,625 pesos. The beginning stockholders' equity in dollars is $32.67 and the foreign entity earned $2, so that the ending stockholders' equity can be expected to be $34.67. The actual translated stockholders' equity is $26.25 so there is $8.42 of translation loss.

Computation of Translation Loss

Beginning balance (pesos)	$2{,}450 \times \dfrac{1}{75} =$ 32.67 (dollars)
Part of ending balance (pesos)	$2{,}450 \times \dfrac{1}{100} =$ <u>24.50</u> (dollars)
	$ 8.17 loss

Remainder of ending balance
  (the ending balance is 2,625 pesos)

$$175 \times \frac{1}{87.5} = \$2.00$$

$$175 \times \frac{1}{100} = 1.75$$

<u>.25</u> loss
Translation loss = $ 8.42

The parent will show income of $2 for the period, and the loss of $8.42 from translation will be shown as a subtraction in the parent's stockholders' equity section.

The foreign subsidiary's stockholders' equity account increased in terms of pesos by 175 but decreased in terms of dollars by $6.42. This dollar change results from the use of the current exchange rate for all assets and liabilities. The use of a different translation method would change the beginning and ending stockholders' equity dollar balances.

In this example we assumed that the reporting currency was dollars and that the functional currency was pesos. How do we determine the functional currency? The functional currency should be the currency of the primary economic environment that the foreign entity is operating in.

If the foreign entity is only selling to its U.S. parent, then the functional currency should be the dollar. If the functional currency is the dollar, then the method of translation changes from the use of the current exchange rate for all asset and liability account to the use of a mixture of current and historical exchange rates as described in FASB No. 8. This same method of translation is used if the foreign entity is operating in a country where the inflation rate is larger than 100 percent over a three-year period.

A study of FASB No. 52 reveals that it is a very complex set of rules for translating foreign currencies. The objective in issuing FASB No. 52 was to correct the deficiencies of FASB No. 8. It corrected some of the causes of complaints by business executives (e.g., the gain or loss from exchange rate changes does not affect the period's income), but it multiplied the degree of complexity and left other deficiencies that raise the potential for future complaints. We can expect there to be changes in the future in the way in which the transactions involving different currencies are recorded.

The financial executive should realize that each transaction involving more than one currency has two elements: one is the economic consequences of the transaction; the second is how the transaction will affect the accounting statements.

Special Risks

There are special risks when a company does business in several different countries. We have stressed the exchange risk. There are also political risks, including the possibility of confiscation, the passage of laws that make it difficult to do business profitably, as well as the risk that profits will not be allowed to be transferred out of the country.

Although it is true that all these risks are present, it is also true that doing business in Country B may be more risky than doing business in the United States, but a U.S. firm might still reduce risk by doing business in Country B. Not only is the variance of outcomes of doing business in B important, but also the covariance of the outcomes of doing business in B with the outcomes of doing business in the United States. Finally, the correlation of doing business in B with the other overall business activity in the United States is important for well-diversified investor. Thus it is too simple a solution to state that "Country B has more political risk than does the United States." The effect on the total risk to firm and investors must be considered.

A Strong Dollar

What does it mean when the daily newspaper states that the dollar is strong compared with the Japanese yen? Assume that the current exchange rate is $.004266 and that it takes 234.41 yen to buy one dollar. If a Japanese firm wants to buy a machine tool made in the United States that sells for $1,000,000, it will cost the firm 243,410,000 yen.

Now assume that the dollar strengthens so that the exchange rate goes to .004 and it now takes 250 yen to buy $1. The cost of the machine tool is now 250,000,000 yen and it costs the Japanese firm 6,590,000 more yen.

A strong dollar currency harms exports since dollars are expensive for foreigners. On the other hand, consumers in the U.S. benefit since they can buy foreign goods and services at a lower cost in dollars.

Zero-Coupon Bonds and International Finance

In the early 1980s zero-coupon bonds became a popular method of financing for large financially strong firms. Over $4 billion of these bonds were issued by firms such as J. C. Penney, Allied Corporation, Exxon, and IBM.

About half of these zero-coupon bonds were purchased by Japanese investors. If the bond was sold prior to maturity, the "capital gain" was not taxed.

Important conclusion: Taxes are an important factor in international finance just as they are in domestic finance.

How can a currency become strong? Consider a situation in which the real interest rate in the United States is very high compared to the real interest rate elsewhere. Money flows into the United States seeking the high interest rate and the price of the dollar increases so that it takes 250 yen to buy a dollar and the exchange rate for yen goes down to $.004. Japan might not object to this development since the change makes Japanese exports to the United States cheaper, and it makes the U.S. goods more expensive in Japan, thus discouraging their import.

Assume that a Japanese worker is currently earning 2,000 yen per hour and that this is equivalent to $8 per hour (the exchange rate is $.004). If the exchange rate were to change to $.005 as the yen became stronger, this would be equivalent to $10 per hour. Obviously, the ability of firms to sell their products on the international market depends to a large extent on the current exchange rates. At the labor rate of 2,000 yen per hour, a Japanese firm has a significant edge in labor costs if the exchange rate is $.003 (the cost is $6 per hour). But if the yen became stronger so that the exchange rate is .005 (the cost is $10 per hour), the advantage has to a large extent been eroded.

Although the equilibrium models defining interest rate and purchasing power parity are necessary to understand international finance, at any moment in time, international trade is being affected by interest rates and exchange rates that may not be in equilibrium.

Conclusions

Very few major corporations operate solely within the boundaries of one country. We can expect the importance of international finance to grow as foreign trade and investments increase, but even today, international finance is of significant importance to operating financial managers.

Countries have different inflation rates. The first step in the analysis is to tie the nominal interest rate of each country to the inflation rate using the relationship $k = r + j + rj$.

There are a wide range of forms for relating the difference in nominal interest rates and differences in inflation rates of two countries. Two of the more useful forms are

$$k - k' = (1 + r)(j - j') \tag{22.5}$$

and

$$\frac{k - k'}{1 + k'} = \frac{j - j'}{1 + j'} \tag{22.6}$$

Starting with current prices (which determines the current exchange rate), we next look at the inflation rates of the two countries to determine the nominal interest rates as well as the exchange rates. The inflation rates help to determine the nominal interest rates.

Do the formulas illustrated in this chapter define the exact relationships found in the real world? Given the fact that we need the expected inflation rates rather than the observed inflation rates to determine the next period's interest rates and exchange rates, it would be surprising if historical data exactly verified the relationships. On the other hand, it would also be surprising if interest rates and changes in exchange rates were independent of inflation rates.

Review Problem 22.1

Assume that the real interest rate is .05 and that there is expected to be .06 inflation in the United States. Assume also that the spot rate for pesos is $.20 and that the expected inflation rate in Mexico is .35.
(a) With equilibrium, what will be the nominal interest rates in the two countries?
(b) What will be the one-year forward rate?

Solution to Review Problem 22.1

(a) In the United States,

$$k = .05 + .06 + .003 = .113$$

In Mexico,

$$k = .05 + .35 + .0175 = .4175$$

(b) $F = \dfrac{1 + j}{1 + j^1} S = \dfrac{1.06}{1.35}(\$.20) = \$.157$

PROBLEMS

1. Assume that the real interest rate is .04 and that there is expected to be .25 inflation.
   (a) What would you expect the nominal interest rate to be?
   (b) If the inflation rate is .05, what would you expect the nominal interest rate to be?

2. If the inflation rate is .25 and the nominal interest rate is .325, what real return will an investor earn?

3. (Problem 2 continued) With equilibrium, and with a real interest rate of .06, what nominal return would you expect to earn in a country with a .05 inflation rate?

4. If a Canadian dollar costs $.8086 (this is the spot exchange rate), how many Canadian dollars does it take to buy one U.S. dollar?

5. Assume that the spot exchange rate for a Canadian dollar is $.8086 and the one-year forward rate is .8200.
   If the U.S. interest rate is .12, what would you expect the Canadian interest rate to be?

6. (Problem 5 continued) Compute the number of dollars held after one year.
   (a) if $100 is invested in the United States.
   (b) if $100 is translated into Canadian dollars and invested for one year and then exchanged into U.S. dollars.

7. (Problems 5, 6 continued) If the Canadian inflation rate is expected to be .06, what inflation rate is being projected by the market for the United States?

8. Assume that the spot rate is $S = \$2.50$. If the inflation rate in the United States is .05 and .25 in the foreign country, what would be the one-year forward rate?

9. In equilibrium

$$\frac{F - S}{S} = \frac{k - k'}{1 + k'} = \frac{j - j'}{1 + j'}$$

Using the information from Problems 1 and 8, verify that the equalities hold.

10. Assume the current price level in the United States is 100 and that in a foreign country it is .40. The facts of Problems 1 and 8 apply. Assume that the United States has a .05 inflation rate.

    Prepare a table showing the price levels for the next three years and the spot or forward prices.

11. With the facts as given in Problems 1 and 8, what will be the expected spot rate three years from now?

12. Assume that funds can be borrowed at a cost of .092 in the United States where there is a .05 inflation rate. They can also be borrowed in a foreign country at a nominal cost of .25. The inflation rate is .25 in that country.

    In which country should the funds be borrowed?

13. For the Japanese manufacturing industry as of 1974 approximately 82 percent of the companies' capital was debt and 18 percent was stock equity.

    Is this degree of debt an advantage or disadvantage as Japanese firms engage in international competition or business?

14. Assume a $30 billion trade deficit for the United States.
    Describe some of the ways that the trade deficit is paid for.

15. Professor Smith is the best teacher of finance and economics at the New Haven University's Graduate School of Business.

    How does the dean decide in which area she should teach?

16. Assume that the one-year interest rate in the United States is .092 and that the inflation rate is .05. The inflation rate in the country of Pongo is .20. The real interest rate is the same in both countries.

    What interest rate would you expect to earn (or to pay) in Pongo?

REFERENCES

Aliber, R. L. *Exchange Risk and Corporate International Finance.* New York: Halsted Press, 1978.

Dufey, G. "Corporate Finance and Exchange Rate Variations." *Financial Management,* Summer 1972, 51–57.

Eiteman, D. F., and A. I. Stonehill. *Multinational Business Finance.* Reading, Mass.: Addison-Wesley Publishing Company, 1979.

Polk, J., I. W. Meinster, and L. Veit. "Company Financial Operations." In A. I. Stonehill (ed.), *Readings in International Financial Management.* Columbus, Ohio: Goodyear Publishing Company, Inc., 1970.

Robbins, S. M., and R. B. Stobaugh. "Financing Foreign Affiliates." *Financial Management,* Winter 1972, 56–65.

Rodriguez, R. M., and E. E. Carter. *International Financial Management.* Englewood Cliffs, N.J.: Prentice-Hall, Inc., 1979.

Weston, J. Fred, and B. W. Sorge. *International Managerial Finance.* Homewood, Ill.: Richard D. Irwin, Inc., 1972.

Zenoff, D. B., and Jack Zwick. *International Financial Management.* Englewood Cliffs, N.J.: Prentice-Hall, Inc., 1969.

Chapter 23

Finance and Inflation

Major Topics

1. The definition of inflation.
2. Real and nominal interest returns; real and nominal dollars.
3. Maintenance of real income.
4. Capital budgeting and inflation.
5. Common stock prices and inflation.
6. Accounting and inflation.
7. Inflation, measuring performance, and investment decisions.

Inflation

Throughout the history of the United States there have been periods of rapid price increases. In recent times inflation has been present in the U.S. economy since 1940, but in the last two decades the rate of price increases has become much more rapid than in the past, with the result that managers are much more concerned with incorporating inflation considerations into their decision-making analysis.

Changes in the price level add interesting complexities to financial analysis. While the basic financial techniques discussed in previous chapters still apply, the interpretation of events is somewhat more difficult.

Defining Inflation

In a dynamically growing economy, price changes take place continuously. In the highly organized markets for securities and for some commodities, it is normal for prices to change from one transaction to the next. In other cases, for example, most real estate leases, prices (rents, in the case of a lease) are fixed by contract for a year or a period of years. Sometimes the price of a particular good or service exhibits an upward or downward trend that can last for months, years, or even decades.

The price changes that are the result of shifts in the supply or demand for particular goods and services do not imply any change in the general price level. Increases in the price of some goods or services may be offset by decreases in others, so that the average level of prices can remain more or less constant. A change in the average price level takes place if there is a strong tendency for many prices to move up (or down). Inflation is a rise in the average price level; deflation is a decline in the average price level. In the United States, price-level changes have tended to be inflationary during most of the last half-century; during the preceding half-century, the price-level changes tended to be deflationary.

Although the idea of an average price level is a useful tool, it is important to be aware of its limitations. The statisticians who construct price-level indexes must decide what goods to include in the index and what weight to assign to each. A commonly used index, the consumer price index, is designed to measure the average price of the goods consumed by an average-sized middle-income urban family. It is a reasonable measure for this purpose, but the price level it records may not accurately reflect the buying habits of a specific family or of a business enterprise. Many families and almost all business organizations will have important components of their revenues or expenses whose movements are not closely tied to the average price level of consumer goods. In these circumstances, careful consideration of the prices of specific goods and services of particular importance to the decision makers is required. In evaluating capital budgeting decisions, a manager must consider the effect of long-run trends in the relative prices of products and of important categories of expenditures.

This point is particularly important because the prices of many of the most important goods and services purchased by firms are not directly included in the commonly used price indexes. Labor is the prime example. Wage and salary payments are a major expense item for almost every business. Yet wage rates are not directly included in price indexes used to measure the rate of inflation or deflation. Labor costs, however, are reflected in the costs of the consumption goods and services that are included in the price indexes.

We define inflation to be an increase in the general price level. Inflation is easier to define than to measure because several difficulties exist. Not all prices increase proportionally, thus quantitative weights have to be determined for different products. The determination of weights is made more complex by change in consumption patterns. Also, product quality changes make it difficult to define what is a given product through time. The two more commonly used measures of the U.S. price level are the consumers price index and the GNP price deflator.

If your paycheck is for $1,100 per week this year and it was $1,000 per week last year, then you had a $100 per week pay increase. But these measures are all nominal dollars. Nominal dollar measures are apt to be misleading if there are significant price-level changes and these changes are not included in the analysis.

Let us assume that the price index was at 100 percent last year and is at 120 percent this year. Prices (e.g., the consumer price index or the gross national product price deflator) have gone up by 20 percent. If we take last year's wages of $1,000 as a reference point in terms of purchasing power, then this year's wages of $1,100 in dollars of the same purchasing power are the equivalent of

$$\frac{\$1,100}{1.20} = \$917$$

Note that we divide the nominal dollars by one plus the relative change in price level to obtain a real dollar measure (in terms of beginning-of-the-period dollars).

The real wages were $1,000 last year and are now $917. The decrease in purchasing power was $83 (in terms of last year's purchasing power). A comparison of the two wages may be made in terms of nominal or real dollars.

Year	Nominal Dollars	Real Dollars, Assuming 20% Inflation
Wages last year	$1,000	$1,000
Wages this year	1,100	917

Which comparison is more useful? For many purposes, the "Real Dollars" column presents more information. Consider the question, "Is the wage earner better off this year or last year?" The "Real Dollars" column answers this question if we have faith in the usefulness of the price index being used. If we question the validity of the price index, we might prefer the nominal dollar measures or a third calculation.

EXAMPLE 23.1 ───────────────────────────────────────

Assume a price index that is 100 as of January 1, 1980 and that the following information applying to the year 1985.

	Price-Level Index	Cash on Hand
January 1	122	$105,000
December 31	137	108,000

Compare the cash on hand for the two moments in time.

The nominal dollars are multiplied by price index at the beginning of the year and are divided by the index at the end of the year to obtain the equivalent of beginning-of-the-year dollars:

$$\$108,000 \times \frac{122}{137} = \begin{array}{ll} \$105,000 & \text{beginning-of-year balance} \\ \underline{96,175} & \text{end-of-year balance} \\ \$8,825 & \text{decrease in real dollars} \\ & \text{(expressed in January 1 dollars)} \end{array}$$

Using the base index of 100 purchasing power, we obtain

$$\$105,000 \times \frac{100}{122} = \$86,066 \quad \text{beginning-of-year balance}$$

$$\$108,000 \times \frac{100}{137} = \begin{array}{ll} \underline{\$78,832} & \text{end-of-year balance} \\ \$7,234 & \text{decrease in real dollars (expressed in} \\ & \text{dollars when the index was 100)} \end{array}$$

An alternative solution is to use nominal dollars to analyze the change in cash:

$105,000	beginning of year
$108,000	end of year
$ 3,000	increase in nominal dollars

Nominal dollars of cash increased, but real purchasing power decreased. Other comparisons are also feasible.

Perfectly Anticipated Inflation

Let us assume that the inflation rate is j and that the money market with zero inflation would require a return of r. The nominal interest rate k gives a return $(1 + k)$, and when this return is deflated by $(1 + j)$ the inflation factor interacting with the nominal return of k leads to a real return of r. Expressed algebraically, we have

$$\frac{1 + k}{1 + j} = 1 + r \tag{23.1}$$

Solving for k,

$$k = r + j + rj \tag{23.2}$$

The nominal interest rate is equal to the real rate, r, plus the inflation rate, j, plus the product, rj (the last term is sometimes incorrectly omitted). Not only do we assume that the inflation is perfectly anticipated, but in addition, it is assumed that the investor has investment opportunities that yield a real return of r and a nominal return of k. Thus, if the real interest rate is $r = .05$, and the inflation rate is $j = .20$, we have for the equilibrium nominal return k

$$k = .05 + .20 + .01 = .26$$

For example, a one-period $1,000 debt will have to pay .26 percent, or $260, if the investor is to earn a real return of .05.

The investor buying the $1,000 loan at time 0 receives at time 1 $1,260. In terms of beginning-of-the-year purchasing power, this is

$$\frac{\$1,260}{1.20} = \$1,050$$

which is a .05 real return on the investment of $1,000. There is a .26 nominal return and a .05 real return.

A common dollar accounting procedure for the issuer of the debt would report a monetary gain associated with the debt of $200, but the inflated interest cost of $260 would balance out the monetary gain and result in a net cost of $60 in terms of nominal money and a $50 real cost in terms of beginning-of-the-period dollars. With perfectly anticipated inflation and with the nominal interest rate in equilibrium, a firm would not borrow funds just because of inflation since the inflation factor is fully incorporated into the interest rate that borrowers demand (there may be other reasons for borrowing).

Also, if the actual inflation rate is not equal to the projected inflation rate, a gain or loss may be incurred (this will be discussed later).

Solving for the Real Return

Assume that the nominal return for an investment is .26 but that the actual inflation rate is .10 rather than .20. What real return will the investor earn? We need to solve equation (23.1) for r.

$$k = r + j + rj \tag{23.1}$$

Rearranging we obtain

$$r = \frac{k - j}{1 + j} \tag{23.3}$$

Since $k = .26$ and $j = .10$, we have

$$r = \frac{.26 - .10}{1.10} = .1455$$

The real rate of interest is .1455 with the facts as given. At the end of a year the $100 investment will grow to $126. This is $126/1.10 = $114.55 in real dollars, which is a .1455 real return.

If the inflation rate is .14 and the nominal interest rate is .12, the real interest rate is negative. This is an unstable situation and is not likely to persist for a long period of time. Investors will tend to flee securities yielding a nominal return of .12 and will purchase real assets. Any time the nominal interest rate is lower than the expected inflation rate, we can expect investors to be unwilling to purchase securities such as bonds or preferred stock with fixed contractual interest payments.

Tax Considerations

We start with the basic zero tax relationship

$$1 + k = (1 + j)(1 + r)$$

If we believe that the nominal market interest rate will adjust so that an investor being taxed at the rate t will earn the same after-tax real return as if there were no inflation, then the nominal interest rate must satisfy the following relationship.

$$1 + (1 - t)k = (1 + j)[1 + (1 - t)r]$$

Solving for k,

$$k = r + rj + \frac{j}{1 - t} \tag{23.4}$$

As shown in equation (23.4), the nominal interest rate required to protect a taxpaying investor against inflation depends on the marginal tax rate of the investor. High tax rate investors require higher nominal before-tax rates of return to achieve the same after-tax returns that they could have achieved with no inflation. If the real interest rate would have been 5 percent with no inflation, and there is actually a 10 percent of inflation, an investor in the zero tax bracket needs a nominal .155 return to earn a real return of 5 percent. In the same circumstances, an investor in the 50 percent tax bracket would require a nominal before-tax interest rate of .255 to be as well off as if there were no inflation. Thus, whatever the nominal market rate of interest, in the presence of inflation some investors will tend to be relatively better off and others relatively worse off than they would have been with no inflation.

To some extent these effects are mitigated by the presence of tax shelters. Suppose that with no inflation the best available default-free investment for an investor in the zero tax bracket was a U.S. government note with a taxable 5 percent nominal return, and for an investor in the 50 percent bracket, a tax exempt 4 percent nominal return from a municipal obligation. With a 10 percent rate of inflation, in order for each of the investors to earn the same after-tax real return, the nominal rate on the taxable note would have to increase from 5 percent to 15.5 percent and the nominal rates on the tax exempt note would have to increase from 4 percent to 14.4 percent.

EXAMPLE 23.2 ───

Let the investor's tax rate be $t = .6$. The before-tax real rate of interest is again .05. The after-tax real rate is

$$r = (.05)(1 - .6) = .02$$

To maintain the same after-tax real return to this investor, the before-tax nominal return must be

$$k = r + rj + \frac{j}{1 - t}$$

With .20 inflation,

$$k = .05 + .20(.05) + \frac{.20}{1 - .6}$$

$$= .05 + .01 + .50 = .56$$

To earn .02 real after-tax, one must earn .56 nominal before-tax. Assume that an investment of $100 earns .56. The investor has $156 after one period.

Total return	$156.0	$156.0	Total return
Principal	− 100.0	− 33.6	Tax
Taxable income	$ 56.0	$122.4	After-tax income
Tax rate	.6		
Tax	$ 33.6		

We adjust the $122.40 for .20 inflation:

$$\frac{\$122.4}{1.2} = \$102$$

This is a .02 after-tax real return on the initial investment of $100.

Inflation and Maintenance of Real Income: The Wage Earner

Given a wage of $20,000, an inflation rate of 10 percent, and an average and marginal tax rate of .4, what do wage earners need in the way of wage increases to maintain their real income?

The answer may be surprising to you. Before the inflation, the after-tax income is $12,000 with $20,000 of pretax income. After the 10 percent inflation, the after-tax income only has to be increased by 10 percent to $13,200 to maintain real income. If we add 10 percent to $20,000, we obtain $22,000. The after-tax income is $22,000(1 − .4) = $13,200. The $13,200 deflated by 10 percent inflation is

$$\frac{\$13,200}{1.10} = \$12,000$$

Thus the before-tax income only has to increase at the same rate as the inflation rate to maintain the real income of the wage earner. If the average tax rate were to change with the increased dollar income, the amount of required increase would change. With progressive income tax rates, a larger percentage increase in income than the inflation rate is needed to maintain purchasing power.

Capital Budgeting and Inflation

The basic principles of capital budgeting are applicable when there is a risk of inflation as well as when the risk of inflation is negligible. However, it is not always easy to apply these principles correctly when the risk of inflation is of primary importance. When inflation is likely, future cash flows may differ not only in their timing but in their purchasing power. In addition, selecting an appropriate discount rate in the presence of inflationary risks is more complex. The principal conclusion of the next section will be that investments can be analyzed using either money cash flows or purchasing power flows, as long as the analysis is done in a consistent manner.

Measuring Cash Flows

There are several ways of incorporating inflation forecasts into cash flow forecasts. The most straightforward method is to forecast the rate of inflation and the effect that the price-level change will have on the cash flows. If a 10 percent increase in prices will cause a 10 percent increase in cash flows, and if the cash flow of period 1 is $100, we would forecast $110 for period 2 if there are no other changes. Instead of a 10 percent inflation causing a 10 percent increase in the cash flows, we could have the 10 percent inflation cause an x percent increase in the cash flows of the firm, where x is determined by detailed economic analysis relative to the specific situation.

Rather than use the forecast of the nominal dollars to be received, some analysts prefer to deflate the forecasted dollars into dollars of common purchasing power (or "real" dollars). For example, if $220 is to be received at time 1 when the price level has increased by 10 percent, the $220 forecast would be divided by 1.10 and changed into $200 of today's purchasing power. The analyst is concluding that the real value of the product being sold will stay constant at $200, and it is easier to use a constant $200 and measure the real flows than to predict the inflation rate and the resulting nominal dollar measure. The real dollars cannot then be discounted by observed market rates of interest, but rather an appropriate real rate of interest must be used.

Money values are converted into real values by dividing the monetary value by an appropriate price index relative. For example, suppose that an investment promises to return $100 per year for the next two years and that the cash proceeds measured in money values are certain. At 9 percent, the present value of the monetary value is $175.91. Suppose that the price index for the current period is 140; it is expected to be 145.6 next year and 151.424 the following year. We wish to convert the money values in all three years to real values in terms of this year's price level. To do this, the first step is to construct price index relatives for each of the three years. A price index relative is a ratio of two price index values. The value in the numerator is the value of the price index for the year in which the cash flows will occur. The denominator is the price index of the base period (the real values are to be expressed in terms of the purchasing power of that period). The price relatives are $140/140 = 1$ for the current period, $145.6/140 = 1.04$ for next year, and $151.424/140 = 1.0816$ for the following year.

To convert money values to real values, the money values for a given period are divided by the price index relative for that period. The real value of the $100 to be received next year is $96.154 ($100/1.04), and the real value of the $100 to be received the following year is $92.456 ($100/1.0816). If real cash flows are used, it is not appropriate to use the nominal observed market costs of capital as a discount rate. A "real" cost of money must be estimated using the observed nominal rate and expected inflation rate. If the decision maker is a taxpaying entity, the real cash flows must be on an after-tax basis, and the discount rate must measure the real after-tax opportunity cost of the decision maker.

Expected Nominal Dollars and Nominal Discount Rates

We shall consider here the use of expected nominal cash flows and the observed borrowing rate. In this formulation, the expected cash flows should reflect the forecast of inflation. Each component of the cash flow should be adjusted based on reasonable expectations of cash flows that will be affected by the inflation.

For example, assume that an investment costs $200 and is expected to have a life of two years. It is expected that there will be 7 percent inflation. Based on the inflationary forecast, the cash flows of period 1 are expected to be $110 and of period 2 to be $121.

This investment has an internal rate of return of 10 percent based on the expected nominal cash flows. If funds can be borrowed at a cost of less than 10 percent, the stockholder's position will be improved if there is no uncertainty. If funds are borrowed at a cost of 10 percent, the firm will just break even. For example, if the funds are borrowed at 10 percent and the funds generated by the investment are used to repay the loan, we would exactly break even:

Initial debt	$200
Interest period 1	+ 20
Owed after period 1	$220
First payment	− 110
Debt at time 1	$110
Interest period 2	+ 11
Owed after period 2	$121
Second payment	− 121
Amount owed at time 2	$ 0

To analyze this investment, the cash flow forecasts had to incorporate the effects of the expected level of price changes. It was not necessary to convert the cash flows into dollars of common purchasing power.

In the example, the funds used were borrowed; thus it was only necessary to determine whether the internal rate of return of the investment was larger than the borrowing rate. If the funds used were supplied by the stockholders, we have not determined whether or not stockholders are better off at the end of the investment period compared to the beginning in real terms. We would need to define the stockholders' required return.

The method of analysis is easily described. It is theoretically correct to use the actual cash flows forecasted (including the effects of the inflation forecasts) and the nominal (actual) costs of money (not the real required return) to obtain a workable method of capital budgeting under inflationary conditions. For taxpaying entities, both the cash flows and the discount rates should be on an after-tax basis.

EXAMPLE 23.3

Assume that an investment to be financed with new capital would have the following cash flows with an internal rate of return of .10 if the forecast is a zero price change. The "real" interest is estimated to be .03. If the cost of new capital is less than .10, this is a desirable investment.

Time	Cash Flow
0	− $3,000
1	1,300
2	1,200
3	1,100

But now assume that a general price level increase of .15 per year is fore-casted for the next three years, so that if the cash flows of the investment increased by the same .15 per year we would have

Time	Cash Flow	Price-Level Adjustment	Adjusted Cash Flow
0	− $3,000	$(1.15)^0$	− $3,000
1	1,300	$(1.15)^1$	1,495
2	1,200	$(1.15)^2$	1,587
3	1,100	$(1.15)^3$	1,673

The adjusted cash flows would be used to evaluate the investment unless management were willing to forecast the specific effects of inflation on the prices and costs of its products, rather than using the general price-level increase. If the inflation rate is .15 and if investors want a real return of .03, then using equation (23.2) it is necessary for the investment to return

$$k = .03 + .15 + (.03)(.15) = .1845$$

For example, with a one-period investment of $10,000, one would have to receive $11,845. The $11,845 converts $11,845/1.15 = $10,300 of price-level deflated dollars. The $10,300 leads to a .03 real return on the $10,000 initial investment.

Equivalence of the Two Methods

Discounting a real cash flow (price-level adjusted) at a real interest rate gives the same present value as discounting a nominal cash flow at a nominal discount rate.
    Let

j = the constant inflation rate
C_t = the nominal cash flow at time t, so the real cash flow is

$$\frac{C_t}{(1 + j)^t}$$

k = the nominal interest rate

r = the real interest rate where

$$1 + r = \frac{1 + k}{1 + j}$$

Using the real cash flow and the real interest rate, we find that the present value of any nominal cash flow C_t is

$$PV \text{ (real)} = \frac{C_t}{(1 + j)^t} (1 + r)^{-t} = \frac{C_t}{(1 + j)^t} \times \left(\frac{1 + j}{1 + k}\right)^t = \frac{C_t}{(1 + k)^t} \qquad (23.5)$$

Thus PV (real) is equal to the present value of the nominal cash flows using the nominal interest rate.

For example, with .15 inflation, we obtained

Time	Cash Flow (real)	Inflation-Adjusted Cash Flow (nominal)
0	− $3,000	− $3,000
1	1,300	1,495
2	1,200	1,587
3	1,100	1,673

Let us assume that the real interest rate is .03 and that the nominal interest rate is .1845. We then have, using the real measures,

$$\text{real net present value} = -\$3,000 + \frac{\$1,300}{1.03} + \frac{\$1,200}{(1.03)^2} + \frac{\$1,100}{(1.03)^3} = \$400$$

Using the nominal cash flow measures and nominal discount rate, we again have a net present value of $400:

$$\text{nominal net present value} =$$

$$-\$3,000 + \frac{\$1,495}{1.1845} + \frac{\$1,587}{(1.1845)^2} + \frac{\$1,673}{(1.1845)^3} = \$400$$

A relationship similar to equation (23.5) also holds if taxes are considered. The present value of the real after-tax cash flows discounted at the real after-tax discount rate can be shown to be equal to the present value of the nominal after-tax cash flows discounted at the nominal after-tax discount rate provided. This will be true provided that the relation between the real and nominal discount rates satisfies equation (23.4).

Inflation and Real Assets

Holding real assets during inflation may well be desirable, but there is the negative feature of having the tax deduction for depreciation expense based on historical cost and not adjusted for inflation. The real value of the depreciation deductions decreases through time. For example, assume that a firm undertakes a one-period investment that costs $1,000. The investment is expected to earn revenue of $1,167 at time 1 and earn after-tax cash flows of $1,100 (the tax rate is .40 and the tax on the $1,167 revenues is $67 since the before-tax income is $167). The firm earns a .10 real after-tax return.

Now assume that there is actually a 20 percent inflation and that the revenues grow by 20 percent to $1,400. The taxable income is now $400 (the depreciation expense is still $1,000) and the tax is .4 of $400 or $160. The after-tax cash flows at time 1 are $1,240. This is a 24 percent rate of return on the investment of $1,000. Thus an after-tax rate of return of 10 percent increases to 24 percent as the result of a 20 percent inflation, where the asset's revenues and out-of-pocket expenses are perfectly correlated with the inflation rate. The 24 percent is a rate of return of nominal cash flows. One might guess (incorrectly) that the rate of return would increase to approximately 30 percent because of the 20 percent inflation rate.

Converting the $1,240 after-tax nominal cash flows to real dollars, we obtain $1,240/1.2 = $1,033 in real dollars. Thus with 20 percent inflation, the real return decreases from 10 percent to 3.3 percent. The depreciation tax deduction loses some of its real value with inflation. The $1,000 tax deduction is worth $400 in nominal dollars and $400/1.20 = $333 in real (beginning-of-year) dollars.

Common Stock Prices and Inflation

Assume that stock prices are set using the following model:

$$P = \frac{D}{k - g}$$

where

D = the expected dividend
k = the required return
g = the dividend growth rate

EXAMPLE 23.4 ─────────────────────────────────────

Assume that without inflation the following facts apply:

$$D = \$2$$
$$k = .09$$
$$g = .05$$

$$P = \frac{D}{k - g} = \frac{2}{.09 - .05} = \$50$$

With inflation we can expect k to increase. Assume that there is .05 inflation and that k changes to .14. We now have

$$P = \frac{D}{k - g} = \frac{2}{.14 - .05} = \$22$$

If there were no change in g, the stock price would be reduced from \$50 to \$22 as a result of the inflation. We might also expect the dividend growth rate to change. Whether the growth rate increases or decreases will depend on the economic position of the firm. We can easily argue that inflation will increase the value of k, but we cannot be sure that it will also increase the value of g by the same amount. If k and g increase by the same amount, the value of P will be unchanged.

Accounting and Inflation

The basic accounting reports of firms use dollar terms not "real" measures, and in addition accounting practice is "cost based." This means that the accounting measures of income and financial positions are the result of accounting conversions and in no sense measure the income or financial position in real terms.

For example, consider a firm that has \$1,000 of cash at the beginning of the period financed completely with common stock and has the same number of dollars in cash at the end of the period. The conventional accountant would report zero income and the same balance sheets at the beginning and end of the period. However, if there has been a 100 percent inflation, the \$1,000 of cash at the end of the time period is only worth \$500 in terms of the beginning-of-the-period purchasing power. In real terms, there has been a loss of \$500 in the value of the cash (measured in beginning-of-the-period dollars).

There are also accounting problems with long-lived assets and inventory that are accentuated when there are changes in the price level. These problems are periodically being studied by the accounting profession.

Inflation and Measuring Performance

If the inflation was expected by management and was incorporated into the cash flow stream on which the investment decision was based, then no adjustment for inflation is necessary in computing income and return on investment.

EXAMPLE 23.5

Assume that the following nominal cash flows with a .20 internal rate of return were forecasted based on a .10 inflation rate. A .20 internal rate of return is required by the firm for an investment to be acceptable.

Time	Cash Flow
0	− $3,000
1	1,600
2	1,400
3	1,200

If the forecasted .10 inflation rate actually occurs, it would not be correct to adjust the cash flows for the price-level changes. The inflation that was forecasted was part of the decision analysis to accept the investment.

With no adjustment, if the actual results were exactly as forecasted, in this very special situation using straight-line depreciation, we would have a constant return on investment (ROI) of .20:

Period	Cash Flows	Depreciation	Income	Beginning Investment	ROI
1	$1,600	$1,000	$600	$3,000	.20
2	1,400	1,000	400	2,000	.20
3	1,200	1,000	200	1,000	.20

In each year management earns the required return of .20.

Now we adjust both the depreciation expense and the investment for .10 inflation per year:

Year	Depreciation	Beginning Investment
1	$1,000(1.10)^1 = $1,100$	$3,000
2	$1,000(1.10)^2 = $1,210$	2,200
3	$1,000(1.10)^3 = $1,331$	1,210

We have adjusted each year's depreciation for .10 inflation per year. The beginning investment at time 0 is not adjusted. The incomes and ROIs using the adjusted depreciation and adjusted investments are

Period	Cash Flow	Depreciation	Income	Beginning Investment	ROI
1	$1,600	$1,100	$500	$3,000	.167
2	1,400	1,210	190	2,200	.086
3	1,200	1,331	−131	1,210	Negative

In no year is the .20 required return earned.

To avoid a negative performance report, operating management will require an investment to earn an internal rate of return larger than .20 if it is to be accepted. But .20 is the return that top management has defined for acceptance. Good investments will be rejected by operating management if the foregoing adjustments for inflation are made. Price-level adjustments of depreciation and investment do not provide more useful information than the use of costs, if the expected inflation used in the calculation of the forecasted cash flows actually occurs.

Now assume that .10 inflation was forecasted but that zero inflation actually takes place. If the cash flows of period 1 are less than $1,600, one explanation can be that the inflation was less than forecasted. Whether or not this explanation is accepted by top management will be a matter of taste.

If the actual inflation rate is larger than the forecasted .10, the actual cash flows may exceed those that were forecasted. Again, top management has the

---

The "Giscard" Bonds

In 1973 French Finance Minister Valery Giscard d'Estaing issued $666 million of bonds. Both the principal and interest payments were linked to the price of gold. The objective was to reduce the real interest cost of the bonds by eliminating the inflation risk.

In 1985 the French government paid out $440 million in interest.

By maturity in 1988 the investors will have received approximately $11 billion.*

*The Wall Street Journal, January 16, 1985.

---

choice of adjusting the unexpected profits for the inflationary effects or giving management credit for the improvement, even though the cause of the good performance may not have been in management's control.

When the inflation has been accurately incorporated into the forecasted cash flows, there is no necessity to adjust the investment basis. The present value of the cash flows at all moments in time reflect the expected inflation.

Conclusions

During periods of rapidly changing prices, managers tend to question the use of dollar cash flows. The maintenance of purchasing power becomes an objective. Investments can be analyzed using either money cash flows or purchasing power flows, but the analysis must be done in a consistent manner. If real purchasing power units are used (dollars adjusted for purchasing power changes), a real discount rate must be used and the nominal (observed) discount rates cannot be used. If the expected dollars unadjusted for purchasing power changes are used, the nominal rate must be used.

Although the maintenance of real purchasing power may be considered desirable, an investment may still be acceptable in the absence of uncertainty if its return is larger than the cost of money (e.g., the borrowing rate) without considering the purchasing power changes. If the money market thinks that there will be inflation, we can look for this expectation to be built into the interest rates that are demanded on debt. With perfectly anticipated inflation, the monetary gains from being in debt merely reduce the interest cost to a real net cost that is economically significant.

Review Problem 23.1

Company X can borrow funds at .14. It is considering an investment that has an outlay of $20,000 and $23,200 of benefits at time 1 in nominal dollars. There is forecasted an 11 percent inflation for the next year.

   Should the investment be undertaken?

Solution to Review Problem 23.1

(a) Using nominal dollars, we have

$$\text{NPV} = -\$20,000 + \frac{\$23,200}{1.14} = \$350.88$$

(b) Using real dollars and a real discount rate, we have

$$\text{real dollars} = \frac{\$23,200}{1.11} = \$20,900.90$$

Solving for the real interest rate, we obtain

$$.14 = .11 + r + .11r$$

$$1.11\,r = .03$$

$$r = .027027$$

$$\text{NPV} = -\$20,000 + \frac{\$23,200}{(1.11)(1.027027)}$$
$$= -\$20,000 + \$20,350.88 = \$350.88$$

Both procedures give the same positive net present value. Accept the investment.

PROBLEMS

1. An investment costs $1,000, and with no inflation, the expected cash flows are $1,100. With a .20 inflation the cash flows are expected to be $1,180. It is expected that there will be .20 inflation. Funds can be borrowed at a cost of .15.

   (a) Using the borrowing rate, what is the NPV?

(b) What real return does the investment earn?

(c) Should the investment be accepted?

2. Company A can borrow funds at .15. It is considering an investment that has an outlay of $1,000 and $1,100 of benefits in real purchasing power terms at time 1. A 20 percent inflation is forecasted.

   Should the investment be accepted?

3. Assume that investors want a real return of .04 and that there is an inflation rate of .16.

   What nominal rate of return must be earned?

4. Assume that there is a .16 rate of inflation. A $1,000 investment earns a rate of return of .2064.

   What real rate of return is earned?

5. Assume that a firm has borrowed $1,000 and is paying .2064 interest per year. There is a .16 inflation rate.

   What is the real cost of the borrowed funds?

6. Does a firm benefit from using fixed rate debt instead of common stock during a period of inflation?

7. Miss Smith is currently earning $30,000 and is paying an average tax rate of .4 and a marginal rate of .7.

   With an inflation rate of .10, what pay increase does Miss Smith require to maintain her standard of living?

8. (Problem 7 continued)   Miss Smith would like to earn a real return of .04 before tax and $(1 - .7)(.04) = .012$ after tax.

   What interest rate would she have to earn if the marginal tax stays at .7 and if there is an inflation rate of .10?

9. Assume that the price level is expected to increase by .05 in the coming year.

   What rate of return do you have to earn on an investment of $100 to earn .06 on your investment in terms of real purchasing power?

10. A one-year $100 debt security is issued to yield .10. It is expected that there will be .08 inflation during the next year.

    What rate of return, in real terms, will the security earn if the prediction of price-level change actually is fulfilled?

11. A three-year $100 zero coupon debt is issued to yield .10 ($133.10 will be paid after three years). It is expected that there will be .08 inflation per year during the time period.

    What internal rate of return, in real terms, will the security earn if the prediction of price-level change actually occurs?

12. The ABC Company is building a plant that is expected to cost $10 million to service the capacity needs of the firm for the next three years. For another $2 million, it can build excess capacity that is expected to fill the needs for an additional seven years. It is expected that there will be .09 inflation and that it would cost $3 million to make the identical changes three years from now. The firm's cost of money is .10.

    Should the excess capacity be purchased?

13. The UVW Company is considering an investment costing $1 million that is expected to yield .04. Debt funds can be obtained to finance this investment at a cost of .05. The justification offered for the investment is that there is expected to be inflation; thus there will be a gain at the expense of the bondholders (they will be holding fixed dollar claims). The .04 yield of the investment includes appropriate adjustments in cash flows because of the expected inflation. The lives of the investment and the debt are comparable.

    Can the investment be justified?

14. Assume that a firm expects a 9 percent per year increase in wage rates and in the price level and a 10 percent time value factor (costing of borrowing). A piece of equipment costing $331,210 will save 5,000 hours of labor per year. Initially, each hour is worth $20. The life of the equipment is four years.

    Should the equipment be purchased? There are zero taxes.

15. Continuing Problem 14, assume that the 9 percent applies to the firm but there is a 15 percent inflation in the economy. The firm wants to translate future dollars into current purchasing power and make the following calculations:

$100,000	$= \$100,000 \times 1.10^{-1} =$	90,900
$\$109,000 \times 1.15^{-1} =$	$\$ 94,800 \times 1.10^{-2} =$	78,300
$\$118,000 \times 1.15^{-2} =$	$\$ 89,800 \times 1.10^{-3} =$	67,500
$\$129,503 \times 1.15^{-3} =$	$\underline{\$ 85,200} \times 1.10^{-4} =$	$\underline{58,200}$
	$\$369,800$	$\$294,900$

    The NPV $= -\$331,210 + \$294,900 = \$36,310$.
    The investment was rejected. Evaluate

16. Assume a real interest rate of .04 and an expected inflation rate of .10.

    What is the nominal rate of interest that will be equivalent to the .04 real rate for a tax exempt investor?

17. (Problem 16 continued)   If an investment of $1,000 earned $1,144 at time 1, what real rate of return will be the investment have earned?

18. Compute the net present value of the following cash flows:

Time	Cash Flow
0	− $1,000
1	+ 1,300

Use nominal and real measures. Assume that the interest rate factors of Problem 16 apply.

19. Debtholders and stockholders will both accept a .16 return if there is zero operating risk. Assume that a corporation uses .35 debt and .65 common stock.
    (a) If an investment is to be financed by that mixture of debt and common stock, what after-tax internal rate of return will it have to earn? The corporate tax rate is .46.
    (b) Assume a $1,000 investment with a one-year life. Show the total revenues at time 1, the taxes, and the distributions to debt and common stock. All earn the exact required return.
    (c) If both debt and common stock are taxed at a .4 rate and if the inflation rate is .09, an investor will earn an after-tax real return of

    _____ .

20. Assume that the expected inflation rate is .12 and that the nominal rate of interest is .176.
    (a) A zero tax investor earning .176 will earn what real return?
    (b) Assume that an investor has a tax rate of .55. If the expected inflation rate is .12 and the investor wants to earn a real after-tax return of .05,

    the before-tax nominal return will have to be _____ .

21. Con-Chem-Co. has specified standard methodology for evaluating investments. They specified in 1980 a 26 percent internal rate of return "regardless of the project or division."

    One of the directions given in the manual is "Deflate the current dollar cash flows to obtain the results in today's dollars." Annual deflators were supplied. The deflators to be used for the five years starting in 1980 are

1980	1.0
1981	.90
1982	.80
1983	.73
1984	.68
1985	.63

Assume that the five-year debt costs Con-Chem-Co. .14, that there is a .46 tax rate, and that the after-tax cash flows (current dollars) of an investment are

1980	− $1,000
1981	+ 200
1982	+ 200
1983	+ 200
1984	+ 200
1985	+ 1,200

The cash flows are certain.
(a) Prepare the analysis as it would be prepared by Con-Chem-Co.
(b) Should the investment be undertaken?

22. (Problem 21 continued)   The company requires a .26 "real return." With a .15 inflation rate, what nominal (current dollar) return must the firm earn?

23. Suppose that a riskless investment with an initial outlay of $2 million and a life of two years is being contemplated. With zero price changes or inflation, the projected contribution margin would be $1.2 million per year. The current yield to maturity on a two-year government bond is 7 percent, and general inflationary expectations are 4 percent per year. Funds can be borrowed to finance the investment at a cost of 8 percent. If accepted, the investment will be financed with debt. Competition and a new labor agreement are expected to limit the increase in the contribution margin to 3 percent annually, even though there is expected to be a 4 percent overall inflation. The corporate tax rate is 40 percent, and straight-line depreciation for tax purposes would be used. The contribution margin excludes the depreciation expense. There is zero investment tax credit.
    Should the investment be undertaken?

REFERENCES

Bodie, Z. "Common Stocks as a Hedge Against Inflation." *Journal of Finance,* May 1976, 459–470.

Fama, E. F. "Interest Rates and Inflation: The Message in the Entrails." *American Economic Review,* June 1977, 487–496.

———, and M. R. Gibbons, "Inflation, Real Returns and Capital Investment," *Journal of Monetary Economics,* May 1982, 299–323.

————, and G. W. Schwert. "Asset Returns and Inflation." *Journal of Financial Economics*, November 1977, 115–146.

Ibbotson, R. G., and R. A. Sinquefield. *Stocks, Bonds, Bills and Inflation: The Past and the Future.* Charlottesville, Va.: The Financial Analysis Research Foundation, 1982.

Jaffe, J. F., and G. Mandelker, "The 'Fisher Effect' for Risky Assets: An Empirical Investigation." *Journal of Finance,* May 1976, 447–458

Modigliani, F., and R. A. Cohn. "Inflation, Rational Valuation, and the Market," *Financial Analysts Journal,* March–April 1979, 3–23.

Nelson, C. R. "Inflation and Rates of Return on Common Stocks." *Journal of Finance,* May 1976, 471–482.

————, and G. W. Schwert. "Short-Term Interest Rates as Predictors of Inflation: On Testing the Hypothesis That the Real Rate of Interest Is Constant." *American Economic Review,* June 1977, 478–486.

Von Furstenberg, G. M., and B. G. Malkiel. "Financial Analysis in an Inflationary Environment." *Journal of Finance,* May 1977, 575–587.

Wilcox, J. A. "Why Real Interest Rates Were So Low in the 1970's," *American Economic Review,* March 1983, 44–53.

Chapter 24

Mergers and Acquisitions

Major Topics

1. Reasons for mergers.
2. A merger motivation if cash is available.
3. Pooling and purchase accounting.
4. Methods of valuation for acquisition.
5. The mathematics and power of using debt for acquisitions.
6. The P/E ratio before and after merger.
7. The cost of an acquisition.
8. Conservation of risk; how an acquisition affects risk.
9. Greenmail.
10. Golden parachutes.

Mergers

Two firms may join together to form a new joint firm, or one dominating firm may acquire all the common stock of another firm and digest it. With either transaction two firms are converted into one firm, and economically the transactions are very similar. Almost all firms are either actively engaged in merger activity or are worried about being acquired. Thus the topic is important.

Mergers and acquisitions occur for many different reasons ranging from the desire for risk reduction to the necessity of doing something with extra cash currently held for which the firm has no special plans. Consider the following four acquisitions of oil companies:

1. Socal (now Chevron) acquired Gulf Oil for $13.2 billion in 1984.
2. Texaco acquired Getty Oil for $10.2 billion in 1984.
3. Du pont acquired Conoco for $7.4 billion in 1981.
4. U.S. Steel acquired Marathon Oil for $6.5 billion in 1981.

All four acquisitions occurred because the management of the acquiring firm thought that the oil reserves were undervalued by the market. Socal and Texaco were seeking additional oil reserves needed for their distribution systems. Du pont and U.S. Steel were diversifying out of their basic industries because they saw relatively low profits and high risks in those industries (chemicals and steel).

Reasons for Mergers

Obtaining Resources

Many specific reasons are given for mergers and acquisitions. For example, if a firm wants to start a new activity, an acquisition may be quicker than doing it from scratch. Another reason for mergers is that retention of earnings saves investor taxes; thus it is a sensible strategy compared to a cash dividend and may be the best internal use of resources.

One of the more important reasons for a merger is that it will lead to the acquisition of resources such as

1. Management talent.
2. Markets.
3. Products.
4. Cash or debt capacity.
5. Plant and equipment (replacement cost is less than price).
6. Raw material.
7. Patents.
8. Know-how (processes or the people teams).

Diversification

Another reason for mergers and acquisitions is diversification for risk reduction. Risk diversification is a difficult objective to evaluate. Individual investors can diversify for themselves. A corporation does not have to diversify for its investors—the investors can diversify relatively cheaply. On the other hand, managers and labor find it difficult to diversify their careers, since they are generally tied to a firm and an industry.

Synergy

A popular reason offered for mergers is that the two firms joined together will be more valuable than the sum of the values of the two independent firms. There will be synergy.

Synergy is a process whereby when one and one are added more than two is obtained. Two firms joined together may be worth more than they are worth individually. There are several reasons why a merger of the two firms may result in total profits larger than the sum of the two individual profits:

1. One firm may be badly managed, and the second firm may be able to improve the level of management skills of the total operation.
2. Vertical integration may allow better planning, the saving of some selling effort, and improved distribution of product in process.
3. Horizontal integration may allow efficiencies in market coverage.

All of the foregoing might lead to operating efficiencies (lower costs). The horizontal integration might also lead to decreased competition, which, although not socially desirable, might well be welcomed by management (this type of merger would tend to be discouraged by governmental bodies).

A form of synergy can be derived from the market's respect for size. A firm of large size tends to be able to obtain capital at a lower cost. Consistent with this is management's hope that the market will pay a higher P/E for the stock of a larger, less risky firm.

Profits may also increase when a resource-poor company acquires a resource-rich company because the marginal value of that resource is greater for the resource-poor company. Thus we find oil companies with wide distribution networks acquiring firms with large amounts of oil reserves but inadequate distribution systems.

Tax Implications

A tax-loss company might acquire a profitable company in order to use its tax loss, or a profitable firm might acquire a tax-loss company. (To take advantage of the loss, the loss company must be operated; it cannot be acquired just for the tax loss.)

The tax motivation is sometimes not apparent to the public since both firms involved are reporting incomes. It should be remembered that a firm with accounting income might still have a tax loss.

Frequently, acquisitions occur because the owners of the acquired firm want to prepare their estates for the inevitable moment of death. There are advantages to an estate in having marketable stock whose value is relatively easily determined, rather than having partial ownership in a privately owned corporation. In the latter case, it is necessary to estimate the value of the firm, and this process is far from being as objective as a stock market price.

Growth

The question might be asked as to why a firm would acquire another firm when the acquiring firm could enter the industry by developing its own product and productive facilities. Acquisition is much faster and sometimes safer than "doing it yourself." Management has its own reasons for wanting rapid growth. Growth through merger and acquisition means more power and prestige and the potential for higher salaries and bonuses.

Size

Size itself may be one of the reasons for a merger (not the only reason, it is hoped). Size is thought to reduce financing costs and may offer bargaining power in negotiating with suppliers.

It is also possible that some managers value size as reflecting a type of personal achievement, but this is not likely to be a significant factor as a general explanation of mergers.

Anti-raiding Maneuver

Some mergers take place in order to fight off other raiders. A reluctant bride might well prefer a friendly marriage to a white knight rather than succumb to a raid by a black knight. Managers are people, and it is reasonable to expect that they will have preferences when they fear that they will not be able to continue as they did in the past. They would like to choose their next boss. This desire may give rise to a merger with a friendly firm (a white knight) even though the number one choice (if feasible) would be to continue with unchanged operations.

Different Expectations

If the managements and owners of two firms have different expectations, they will compute different values, and this might create a situation where an exchange can take place.

Other factors helping to create such a situation are different perceptions of the time value of money (or different actual time values) and different risk attitudes. Different opinions help to create mergers.

Summary: Reasons for Mergers

There are many reasons for firms to want to merge. Advantages of size have been described, but one should also remember that size frequently results in a loss of flexibility and the ability to react quickly. Assuming that the government's antitrust activities create a climate conducive to competition, we would expect competition to limit the size of firms and the tendency of firms to merge.

Antitrust Considerations

Both the U.S. Justice Department and the Federal Trade Commission act as watchdogs to prevent mergers that tend to lessen competition or tend to create a monopoly. There are some who also would like them to prevent the largest firms in the economy from acquiring any smaller firms in any industry.

Because it tends to lessen competition or to create a monopoly, the prevention of any merger or acquisition will obviously be a judgment call if the two firms involved are in the same industry. Well-defined distinctions between legal or illegal mergers are very difficult to define. The applications of laws depend to a large extent on political and philosophical leanings of the persons administering the law.

It is reasonable to expect that a conglomerate acquisition (unrelated businesses) will be more likely to be approved than will a horizontal acquisition (say, a department store chain acquires another department store chain). A vertical integration (either integrating backward by acquiring a material or parts supplier or forward by acquiring a sales outlet) will .tend to be less acceptable than will a conglomerate acquisition but more acceptable than a horizontal acquisition.

An Acquisition for Cash

A firm finding itself with extra cash above that required for normal operations essentially has four choices:

1. Expand *present* activities.
2. Add *new* activities.
   (a) Do it yourself with basic building blocks.
   (b) Acquire an ongoing activity by the merger and acquisition process.
3. Give the excess cash to stockholders via the following methods.
   (a) Dividends.
   (b) Other cash distributions (such as the acquisition of shares by the firm).
4. Retire debt.

If the cash is not available, any of the foregoing can also be financed by raising new capital.

We will concentrate in this section on the merger alternative using either cash or new capital. The objective is assumed to be to increase profit (after all capital costs). The first step will be to determine the premium that the acquiring firm can afford to pay.

Determining the Premium

We want to determine how much cash a firm can offer for an acquisition when as an alternative it can pay a cash dividend and its investors can buy shares of the same firm in the capital market. We will assume that the investor's objective is to acquire the shares of common stock in the firm being acquired.

Let P_0 be the current market price of the firm to be acquired and x equal the stock price multiplier. The investor's tax rate is t_p. The bid price is defined to be

$$\text{bid price} = xP_0$$

Assume that a firm has D available either for reinvestment or for a cash dividend. To make the investor indifferent to retention or a dividend, we want the same number of shares purchased with retention as with dividend (we initially assume that capital gains and dividends earned by a corporation are not taxed).

The shares to be purchased by the investor with the after-tax proceeds of a cash dividend of D are

$$\Delta N = \frac{D(1 - t_p)}{P_0}$$

where P_0 is the current common stock price and t_p is the tax on the investor's ordinary income.

With retention and a bid price of xP_0, the shares purchased by the firm with the D dollars are

$$\Delta N = \frac{D}{xP_0}$$

Equating the two equations yields

$$\frac{D(1 - t_p)}{P_0} = \frac{D}{xP_0}$$

And solving for x, we obtain

$$(1 - t_p) = \frac{1}{x}$$

or

$$x = \frac{1}{1 - t_p}$$

EXAMPLE 24.1 ————————————————————————————

Assume that the stock being acquired is actually selling for $40 and that this is its value. Let $t_p = .6$. To compare a dividend and firm acquisition, we first compute the stock price multiplier:

$$x = \frac{1}{1 - t_p} = \frac{1}{.4} = 2.5$$

Bid price $= xP_0$:

$$2.5 \times \$40 = \$100 \text{ per share}$$

With a *dividend of $100*, the investors net $40 after tax. The cash buys 1 share with a tax basis of $40. With *retained earnings of $100*, the firm can pay $100 per share for 1 share. The tax basis is $0 for the investors and $100 for the corporation.

If the $100 is retained and $100 is paid for a share, then one share can be purchased. If the $100 is paid as a cash dividend, the $60 of tax is paid and a share can be purchased for $40. The company can pay 2.5 times the current market price and leave the taxable investor with the same number of shares of stock of the acquired firm as if the investor had purchased the stock directly.

This analysis ignores the capital gains tax that would take place on sale and assumes that the alternative to retention by the firm is a cash dividend. If enough of the common stock is acquired so that the purchasing corporation does not pay taxes on the dividends (or cash flows) received from the acquired firm, then the investors can receive the same dividend as they would receive if they bought the one share of stock.

Analysis with Capital Gains

With a cash dividend, the change in value for the investor is

$$\Delta V = (1 - t_p)D$$

With retention, the firm can buy D/xP_0 shares. Each share has a value of P_0; thus the total value of the acquisition is

$$\text{value} = P_0 \left(\frac{D}{xP_0} \right) = \frac{D}{x}$$

If we assume retention and then an immediate sale (a worst case situation) with a capital gain of D/x and a capital gains tax of $t_g(D/x)$, the after-tax value is

$$\text{after-tax value} = (1 - t_g)\frac{D}{x}$$

By equating the two values (dividends and retention with purchase and sale of stock),

$$(1 - t_p)D = (1 - t_g)\frac{D}{x}$$

Solving for x we find that

$$x = \frac{1 - t_g}{1 - t_p}$$

EXAMPLE 24.2 —————————————————————————————————

If $t_p = .6$ and $t_g = .20$, we have

$$x = \frac{1 - t_g}{1 - t_p} = \frac{.8}{.4} = 2.0$$

Instead of paying $100 per share, now that we assume immediate sale, the firm can offer a maximum of $80 per share:

$$2(\$40) = \$80$$

If instead of a cash dividend taxed at t_p the cash distribution were taxed at t_g, we would have

$$(1 - t_g)D = (1 - t_g)\frac{D}{x}$$
$$x = 1$$

With the assumption that the initial cash distribution were taxed at t_g, the firm could not pay a premium. At the other extreme, if the D/x of value were not taxed, but the cash distribution were taxed at a rate of t_g,

$$(1 - t_g)D = \frac{D}{x}$$

$$x = \frac{1}{1 - t_g}$$

If $t_g = .20$, then

$$x = \frac{1}{1 - .20} = 1.25$$

Pooling and Purchase Accounting

A firm engaging in mergers and acquisitions will use one of two accounting methods. These methods are the pooling and the purchase methods. With pooling, the two sets of accounts are merely added. With purchase, the specific assets are recorded at their estimated value and the difference, if any, with the purchase price is recorded to a goodwill account. Pooling can only be used if certain conditions exist (the stockholders of the acquired firm must also be stockholders of the new firm).

Consider the following example.

EXAMPLE 24.3

	Parent P	Subsidiary S	After Acquisition	
			Pooling	Purchase
Assets	$400,000,000	$50,000,000	$450,000,000	$450,000,000
Goodwill				70,000,000
Liability	100,000,000	20,000,000	120,000,000	120,000,000
Stockholders' equity	300,000,000	30,000,000	330,000,000	400,000,000

Assume that P has a stock price of $40 before the acquisition and that an acquisition of S firm's common stock would require the issuance of 2,500,000 shares. The book value of the stock equity of the firm being acquired is $30,000,000.

1. What is the cost of S's stock if pooling of interests is used?
2. What is the cost of S's stock if the purchase method is used?

The cost of S's stock is $40(2,500,000) = $100,000,000 independent of the method of accounting. Assume that S firm is acquired and that pooling is used, but that all the assets are sold after one year for $55,000,000. The buyer assumes the liabilities.

1. What was the gain or loss?
2. Does your answer change if the firm is "sold" over a period of 30 years?

Parent firm P effectively paid $100,000,000 and then sold S for $55,000,000. There is an economic loss of $45,000,000.

If pooling is used, there is a gain of $25,000,000 since the stockholders' equity of S is recorded at $30,000,000, and it is sold for $55,000,000. If the purchase method is used, the assets and stockholders' equity are recorded at $100,000,000 and there is a $45,000,000 loss. If instead of selling after 1 year the firm operates for 30 years, the same types of results occur. Pooling tends to inflate the future incomes by understating costs when more than book value is paid for the assets.

A Holding Company

Although holding companies are not a widely used form of business organization, it is not unusual to see a chain of firms owning each other.

EXAMPLE 24.4

Assume A owns B which owns C which owns D which owns E. The common stock of A is $10,000. Mr. Jones owns 51 percent of A's common stock financed with borrowed funds.

	A	B	C	D	E
Assets	$50,000	$500,000	$5,000,000	$50,000,000	$500,000,000
Debt	40,000	400,000	4,000,000	40,000,000	400,000,000
Common stock	10,000	100,000	1,000,000	10,000,000	100,000,000

Now assume that

1. A owns 50 percent of B's common stock.
2. B owns 50 percent of C's common stock.
3. C owns 50 percent of D's common stock.
4. D owns 50 percent of E's common stock.

Common stock E is $500,000,000 of assets, and Jones controls it all with an investment of $5,100 financed with the bank's money.

The consolidated balance sheet shows the immense amount of debt.

Consolidated Balance Sheet

Debt	$444,440,000
Common stock, minority interest	55,550,000
Common stock	10,000
	$500,000,000

This is an extreme case, since all of A's assets consist of stock in B; all of B's assets consist of stock in C, etc.

Valuation for Acquisition

The four basic methods of valuating a firm are

1. cash flow
2. earnings $\underset{\text{P/E multiplier or earnings}}{\overset{\text{present value}}{\diagdown}} \times \dfrac{1 - b}{k - g}$

3. assets − liabilities $\overset{\text{book value}}{\underset{\text{replacement cost}}{\diagup\!\!\!\longleftarrow\!\!\!\diagdown}}$ market values (liquidation value)

4. stock price: present and past

The cash flow approach to valuation treats a firm being considered for acquisition to be the same as any real asset. The cash flows are the relevant input.

Since a firm has an earnings history, there is a temptation to use the earnings as the input. One can compute the present value of the earnings. If interest on all capital is subtracted in computing the earnings of each year, the present value of the earnings will be the same as the net present value of the cash flows.

A second valuation approach using earnings is to multiply the earnings by a price earnings multiplier. The basic valuation model is

$$P = \frac{D}{k - g} = \frac{(1 - b)E}{k - g}$$

If we multiply E (the earnings per share) by $(1 - b)/(k - g)$, where

$1 - b$ = the retention rate
k = the required return
g = the growth rate

we obtain the value of a share. This can be made to be equivalent to computing the net present value of the cash flows and the present value of the earnings, if all the inputs are consistent, but the equivalency should not be assumed. If we divide both sides by E, we have

$$\mathrm{P/E} = \frac{1 - b}{k - g}$$

Instead of using the income flows, some analysts prefer to value the assets and the liabilities. The easy measures are the book values (the data are readily available), but either market values (including liquidation values) and replacement costs are likely to be more useful.

With the acquisition of a firm whose stock is traded on a market, the present and past stock prices are relevant. Investors will consider any offer in relation to the current stock price and are likely to compare any offer to the recent past prices (even though past prices are not relevant in a theoretical economic sense).

Other Factors

The existence of assets that can be sold, or debt capacity that is available, will affect the value of an acquisition. Some assets will not be recorded (e.g., recent knowledge acquired through research) or will be stated on the financial statements at understated costs (e.g., land).

An important consideration for management is an analysis of the effect of the acquisition on the riskiness of the firm. This will be high on management's list of relevant considerations.

The Mathematics of Leverage

Assume that there are zero personal taxes, that the investor can earn k_i (this is the investor's opportunity cost), and that this is also the borrowing rate of the firm.

Let X be the before-tax earnings, a perpetuity

t = the corporate tax rate
B = the amount of debt
V_U = the value of the unlevered firm
V_L = the value of the levered firm

The Unlevered Firm

If we assume constant earnings of X, to the investor, the unlevered firm has a value of

$$V_U = \frac{X(1-t)}{k_i}$$

The Levered Firm

Add an amount B of debt paying $k_i B$ interest. The cash flows to the capital contributors are

To Stockholders	To Debtholders	
$(X - k_i)(1-t)$ +	$k_i B$	$= X(1-t) + k_i Bt$

The amount $k_i Bt$ is added to the cash flows when B of debt is used. The present value of the cash flows using k_i to discount the perpetuities is

$$V_L = \frac{X(1-t)}{k_i} + \frac{k_i Bt}{k_i} = V_U + Bt$$

We start with a value of V_U, and if B of debt is substituted for common stock, the value of the firm increases by Bt. This analysis assumes zero personal taxes and no bankruptcy costs.

It shows the power of using debt financing. If a prospective acquisition is currently using zero debt, its value can be changed to

$$\frac{V_u}{1-t}$$

by using a maximum amount of debt.

EXAMPLE 24.5

$X = \$1,000,000$

$k_i = .10$

$t = .4$

$$V_U = \frac{X(1-t)}{k_i} = \frac{\$600,000}{.10} = \$6,000,000$$

The maximum value (using $10,000,000 of debt) is

$$V_L = \frac{V_U}{1 - t} = \frac{\$6{,}000{,}000}{.6} = \$10{,}000{,}000$$

With $7,000,000 of debt, the value of the firm is

$$
\begin{aligned}
V_L &= V_U + Bt \\
&= \$6{,}000{,}000 + .4(\$7{,}000{,}000) \\
&= \$8{,}800{,}000
\end{aligned}
$$

The increase in the value of the firm is

$$Bt = \$7{,}000{,}000(.4) = \$2{,}800{,}000$$

The value of the firm to a zero-tax investor ranges from $6,000,000 with zero debt to $10,000,000 with $10,000,000 of debt.

Adding Personal Taxes

Personal taxes make the valuation analysis much more complex and more difficult to reach definite conclusions. However, personal taxes must be considered.

Common stock is more desirable than is debt if debt returns are taxed at t_p and common stock returns are taxed at t_g if

$$(1 - t)(1 - t_g) > (1 - t_p)$$

EXAMPLE 24.6

$t = .46, \quad t_g = .20, \quad t_p = .6$
$X = \$100$

	Common Stock	Debt
Profits before interest and taxes	$100.00	$100
Corporate tax	46.00	0
Net income before interest	$ 54.00	$100
Personal tax	10.80	60
Net	$ 43.20 >	$ 40

Common stock is more desirable than debt with these facts. We have

$$(1 - t) = .54 \qquad (1 - t_g) = .80 \qquad (1 - t_p) = .4$$

which is

$$(1 - t)(1 - t_g) > (1 - t_p)$$
$$.54(.80) = .432 > .4$$

Since $(1 - t)(1 - t_g)$ is larger than $(1 - t_p)$, the firm should use common stock.

Most firms will have some investors paying zero tax and some investors paying taxes at a rate over .5. A wide range of securities is sensible for such firms.

The P/E Ratio

We want to investigate the financial effects of a high-P/E ratio firm (P) acquiring a low-P/E firm (S). Table 24.1 shows the financial information for the two firms and for their combination.

EXAMPLE 24.7

TABLE 24.1

	The Merger of P and S		Pro Forma
	P	S	(P + S)
Total market value	$8,000,000	$2,000,000	$10,000,000
Total earnings	$1,000,000	$400,000	$1,400,000
Number of shares	100,000	100,000	125,000
Earnings per share	$10	$4	$11.20
Market price	$80	$20	$80
P/E ratio	8×	5×	7.143×

If P gives 25,000 shares having a market price of $80 per share (having a total value of $2,000,000) for S, there will be 125,000 shares outstanding. What is their value if the earnings per share is $11.20?

It is incorrect to argue that the P/E of P + S will be the same as the P/E of P leading to a price of $11.20 times 8 or $89.60. The new price/earnings ratio can be expected to be a weighted average of the old P/E ratios, where the weights are the total earnings of each of the companies divided by the total earnings of both companies.

$$\text{New P/E} = \frac{E_P}{E_P + E_S} \text{ (P/E of P)} + \frac{E_S}{E_P + E_S} \text{ (P/E of S)}$$

$$= \frac{\$1,000,000}{\$1,400,000} \text{ (8)} + \frac{\$400,000}{\$1,400,000} \text{ (5)}$$

$$= 5.714 + 1.429 = 7.143$$

This leads to a market value of a share of P + S equal to 7.143(11.20) = $80. The total market value is

$$\$80(\$125,000) = \$10,000,000$$

which is equal to the sum of the values of firms P plus S. Value is neither being created nor destroyed by the acquisition.

With no change in operations, expectations, or payouts, the postacquisition P/E ratio should be a weighted average of the preacquisition P/Es, where the weights are the relative amounts of earnings of each component.

To understand better the logic of why the P/E of firm P + S is less than firm P, we will determine the implied growth rates for P and for S. Table 24.2 shows the current dividend, the cost of equity, and the retention rate. For example, P earned $10 and paid a $6 dividend; therefore, the retention rate is .4.

Using the one-stage growth model,

$$P = \frac{D}{k_e - g}$$

TABLE 24.2   Additional Information

	P	S
Current dividend	$6.00	$2.00
Cost of common stock equity (k_e)	.15	.15
Retention rate (b)	.4	.5

and if $D = (1 - b)E$, then

$$P = \frac{(1 - b)E}{k_e - g}$$

Solving this relationship for g, we obtain the implicit growth rate:

$$g = k_e - (1 - b)\frac{E}{P}$$

For firm P we have

$$g = .15 - \tfrac{1}{8}(1 - .4) = .15 - .075 = .075$$

With zero debt, and a return on investment of r for new investments, then

$$g = rb$$
$$.075 = .4r$$
$$r = .1875$$

For firm S we have a lower implied growth rate:

$$g = k_e - \frac{E}{P}(1 - b)$$

$$= .15 - \frac{1}{5}(1 - .5) = .05$$

The implicit return on new investments is

$$g = rb$$
$$.05 = .5r$$
$$r = .10$$

Firm S has a lower growth rate than does P; we also see that S is expected to earn only .10 on new investments, whereas P is expected to earn .1875. P's higher P/E ratio implies that the market is more optimistic about its future growth and earnings opportunities.

Each P/E ratio and dividend retention percentage implies a different growth rate (and thus a different return on new investment). Table 24.3 gives a few illustrative values for a retention rate of .6 and a .15 cost of equity capital.

TABLE 24.3   Implied Growth Rates and Returns

$$b = .4, k_e = .15, g = k_e - (1 - b)\frac{E}{P}, g = rb$$

P/E	$\frac{E}{P}$	$.60\frac{E}{P}$	$g = .15 - .60\frac{E}{P}$	$r = \frac{g}{.4}$
20	.05	.03	.12	.30
10	.10	.06	.09	.225
5	.20	.12	.03	.075
4	.25	.15	0	0

The relationship $g = rb$ assumes that there is zero debt. If we changed that assumption, the growth rate formulation would be somewhat more complex.

Thus, assuming that a firm can be acquired for its current market value, it is not important if the current P/E of the candidate for acquisition is above or below the acquirer's P/E. It is important whether the acquisition can be expected to result in an increase in acquirer's P/E as a result of a change in operations (changing retention rates or debt utilization), a decrease in financing costs (k_i or k_e), or real synergistic effects such as better rates of return on reinvestment or direct reduction of cost (higher current earnings). If the weighted average postacquisition P/E ratio exceeds the weighted average preacquisition P/E ratio, or if earnings improve, the acquisition will tend to be beneficial to stockholders of both the acquired and acquiring firms.

Dilution of Earnings

Assume that earnings per share are now $1.20 and that they are growing at 5 percent per year. If the acquisition takes place, the earnings per share will only be $.80, but the expected growth rate will now be 10 percent per year. The earnings per share are diluted.

How long will it take for the earnings with the acquisition to exceed the earnings without the acquisition? Let both sets of earnings grow for n years so that the two earnings are equal:

$$(1.05)^n 1.20 = (1.10)^n .80$$

$$\left(\frac{1.10}{1.05}\right)^n = 1.5$$

$$n \ln (1.0476) = \ln 1.5$$

$$n = \frac{.405465}{.04652} = 8.716 \text{ years}$$

After 8.716 years without the acquisition, the earnings will be

$$(\$1.05)^{8.716}(\$1.20) \;=\; 1.53(\$1.20) \;=\; \$1.84$$

After 8.716 years with the acquisition, the earnings will be

$$(\$1.10)^{8.716}(\$.80) \;=\; 2.295(\$.80) \;=\; \$1.84$$

Many managers would state that 8.716 years is too long to wait for an uncertain improvement in earnings per share and would reject the acquisition.

The Cost of an Acquisition

If the acquisition requires the issuance of 1,000,000 shares, where the shares of the acquiring firm before the acquisition announcement were selling at $80 per share, the cost of the acquisition can be defined to be

$$\$80(1,000,000) \;=\; \$80,000,000$$

If there are 3,000,000 shares outstanding before the acquisition, and 4,000,000 shares after, and if the total value of the postacquisition firm's stock is $400,000,000, we could define the cost to be

$$\$400,000,000 \times \frac{1,000,000}{4,000,000} \;=\; \$100,000,000$$

since one-fourth of the shares are being given away to achieve the acquisition. But this is stretching the definition of cost, since the firm would not be worth $400,000,000 without the acquisition.

If the 3,000,000 shares were worth

$$\$80(3,000,000) \;=\; \$240,000,000$$

before the acquisition and $300,000,000 after the acquisition, the original stockholders will have a $60,000,000 improvement in their wealth position (before tax). The total value of the firm after the acquisition is assumed to be $400,000,000.

Although common stock is frequently issued for an acquisition since the transaction can be nontaxable to the investors, cash, debt, and preferred stock are also used.

If instead of issuing new common stock shares, in the example, a purchase price of $80,000,000 cash is paid and if the firm's value after acquisition is $320,000,000 (equal to $400,000,000 minus the $80,000,000 purchase price), then the stockholder's position will now improve from $240,000,000 to $320,000,000, for a gain of $80,000,000.

Conservation of Value

We want to illustrate the fact that if the outcomes of two firms are independent, there is a conservation of value* that takes place. The total value is not changed, but there can be shifting of value among the different capital suppliers.

EXAMPLE 24.8 —————————————————————————————

Assume that a firm has a .9 probability of making $500 and a .1 probability of losing $500. The expected value of the two outcomes is $400. The firm has $240 of debt payments coming due. If the firm loses $500, the debtholders will not be paid.

The debtholders have .1 probability of no payment. The expectation for debtholders is:

(1) Probability	(2) Outcome	(1) × (2)
.9	$240	$216
.1	0	0
		Expected value = $216

The expectation for stockholders is

(1) Probability	(2) Outcome	(1) × (2)
.9	$260	$234
.1	0	0
		Expected value = $234

* L. Joseph Thomas helped to develop the logic of this section

The sum of the expected value to both sets of investors is $450.

Now assume that a firm, whose results are independent of but identically distributed to the first firm, merges with the original firm. Figure 24.1 shows the results of operations, before debt payments, of the merged firm. The debtholders now only are paid if the top path is followed; thus they now have a .19 probability of no payment. The debt has an expected value of $389 (that is, .81 × $480).

The debtholders of Firm 1 hold half the debt; thus their expected value is one half of $389.00 or $194.50 (compared to $216.00 before the merger). The expected return to the stockholders is $421.00 (that is, .81 × $520), and one half of this is $210.50 (compared to $234.00 before the merger). Both the debtholders and stockholders have lower expected values than before the merger. Both sets of investors lose as a result of the merger.

Although the debtholders and the stockholders are harmed by the merger, the trade creditors do better with the merger. A "conservation of total value" principle is at work as well as limited liability. Payments are being shifted from debtholders and stockholders to trade creditors. Without the merger, the trade creditors lost $500 with .1 probability, an expectation of negative $50. With the

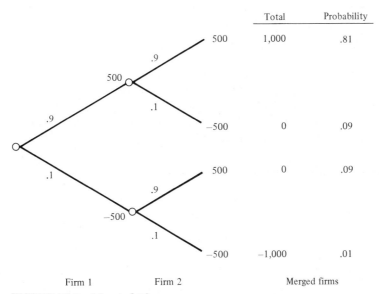

		Total	Probability
	500	1,000	.81
	−500	0	.09
	500	0	.09
	−500	−1,000	.01

Firm 1   Firm 2   Merged firms

FIGURE 24.1   Merged Firms

TABLE 24.4   Expected Values for One Firm

	Without Merger	With Merger
Expected value of debt	$216	$194.50
Expected value of common	234	210.50
Expected loss of creditors	−50	− 5.00
Net to all investors	$400	$400.00

merger the trade creditors of the one firm lose $\frac{1}{2}(\$1000).01 = \$5$ on the average. Table 24.4 shows that the net of all investors is $400 and is not changed by the merger.

Mergers do not necessarily decrease risk to stockholders and debtholders. Even if the return outcomes of the firms involved in a merger are independent and indentically distributed, there can be decreased expected return and increased risk to both debtholders and stockholders. The effects of a merger have to be computed. They should not be assumed.

Leveraged Buyouts

Leveraged buyouts (LBOs) are not new, but the increase in the size of the firms being bought out has risen dramatically. In a leveraged buyout, a firm is acquired by a group of investors. The financing is characterized by the use of a large amount of debt.

There are two basic types of leveraged buyouts. One type is engineered by the current management whose members become significant stockholders in the new firm. The second type is structured by outsiders, but almost invariably they will attempt to retain the more important members of management.

A very large LBO of the first type was the acquisition of Metromedia Broadcasting Corporation by a group called J. W. K. Acquisition Corporation. The acquisition price was over $1 billion. In fact, Metromedia itself issued $1.3 billion of high-yield bonds to help finance the acquisition (the funds were used to buy back the company's common stock). To place this amount of debt in perspective, the total assets of Metromedia was $1.3 billion. J. W. K. Acquisition Corporation was controlled by the management of Metromedia.

As long as banks and other investors are willing to finance very highly leveraged acquisitions, LBOs will prosper. They are a very important financial development of the 1980s.

Greenmail

In the early 1980s, as the merger and acquisition movement accelerated, a new phenomenon came into being. A corporation (or a corporate management) finding that it was pursued by a undesirable suitor (a black knight) would arrange to buy at a premium price the shares held by the black knight. Thus St. Regis Corporation, finding that over 6 percent of its stock was held by a person who had a reputation for dismembering firms, acquired these shares at a price of $52 when its stock was ranging in price between $30 and $40. Two other raiders immediately started to expand their positions in St. Regis common stock, putting the firm back into jeopardy. (St. Regis finally sought a white knight, a friendly acquirer.)

The intentions of the raider may be perfectly honorable, but the perceptions of the management might be different. The fairness of the greenmail process has been questioned by many observers. It is not fair to all shareholders for one select group of investors to be given the opportunity to sell at a premium price. One solution that has been suggested is to have the same offer go to all shareholders if the firm is buying out one group of investors.

Greenmail is not desirable for the majority of stockholders. They are harmed when a group of investors gain a negative reputation, then exploit this reputation by buying a significant stock position, and finally have the firm buy its freedom to operate by buying the stock back at a premium price. At a minimum, other shareholders should also be given the opportunity to sell their shares at the same price.

Golden Parachutes

If the defensive tactics (including greenmail) have not worked, then management's final option is to have a safety net. A contractual agreement is prepared that guarantees a manager a given sum if his or her employment is terminated because of an acquisition or merger.

The federal government has taken action limiting the amount of tax write-off associated with golden parachute payments, but we expect to see such arrangements continue in the future.

Divestments

The Wall Street Journal headline read*

ITT IS PLANNING TO SELL $1.7 BILLION
OF ITS ASSETS IN STREAMLINING MOVE

Effort Is Aimed at Focusing on Telecommunications,
Insurance, and Technology

In 1985 ITT sold its Continental Baking Co. Some investors theorized that the sum of the parts of the company was worth more than the market valued ITT. Among ITT's businesses were

Telecommunications equipment.
Insurance.
Sheraton Hotels.
Publishing.
Education services.
Seed companies.
Oil.
Forest products.
Automotive products.
Semiconductors.
Pipes and valves.

Although the company's debt/equity ratio as of the end of 1984 was only 37.5 percent, this measure omitted a very large amount of nonreported (nonconsolidated) debt. Thus one objective was probably to reduce the total amount of debt.

The second reason for divesting was that if enough investors thought that ITT was worth less than the sum of its parts, a raider would likely be attracted with the objective of breaking it up (using the sale of the assets to pay for the acquisition). Management has an incentive to make the company more attractive.

Harold Geneen was a business genius who had built ITT into a very large international conglomerate using the international communications business as the foundation for raising capital. Since Geneen had retired, it was difficult to see how the pieces fit together. Ordinary business managers do not see synergy in a company whose businesses ranged from grass seed to semiconductors.

* *The Wall Street Journal*, January 17, 1985.

Greenmail Example

The following "greenmail" deals made in 1984 illustrate the magnitude of this phenomenon:

Texaco, Inc., paid $1.28 billion to Bass Brothers.
Phillips Petroleum Co. paid $472 million to Mesa Partners.
Walt Disney paid $325 million to the Saul P. Steinberg group.

In March 1984 St. Regis Corporation paid $52 a share for the common stock owned by a group headed by Sir James Goldsmith. During 1983, St. Regis sold for a low of $24 and a high of $36⅝. During the first half of 1984 the highest price reached was $44¼.

There is a happy ending. In August 1984, Champion International bought St. Regis at $55.50 per share.*

*The New York Times, January 2, 1985.

One reason for divesting a unit is that it does not earn a profitable return. The problem is that the market also perceives the low profitability and bids accordingly. In 1985 forest products were not doing well, so it was logical for ITT to want to sell its forest product company (Rayonier). However, if it sold Rayonier, it would get a "bad" price, since the depressed market conditions for forest products was well known.

Conventional wisdom is that a company should divest those components that are not doing well. Leaving out long-run strategy (product line) considerations, a company should divest that unit whose sale price exceeds its present value as an operating unit by the largest amount. A more likely decision rule to be followed in practice is to divest the unit that is earning the lowest return on investment. This choice can be wrong depending on the sale price and the forecast of future profitability.

Conclusions

The acquisition of a corporation by another corporation is an investment decision. If one is convinced that investments should be evaluated using the net present value method, it would be disconcerting if an investment decision involving the acquisition of a corporate entity could be correctly made using a simplistic device such as the P/E ratio. It is not clear that a management is able to acquire a firm with a low P/E (such as a firm with low growth opportunities) and fold it into a firm with a high P/E and obtain a benefit, unless the market assumes that the growth rate will change under the new management.

We can expect that the prospect of quick and easy profits arising from financial wheeling and dealing will sometimes give rise to decisions made from the point of view of short-run considerations rather than from the long-term profitability of the decision. We cannot force management to set objectives of one type or another. We can hope that a better understanding of the significance of mergers will lead to better analysis on which to base decisions. Just combining two firms does not automatically lead to an increase in value.

Review Problem 24.1

(a) If the common stockholders of ABD Corporation are taxed at .52 and if they buy XYZ stock at $100, how much could the corporation ABD pay for XYZ stock and have the investors indifferent? They will hold and not sell.

(b) If the investor in (a) were to sell after retention and be taxed at a capital gains rate of .20, how much of a premium could ABD pay? The alternative is to pay a cash dividend. Assume that the XYZ stock will have a value of $100 independent of the price paid by ABD.

Solution to the Review Problem 24.1

(a) $x = \dfrac{100}{1 - t_p} = \dfrac{100}{1 - .52} = \$208.33$

(b) $(1 - t_p)D = (1 - t_g)\dfrac{D}{x}$

$x = \dfrac{1 - t_g}{1 - t_p} = \dfrac{.80}{.48} = 1.6667$

$x(\$100) = \$166.67$

PROBLEMS

1. (a) The ABC Company has a simple capital structure. Management wants to substitute $100 million of .12 debt for common stock.

     What effect will the change have on the value of the firm to a zero-tax investor? The corporate tax rate is .46.

   (b) The XYZ Company is thinking of acquiring a firm that is earning before tax $100,000 a year. The borrowing rate of XYZ is .10, and its tax rate is .46. Thus its after-tax borrowing rate is .054. The investment in the firm will be financed with sufficient debt to cause the amount of income taxes paid to be zero on this investment.

     What is the maximum amount that XYZ could afford to pay for the firm?

2. The following facts apply to two companies, A and B, whose operations are completely independent.

	A	B
P/E	20	5
Earnings per share	$1	$2
Shares outstanding	10,000,000	1,000,000

   Assume that A acquires B in exchange for 500,000 shares of common stock.

   (a) What will be the new earnings per share (EPS) for A?

   (b) What would you expect the new P/E of A (after acquisition) to be? Assume a rational market.

   (c) What will be the total market value of A's common stock after the acquisition? Assume a rational market.

3. The ABC Company is considering acquiring the Doggy Corporation. The Doggy Corporation is earning before interest and taxes $2 million per year and expects to continue to earn that (for perpetuity) and it has zero debt.

   The ABC Company can borrow at a cost of .10 and would have a capital structure of 100 percent debt for the Doggy Corporation if it acquired it. The corporate tax rate is .4.

   Consider only corporate taxes. What is the present value of the Doggy Corporation to the ABC Company? Assume that the following calculation is accepted for V_U:

$$V_U = \frac{X(1 - t)}{.10} = \frac{\$1,200,000}{.10} = \$12,000,000$$

where .10 is the appropriate discount factor for the zero-debt cash flows.

4. Problems (a), (b), (c) are True or False.

   (a) _____ Firm A with a high P/E acquires Firm B with a low P/E. The EPS of A will increase immediately as a result of the acquisition.

   (b) _____ Continuing (a), the EPS for a period 10 years from now will certainly be larger for A as a result of the acquisition.

   (c) _____ Either cash flow or earnings can be used to value an acquisition if earnings reflect all capital costs, but the two present values (unadjusted) of earnings and cash flows of the prospective acquisition will not be equal.

5. The RS Company is currently earning $10 per share and expects to grow at a rate of .05 per year. If RS merges with T Company, which is growing at .14, the earnings will be reduced to $8 per share and the growth rate will be .09.

   In how many years will the earnings per share of the merged firms equal the earnings per share of RS without the merger?

6. The ABC Company has the following capital structure:

	Proportion	Cost	Weighted Cost
Debt	.8	.10	.080
Common stock	.2	.16	.032
			.112

The common stock of a company with the identical operating risk can be acquired for $1,000,000. The stockholders' equity cash flows of the acquisition are

0	1	2	
− $1,000,000	$120,000	$120,000	The benefits are a perpetuity.

The firm has $200,000 of debt (net of any disposable assets) paying .06 ($12,000) per year. There are zero taxes.

   Should the acquisition be accepted?

REFERENCES

Alberts, W. W., and J. E. Segall. *The Corporate Merger*. Chicago: University of Chicago Press, 1966.

Austin, D. V. "The Financial Management of Tender Offer Takeovers." *Financial Management*, Spring 1972, 37–43.

Bierman, Harold, Jr., and Jerome E. Hass. "The Use and Misuse of the P/E Ratio in Acquisition and Merger Decisions." *Financial Executive*, October 1970, 62–68.

Butters, J. K., J. Lintner, and W. S. Cary. *Effects of Taxation, Corporate Mergers*. Cambridge, Mass.: Harvard University Press, 1951.

Cheney, R. E. "What's New on the Corporate Takeover Scene." *The Financial Executive*, April 1972, 18–21.

Cohen, M. F. "Takeover Bids." *Financial Analysts Journal*, January–February 1970, 26.

Dodd, P. and R. Ruback. "Tender Offers and Stockholder Returns." *Journal of Financial Economics*, November 1977, 351–373.

Elgers, P., and J. J. Clark. "Merger Types and Shareholder Returns: Additional Evidence." *Financial Management*, Summer 1980, 66–72.

Hayes, S. L., and R. A. Taussig, "Tactics of Cash Takeover Bids." *Harvard Business Review*, March–April 1967, 135–148.

Kummer, D. R., and J. R. Hoffmeister. "Valuation Consequences of Cash Tender Offers," *Journal of Finance*, May 1978, 505–516.

Mueller, Dennis C. "A Theory of Conglomerate Mergers." *Quarterly Journal of Economics*, November 1969, 653–659.

Smalter, D. J., and R. C. Lancey. "P/E Analysis in Acquisition Strategy." *Harvard Business Review*, November–December 1966, 85–95.

Vance, J. O. "Is Your Company a Take-over Target?" *Harvard Business Review*, May–June 1969, 93–98.

Wansley, J. W., W. R. Lane, and H. C. Yang, "Abnormal Returns to Acquired Firms by Type of Acquisition and Method of Payment." *Financial Management*, Autumn 1983, 16–22.

Chapter 25

Convertible Bonds

Major Topics

1. The basic definition of a convertible bond.
2. The computation of a conversion premium.
3. Valuation of a convertible with certainty and uncertainty.
4. Comparing an investment in a convertible with other investments.
5. Trading-off interest rate and conversion premium.
6. Considerations of an issuing firm.

Definition of a Convertible Bond

There are securities that do not classify neatly as being either debt or stock equity, since they are hybrids of the characteristics of several securities. These hybrid securities tend to be difficult to value. In fact, one of the advantages of these securities is that the company issuing them, and the investors considering them, may have entirely different estimates of value (this can be useful in negotiations for firms acquiring other firms). We shall consider in this chapter debt securities that are convertible at the option of the owner into a given number of common stock shares.

Convertible securities are popular among investors who want a fixed (well-defined) interest income but also a large upside potential. The convertible feature opens up the possibility of large gains for investors if the stock rapidly appreciates in value and there is only a small probability of large losses because of the security's bond characteristics. The bond feature tends to guarantee periodic interest payments and the payment of principal at the given maturity date (if the bond is not retired or converted prior to that date) if the stock price does not increase sufficiently to justify conversion. These conversion features are not without a cost to investors; convertible bonds carry a lower interest rate than do comparable bonds without the conversion feature.

Both convertible bonds and preferred stock are convertible into a common stock at a fixed ratio of shares of common stock to the senior security. This discussion of convertible securities will be in terms of convertible bonds, even though the discussion also applies to convertible preferred stock.

Consider a $1,000 face value or par value $1,000 bond that is convertible into 20 shares of common stock. The conversion price is $50 per share (equal to the face value of $1,000 divided by 20). If the common stock price goes above $50 and interest rates have not fallen drastically since issuance, then the conversion privilege is of the value to the investor who has to sell. For example, if the common stock is currently selling at $60 per share, the conversion value of the bond is $1,200 and the holder of the bond can realize at least $1,200 on the sale of the bond. Without the conversion feature and with no change in interest rates, an investor would only realize $1,000 on sale (if interest rates had fallen significantly, the investor might be able to realize $1,200 or more, even without the conversion feature).

A person buying a convertible bond is receiving the rights to future interest and principal payments plus the privilege of converting to common stock if it is desirable. If the price of the common stock increases sufficiently to justify the conversion, the bondholder benefits from the conversion feature. The issuing corporation benefits from the conversion feature by being able to issue debt with a lower interest rate than it would otherwise have to pay. In addition, at some time in the future it may be able to force conversion of the debt into common stock, thus decreasing the amount of debt outstanding, without making a cash outlay for the principal. Also, regulated institutional investors are generally allowed to purchase convertible bonds even where they are prevented from buying common stock of the same corporation. Fringe benefits to the investors are that they can borrow more using the bonds as collateral than with stocks (lower margin requirements) and lower transaction costs than those associated with the purchase of common stock.

Conversion terms may change through time either because of built-in conditions in the bond indenture or because of stock dividends and stock splits. Informed investors in convertible bonds will insist on protection against stock dividends and splits.

The period of time during which the conversion features apply may not be the same as the bond maturity. It is important that the contract be read carefully by an investor considering purchase so as to reduce or eliminate the number of unpleasant surprises.

Description of Convertible Bond

A convertible bond can be described in three different ways:

1. It is a bond with an option to convert to common stock.
2. It is the sum of its expected value as debt plus the expected value as stock.
3. It is common stock with downside insurance if the common stock does not go up sufficiently to warrant conversion.

Let us assume that a very risky company wants to raise debt money, but it cannot find investors unless it pays more interest than it can afford. Adding a conversion feature will attract investors. For example, if the stock price is $40, the bonds can be defined to be convertible into 20 shares (there is a 25 percent conversion premium).

A convertible bond is truly a hybrid. It is a debt, but if the stock price goes up to $50 (a .25 increase) by maturity, the investor will have an option of converting into 20 shares of common stock. If the bond is not callable for a period of time, the investor has some probability of large gains. If the stock price does not go up, the investor has the fallback position of receiving $1,000 at maturity.

One of the important advantages of convertible bonds is that is offers interesting risk possibilities. There is only a very small probability of losing large amounts, and there is a probability of large gains (if the common stock increases in value rapidly). There is also a high probability of a small loss. This is an opportunity loss arising from accepting lower interest than with straight debt, and the conversion feature turns out to have little or no value. Since it is an opportunity loss, it is implicit rather than explicit (larger interest payments could have been earned on bonds without the conversion feature); therefore, it is not apparent to many investors.

A second advantage of convertible bonds for a speculator is that the bonds sometimes have a smaller margin requirement than stock. Thus the investors can lever their investment with more dollars invested in bonds than they can invest in common stock.

Conversion Premiums

Basic Relationships

We first establish basic convertible bond relationships that are useful for analysis. Let

B = the face value of the debt

s = the number of shares of common stock into which a bond can be converted; the conversion ratio

B_0 = the value now of the security as straight debt

M_0 = the convertible bond's market value now

P_0 = the common stock's market value now

Investors are frequently interested in two measures: the premium over bond value and the conversion premium. We shall compute these measures as percentages, although they are sometimes presented in dollar amounts.

The premium over straight bond value incurred by buying the convertible bond is defined as

$$\frac{M_0 - B_0}{B_0} \tag{25.1}$$

The conversion premium is defined as

$$\frac{B - sP_0}{sP_0} \tag{25.2}$$

This gives the percentage increase in common stock price required for the bond (as common stock) to be worth as much as the common stock that could be purchased.

EXAMPLE 25.1

An 8 percent $1,000 bond is convertible into 20 shares of common stock. The stock is currently selling at $45 per share and the bond is selling at $1,200. Assume that the bond as straight debt would have a value of $800. The premium over straight bond value is

$$\frac{M_0 - B_0}{B_0} = \frac{\$1,200 - \$800}{\$800} = \frac{\$400}{\$800} = .50$$

The conversion premium is

$$\frac{B - sP_0}{sP_0} = \frac{\$1,000 - 20(\$45)}{20(\$45)} = \frac{\$100}{\$900} = .11$$

The bond is currently selling at 50 percent over its value as straight debt and has an 11 percent conversion premium.

Other factors of interest to the investor are the call premium and the period of no call (the issuing firm cannot call during this period). The higher the call premium and the longer the period of no call, the more protection the investors have against being forced to sell or to convert their bonds before they want to. During the period that the issuing corporation cannot call, the investor's potential gains are unlimited. If the issuing corporation can call, the potential gain is limited by the likelihood of the firm calling. A called convertible bond can always be converted within a given time period into common stock if an investor so desires. One criterion used when determining whether or not to call is the drain on cash resulting from the dividends on stock compared to the cash drain of the interest payments. Equally important is whether or not the conversion value of the bond is above the call price.

If the common stock in Example 25.1 were paying $1 per share per year, conversion would mean cash dividends of $20 per year compared to $48 per year of after-tax interest (assuming a 40 percent corporate tax rate, the after-tax cost of the $80 contractual interest is $48). Let the stock price at time t be P_t. The corporation might well decide that conversion was desirable as soon as the conversion value (sP_t) went above the call price (or enough above so that the investors would convert rather than take advantage of the opportunity to liquidate their investment without transaction costs at the call price). The investors for their part, would compare $80 of interest and $20 of common stock dividend, the taxes on these returns, and the safety given by the bond feature by the security and would likely decide to postpone conversion until the cash dividend were increased or they were forced to convert by the bonds being called.

Value of a Convertible Bond

Certainty Case

If all the future stock prices, P_t, were known with certainty, the present value of a convertible bond, V_0, can be expressed in terms of the present value of the interest and principal or the present value of the conversion value. If P_t never goes above the conversion price, the face value of the bond is used as the estimate of future value (there will be no conversion) and the bond is valued as straight debt. If P_t goes above the conversion price, we can assume that the bond is converted at time t, where t is chosen to maximize the net present value. If the second calculation (value with conversion) is larger than the value as straight debt, the conversion feature has some value.

EXAMPLE 25.2

A 30-year, .08 bond ($1,000 face value) is convertible into 25 shares of common stock. The price of the common stock is currently $50 per share, and the common stock price is expected to increase steadily to $391 at the end of year 30 (a 7 percent growth rate). The common stock is paying a $2-per-share dividend that is expected to continue for the entire 30 years. The yield for comparable bonds without a conversion feature is .09. We want to determine the present value of the convertible bond if it is converted just before maturity. Assume that the investor does not pay taxes.

The value of the convertible bond with conversion in 30 years using the .09 as the opportunity cost and the common stock price of $391 per share is

$$\sum_{t=1}^{30} \$80(1.09)^{-t} + 25(\$391)(1.09)^{-30} = (\$80 \times 10.2737) + (\$9,775 \times .0754)$$

$$= \$821.90 + \$737.07$$

$$= \$1,558.94$$

The value of the security as a straight bond is $897.30; using .09 present value factors:

$$\$1,000 \times .0754 = \$\ 75.40$$
$$\$80 \times 10.2737 = \underline{\ \ \ 821.90}$$
$$\$897.30$$

The total value of the bond is equal to the sum of the straight bond plus the value of the conversion feature. If the price of the bond is $1,558.94, the value being placed on the conversion privilege is

$$\text{value of conversion privilege} = \$1,558.94 - \$897.30 = \$661.64$$

on the basis of converting in 30 years.

Uncertainty Case

Let us now turn to the case where there is uncertainty and the future stock price at time n, P_n is a random variable. Two factors set the lower limit on the value of a convertible bond. A convertible bond must sell for at least as much as the greater of its current conversion value:

$$sP_0 \qquad\qquad\qquad (25.3)$$

or its value as a straight bond if held to maturity:

$$\sum_{t=1}^{n} I(1 + k_i)^{-t} + B(1 + k_i)^{-n} \qquad (25.4)$$

where k_i is the interest rate on straight debt.

Consider now the possibility of converting at time n. This value is relevant if it is larger than the value as straight debt. The present value of s shares of common stock at time n is $sP_n(1 + k_i)^{-n}$, and the value today of the bond based on conversion at time n is

$$\sum_{t=1}^{n} I(1 + k_i)^{-t} + sP_n(1 + k_i)^{-n} \qquad (25.5)$$

If the conversion value (sP_n) were greater than the market value (M_n) of the bond, arbitragers would ensure that M_n would adjust so that $M_n \geq sP_n$; thus conversion will not take place voluntarily because of stock price changes. A stock price increase will not cause investors to convert, since the bond market value must also increase.

Now let us consider the cash flows. Investors need to compare the dividend resulting from holding stock and the interest flow resulting from holding the bonds. They will not convert as long as the annual interest flow from holding the debt exceeds the annual dividends. If common stock dividends exceed interest, the investor must consider the additional cash flow return balanced against the additional risk associated with holding stock rather than debt. To save cash flow, low-dividend-paying corporations frequently force conversion by calling the bonds (this also reduces risk) as soon as the conversion value sufficiently exceeds the call price (assuming they can call) so the bonds will be converted.

The Investment Decision

Comparing Convertibles and Debt

How does one approach the decision to buy a convertible bond? We shall consider two different tacks. First, we shall compare the convertible bond to straight debt; then we shall compare buying a convertible bond or common stock of the same firm.

Assume that straight debt is paying k_i and that the convertible debt will pay k. Assume that the call premium of C will be received at time n if the convertible bond is purchased. The incremental net present value (NPV) of the cash flows from investing in the convertible bond rather than the straight debt is

$$\text{NPV} = [B(k - k_i)]B(n, k_i) + C(1 + k_i)^{-n} \tag{25.6}$$

The investor in the convertible receives $(k - k_i)B$ less interest for n years than the investor in straight debt, but does receive C(the call premium) at time n that the straight debt does not pay.

Setting the NPV equal to zero, we can solve for n, the number of years that can pass with the investor earning at least a return of k_i if the bond is called on or before n years have passed. If the bond is called after n years has passed, and if the conversion value is not larger than call price, the investor will earn less than k_i. Solving for n, we obtain

$$n = \frac{\ln\left[\dfrac{k_i C}{B(k_i - k)} + 1\right]}{\ln(1 + k_i)} \tag{25.7}$$

EXAMPLE 25.3

Assume that a convertible bond is callable at a price of $1,090 ($C = \$90$). The convertible yields .082 and comparable straight debt yields .10. The investor is zero tax.

Solving for n,

$$n = \frac{\ln\left[\dfrac{k_i C}{B(k_i - k)} + 1\right]}{\ln(1 + k_i)} \tag{25.7}$$

$$= \frac{\ln\left[\dfrac{.10 \times 90}{.018(\$1,000)} + 1\right]}{\ln(1.10)} = \frac{\ln 1.5}{\ln 1.10} = \frac{.40547}{.09531} = 4.25$$

Assume that the bond is callable after two years. In the first two years, the investor can earn unlimited returns (the firm cannot call). In years 2.0 to 4.25, the investor can earn more than k_i, but the gains are limited by the fact that the firm can call any time after 2.0 years.

Assuming that the conversion value at time 4.25 is less than the call price and that the firm will call as soon as the conversion value equals the call price, the investor will earn a return after year 4.25 that is less than k_i. If the bond is held to maturity, without call or a conversion taking place, the investor will earn $k = .082$. This is the contractual rate on the convertible bond originally issued at par.

Now assume that the firm can only call after year 6. The investor can earn unlimited gains until year 6 (n is less than 6, so the exact value of n does not affect the value of the bond to the investor). However, since n is less than 6, we know that the stock price has to go above the conversion price prior to year 6 or the investor will earn less than k_i.

The primary importance of the model [equation (25.7)] is that it highlights the importance of k, k_i, C, and the period during which the firm cannot call. Also, because the likelihood of the stock increasing above the call price before n time periods is of importance, the conversion premium that is set is of concern to the investor.

Comparing Convertibles and Common Stock

Instead of comparing the convertible bond and straight debt, investors frequently compare investing in the convertible debt and investing in common stock. There are several approaches, but we will compare buying a bond convertible into s shares of common or buying s shares of common.

EXAMPLE 25.4

$k_i = .10, k = .09, s = 20$, and there are no taxes
$B = \$1,000$ (cost of convertible bond)
$P_0 = \$42$, dividend = $2 per share

Since $s = 20$, assume that we buy 20 shares of common stock. Twenty shares of common stock will cost

$42 \times 20 = \$840$

They will pay dividends of

$2 \times 20 = \$40$ per year

Buying the convertible bond costs an extra $160:

$1,000 - \$840 = \$160$

and this bond will earn an extra $50 of interest per year compared to the $40 common stock dividend:

$90 - \$40 = \$50$

The net present value from investing in the convertible bond rather than the common stock, assuming the interest advantage lasts forever, is

$$\text{NPV} = -\$160 + \frac{\$50}{.10} = \$340$$

We can determine how long the interest advantage has to exist for the initial $160 investment to be recovered:

$$-\$160 + \$50 \, B(n, .10) = 0$$
$$B(n, .10) = 3.2$$
$$n = 4.05 \text{ years}$$

We can also solve for n more generally. Let C_0 be the additional outlay resulting from buying the bond instead of the stock:

$$-C_0 + (\text{Int} - \text{Div})B(n, k_i) = 0$$

Solving for n yields

$$n = \frac{\ln\left[\dfrac{\text{Int} - \text{Div}}{\text{Int} - \text{Div} - k_i C_0}\right]}{\ln(1 + k_i)} \tag{25.8}$$

For the example, we have

$$n = \frac{\ln\left(\dfrac{\$50}{\$50 - \$16}\right)}{\ln 1.10} = \frac{.3857}{.0953} = 4.05 \text{ years}$$

Some investors like to compute a payback period for the extra $160 investment:

$$\frac{\$160}{\$50} = 3.2 \text{ years}$$

This measure is widely used on Wall Street to evaluate the investment desirability of a convertible.

The 4.05 years previously determined takes into consideration the time value of money. The 3.2 does not consider the time value of money.

So far we have assumed a constant common stock dividend. If the dividend is increasing, then we decrease the net present value of investing in the bond compared to investing in the common stock.

The advantage of comparing an investment in the convertible bond and an investment in the common stock is that it holds the common stock price appreciation neutral (it is present with both buying alternatives) so that we can concentrate on the characteristics of the convertible debt.

Interest Rate and Conversion Premium

The price that is set for a convertible bond is a function of the interest rate on the bond and the conversion premium. The smaller the conversion premium, the smaller the interest rate on the convertible bond has to be. Conversion premiums are usually between 20 and 30 percent.

EXAMPLE 25.5 ───────────────────────────────────

Let us analyze the following two alternatives for a 20-year bond. The stock price is now $40.

	Interest Rate	Shares	Conversion Premium	Conversion Price
Alternative 1	.08	25	$\dfrac{\$1{,}000 - 25(\$40)}{25(\$40)} = 0$	$40
Alternative 2	.10	20	$\dfrac{\$1{,}000 - 20(\$40)}{20(\$40)} = .25$	$50

Which alternative is better for the issuing firm?

Alternative 2 has an extra $20-per-year interest on a $1,000 bond. But it saves 5 shares at the time of conversion. If the stock price is $40 or less and conversion does not take place, alternative 2 leads to an extra $20-per-year (before-tax) cost and zero benefits. The bonds are not converted with either alternative. Alternative 2 is inferior to alternative 1.

If the stock price goes to P_n where P_n is larger than $50, then alternative 2 saves 5 shares worth P_n each. For the issuing firm we have a NPV of

$$\text{NPV} = -20B(n, k_i) + 5(P_n)(1 + k_i)^{-n}$$

If the stock price is between $40 and $50, then at time n alternative 1 costs $25P_n$ while alternative 2 costs $1,000.

The NPV of alternative 2 compared to alternative 1 is

$$NPV = -20B(n, k_i) + (25P_n - \$1,000)(1 + k_i)^{-n}$$

If $P_n = \$40$, the NPV is a negative $20B(n, k_i)$, and alternative 1 is preferred. If $P_n = \$50, n = 20$, and $k_i = .10$, we have

$$NPV = -20(8.5136) + (\$1,250 - \$1,000)(.1486) = -170 + 37 = -133.$$

Alternative 1 is better than alternative 2.

With $n = 20$, P_n has to be at least as large as $229 for alternative 2 to be better:

$$NPV = -20(8.5136) + 5P_n(.1486) = 0$$

$$5P_n = \frac{\$170}{.1486} = \$1,144$$

$$P_n = \$229$$

The analysis should also be done for different values of n and different call strategies. An earlier conversion will increase the importance of the extra 5 shares.

Convertible Debt: More Like Equity

The bonds discussed in the preceding section were debt with an option to convert to common stock. We shall now consider types of convertible debt securities that are more like common stock with downside protection than like debt.

The definition of any security for tax purposes is an important element in determining the desirability of the security for the issuing firm. The Internal Revenue Service has been unable to distinguish exactly whether capital is debt or stock. This has confused the determination whether a convertible bond or note is equity or debt of the issuing corporation. In truth, it is not possible to distinguish between convertible securities that are debt and those that are equity since they are always a combination of both. However, it is possible to affect whether the security is more like debt or equity.

In 1982 and 1983, a convertible security was issued that had some distinctive features. These adjustable rate convertible notes (ARCNs) survived the market test, having been issued by several corporations (e.g., Borg-Warner issued $100 million in 1982, and Mapco, Inc., issued $50 million in 1983), and were in conformance with proposed tax regulations, but they failed to survive the scrutiny of the IRS. The IRS classified them as equities. These securities stretched the patience of the IRS on several issues because they

1. Were convertible into common stock with a low conversion premium.
2. Paid an interest amount that was equal to or larger than the current dividend on the common stock. The interest rate was not a fixed amount but was tied to the dividends on the common stock.
3. Were callable during most (or all) of their lives at a price that was significantly less than the issue price of the security. The maturity price was significantly less than the issue price.
4. Were callable immediately or nearly immediately.
5. Were subordinate to other creditors.

The issuing firm's objective is to have a security that is better than common stock for investors and offers significant benefits (mixed with minor costs) to the corporation. The corporation can vary any of the following variables— (conversion premium, interest payment, no-call period, call price, time till maturity, seniority, and maturity payment)—with an aim at making the security more marketable or to make the security more acceptable to the IRS as debt.

The IRS objected to having the interest payment calculated using the dividend on common stock and having the minimum annual return low compared to returns on comparable conventional debt. To correct this, we have three alternatives. One is to have the interest payment a function of income rather than dividends. Another is to compute the interest rate using some other variable such as the Treasury bill rate. A third is to fix the interest rate at a certain amount.

The Investor

Why should an investor buy a convertible note or bond? We shall assume that the investor has already decided to invest in the common stock of the corporation. We consider only the question as to whether or not this proposed convertible debt is a better investment than the common stock.

To simplify the analysis for both the investor and the issuing firm, we will assume that

1. There is zero conversion premium.
2. The interest payment per period will initially be larger than the cash dividend on the common stock.

3. There is antidilution protection (the number of shares the bond is convertible into is adjusted for stock dividends and stock splits).

The remainder of the security's characteristics will affect the value of the security but will not affect whether or not the security is better than common stock. With these assumptions, the convertible debt is a better investment than common stock. None of the assumptions is necessary for the security to be a desirable investment, but they do simplify the presentation and allow us to reach a definite conclusion. If we change the assumptions, we can move to a situation where the security has both advantages and disadvantages, but it is still worthy of consideration.

Assume that the convertible bond is being issued at a price of $40 and that it is convertible into one share of common stock currently selling at $40 per share. The bond pays $4 interest per year and the stock pays $3 of dividends per year. Should the investor buy the bond or the stock?

The convertible security just described is better than the purchase of an equivalent number of shares of common stock in the same company for a zero-tax investor or for an individual. The most significant advantage occurs because the contractual interest payment is larger as well as safer than the cash dividend. For the investor, the bond dominates the common stock because there is no possible way in which it can be inferior. If the stock price goes up and the cash dividend exceeds the interest being paid, the investor might want to convert and thus will hold the common stock (the same number of shares will be held as if the common stock had been purchased initially). If the common stock price falls below the conversion value, the call price and the maturity value supply some protection (the existence of a maturity date ensures that the investor will at least receive the maturity value). But this protection is merely an extra bonus given that we had already established the relative merits of the bond and the common stock.

Despite the fact that the value of the downside protection of the bond was not important to the decision in this example being considered, normally the investor will consider this value to be a major reason for purchasing the security. If the conversion value falls below the maturity price, the investor has downside protection.

If the firm wants to avoid the interest payments and if the conversion value exceeds the call price, the firm can call and force conversion. However, if the firm wants to avoid the interest payments, and the call price exceeds the conversion value, then a call by the firm will require a cash outlay. Unfortunately, the same factors (unprofitable operations) that might cause the firm to want to avoid paying the interest will also tend to prevent it from calling the bonds prior to maturity, if calling the bonds causes a cash outlay to take place.

If the firm can pay the interest because of adequate cash flow but cannot use the interest tax shield because of low taxable profits, the firm might wish to call the debt to convert the interest payment into the smaller cash dividend.

A conversion value larger than the call price combined with an expectation that the interest tax shield could not be used in the future would simplify the decision to call. But even with forced conversion, the investor is at least as well off as if the common stock had been purchased initially.

If the conversion value is currently larger than the call price, the issuing firm might call now if there is a probability of a future change in the firm's well-being and a resultant decrease in stock price, so that the firm would not be able to force conversion in the future. The investor is no worse off than if common stock has been purchased originally.

The Issuing Firm's Perspective

The negative features of the convertible security from the viewpoint of the issuing firm is that it promises to pay interest periodically and there is an amount due at maturity. The interest payment is contractual and thus has more risk to the firm than do common stock dividends. Also, if the interest payment is larger before taxes than the common stock dividend, and if the firm's tax status were to change so that the firm could not use the tax shield, the debt could become more costly. If the stock price drops below the call price, a calling of the bond would result in a cash outlay, thus forcing conversion might be impossible for a firm with cash problems.

Another way of describing this difficulty is to define it in terms of the downside protection being offered to the investors. Although the downside protection is an advantage to the convertible bond purchaser, it is a disadvantage to the common stockholders (it increases their risk).

Theoretically, the call price can be set at zero dollars, or if that is too dramatic, the call price can be set at an amount that is very close to zero (the Mapco notes were issued at a price of $1,000, were callable at $550, and had a maturity value of $550). Aside from IRS considerations, the company will want to have a call price as close to zero as is feasible. The opportunity to force conversion to common stock reduces the risk to the company of having to pay interest when it cannot afford to pay interest or to pay a large call price when it would rather have the debt converted into common stock.

The company will also want to have the right to call the bonds as soon as feasible so that the risk of having debt outstanding when the firm wants it converted into common stock is reduced. But these characteristics will tend to cause the IRS to classify the security as equity.

The only real advantage for the issuing firm of this type of convertible security compared to common stock is the tax deductibility of the interest. If $100 million of convertible debt is paying $10 million of interest instead of $10 million of common stock dividends, the firm with a .46 tax rate will save $4.6

million per year. This is a significant incentive for using the convertible security rather than common stock. But this advantage exists for all securities classified as debt.

The IRS will object to debt that is too much like common stock and will attempt to block the use of the interest payment as a tax deduction. However, any convertible debt is part debt and part common stock, so the issue is already on the table. The only question is the extent to which the logical use of convertible debt can be extended by the use of securities that have desirable characteristics from the issuing firm's viewpoint. The basic fault is in a tax code that attempts to distinguish in a substantive manner between the cash distributions of common stock and debt. It is not possible to distinguish between them with a hybrid security.

The issuing firm will be happy with its decision to issue the convertible debt rather than common stock as long as the after-tax cost of the interest is less than the cash dividend that would have been paid, and if at the time of call or maturity the conversion value is marginally larger than the call price.

Suppose that the price of the common stock falls and that the debt is called when the conversion value is less than the call price so that the firm has to make a cash outlay. In that case it is possible that the issuance of common stock would have been better. However, if the time of call is reasonably long after the time of issue, it is likely that the cash savings from the interest tax shield will have a larger present value than will the cost of the call (the difference between the call price and the value of the equivalent shares of the common stock at time of call, when the call price is larger than the conversion value).

If the call price can be set relatively low, there is likely to be a very small probability that the firm will regret the issuance of the convertible debt compared to the issuance of an equivalent number of common stock shares. The guidelines that will be established by the Treasury or by Congress as to what is acceptable debt (thus the interest payments will be tax deductible) will be crucially important in determining how close a firm can move to the theoretically optimum security (a zero call price and a small conversion premium at time of issuance).

Bonds with Warrants

A warrant gives the investor the right to buy a share of stock (or a fraction of a share) at a given exercise price. The exercise price is paid to the issuing corporation. In addition to convertible bonds, bonds with detachable warrants are also used by corporations. The advantage of the detachable warrant is that, upon exercise, the investor still has a bond investment with its fixed return and the corporation has debt outstanding. If the number of shares of stock associated with each bond is less with detachable warrants than with a conversion feature, there would tend to be less dilution of the current stockholders' position. A possible drawback from the corporation's point of view is that, after the exercise of the warrants, there is still debt outstanding, and this reduces the debt issuing ability of the firm (assuming that it wants to issue more debt). To solve this objection the face value of the bond may be accepted for the exercise price.

One advantage of issuing bonds with warrants is that the issue price is split between debt and stock equity (the value of the warrant is classified as stock equity). The issue price of a convertible bond is classified as debt.

The two types of securities (convertible bonds and bonds with detachable warrants) are very similar, and it is difficult to describe substantive differences aside from differences in accounting.

Dilution

Dilution for the present shareholders takes place when their percentage of ownership is reduced by the issuance of new shares or new securities. Convertible securities are attractive to issuers, since the conversion feature tends to reduce the explicit interest cost. But a convertible security carries with it a threat of dilution of the stockholders' equity that is not present with straight debt. However, the dilution may be less than if common stock were issued immediately or if warrants were sold. Also, there is always the chance that the bonds will not be converted, and the corporation will have raised funds at a lower expost cost than straight debt. (This means that the stock price failed to rise above the conversion price, so stockholders may still be unhappy.)

EXAMPLE 25.6

Assume that a corporation is considering issuing 1 million shares of common stock at a price of $40 or 40,000 convertible $1,000 bonds with a 20-year maturity. Each bond would be convertible into 20 shares of common stock. There are currently 5 million shares of common stock outstanding.

As long as there is a positive conversion premium (it is 25 percent), the bonds will lead to less potential dilution than will the issuance of common stock. The purchaser of the bond is paying a price for the downside protection offered by the bond features.

Whether convertible bonds or bonds with warrants attached will lead to more dilution will depend on the terms of the specific securities. We might

> ## U.S. Leasing International
>
> In 1980 U.S. Leasing International, Inc., wanted to raise capital. To do this, it had its subsidiary U.S. Leasing Corporation issue convertible senior subordinated debentures, because the subsidiary had a stronger credit rating than the parent. The debentures were convertible into common stock of U.S. Leasing International, Inc.

expect detachable warrants to lead to less dilution since the investor will have a debt security no matter what happens with the warrant. On the other hand, the warrant will require an additional cash investment; thus we cannot guess at the potential dilution.

Convertible Bonds and the Black–Scholes Model

Since a convertible bond is a combination of a conventional bond and an option to convert into common stock, it follows that methods of valuing options are also of interest in the valuation of convertible bonds. An important step in convertible bond valuation is the application of the Black–Scholes model to valuation of both the option feature and bond feature of convertible debt as an investment.*

Conclusions

The value of warrants, options, calls, and the conversion feature of convertible securities are all governed by the same economic rationale. If they can be converted immediately, their minimum value as common stock is set by their immediate conversion value. Their actual value will depend on a host of factors, among which are the current common stock market price, the distribution of future stock prices, the time value of money, and the risk preferences of the market.

Convertible bonds may be an attractive investment in a common stock growth situation (thus tending to ensure conversion) and as a substitute for

* The Black–Scholes model is a mathematical model for the valuation of an option. See F. Black and M. Scholes, "The Valuation of Option Contracts and a Test of Market Efficiency," *Journal of Finance*, May 1972, pp. 399–417; Black and Scholes, "The Pricing of Options and Corporate Liabilities," *Journal of Political Economy*, May–June 1973, pp. 637–654; and Chapter 26 of this book.

common stock where there is a possibility of the growth not taking place (thus investors are willing to pay for the downside protection). If there were no common stock growth possibilities, the investor would prefer straight debt. If there were certainty of growth (no risk of the conversion feature being worthless), the investor is likely to do better investing in the common stock or warrants or calls. Thus a convertible bond is a type of security that fills the needs for an investor with a risk preference for a chance of a large gain, a very small chance of a large loss, but with a large chance of a small loss (an opportunity cost).

Review Problem 25.1

Assume a $1,000 20-year convertible bond that has a contractual interest rate of .10. Straight debt pays .12. The corporate tax rate is .46.

The stock price at time of issue is $20. The bond is callable at a price of $1,100 after one year.

(a) If the conversion premium at time of issue is .25, the conversion price

per share is ——————— . The bond is convertible into ———————

shares.

(b) A zero-tax investor will earn more than .12 if the bond is called prior

to ——————— years.

(c) Assume that a .10 bond is convertible into 25 shares of common stock currently selling at $40 per share. The stock is paying $3 per share dividend. The bond is being issued at a price of $1,000.

Would you buy the common stock or the convertible bond, assuming you (an individual) are going to buy one or the other? Explain.

Solution to Review Problem 25.1

(a) $20(1.25) = 25 conversion price

$$\frac{\$1,000}{\$25} = 40 \text{ shares}$$

(b) $n = \dfrac{\ln\left[\dfrac{Ck_i}{B(k_i - k)} + 1\right]}{\ln(1 + k_i)} = \dfrac{\ln\left[\dfrac{\$100(.12)}{\$20} + 1\right]}{\ln 1.12}$

$= \dfrac{\ln 1.6}{\ln 1.12} = \dfrac{.47}{.1133} = 4.15 \text{ years}$

The basic formulation is

$$C(1 + k_i)^{-n} - B(k_i - k)B(n, k_i) = 0$$

(c) Buy the bond. It is at least as good as the common stock costing the same for the same number of shares, plus
  (1) $100 interest > 75 dividend today
  (2) Downside protection
  (3) Same upside potential

PROBLEMS

1. A $1,000 bond can be converted into 20 shares of common stock. The stock is now selling at $36.
   What is the bond's converison premium?

2. (Problem 1 continued)   If the stock price were to increase 38.9 percent, what would be the conversion value of the bond?

3. (Problem 1 continued)   If the present value of the convertible bond as straight debt is $780, what is the bond's premium on straight bond value if the market price of the bond is $940.

4. (a) Assume that a 20-year convertible bond is paying .06 interest per year. Straight debt is yielding .10.
       What is the value of the convertible as straight debt?
   (b) If the bond is selling for $940, what value is the market placing on the conversion feature?

5. (Problem 4 continued)   Assume that the bond is expected to be called after five years at a price of $1,090.
   What is the net present value of the investment in the convertible bond at time 0, assuming a zero-tax investor who paid $1,000 for the bond?

6. (Problems 4 and 5 continued)   What is the net present value at time 0 if the bond is convertible into 20 shares and the stock is selling at $70 per share when the bond is called at time 5?

7. The ABCD Company is issuing 7 percent, 20-year convertible debt callable at a price of $1,080 at any time. The conversion price has been set at a 30 percent price premium over the current stock price. The bonds have been recommended to a pension fund manager. The argument has been made, "You will earn a high return since we can expect the stock price to easily

double within the next 10 years." However, it is agreed that it is unlikely that the annual rate of growth in stock price will exceed 10 percent per year. Comparable-risk straight noncallable debt is being issued at a yield of 11 percent

Should the bonds be bought if they sell at par? Explain.

8. A zero-tax investor is considering purchasing either straight debt or a convertible bond issued by firms of identical risk. The straight debt has a coupon of .12 and the convertible debt .05. The call price of the convertible bond is $1,140 and the bond can be called at or after time 2. Both bonds can be bought at par.

   The investor expects the common stock price to increase, so that the stock price is larger than the conversion price at and after time 3, but not prior to that time.

   (a) Which security should be purchased? Why?
   (b) How long can it be (maximum time) before the stock price forces the bond price above the call price, if the investor is to earn more than .12?

9. The ABC Company has been given two choices by an investment banker; one is to issue 5 percent convertible 20-year bonds ($1,000 par). The stock price is now $10 per share, and the conversion premium would be 100 percent. The other alternative would be a 4 percent interest rate and a 25 percent conversion premium.

   The bonds would be noncallable. The company does not pay a cash dividend on its stock, and it does not intend to start in the near future.

   The company has recently issued 20-year straight debt costing .10. The company has a .40 tax rate.

   Which of the two alternatives should the company prefer? Explain.

10. There are zero taxes. Straight debt can be purchased at par with a 15 percent coupon, and a convertible bond can be purchased at par with a 10 percent coupon. The call premium for a convertible $1,000 bond is $90.

    The bonds can be called immediately. The company will call as soon as the conversion value is at least as large as the call price.

    (a) What is the latest time that the bonds can be called and the investor earn a return of .15?
    (b) Assume that the bonds are called at time 2 after the interest payment and the conversion value and call price are both $1,090.
    What return did the investor earn?

11. Company F is considering the terms of a convertible bond that it is going to issue. The following facts apply:

Alternative	Interest	Conversion Premium
1	.08	.15
2	.09	.20

The bond issue size is $10 million. The bonds will have a maturity of 10 years and will be noncallable. The tax rate is .46. The stock price is $50.

(a) How many shares would the bond be convertible into with the .15 premium?

(b) Into how many shares would the bond be convertible with the .20 premium?

(c) With the .20 conversion premium, there is an extra after-tax cost of

$_____ per year.

(d) What does the price of the common stock have to be at time 10 for alternative 2 to be preferred? Assume the firm has an opportunity cost of money of 10.

12. A $1,000 convertible bond is to be issued with a call premium of $90 and a coupon of .12. Straight debt could be issued at a cost of .16. The bond is callable any time after year 4.

Is this convertible bond a good investment, compared to straight debt, if a zero-tax investor thinks that the bond will be called at year 5? Explain with numerical justification.

13. Assume that the stock price is above the conversion price.

When should an investor holding the convertible bond voluntarily convert into common stock? List three necessary conditions (not necessarily sufficient conditions).

14. Design a convertible bond that is very much like debt.

15. Design a convertible bond that is very much like common stock.

REFERENCES

Black, F., and M. Scholes. "The Pricing of Options and Corporate Liabilities." *Journal of Political Economy*, May–June 1973, 637–654.

———. "The Valuation of Option Contracts and a Test of Market Efficiency," *Journal of Finance*, May 1972, 399–417.

Brennan, M. J., and E. S. Schwartz. "Convertible Bonds: Valuation and Optimal Strategies for Call and Conversion." *Journal of Finance*, December 1977, 1699–1715.

Brigham, E. F. "An Analysis of Convertible Debentures: Theory and Some Empirical Evidence." *Journal of Finance*, March 1966, 35–54.

Cootner, P. *The Random Character of Stock Market Prices.* Cambridge, Mass. M.I.T. Press, 1964.

Hayes, S. L., III, and H. B. Reiling. "Sophisticated Financing Tool: The Warrant." *Harvard Business Review*, January–February 1969, 137–150.

Ingersoll, J. "A Contingent-Claims Valuation of Convertible Securities." *Journal of Financial Economics* January 1977, 289–322.

———. "An Examination of Corporate Call Policies on Corporate Securities." *Journal of Finance*, May 1977, 463–478.

Jennings, E. H. "An Estimate of Convertible Bond Premiums." *Journal of Financial and Quantitative Analysis*, January 1974, 33–56.

Samuelson, P. "Rational Theory of Warrant Pricing." *Industrial Management Review*, Spring 1965, 13–22.

Shelton, J. P. "The Relation of the Price of a Warrant to the Price of Its Associated Stock." *Financial Analysts Journal*, May–June 1967, 143–151.

Stone, B. "Warrant Financing." *Journal of Financial and Quantitative Analysis*, March 1976, 143–153.

Chapter 26

Valuation of Options

Major Topics

1. Minimum and maximum values of an option.
2. A binomial model of option pricing.
3. Designing a riskless hedged portfolio.
4. The Black–Scholes option valuation formulation.

Options

One can cite the managers of the XYZ Company who receive options over the course of their careers worth many millions of dollars and value the options at the current common stock market price rather than at their value when issued. This ignores the fact that the stock had appreciated in value over time but that it could have gone down. This method of valuation is similar to that used by a state offering to buy back for $2 (giving the owner 100 percent profit) the lottery ticket it had sold for $1 after the ticket had won the $1 million prize. The after-the-fact value may be of interest, but even more important and difficult to measure is the value of an option to purchase stock before the option has expired or has been exercised.

If you are a manager and have a choice between a given level of dollar wages and a lower level of dollar wages plus a stock option plan, how do you place a value on the stock option plan? There is a valuation problem from the point of view of management administering the stock option plan (or setting the terms of warrants to be attached to bonds to be issued).

Warrants, call options, and stock options all give their holders (owners) the right to purchase a specified number of shares of common stock of a particular corporation at a given price, called the exercise price, at specified times. In the case of an American option, the owner can purchase the shares any time before the option expires; with a European option, the owner can purchase the shares only on the day the option expires. If the price of the common stock goes up above the exercise price during the allowed time period, the owner of the American warrant or option can exercise the right to buy, pay the exercise price, and receive the specified shares of common stock that at the time of exercise have more market value than the exercise price. (A better strategy may be to sell the option or to hold it until maturity.) A warrant may have a finite or infinite life, and the exercise price may be constant or changing over time. Warrants will tend to have longer lives than options and call options.

Warrants may be issued to investors in return for cash or services (such as investment banking services) or for other assets (as in a merger or acquisition). They are also sold in conjunction with the issuance of other securities, such as bonds or preferred stock. A "detachable" warrant may be sold by an investor while retaining the companion security. Warrants provide a form of delayed and contingent equity financing for the issuing firm.

Stock options are awarded to management in place of monetary compensation for services. For many years stock options awarded to members of management offered possible tax advantages (realized gains were taxed at capital gains rates). Managers liked the options since they offered tax advantages and the opportunity to buy stock at a discount. Corporations liked them because they did not require cash outlays and did not decrease profits unlike salary payments (because of accounting permissiveness). They also tended to tie managers to the firm and to provide consistency between the objectives of management and the stockholders. Successive changes in the tax laws have closed the desirability gap between stock options and cash payment; in addition some managers have seen their options become worthless (ex post) because of nonincreasing stock prices. These factors have combined to lessen the attractiveness of conventional stock options to managers relative to direct cash payments, but they are still a popular form of compensation.

Although stock options are not marketable, since they are granted only to the individual being remunerated, warrants are traded on stock exchanges and on the over-the-counter market. Aside from the marketability aspect, however, the value of and decisions regarding warrants and options are governed by the same economic rationale.

A convertible bond is a bond that is convertible into a given number of shares of common stock. The conversion feature of such a bond has the same characteristics as an option. Thus option theory is applicable to stock options awarded to management, warrants, call options, and convertible bonds as well as to any other right to purchase common stock at a given price over a period of time. In fact, option theory has much broader applications.

A call option is written by the owner of a stock (or by a person who does not own the stock, but is obligated to buy the stock if the call is exercised); thus no new shares are issued when the call is exercised. Call options tend to be for periods of less than a year.

A Put

The buyer of a call option has the right to buy a share of stock at the exercise price. The buyer of a put option has the right to sell a share of stock at a given price.

Assume that you own 100 shares of stock selling at $60 per share and you fear that the price is likely to go down; because of income tax reasons, however, you do not want to sell now. If you buy a put to sell 100 shares at $60, you will now lose with a price decrease from holding the common stock, but you will gain from owning the put (the right to sell at $60 even if the price is less than $60). To be fully protected, you might need to hold a put for a different number of shares than 100.

Leverage

One of the most important reasons for an option to have value is that it enables the purchaser to lever a given dollar investment compared to buying the stock outright. If investors know that the price of the stock will immediately rise above the exercise price of option, they will purchase options rather than common stock in order to take advantage of the price increase over more shares of stock. However, an investor does not usually know that a stock price is going to rise, and there is likely to be more risk accompanying a speculative purchase of options compared to the purchase of common stock. If the price rise does not materialize, the options will be worthless at maturity. Even if the stock price falls, the stock investment will still have value equal to its fallen market price.

EXAMPLE 26.1

Assume that an individual has $1,000 to invest. The current price of a stock is $10. Options to purchase 100 shares of the stock at an exercise price of $20 per share can be purchased at a price of $500, or $5 per share. Thus, the investor can buy either 100 shares or 200 options with the $1,000. Suppose that the stock is expected to pay no dividend and the stock price is to rise to $50 before the options expire. If the stock price does reach $50 on the exercise date, the options will have a value of $30 each and the 200 options will be worth $6,000. If the investor had purchased the stock, 100 shares would be worth only $5,000. Thus holding the options creates the possibility of earning more on the investment than the outright purchase of stock. This form of investor leverage does have risk. If the stock price only increases from $10 to $18 over the exercise period, the 100 share will be worth $1,800, an increase in value of $800. The options will be worthless at the time of expiration of the exercise period since the stock can be acquired cheaper through open market purchase ($18) than through the exercise of an option (the exercise price is $20).

Valuing an Option

An option cannot have a negative value. It will have a positive value so long as there is a positive probability that the price of the common stock will be higher than the exercise price some time during the exercise period. Other factors such as the dividends forgone by purchasing options rather than purchasing stock play an important role in the valuation process. To examine the process systematically, we shall first examine the minimum value of an option (called somewhat misleadingly its "theoretical value"). We shall then determine its maximum value. Finally, we shall examine its behavior between these ranges as a function of the uncertain future stock prices and other factors.

Throughout this chapter we shall assume that an option gives the owner a right to acquire *one* share of common stock. Although options may be for more or less than one share, the assumption enables us to simplify notation somewhat.

Minimum and Maximum Values of an Option

The "theoretical" value of an option is conventionally defined to be the difference between the market value of the common stock and the exercise price times the number of shares of common stock that may be purchased using one option (and a payment of cash equal to the exercise price). We shall modify the definition slightly. Let

C_{min} = the minimum (theoretical) value of an option
S = the market value of a share of common stock now
K = the exercise price

Then the theoretical value of an option is

$(S - K)$ if $S > K$ and zero if $S \leq K$

The "theoretical" value is by no means the theoretically correct value of an option. It does, however, set a minimum value for an option if the option could be exercised immediately and the gain realized. The market value of the option will either be equal to or larger than the theoretical value. If the common stock price is $20 and the exercise price is $15, the option cannot sell at less than $5. If the option sold for $3 one could buy the option, exercise it, and sell the stock for $20 and make $2 profit. $(S - K)$ defines the minimum value of the option. C_{min} depicted in Figure 26.1 is the "theoretical" value.

At the other extreme, the absolute maximum value of an option at any time is the market value of the stock at that time. The option will allow the holder to purchase at the exercise price, but the stock itself can always be purchased on the open market. This price, labeled C_{max}, is also shown in Figure 26.1. If the common stock can be purchased for $20 per share, an investor will not pay as much as $20 for an option to buy a share if the exercise price is some positive amount.

For any current price, the actual value of the option, C, will fall between these two boundaries. C depends on the exercise price, the maturity date of the option, and the distribution of the future prices of the common stock. A longer maturity will increase the option value (move it closer to C_{max}).

In the next section we shall develop a method of valuing an option that is based on an arbitrage model. Although it is a simplified model, it does illustrate the basic logic behind modern option pricing theory.

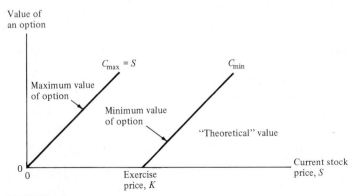

FIGURE 26.1

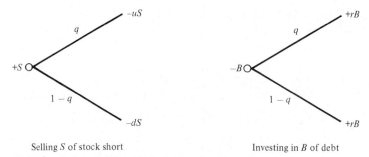

Selling *S* of stock short   Investing in *B* of debt

FIGURE 26.2   Selling Short and Investing in Debt

Option Pricing: A Binomial Model

We shall develop a single-period option pricing model where the stock price can take on only two values in the next period.* In the next period, a stock currently selling for a price *S* will sell for *uS* with probability *q* or *dS* with probability (1 − *q*); *uS* is larger than *dS*.

B of debt can be borrowed or lent at a rate of r_f, and *r* is defined as

$$r = 1 + r_f$$

There is zero risk on the debt investment earning r_f. The value of *r* is larger than *d*, but it is less than *u*. This is necessary so that there are not riskless profit opportunities involving only the stocks and debt. For example, if both *u* and *d* were larger than *r*, an investment in the stock financed by debt would lead to a certain profit (no risk).

Also, if *r* were larger than both *u* and *d*, an investor could make riskless profit by investing in bonds and selling an equal amount of stock short (assuming that the proceeds from short sales are immediately available and there are no transaction costs). This situation is shown in Figure 26.2.

No matter what the outcome, the investor wins if *rB* > *uS* and *rB* > *dS* since *B* = *S* and *r* is larger than *u* and *d*. To prevent these riskless profit situations, we define *u* > *r* > *d*.

We shall define a call option on the stock with an exercise price of *K* expiring in one period to have a value at time 0 of *C*. If the stock goes to *uS*, the value of the call will be C_u, and if the stock goes to *dS*, the value of the call will be C_d. In either case, immediately before expiration the value of the

---

* This section is based heavily on J. C. Cox, S. A. Ross, and M. Rubinstein, "Option Pricing: A Simplified Approach," *Journal of Financial Economics*, September 1979, pp. 229–263, for the multiperiod case.

call will be the larger of zero (the call value cannot be negative) or the difference between the stock price and the exercise price.

Constructing a Hedged Portfolio

The investor who wants to construct a hedged portfolio will:

1. Buy ΔS common stock (or sell the stock).
2. Invest B in debt (or borrow B to finance the common stock).
3. Write (sell) a call with a value of C on the common stock (buy a call).

Assume that ΔS of stock is purchased, that B is invested in debt, and that C is received from the writing of a call. This is shown in Figure 26.3.

We can select ΔS and B so that the sums of the beginning- and end-of-period outcomes are equal to zero. Using Figure 26.3, the two possible end-of-period outcomes are

$$\Delta uS + rB - C_u = 0 \tag{26.1}$$
$$\Delta dS + rB - C_d = 0 \tag{26.2}$$

Solving the two equations for Δ, we have

$$\Delta S(u - d) - (C_u - C_d) = 0$$

$$\Delta = \frac{C_u - C_d}{(u - d)S} \tag{26.3}$$

This value of Δ is called the hedge ratio because it defines the number of shares of stock to be purchased to balance the return from one call.

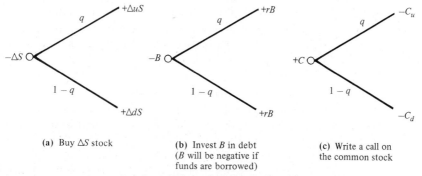

(a) Buy ΔS stock

(b) Invest B in debt (B will be negative if funds are borrowed)

(c) Write a call on the common stock

FIGURE 26.3   Investing in Stock and Debt and Writing a Call

Solving equations (26.1) and (26.2) for B,

$$B = \frac{uC_d - dC_u}{(u - d)r} \qquad\qquad (26.4)$$

The portfolio consisting of one call, B debt, and Δ shares of stock has a zero payoff in each possible state. Therefore in equilibrium, the initial value of the portfolio must be zero. This requires the following equation to be satisfied.

$$C - \Delta S - B = 0$$

Rearranging, we find the equilibrium value of one call is

$$C = \Delta S + B \qquad\qquad (26.5)$$

Note that the value of the call, C, must be equal to $\Delta S + B$, or there is an opportunity for profits to be made. There is an important fact hidden in the foregoing relationships. The value of C does not depend on the value of q or $(1 - q)$. The value of the call option does not depend on the probabilities of the stock price outcomes. The spread of the outcomes (u and d) does affect the value of the call as does the interest rate. Because each outcome is perfectly hedged, it does not make any difference as to which outcome is more likely to occur.

An individual investor might think the stock is going up to uS with a higher probability than q and thus find the call an attractive investment. But this is speculation; it is not creating a hedged portfolio. Because the portfolio is hedged, the risk preferences of the investors do not affect the call price.

We now illustrate the use of the model to determine the hedged portfolio and the value of a call option for a given set of facts.

EXAMPLE 26.2 ─────────────────────────────────

$$S = \$100, \qquad u = 1.5, \qquad d = 1.0, \qquad k = \$120$$
$$C_u = \$30, \qquad C_d = 0, \qquad r_f = .10, \qquad r = 1.10$$

The call option expires in one time period.

The stock price is currently $100, and after one period, the price will be either $150 or $100.

$$uS = 1.5(\$100) = \$150$$
$$dS = 1.0(\$100) = \$100$$

With the call having an exercise price of $120, the value of the call at the end of the period will be either $30 (with a stock price of $150) or $0 (with a stock price of $100).

We want to solve for Δ and B. Since $(u - d) = .5$ and $(C_u - C_d) = 30$,

$$\Delta = \frac{C_u - C_d}{(u - d)S} = \frac{\$30}{.5(\$100)} = \frac{\$30}{\$50} = .60$$

$$B = \frac{uC_d - dC_u}{(u - d)r} = \frac{-1(\$30)}{.5(1.1)} = \frac{-60}{1.1}$$

The negative value for B indicates that funds should be borrowed.

For each call, .6 of a share or .6($100) = $60 of common stock should be purchased and $60/1.1 = $54.55 should be borrowed (the payment of the debt at time 1 will be $60). If u occurs, the value of the portfolio will be

Common Stock	Debt: rB	C_u	Sum of Outcomes
$150(.6) = $90	− $60	− $30	$0

If d occurs, the value of the portfolio will be

Common Stock	Debt: rB	C_d	Sum of Outcomes
$100(.6) = $60	− $60	$0	$0

The initial value of the call is

$$C = \Delta S + B = \$60.00 - \$54.55 = \$5.45$$

The .6 of a share of stock costs $60, of which $54.55 is borrowed at an interest cost of .10 and $5.45 is obtained by selling a call on the stock. No matter which of the two outcomes occurs, the investor exactly breaks even.

If the call is selling at a market price different from $5.45, then an arbitrager could make a riskless profit. For example, if the call is sold for $10 but the investor buys $60 of stock and borrows $54.55 of debt, then the initial cash flows are

$$-\$60.00 + \$54.55 + \$10.00 = \$4.55$$

and the investor has $4.55 of riskless profit since the outcome at time 1 is zero. Arbitrage will tend to eliminate riskless profit opportunities.

The value of the call is determined so that the purchase of the stock, the use of debt, and the selling of a call lead exactly to zero outcomes for each of the possible events and have an initial zero cost.

If we were studying a multiperiod case, the portfolio (stock, debt, and calls) would have to be adjusted so that the appropriate amounts of each were held so that the portfolio was always hedged. If the time periods become very small and trading is continuous, we are then led to the Black–Scholes model of option valuation. The Black–Scholes model is consistent with the binomial model of this section, if we let the time periods become very short and allow continuous trading.

Black–Scholes

In 1973 F. Black and M. Scholes published a paper titled "The Pricing of Options and Corporate Liabilities" in the *Journal of Political Economy*. The model presented in that paper has drastically changed the approach to studying options as well as other securities. Based on an equilibrium analysis, they derive a valuation formulation for an option where all the inputs may be observed except one, and for that one input, reasonable estimates can be computed.

Black and Scholes make many assumptions in their derivation, not all of which are obviously necessary (relaxing of the assumptions will be tested by future researchers). Among these assumptions are

1. The volatility (standard deviation) of the stock's return may be estimated.
2. There is a risk-free rate that is constant through time.
3. There are no transaction costs and the seller receives the proceeds immediately.
4. Taxes are not relevant.
5. There are no dividends.
6. The stock price follows a random walk and the price at time t is log normally distributed.

Black and Scholes use a very clever device to derive the value of an option. They create a hedged position that must, over time, lead to a certain return. Since there is no risk, the certain return is equal to the return earned on other risk-free investments.

The investor can go long on the common buying one share of common stock and then writing enough calls so that if, in a short period of time the price of the common stock increases $1, the value of the calls will also, re- sulting in a loss of $1. The dollar investment in common stock will be greater than the dollars received by selling the calls, so the investor has a net equity position that can be financed by debt. It is this equity position that, through time, will yield a return equal to the return of a risk-free security. Applying this basic situation and then solving for the value of an option, Black and Scholes find the value of an option C to be equal to

$$C = SN(h_1) - (r^{-T})KN(h_1 - \sigma\sqrt{T}) \qquad (26.6)$$

where

$$h_1 = \frac{\ln \dfrac{S}{K} + \left[\ln r + \dfrac{\sigma^2}{2}\right]T}{\sigma\sqrt{T}} \qquad (26.7)$$

$N(h_1)$ = the cumulative normal probability distribution (left tail) for h_1 standard deviations

K = the exercise price

S = the stock price now

ln = the natural logarithm

$r = 1 + r_f$ = the interest rate plus 1

T = the time till maturity

σ = the standard deviation of the rate of return of the common stock (this is the only input that cannot be observed)

The Black–Scholes model assumes that the future stock prices will be log normally distributed with a fixed standard deviation, but that is the extent of the assumption about the expected return on the common stock. The ex- pected return of the common stock does not affect the value of the option in this model.

EXAMPLE 26.3 ───────────────────────────────────

S = $41.50 stock price now

K = $40.00 exercise price

T = .4 time till maturity is .4 of a year

$r = 1 + r_f$ = 1.05 = interest rate plus 1

r_t = return earned in t period

Assume that the weekly price observations for six weeks are

S_t	$1 + r_t = S_t/S_{t-1}$	$\ln (1 + r_t)$	$\ln (1 + r_t) - u$	$[\ln (1 + r_t) - u]^2$
41.0				
40.0	.9756	$-.0247$	$-.0271$	.00074
40.2	1.0500	.0050	.0026	.00001
40.8	1.0149	.0148	.0124	.00015
41.2	1.0098	.0098	.0073	.00005
41.5	1.0073	.0073	.0048	.00002
Totals		.0121		.00097

We are only using six weeks to simplify the computations. In actual practice, many more observations should be used than six.

The summation of the squared deviations are divided by $(n - 1)$, where n is the number of terms so that the estimate of σ is unbiased. The weekly estimate of σ is annualized by multiplying by 52. Define

$$u = \frac{\Sigma \ln (1 + r_t)}{n}$$

$$u = \frac{.0121}{5} = .0024$$

$$\sigma^2 = \frac{.0009725}{4} \times 52 = .0126$$

$$\sigma = .1124$$

$$\frac{S}{K} = \frac{41.50}{40} = 1.0375,$$

$$\frac{\sigma^2}{2} = .0063$$

$$\ln r = \ln 1.05 = .0488$$

$$\ln \frac{S}{K} = \ln 1.0375 = .0368$$

$$T = 0.4 \text{ years}$$

$$\sigma\sqrt{T} = .0711$$

$$r^{-T} = .9807$$

A Different Language

The languages of puts and calls is exotic. For example,

Straddle—Buy a call to buy at K; buy a put to sell at K.
Strip—Add a second put to a straddle.
Strap—Add a second call to a straddle.

Frequently, complex combinations are motivated by the tax law. Combining short-term losses and long-term gains is advantageous.

We need to determine the value of h_1:

$$h_1 = \frac{\ln \frac{S}{K} + [\ln (r) + (\sigma^2/2)]T}{\sigma\sqrt{T}} = \frac{.0368 + (.0488 + .0063)\,.4}{.0711}$$

$$= .8277$$

$$h_1 - \sigma\sqrt{T} = .8277 - .0711 = .7566$$

$$C = SN(h_1) - r^{-T} KN(h_1 - \sigma\sqrt{T})$$

$$= \$41.50\, N(.8277) - .9807(\$40.00)N(.7566)$$

$$= \$41.50(.7973) - .9807(\$40.00)(.7838)$$

$$= \$33.00 - \$30.74 = \$2.26.$$

Assume that the Black–Scholes model is applied to actual data and that a difference is observed between the Black–Scholes value and the market price of the option. One explanation can be that the market has set an incorrect value and that there are profits to be made by applying the formula. A second possibility is that the value obtained by application of the formula is incorrect. The two most likely causes of error are an incorrect estimate of the standard deviation of the stock's returns and the fact that the formulation itself is in error because of unrealistic assumptions (e.g., the stock maybe paying a cash dividend and the model assumes zero dividend). Since the value of an option is sensitive to the volatility of the stock, we can expect different estimates of the standard deviation to affect significantly the value placed on an option.

Conclusions

The primary importance of the Black–Scholes model is that it can be applied to other types of securities and situations than options and warrants. It can be applied to bonds, convertible bonds, common stock, and some real assets. The general applicability of the model means that there will be numerous applications in the finance literature in the future to a wide range of situations and problems. The fact that the model avoids subjective evaluations of future events enhances its attractiveness to both practicing finance persons and academic researchers. Note that to have an option valued using the Black–Scholes model, it was necessary to be able to arbitrage the situation by writing (or selling) a call. This opportunity is a necessary condition for treating a situation as being the equivalent of an option.

Review Problem 26.1

Determine the equilibrium value of a call if the stock is now selling at $80 and after one period it will sell at either $100 (with .8 probability) or $56 (with .2 probability). The exercise price is $95. Funds can be borrowed or lent at zero risk at .10. The call option expires in one time period.

Solution to Review Problem 26.1

$$S = \$80, \quad U = 1.25, \quad d = .70, \quad K = \$95$$
$$C_u = 5, \quad C_d = 0, \quad r = 1.10$$

$$\Delta = \frac{C_u - C_d}{(u - d)S} = \frac{5}{(1.25 - .70)\$80} = \frac{5}{\$44}$$

$$= .113636 \quad \text{and} \quad \Delta S = \$9.09$$

$$B = \frac{uC_d - dC_u}{(u - d)r} = \frac{-.70(5)}{(.55)1.10} = -5.785$$

$$C = \Delta S + B = \$9.09 - \$5.79 = \$3.30$$

If a stock price of $100 occurs, we have

$100(.113636) = \$11.36$ common stock value
$5.785(1.10) = -6.36$ debt value
$C_u = \underline{-5.00}$ option value (lost because of call)
 Sum $= 0$

If a stock price of $56 occurs, we have

$56(.113636) = \$6.36$ common stock
$5.785(1.10) = -6.36$ debt
$C_d = \underline{0}$ option
 Sum $= 0$

PROBLEMS

1. A warrant gives the holder the right to purchase a share of common stock any time in the next five years at a price of $20 per share. The current market price of the stock is $15 per share. No dividends are anticipated, and the stock price is expected to grow to $30. The time value of money is 12 percent.
   (a) What is the minimum value of the warrant?
   (b) What is the maximum value of the warrant?
   (c) What is the present value of the warrant based on a common stock price of $30 at time 5?

2. Assume the same facts as in Problem 1 except that an investor believes that the stock price will increase to $40 per share five years from now.
   What effect will this have on the three warrant values calculated in Problem 1?

3. Assume the same facts as Problem 1 where an investor believes the stock price will rise to $30, five years from now. The stock pays zero dividends.
   (a) Would an expected present value–maximizing investor buy the warrant at a price of $5 or the stock at a price of $15 per share?
   (b) Would you prefer to buy one share of common stock or three warrants?

4. Assume the same facts as in Problem 3 except that a $1 dividend per share is anticipated each year.
   What effect will this have on the buy stock versus buy warrant decision?

5. Suppose that the warrant in Problem 4 could be purchased for $5 and that a common stock price rise to $45 was expected to occur within days.

   What effect will this have on the intrinsic present value and maximum price of the warrant?

6. A stock is now selling at $80 per share. You buy a put to sell the stock at $75. The cost of the put is $4. The stock goes down to $72 just before the put expires.

   What was the profitability of buying the put?

7. Assume that an investor has $10,000 to invest. Stock can be purchased at $20 per share (500 shares can be purchased). Call options to purchase 100 shares at a price of $25 can be purchased for $500 (options to purchase 2,000 shares can be purchased).

   Compare the change in the investor's wealth from buying the stock and buying the options if the stock price at the expiration of the option is

   (a) $35.

   (b) $24.

8. Determine the equilibrium value of a call if the stock is now selling at $100 and after one period it will sell at either $160 (with .5 probability) or $80 (with .5 probability). The exercise price is $120. Funds can be borrowed or lent at zero risk at .20. The call option expires in one time period.

9. (Problem 8 continued) Determine the value of the portfolio after one period for an investor who sold (wrote) a fully hedged call option at the equilibrium price at time zero:

   (a) If the stock price is $160.

   (b) If the stock price is $80.

10. If the probability of the stock price going to $160 is .9 instead of .5 and .1 probability of $80 instead of .5, how does this affect the answers to Problems 8 and 9?

11. Assume that an investor has computed

   $$\Delta S = \$50.00$$

   $$B = -\$33.33$$

   for a perfectly hedged portfolio. The call option is selling at a price of $20.00.

   (a) What should the investor do?

   (b) What risk does the investor have?

12. Using the Black–Scholes formulation, compute the value of a option that expires in one year ($T = 1$) if the following facts apply:

$$S = \$45 \text{ stock price now}$$
$$K = \$40 \text{ exercise price}$$
$$r = 1.20 \ (r_f = .20)$$
$$\sigma^2 = .0225$$
$$\sigma = .15$$

REFERENCES

Black, M., and M. Scholes. "The Pricing of Options and Corporate Liabilities." *Journal of Political Economy*, May 1973, 637–659.

Cox, J. C., S. A. Ross, and M. Rubinstein. "Option Pricing: A Simplified Approach." *Journal of Financial Economics*, September 1979, 229–263.

Cox J. C., and M. Rubinstein. *Option Markets*. Englewood Cliffs, N.J.: Prentice-Hall, Inc., 1985.

Merton, R. C. "The Relationship Between Put and Call Option Prices: Comment. *Journal of Finance*, 28, March 1973, 183–184.

———. "Theory of Rational Option Pricing." *Bell Journal of Economics and Management Science*, Spring 1973, 141–183.

Smith, C. W. "Option Pricing: A Review." *Journal of Financial Economics*, March 1976, 3–51.

Cases: Part V

Case 1. The Beta Corporation

In 1979 the Beta Corporation, a major Mexican conglomerate, needed to raise $100 million to finance its acquisition program. The management of Beta was very sophisticated in matters of engineering and production, but it felt less comfortable with international finance.

There was no question that Beta could raise the capital. The only issue was where the borrowing was to take place.

The following information was obtained:

Location of Bank	Currency of Repayment	Annual Cost (percent)	Expected Inflation Rate (percent)
Mexico City	Peso	25%	20%
New York	U.S. dollar	12	10
London	Pound	15	12
Frankfurt	Mark	10	4

The funds when obtained would be used to finance the acquisition of a U.S.-based firm doing 100 percent of its business in the United States.

QUESTIONS

(a) Where should Beta obtain its $100 million?

(b) What other information would you like to have?

Case 2. American Manufacturing Company

The top management of the American Manufacturing Company (AMC) was upset. While conventional accounting reports had indicated operations of a satisfactory profit level, John Johnson, the financial vice-president, had just dropped a bomb in the board room. Using the price-level–adjusted data, the firm had earned a lower return on equity than could have been earned on an investment in U.S. government securities. In fact, for 1983 the company had a loss from continuing operations (see Exhibit 1).

Exhibit 2 shows the calculations that were made to adjust $113,900,000 of depreciation expense to $161,700,000.

Tom Layton, the president of AMC, was displeased with the results as presented in Exhibit 1. He decided that decisive action was needed and asked John Johnson to prepare information similar to that shown in Exhibit 1 by division.

Exhibit 3 shows the information that was prepared for the Housewares Division.

While the conventional financial data indicated that the Housewares Division was making $2,000,000, the data adjusted for inflation showed a loss of $10,000,000.

Since the total firm's loss (price level adjusted) was only $3,200,000, it was

EXHIBIT 1   Statement of Income Adjusted for Inflation
(millions, except per share amounts)

	1983 Average Dollars		
	1983 Historical Cost	Adjusted for General Inflation	Adjusted for Changes in Specific Prices
Revenues	$2,826.8	$2,826.8	$2,826.8
Costs of products sold	2,304.0	2,314.6	2,313.4
Depreciation, depletion, amortization	113.9	161.7	204.3
Selling and administrative expenses	249.4	249.4	249.4
Interest	72.2	72.2	72.2
Provision for losses on divestiture of assets	15.0	15.0	15.0
Provision for income taxes	17.1	17.1	17.1
Total expenses	$2,771.6	$2,830.0	$2,871.4
Net earnings (loss)	$ 55.2	$ (3.2)	$ (44.6)

EXHIBIT 2   Adjusting Depreciation Expense

CPI	Price Index of 1983 Inflators (index of year)	Accounting Depreciation for Asset Required in Year	Price-Level–Adjusted Depreciation
1960 89	3.348	$ 11,800,000	$ 39,400,000
1979 217	1.373	40,000,000	54,900,000
1980 247	1.206	20,000,000	24,100,000
1981 272	1.096	10,000,000	11,000,000
1982 289	1.031	5,000,000	5,200,000
1983 298	1.000	27,100,000	27,100,000
		$113,900,000	$161,700,000

clear to Layton that if the firm divested Housewares the firm would turn the corner.

The simplified balance sheet for Housewares is shown in Exhibit 4.

The Housewares Division has recently modernized its plant and no additional capital expenditures are on the horizon (a 10-year planning period).

Of the $12,000,000 selling and administrative expenses charged to Housewares, $7,000,000 are directly identified with Housewares and $5,000,000 are cost allocations of general corporate overheads. The $5,000,000 interest expense is the estimated cost of the $50,000,000 liabilities allocated to the division.

AMC requires that new investments earn a .15 internal rate of return and estimates its weighted average cost of capital to be .12. The riskiness of Housewares is considerably less than the risk of the AMC's other divisions if risk is defined to be the ability to forecast the future cash flows of the division.

Tom Layton called the firm's investment banker, who reassured him that despite the division's current operating loss, a buyer could be found. The investment banker estimated that a purchase price of between $5,000,000 and

EXHIBIT 3   Statement of Income, Housewares Division

	Historical Cost	Adjusted for Inflation
Revenues	$100,000,000	$100,000,000
Costs of products sold	70,000,000	70,000,000
Depreciation	10,000,000	22,000,000
Selling and administrative expense	12,000,000	12,000,000
Interest expense	5,000,000	5,000,000
Income taxes	1,000,000	1,000,000
Income (loss)	$ 2,000,000	(− $ 10,000,000)

EXHIBIT 4   Simplified Balance Sheet, Housewares Division

Assets		*Liabilities and Stockholders' Equity*	
Current	$ 30,000,000	Liabilities	$ 50,000,000
Long-lived assets	120,000,000	Stockholders' equity	100,000,000
	$150,000,000		$150,000,000

$10,000,000 could be obtained, with the buyer taking all the assets and assuming the liabilities.

Tom Layton thinks that the opportunity to unload the operating loss and actually receive between $5,000,000 and $10,000,000 of cash should be grabbed. However, before telling the investment banker to go ahead and find a buyer, he thought it desirable that John Johnson prepare an analysis confirming the desirability of selling for presentation to the firm's board of directors.

John Johnson has given you the task of preparing the analysis.

Case 3.   The Bendix–Marietta–Allied Acquisition. The Pac Man Caper*

August 1982 marked the beginning of a unique adventure in American industrial activity. The Bendix Corporation made an offer to acquire enough shares of Martin Marietta to gain control. This announcement triggered a sequence of events that are worthy of consideration.

There are a few background facts with which one should be familiar.

The chief executive of the Bendix Corporation was Bill Agee. He had within the year married a young MBA graduate by the name of Mary Cunningham, currently employed by Seagrams, who had previously been a successful manager at Bendix and whose success received a great deal of press coverage.

Bill Agee was born in Boise, Idaho, received his MBA from Harvard Business School, and immediately on graduation took a position with Boise Cascade. Eight years later, he was a senior vice-president of that firm. At age 36 he shifted to Bendix to be executive vice-president. In 1977 he as named chief operating officer.

He followed a strategy that shifted Bendix from automotive parts to aerospace and electronics and engaged in some successful acquisitions. Among his acquisitions were 20 percent of the outstanding shares of Asarco, Inc., a major metals producer (he sold the shares for a large profit near the peak of their value); timberland (he sold for a large profit immediately before a major price decline); and shares of RCA, which started a minor but nasty war be-

---

* *The New York Times* and *The Wall Street Journal* were used as sources for many of the facts. Conversations were held with executives from Allied, Bendix, and investment banking firms.

tween Agee and RCA. RCA did not want to be acquired by a Agee-managed firm. It was not acquired. Failing to acquire control of RCA, Bendix merely sat on the stock.

The chief executive officer of Martin Marietta was Thomas G. Pownall. Pownall was a graduate of the U.S. Naval Academy and an ex-football player. He is said to have arm-wrestled Jack Kemp (ex–pro football quarterback) to a draw. His favorite (or at least most famous) tie sported the famous U.S. Navy directive (issued by Captain Lawrence) from the War of 1812, "Don't Give up the Ship." He enjoyed his job.

At Allied Corporation, Ed Hennessey was chief executive officer. He had worked for Harry Gray of United Technologies but unhappily did not seem to be in line for the number one position when Gray retired. He looked at his job at Allied as being to move the company from generic chemicals and foreign oil into a more diversified product mix with the prospect of high profit margins. One of this first acts at Allied was a wholesale firing of expendable managers.

The sequence of events that we want to consider started with a decision by Agee that an acquisition of Martin Marietta would fit with the interests of Bendix, moving Bendix farther away from its excessive dependence on the health of the U.S. automobile industry. As the result of the sale of both Asarco and the timberland, Bendix had a lot of excess cash (approximately $500 million); in addition the RCA stock (another $300 million) was clearly expendable.

A diary of events follows.

August 25, 1982

Bendix already holding 4.5 percent of Martin Marietta's stock announces that it intends to take over Martin Marietta for about $1.5 billion in cash and stock. It would buy 45 percent of Martin Marietta's 37.5 million shares for $43 each and would swap Bendix shares for the remainder. Bendix stock drops $2.50 and closes at $50. Martin Marietta closes at 39¼, up 6⅛ points.

August 30, 1982

Martin Marietta rejects the Bendix offer and in a defensive move offers $75 per share for 50.3 percent of Bendix shares (11.9 million shares). The remaining Bendix shares (11.7 million) would be acquired at about $55 a share via a swap for Marietta shares.

Thomas G. Pownall of Marietta indicates that a policy would be followed that would result in Martin Marietta being an independent company.

September 7, 1982

United Technologies Corp. teams up with Martin Marietta and offers $75 a share for 50.3 percent of Bendix shares (11.9 million shares) to be followed by a stock swap for remaining shares. The assets of Bendix were to be split between the two firms, independent of which firm won Bendix.

September 7, 1982

Bendix raises its offer price by $5 from $43 to $48. Marietta says the bid is still not acceptable.

September 7, 1982

The Bendix board of directors approves "golden parachutes" for 16 of Bendix's top executives. Agee receives five years of protection, and the others receive three years of protection. Marietta had already given parachutes to 29 Marietta executives.

Wall Street analysts interpret the giving of parachutes to the Bendix officers as a sign of weakness on the part of Bendix in the face of Marietta and UT's counterattack.

Bendix stock, which has been selling in the low fifties in August, rises $6.00 to $62.50 on September 8 after UT joins Marietta. United Technologies' common stock closes down $2.875. Its cost of acquiring Bendix would be $1.45 billion.

September 8, 1982

The following advertisement is published.

Notice of Offer to Purchase for Cash

Up to 11,900,000 Shares of Common Stock

of

The Bendix Corporation

at

$75.00 Net Per Share

by

United Technologies Corporation

> **The Proration and Withdrawal Deadline is 12:00 Midnight, New York City Time, on Tuesday, September 28, 1982. The Offer Will Expire on Tuesday, October 5, 1982, at 12:00 Midnight, New York City Time, Unless Extended.**

United Technologies Corporation, a Delaware corporation (the "Purchaser"), is offering to purchase up to 11,900,000 shares of Common Stock, par value $5 per share (the "Shares") of The Bendix Corporation, a Delaware corporation (the "Company"), for $75.00 per Share, net to the seller in cash, upon the terms and subject to the conditions set forth in the Offer to Purchase dated September 8, 1982 (the "Offer to Purchase") and in the related Letter of Transmittal (which together constitute the "Offer").

The Offer is not conditioned upon any minimum number of Shares being tendered.

The purpose of the Offer is to acquire for cash a sufficient number of Shares so that the Purchaser would have voting control over a majority of the outstanding voting securities of the Company as a first step in acquiring control of the business of, and the entire equity interest in, the Company. The Purchaser intends to acquire or influence control of the business of the Company.

If more than 11,900,000 Shares are properly tendered prior to 12:00 Midnight, New York City time, on September 28, 1982 (the "Proration Date") and not withdrawn, the Purchaser, upon the terms and subject to the conditions of the Offer, will purchase 11,900,000 Shares, on a pro rata basis (with adjustments to avoid purchases of fractional Shares) according to the number of Shares properly tendered by each stockholder prior to Midnight on the Proration Date and not withdrawn, and Shares tendered after the Proration Date will not be purchased. If fewer than 11,900,000 Shares are properly tendered prior to Midnight on the Proration Date and not withdrawn, upon the terms and subject to the conditions of the Offer, all Shares so tendered will be purchased, and any Shares properly tendered thereafter and prior to the expiration of the Offer and not withdrawn, will, upon the terms and subject to the conditions of the Offer, be purchased in the order in which they are tendered until 11,900,000 Shares shall have been purchased.

For purposes of the Offer, the Purchaser shall be deemed to have accepted for payment tendered Shares as, if and when the Purchaser gives oral or written notice to the Depositary of its acceptance of the tenders of such Shares. The period of time during which the Offer is open may be extended by the Purchaser, at any time or from time to time, by giving oral or written notice of such extension to the Depositary and by making a public announcement thereof.

Tenders of Shares made pursuant to the Offer are irrevocable, except that Shares tendered pursuant to the Offer may be withdrawn at any time prior to 12:00 Midnight, New York City time, on September 28, 1982, and, unless theretofore accepted for payment by the Purchaser, may also be withdrawn at any time after November 6, 1982. In addition, if any person (other than the Company) makes a tender offer for any Shares, Shares not theretofore accepted for payment by the Purchaser may be withdrawn on the date of, and for 10 business days after, the commencement (other than by public announcement) of such competing offer, provided that the Purchaser has received notice or otherwise has knowledge of such competing offer. For a withdrawal to be effective, a written, telegraphic, telex or facsimile transmission notice of withdrawal must be timely received by the Depositary at its address set forth in the Offer to Purchase. Any notice of withdrawal must specify the name of the person having deposited the Shares to be withdrawn, the number of Shares to be withdrawn and the name in which the certificates representing such Shares are registered, if different from that of the tendering stockholder. If certificates have been delivered or otherwise identified to the Depositary, then prior to the release of such certificates the tendering stockholder must also submit the serial numbers shown on the particular certificates evidencing such Shares, and the signature on his notice of withdrawal must be guaranteed by a firm which is a member of a registered national securities exchange or of the National Association of Securities Dealers, Inc., or by a commercial bank or trust company in the United States.

September 13, 1982

Thomas Pownall vows to seek the control of Bendix even if Bendix gained control of Marietta. Agee responds, "Our resolve to proceed with our offer for Martin Marietta has not changed as a result of their statement."

September 14, 1982

Bendix has acquired 54 percent of Marietta stock at a price of $48. (By federal law, Marietta has to wait until September 23 to buy the Bendix shares. UT has to wait until September 28. Marietta has been offered 75 percent of Bendix's shares.) The U.S. Justice Department gives Bendix a green light in its attempt to acquire Marietta. By implication, this also allows Marietta to acquire Bendix. Justice does not clear UT's attempt to acquire Bendix.

September 20, 1982

Approximately 14,490,000 shares of Bendix (75 percent of outstanding shares) are tendered to Marietta by this date. Marietta has offered to buy 11,900,000 shares. Bendix purchases 70 percent of Marietta stock (25,600,000 shares) at $48 a share, for approximately $1.2 billion.

September 21, 1982

Agee, his wife Mary Cunningham, and staff visit Bethesda, Maryland, to present a friendly merger plan to the Marietta board. The board adjourns before Agee was invited to talk with Pownall. Agee states to reporters that he feared a possibility where Bendix and Marietta would own each other.

September 22, 1982

Allied Corporation offers to buy all of Bendix for cash and securities valued at $80 a share and also to buy 39 percent of Martin Marietta.

The acquisition of Bendix would move Allied's debt-to-capital ratio from 23 percent to 44 percent. The cost of the Bendix acquisition to Allied was reported to be approximately $1.9 billion. Newspapers report that Allied would pay $85 a share for 51 percent of Bendix's stock and $77.50 in Allied securities for the remaining shares.

At the time, Martin Marietta owns 42.4 percent of Bendix's common and

Bendix owns 70 percent of Martin Marietta. Martin Marietta had borrowed $900 million to acquire the Bendix shares.

September 23, 1982

Marietta buys 45 percent of Bendix stock and announces that it intends to increase this to 50.3 percent (11,900,000 shares).

The original Allied-Bendix offer is modified. Allied would own 100 percent of Bendix and 39 percent of Martin Marietta (which now has an agreement that it would retain its independence). Allied agreed that it would not expand its Marietta holdings without Marietta's approval for 10 years, and it also agreed to a schedule of prices at which Marietta could buy back its shares.

The Bendix board votes to accept Allied's offer. Four Bendix directors resign in protest before the vote.

December 1982

Martin Marietta swaps the 11,900,000 shares of the Bendix Corporation (50.3 percent of Bendix's shares) that it owned for 19,128,000 shares of its common stock (54 percent of its shares) held by Bendix Corporation. Bendix had acquired 25,600,000 or 70 percent of Marietta's shares. Bendix (or, more accurately, Allied) retains 6,472,000 of Marietta's shares (39 percent). After the swap, there are 16,400,000 shares outstanding. After exchanging shares with Bendix, Martin Marietta's shareholders' equity is reduced to $324 million.

January 31, 1983

Stockholders of Allied vote to approve the $1.8 billion merger with Bendix. The Bendix stockholders also approve. Some 50.3 percent of Bendix stock (11,900,000 shares) will be acquired at a cost of $892,000,000. New securities in the amount of $926,000,000 will be issued by Allied for the remainder of the common stock (approximately 11.7 million shares). Bendix will be paid $301,000,000 or $46.66 per share for 39 percent of Martin Marietta.

The $892,000,000 will be paid to Martin Marietta for the Bendix shares that it holds. Marietta will pay Bendix $892,000,000 for 19,128,000 shares held by Bendix. Bendix will retain 6,472,000 shares. These shares will be "purchased" by Allied at $46.66 per share. The $892,000,000 will be lent by Bendix to Allied.

February 1, 1983

An Allied advertisement in *The Wall Street Journal* asks, "Was Allied crazy to acquire Bendix?" The text went on.

> *Apparently a lot of people thought so, because they didn't think we had a strategy.*
> *But.*
> *We said we wanted to expand in electronics, one of the fastest-growing industries in the world.*

With Bendix, we did.
We said we wanted to advance our technology.
With Bendix, we did.
We said we wanted to balance oil and gas profits with improved profits from domestic businesses.
With Bendix, we did.
And with Bendix, we even got a bonus. Overnight, we became a leading manufacturer of automotive, aerospace, and industrial equipment.
All in all, we acquired a well-run $4 billion company with 61,000 talented employees to help our earnings grow faster. This acquisition fits our strategy and then some.
Crazy? No. Just good business.

February 7, 1983

A. L. McDonald, the president of Bendix and a friend of Bill Agee, resigns. The next day Agee resigns as president of Allied and chairman of Bendix. He had been told by Hennessey, chairman of Allied, that Allied was looking for a chief operating officer and he was not in the running.

In discussing the Bendix–Marietta takeover battle, Hennessey had said, "The whole thing was a pretty sorry spectacle for American business."

Agee owns 47,055 shares of Bendix valued at $85 a share cash ($3,999,675); in addition, Agee has a golden parachute ($825,000 a year for five years).

QUESTIONS

(a) Who won? Who lost? Who made mistakes?
(b) What corporate strategies were being followed?
(c) What public policy implications are there?

Case 4.   The Xray Oil Company

The Xray Oil Company has an opportunity to buy an option on 1,000 acres of land for $15 million. A study has already been made on the decision to buy the land at a cost of $80 million. The net present value is a positive $20 million, but there is a large amount of risk.

Consider the simplified decision tree.

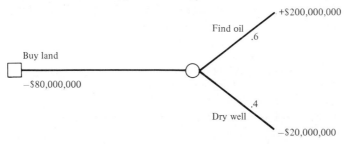

If the company finds oil, the property can be sold for $200 million. The drilling costs are $20 million; thus, if successful, the firm will net $180 million from the sale. If the well is dry, the company will lose $20 million.

The expected present value is

$200,000,000 × .6 =		$120,000,000
Less: Drilling costs	$20,000,000	
Land costs	80,000,000	100,000,000
Net		$ 20,000,000

Equivalently,

$180,000,000 × .6 =	$108,000,000
− $20,000,000 × .4 =	− 8,000,000
	$100,000,000
Land costs	80,000,000
Net	$ 20,000,000

The company does not want to risk losing $100 million with a dry well that has a .4 probability.

It can pay $15 million for the option to buy the land, but the purchase price of the land will be increased to $102 million (the $15 million paid for the option will be applied to the purchase price).

QUESTION: Assume that after buying the option and before buying the land, tests can be conducted that are 100 percent accurate in predicting the presence of oil. The tests cost $3 million. They can only be conducted if the option is purchased or the land is owned. Should the option be purchased?

Case 5.   Owens-Corning Fiberglas Corporation

The Owens-Corning Fiberglas Corporation's "Notice of Annual Meeting of Stockholders and Proxy Statement" of April 16, 1981, included the following statement:

   a. *The principal executive officers of the Company participate in the Company's stockholder-approved Additional Compensation Plan which provides for payment of additional compensation to participants based upon income before taxes of the Company in excess of $12\frac{1}{2}\%$ of capital invested. Some officers participate in part in this Plan and in part in other incentive* *compensation plans, or solely in those incentive compensation plans, which are based upon achievement of performance goals set each year. All numbers in this column include payments under these plans for 1980.*

The Owens-Corning Fiberglas Corporation's "Notice of Annual Meeting of Stockholders to be held on April 15, 1982" included the following statement:

The Board of Director terminated the Additional Compensation Plan effective for 1982. The Board concluded that this annual incentive compensation plan, first adopted in 1946, no longer served the best interest of the Company. All officers participate in one or more other incentive compensation plans, which are based generally upon achievement of performance goals set each year. All number in this column include payments under these plans for 1981.

In 1980, the stockholders of the Company adopted the Owens-Corning Fiberglas Corporation Long-Term Incentive Plan ("Plan"). The Compensation Committee of the Board of Directors selected participants in the Plan for the 1980–1983 and 1982–1985 Performance Periods and granted each participant a Target Award for each period based on the participant's level of responsibility and the impact of his job on the Company's success. The Committee also established target levels of Company performance at which the Target Awards, and lesser or greater amounts, could be earned. The performance criteria for the 1980–1983 Performance Period are based upon both compounded growth in the Company's annual earnings per share, compared with the average earnings per share for the years 1978 and 1979, and average annual return on the Company's gross assets over the four-year period. The performance criteria for the 1982–1985 Performance Period are based upon both total net income and average annual return on the Company's gross assets over the four-year period. Target Awards are payable from 50 percent to 150 percent if compounded annual earnings per share or total net income and average annual return on gross assets reach specified levels for each Performance Period. Target Awards payable may be adjusted up or down by 20 percent to reflect individual performance. In addition, any awards paid will be increased or decreased by one-half of the percentage change in the fair market value of Common Stock from the beginning to the end of the applicable Performance Period. Each officer is a participant in the Plan for the 1980–1983 and 1982– 1985 Performance Periods. No amounts were accrued under the Plan in 1981.

QUESTION: Evaluate the old and the new plans. Are the goals of the managers and the stockholders likely to be congruent?

Case 6.   Phillips Petroleum, Mesa, and Icahn

Late in 1984 T. Boone Pickens through his firm Mesa Petroleum started to accumulate the common stock of Phillips Petroleum Corporation when the stock price was $40. By December 1984 Pickens and his partners had accumulated 8.9 million shares of Phillips stock. Mesa partners then offered to buy as many as 23 million Phillips shares at a price of $60 per share. The Phillips stock price went to $55 per share. There were then 154.6 million shares outstanding.

In January 1985 Phillips made an offer to Pickens and to the rest of its stockholders that caused Pickens to withdraw his offer. Phillips offered its common stockholders the following package:

1. It would buy Mesa's 8.9 million shares of Phillips' stock at $53 per share (Mesa did not have to accept).
2. The remaining shareholders would receive:

   .62 of a common stock share
   $22.80 of debentures

3. Stockholders would receive a dividend of $3.32 of preferred stock.
4. The common stock dividend of $2.40 would be maintained.
5. The firm would tender 20,000,000 shares at $50 per share (there would be 145.7 million shares outstanding so that 13.7 percent of the shares would be acquired).
6. The company's ESOP (Employee Stock Ownership Plan) would buy 24 million shares over the course of a year.

The $22.80 of debt consisted of the following:

Amount		Interest
$11.00 of floating rate (initially .10) senior notes	=	$1.10
5.50 of .13 senior notes	=	.715
6.30 of .1375 subordinated debentures	=	.866
$22.80		$2.681

This package was rejected by the shareholders.

The above offer was fought vigorously by Carl C. Icahn. The company valued the offer at $53 a share, but Icahn said that the recapitalization was worth only $42 a share. He offered an alternative plan where he would acquire the company's shares at $55 a share (the stockholders would receive an equal amount of cash and securities).

Phillips attempted to stop the Icahn bid by legal means as well as by using a poison pill. The poison pill consisted of a right entitling each common stock to be swapped for $62 face amount of a 15% note. The right expired if the recapitalization plan was approved by the shareholders. The potential increase in debt was meant to discourage Icahn. By the end of February, Icahn had raised the price he was willing to pay to $60 for 70 million shares. The remainder of the shares would be purchased at $50 a share using debt securities. After this offer the Phillips stock sold at about $48 per share. Phillips management was stating that the value per share was $62. On March 4, 1985, Phillips offered a new proposal that it said was worth in excess of $60.

The package consisted of the following:

1. The Company would buy Mesa's shares at $53 per share (Mesa did not have to accept). Mesa and Icahn each received $25,000,000 to cover their expenses.
2. The shareholders who tendered would receive $4,500,000,000 of debentures in exchange for 72,580,000 shares. The debenture package was valued at $62 per share.
3. Stockholders would receive a dividend of $300,000,000 preferred stock (based on 73.1 million shares still outstanding after the purchase of 72.6 million shares, this would be worth $4.10 a share).
4. The common stock dividend of $2.40 would be increased to $3.00.

For each common stock share tendered, the debenture offer consisted of:

		Interest
$29 floating rate (currently paying .1125)	=	$3.2625
18 paying .13875	=	2.4975
15 paying .1475	=	2.12125
$62		$7.88125 interest

Assume that 100% of the shares are tendered and 50% accepted; the $3 dividend and the $7.88 of interest leads to an average cash distribution of $5.44 per year per share compared to the current dividend of $2.40. The $7.88 of interest has an after-tax cost of $7.88(1 - .46) = 4.255 so that the average after-tax cost is

$$\frac{4.255 + 3}{2} = \$3.63 \text{ per current share}$$

Evaluate the sequence of events and the two offers made by Phillips.

QUESTIONS

1. In response to the Mesa challenge, Phillips made an offer which was rejected. It then made a second offer which was accepted.
   a. What was the cash flow to a single share stockholder before either offer?

b. What was the cash flow to a single share stockholder from either offer, assuming tendering whenever an offer is made? The following table may help structure your answer:

	Rejected Offer	Accepted Offer (Assuming everyone tenders)
Interest on debt		
Dividend on remaining fractional share		
Earnings from fraction of share tendered @ $50 (rejected offer)[a]	_____	_____
Total first year C.F.		

[a]Assume the funds can earn .1375.

2. Using the theoretic valuation formula, $V_L = V_U + t_cB$, estimate the increase in market value of Phillips securities (total capital). Assume $t_c = .46$ and the number of shares outstanding before the accepted offer was 154.6 million.

   Under the accepted offer, how many shares will be outstanding if Pickens accepts the swap and all other shareholders tender? What is the expected value per share of common after the smoke clears? How much did each original single share owner receive in value? Was the "restructuring" worth it? Who won? Pickens? Stockholders?

3. As a stockholder, did the issuance of the preferred stock enhance either offer?

   Did the increase in the common stock dividend from the first offer to the second (on an original share basis the dividend went from $1.158 to $1.51) enhance the attractiveness of the offer?

   Icahn insisted that Phillips promise to split the stock after the swap. What do you think of this condition?

Appendix Tables

TABLE A Present Value of $1.00^a (1 + r)^{-n}$

n/r	1.0%	2.0%	3.0%	4.0%	5.0%	6%	7%	8%	9%	10%	11%	12%	13%	14%	15%
1	.9901	.9804	.9709	.9615	.9524	.9434	.9346	.9259	.9174	.9091	.9009	.8929	.8850	.8772	.8696
2	.9803	.9612	.9426	.9246	.9070	.8900	.8734	.8573	.8417	.8264	.8116	.7972	.7831	.7695	.7561
3	.9706	.9423	.9151	.8890	.8638	.8396	.8163	.7938	.7722	.7513	.7312	.7118	.6931	.6750	.6575
4	.9610	.9238	.8885	.8548	.8227	.7921	.7629	.7350	.7084	.6830	.6587	.6355	.6133	.5921	.5718
5	.9515	.9057	.8626	.8219	.7835	.7473	.7130	.6806	.6499	.6209	.5935	.5674	.5428	.5194	.4972
6	.9420	.8880	.8375	.7903	.7462	.7050	.6663	.6302	.5963	.5645	.5346	.5066	.4803	.4556	.4323
7	.9327	.8706	.8131	.7599	.7107	.6651	.6227	.5835	.5470	.5132	.4817	.4523	.4251	.3996	.3759
8	.9235	.8535	.7894	.7307	.6768	.6274	.5820	.5403	.5019	.4665	.4339	.4039	.3762	.3506	.3269
9	.9143	.8368	.7664	.7026	.6446	.5919	.5439	.5002	.4604	.4241	.3909	.3606	.3329	.3075	.2843
10	.9053	.8203	.7441	.6756	.6139	.5584	.5083	.4632	.4224	.3855	.3522	.3220	.2946	.2697	.2472
11	.8963	.8043	.7224	.6496	.5847	.5268	.4751	.4289	.3875	.3505	.3173	.2875	.2607	.2366	.2149
12	.8874	.7885	.7014	.6246	.5568	.4970	.4440	.3971	.3555	.3186	.2858	.2567	.2307	.2076	.1869
13	.8787	.7730	.6810	.6006	.5303	.4688	.4150	.3677	.3262	.2897	.2575	.2292	.2042	.1821	.1625
14	.8700	.7579	.6611	.5775	.5051	.4423	.3878	.3405	.2992	.2633	.2320	.2046	.1807	.1597	.1413
15	.8613	.7430	.6419	.5553	.4810	.4173	.3624	.3152	.2745	.2394	.2090	.1827	.1599	.1401	.1229
16	.8528	.7284	.6232	.5339	.4581	.3936	.3387	.2919	.2519	.2176	.1883	.1631	.1415	.1229	.1069
17	.8444	.7142	.6050	.5134	.4363	.3714	.3166	.2703	.2311	.1978	.1696	.1456	.1252	.1078	.0929
18	.8360	.7002	.5874	.4936	.4155	.3503	.2959	.2502	.2120	.1799	.1528	.1300	.1108	.0946	.0808
19	.8277	.6864	.5703	.4746	.3957	.3305	.2765	.2317	.1945	.1635	.1377	.1161	.0981	.0829	.0703
20	.8195	.6730	.5537	.4564	.3769	.3118	.2584	.2145	.1784	.1486	.1240	.1037	.0868	.0728	.0611
21	.8114	.6598	.5375	.4388	.3589	.2942	.2415	.1987	.1637	.1351	.1117	.0926	.0768	.0638	.0531
22	.8034	.6468	.5219	.4220	.3418	.2775	.2257	.1839	.1502	.1228	.1007	.0826	.0680	.0560	.0462
23	.7954	.6342	.5067	.4057	.3256	.2618	.2109	.1703	.1378	.1117	.0907	.0738	.0601	.0491	.0402
24	.7876	.6217	.4919	.3901	.3101	.2470	.1971	.1577	.1264	.1015	.0817	.0659	.0532	.0431	.0349
25	.7798	.6095	.4776	.3751	.2953	.2330	.1842	.1460	.1160	.0923	.0736	.0588	.0471	.0378	.0304
26	.7720	.5976	.4637	.3607	.2812	.2198	.1722	.1352	.1064	.0839	.0663	.0525	.0417	.0331	.0264
27	.7644	.5859	.4502	.3468	.2678	.2074	.1609	.1252	.0976	.0763	.0597	.0469	.0369	.0291	.0230
28	.7568	.5744	.4371	.3335	.2551	.1956	.1504	.1159	.0895	.0693	.0538	.0419	.0326	.0255	.0200
29	.7493	.5631	.4243	.3207	.2429	.1846	.1406	.1073	.0822	.0630	.0485	.0374	.0289	.0224	.0174
30	.7419	.5521	.4120	.3083	.2314	.1741	.1314	.0994	.0754	.0573	.0437	.0334	.0256	.0196	.0151
35	.7059	.5000	.3554	.2534	.1813	.1301	.0937	.0676	.0490	.0356	.0259	.0189	.0139	.0102	.0075
40	.6717	.4529	.3066	.2083	.1420	.0972	.0668	.0460	.0318	.0221	.0154	.0107	.0075	.0053	.0037
45	.6391	.410	.2644	.1713	.1112	.0727	.0476	.0313	.0207	.0137	.0091	.0061	.0041	.0027	.0019
50	.6080	.3715	.2281	.1407	.0872	.0543	.0339	.0213	.0134	.0085	.0054	.0035	.0022	.0014	.0009

$^a r$ is the rate of discount and n is the number of time periods.

Source: H. Bierman, Jr., and S. Smidt, The Capital Budgeting Decision, 6th ed. (New York: Macmillan Publishing Company, 1984), pp. 531–532.

TABLE A   Present Value of $1.00 (cont'd)

n/r	16%	18%	20%	22%	24%	26%	28%	30%	32%	34%	36%	38%	40%	45%	50%
1	.8621	.8475	.8333	.8197	.8065	.7937	.7813	.7692	.7576	.7463	.7353	.7246	.7143	.6897	.6667
2	.7432	.7182	.6944	.6719	.6504	.6299	.6104	.5917	.5739	.5569	.5407	.5251	.5102	.4756	.4444
3	.6407	.6086	.5787	.5507	.5245	.4999	.4768	.4552	.4348	.4156	.3975	.3805	.3644	.3280	.2963
4	.5523	.5158	.4823	.4514	.4230	.3968	.3725	.3501	.3294	.3102	.2923	.2757	.2603	.2262	.1975
5	.4761	.4371	.4019	.3700	.3411	.3149	.2910	.2693	.2495	.2315	.2149	.1998	.1859	.1560	.1317
6	.4104	.3704	.3349	.3033	.2751	.2499	.2274	.2072	.1890	.1727	.1580	.1448	.1328	.1076	.0878
7	.3538	.3139	.2791	.2486	.2218	.1983	.1776	.1594	.1432	.1289	.1162	.1049	.0949	.0742	.0585
8	.3050	.2660	.2326	.2038	.1789	.1574	.1388	.1226	.1085	.0962	.0854	.0760	.0678	.0512	.0390
9	.2630	.2255	.1938	.1670	.1443	.1249	.1084	.0943	.0822	.0718	.0628	.0551	.0484	.0353	.0260
10	.2267	.1911	.1615	.1369	.1164	.0992	.0847	.0725	.0623	.0536	.0462	.0399	.0346	.0243	.0173
11	.1954	.1619	.1346	.1122	.0938	.0787	.0662	.0558	.0472	.0400	.0340	.0289	.0247	.0168	.0116
12	.1685	.1372	.1122	.0920	.0757	.0625	.0517	.0429	.0357	.0298	.0250	.0210	.0176	.0116	.0077
13	.1452	.1163	.0935	.0754	.0610	.0496	.0404	.0330	.0271	.0223	.0184	.0152	.0126	.0080	.0051
14	.1252	.0985	.0779	.0618	.0492	.0393	.0316	.0253	.0205	.0166	.0135	.0110	.0090	.0055	.0034
15	.1079	.0835	.0649	.0507	.0397	.0312	.0247	.0195	.0155	.0124	.0099	.0080	.0064	.0038	.0023
16	.0930	.0708	.0541	.0415	.0320	.0248	.0193	.0150	.0118	.0093	.0073	.0058	.0046	.0026	.0015
17	.0802	.0600	.0451	.0340	.0258	.0197	.0150	.0116	.0089	.0069	.0054	.0042	.0033	.0018	.0010
18	.0691	.0508	.0376	.0279	.0208	.0156	.0118	.0089	.0068	.0052	.0039	.0030	.0023	.0012	.0007
19	.0596	.0431	.0313	.0229	.0168	.0124	.0092	.0068	.0051	.0038	.0029	.0022	.0017	.0009	.0005
20	.0514	.0365	.0261	.0187	.0135	.0098	.0072	.0053	.0039	.0029	.0021	.0016	.0012	.0006	.0003
21	.0443	.0309	.0217	.0154	.0109	.0078	.0056	.0040	.0029	.0021	.0016	.0012	.0009	.0004	.0002
22	.0382	.0262	.0181	.0126	.0088	.0062	.0044	.0031	.0022	.0016	.0012	.0008	.0006	.0003	.0001
23	.0329	.0222	.0151	.0103	.0071	.0049	.0034	.0024	.0017	.0012	.0008	.0006	.0004	.0002	.0001
24	.0284	.0188	.0126	.0085	.0057	.0039	.0027	.0018	.0013	.0009	.0006	.0004	.0003	.0001	.0001
25	.0245	.0160	.0105	.0069	.0046	.0031	.0021	.0014	.0010	.0007	.0005	.0003	.0002	.0001	.0000
26	.0211	.0135	.0087	.0057	.0037	.0025	.0016	.0011	.0007	.0005	.0003	.0002	.0002	.0001	
27	.0182	.0115	.0073	.0047	.0030	.0019	.0013	.0008	.0006	.0004	.0002	.0002	.0001	.0000	
28	.0157	.0097	.0061	.0038	.0024	.0015	.0010	.0006	.0004	.0003	.0002	.0001	.0001		
29	.0135	.0082	.0051	.0031	.0020	.0012	.0008	.0005	.0003	.0002	.0001	.0001	.0001		
30	.0116	.0070	.0042	.0026	.0016	.0010	.0006	.0004	.0002	.0002	.0001	.0001	.0000		
35	.0055	.0030	.0017	.0009	.0005	.0003	.0002	.0001	.0001	.0000	.0000	.0000			
40	.0026	.0013	.0007	.0004	.0002	.0001	.0001	.0000	.0000						
45	.0013	.0006	.0003	.0001	.0001	.0000	.0000								
50	.0006	.0003	.0001	.0000	.0000										

TABLE B Present Value of $1 Received per Period $\dfrac{1 - (1 + r)^{-n}}{r}$

n/r	1.0%	2.0%	3.0%	4.0%	5.0%	6%	7%	8%	9%	10%	11%	12%	13%	14%	15%
1	.9901	.9804	.9709	.9615	.9524	.9434	.9346	.9259	.9174	.9091	.9009	.8929	.8850	.8772	.8696
2	1.9704	1.9416	1.9135	1.8861	1.8594	1.8334	1.8080	1.7833	1.7591	1.7355	1.7125	1.6901	1.6681	1.6467	1.6257
3	2.9410	2.8839	2.8286	2.7751	2.7232	2.6730	2.6243	2.5771	2.5313	2.4869	2.4437	2.4018	2.3612	2.3216	2.2832
4	3.9020	3.8077	3.7171	3.6299	3.5459	3.4651	3.3872	3.3121	3.2397	3.1699	3.1024	3.0373	2.9745	2.9137	2.8550
5	4.8534	4.7135	4.5797	4.4518	4.3295	4.2124	4.1002	3.9927	3.8897	3.7908	3.6959	3.6048	3.5172	3.4331	3.3522
6	5.7955	5.6014	5.4172	5.2421	5.0757	4.9173	4.7665	4.6229	4.4859	4.3553	4.2305	4.1114	3.9975	3.8887	3.7845
7	6.7282	6.4720	6.2303	6.0020	5.7864	5.5824	5.3893	5.2064	5.0330	4.8684	4.7122	4.5638	4.4226	4.2883	4.1604
8	7.6517	7.3255	7.0197	6.7327	6.4632	6.2098	5.9713	5.7466	5.5348	5.3349	5.1461	4.9676	4.7988	4.6389	4.4873
9	8.5660	8.1622	7.7861	7.4353	7.1078	6.8017	6.5152	6.2469	5.9952	5.7590	5.5370	5.3282	5.1317	4.9464	4.7716
10	9.4713	8.9826	8.5302	8.1109	7.7217	7.3601	7.0236	6.7101	6.4177	6.1446	5.8892	5.6502	5.4262	5.2161	5.0188
11	10.3676	9.7868	9.2526	8.7605	8.3064	7.8869	7.4987	7.1390	6.8051	6.4951	6.2065	5.9377	5.6869	5.4527	5.2337
12	11.2551	10.5753	9.9540	9.3851	8.8632	8.3838	7.9427	7.5361	7.1607	6.8137	6.4924	6.1944	5.9176	5.6603	5.4206
13	12.1337	11.3484	10.6350	9.9856	9.3936	8.8527	8.3577	7.9038	7.4869	7.1034	6.7499	6.4235	6.1218	5.8424	5.5831
14	13.0037	12.1062	11.2961	10.5631	9.8986	9.2950	8.7455	8.2442	7.7862	7.3667	6.9819	6.6282	6.3025	6.0021	5.7245
15	13.8650	12.8493	11.9379	11.1184	10.3797	9.7122	9.1079	8.5595	8.0607	7.6061	7.1909	6.8109	6.4624	6.1422	5.8474
16	14.7179	13.5777	12.5611	11.6523	10.8378	10.1059	9.4466	8.8514	8.3126	7.8237	7.3792	6.9740	6.6039	6.2651	5.9542
17	15.5622	14.2919	13.1661	12.1657	11.2741	10.4773	9.7632	9.1216	8.5436	8.0216	7.5488	7.1196	6.7291	6.3729	6.0472
18	16.3983	14.9920	13.7535	12.6593	11.6896	10.8276	10.0591	9.3719	8.7556	8.2014	7.7016	7.2497	6.8399	6.4674	6.1280
19	17.2260	15.6785	14.3238	13.1339	12.0853	11.1581	10.3356	9.6036	8.9501	8.3649	7.8393	7.3658	6.9380	6.5504	6.1982
20	18.0455	16.3514	14.8775	13.5903	12.4622	11.4699	10.5940	9.8181	9.1285	8.5136	7.9633	7.4694	7.0248	6.6231	6.2593
21	18.8570	17.0112	15.4150	14.0292	12.8211	11.7641	10.8355	10.0168	9.2922	8.6487	8.0751	7.5620	7.1015	6.6870	6.3125
22	19.6604	17.6580	15.9369	14.4511	13.1630	12.0416	11.0612	10.2007	9.4424	8.7715	8.1757	7.6446	7.1695	6.7429	6.3587
23	20.4558	18.2922	16.4436	14.8568	13.4886	12.3034	11.2722	10.3711	9.5802	8.8832	8.2664	7.7184	7.2297	6.7921	6.3988
24	21.2434	18.9139	16.9355	15.2470	13.7986	12.5504	11.4693	10.5288	9.7066	8.9847	8.3481	7.7843	7.2829	6.8351	6.4338
25	22.0232	19.5235	17.4131	15.6221	14.0939	12.7834	11.6536	10.6748	9.8226	9.0770	8.4217	7.8431	7.3300	6.8729	6.4641
26	22.7952	20.1210	17.8768	15.9828	14.3752	13.0032	11.8258	10.8100	9.9290	9.1609	8.4881	7.8957	7.3717	6.9061	6.4906
27	23.5596	20.7069	18.3270	16.3296	14.6430	13.2105	11.9867	10.9352	10.0266	9.2372	8.5478	7.9426	7.4086	6.9352	6.5135
28	24.3164	21.2813	18.7641	16.6631	14.8981	13.4062	12.1371	11.0511	10.1161	9.3066	8.6016	7.9844	7.4412	6.9607	6.5335
29	25.0658	21.8444	19.1884	16.9837	15.1411	13.5907	12.2777	11.1584	10.1983	9.3696	8.6501	8.0218	7.4701	6.9830	6.5509
30	25.8077	22.3965	19.6004	17.2920	15.3724	13.7648	12.4090	11.2578	10.2737	9.4269	8.6938	8.0552	7.4957	7.0027	6.5660
31	26.5423	22.9377	20.0004	17.5885	15.5928	13.9291	12.5318	11.3498	10.3428	9.4790	8.7331	8.0850	7.5183	7.0199	6.5791
32	27.2696	23.4683	20.3888	17.8735	15.8027	14.0840	12.6466	11.4350	10.4062	9.5264	8.7686	8.1116	7.5383	7.0350	6.5905
33	27.9897	23.9886	20.7658	18.1476	16.0025	14.2302	12.7538	11.5139	10.4644	9.5694	8.8005	8.1354	7.5560	7.0482	6.6005
34	28.7027	24.4986	21.1318	18.4112	16.1929	14.3681	12.8540	11.5869	10.5178	9.6086	8.8293	8.1566	7.5717	7.0599	6.6091
35	29.4086	24.9986	21.4872	18.6646	16.3742	14.4982	12.9477	11.6546	10.5668	9.6442	8.8552	8.1755	7.5856	7.0700	6.6166
40	32.8347	27.3555	23.1148	19.7928	17.1591	15.0463	13.3317	11.9246	10.7574	9.7791	8.9511	8.2438	7.6344	7.1050	6.6418
45	36.0945	29.4902	24.5187	20.7200	17.7741	15.4558	13.6055	12.1084	10.8812	9.8628	9.0079	8.2825	7.6609	7.1232	6.6543
50	39.1961	31.4236	25.7298	21.4822	18.2559	15.7619	13.8007	12.2335	10.9617	9.9148	9.0417	8.3045	7.6752	7.1327	6.6605

Source: H. Bierman, Jr., and S. Smidt, *The Capital Budgeting Decision*, 6th ed. (New York: Macmillan Publishing Company, 1984), pp. 533–534.

TABLE B Present Value of $1 Received per Period (cont'd)

n/r	16%	18%	20%	22%	24%	26%	28%	30%	32%	34%	36%	38%	40%	45%	50%
1	.8621	.8475	.8333	.8197	.8065	.7937	.7813	.7692	.7576	.7463	.7353	.7246	.7143	.6897	.6667
2	1.6052	1.5656	1.5278	1.4915	1.4568	1.4235	1.3916	1.3609	1.3315	1.3032	1.2760	1.2497	1.2245	1.1653	1.1111
3	2.2459	2.1743	2.1065	2.0422	1.9813	1.9234	1.8684	1.8161	1.7663	1.7188	1.6735	1.6302	1.5889	1.4933	1.4074
4	2.7982	2.6901	2.5887	2.4936	2.4043	2.3202	2.2410	2.1662	2.0957	2.0290	1.9658	1.9060	1.8492	1.7195	1.6049
5	3.2743	3.1272	2.9906	2.8636	2.7454	2.6351	2.5320	2.4356	2.3452	2.2604	2.1807	2.1058	2.0352	1.8755	1.7366
6	3.6847	3.4976	3.3255	3.1669	3.0205	2.8850	2.7594	2.6427	2.5342	2.4331	2.3388	2.2506	2.1680	1.9831	1.8244
7	4.0386	3.8115	3.6046	3.4155	3.2423	3.0833	2.9370	2.8021	2.6775	2.5620	2.4550	2.3555	2.2628	2.0573	1.8829
8	4.3436	4.0776	3.8372	3.6193	3.4212	3.2407	3.0758	2.9247	2.7860	2.6582	2.5404	2.4315	2.3306	2.1085	1.9220
9	4.6065	4.3030	4.0310	3.7863	3.5655	3.3657	3.1842	3.0190	2.8681	2.7300	2.6033	2.4866	2.3790	2.1438	1.9480
10	4.8332	4.4941	4.1925	3.9232	3.6819	3.4648	3.2689	3.0915	2.9304	2.7836	2.6495	2.5265	2.4136	2.1681	1.9053
11	5.0286	4.6560	4.3271	4.0354	3.7757	3.5435	3.3351	3.1473	2.9776	2.8236	2.6834	2.5555	2.4383	2.1849	1.9769
12	5.1971	4.7932	4.4392	4.1274	3.8514	3.6059	3.3868	3.1903	3.0133	2.8534	2.7084	2.5764	2.4559	2.1968	1.9845
13	5.3423	4.9095	4.5327	4.2028	3.9124	3.6555	3.4272	3.2233	3.0404	2.8757	2.7268	2.5916	2.4685	2.2045	1.9897
14	5.4675	5.0081	4.6106	4.2646	3.9616	3.6949	3.4587	3.2487	3.0609	2.8923	2.7403	2.6026	2.4775	2.2100	1.9931
15	5.5755	5.0916	4.6755	4.3152	4.0013	3.7261	3.4834	3.2682	3.0764	2.9047	2.7502	2.6106	2.4839	2.2138	1.9954
16	5.6685	5.1624	4.7296	4.3567	4.0333	3.7509	3.5026	3.2832	3.0882	2.9140	2.7575	2.6164	2.4885	2.2164	1.9970
17	5.7487	5.2223	4.7746	4.3908	4.0591	3.7705	3.5177	3.2948	3.0971	2.9209	2.7629	2.6206	2.4918	2.2182	1.9980
18	5.8178	5.2732	4.8122	4.4187	4.0799	3.7861	3.5294	3.3037	3.1039	2.9260	2.7668	2.6236	2.4941	2.2195	1.9986
19	5.8775	5.3162	4.8435	4.4415	4.0967	3.7985	3.5386	3.3105	3.1090	2.9299	2.7697	2.6258	2.4958	2.2203	1.9991
20	5.9288	5.3527	4.8696	4.4603	4.1103	3.8083	3.5458	3.3158	3.1129	2.9327	2.7718	2.6274	2.4970	2.2209	1.9994
21	5.9731	5.3837	4.8913	4.4756	4.1212	3.8161	3.5514	3.3198	3.1158	2.9349	2.7734	2.6285	2.4979	2.2213	1.9996
22	6.0113	5.4099	4.9094	4.4882	4.1300	3.8223	3.5558	3.3230	3.1180	2.9365	2.7746	2.6294	2.4985	2.2216	1.9997
23	6.0442	5.4321	4.9245	4.4985	4.1371	3.8273	3.5592	3.3253	3.1197	2.9377	2.7754	2.6300	2.4989	2.2218	1.9998
24	6.0726	5.4509	4.9371	4.5070	4.1428	3.8312	3.5619	3.3272	3.1210	2.9386	2.7760	2.6304	2.4992	2.2219	1.9999
25	6.0971	5.4669	4.9476	4.5139	4.1474	3.8342	3.5640	3.3286	3.1220	2.9392	2.7765	2.6307	2.4994	2.2220	1.9999
26	6.1182	5.4804	4.9563	4.5196	4.1511	3.8367	3.5656	3.3297	3.1227	2.9397	2.7768	2.6310	2.4996	2.2221	1.9999
27	6.1364	5.4919	4.9636	4.5243	4.1542	3.8387	3.5669	3.3305	3.1233	2.9401	2.7771	2.6311	2.4997	2.2221	2.0000
28	6.1520	5.5016	4.9697	4.5281	4.1566	3.8402	3.5679	3.3312	3.1237	2.9404	2.7773	2.6313	2.4998	2.2222	2.0000
29	6.1656	5.5098	4.9747	4.5312	4.1585	3.8414	3.5687	3.3316	3.1240	2.9406	2.7774	2.6313	2.4999	2.2222	2.0000
30	6.1772	5.5168	4.9789	4.5338	4.1601	3.8424	3.5693	3.3321	3.1242	2.9407	2.7775	2.6314	2.4999	2.2222	2.0000
31	6.1872	5.5227	4.9824	4.5359	4.1614	3.8432	3.5697	3.3324	3.1244	2.9408	2.7776	2.6315	2.4999	2.2222	2.0000
32	6.1959	5.5277	4.9854	4.5376	4.1624	3.8438	3.5701	3.3326	3.1246	2.9409	2.7776	2.6315	2.4999	2.2222	2.0000
33	6.2034	5.5320	4.9878	4.5390	4.1632	3.8443	3.5704	3.3328	3.1247	2.9410	2.7777	2.6315	2.5000	2.2222	2.0000
34	6.2098	5.5356	4.9898	4.5402	4.1639	3.8447	3.5706	3.3329	3.1248	2.9410	2.7777	2.6315	2.5000	2.2222	2.0000
35	6.2153	5.5386	4.9915	4.5411	4.1644	3.8450	3.5708	3.3330	3.1248	2.9411	2.7777	2.6215	2.5000	2.2222	2.0000
40	6.2335	5.5482	4.9966	4.5439	4.1659	3.8458	3.5712	3.3332	3.1250	2.9412	2.7778	2.6316	2.5000	2.2222	2.0000
45	6.2421	5.5523	4.9986	4.5449	4.1664	3.8460	3.5714	3.3333	3.1250	2.9412	2.7778	2.6316	2.5000	2.2222	2.0000
50	6.2463	5.5541	4.9995	4.5452	4.1666	3.8461	3.5714	3.3333	3.1250	2.9412	2.7778	2.6316	2.5000	2.2222	2.0000

Subject Index

Name Index